Security Assistance in the Middle East

Security Assistance in the Middle East

Challenges . . . and the Need for Change

edited by
Hicham Alaoui and
Robert Springborg

LYNNE
RIENNER
PUBLISHERS

BOULDER
LONDON

Published in the United States of America in 2023 by
Lynne Rienner Publishers, Inc.
1800 30th Street, Suite 314, Boulder, Colorado 80301
www.rienner.com

and in the United Kingdom by
Lynne Rienner Publishers, Inc.
Gray's Inn House, 127 Clerkenwell Road, London EC1 5DB
www.eurospanbookstore.com/rienner

© 2023 by Lynne Rienner Publishers, Inc. All rights reserved

Library of Congress Cataloging-in-Publication Data
Names: Moulay Hicham, Prince of Morocco, 1964– editor. | Springborg, Robert, editor.
Title: Security assistance in the Middle East : challenges . . . and the need for change / edited by Hicham Alaoui and Robert Springborg.
Description: Boulder, Colorado : Lynne Rienner Publishers, Inc., 2023. | Includes bibliographical references and index. | Summary: "Evaluates the costs and benefits to the main providers and recipients of security assistance in the MENA region and explores alternative strategies to improve outcomes for both"— Provided by publisher.
Identifiers: LCCN 2022038447 (print) | LCCN 2022038448 (ebook) | ISBN 9781955055802 (hardcover) | ISBN 9781955055994 (ebook)
Subjects: LCSH: Military assistance, American—Middle East. | Military assistance, European—Middle East. | Security, International—Middle East. | Middle East—Military relations—United States. | United States—Military relations—Middle East. | Middle East—Military relations—Europe. | Europe—Military relations—Middle East.
Classification: LCC UA832 .S434 2023 (print) | LCC UA832 (ebook) | DDC 355/.033056—dc23/eng/20221223
LC record available at https://lccn.loc.gov/2022038447
LC ebook record available at https://lccn.loc.gov/2022038448

British Cataloguing in Publication Data
A Cataloguing in Publication record for this book
is available from the British Library.

Printed and bound in the United States of America

∞ The paper used in this publication meets the requirements of the American National Standard for Permanence of Paper for Printed Library Materials Z39.48-1992.

5 4 3 2 1

Contents

Acknowledgments vii

1 First, Do No Harm: Curing What Ails Security Assistance to the Middle East 1
   Hicham Alaoui and Robert Springborg

2 Security Assistance in a Changing Region 17
   Anthony H. Cordesman

3 Political Drivers of Demand for Security Assistance 47
   Glenn E. Robinson

PART 1   SHARED CHALLENGES, SHARED RESPONSES

4 Tunisia: A Reframed Security-Centered Approach 69
   Noureddine Jebnoun

5 Lebanon: Assessing US-Led Capabilities Development 93
   Aram Nerguizian

6 Egypt: Reconsidering the Political Value of US Assistance 111
   Zeinab Abul-Magd

PART 2   THE ROLE OF MULTILATERAL AND REGIONAL ACTORS

7 EU and Member States' Security Assistance: Complementary or Contradictory? 133
   Florence Gaub and Alex Walsh

Contents

8	The Politics of Security Assistance by "European NATO" *Kevin Koehler*	149
9	The Gulf Monarchies: Security Consumers and Providers *Zoltan Barany*	171
10	Regional Entanglements: MENA States as Providers of Security Assistance *Simone Tholens*	191

PART 3 CIVIL-MILITARY RELATIONS

11	US Security Assistance in Jordan: Militarized Politics and Elusive Metrics *Sean Yom*	211
12	Security Assistance and Public Support for Arab Militaries *Lindsay J. Benstead*	231
13	Civilians in Arab Defense Affairs: Implications for Providers of Security Assistance *Yezid Sayigh*	255

PART 4 PRACTITIONER PERSPECTIVES

14	US Security Assistance to Egypt: The Importance of Framing a Relationship *F. C. "Pink" Williams*	273
15	Subjectivity and Objectivity in Assessing Security Assistance *John J. Zavage*	291

PART 5 CONCLUSION

16	Quit Trying, or Try to Cure? *Hicham Alaoui and Robert Springborg*	313

List of Acronyms	341
Bibliography	345
List of Contributors	377
Index	381
About the Book	397

Acknowledgments

THIS BOOK WAS CONCEIVED BY HICHAM ALAOUI, LINDSAY BENSTEAD, Sean Yom, and Robert Springborg in 2019 as a successor volume to *The Political Economy of Education in the Arab World*, also supported by the Hicham Alaoui Foundation and published by Lynne Rienner. We selected the topic of Western security assistance given its many problems, which both the policy and academic literatures had not adequately addressed. The ratio of costs-to-benefits of security aid for many countries in the Middle East and North Africa had drastically deteriorated. Simply put, financing and arming allied militaries of the region is a pillar of Western—and particularly US—foreign policy. Yet, this has sown immense problems related to institutional stability, deepening authoritarianism, geopolitical conflict, and economic underdevelopment.

How, then, do we reform security assistance, and indeed is it worth reforming at all? These questions motivate this book, which provides both theoretical and empirical analysis about why Western security assistance is provided, how it is absorbed in recipient countries, and what dilemmas have emerged in its proliferation across the region. It is intended for academics, policymakers, and even lay audiences. Our contributors have regional expertise gleaned from many decades of observing local politics and military affairs; some also bring direct experience in managing, overseeing, or implementing security assistance programs. They are not only impressive in the scope and depth of their knowledge, but also have been remarkably responsive in their writing and revisions.

Just as the project was commencing, the Covid-19 pandemic hit, causing us to cancel all in-person conferences. All of our interactions were thus virtual, making it a bit more difficult—though not impossible—

to engage one another intellectually by sharing ideas, circulating drafts, and suggesting revisions. Then, as we finalized our chapters, Russia invaded Ukraine, forcing many of the authors to take this new crisis into account in their analyses. Both the pandemic and the Ukrainian conflict delayed publication of the book by some months, but we feel that the wait was worth it. Though other excellent studies and works on Western security assistance in the Middle East exist, we feel that this book is unique in its region-wide scope, country-based details, and eclectic mix of contributors.

As editors, we must thank the tireless support and interest of Lynne Rienner, and the fastidious work of her staff, among them Moorea Corrigan. From the outset, Lynne helped us to visualize our book as a coherent, integrated whole rather than a disparate collection of individual expositions. Readers can judge whether that objective has been realized. If it has not, the blame lies with us, not Lynne.

—Hicham Alaoui and Robert Springborg

1

First, Do No Harm: Curing What Ails Security Assistance to the Middle East

Hicham Alaoui and Robert Springborg

HIPPOCRATES'S ADMONITION IS RELEVANT TO SECURITY ASSISTANCE (SA) in the Middle East and North Africa (MENA). Considerable evidence suggests that SA is part of the problem of the region's insecurity, rather than a solution to it. By virtually all relevant per capita indicators, ranging from battle deaths and displaced persons to military personnel and expenditures, the region is the world's most insecure and militarized. Of the 10 most militarized countries of the 151 ranked on the Global Militarization Index, 6 are in MENA, as are 10 of the top 20.[1] Five of the 20 least peaceful countries of the 163 ranked by the Global Peace Index are in MENA.[2] Polling data reveals that worries about security typically rank among the very highest concerns of the region's residents. MENA is also the region that receives the greatest absolute amount of security assistance and the highest ratio of it in overseas development assistance (ODA). Between 2000 and 2018, 55 percent of all US aid to MENA was military-related assistance, compared to one-third for all US foreign assistance.[3] The first foreign affairs budget of the Joe Biden administration raised security assistance's proportion of total aid to MENA to 76 percent.[4] Afghanistan illustrates the profound disproportion between ODA and military assistance. In 2019, Afghanistan received $114 per capita of the former, while in the following year the United States spent $1,060 per Afghan on its military intervention there.[5] The negative correlation between ODA and the growth rate of gross domestic product

(GDP), which obtains globally, is particularly strong in MENA, possibly reflecting the preponderance of SA.

If the relative overweighting of SA to MENA exerts a drag effect on the region's economic development, it might also contribute indirectly to the securitization and growing authoritarianism of the region. The region's comparatively low economic growth rate for a generation, coupled with it having the world's second-highest rate of population expansion, has placed huge pressure on virtually all the region's governments, which have responded in lockstep by imposing ever greater repression, thereby stimulating spirals of state-society violence. The region's abysmal human rights record and its democratic backsliding reflect this trend. In the latter case MENA may reflect the global trend of countries with formal or implied security assistance agreements with the United States, of which there are forty-one, accounting for 36 percent of all democratic backsliding and only 5 percent of cases of increasing democratization. In US-allied countries, the quality of democracy declined by almost double the rate in nonallied countries.[6]

In addition to the indirect effects of retarding economic growth and contributing to repressive governance, SA also seems to be "doing wrong" in direct ways. Provision of equipment to suppress demonstrators and monitor social media is the most visible but not the most substantive contribution of SA to authoritarian governance. The imbalance of civil-military relations in favor of the latter in most MENA nation-states is one such wrong. As recipients of the preponderance of aid provided to their countries, militaries, which in virtually all cases receive such assistance directly rather than through and with oversight by civilian institutions such as parliaments, necessarily outgun those institutions. In many cases SA has facilitated expansion of military influence over domestic economies and even direct involvement in them by military-owned enterprises, thus tilting the balance of financial power away from civilians and their institutions toward officers and theirs. The relative prosperity of militaries has contributed to their popular appeal, in part because of well-financed public relations, rendering militaries the most trusted institution in virtually all MENA countries, whatever the magnitude of their economic and political indiscretions.

MENA states' external relations appear also to have been negatively impacted by SA, which, as with domestic civil-military relations, has tilted those relations toward militaries. The most obvious manifestation of that imbalance is the MENA arms race, the most intense of any global region. Absorbing the greatest share of weaponry in world trade, the region is armed to the teeth, including with technically advanced, expensive manned and unmanned aircraft; surface-to-air, sea, and surface missiles; and both underwater and surface naval vessels, including aircraft carriers. The arms race exacerbates the region's fissiparous tendencies, which are reflected in its dearth of effective regional integration associations, whether economic, political, or functionally specific in such areas as telecommunications, electricity, tourism, and so forth. The primary causes of national autarchy in MENA result from pursuit of the political and economic interests of the political elites who have captured its states and established limited access orders. Such orders thrive off autarchy and are threatened by integration, which can render polities and economies more competitive.[7] Arms races exacerbate the problem by magnifying the security dimension in interstate relations, thus impeding the emergence of effective functionally oriented associations. The centrality of military power to interstate relations also inflates officers' roles in foreign policy decisionmaking. The power-projection capacities of contemporary weaponry, including aircraft carriers, submarines, and ballistic missiles, expand the geographic range of national security interests, which for many MENA countries now extend well beyond the traditional borders of the region into the Horn of Africa and the Sahel and throughout the southern and eastern Mediterranean.[8]

The plague of proxy wars afflicting MENA is also due, in considerable measure, to SA. Libya, Syria, Yemen, and to some extent Iraq are presently experiencing conflicts that have sucked in military advisors, combatants, and weaponry from global and regional actors. While proxy wars have long occurred in MENA, not only have they become more common, but the roles of external actors have expanded. The UN special representative to Libya, Ghassan Salame, for example, observed that during the Lebanese civil war from 1975 to 1989, the principal combatants were Lebanese themselves, although Syrian and Israeli troops became directly involved in 1982. By contrast, in Libya, within a few years of the fall of Mu'ammar Gadhafi, most frontline fighters were foreigners, including Turks, Russians, Egyptians, Emiratis, and mercenaries drawn from Syria, Iraq, Sudan, and elsewhere.[9] MENA is becoming truly Hobbesian, with internal conflicts sucking in outsiders willing to provide SA in pursuit primarily of their own region-wide or even global objectives, whatever the consequences for the host country and its citizens.

This does not imply, however, that security assistance is adequately serving those objectives of its providers. Indeed, back-of-the-envelope cost/benefit analyses of it in the United States suggest it is not. Popular dissatisfaction with forever wars that have ended in defeats, provision of taxpayer dollars to Middle Eastern autocrats rather than needy Americans, and growing challenges from China and Russia making ever greater claims on US security and other resources has produced the rare outcome of a Washington policy consensus between Republicans and Democrats. That consensus is to scale back American SA commitments in the region, although disagreements remain over where, how, and to what extent that should be done. The European Union and relevant European states, aware of the likely US drawdown, are debating how to respond, so far without reaching a definitive conclusion. For their part virtually all MENA states, including Israel, have, in the wake of Russia's invasion of Ukraine, doubled down on hedging strategies adopted in response to the anticipated US drawdown, thereby calling into question whether Western security assistance was securing their loyalty. In sum, security assistance—which, as recently as the early years of the new millennium, appeared to offer substantial benefits coupled with reduced costs to providers—is no longer almost universally viewed in the United States as an appropriate alternative strategy to boots on the ground in MENA. The emerging preference prior to Russia's invasion of Ukraine was for few boots and little SA, if any of either, a preference yet to be noticeably impacted by that invasion.

Were Hippocrates still with us, he might have concluded that SA certainly risks "doing wrong" to its recipients, while providing inadequate benefits for its providers. But as a wise Greek, he might also have observed that it has the potential to do good and at lower cost. Assuming that to be so, the question becomes not whether but whither SA—that is, not should it be discontinued, but how can its costs be reduced and its benefits enhanced? That question is central to this book, which assumes that SA as provided by Western powers can benefit both them and recipients, but given new regional and global contexts and changing weapons technologies, changes will be needed if the cost/benefit ratio is to be substantially improved.

Impacts of Regional Context

Benefits claimed for Western-provided SA typically rest on assumed "stateness" of recipients linked together in a Metternichian system of interstate relations, whether conflictual or consensual. The postcolonial MENA did indeed replicate the nineteenth-century European prototype and structured Cold War competition in the region between the superpowers. The United States and USSR competed for favor and influence within the MENA state system, with weapons supplies constituting but one component of their all-embracing SA and their bilateral relations more generally. Other aspects of those relationships included economic aid, efforts to facilitate adoption of either communist- or capitalist-inspired development models, cultural exchanges, inclusion in superpower-instigated and -centered alliances, membership in trading blocs, and so on. SA thus was intended by providers to serve a mix of military and nonmilitary purposes in pursuit of the overall objective of influence over states and their policies, the hoped-for apotheosis of which was integration of the recipient state into the relevant superpower's camp. While development of military capacities was important to providers, it was not the only measure of success of SA, which included intangibles such as access to decisionmaking elites, linking them to elites of other friendly states, and conveying positive public images of the provider, as well as more military-relevant, tangible measures, such as interoperability and complementarity, although even in these cases those objectives were both political and military. They were intended to recruit and retain states in the respective blocs. As for actual combat, all parties assumed it would pit states against states. The Cold War–model military, replete with main battle tanks, bomber aircraft, and vast standing armies, was thus directly relevant and could be transferred intact through SA to recipients.

All of this has changed. Despite Russia's invasion of Ukraine, if a new Cold War ensues, it will not replicate the original. Russian reassertion is on a narrower front than when the USSR was seeking to remake the region along communist lines. Western objectives have also become more modest. For both, SA is becoming less strategic and more tactical in nature, with weapons sales assuming greater, even central importance. The MENA state system is under duress, with some of its members having already transited through fragile to failed status. Virtually all are consumed with containing domestic threats to their existing, shaky orders. Nonstate actors, which other than the Palestinian Liberation Organization played no significant role in regional affairs during the Cold War, have arisen in geopolitical spaces abandoned by retreating states and, as in the case of the Islamic State, assumed near-statehood. Accordingly, the salience of interstate warfare has diminished, while that of intrastate conflict has increased.

The military impact of this "de-statification" is reinforced by the emergence of new weapons technologies, some of which are embedded in so-called hybrid or asymmetric warfare, also known as grey zone operations. As states have been more thoroughly penetrated and borders between them become more porous, so has the black-and-white clarity of major land battles between states given way to the ambiguity of grey zone warfare, which relies on fifth column elements, permits deniability, utilizes asymmetric weaponry, incorporates means of disruption such as cyberwarfare and disinformation, and assumes that outcomes are unlikely to be definitive and sudden (such as in the Six Day War of 1967) but instead will be achieved gradually and incrementally. The war in Ukraine has further illustrated the potency of new, relatively inexpensive weapons, ranging from antiship and handheld antiaircraft and antitank missiles to armed drones, many of which are already in MENA armories.

MENA, in other words, has entered a stage of permanent, if intermittent, low-level conflicts, accompanied by shifting tactical alliances and hostilities between states and nonstate actors. This Hobbesian world has rendered the SA of the Cold War era largely irrelevant and ineffective. As Anthony Cordesman notes in Chapter 2, the United States no longer has a comprehensive strategy for the ever more complex MENA. Instead, it pursues its interests on case-by-case, country-by-country, or, at best, subregional bases. While the complex regional context may dictate this tactically driven US approach to security assistance, the absence of an overarching strategy renders more difficult both the upstream of policy formation and the downstream of its implementation. Moreover, as Zeinab Abul-Magd argues in Chapter 6, US and Western influence more generally over military, security, and foreign policies in even once critically important Egypt has receded in tandem with the decline since the early 1980s in security and development assistance as a proportion of that country's defense budgets, government revenues, and GDP. The SA operational consequences of that declining influence are illustrated in this book by General F. C. Williams, whose lengthy, multirole career in delivering SA to Egypt made him an ideal observer of the ebbing away of American influence in Cairo.

Yet it does not follow that reduced US or other external actors' leverage and even influence results in SA doing less harm. Two chapters in this book directly address the distortions that SA can inflict on MENA militaries and overall political economies in countries with strong connections to the West. Sean Yom describes how in Jordan the monarch's dependence on SA to sustain the loyalty of his core East Bank constituency has helped sustain authoritarianism, impede national integration, undermine economic development, and even militate against improvements that would enable the Jordanian Armed Forces effectively to project power or even adequately defend Jordan's borders.

Similarly, Noureddine Jebnoun traces the ripple effects in Tunisia on its military and state-society relations of the concentration of SA on counterterrorism and border control. The latter has disrupted long-established localized political economies based on cross-border interactions, while the former has posed obstacles to consolidating the on-again, off-again democratic transition, which came to a complete, if hopefully temporary, halt with Kais Saied's assumption of ever-greater personal power from July 2021.

Implications for Tactics and Strategies

Regional, technical, and economic changes have given rise to fundamental questions about SA. A key tactical one is whether Western SA should "go over to the dark side," meaning whether it should more systematically emulate grey zone approaches utilized by Iran and Russia, which have undeniably met with considerable success. Until now the West as the status quo power in MENA has sought to reinforce the region's states and to bolster relations between them. While that has in many cases necessitated shifts in SA focus from interstate battles to counterterrorism, the primary concern with institutionalized state military capacities, replicating those of the SA provider, has endured. Western military contractors, for example, remain tethered to that model rather than becoming equivalents to Russia's mercenaries or Iran's sponsored militias in Iraq, Syria, Lebanon, and Yemen.[10] Although Iranian operatives have been assassinated, including through the use of unmanned aerial vehicles, and cyberattacks have been launched against Iran's nuclear facilities, major Western SA efforts to contain Iran remain devoted primarily to developing Arab state military capacities. Emulating grey zone activities could provide operational dividends, but possibly at the cost of further undermining already weakened states and the informal alliances in which some are enmeshed. Moreover, grey zone warfare might further erode rule of law and formal institutions, so begs the question of whether tactical successes might be offset by strategic costs to stateness, which theoretically at least underpins rule of law and institutionalization of governance.

The accompanying strategic questions are if and how the West should try to resolve the incongruity of it providing SA to authoritarian states, which by their nature are more akin to other authoritarian states, such as Russia or China. The salience of this inherent contradiction is enhanced by reflecting on Cold War precedents, during which efforts were made by the superpowers and their allies to convert recipients of SA to their prevailing ideologies and models. Presently there are few, if any, such underpinnings to provider-recipient relationships in SA or even attempts to establish them. The strength of relations between Western providers of SA and MENA recipients would be stronger if the latter were democratic or at least aspire to being so and considered themselves normatively allied with Western democracies in their intensifying global competition with authoritarian, antidemocratic states. The unwillingness of all key MENA states to openly side with the West against Russia's invasion of Ukraine illustrates the problem. As MENA states continue their drift toward greater authoritarianism, they presumably will find more common ground with other authoritarian states, whether developmental, as in China, or stagnating but aggressive, as in Russia. While major ruptures in relationships that bridge the democratic-authoritarian divide may not occur, irritations and interruptions are likely to increase, as they have presently, for example, in the Saudi-American relationship. The absence of substantial ideological and systemic underpinnings for relationships between Western providers and MENA recipients pushes the region ever closer to being simply an arms bazaar, with buyers and sellers motivated more by immediate material and security benefits than by long-term strategic objectives.

These questions are not just academic. They lie at the heart of current debates in Western countries about the provision of SA to MENA. The tactics of grey zone warfare are controversial, as debates about the appropriateness of the US assassination of Qassem Suleimani and alleged support for Israel's killing of Iranian nuclear expert Mohsen Fakhrizadeh reflect.[11] A closely related issue is whether, by engaging in grey zone activities, security providers invite retaliation, such as by Iranian use of cyberattacks against European and American targets in reaction to the Stuxnet and other cyberattacks on Iranian nuclear facilities. At a more general level, the issue of grey zone warfare's possible contravention of Western legal codes, to say nothing of underlying morals and ethics, is also pertinent. One position in these debates is that if the West must stoop to such methods to compete in MENA, it would be preferable to abandon the region to its fate, whatever it might be. The same logic has been applied to the question of whether support should be given to authoritarian states, as evidenced by strong criticism in the United States against provision of SA to Egypt and Saudi Arabia. Since the occasional withholding of SA has not induced policy or structural changes in these states, the implied and sometimes stated answer is to terminate the relevant SA.

The contributors to this book are skeptical of the democratization potential of even a revised SA, which historically has supported MENA authoritarianism but is not its only cause. They do believe, however, that SA could assist democratization at least indirectly, primarily by impacting the quality of governance, especially within the defense sector. Yezid Sayigh's analysis of civil-military relations sees civilianizing defense institutions as a possible initial step on the path to developing capacities for control of militaries. Given the central role of militaries in MENA states, infusing their institutions with meritocratic norms and professionalizing their armed forces might have spillover effects on other institutions of governance. Florence Gaub and Alex Walsh in Chapter 7 and Kevin Koehler in Chapter 8 describe multilateral SA as provided by the European Union and the North Atlantic Treaty Organization (NATO), respectively, as focusing on this type of soft military-capacity building.

Western SA to MENA has come to a crossroads. Enmeshed in what is essentially a revised but still dated model that has proven ineffective even in confronting the old Cold War enemy Russia, it is neither popular at home nor particularly effective in the region. It is based heavily on the questionable assumption that a Metternichian state system, which is structurally inherently favorable to the West, still obtains. Both tactical and strategic changes to SA seem necessary. That some changes envisioned are profound reflects widespread frustration with the current state of Western SA. Accelerating the present drift toward grey zone warfare implies adopting tactics relevant to modernized total war, likely inconsistent with at least idealized Western norms, practices, and aspirations. Elevating concerns for democracy, governance, and human rights in recipient countries over calculations of threats to their stability and contributions to Western geostrategic interests amounts to abandoning traditional justifications and methods of SA. While tactical and strategic changes of this magnitude are unlikely, that they are on relevant tables for debate indicates how deeply felt and widespread the need for change to SA is.

Truth in Packaging Security Assistance

Terminology reveals, conceals, and confuses. One person's security assistance is another person's support for terrorism. Detailed clarification of the SA vocabulary would be a useful endeavor but is beyond the scope of this book. Instead, we shall fall back on American usages despite the inclusion of the non-American, European and MENA SA providers. We do so primarily because the United States is the elephant in the room of SA, the amount it provides to MENA dwarfing all others combined. But it is not just quantity that is determinative. While other providers' objectives and practices of SA do differ from the American model, they must all take account of it, and many emulate it.

This is not to say, however, that the US SA lexicon is standardized. Even the term *security assistance* can be seen as misleading—or at least its common usage as departing from the official definition. The US Joint Chiefs of Staff define SA as "a group of programs, authorized under Title 22 authorities, by which the United States provides defense articles, military education and training, and other defense-related services by grant, loan, credit, cash sales, or lease, in furtherance of national policies and objectives."[12] *Security cooperation*, which might be seen as a politically more acceptable term, covers a broader range of activities, as it "encompasses all Department of Defense (DOD) interactions, programs, and activities with foreign security forces (FSF) and their institutions to build relationships that help promote US interests; enable partner nations (PNs) to provide the US access to territory, infrastructure, information, and resources; and/or to build and apply their capacity and capabilities consistent with US defense objectives."[13] Relevant academic and policy-oriented literature uses both terms more or less interchangeably. We have chosen to use *security assistance* as it seems to more correctly characterize flows of resources and the actual nature of the relationship between providers and recipients, at least in MENA.

As one wades further into the topic, yet more terminological ambiguities arise, as Simone Tholens notes in Chapter 10. She argues that the characterization of SA as a relationship between provider and recipient—also referred to as principal and agent or even patron and client—is misleading, especially in MENA. There, complex intraregional interactions, which increasingly involve extraregional actors, "challenge binary logics of patron-client, international-local, or state-nonstate." Her preferred term is *entanglement*, which may better describe current MENA complexities than the commonly used provider-recipient or principal-agent dyads, which rest on the primacy of bilateral rather than multilateral relationships. These complexities are illustrated by the hedging strategies in reaction to the war in Ukraine of both MENA states nominally allied with the West (e.g., Saudi Arabia, the United Arab Emirates, and Egypt) and even, to some degree, Iran and Turkey, the former closely associated with Russia and the latter enmeshed with it in bilateral cooperative undertakings such as in Libya and in some measure Syria. But as in the cases of security cooperation and security assistance, we have chosen to employ current usage of the terms *principal* and *agent* precisely because it is current and because our interest is, through comparative case studies, to focus on SA effects and to explore how they might be rendered more positive for both parties.

Building partner capacity (BPC) is another term whose use can structure how activities are conceptualized and conducted. It "refers to a broad set of missions, programs, activities, and authorities intended to improve the ability of other nations to achieve those security-oriented goals they share with the United States."[14] It is frequently used as a synonym for *security assistance* or even the officially broader term *security cooperation*. This sematic confusion could be dismissed as irrelevant if it did not have actual consequences. John Zavage's detailed treatment of assessments, mandated by Congress and the US Department of Defense, of BPC in those MENA theaters where he was deployed points to such consequences. While he focuses on the limitations of empirical, check-list assessment mechanisms, as opposed to more in-depth evaluations that take into account context and extend over longer periods, he also highlights the costs of the narrow focus of BPC assessments. Building a partner's capacity is typically only one objective of a US SA program in any given MENA country. Most others can be subsumed under the generic label of *relationship building*; they range from such objectives as access and trust, which imply a weak or nonexistent power dimension, to leverage, in which power is substantial and manifest. These important objectives, however, are not susceptible to measurement or even consideration by the official assessment tools created in order to be accountable to Congress and ultimately the American public, as the cases of BPC in Iraq and Afghanistan so amply demonstrate. Sean Yom's analysis of BPC in Jordan suggests it is more a point of entry for US geostrategic interests in the country and region than a principal objective.

The failure of formalized assessments to capture the multiple objectives of SA and thus their potential to provide more optimistic accounts than warranted is not a new development. Secretary of Defense Robert McNamara's obsession with empirical assessments of performance in the Vietnam War resulted in misleading metrics such as body counts and pacified villages, enabling the US military to claim success almost to the moment of defeat. That the misleading metric approach subsequently became embedded in the Department of Defense is suggested by a similar outcome in Afghanistan. Virtually until the end of that war, the metric of territory held painted a profoundly misleading picture of the actual balance of power between the Taliban and Western-backed Afghanistan government forces.

The terminology of security assistance, in sum, is not neutral and needs to be employed with awareness of its implications and consequences. MENA is a particularly arduous testing ground for this lexicon. When is security assistance better described as support for terrorism? Is the former reserved for Western providers and the latter for, say, Iran? When is security assistance better characterized as military intervention? Behind these terminological matters lurk not only political commitments and preferences but history. The West has been providing SA to MENA for some two centuries, whereas local providers, such as Iran, Turkey, the UAE, and Saudi Arabia have been doing so for about a generation at most, with Israel having recently joined that list. Moreover, the assistance they provide tends to be more tactical, limited in scope, concentrated on kinetic rather than institutional capacity building, more likely to be provided to nonstate actors, and short-lived. Clearly there are substantial differences in SA as provided by regional as opposed to external actors. We leave it to the reader to grapple with the relevance of these terms for SA extended by different providers, concentrating here instead on conveying relevant information, most especially in the chapters by Zoltan Barany on security assistance by Gulf Cooperation Council (GCC) states and Simone Tholens on SA extended by Iran and Turkey.

Purpose and Organization of the Book

This book addresses the debate over the future of Western SA to MENA. It does so by investigating the key challenges facing SA as presently conceived and delivered. It then draws upon this information to evaluate alternative ways and means to improve SA by reducing the harm it causes, while increasing the benefits to both providers and recipients, the latter being not just states but their citizens as well.

The book consists of five parts preceded by two stage-setting introductory chapters by Anthony Cordesman and Glenn Robinson. The former addresses the challenges of providing SA not only in the face of regimes' perceived needs, as subsequently analyzed in more detail by Glenn Robinson, but also in light of rapid, dramatic changes that have occurred since 2011 in the various dynamics of the region. After reviewing the region's security context in that year, Cordesman notes that "none of those things are true. The Arab Spring has . . . turn[ed] the

MENA region into a fragmented mess." After describing that mess, he takes up the challenges it and rapidly developing symmetric and asymmetric weapons technologies pose to providers of SA, the ever-greater number of which further complicates matters.

Cordesman's chapter is followed by Robinson's analysis of how demand for SA and the effectiveness of its utilization are shaped by regime needs in three types of MENA states: oil monarchies, repressive republics, and flawed democracies. Only in the last type of state is SA used reasonably effectively. In oil monarchies SA serves primarily as insurance premiums for US support, while in repressive republics it is primarily sought to assist coup-proofing.

The classic bugbear of SA, which is the principal-agent problem consisting, according to Stephen Biddle, of "interest misalignments between the provider and the recipient, difficult monitoring challenges, and difficult conditions for enforcement," is the topic of Part I.[15] Noureddine Jebnoun focuses in Chapter 4 on the "interest misalignment" resulting from the US preference for Tunisian security efforts to concentrate on counterterrorism and border control in the face of the Tunisian military's desire to develop broader capacities and the state's need for economic and other support for democratization. The Lebanese Armed Forces, analyzed by Aram Nerguizian in Chapter 5, paradoxically illustrate that a military more or less quarantined by the jealous and fearful political elite that controls the state has been able to develop considerable capacities despite severe limits imposed on its procurement of weaponry. But its operational abilities remain constrained by that state and the confessional balance that underlies it. Unlike, say, Egypt and Algeria, where it can be argued that the states are extensions of their militaries, the Lebanese Armed Forces constitute a symbol, not the backbone, of the nation-state. In Chapter 6 Zeinab Abul-Magd documents the limitations to a principal's influence over an agent resulting from the declining relative monetary value of assistance provided by the US to Egypt.

Part II investigates multilateral, European, and regional providers of SA. Florence Gaub and Alex Walsh show in Chapter 7 how EU SA efforts are confined mainly to enhancing soft power, whereas those of its member states concentrate on building hard power. Whether this division of labor creates the basis for more effective SA, because a considerable portion of the European total is necessarily devoted to defense institution building coupled with military professionalization, is a question that concerns both them and Kevin Koehler. In Chapter 8 he describes the limitations faced by NATO in seeking to provide SA in MENA, the key one being that it is driven by demand from recipients, thus reducing input from providers, who are in any case hampered by conflicting interests with their own governments. Zoltan Barany's Chapter 9 on GCC states describes their varying degrees of effective utilization of SA, while also investigating how the UAE and Saudi Arabia simultaneously serve as providers of SA, or possibly only as interveners, in the region. Simone Tholens's Chapter 10 contextualizes Iran and Turkey's efforts to expand their influence in MENA through SA and military intervention. She evaluates the comparative advantages and disadvantages of SA provided by these actors, noting their disruptive impacts on bilateral models of SA as well as the normative dimensions of SA lexicons.

Part III takes up the impact of SA on civil-military relations in recipient countries. Sean Yom's analysis of US SA to Jordan in Chapter 11 reveals that it has failed to create a proficient military, but combined with a massive amount of financial aid, it has reinforced the coercive apparatus and the underlying tribal socioeconomic base upon which the authoritarian client state rests. Lindsay Benstead's Chapter 12 draws upon public opinion data, most notably in Tunisia, to assess causes of relatively high popular support for militaries, including the impacts of security assistance. In Chapter 13 Yezid Sayigh addresses the causes and consequences of SA providers' belief that their assistance can upgrade, even transform, recipient's capabilities without an equivalent shift in the recipient's political, institutional, and social frameworks. He speculates on the consequences of SA for civil-military relations and notes that it provides inadequate support for defense institution building, valuable in its own right, but also as a model for better governance more generally and possibly even as an initial step on a path to democratization.

Part IV presents practitioners' perspectives on providing security assistance. US Air Force General F. C. Williams (Ret.) and US Army Colonel John Zavage (Ret.) present their insights as longtime participants in delivering US SA to MENA countries. General Williams describes a range of principal-agent problems in the US-Egyptian relationship and offers recommendations as to how they might best be dealt with. Colonel Zavage draws upon his experience as a military advisor in Iraq, Jordan, and Yemen/Saudi Arabia in demonstrating the limits of evaluation tools mandated by Congress and the Department of Defense, while offering suggestions on how to improve those tools.

In the conclusion in Part V, Hicham Alaoui and Robert Springborg draw upon the preceding chapters to address the question of whether SA in MENA may be inherently harmful or ineffective and thus best replaced or supplemented by other policies, such as the United States withdrawing completely from MENA, engaging in offshore balancing, conducting coercive diplomacy, or intensifying grey zone activities.

In sum, this book provides multidimensional analyses of the costs and benefits to American, European, and regional providers of SA and assesses the impacts of that SA on various MENA actors, key among them being the Arab states. By so doing it provides empirical and analytical bases upon which recommendations are made for reducing harm caused by SA while increasing its benefits to both providers and recipients.

Notes

1. Global Militarization Index (http://gmi.bicc.de).
2. Institute for Economics & Peace, *Global Peace Index 2021*.
3. Zuaiter, "The Middle East's Addiction to Foreign Aid."
4. Binder, "Report."
5. Hausmann, "How Afghanistan Was Really Lost."
6. The data is produced by V-Dem, a Swedish NGO, cited by Fisher, "U.S. Allies Drive Much of World's Democratic Decline."
7. On limited access orders in MENA and their negative consequences for regional integration associations, see Springborg, *Political Economies in the Middle East and North Africa*.
8. Lynch, "The End of the Middle East."
9. Salame made this comparison in his address to the Mediterranean Dialogue Conference of the Italian Institute for International Studies.
10. Marten, "Russia's Use of Semi-state Security Forces."
11. On the latter, see Bergman and Fassihi, "The Scientist and the A.I.-Assisted Remote Control Killing Machine."
12. *Security Cooperation* (Joint Publication 3-20), 5.
13. Ibid.
14. Congressional Research Service, "What Is 'Building Partner Capacity'?"
15. Biddle, Macdonald, and Baker, "Small Footprint, Small Payoff," 89–142; Biddle, "Building Security Forces and Stabilizing Nations," 126–138.

2
Security Assistance in a Changing Region

Anthony H. Cordesman

THE UNITED STATES FACES MAJOR CHALLENGES IN SHAPING ITS SECUrity relations with each state in the Middle East and North Africa (MENA) as well as in dealing with key neighboring nations outside the MENA region like Turkey. The United States is still the dominant outside power in the region, but the security dynamics of the Middle East and North Africa have changed radically over the last decade, and their forces are now undergoing a process of modernization that will be equally radical over the coming decade. US security assistance must adjust to both the broader strategic shifts in the region and the need to help regional partners restructure their forces and create new forms of interoperability.

The United States also faces growing competition for regional influence from China and Russia, new types of military threats from regional powers like Iran, and the need to modernize and change its own forces in ways that will force it to create new levels of interoperability, joint warfare capabilities, and all-domain command and control in operating with its MENA strategic partners.

This will require new approaches to security assistance in the region. The United States must also tailor its security assistance to suit each MENA state's different character and strategic importance, and it will need to consider the different capability of each to take on new approaches to future military cooperation and modernization. The

United States must also tie these efforts to balancing the different and sometimes conflicting goals that security assistance can help to achieve, while dealing with the fact that some MENA states are threats rather than partners, others are torn apart by internal or local conflicts, and still others have no interest in becoming strategic partners.

Dealing with the Reality vs. the Rhetoric of Security Assistance

The United States must make these changes because the primary goal of security assistance is to serve US strategic interests with partners that have very different cultures and political systems. The official rhetoric the United States uses to justify its strategic partnerships and security assistance efforts does not always reflect this reality. The United States does have an interest in using such partnerships in ways that preserve human rights and help each partner state improve its governance and approach to economic development. As the ongoing military conflicts and tensions in the region show all too clearly, however, such interests need to be balanced against the fact that the primary goal behind security assistance is to serve US strategic interests by helping partner states create more effective military and internal security forces to meet very real outside and internal threats.

The other key goals in providing security assistance are to help create regional stability and to link the security posture of a given partner country to the United States rather than to hostile regional states and competitors like China and Russia. Moreover, only a limited number of MENA states can develop modern and effective military forces that are interoperable with the United States or offer major basing and other strategic advantages. The United States must give priority to using security assistance to maintain US strategic access and power-projection capabilities in such partner states and to enhance their effectiveness in joint operations or deterring and defending against common threats.

The Changing Strategic Environment for Security Assistance

US security assistance efforts must also be based on the region's political realities. Most MENA regimes are not democratic, and those that do have some form of democracy are often deeply divided on an ethnic and sectarian level. Even where the United States can use security assistance to support humanitarian values, creating personal security and a more just rule of law often has a higher priority in human terms than encouraging democracy. The same is true of giving priority to progress in economic development and equality of opportunity.

Moreover, the recent history of the MENA region has made all too clear that security assistance must help partner states deal with internal instability and unpredictable crises. MENA state after MENA state has recently gone through a period of crisis, instability, popular uprising, and sometimes civil war. Other regimes and factions, like the government of Iran, the Houthis in Yemen, the parts of Syria controlled by Bashar al-Assad, and Hezbollah in Lebanon, have come to pose new threats in the form of missiles and irregular warfare, and the causes of extremism and terrorism have tended to grow rather than diminish.

These realities pose major challenges, as the recent history of the need for security cooperation has thrown into relief. At the beginning of 2011, most MENA nations were at peace and seemed relatively stable. North African countries were at peace under authoritarian leaders. The Arab-Israeli conflicts were limited to low-level clashes between Israel and Palestine. Egypt acted as a stable major regional power. Iraq's Islamic extremists seemed to be defeated. Iran was a weak military power dependent on low-grade and dated weapons. The other Arab Gulf states appeared to be unified in a Gulf Cooperation Council (GCC). Yemen was poor and could not meet the needs of many of its people, but the country still seemed stable. Military spending and arms purchases were high by global standards but placed only a moderate burden on local economies.

Today, as the chapters that follow show, none of those things are true. The Arab Spring has created new regional rivalries, extremism, and political uprisings and civil conflicts, turning the MENA region into a fragmented mess. What appeared to be a relatively stable pattern of national security developments and outside support before the political upheavals that began in 2011 has become the scene of local power struggles, internal conflicts, new battles with extremist movements, and major civil wars in Iran, Libya, Syria, and Yemen.

Instead of a shifting toward democracy, many regimes have become more repressive and authoritarian. Efforts at reforming governance and the economy have fallen far short of the needs of most states. Moreover, only a few of the major petroleum-exporting states in the Gulf have avoided major economic challenges as a result of Covid-19, poor governance, and civil tensions, and even they faced serious financial challenges before the war in Ukraine placed limits on Russia's exports.

Far too many MENA states face new internal or external military threats that affect the kind of security assistance the United States should provide. Tensions have revived between Morocco and Algeria over the Western Sahara. Libya remains divided and on the edge of civil conflict. Tunisia remains politically unstable. Egypt seems relatively stable but at the cost of a more authoritarian regime. Tensions, civil violence, and serious clashes continue between Israel and the Palestinians. The government of Lebanon has collapsed, leaving Hezbollah the major power in the country. The Assad regime continues to make slow gains in the Syrian civil war and now controls most of the country, although it still faces challenges from Turkey in Idlib and from a Kurdish enclave in the east that has some US military support.

US military interventions in Afghanistan and Iraq have created further problems. The US invasion of Iraq in 2003, the fall of Saddam Hussein's regime, and the resulting struggle to defeat extremists and end factional struggles created a civil war that led to a prolonged US military occupation. This fighting seemed to be coming to a close in 2011 and to be leading to the withdrawal of US combat forces. In practice, however, it resulted in a new struggle between a faltering Iraqi government and the Islamic State of Iraq and Syria (ISIS) that led to another decade of direct US participation in active combat and combat support of Iraqi government forces.

Despite US claims of victory against ISIS in 2020 and 2021 and the major US withdrawals from Iraq, ISIS has not been fully defeated. Moreover, Iran has been able to maintain a significant security presence in Iraq, which remains deeply divided and unstable. Iran has also emerged as a far more serious military threat in the Gulf.

At the same time, a civil war in Yemen has made the Houthis the most dominant political and military force in the country, one that has used Iranian-supplied missiles to attack key military and infrastructure targets in Saudi Arabia and the United Arab Emirates. Moreover, US security assistance must deal with the threat posed by the Assad forces in Syria, Hezbollah in Lebanon, the pro-Iranian Popular Mobilization Forces (PMFs) in Iraq, and the Houthis in Yemen. These threats form a loose coalition of hostile powers that threaten US interests and those of all its strategic partners.

The United States must also provide advanced forms of security assistance in a region where weak or failed governance is more the rule than the exception. In far too many cases—as the following chapters show—MENA states have failed to make their governments more honest and effective, meet the needs of their peoples and growing populations, and develop their economies at the rate needed to ensure the civil side of security. Some countries are divided by civil conflict, ethnic and sectarian tensions, and the threat posed by extremist groups—and they all face challenges from the impact of Covid-19. Many, if not most, have internal security forces and security efforts that are repressive or abuse the power of the state, becoming a source of the very extremism and hard-line opposition they are trying to suppress. Most states barely tolerate peaceful and legitimate opposition or dissent—if at all.

The United States does continue to deploy forces and security assistance efforts in many countries in the region, including Morocco, Egypt, Israel, Jordan, Iraq, Kuwait, Bahrain, Qatar, Saudi Arabia, and the UAE. The United States has, however, withdrawn the forces it deployed in the MENA region to support the war in Afghanistan and most of the forces it deployed to fight ISIS in Iraq and Syria. While the United States has continued to deploy significant forces to support its partners and power-projection options in the region, it is now reexamining its global commitments. This reexamination of US global security priorities includes its support of MENA security partners and the value of maintaining US forces in the MENA region compared to relying on power-projection forces from the United States. It also includes an examination of human rights issues. At the same time, President Joe Biden has taken a much stronger stance on human rights issues that affects security assistance to key partners like Egypt, Saudi Arabia, and the UAE.

The Role of Outside Powers: Europe, Russia, and China

The United States also must deal with major changes in the role of outside powers in providing security assistance. The United States in the MENA region is receiving less support from Europe. More importantly, Russia and China pose growing challenges.

The Impact of Europe

The United States still receives some security assistance from its European allies in the Mediterranean and North Africa, and European powers provide more significant help in security assistance to some Gulf countries. The United Kingdom and France still play an important role in the Gulf, particularly in Qatar, Saudi Arabia, the UAE, and Oman. However, European powers focus more on immigration issues than

MENA security, and the roles of the United Kingdom and France have increasingly been tied to arms sales, while key aspects of their power-projection capabilities have continued to slowly decline. Turkey is a somewhat different story. While Turkey remains an ally, it is playing an active military role in Libya, Syria, and Iraq, and it has tilted away from the North Atlantic Treaty Organization (NATO) and Europe to play a growing role in the MENA region.

As for the rest of Europe, a number of countries provide support through arms transfers and through their efforts to limit migration. More broadly, the European Union did discuss the possibility of creating its own intervention force before Russia invaded Ukraine, but the EU only discussed a force of 5,000 personnel, which is less than one full brigade plus support. This force creation also did not involve discussions of strategic life and sustainability, equipment and technology, or supporting air and missile power.[1]

The Impact of Russia

Russia and China pose growing challenges in the MENA region, although the United States has focused on the threat they pose in Europe and Asia. The United States announced a series of new national strategies during the Donald Trump and Joe Biden administrations that focused on a direct threat from Russia and possible conflict with China. These strategies called for the United States to deter and defend against direct threats from each major power, but both Russia and China are playing a growing security role in the MENA region.

The Stockholm International Peace Research Institute (SIPRI) reports that the United States still accounted for 53 percent of all arms sales to the MENA region from 2017 to 2021; France sold another 12 percent, and Russia rose to the third-largest seller with 11 percent of all sales—with major sales to Algeria and Egypt.[2] Russia began to reassert itself as a major power and competitor in the MENA region when it intervened in the Syrian civil war in September 2015. It has since resumed active naval activity in the Mediterranean and established naval and air facilities in Syria. Russia has built up new commercial ties to the Arab oil-exporting states. At the same time, Russia has played a major security role in the Libyan civil war and in providing major arms transfers to Egypt. Russia is clearly seeking region-wide influence and will almost certainly be far more aggressive in challenging the United States in the MENA region as a result of the new tensions unleashed by the war in Ukraine.

The Impact of China

China is emerging as a major global power that is substantially larger than Russia and can compete directly with the United States. China is a growing competitor in the MENA region—which it sees as a key source of oil and gas imports through 2050. China has a growing presence in the Indian Ocean and now has a small naval base in Djibouti on the southern coast of the Red Sea.

China also is actively trying to market its new and more advanced arms and military technology to MENA states, and it is reported to be marketing these arms to the Arab Gulf states, seeking a military facility in Abu Dhabi, and developing a new surface-to-surface missile production facility in Saudi Arabia. While such reports are uncertain and the sales involved are small in comparison with the US sales to the same countries, China is reported to have increased its arms exports to Saudi Arabia from $35 million between 2011 and 2015 to $170 million from 2016 to 2020. China also increased its exports to the UAE from $45 million to $121 million during the same period. Other reports indicate that China became one of the five largest arms suppliers to Qatar between 2000 and 2019.[3]

As discussed later, China has also signed a major economic and security agreement with Iran, which may greatly expand its role in that country as well as create new commercial links to oil field development in Iraq.[4]

Challenges by MENA Subregion and Country

If one looks across the entire MENA region, the shifts in security and political stability since 2011 have led to important shifts in the civil side of security and stability in ways that have made many national security structures more controlling and repressive. At the same time, Algeria, Libya, Tunisia, Egypt, Syria, Lebanon, Iraq, Iran, and Yemen have spent so much on war or on building up their militaries and internal security forces that their military budgets now come at a serious cost to adequate civil and economic development. Since the beginning of 2020, the Covid-19 crisis has made this situation much worse in at least half the states in the MENA region.

It must be stressed, however, that security assistance demands and trends vary sharply by country and subregion within the MENA region. There is no easy way to illustrate the range of differences involved, but security developments in the MENA region can be broadly organized by three major subregions: North Africa, the Greater Levant, and the Persian/Arab Gulf. Each presents a somewhat different range of new problems and security assistance requirements that now drive US security assistance efforts.

The North African Subregion

Morocco and—to a lesser degree—Tunisia are America's key security partners in the North African subregion. They are nations where the main goal of US security assistance is to aid in providing stability and internal security, maintain US influence in Morocco and Tunisia, and work with European states to both preserve stability and bring an end to the Libyan civil war. Morocco has made progress in developing its military security forces, encouraging economic reform, and dealing with its Islamic extremists, but it still faces major challenges from poverty and a limited challenge from Polisario rebels in its south. Tunisia seems to have made some progress toward reform, but it remains unstable and could still be the scene of additional civil conflicts.

Algeria is a very different story. Ever since its independence from France, Algeria has been more of an army with a country than a country with an army. It also has long been dependent on Russia for its arms and some aspects of security assistance. The Arab Spring did pose major challenges to its ruling military junta, and protests led to some increases in the government's civil role. However, the military still remains the key power, Algeria still supports the Polisario against Morocco, and Russia remains its major source of arms and outside military support.

The volume of arms transfers to a given country provides a rough picture of one key aspect of its total effort in security assistance to a given recipient. A report by the Congressional Research Service indicates that Algeria has been the third-largest arms importer from Russia after India and China and that Algeria has bought advanced weapons systems, like the Iskander surface-to-surface missile, T-90S tank, Su-300PMU2 surface-to-air missile, Su-30MK fighter, and Project 636 submarine.[5] SIPRI estimates that Algeria was the eleventh-largest arms importer in the world from 2017 to 2021 and that 81 percent of its imports came from Russia versus 6.4 percent from Germany and 3.7 percent from France.[6]

Libya has steadily divided into competing hostile factions since the fall of Mu'ammar Gadhafi in 2011. It also is a country where the United States has not played any coherent role in security assistance since the assassination of the US ambassador and other US officials in 2012. While peace efforts continue, Libya plunged in 2014 into a state of civil war that has turned it into a divided, violent mess. The country is now split in two, with General Khalifa Haftar's parliament in the east and current prime minister Abdul Hamid Dbeibeh's internationally recognized government in the west.

The forces in eastern Libya are centered around the Libyan National Army (LNA), led by General Haftar, and have support from air strikes by Egypt and the UAE, as well as extensive support from both Russian and Syrian mercenaries and possibly from small elements of US commercial mercenaries. Egypt has provided fighter jets, arms, drones, and surface-to-air missiles.[7] Over 330 Russian flights provided arms, drones, and Russian and Syrian mercenary fighters during the eighteen months before early February 2020.[8]

The current Government of National Unity (GNU) is the predecessor of the General National Accord, which is composed of a mix of changing militias that are not bound by loyalty to the GNU but are rather anti-LNA. This faction has received large amounts of aid from Qatar and Turkey and some from Sudan. Turkey has provided combat ships, an airlift with at least 145 flights in 2020, armed drones, armored troop carriers, surface-to-air missiles and antiaircraft guns, some helicopter support, and extensive electronics and electronic warfare equipment, including jammers and air combat aids—as well as help in improving airbases.[9]

The Greater Levant Subregion

The US security partners in the Greater Levant subregion include Egypt, Israel, Lebanon, and Jordan, each of which is highly independent and pursues its own security interests. Israel is a close US security partner and has the most advanced military forces in the MENA region, but it is heavily dependent on US security assistance. At present, the risk of another major Arab-Israeli war seems limited, although continued sporadic clashes between Israel, various Palestinian elements, Hezbollah in Lebanon, and Assad's Syrian forces seem all too likely. As described later in this book, Egypt and Jordan represent challenges in terms of preserving US influence and their internal security, but the risk of a serious war occurring seems minimal.

Israel remains a strong, modern military power and economy that is closely tied to the United States and receives major security assistance in modernizing its forces, like the transfer of advanced F-35 fighters and support of its new air and missile defenses. Although Israel is the only MENA state with a major modern military industry, SIPRI estimates that it was the fourteenth-largest arms importer from 2017 to 2021 and that 92 percent of its arms came from the United States versus 6.9 percent from Germany and 1.0 percent from Italy.[10] Israel has improved relations with its Arab neighbors in the Gulf—and was openly recognized by Bahrain, the UAE, Sudan, and Morocco in 2020. However, Israel is deeply divided politically, and there no longer is any clear path toward a full peace with the Palestinians. Annexation has become a key issue in Israeli politics, and the Palestinian movement is deeply divided between a radical Hamas-controlled government in the Gaza—which repeatedly clashes with Israel and supports Palestinian violence in Israel proper and Jerusalem—and a Palestinian Authority that is weak and corrupt and whose security forces no longer seem to provide a basis for building an independent West Bank. The United States no longer focuses on a two-state solution and has even moved its embassy to Jerusalem. Meanwhile, Israel seems more focused on annexing more of the West Bank than revitalizing peace negotiations.

Jordan has made some reforms and remains relatively stable despite rifts within the ruling elite that manifested in spring 2021. Its military and internal security forces are effective in meeting its internal security needs, it does not face major security challenges, and it could probably count on US diplomatic and power-projection assistance if such threats emerged. It is, however, now focused heavily on special forces and has only had limited modernization of its airpower and heavy armor and artillery.

As for the other states in the Greater Levant, Egypt's popular uprising in 2011 failed to bring lasting new elements of democracy and civil rights. Like Algeria, it remains an army with a country rather than a country with an army. As Chapter 14 by General F. C. Williams shows, Egypt does remain a major US security partner, but it has shown that it can turn to France and Russia when the United States attempts to pressure it on political reform by limiting arms transfers and aid, and there is significant tension between the United States and Egypt over democracy and human rights issues.

Russia has exploited this situation to sell Egypt advanced fighters like the Mig-29M, K-52 attack helicopter, and S-300VM surface-to-air missile, and Egypt is considering the purchase of the T-90S tank and Su-35 fighter.[11] SIPRI estimates that Egypt was the third-largest arms importer in the world from 2017 to 2021 and that 41 percent came from Russia, 21 percent from France, and 15 percent from Italy. The United States did not rank among the top three.[12]

Lebanon's government has virtually disintegrated, and its economy has collapsed. Chapter 5 by Aram Nerguizian shows that Lebanon's military forces do continue to receive US and French aid, which has played a constructive role in preserving internal security, but that Hezbollah has become the nation's dominant military force—with its own steadily more advanced missile forces—and Hezbollah has ties to Iran, Syria, and Russia. Considering that Hezbollah maintains power in a deeply divided country with its own major missile forces, it is far from clear how any new government of Lebanon can achieve a level of unity, honesty, and effectiveness to bring economic reform, much less create an effective security structure that unites the country's divided factions.

Syria is still fighting one of the most destructive civil wars in modern history. However, this civil war has been going on since 2011; the Assad regime has survived and in 2022 seems to be on the edge of winning. Assad has secured victory by becoming steadily more repressive and authoritarian, by ruthlessly employing more Russian advanced air power and weapons against his own population, by relying on the use of state terrorism, and by turning to Iran, Russia, and Hezbollah for military and financial support.

Russian security assistance has played a critical role in preserving Assad's rule by providing active military support in war fighting. Russia intervened in the Syrian civil war in September 2015 and declared an established and lasting presence in December 2017. It has carried out numerous air strikes in support of pro-Assad forces, including strikes on civilians and urban areas. It has deployed Tu-95, Tu-160, and Tu-22 bombers; combat aircraft like the Su-24, Su-25, Su-34, Su-35, Su-57, MiG-29K, and IL-20; and precision-guided air weapons.[13] Russia now has lasting rights to use Hmeimim Air Base as well as use of a Syrian naval base, and it has made extensive use of Syrian bases to airlift forces and weapons to Libya.

The Assad regime has also received extensive support from Iran in terms of arms, funds, al-Quds forces, and volunteers, as well as support from the Lebanese Hezbollah. Experts differ on the levels of coordination between Iranian and Russian security assistance efforts and on the effectiveness of Iranian training efforts, but the combination of Russian, Iranian, and Hezbollah support has given the Assad regime control of most of Syria, aside from Turkish-occupied areas in the north, a small and shrinking rebel enclave in Idlib, US-supported Kurdish/Arab territories in northeast Syria, and a small Arab rebel enclave near the Jordanian border. Syrian economic development has virtually collapsed, however, and Assad still faces challenges from rebel forces in the country's northwest, a Kurdish-Arab coalition in its northeast, and pressure from Turkey on its northern border.

So far, the United States has not established any kind of clear strategy or overall security assistance effort to deal with Hezbollah, Assad's survival and the Russian presence in Syria, Iranian influence in the subregion, or Turkey's growing role in Syria, Iraq, and the region. The United States has sharply reduced its support of the Kurdish-Arab forces in Syria that helped it defeat the ISIS "caliphate." There are no clear indicators of what long-term posture Russia will deploy or what Syrian forces it will support if Assad regains full control of Syria. So far, China has no significant military presence in the subregion and has made only limited arms sales.

The Persian and Arab Gulf Subregion

In the Persian and Arab Gulf subregion, the United States has long established security partnerships with Bahrain, Oman, Qatar, Saudi Arabia, and the UAE. In theory, these states are united in a Gulf Cooperation Council (GCC). In practice, each state's military development, plans, and operations remain highly independent. Each pursues its own security interests and largely develops its own forces in its own ways. At the same time, the United States has largely withdrawn its combat forces from Iraq and Syria but still plays a direct role in aiding the Arab Gulf states in deterrence and defense against Iran and in dealing with extremism. The US naval command in Bahrain, the US air command in Qatar, and the US advisory and contract teams in Bahrain, Kuwait, Oman, Qatar, Saudi Arabia, and the UAE all play a key role in supporting each nation's security efforts and in providing aid for training, sustainability, operations, and interoperability in different forms tailored to each country's own approach to developing its security forces.

This US role in security assistance—supported by the United Kingdom and France—remains critical to the subregion's stability. The Arab Gulf states have spent decades as some of the largest arms importers in the world, and most of their recent arms purchases have come from the United States—but they are also purchases that these Arab Gulf states cannot properly maintain, operate, or support in combat without significant outside aid and support. The sheer scale of US security assistance efforts is better illustrated by the scale of US arms exports to the key Gulf military powers—all of which require major US contract support efforts to maintain the equipment, help with modernization, and create sustainable forces. While the exact numbers are uncertain, all sources agree that

Saudi Arabia is one of the world's largest arms importers, and SIPRI indicates it was the second-largest importer in the world between 2017 and 2021. The critical security assistance role of the United States is indicated by SIPRI's estimate that 82 percent of total Saudi arms are from the United States, 5.1 percent from France, and 5 percent from the United Kingdom.[14] The United States has since limited the sale of some air weapons to Saudi Arabia, which nonetheless remains a major customer.

Qatar ranked sixth in the world between 2017 and 2021, and it imported 46 percent of all its arms from the United States, 36 percent from France, and 15 percent from Italy.[15] The UAE ranked ninth in the world; it imported 61 percent of all its arms from the United States, 6.2 percent from France, and 5.3 percent from Russia.[16] Iraq, whose forces were largely Russian equipped until 2003, ranked twenty-first in the world; it imported 44 percent of all its arms from Russia, 35 percent from the United States, and 10 percent from Italy.[17] Kuwait ranked twenty-eighth in the world; it imported 56 percent of all its arms from the United States, 26 percent from France, and 9.4 percent from Italy.[18] The only major Gulf importer that did not import from the United States was Oman, which received 63 percent of all its arms from the United Kingdom, 16 percent from Turkey, and 8.1 percent from Norway.[19]

The effectiveness of US support to the Arab Gulf states is of major importance because Iran presents a major risk of war. The United States and its partners now face only limited contingency threats in North Africa and the Levant, but in the Persian and Arab Gulf subregion, the United States faces a major threat of war with Iran in addition to the threats posed by extremism, gray area operations, proxy warfare, and low-intensity clashes and combat. The United States also faces growing uncertainties as to how Iran's ties to other state and nonstate actors will evolve and how Iran will develop its future alignment and military capabilities in Syria, Iraq, and Yemen.

Iran may still acquire nuclear weapons. The Biden administration is attempting to reverse Trump's withdrawal from the Joint Comprehensive Plan of Action (JCPOA) nuclear agreement with Iran, but the success of such efforts remains uncertain, and Iran is coming steadily closer to a breakout capability to deploy nuclear weapons. This could lead the wealthier Arab Gulf states to seek their own nuclear weapons, thus affecting Israel's nuclear strategy and targeting. The United States must also consider the fact that Iran and Syria—and possibly Israel and Egypt—have chemical weapons and that the more advanced MENA states are acquiring the technology and manufacturing base to develop biological weapons.

The most immediate challenge Iran presents to the outside world, however, is its rapidly improving precision-strike capability using conventional warheads and ballistic missiles, cruise missiles, and drones—as well as new antiship missiles, submersibles, and "smart mines." Iran poses a steadily growing major missile and hybrid warfare threat to US interests in the Gulf subregion and to those of America's Arab security partners and Israel. While many of Iran's conventional military forces are still dated and lack accuracy and lethality, Iran now has a steadily growing family of precision-guided ballistic missiles and drones and highly capable irregular naval/air/missile forces in the Gulf region and the Gulf of Oman, as well as strong ties to Hezbollah in Lebanon, the Assad regime in Syria, and the Houthis in Yemen.

As a result, the southern Gulf Arab states—Bahrain, Kuwait, Oman, Qatar, the UAE, and Saudi Arabia—along with the United States, the United Kingdom, and France, must continue to prepare for a major war with Iran in which Iran can use steadily more capable missile forces, advances in antiship missiles, and hybrid naval warfare against partner and US forces and bases as well as against civil economic targets ranging from petroleum export facilities to desalination plants.

As Zoltan Barany shows in Chapter 9, "The Gulf Monarchies: Security Consumers and Providers," the Arab Gulf states continue to make massive arms imports, and the United States must not only improve its own forces but try to compensate for the lack of real-world cooperation and interoperability between the Arab Gulf states. Following the Saudi-Emirati-Bahraini-Egyptian-led boycott of Qatar that began in 2017 and ended in early 2021, senior leaders have since been carefully photographed as "friends." Nevertheless, the GCC remains a military fiction with little effective military integration and interoperability. The GCC cannot fight cohesively except under US leadership and by relying on US command-and-control as well as intelligence, surveillance, and warning capabilities.

As yet, Russia and China do not play a major military or security assistance role in Iran, but they do export arms—and their security relations may be changing. Iran has recently procured Russian aid in modernizing its land-based surface-to-air missile forces and air defense systems, and UN sanctions against conventional arms transfers to Iran expired in late 2020.[20] Russia and China can now export far more advanced weapons and military systems, and both China and North Korea seem to have played an important role as the sources of Iran's family of missiles and drones in the past.

More broadly, Iran is actively competing with the United States for influence in Iraq—a competition where Iranian success could create an axis of influence that extends from Iran, through Iraq, Syria, and Lebanon, to Yemen. The United States has worked with the government of Iraq to defeat the efforts of ISIS to dominate Iraq and eastern Syria—effectively "winning" a second war against extremism from 2015 to 2018 that matches its victories between 2005 and 2011.

Although the Biden administration has tried to forge a more stable and strategic partnership with Iraq as a priority, it has not advanced any major successful initiatives, and Iraq's future status is increasingly uncertain. The United States provided critical ground and air support as well as advisory support and arms to Iraqi military operations against ISIS after 2014, when ISIS conquered parts of Iraq and eastern Syria to establish a proto-state or "caliphate." The United States has not, however, established any clear, lasting security partnerships since it helped to defeat the "caliphate" in 2017 and 2018.

This defeat of the ISIS "caliphate" in eastern Syria and western Iraq has produced limited effects and has not prevented ongoing attacks by the remnants of ISIS's forces. It also has not united Iraq or led to more effective Iraqi governance or broad economic recovery. It has instead led to growing competition between the United States and Iran for political and military influence in Iraq.

The United States also has not reached any agreement with the Iraqi government on a future strategic partnership. The United States has repeatedly discussed creating such a partnership with senior Iraqi officials, but it has not reacted decisively to attacks from pro-Iranian PMFs. The United States also left most of its joint basing facilities in Iraq in 2020, stating that it had reduced its active military presence in both Iraq and eastern Syria to a nominal 2,500 personnel in January 2021, and it seems to have made major further cuts since that time.[21]

US arms transfers to the Iraqi army and air force have produced only limited success, and they have experienced major problems in support and sustainment. SIPRI reports that Russia is now Iraq's major arms supplier, that Iraq ranked as the world's twenty-first-largest importer from 2017 to 2021, and that Russia provided 44 percent of its arms, the United States 35 percent, and Italy 10 percent.[22] As for the future, Iran may become the major outside presence in Iraq, although Turkey has a major influence in the country's north.

An Emerging Red Sea Subregion?

The Red Sea has long been an unstable region, and the Yemen Arab Republic is a desperately poor country that has suffered from repeated civil wars and civil conflicts. It was formerly divided into the Yemen

Arab Republic (North Yemen), and the People's Democratic Republic of Yemen (South Yemen) that fought repeated border wars. Its fragile unity only occurred in May 1990 due to the internal political and economic collapse of the People's Democratic Republic of Yemen.

It is now in a state of civil war that began with the fall of Ali Abdullah Saleh—the country's former dictator, or "president"—in February 2012. This led to a series of power struggles that divided the country into warring factions. The key faction that came to dominate the western part of the country was the Houthis, a Shi'ite tribal faction backed by Iran. The Houthis' main opponent has since been Saudi Arabia and the UAE as well as their military forces and airpower, although the Houthis' official opponent has been a rival Yemeni government in exile. This government was led by Saleh's former vice president Abdrabbuh Mansur Hadi until 2021, but Hadi proved to be as ineffective as he was unpopular, and he resigned without any effective replacement. A number of other factions—including al-Qaeda in the Arabian Peninsula and a complex mix of other tribal and extremist factions—are fighting in other regions of the country, along with factions that call for an independent South Yemen.

Saudi Arabia and the UAE supported the Hadi faction—with US support in the form of arms transfers, intelligence and targeting support, and airborne refueling—until 2021, but their efforts have largely failed. The UAE and Saudi Arabia never cooperated effectively, and the UAE has since limited its involvement while pursuing a strategy intended to solidify its position around the Bab el-Mandeb Strait. The United States ceased to provide targeting, precision-guided air munitions, and refueling support to Saudi Arabia in February 2021 because of Saudi air strikes on civilians and what many in the United States felt was the Saudi and Emirati role in creating a rising humanitarian crisis.

In contrast, Iran successfully backed the Houthis, who came to dominate Yemen's heavily populated northwest and threatened the limited areas controlled by the Hadi forces. The Houthis have outfought the Saudis in the Saudi-Yemeni border area, and Iran has helped to create a new threat from Houthi-operated precision-guided missiles and drones. In the process, Iran's support of the Houthis gave it a growing role in the Red Sea/Bab el-Mandeb area.

While various peace negotiations continue, the end result may become a new Red Sea subregion in the MENA military balance. Given the instability of the African Red Sea states—which include an unstable Sudan, a warring Ethiopia in a brutal civil war, and an unstable Eritrea—the security of the Red Sea is increasingly unpredictable. So is the role of outside powers. China has acquired a new port and naval base in Djibouti, and Russia deployed paramilitary forces to Sudan and signed an agreement with the Sudanese government to build a naval base there in February 2021. As a result, the United States has discussed some new areas of security assistance with both Djibouti and Sudan, although it has not announced any major plans to deal with such threats.

Adapting Security Assistance to an Ongoing Revolution in Security Forces

What all the countries in the MENA region do have in common is the need for security assistance in creating new forms of military forces. Some of these changes have been touched on earlier, and needs do vary by country, but MENA military forces are all entering a different world.

From roughly the end of the colonial era after World War II through the First Gulf War in 1991, MENA countries focused on developing conventional military forces and fighting conventional wars. Post–World War II security and military developments began largely as efforts to develop modern land, air, and naval forces for the first time. Military development then focused on actual war fighting in the case of the major Arab-Israeli wars through 1982 and in the Persian/Arab Gulf states after the start of the Iran-Iraq War in 1980. Finally, the deployment of major outside combat forces for joint warfare and strategic partnerships with MENA countries occurred in liberating Kuwait, fighting in Iraq, and dealing with contingency plans of a major conflict with Iran.

These military dynamics have changed steadily since the First Gulf War in 1991. So has the role of outside states in deploying forces in the region, projecting power, and providing security assistance. Outside support has gone far beyond arms transfers, limited security financing, training and education, and the peacetime support of conventional forces. The role of security assistance has steadily broadened, and several trends are affecting most of the region.

The MENA Region and the Ongoing Revolutions in Military Affairs

The most advanced MENA military forces are realizing that the ability to manage joint warfare, use advanced sensors, and integrate their battle management is essential to the effective use of their major combat elements. Like their US counterparts, some of the planners involved feel that such changes can be more important than acquiring even the most advanced major combat platforms at a time when many states are becoming increasingly vulnerable unless they maintain advanced joint warfare and battle-management capabilities.

Most MENA states still lag in such areas, but several MENA states—most notably the UAE—are seeking US and other outside aid in acquiring a wide range of new systems for multidomain warfare, space capabilities, battle management, secure communications, and combat intelligence and targeting. These systems can provide far more interoperability between national forces and can improve a given MENA nation's ability to conduct more effective joint warfare.

Outside powers increasingly provide military and security assistance in the form of advanced training aids, readiness indicators, and command post and field training exercises. This form of security assistance can range from advanced simulators to support in training for large-scale and high-technology combat—providing capabilities, equipment, and experience that many recipient countries lack or are too small to develop on their own.

The United States, major European powers, and Russia use military advisors and the equivalent of contractors to support both the most advanced weapons and the full range of military technology and systems over their entire life cycle. It is also clear that supporting such systems during intense combat will be a critical part of security assistance. This reflects the fact that modern weapons need to be procured, upgraded, and supported on a far more intensive and expensive life cycle basis than in the past.

The cost of such support and modifications over the life of a weapon—while rarely reported—can now exceed the original procurement cost of the system. The ongoing modification and improvement of weapons—sometimes called the multi-stage improvement program—has become more the rule than the exception, as there is a need for outside aid in maintaining complex systems and supporting them once they are engaged in combat.

Long-Range Precision-Guided Missiles and Weapons

The Iranian and Houthi use of long-range precision-guided weapons against industrial targets in Saudi Arabia—as well as the increasing development and deployment of precision-guided missiles, cruise missiles, and drones throughout the world—is leading to another major change taking place in MENA forces and their need for security assistance. As the fighting in Ukraine and between Armenia and Azerbaijan has shown, precision-guided and "smart" missiles of all ranges, as well as unmanned combat aerial vehicles (UCAVs), can inflict serious strategic damage to armor, ships, aircraft, key military facilities, and civil/economic infrastructure facilities. This development has created a broad demand for more complex and advanced missile and air defense systems throughout the MENA region—all of which require substantial changes in security assistance.

Missile Defense and "Layered" Artillery, Rocket, and Air Defense Weapons

As purchases by Israel, Saudi Arabia, the UAE, and Iran have shown, these advances in ballistic and cruise missiles—coupled with the proliferation of shorter-range precision rockets, artillery weapons, and air-launched systems—are leading MENA countries both to buy more advanced air and missile defense systems and to examine new mixes of missile, air, and counter-artillery-rocket defenses.

Advances in defense, however, lead to increases in the use of offensive systems, particularly those designed to exploit any gaps in layered defenses. Every advance in defense will lead to an interaction against the steadily rising mixes of new UCAVs, more accurate rockets, and missiles with precision-strike capabilities. They too are leading some MENA countries to examine new mixes of missile and air defenses.

Short-Range Precisions-Guided and Smart Systems

As weapons like the javelin have shown during the fighting in Ukraine, other "smart" weapons are coming to supplement or replace major weapons platforms, and they are increasing the need for complex battle management, command and control, and joint all-domain operations. These include some shorter-range systems like antiarmor guided weapons, man-portable antiair missiles, antiship missiles, and "smart mines." These systems are increasingly being used to arm drones and unmanned air, land, and naval platforms—creating a steadily increasing risk that major weapons platforms can enhance the ability to arm non-state actors, light forces, and extremists/terrorists more effectively and at a lower cost. The arming of Iranian forces with more effective antiship missiles and smart mines and the steadily increasing use of relatively low-cost drones throughout the MENA region are only a few examples of such changes.

Cyber and Information Warfare

Most MENA states are creating some capability to wage cyber, internal security, and information operations and warfare. Depending on the country, they may rely heavily on outside support—often on commercial vendors and contractors that come from a wide variety of different countries. Some countries, like Israel and Iran, have developed relatively advanced domestic capabilities for cyber and information operations—often with links to intelligence. Some have sought support from the United States and European states. Others have bought at least some support from other sources—not always knowing the level of control or influence from outside governments—to enhance internal security efforts and public information campaigns in developing technical sophistication, sensor coverage, and software. Reporting on the levels of such activity, however, remains limited.

Security Assistance and Access to Advanced Weapons

In the past, the United States and its MENA, European, and Asian strategic partners have benefited from privileged access to advanced weapons and military technology. This includes access to the most advanced combat aircraft as well as to the full range of precision-guided conventional weapons from man-portable to long-range land and naval attack systems that can destroy high-value targets anywhere in another country's territory.

So far, this privileged access to US weapons and military technology has given US strategic partners a major advantage, but there is no guarantee that US security assistance efforts will continue or that US strategic partners can count on such advantages in the future. Russia and China can also sell or provide advanced weapons, and nations like Iran or nonstate actors like Hezbollah and the Houthis have shown that they too can acquire and successfully operate these weapons.

Much will depend on Russian and Chinese willingness to provide such weapons and technology in the future and whether they will do so at a relatively low cost in order to exploit countervailing powers and to carry out "spoiler" operations where the objective is to increase the threat and the cost to the United States and its partners rather than to "win" tactical or strategic victories.

Security Assistance to Irregular Forces

Other kinds of change are also affecting security assistance. A variety of new forms of nonstate actors and paramilitary forces are appearing in the MENA region. The United States has helped to create such forces in eastern Syria. Russia has deployed state-controlled mercenaries, specifically the Wagner private military company, to Libya. Iran has deployed "volunteers," including both non-Iranian mercenaries and Iranian elements, to Syria. Syria and Iran work alongside and arm the Lebanese Hezbollah. Iran arms the Houthis in Yemen and supports PMFs in Iraq. The United States and Arab states have funded, trained, and armed Syrian rebel groups. MENA countries and outside powers increasingly make use of proxies and nonstate actors, while proxies and nonstate actors increasingly make use of MENA countries and outside powers.

Population and Population Warfare

Wars in the MENA region have always had an impact on the civil population. The wars that led to Israel's creation as a state displaced numerous Palestinians, and the six day Arab-Israeli War of 1967 gave Israel control of a divided Jerusalem and the Palestinian areas in the West Bank and Gaza. The Lebanese civil war restructured that country's political system, the Algerian civil war had a major impact on its citizens, and the Iran-Iraq War affected many Iraqi and Iranian civilians and was fought, to some extent, along sectarian lines.

The 2003 invasion of Iraq and the creation of a war between the US forces and the new Iraqi government with Sunni extremist factions established a different precedent. It had a direct war-fighting impact on civilians. This includes fighting that temporarily partitioned Baghdad, major urban warfare in western Iraq, the near destruction or exile of religious minorities, and crippling damage to the Iraqi economy. This focus on using civilians as human shields and fighting directly in highly populated areas was then repeated in the war against ISIS, with even more serious urban warfare and economic impacts.

Population warfare in the Syrian civil war that began in March 2011 created even more civilian casualties, refugees, and internally displaced persons. It has led to the systematic use of air and helicopter strikes on civilian populations and targets, the use of poison gas, a long series of brutal urban battles against Syrian rebels, and the deliberate creation of new groups of refugees and displaced persons. It also created a series of rebel enclaves where civilians have often been targets, humanitarian aid has been blocked, medical facilities and infrastructure have been attacked, and the population has been forced to leave.

At the same time, the MENA region's military dynamics and security assistance needs have been affected by the fact that extremist and terrorist factions, as well as a wide range of rebel groups, can hide among the general population and essentially use civilians as human shields. This has led to the extensive use of precision-guided air and missile strikes in areas where civilians are present, and there is often no clear military alternative to striking at targets that do not present a risk to civilians. Any effort to substitute ground forces and ground warfare will almost inevitably lead to far more serious civilian casualties and collateral damage.

So far, there is a tendency inside the United States and in many European powers to deny the reality of this dilemma and the fact that population warfare means having to target opponents that use civilians as defensive weapons. Libya, Syria, Iraq, and Yemen, however, have all shown that population warfare has become a key military dynamic in the MENA region, and security assistance must adjust to help US partners fight in ways that target the enemy with far fewer civilian casualties and far less civilian damage.

Counterproliferation

Finally, the proliferation of weapons of mass destruction involves security assistance as well. This can take the form of security assistance in arms control, providing defenses, and extending deterrence. Counterproliferation also raises serious questions about the current efforts to provide MENA nations with nuclear power reactors and about the steadily widening scale of national biotechnology and chemical production facilities.

So far, the region faces only moderate near-term nuclear threats. Israel has long had nuclear-armed missile systems. Iran is acquiring the capability to build and deploy a wide range of such missiles and drone systems, and it still has many elements of a nuclear weapons program. Iraq made extensive use of chemical weapons during the Iran-Iraq War. The Assad regime in Syria has used chemical weapons repeatedly in the Syrian civil war while also attempting to covertly build a nuclear reactor that was destroyed by Israel in 2007. Israel and Egypt seem to have both a biological and chemical weapons development program, although those may be largely defensive in character.

Here, it should be noted that while international controls on nuclear technology remain significant—and the JCPOA would have produced a major impact on Iran's efforts—the US withdrawal from the JCPOA led Iran to take steps that radically cut the time it would take to actually produce nuclear weapons, and it is far from clear that the negotiations over renewing the JCPOA will produce meaningful results. Countries like Pakistan are producing weapons at rates that could allow them to start selling such weapons. Egypt and a number of Arab Gulf countries are procuring nuclear reactors or have shown an interest in nuclear power plants that make little sense when used as cost-effective sources of power and instead could be a prelude to proliferation if Iran actively resumes its full nuclear weapons program. As for chemical weapons, Syria has used such weapons against its rebels and even its own population. Iran declared that it had chemical weapons when it joined the Chemical Weapons Convention, and Egypt and Israel may have such weapons.

There are no reliable data on biological weapons holdings and development efforts, but it seems likely that Egypt and Israel have explored such weapons at least as part of their biological defense efforts, and—as with the technology needed for chemical weapons—most transfers do not require security assistance as they are now available through open, commercial transactions. Iraq made extensive use of chemical weapons against Iran and Iraq's Kurds during the Iran-Iraq War, and it is clear that the days when effective international controls existed on many key aspects of the technology and equipment used in biological and chemical weapons are long over.

Changing the Security Assistance Role and Impact of the United States

So far, US security assistance efforts have only begun to address these issues as the US military tries to come to grips with the need to change its own forces to meet all of the same challenges in new forms of warfare, and the United States has focused more in recent years on reducing its presence in the MENA region than on meeting these new challenges. This prior buildup in the MENA area has been followed by something of a "build-down," although this has been driven more by the end of the fighting in Afghanistan and the war against ISIS in Iraq than by cuts in the more lasting aspects of US presence and security assistance efforts.

The fall of the shah in 1979, the 1980–1988 Iran-Iraq War, and Saddam Hussein's invasion of Kuwait in 1990 led the United States to deploy a mix of military forces, advisors, and arms transfers that made US strategic partnerships in the Gulf the de facto equivalent of active military alliances.

After the beginning of the Iran-Iraq War in 1980—and certainly after the massive buildup of US forces to liberate Kuwait in the First

Gulf War in 1991—the United States built up a major set of US deployments and contingency bases in the Gulf region. It focused on building up its Gulf Arab strategic partners through massive arms sales, training, and joint exercises. And the United States created major naval battle-management and command centers for the 5th Fleet in Bahrain, including advanced air warfare command centers in Saudi Arabia and then at Al Udeid Air Base in Qatar.

The United States further expanded these contingency bases and facilities after the al-Qaeda attacks on the Pentagon and World Trade Center in 2001 to help support the war in Afghanistan, and the United States simultaneously expanded its security assistance to cover a wide range of new counterterrorism and counterextremism activities throughout the region. The United States again expanded its presence, contingency agreements, arms sales, and advisory roles from 2003 onward as a result of the US-led invasion of Iraq. This invasion brought the United States into two major cycles of war in Iraq as an attempt to create effective Iraqi national forces and to expand country-by-country efforts to deal with the consequences of the political uprisings in the region that began in 2011.

Most of these developments, however, were ad hoc efforts to deal with each developing crisis. The United States largely reacted to outside events over a period of nearly three decades. It did not develop cohesive structures or strategies for most such efforts. The individual US security assistance efforts in the MENA region were divided and constantly changing, although military progress still took place. The United States also did not develop lasting structures for strategic partnerships once ISIS seemed to be largely defeated and the United States no longer needed to support the war in Afghanistan.

The level of US commitment and security assistance to the MENA region then became significantly more uncertain after the Trump administration announced a new national security strategy in 2017 and a national defense strategy in 2018, but these were both focused on China and Russia.[23] Both named Iran as a threat, but neither advanced any practical strategy, force plans, programs, or budgets for dealing with the MENA region. The Trump administration did cut US combat forces after defeating the ISIS "caliphate" in Iraq, but it never really defined what a future US regional security presence and assistance effort should be.

As of the spring of 2022, the United States still had no clear plans for shaping its future force posture and security assistance efforts in the region. The Biden administration stated it was developing a new strategy soon after it came to office, and it announced an interim national security strategic guidance document in March 2021. It called for a renewal of the US emphasis on strategic partnerships, which the Trump administration had seriously undercut, but had the same focus on Russia and China as the Trump administration and limited its comments on the MENA region to saying that the United States would leave Afghanistan and that

> as we position ourselves to deter our adversaries and defend our interests, working alongside our partners, our presence will be most robust in the Indo-Pacific and Europe. In the Middle East, we will right-size our military presence to the level required to disrupt international terrorist networks, deter Iranian aggression, and protect other vital U.S. interests. A Global Posture Review will guide these choices, ensuring they are in keeping with our strategic objectives, values, and resources. And we will make these adjustments consistent with the safety of our personnel and in close consultation with our allies and partners.[24]

The Biden administration stated later that it would advance a full national strategy in late 2021 or spring 2022, but it submitted its Fiscal Year 2023 defense budget request in March 2022 without any indication that such a document was nearing completion. The need to respond to the Russian invasion of Ukraine may have led the administration to delay issuing such a document, but there has been no clear indication of how the United States would deal with either a broad security assistance policy or the MENA region.

As of April 2022, the administration was still focused largely on renewing the JCPOA, although it received both uncertain support from Congress in making such changes and questionable support from Russia and China. The Biden administration and major elements of Congress also had serious differences over human rights issues with key strategic partners like Egypt, Saudi Arabia, and the UAE. Furthermore, some of America's partners have made it informally clear that they had growing doubts about the US commitment to an enduring military presence and security commitment in many countries in the MENA region.

The Impact of the Uncertain Trends in US Strategy and Security Assistance

The United States also needs to understand that America's strategic partners in the region have reason for concern. From 2019 onward, the Trump and Biden administrations have sought to minimize the US military presence and security assistance efforts in Syria, Iraq, and Afghanistan. These policies led to major cuts in the US military presence in Syria and Iraq. The number of US troops in Iraq had peaked at 170,300 in 2007. It dropped to 47,305 in 2010, dipped to a low of around 1,000 in 2014, rose back to some 3,500 by December 2015, and then increased to 5,000 forces by April 2015. In December 2019—at the point when the ISIS "caliphate" had been defeated—it was well over 6,000 in Iraq and Syria. This number did not include the large numbers of civilians and contractors, some special forces and other combat personnel, and civilian intelligence officers.[25] This total was reduced to 3,000 by late 2020, and it further dropped to a nominal 2,500 personnel by January 15, 2021—although the real totals included some 750 to 1,000 added troops in both cases.[26]

The full details of the Biden administration's withdrawal of US forces from Afghanistan and forces in Syria and Iraq since early 2021 remain unclear, as do the levels of contractor effort and the deployment of some elements of special forces and intelligence personnel.

Accordingly, America's strategic partners in MENA have reason to be uncertain about the continuing level of US commitment to strategic partnerships in the region and to push back when US pressure affects their military and political priorities. Moreover, if the United States often had valid reasons to question individual MENA military and internal security priorities, MENA states have good reasons to question US resolve and capabilities given US actions in Libya, Syria, Iraq, and Yemen.

At the same time, such concerns need to be kept in careful perspective. The net US presence has actually increased in some MENA countries. It is also important to point out that the figures the United States announces for its personnel levels in the MENA countries only cover military and civilian personnel assigned on a lasting basis and do not cover the personnel onboard ships, the large volumes of commercial contractors, the personnel deployed for military exercises, the civilian intelligence personnel, or the special forces and other military personnel deployed for special missions.

Moreover, some official documents issued by the Biden administration indicate that any near-term cuts to US forces, facilities, and security assistance in the MENA region may be limited and that US capabilities to rapidly project power into the MENA region will actually increase. The 2021 *Annual Threat Assessment of the U.S. Intelligence Community* makes clear that the United States does continue to see Iran and extremist and terrorist groups as major threats.[27]

While the details of the Biden administration's efforts to make a full assessment of its strategy and security assistance plans for the MENA region remain classified, a November 29, 2021, press statement issued by the Department of Defense on the global force posture does seem to indicate that there are no plans to make major further cuts in the US posture in the MENA region and that the administration does plan to increase conventional US air and missile precision-strike capabilities in ways that could potentially provide major new forms of support to its strategic partners.[28]

Less clear is whether the Biden administration can deal with all the challenges in funding US military and security assistance activities in the MENA region as well as a new force that can meet the growing challenges from China and Russia and the civil challenges from Covid-19 in the face of the political "war fatigue" caused by America's "long wars" in Iraq and its defeat in Afghanistan. Such a new force may not be cheap. Iran remains a major military challenge. The Russian presence in Syria may well result in a final victory of the Assad regime and a new Syrian threat. There is a real risk that Iraq may align with Iran and Syria. The civil war in Yemen continues. Moreover, the risk of nuclear proliferation remains.

President Biden also needs to be more realistic about his emphasis on human rights and political reform. The United States must accept the real-world limits to what it can actually accomplish. Success means dealing with each partner on the basis of its own priorities, national political structure, and approach to security—which often has an authoritarian character. The United States will have to adapt its efforts in dealing with a given country to suit the wishes of its ruling elite and the character of its political system and internal security system—often authoritarian and repressive. The United States can urge countries to make reforms, be more liberal and less repressive, and focus on popular needs and freedoms, but it can scarcely compel them. It must adapt to their priorities in reshaping and equipping their security forces, accept the fact they often have different approaches to human rights and the rule of law, focus on the areas where US influence can have a positive effect, and make many compromises in the process.

Shaping an Uncertain Future

In summary, much will depend on the Biden administration's ability to develop convincing, real-world plans for both a new US posture in the

MENA region and a new approach to security assistance. The United States must restore confidence in its willingness to maintain its commitments in the MENA region—particularly in the Gulf. It must show it can aid its strategic partners in times of war or crisis and provide them with effective security assistance.

This may take at least several years. As of spring 2022, US strategy focused on areas outside the MENA region and the challenges of security assistance within it. The Russian invasion of Ukraine led to a major revival of the US focus on NATO, while the Biden administration continued the Trump administration's strategic focus on building up the US capability to deal with China in the Indo-Pacific. It was also clear that the United States would have to make major changes in its force posture as a result of the war in Ukraine. Yet, it was far from clear what these costs would be or how they would affect US attention and resources devoted to the MENA region.

Clearly the military and security forces in every MENA country will continue to change in size, structure, and force posture as the world goes through a continuing revolution in military affairs. Every MENA state that is not consumed by civil war is already adapting its military forces to new military tactics and technology, including more advanced forms of battle management, intelligence, surveillance, targeting, communication, and use of artificial intelligence. Each current US strategic partner in the MENA region is also aware that cooperation with the United States and with other military forces in the region will require it to adapt to the new forms of joint all-domain warfare that are reshaping the capabilities of the United States, China, Russia, and the rest of the world's more advanced military powers.

These shifts are transforming the security assistance needs of every MENA partner state. As a result, every partner country will need help in creating its own approach to creating new systems of command and control, battle management, secure communications, dependence on space systems, and capabilities for joint all-domain operations. Each partner must be helped to find its own path to dealing with the advances in military software, in uses of artificial intelligence, and in all the other aspects of what the United States has come to call joint all-domain operations.

Notes

1. Emmott, "EU Rapid Deployment Force."
2. Wezeman, Kuimova, and Wezeman, *Trends in International Arms Transfers, 2021.*

3. Shanif, "Strategic Maneuvering."
4. Tiezzi, "China-Iran Strategic Cooperation Agreement."
5. Bowen, "Russian Arms Sales and Defense Industry."
6. Wezeman, Kuimova, and Wezeman, *Trends in International Arms Transfers, 2021.*
7. Roblin, "You Missed This."
8. Miller et al., "At the Mercy of Foreign Powers."
9. Ibid.
10. Wezeman, Kuimova, and Wezeman, *Trends in International Arms Transfers, 2021.*
11. Bowen, "Russian Arms Sales and Defense Industry."
12. Wezeman, Kuimova, and Wezeman, *Trends in International Arms Transfers, 2021.*
13. Jones et al., "Moscow's War in Syria."
14. Wezeman, Kuimova, and Wezeman, *Trends in International Arms Transfers, 2021.*
15. Ibid.
16. Ibid.
17. Ibid.
18. Ibid.
19. Ibid.
20. Czulda, "Is Iran Going on an Arms Shopping Spree"; SIPRI, "UN Arms Embargo on Iran, April 7, 2021, https://www.sipri.org/databases/embargoes/un_arms_embargoes/iran.
21. Garamone, "U.S. Complete Troop-Level Drawdown."
22. Wezeman, Kuimova, and Wezeman, *Trends in International Arms Transfers, 2021.*
23. White House, "National Security Strategy of the United States of America"; Mattis, "Summary of the 2018 National Defense Strategy of the United States of America."
24. White House, "Interim National Security Strategic Guidance."
25. Berger, "Invaders, Allies, Occupiers, Guests."
26. Garamone, "U.S. Complete Troop-Level Drawdown"; Lead Inspector General, *Quarterly Report to Congress, October 1, 2020, to December 31, 2020,* SIGAR, https://www.sigpr.gov/sites/sigpr/files/2021-02/SIGPR-Quarterly-Report-to-Congress-December-31-2020.pdf.
27. Office of the Director of National Intelligence, *Annual Threat Assessment,* 12, 15, 25.
28. US Department of Defense, "DoD Concludes 2021 Global Posture Review."

3

Political Drivers of Demand for Security Assistance

Glenn E. Robinson

MANY YEARS AGO, I HAD A STUDENT—A MILITARY OFFICER FROM ONE of the small Arab monarchies of the Persian Gulf—who thought it a waste for his country to be spending so lavishly on purchases of top-end weapons systems. Given its small size, he reasoned, it could not withstand an invasion by any of its big neighbors, no matter how many of the latest American fighter jets it purchased. The Americans, he argued, would not want to see any of the powerful countries of the region swallow up his country in a military campaign, so the best and most efficient use of resources would be to make sure his country's defense infrastructure was completely interoperable with American systems and logistics. His strategy was to turn his country into something akin to a forward operating base that the Americans could use at any moment to repel an invasion, to complement the US forces already stationed there. This would be far cheaper than buying large amounts of top-quality military hardware in what would be a vain attempt at self-defense. The savings could be used for social advancement.

This story succinctly captures the common disconnect in the Middle East and North Africa (MENA) between realistic defense strategies and the demand for security assistance. Often, weapons purchases by MENA countries do not seem to address obvious and real national security vulnerabilities. National security strategies, which should guide demand for relevant assistance from the United States and other countries, often appear either nonexistent or irrelevant to the desired forms of security assistance sought by MENA regimes. Sought-after and prestigious weapons systems are rarely consistent with actual national security needs and strategies.

This chapter makes two broad arguments with regard to security assistance to MENA countries. First, in order to understand this common disconnect between specific demands for security assistance and actual national security needs, I argue that the demand for security assistance in recipient countries is largely driven by political considerations, not actual security requirements. Specifically, demand is largely determined by internal political calculations about what best serves regime interests, including regime survival against potential internal foes from within and without the regime. Those political calculations are fundamentally shaped by regime type, of which the three dominant types are identified and discussed: oil monarchies, repressive republics, and flawed democracies.

Second, the capacity to reform this mismatched system is not found in the recipient countries as those regimes have every interest in continuing the current system that serves their narrow political interests. Rather, the capacity for reform is only meaningfully found on the supply side, primarily in the United States (as the preeminent supplier of security assistance to MENA). But even on the supply side, there are serious obstacles to real reform in the security assistance system even though there is wide agreement that enhanced national security of allied countries is (or should be) the foremost objective of security assistance.[1] Thus, there are conflicting fundamental objectives between the supply and demand sides of security assistance: each side wants something quite different from the arrangement—a historical paradox identified by Stephanie Cronin.[2] This disconnect between party goals is not just a scholarly concern but impacts how practitioners do their jobs, as both F. C. "Pink" Williams and John Zavage demonstrate in Part 4 of this book.

This disconnect between the forms of security assistance sought by MENA regimes and the nature of actual national security threats that are not meaningfully addressed by the forms of security assistance deepens further upon inspection. Specifically, large amounts of security assistance have only periodically led to enhanced effectiveness on the battlefield. By many measures, MENA is the most heavily armed region in the world. For example, MENA countries represent nine of the thirteen countries around the world with the highest military spending as a share of gross domestic product (GDP) in 2019.[3] Indeed, the top five, and six of the top seven, are all MENA countries: Oman, Saudi Arabia, Algeria, Kuwait, Israel, and Jordan. A similar story is told when looking at major arms imports around the world in the 2016–2020 period: five of the nine largest arms importers around the globe are MENA countries (Saudi Arabia, Egypt, Algeria, Qatar, and the United Arab Emirates). These five MENA countries alone accounted for 28 percent of all arms purchases around the world between 2016 and 2020. And the relative pace of arms purchases has grown much more rapidly in MENA than anywhere else in the world over the past decade: from 2011 to 2015, the MENA countries accounted for 26 percent of all major arms imports around the world, a share that rose to 33 percent in the 2016–2020 period.

These figures do not even account for all of the security assistance purchased or otherwise provided by suppliers. For example, US security assistance to MENA goes well beyond foreign military sales to include the US military presence in the region (primarily in the Gulf), which is designed, in part, to protect allied regimes; foreign internal defense (FID) assistance, which is often designed to train local forces in counterterrorism (CT) and counterinsurgency techniques; and a significant web of nongovernmental American contractors who help train local military and security forces.

This level of security assistance to MENA countries from the United States and other actors has only occasionally enhanced the effectiveness of MENA forces to fight and defeat foreign adversaries. Examples of poor military performance in spite of abundant armaments include Saudi Arabia, which, with the richest collection of top-end American weapons systems available, has been unable to defeat the ragtag Houthi forces in Yemen since initiating a war there in 2015.[4] Indeed, the Saudi military has periodically engaged Houthi forces since 2004 and has invariably come up short.[5] Cutting-edge US military communications systems have not compelled Saudi land forces to effectively communicate with their air forces. Nor did UAE forces fare particularly well in Yemen, despite being stocked with advanced American weapons systems; it should be noted, however, that the UAE had different strategic goals in Yemen than did the Saudis.[6] Further north, the rebuilt Iraqi military—at a cost of billions of dollars—folded and fled in 2014 at the first sight of a few hundred Islamic State of Iraq and Syria (ISIS) fighters on the outskirts of Mosul. It took concerted American and Iranian assistance over the next three years to rebuild the Iraqi army (yet again) to the point where it could drive out a band of fighters with no air force, no navy, little in the way of heavy armor (only what they could capture), and even less in the way of professional training.[7] Syria's military, never a match for Israel, had to resort to barrel bombs, chemical weapons, and the Russian air force to (mostly) defeat an insurrection among its civilian population.[8]

Egypt's military, the largest in the Arab world, is widely seen among external professionals to have a low capacity to fight a war, as Williams suggests in Chapter 14. Egypt's assistance to General Khalifa Haftar's forces in Libya, fighting against the internationally recognized government in Tripoli, did not save Haftar's forces from defeat.[9]

This paradox of heavily armed states with low capacities to fight and win wars and low-intensity conflicts is best explained by the political nature of the demand for weapons systems, although other explanations are occasionally proffered. For example, some studies have usefully focused on the low professionalization of many officer corps in the Arab world; while individual officers may be excellent, the structural conditions in those corps may encourage low capacity. The most obvious example of this is when officers are recruited based not on their abilities but rather on their ethnic, religious, tribal, or other immutable characteristics. Famously, the Syrian officer corps is overwhelmingly drawn from the 'Alawi ethnoreligious population from which the ruling Assad family hails, in spite of the 'Alawis constituting just 12 percent of Syria's population. When Jordan converted to an all-volunteer military in the early 1990s, one result—almost certainly intended—was that the officer corps shifted over time from one that included both East Bank and Palestinian Jordanians to one with only a tiny percentage of Jordanians of Palestinian heritage, even though they make up a majority of the country's population.[10] The officer corps in Iraq under Saddam Hussein was overwhelmingly Tikriti; in the post-Hussein period, it has transitioned to a primarily Shia officer corps, backed up by an exclusively Shia militia (*al-hashd al-sha'bi*). Tribal affiliation is a critical criterion for the construction of the officer corps for all armies on the Arabian Peninsula, as Zoltan Barany demonstrates in Chapter 9.

The incentive structure in these circumstances is tribal or ethnic loyalty, not capacity building under a genuinely national army. But such parochialized armies are not always the case in MENA, as some countries have built armies that are widely seen as national in their composition, not merely representative of a dominant group. Egypt and Tunisia, for example, have militaries that are much more representative of their national populations, so that parochial loyalty to an ethnic group or tribe is not a characteristic of the incentive structures for officers. Compare these two cases with Syria, and one can more readily understand why the Arab Spring events in 2011 quickly went massively violent in Syria in a way that they never did in Tunisia and Egypt.

But the more compelling answer to our paradox is based on the inherently political—not strategic—nature of the demand for security assistance. That is, MENA regimes often make security assistance decisions based on calculations about what is in the regime's best political interest rather than what is in the national strategic interest. Finely calculated strategic threat assessments tend to give way to calculations of regime survival, of coup-proofing, and of mitigating social or military unrest. Thus, there is often a disconnect between the kind of military that is built and how it is supplied, on the one hand, and the requirements for fighting and winning wars, on the other. In some cases, top regime leaders seek to placate military leadership through the purchase of prestige US weapons systems, not because of a particular national security threat but rather for domestic political tranquility within the regime. Political strategies for security assistance that focus on coup- or rebellion-proofing will concentrate demands for assistance more on FID systems than big-ticket prestige armaments. Conversely, regimes that are more democratic and thus more politically secure tend to have demands for security assistance more closely tied to national strategic requirements, not internal political needs.

This chapter argues that not only are the drivers of security assistance often political rather than strategic, but the nature of those political drivers is strongly linked to regime type and its resulting forms of civil-military relations. I provide a conceptual framework that links regime type to variation in demands for security assistance and related issues of civil-military relations. Specifically, I argue that there are three primary regime types in the MENA region, and each type creates its own cluster of drivers of security assistance, type of civil-military relations, and resulting operational military effectiveness.[11] The three primary regime types in MENA are oil monarchies, repressive republics, and flawed democracies. Each of these regime types has a relatively unique cluster of characteristics when it comes to demands for security assistance, the internal rationale for those demands, the dominant forms of civil-military relations, and the relationship between security assistance and military effectiveness.

Oil Monarchies

The oil monarchies of MENA are all located on the Arabian Peninsula: Saudi Arabia, Kuwait, the UAE, Qatar, and, to a lesser degree, Bahrain and Oman. They all share two fundamental characteristics. First, each is a rentier state that derives virtually all governmental funds from the sale of oil and gas on the international market (not from domestic taxation).

The politics of rentier states have been robustly studied, including their tendency to promote authoritarianism.[12] Only in rare cases where democratic institutions were firmly established prior to the discovery of large quantities of oil and gas has democracy been possible in rentier states (e.g., Norway). In the absence of strong preexisting democratic institutions, rentier states almost always move in the direction of authoritarianism, often at the expense of nascent democratic institutions. For example, Venezuela used to have many attributes of democracy, but the discovery of large quantities of oil helped weaken democratic institutions and promote personalized authoritarianism.[13]

The second shared characteristic of these oil monarchies is, as the name implies, that they are all family-run regimes, although Saudi Arabia and the UAE appear to be transitioning to the more usual autocratic rule of one man rather than a family-corporate enterprise.[14] These are not monarchies with deep history; rather, they trace their monarchical roots to British imperial interests in the nineteenth and early twentieth centuries (in spite of the national myths that often get told of more ancient roots).[15]

Both of these facts suggest a limited amount of regime legitimacy. The rentier nature of these states creates a dynamic of weak state-society relations, as regimes do not need their own populations to finance state institutions and policies. Moreover, many state institutions remain significantly underdeveloped in rentier states, again limiting the ties that bind state to society. The presence of substantial noncitizen populations in these oil monarchies further complicates the issue of state-society relations.

Like in other rentier states, oil monarchies on the Arabian Peninsula tend to rely on utilitarian calculation more than moral legitimacy to maintain popular support within society and even among elements of the state. As long as the regime is "delivering the goods," it is in the self-interest of actors to not be involved in public political criticism. The relative lack of bread-and-butter political arguments in the public square in these oil monarchies has long been noted; those arguments have been replaced, often, by cultural wedge issues in the public discourse. This is true even in the most active of all parliaments among the oil monarchies: Kuwait. Kuwait's parliament lacks meaningful budgetary power-of-the-purse authority, so bread-and-butter issues, which require budgetary action, tend to be pushed aside and replaced by non-budgetary debates on cultural issues instead.[16]

The utilitarian nature of support for the regime is the foundation upon which the primary political driver of security assistance rests: the need to placate military leadership with prestige American weapons systems. Such systems are not usually linked to actual strategic requirements but rather demonstrate regime support for powerful actors who could potentially create significant problems for the regime. Buying shiny new—if often unnecessary—prestige weapons systems serves two purposes for oil monarchies that help stabilize regimes. First, many of the top officers come from royal families, and many more come from privileged tribal networks tied to the regimes. Essentially, these officers demand to receive the honor and patronage due other leading members of the royal family, and that status is conveyed, in part, through top-end American weapons systems put under their control. Intrafamily rivalries are often more damaging to ruling families in the oil monarchies than external threats, and thus the regimes have a vested interest in placating potential powerful family members leading the officer corps.[17] And second, for those officers not hailing from royal or other powerful families in the oil monarchies, such prestige weapons systems help raise their status locally and mitigate potential political jealousies they may hold.

These oil monarchies purchase both prestige weapons systems and vast quantities of armaments in general. Saudi Arabia was the world's largest arms importer from 2016 to 2020 and has pledged to buy tens of billions of more arms from the United States.[18] But such weapons' only actual use in the field appears to be to pulverize the Yemeni population without actually winning the war. These weapons systems have not been effective at stopping low-cost Iranian provocations against Saudi, such as the 2019 drone attack against the huge oil-processing plant in Abqaiq. The UAE is another major arms importer, ranked tenth in the world during the 2016–2020 period by SIPRI, in spite of the fact that it is a tiny country with slightly over one million citizens who constitute less than 12 percent of the overall population living in the country. In exchange for its diplomatic recognition of Israel in 2020, the UAE was allowed access to many of the most advanced US weapons systems, including F-35 fighter jets, of which it ordered fifty at a cost of $23 billion.[19] It is not at all clear what strategic objective is served by purchasing the most sophisticated fighter jet in the world. The often-stated rationale is the threat from Iran, but it is not apparent how the UAE would use such fighters in a conflict with that county. With its population of eighty-five million people, Iran could probably overwhelm the UAE in the unlikely event that it ever decided to do so. More obviously defensive weapons systems would seem to be more relevant in such a scenario, but such weapons systems are typically much less sexy—and less expensive. Nor are F-35s so obviously useful for the UAE's port-and-base strategy around the Arabian Sea and Bab el-Mandab region that cheaper alternatives could not suffice.[20] In 2019, Oman was the largest spender on the military as a share of GDP in the world, with Kuwait ranked fourth. Qatar is among the top ten weapons importers worldwide. All three of these big spenders also focused on the purchase of prestige weapons systems, almost all American made with some European weapons as well.

Total military expenditures in MENA are heavily weighted toward the oil monarchies. For example, according to the International Institute for Strategic Studies' authoritative *Military Balance 2021*, over 42 percent of all defense spending in MENA in 2020 was done by Saudi Arabia and the UAE alone.[21] There is no reason to believe this trend will change any time soon.

Civil-military relations in these oil monarchies vary from those found in other regime types (such as in the repressive republics) that likewise premise security assistance on placating military and security leaders as a form of political insurance. Oil monarchies typically put members of the royal family among the officer corps, as well as in positions of direct authority within the chain of command. For example, Mohamed bin Zayed Al Nahyan, the longtime crown prince and now ruler of the UAE, has held a series of military commands, including as a pilot and then commander of the UAE air force and subsequently as deputy supreme commander of the UAE Armed Forces. He holds the rank of lieutenant general in the military while also running the civilian government. His protégé, Mohammed bin Salman in Saudi Arabia, likewise wears two hats: crown prince and de facto ruler, on the one hand, and minister of defense on the other.

Military effectiveness in oil monarchies is routinely poor primarily because of the deeply political nature of all major military and security decisions. This includes the demands for security assistance in oil monarchies, which are rarely linked to actual strategic or defense needs and are most often tied to political considerations from family regimes who rely on oil revenues more than political legitimacy to stay in power. None of these leaders have ever been elected, so none enjoy democratic legitimacy; none of the ruling families have the historical legitimacy that comes from being in power for centuries;[22] none have specific charismatic or religious legitimacy that could justify their positions of power as a sanctification by God.

Fighting effectiveness is also often limited in oil monarchies due to the rentier nature of the political economy. As noted above, rentierism creates a dynamic that weakens state-society relations by slowly replacing more traditional ties (e.g., tribalism, religion) with a cash nexus of utilitarian calculation. Creating a sense of strong national identity and societal commitment to national goals under such circumstances is difficult. It is never quite clear where regime self-interest ends and shared national goals begin. Often, a society-wide crisis such as war or dislocation must occur in order to bolster a shared sense of national identity that would, in turn, help in promoting military cohesion and effectiveness. For example, Russia's invasion of Ukraine in February 2022 appears to have had the effect of strengthening the ties of national solidarity among Ukrainians, even as Russian president Vladimir Putin denied the legitimate existence of Ukraine or Ukrainian nationalism.

Repressive Republics

A second regime type in MENA is the repressive republic. As with oil monarchies, demands for security assistance by repressive republics are primarily political, not strategic, but the underlying political logic and the nature of civil-military relations in repressive republics are distinctive from those of oil monarchies. Repressive republics are essentially military regimes with a thin veneer of civilian control. Egypt, Syria, and Algeria are the most obvious examples of repressive republics, as each has a large and politically active military as well as nominal civilian control. Syria has been a repressive republic since the 1963 Ba'ath Party–military coup and a specifically family-run regime since the Assads took over in 1970. The Syrian regime has organized its military with an eye toward repressing a restless domestic population, especially since the first round of the Syrian civil war in the late 1970s and early 1980s.[23] Egypt has been a military regime with a veneer of civilian control since 1952. With the exception of the brief rule of Mohamed Morsi in 2012 and 2013, all Egyptian presidents have been former military officers who exchanged their fatigues for civilian attire upon becoming president. But all, including current president Abdel Fattah al-Sisi, have ruled Egypt with an authoritarian hand and an eye toward the corporate interests of the Egyptian military. In addition to its political power, the Egyptian military has become the dominant actor in the Egyptian economy. The 1954–1962 Algerian revolution against French colonialism cemented a National Liberation Front party–military alliance that came to power after the defeat of France. Even though the party remained important, the Algerian military became the dominant state actor, especially during the civil war in the 1990s. While a veneer of civilian rule remains in Algeria, the military has clearly captured the state and uses that power, in part, to advance its corporate interests.

In addition to Egypt, Syria, and Algeria, a fair argument can be made that Iran and perhaps Iraq also fall into the category of repressive republics. While this book concerns Arab states, I use Iran here as a comparative example showing that many of the tendencies being explored in this book also have resonance in the wider region. The Islamic Republic of Iran has more actual civilian leadership than its Arab neighbors, but civilian control of the state has begun to wane with the rising power and internal use of the Islamic Revolutionary Guard Corps (IRGC) and the Basij militia that it controls. The political rise of the IRGC and Basij has been especially pronounced since 2009 and the crushing of the "Green Revolution" following a manipulated presidential election. Today, the IRGC and its allies in the clergy control a network of foundations and other economic assets such that they parallel the Egyptian military's control of the national economy. Iraq today, with some credible electoral politics, is a more marginal example of a repressive republic, although it had a long history as such under the Ba'ath Party. Iraq's civilian control over the military is more than mere tokenism, but add in the Shia Popular Mobilization Forces (*al-hashd al-sha'bi*), and the similarities with other repressive republics begin to mount. Iraq also has the relatively unique situation of extensive external influence among its various armed forces by Iran and the United States. Yemen, before its descent into both civil and regional war, could also have been classified as a repressive republic.

Demands for security assistance in repressive republics are likewise often political, not strategic, but there are notable differences in form and purpose. The first obvious difference is that repressive republics all have very large militaries, as opposed to the relatively small (and even mercenary) ones in oil monarchies. Tables 3.1 and 3.2 compare the size of the militaries in the repressive republics to those in the oil monarchies.[24] As Table 3.1 shows, the militaries in the repressive republics are quite large. Also, the percentage of the population under arms in some capacity (active duty + reserves + paramilitary) averages roughly 1.2 percent—a significantly higher percentage than in the oil monarchies.

By contrast, Table 3.2 shows that militaries in the oil monarchies are, both in aggregate and on a per capita basis, generally much smaller than those in the repressive republics.

The large militaries in repressive republics are designed primarily for regime security, not national defense, and in some cases, like Egypt and Iran, they are also designed to provide cheap labor for military enterprises (Yemen also used this formula prior to its civil war). The militaries tend to be organizationally fragmented, with lines of communication directly to the national leadership. This organizational structure is a common form of coup-proofing, as the fragmented elements com-

Table 3.1 Size of Militaries in Four MENA Repressive Republics

Country	Active Duty	Reserves and Paramilitary	Total Under Arms	Population of Country	Population Under Arms (percentage)
Syria	169,000	100,000	269,000	20,400,000	1.32
Egypt	438,500	876,000	1,314,500	106,400,000	1.24
Algeria	130,000	337,200	467,200	43,600,000	1.07
Iran	610,000	390,000	1,000,000	85,900,000	1.16

Table 3.2 Size of Militaries in Three MENA Oil Monarchies

Country	Active Duty	Reserves and Paramilitary	Total Under Arms	Population of Country	Population Under Arms (percentage)
Saudi Arabia	227,000	24,500	251,500	34,800,000	0.72
UAE	63,000	0	63,000	9,900,000	0.64
Qatar	16,500	5,000	21,500	2,500,000	0.86

pete among themselves for resources and are less likely to unite against the regime. Elements often spy on each other as part of this competition. Elements viewed as especially loyal and important to the regime—often military intelligence—are handsomely rewarded, while more marginal units are not. In repressive republics, relations between the Ministry of Defense and the Ministry of the Interior—which usually controls its own security forces—can be strained and uncooperative. Large militaries in repressive republics provide significant patronage to average citizens in the form of jobs, and they are structured to maximize regime survival over strategies of national defense.

Demand for security assistance in repressive republics is fundamentally shaped by this same structure in at least two ways. First, and most importantly, the security assistance these regimes desire prioritizes requirements for coup-proofing (within the military) and rebellion-proofing (outside of the military). Assistance focusing on FID is thus prioritized in repressive republics much more than in the oil monarchies. Counterterrorism, counterinsurgency, and intelligence equipment and training are generally prized above prestige weapons systems. But even here, rivalries within and between militaries and security forces often hinder CT implementation. In Tunisia under Zine El Abidine Ben Ali, CT was done by security forces under the Ministry of Interior, not the military, and had less to do with terrorism than political repression.

The Tunisian military, as a result, had a much better and more professional reputation than Tunisia's security forces. Much the same is true in Egypt, where historically the counterterrorism mission was done by security forces, and the military has only recently and begrudgingly taken on this role under American pressure.[25]

The emphasis on FID security assistance has been especially pronounced since the events of the Arab Spring in 2011, which saw various levels of regime change in Tunisia, Egypt, Libya, and Yemen and a serious threat to regime survival in Syria. More recent popular upheavals in Iraq, Algeria, and Sudan suggest the emphasis on security assistance that focuses on regime security will likely continue well into the future.

A second political driver of security assistance in repressive republics occurs when leaders seek to reward themselves with prestige weapons systems, although generally at a lesser rate than in oil monarchies. Egypt under Sisi is the repressive republic most enamored of prestige weaponry. It is important to note, however, that the dynamic involving such systems is substantially different in repressive republics as compared to the oil monarchies. In oil monarchies, civilian rulers provide prestige weapons systems to their militaries as a means to reward family members who run the military and to placate other elements of military leadership against any form of intrafamilial rivalries and discord. Oil monarchies also buy significant amounts of high-end weaponry from US firms as a means to embed their own regime security within a larger American umbrella. By contrast, in repressive republics, the rulers are giving themselves such prestige systems as a form of entitlement, not appeasement, as there is no useful distinction between military and political leadership in such regimes. As well, since prestige systems are purchased at lower levels in repressive republics as compared to oil monarchies, the ingratiation into the US military-industrial complex and related security umbrella tends to be a more marginal phenomenon.

Repressive republics have the worst results of our three state categories in terms of civil-military relations and military effectiveness. The first point is obvious: since the "civilian" leaders in repressive republics tend to be military generals who have now put on a coat and tie, there is no meaningful distinction between civil and military leaders and thus no meaningful civilian control of the military. Rather, the military has effectively captured the state and uses its instruments of power to enhance its own corporate interests as well as the personal interests of its top leaders. In such a situation, civil-military relations in general and civilian control over the military are mirages.

Also, military effectiveness is compromised by the logic of regime security. The militaries of repressive republics are mostly designed to fight their own people, not the armies of neighboring hostile states. At the outset of this chapter, I noted what a poor track record most MENA states have in terms of war fighting. The repressive republics have the worst track records of all, led by Egypt, Syria, and Iraq, none of which has won a war in seventy-five years. While not having fought full-on foreign wars in over thirty years, Iran and Algeria have also clearly focused and structured their coercive capabilities around fighting and winning internal battles for regime survival, not fighting external armies that threaten national security. Force structures in repressive republics further underline the internal security function of many militaries. Compare, for example, the size of paramilitary forces in Algeria (187,200, or .43 percent of the total population), Egypt (397,000, or .37 percent), and Syria (100,000, or .49 percent) to those in Qatar (5,000, or .2 percent), Saudi Arabia (24,500, or .07 percent), and the UAE (0, or 0 percent). In other words, even on a per capita basis, paramilitary forces are at least twice as large in repressive republics as they are in oil monarchies, again testifying to the internal security force structure common in repressive republics.

In summary, repressive republics also privilege internal political calculations in their demands for security assistance but do so in distinctly different ways from the oil monarchies. Repressive republics tend to build extremely large militaries by comparison and with an eye toward regime survival against internal challenges. Security assistance is focused more on FID calculations as a means of coup- and rebellion-proofing, with fewer prestige weapons systems and somewhat different calculations when such systems are attained. While oil monarchies have decent civilian control over the military, no such civil-military relations exist in the repressive republics, where the military *is* the "civilian" regime. Their military effectiveness is generally quite poor when performance is measured against foreign adversaries. Their militaries and armaments are designed primarily to prevail against domestic enemies of the regime, less so against foreign militaries.

This is not to imply that *no* strategic planning is involved in demands for security assistance in repressive republics. Algeria continues to fight a proxy war against Morocco over the Western Sahara; Egyptian military planning continues to factor in possible conflict with Ethiopia over Nile River waters; Syria is overwhelmed with military problems, including having enemies to the south (Israel) and north (Turkey); and the discovery of large deposits of natural gas in the eastern Mediterranean has many countries building up naval capacities for potential conflict. Rather, the point is that domestic political considerations overwhelmingly drive demands within repressive republics concerning the nature and size of security assistance. The drivers of security assistance demand parallel oil monarchies in that they are largely a reflection of domestic political considerations but vary in the nature and expression of those political considerations and the resulting civil-military relations.

Flawed Democracies

A third broad category of states in the Middle East and North Africa is the flawed democracy. Despite their deep flaws, these democracies have consistently better records than either oil monarchies or repressive republics in linking security assistance to strategic needs as opposed to the politics of regime survival. They also have consistently better records of civilian control over the military and a more professional officer corps.

MENA has no true, top-drawer democracy, and only Tunisia among the Arab states might qualify as a democracy at all (and decreasingly so). Given this paucity of democracies in the Arab world, I also include in this section discussions of Turkey and Israel, neither of which is primarily Arab but both of which are important regional actors. I label all three countries as "flawed democracies." Turkey, often not even considered part of MENA, is the original "deep state" in the region, where for decades civilian rule and democratic elections were always shadowed by behind-the-scenes military rule. Civilian leaders knew there were red lines they could not cross without inviting military intervention. Indeed, military coups happened from time to time: 1960, 1971, 1980, and the "soft coup" of 1993. The rise of the Islamist movement in Turkey over the past twenty years, especially under Recep Tayyip Erdogan, has had a significant but mixed impact on democracy in Turkey. On the positive side, Erdogan has ended the era of the deep state in Turkey. No longer are the military and its networks the real rulers in the shadows. While Erdogan has taken numerous steps to undercut the political power of the military, by far the most important (and, some would argue, antidemocratic) of these was his reaction to the failed 2016 coup attempt, which was famously put down via Facetime. Calling the failed coup a "gift from God" that would allow Turkey to "cleanse our military," Erdogan removed thousands of personnel from the ranks of the military, including nearly half of all generals and admirals.[26] By crushing the military deep state, Erdogan advanced the usual democratic goal of cementing civilian control over the military.

That said, Erdogan's authoritarian tendencies and rejection of the concept of dissent have led to growing autocracy, censorship, and democratic rollback in Turkey. While Turkey still holds meaningful elections, there is a reason that it is widely viewed as moving in the wrong direction regarding democratic expansion. This is also why Turkey is often lumped together with Egypt, Hungary, Russia, India, and other countries that promote authoritarianism under a democratic facade, in what Steven Levitsky and Lucan A. Way describe as "competitive authoritarianism."[27]

Israel too is a flawed democracy, widely viewed as moving toward greater authoritarianism under the long premiership of Benjamin Netanyahu that drew to a (temporary?) close in 2021. Israel has many traits of a full democracy, including regular and meaningful elections, broad press freedom, and many individual rights such as speech and assembly. However, two deep structural problems make Israel's democracy significantly flawed. First, Israel's domination of five million stateless Palestinians for nearly sixty years can no longer be said to be a temporary state of affairs awaiting political resolution. The occupation has become permanent. No country can be said to be truly democratic when it keeps nearly 40 percent of the population under its control stateless, without citizenship rights, and thus, in the words of Hannah Arendt, without the right to have rights.[28] Second, looking inward at its own citizens, Israel systematically and legally privileges the rights of Jews, who comprise 75 percent of Israel's citizens, over non-Jews.[29] The systematic privileging of one group over all others by the state in the context of otherwise democratic rule has been insightfully labeled "ethnocracy" by Oren Yiftachel.[30]

The third member in the camp of flawed democracies and the only Arab member, Tunisia, likewise took a large step backward in 2021 when its president, Kais Saied, staged a coup against Tunisia's parliament, sending its democratic future into doubt. Before the coup, Tunisia had spent a decade consolidating democratic rule in spite of numerous problems. The initiators of the Arab Spring movement in December 2010, Tunisians overthrew the quarter-century dictatorship of Zine El Abidine Ben Ali and established a functioning, if flawed, democracy in its stead. Over the ensuing decade, Tunisia held free and fair elections, saw the smooth transition of power following elections, and adopted a progressive and democratic constitution. Its civil society is strong and remains a bulwark for democracy, and civilian control over the military has been healthy. Until the 2021 presidential coup, much had gone right in Tunisia, in spite of setbacks, economic stagnation, and periodic terrorism. Tunisia was clearly the most democratic of all Arab states but must remain in the "flawed" category until it can truly consolidate its democracy over time, including reversing Saied's action. Parliamentary dysfunction and growing alienation and political polarization provided the rationale for the presidential coup.[31] Reflecting the alienation among young people, Tunisia was among the highest per capita contributors of foreign fighters to ISIS.

However flawed their democracies are, Turkey, Israel, and Tunisia have consistently sought security assistance that is in line with plausible strategic needs as opposed to regime survival. As a member of the North Atlantic Treaty Organization (NATO), Turkey shares the interoperable weapons systems (mostly American made) that its alliance partners also have and, as part of its regular planning process, obtains security assistance largely consistent with both its NATO obligations and its national strategy. Despite the sometimes harsh rhetoric between Ankara and its NATO allies and Europe's rejection of Turkey as a potential European Union member, it is likely that Turkey will remain in NATO for the foreseeable future. Consistent with that reality is the likelihood that Turkey's demands for security assistance will also reflect less the regime's political needs and more national and NATO requirements. Erdogan's taming of the Turkish military's deep state has also helped to rationalize security assistance demands and planning.

Israel has by far the greatest percentage of foreign military assistance per capita in the world. Under the current ten-year agreement struck with the Barack Obama administration, Israel receives $3.8 billion in US military assistance every year. Israel also has a history of receiving used American military equipment following "drawdowns" in the region following conflicts, as well as further periodic supplements to its Iron Dome supplies, in addition to the regular flow of security assistance from the United States. That said, the Israeli state has effective civilian control over the military and makes demands for security assistance that generally follow consensus national needs, not the coup-proofing needs of any particular government. That is not to say that Netanyahu did not try to use the Israeli military for his own domestic political needs. He did. Rather, it is to say that Israel's democracy, however flawed, still produces demands for security assistance that are national and strategic in nature and not focused primarily on internal political considerations. And its democracy was healthy enough to vote out Netanyahu and have a smooth transfer of power following the rule of the longest-serving prime minister in Israel's history.

Ben Ali's regime favored the civilian *mukhabarat* as the preferred coercive arm of the regime and largely ignored the small but generally professional Tunisian military. The professionalism of the Tunisian officer corps helped in the success of the 2010–2011 "Jasmine Revolution" and continued during the period of democratization. The professional and apolitical nature of the Tunisian military has been a cornerstone of Tunisian democracy to date. Tunisia's professional officer corps has also been critical in terms of security assistance issues, which, as in Turkey and Israel, have been far more national and strategic than focused on regime survival.

It is not a coincidence that Turkey, Israel, and Tunisia are mostly democratic, on one hand, and have more professional officer corps and established civilian control over their militaries, on the other. Democracies generally insist on military professionalism and proper civil-military relations, and those attributes, in turn, help democracies persist despite many challenges. Often the path to civilian control over the military is a rough one. Erdogan's purge of the officer corps and elimination of the old deep state assisted civilian control over a once dominant military but at the same time generated concerns about subordination of Turkey's military to the ruling Justice and Development Party under Erdogan. Still, as a general rule, these clusters of attributes allow for security assistance planning in flawed democracies to focus more on national and strategic needs as opposed to regime survival as seen in both oil monarchies and, especially, repressive republics.

Finally, because (flawed) democracies make security assistance demands that better reflect national needs than political calculation, they tend to produce better military effectiveness. Turkey has the most powerful conventional military in the region and has utilized its military effectively in various regional conflicts, including in northern Iraq, northern Syria, and northern Cyprus. Israel's conventional forces, particularly its air force, have had little difficulty in fighting and defeating Arab militaries for decades. Like with Turkey and its Kurdish population, Israel's military falls short when it tries to undertake essentially policing tasks vis-à-vis the Palestinian population. Neither military is well trained for these traditionally nonmilitary missions. That said, Turkey and Israel have the best trained and most effective militaries in MENA, which reflects, in part, the democratic nature of their security planning and assistance. While Tunisia's military is professional in nature and its demands for security assistance largely national and rational, the military effectiveness of its small fighting forces (about 35,000 active military personnel) is hampered by an accident of history: the country being wedged between two much larger countries, Algeria and Libya. While it has not been much tested, Tunisia's military could likely inflict significant pain on an attacking adversary, and it certainly has few conventional worries looking toward present-day Libya. Algeria will always remain a serious military challenge for Tunisia in times of conflict.

What Is to Be Done?

It is not at all clear that the current state of affairs serves the interests of the United States, its NATO allies, or the populations of most of the countries in MENA. The most heavily armed region in the world is also the least stable, where vast resources that could fund social and economic development are often instead squandered on prestige weapons systems that do little for a country's national defense. The current state of affairs fails to serve the interests of the populations in MENA and the stated objectives and ideals of American and Western suppliers of armaments.

Changing this pattern of security assistance on either the demand or the supply side will not be easy. The leaderships of oil monarchies and repressive republics rely on the current system to assist in regime survival, so they will not be eager to reduce and rationalize the flow of security assistance to their own countries. But the problem goes beyond the preferences of individual leaders, as state type is a structural condition, meaning that any individual put into leadership in that regime will likely arrive at the same conclusion. The structural conditions of the state provide the logic for calculations of regime survival no matter the individual or cohort that happens to be in charge at any one time.

If the demand side is not a good place to start to try to reform the system of security assistance for the benefit of a more peaceful, prosperous, and stable MENA, then what about the supply side? There is more room to maneuver here, as the provision of security assistance is not a structural condition and is thus more easily changed. Again, though, such change will not come easily, as the corporations that actually sell prestige (and other) weapons systems, either directly to MENA or via the US or other governments, make a great deal of money from those sales and can wield that money in politically powerful ways inside American or European capitals. Often the continuing supply of security assistance to MENA gets caught up in domestic politics on the supply side and is not linked to actual strategic needs in the recipient countries. For example, Donald Trump was publicly and regularly explicit in tying the sale of prestige weapons systems to Saudi Arabia to the creation of American jobs, not to legitimate Saudi (or even American) defense requirements.[32]

Even with those political constraints, large foreign military sales by the United States must be approved by both Department of Defense leadership and Congress, so the possibility of reform does exist. It is certainly possible for both those branches of government to create a wholistic approach to security assistance to MENA that not only is consistent with legitimate national defense needs of the recipient countries but also helps promote good governance and proper civil-military relations in the region.

The first and loudest objection to such a wholistic reformed approach that would necessarily lead to a significant reduction in some forms of security assistance is that American weapons systems would simply be replaced by weapons systems from other countries. This would likely happen, but only to a limited degree. American prestige weapons platforms are not easily replaced; there is a reason they are considered the gold standard. They are also not compatible with Russian or Chinese replacements, so countries would be faced with building a new defense system nearly from scratch if they did not want to cooperate with a reformed US system of security assistance. An entire weapons system, including replacement parts, designed around, say, F-16 or now F-35 fighter planes, cannot simply or easily be converted to accommodate the latest Russian Sukhoi or Chinese Chengdu fighter jet. Even if the American security umbrella begins to be questioned, as it has in Saudi Arabia, for example, wholesale replacement of American prestige systems with lesser Russian or Chinese equipment would be tricky.[33]

While replacing American prestige weapons systems is not so easily done, that calculation is muddied by what may be called the "endorsement factor."[34] The acquisition of prestige weapons systems by MENA countries is complicated by the politics between the supplier and the recipient. Specifically, the recipient regime often views the supply of such prestige systems as a tacit endorsement of the regime and its policies. These are not simple economic transactions but implied political endorsements of a regime by the world's leading military power—at least they are often seen and propagated in those terms by the recipient regimes. While the "endorsement factor" complicates the equation, it actually provides decisionmakers in Washington more leverage to demand reforms. Essentially an American administration is in the position to effectively say, "If you want our tacit endorsement of your regime through the sale or grant of these prestige systems, we require certain reforms be undertaken." US law already demands that recipients of US military assistance abide by certain rules detailed in the Arms Export Control Act, but a great deal more can be done to use security assistance as a vector for recipient reform.[35]

Moreover, there may well be further openings to apply useful pressure on MENA countries to reduce and rationalize their demands for security assistance. When it comes to oil monarchies, most economists believe oil and gas prices have entered into a permanent low range. Of course, periodic spikes in the price of oil will occur in the wake of some major events, such as happened following Russia's invasion of Ukraine.

But, over time, the expectation is continued softening in the price of carbon energy. As more renewables come online, demand for MENA oil and gas will be reduced, further driving down prices. Some places, like Scotland, already meet most of their energy needs through renewable platforms, especially wind power. Renewable energies do not need to replace carbon energy to have a significant impact on softening prices; they only need to increase market share. Oil monarchies will thus have fewer resources now and in the future with which to lavish their militaries with top-end but not very useful prestige weapons systems. That fact provides another opening for American reformers to reduce and rationalize security assistance to MENA.

Regimes in MENA's repressive republics are likewise increasingly vulnerable and can be subject to pressures to reform. Some, like Algeria, Iran, and Iraq, export oil and gas and are thus subject to the same long-term decline in the price of carbon energy. Others, like Egypt, don't have substantial oil and gas reserves but are nonetheless impacted by declining prices. Saudi Arabia has largely kept the Sisi dictatorship financially afloat in Egypt through its largesse to the regime (and the Saudis were rewarded with the transfer to their sovereignty of the small, deserted Egyptian islands of Tiran and Sanafir in the Red Sea). The regimes of the repressive republics are the most vulnerable to upheaval and regime change and are thus the most susceptible to smart pressure for security and political reform. Few analysts would be surprised if the regimes in Egypt and Algeria, for example, were overthrown or otherwise radically altered in the coming decade due to their precarious political positions and limited legitimacy. Now would be an august time to push for far-reaching reform in their security postures in ways that could actually extend the lifespan of these regimes and help ensure that change, when it comes, proceeds gradually and reasonably and not through violent upheaval. Cooperation from repressive republics with calls for reform, however, will likely be limited. Since they are less dependent on prestige weapons systems and more interested in FID-related systems, it is easier for repressive republics to change suppliers if need be.

MENA's flawed democracies are in the least need of immediate reform when it comes to security assistance, but certainly some rethinking is in order. It serves American and European interests to have Turkey inside NATO. A review of that relationship may have to wait for Erdogan's departure from the political scene, as he regularly uses criticism of NATO to advance his own political career. Erdogan likewise responded to Sweden and Finland's requests to join NATO, following Russia's invasion of Ukraine, by threatening to torpedo the request (which must be unanimously approved) unless there was some political payoff to Erdogan. Israel's $3.8-billion-per-year security package from the United States is not helpful to efforts to reduce and reform security assistance for the benefit of the people of MENA. Instead, it acts as an inflator of other countries' demands for bigger and better weapons systems, helping to create a regional arms race. The UAE signed on to the Abraham Accords in part to match Israel in its possession of American-made F-35 fighters. By always looking to preserve Israel's "qualitative edge" in advanced weaponry, the United States causes an ever-increasing inflation of demands for similar weapons elsewhere. A greater reliance on diplomacy over military imbalance may produce better security for all. Assisting in the survival and flourishing of Tunisian democracy should be a high priority for the United States and its democratic allies in Europe.

In sum, reforming the demand side for security assistance is no easy task, because those demands are often caught up in the political calculations of regime survival, and those calculations vary in a significant way depending on the type of regime. These are structural problems that are not easily changed. The expected long-term softening of oil and gas prices—put on hold due to the Russian invasion of Ukraine—does present a window of opportunity on the supply side of security assistance to push for reform and reduction. The current pattern of supply and demand is not tenable over the long term and produces less security and diminished human prosperity. American policymakers and their allies in Europe would do well to take advantage of this window for security assistance reform to enhance the prospects for long-term security, stability, and prosperity in the Middle East and North Africa.

Notes

1. Anthony Cordesman covers some of these challenges inside the United States in Chapter 2 of this book.
2. Cronin, *Armies and State-Building*.
3. Unless otherwise noted, all data on military spending used in this chapter come from the Stockholm International Peace Research Institute.
4. For a good and recent summary of the impacts of Saudi's war on Yemen, see Johnsen, *The End of Yemen*.
5. See Boucek, "War in Saada."
6. Younes, "Analysis." For a deeper analysis of the UAE's port-and-base strategy, of which Yemen is part, see Khalili, *Sinews of War and Trade*.
7. See chapter 3 in Robinson, *Global Jihad*. Simone Tholens covers the Iranian security assistance to Iraq in Chapter 10.
8. For a recent analysis of Syrian government policy toward its civil war, see International Crisis Group, "Silencing the Guns in Syria's Idlib." For an analysis of the Russian military intervention in Syria, see Lavrov, "The Efficiency of the Syrian Armed Forces."

9. For an overview of the external arming of competing sides in Libya, see Saini Fasanotti, "The Biden Administration Inherits a Rapidly Deteriorating Libya."

10. See Sean Yom's Chapter 11 for a more detailed study of civil-military relations in Jordan.

11. See Part 5 for more detailed discussions of civil-military relations in MENA, as well as Chapter 11.

12. The best book on the relationship between oil states and authoritarianism is Ross, *The Oil Curse*.

13. The best early analysis of this oil-generated rise of authoritarianism in Venezuela is Karl, *The Paradox of Plenty*. A more recent and more journalistic analysis of the negative impacts of oil on Venezuelan politics is Gallegos, *Crude Nation*.

14. See Davidson, *From Sheikhs to Sultanism*.

15. For the British role in creating the Arab states of the Gulf in the nineteenth century as an extension of the British Raj in India, see Onley, *The Arabian Frontier of the British Raj*; Rich, *Creating the Arabian Gulf*.

16. The best study of Kuwait's parliament is Herb, *The Wages of Oil*. A recent discussion of Kuwaiti parliamentary debates can be found in Freer and Leber, "The 'Tribal Advantage' in Kuwait Politics."

17. Intrafamily politics among Arabia's royals are notoriously opaque, but a good place to start is Azoulay, *Kuwait and Al-Sabah*.

18. Riedel, "It's Time to Stop US Arms Sales to Saudi Arabia."

19. Tony Cordesman usefully suggests that Russia's war in Ukraine may have impacts on security assistance in terms of what demand-side states request in the future, including the newly tested hypersonic weaponry. See Cordesman, "The Longer-Term Impact of the Ukraine Conflict and the Growing Importance of the Civil Side of War."

20. For an overview of the UAE's drive to build military bases around the region tied in with commercial ports, see Khalili, *Sinews of War and Trade*. See also Telci and Horoz, "Military Bases in the Foreign Policy of the United Arab Emirates"; Vertin, *Red Sea Rivalries*.

21. IISS, *The Military Balance 2021*, 319.

22. The exception is the Omani sultanate.

23. Robinson, "Syria's Long Civil War."

24. Data on the size of militaries come from IISS, *The Military Balance 2021*. Data on population size come from the US Census Bureau (www.census.gov).

25. See Chapter 14 by Pink Williams for more on the Egypt case.

26. Bradley, "Analysis."

27. Levitsky and Way, *Competitive Authoritarianism*.

28. Arendt, *The Origins of Totalitarianism*, esp. chapter 9. Chapter 9 was originally published as an essay in 1946 as "The Rights of Man: What Are They?"

29. See, most recently, Israel's passage of the "nation-state law" in 2018, examined in Ben-Youssef and Tamari, "Enshrining Discrimination."

30. Yiftachel, *Ethnocracy*.

31. Grewal, "Ten Years In, Tunisian Democracy Remains a Work in Progress."

32. See Hartung, Arabia, and Yousif, *The Trump Effect*.

33. See Gause, "Should We Stay or Should We Go?"

34. The term comes from Robert Springborg, private communication, May 26, 2021.

35. For a good short summation of the Arms Export Control Act and related laws, see "US Arms Sales and Human Rights."

4

Tunisia: A Reframed Security-Centered Approach

Noureddine Jebnoun

IN 2019, THE UNITED STATES ALLOCATED MORE THAN $17 BILLION IN military assistance for foreign governments and nonstate actors, with 52.78 percent of this going to the Middle East and North Africa (MENA).[1] The American government seeks to achieve a broad range of goals as part of its foreign military assistance, including using arms supplies as a mechanism to secure leverage in strengthening bilateral relations with foreign actors considered critical players in maintaining regional security.[2] Also, security assistance in the form of arms sales was justified to allegedly sustain domestic US jobs that took "precedence over the need to hold a murderous regime accountable."[3] Security assistance is thought to consolidate US national and international security interests by providing venues to foster recipient-state security cooperation in line with US objectives.

As a precarious and uncertain democratic experiment evolving within a convoluted regional context, Tunisia has been further integrated into the US global security architecture since 2011. Interestingly, the deepening of US security assistance in a democratizing Tunisia faced with social upheavals and security troubles is much in line with the US officials' initial understanding of the democratic transition, in the wake of the fall of the autocratic regime, as a process in which the United States is willing to assist the Tunisian "people and government [to] bring peace and stability."[4]

The attempt to deliver stability through security assistance has led to the empowerment of the state's coercive institutions in ways that risk undermining Tunisians' democratic aspirations. The emphasis on stability in the US official discourse could be explained by the assumption that stability provides external players with the advantage of dealing with a government whose actions are to some extent predictable. From this standpoint, dealing with a dysfunctional polity undergoing political reforms perceived as "destabilizing" is a less suitable scenario. It comes as no surprise that Western actors—not only the United States—are constantly trying to assess the risks threatening the perceived stability across the MENA region, especially if this stability is closely associated with strongman rulers.

The various and diverse definitions of *political stability* demonstrate that the concept is rather controversial. A broad definition of *stability* refers to the nonexistence of domestic civil turmoil and pervasive violence. In this sense, a country can be considered "stable" when no systematic political violence takes place within its boundaries. Such a definition is problematic, since the political situation of a specific country can look stable notwithstanding the fact that the regime may be highly fragile. Another classic interpretation equates stability with regime longevity and durability without regard to whether a ruler is democratically elected or autocratically self-appointed. A serious problem with this definition is that a country like Tunisia since 2011, experiencing socioeconomic turmoil and frequent changes of government, is considered "unstable," even when continuity in governmental policies is maintained by a resilient administrative system in which institutional norms are well embedded. Yet the centrality of stability discourse in US foreign assistance toward democratizing Tunisia has further securitized foreign assistance, leading to a prioritization of security over democratic liberties and the criminalization of popular protests.

This chapter is structured in three sections. The first discusses the literature on Western—mainly US—foreign aid and the use of "securitization" as an analytical framework to capture the consequences of US security assistance to Tunisia. The second charts US security assistance and its implications for shaping Tunisia's defense sector aligned with US strategic interests. The final section examines the security-stability nexus through which US security assistance has been approaching Tunisia's democratization while arguing that US security assistance to Tunisia has contributed to the securitization of the country's marginalized border communities and further criminalized their informal cross-border activities.

Foreign Assistance Through the Lens of Securitization

During the Cold War, US foreign aid policies to developing countries depended on both recipient countries' adherence to the American anti-communism efforts as a nonnegotiable geopolitical stance and the embrace of neoliberal policies through a set of macroeconomic measures established by the Washington Consensus from the 1990s onward. The collapse of the Soviet Union reinforced the uneven neoliberal socioeconomic development and enabled the US military activism to further instrumentalize human rights and democracy promotion.[5] Notwithstanding the US rhetorical promotion of democratic values and human rights discourse, foreign assistance serves as a foreign policy tool to achieve strategic goals, chief among them being maintenance of a regional order secured by autocratic regimes. This approach was consistent with Washington's aid policy toward Hosni Mubarak's regime as both US congressional and government support usually emphasized the promotion of strong leaders and regime stability, constituting a cornerstone of foreign assistance that became tied to Egypt's regional behavior (i.e., Mubarak's alignment with the United States and Israel) regardless of the authoritarian nature of the regime.[6] Yet the discourse of stability gained momentum in the aftermath of 9/11 as clearly displayed in US and EU policies toward Tunisia. In this regard, Brieg Tomos Powel argues that the United States and European Union shared a rhetorical support for democracy in Tunisia that was undermined by a praxis fixation on stability and security.[7] Ironically, this "stability syndrome" turned Zine El Abidine Ben Ali's authoritarian regime into an "attractive" model of governance across the MENA region,[8] as the United States devoted more financial resources "in security-related aid than in sponsoring political reform programs."[9]

The fall of Ben Ali's regime subsequent to the 2010–2011 mass popular uprising not only called into question the stability paradigm as embraced by major Western powers but also problematically reprioritized international donors' policies from support of security-sector reform to raw security assistance stressing performance and effectiveness over security reform.[10] Although intelligence and security services remain closely associated with human rights abuses, they underwent a mending process that sought to improve their operational capabilities through a doctored discourse of technicalities seeking to meet external donors' agendas.[11] By the same token, this performance-centered approach, in the aftermath of the Bardo and Sousse attacks in 2015, has reoriented Tunisia's political reform toward external actors' security agendas, yielding a new era of securitization extending to national infrastructure deemed sensitive (i.e., tourist sites, borders, ports, and airports) and counterterrorism missions.[12] While external donors' rationales departed from the regime-centric security approach emphasized under the fallen autocratic rule, they continued to prioritize stability over a human-citizen security approach as "none of revolutionary goals [related to Tunisia's security governance] (e.g., achieving accountability, anchoring human rights standards and the rule of law in policing, obtaining civilian oversight) had been achieved."[13]

Theoretically speaking, securitization resulting from the US prioritization of securitized foreign aid offers a sound analytical framework to capture the implications for democratizing Tunisia and its military. Securitization theory is associated with the Copenhagen School, which frames security as an intersubjective social paradigm that portrays a given issue as "an existential threat to a referent object [while] the issue is securitized only if and when the audience accepts it as such [through] coercion [and/or] consent."[14] This approach enables actors to circumvent "normal" political procedures and produce "endorsement of emergency measures beyond rules that would otherwise bind."[15] President Kais Saied's imposition of "exceptional measures" on July 25, 2021, exemplifies his deviation from regular procedures to a state of exception. He dismissed the head of government, suspended the parliament, and stripped legislators of immunity, invoking the obvious mismanagement of the Covid-19 pandemic and overall governance failure.[16] He bestowed upon himself unprecedented executive and judicial powers by ruling through presidential decrees and appointing himself as a supervisor of the Office of Public Prosecution.[17] Not only did Saied's power grab overstep his interpretation of Article 80 of the 2014 constitution, but his invocation of "imminent perils" to justify the state of exception is questionable as "exceptional measures are the result of periods of political crisis and, as such, must be understood on political and not juridico-constitutional ground."[18] This departure from regular procedures is grounded in vague national security arguments about handling socioeconomic issues, as the country has already been under a permanent state of emergency since 2011, which enabled the "persistent extension by the President of the far-reaching emergency powers provided to law enforcement officials," while contributing to "de facto normalize[ation of] what should be an extraordinary legal regime."[19]

Popular resistance to the same neoliberal policies implemented by successive governments since 2011 has been dealt with by further criminalization of the people's struggle for social justice. Securitization with US assistance has been instrumental in this process, as it strengthened the Tunisian state's coercive capacity over recognizing the role of the state's policies in fueling grievances in the first place, mainly regional inequality and marginalization, on which social and political violence builds.[20] Still, securitization of aid is as multifaceted as it is instrumental to both donor and recipient countries seeking to justify security measures by "add[ing] a security dimension to policy areas that, at their core, are unrelated to questions of threat and protection," such as socioeconomic issues.[21] However, I argue that securitization construction is a top-down approach, which suggests both the passiveness and submissiveness of the "audience," overlooks people's agency through bottom-up politics, and focuses mainly on policymakers who frame themselves as both legitimate securitizing actors and security providers while they self-define threats as obvious. In the Tunisian context, where people have experienced a tortuous path to democratization punctuated by sharp crises, many citizens strongly reject this truism, particularly among the socially and economically disenfranchised people who live in the heavily securitized and militarized peripheral border areas, who resent securitization's undermining of their livelihoods. These counter-securitization voices can be identified with "resistance [that] is contextually bound to the social and psychological structures that are being resisted"[22] and need to be considered while addressing the implications of US security assistance for Tunisia.

Mapping US Foreign Security Assistance and Its Impacts on Tunisia's Military

The fall of the late Tunisian autocratic ruler Zine El Abidine Ben Ali threw a spotlight on US foreign aid to his regime. This consisted of $19.15 million, with $17.15 million of that in security assistance in the wake of the regime's demise in 2010. In fact, Tunisia was the second-largest recipient of US assistance in North Africa, behind Morocco.[23] Despite the regime's poor domestic human rights records, the US secretary of defense at the time, Robert Gates, argued that by allocating these funds to local clients, the US government would improve its ability to "build partner capacity."[24] Gates overlooked the fact that these regimes are often led by rulers who seek, by positioning themselves as America's allies and obtaining further security assistance, to stay in power against the will of their people.

Notwithstanding the demise of Ben Ali's autocratic rule in January 2011, security and stability considerations have continued to govern US funding rationales, mainly after the establishment of the US-Tunisia Strategic Dialogue in April 2014. This led to the signing of a memorandum of understanding (MOU) between the two countries, paving the way for President Barack Obama's designation of Tunisia as a major non-NATO ally (MNNA) in May 2015.[25] The MOU clearly emphasizes the need to "increase military cooperation through programs aimed at reinforcing Tunisia's security and developing its capacities," including the country's "security needs, counterterrorism, and stability."[26] Stability has been instrumental in US lawmakers' discourse to ensure bilateral assistance to Tunisia. In November 2015, seven months after visiting Tunisia, US Senator Christopher Coons warned in an op-ed that withholding funds could have a negative impact on the country's stability.[27] By the same token, in May 2016, John Desrocher, deputy assistant secretary for Egypt and Maghreb Affairs at the US State Department, solemnly acknowledged before the US Subcommittee on the Middle East and North Africa that US assistance would generate "increased stability and security" in Tunisia.[28] Stability discourse stems from a securitization narrative and reflects a general tendency in the aftermath of 9/11 among the US decisionmakers and lawmakers to use foreign assistance to achieve US national security interests by focusing on a state-centric security approach in recipient countries.[29] Interestingly, in the aftermath of President Saied's power grab, stability discourse and its Western security-assistance-driven agenda have been embraced even by some human rights activists who urgently cautioned US lawmakers against "cutting military and security aid to Tunisia," claiming that such "a misguided decision" could "lead also to the deterioration of the security not only in Tunisia but also in the entire region."[30]

Equally important to the securitization perspective is that US aid to Tunisia has substantially increased since 2011. As of 2020, US foreign assistance to Tunisia has expanded to $191.4 million (a 520 percent increase since 2010), with security assistance representing 56 percent of the total bilateral aid.[31] Accordingly, the number of Tunisian trainees in all American military education and training programs increased by 26 percent in one decade, jumping from 119 (2010) to 151 (2019) with a peak of 659 trainees in 2017.[32] In the same vein, the number of Tunisian officers who have been trained within the International Military Education and Training program rose by 35 percent, from 45 (2010) to 61 (2019), with the highest number of military personnel, 75, recorded in 2016.[33]

In addition to the US military educational exchange programs, Tunisia acquired military equipment under the Foreign Military Sales (FMS) program. This includes eight Sikorsky UH-60 Black Hawk helicopters, valued at $338 million,[34] and eighteen OH-58D Kiowa Warrior Aircraft, valued at $100.8 million, conducted through the Excess Defense Articles program, which grants sales of military items to allies including MNNA countries.[35] In February 2020, the US State Department approved a military sale to Tunisia through the FMS of four AT-6C Wolverine Light Attack Aircraft with an estimated value of $325.8 million.[36] All three of these major arms transfers occurred in the postauthoritarian era and were framed as a means to advance US "foreign policy and national security objectives" by enhancing the defense capability of the Tunisian Armed Forces (TAF) in fighting nonstate armed groups and countering terrorism while enabling Tunisia to serve as an anchor of regional stability.[37]

More significantly, Tunisia benefited from the Section 1206 Train and Equip Program, established under the National Defense Authorization Act (NDAA) for Fiscal Year 2006, which focused on training and equipping foreign military and maritime forces with the main objective of developing their operational capabilities in conducting both counterterrorism and stabilization operations. In 2011, Tunisia secured $12.95 million under Section 1206. Five years later, in 2016, the amount rose to $34.2 million, a 164 percent increase.[38] Under Section 333 of the Fiscal Year 2017 NDAA on building capacity of foreign security forces, which expanded Section 1206, Tunisia received $15.47 million in 2019,[39] including an estimated fund of $4.64 million allocated to a "Tier 1 Counterterrorism Company."[40] The Tier 1 concept aims at establishing elite special forces units, trained by members of the US Special Operations Command (USSOCOM) and tasked with "high-profile missions." This force format is a US-designed model driven by the US Special Mission Unit organization, based on a highly selective process of recruiting operators/personnel.[41]

The US imprint on Tunisia's defense capacity building is already visible with the establishment of the Intelligence Fusion Cell/Center (IFC) following the creation of the Defense Intelligence and Security Agency (DISA) within the Tunisian Ministry of Defense (MOD) in 2014. The IFC is tasked with integrating intelligence and developing interagency coordination between the DISA, the military, and the paramilitary component (i.e., National Guard) of the Internal Security Forces (ISF) in the field. It is an "American operational concept experienced in both Iraq and Afghanistan wars, and recommended by a former member of the U.S. Special Operations forces who served as a DIA [US Defense Intelligence Agency] officer," graduated from Tunisia's Command and Staff College in 2002, and served with many US defense contractors as an advisor to the Tunisian special forces in 2014.[42]

Needless to say, most of the US security assistance funds directed to Tunisia have been devoted to programs and structures focusing on the irregular warfare paradigm (i.e., combating terrorism and low-level insurgencies).[43] These priorities have been a central pillar of the US Global War on Terror since 9/11. As a recipient of small but substantial US security assistance since 2011, Tunisia's military is driven by the Pentagon's agenda, with the main emphasis on counterterrorism operations.[44] This assistance comes with strings attached as Tunisia was pressured to accept the US military deployment of a *footprint*—a vague term to reduce the visibility of US military presence in Tunisia and across Africa—using a Tunisian facility as a launchpad for unmanned aerial vehicles (UAVs) employed for intelligence, surveillance, and reconnaissance (ISR) missions across the region.[45] These ISR-UAVs were reportedly withdrawn in early 2020 from Tunisia,[46] after the 2018 Pentagon decision to close some military "outposts" across Africa,[47] as a part of the US global "interstate strategic competition" prioritizing China and Russia as main competitors.[48] Yet the US active military personnel substantially increased in Tunisia from ten (September 2008) to twenty-two (June 2021), with a majority (thirteen) hailing from the US Marine Corps.[49] The United States has maintained "boots on the ground" from the USSOCOM in many countries, including Tunisia, operating directly against armed groups while partnering with local forces used as surrogates and forming a part of counterterrorism operations conducted under the 127e program. The program uses US trained-equipped local combat forces—regardless of their human rights records—as proxy forces. These local partners are primarily employed in US tailored and ordered missions under broad and loose interpretation of hostilities within the context of irregular warfare in order to target US enemies while serving US national interests.[50] Despite tiresome denials by the Tunisian government, many reports have documented the activities of US Marine Corps Special Operations Forces operating under the USSOCOM, including operations engaging armed groups in fierce combats in western Tunisia near the Algerian border.[51] Interestingly, American commandos deployed in Tunisia and other African countries have seen their missions expand beyond "assisting and advising" to defining operational goals and directing local forces used as "surrogates to hunt militants," including in "direct-action raids" under the 127e authority.[52] Apart from their lack of oversight, these missions fall under the maxim of "It's less 'we're helping you' and more 'you're doing our bidding,'"[53] aligning the recipient country with the strategic interests of the donor while enabling the latter to conduct a war on the cheap.

Although Tunisia's military has struggled to adjust its modus operandi to the new perceived threat environment, US security assistance has led to the development of specific capabilities without consideration of long-term strategic outcomes in Tunisia. The improvement of operational capabilities neither transformed the TAF as a whole nor impacted defense planning, structures, and resources. Rather, Tunisia's military embraced a capability-mending framework that translated into a limited revamped capabilities approach (LRCA) seeking to address security issues with minimum resources on a day-to-day basis while centering the effort on four major axes: strengthening military manpower, acquiring specific tactical assets in line with a counterterrorism logic, adopting new irregular warfare training approaches, and securing international and defense partnership arrangements.[54] However, LRCA is unable to develop a long-term, coherent vision for the format, structures, and organization of Tunisia's military, let alone delink the regional and global strategic priorities of the patron-donor (i.e., the United States) from the local needs of the client-recipient (i.e., Tunisia).

Given that US security assistance is targeting unconventional warfare through niche capabilities identified within the recipient military structures, this trend will likely continue to deepen and lead to further discrepancies in the country's defense apparatus, creating a two-speed military with special forces that are better equipped and trained than regular troops.[55] The narrow focus on nontraditional threats has further eroded the conventional capabilities of the Tunisian military. Yet the uncertainties of the geostrategic dimensions of the Libyan crisis, combined with the unfolding of foreign powers' struggles and the flow of sophisticated weapons in Libya,[56] require a profound reorganization of the armed forces and an upgrade of their conventional capabilities. This need became urgent in the aftermath of the incursion into Tunisian airspace of an outdated Libyan fighter jet that went undetected.[57] Undoubtedly, in its current format, US security assistance is not designed to effectively meet conventional threats that Tunisia might face in the mid- and long-term.

Since 2017, US security assistance to Tunisia has taken on a further institutional dimension through the signing of a five-year Bilateral Country Action Plan (BCAP) with the US Office of Security Cooperation. Decided during the Thirty-First Joint Military Commission in Washington,

DC, in May 2017, the BCAP seeks to enhance Tunisia's military combat effectiveness in dealing with irregular security threats.[58] It outlines a set of distinct programs such as logistics, maintenance, transportation, and intelligence to enable the TAF to operate in an agile, responsive, and sustained mode against insurgency-style warfare. The BCAP prioritized the establishment of a Joint Operations Control Center (JOCC), which became operational in 2019. The JOCC is tasked with "planning, monitoring and integrating operations involving forces from the Army and the Air Force, operating in both the borderland areas contingent to the Algerian border and in the south of the country with the main purpose of fighting terrorism, securing borders and combatting organized crime in its diverse forms."[59] However, the JOCC does not operate at full capacity as there are serious issues hindering the development of jointness, chief among them the parochial interservice command-and-control organizations on the operational level. Still, this structure is more tactically oriented and lacks any structure of joint operations. More significantly, the JOCC has allegedly become "an empty shelf" serving as a "display showcase" for civilian decisionmakers (i.e., president, head of government, and minister of defense). When they occasionally pay a visit to the JOCC, "they fail to ask the right questions about the JOCC's functioning while they seem much impressed by the tailored briefings given to them on site."[60] The JOCC operates in tandem with the Joint Reconnaissance Center (JRC) tasked with "supporting integrated operations, from collecting intelligence on related field activities to identifying targets, from analyzing Battle Damage Assessment to transmitting data in near real-time to the battlefield."[61] However, the JRC and the JOCC neither developed horizontal data integration in real time for operations conducted in different locations nor secured information sharing between deployed military units across the country.[62]

In early September 2020, in line with the BCAP, the United States deployed a security force assistance team (SFAT) as a part of the US Army's Security Force Assistance Brigade (SFAB), tasked with training, advising, assisting, and enabling operational capabilities of partner nations. Yet one could argue that the deployment of the SFAT in Tunisia cannot be taken out of the volatile regional context. In May 2020, General Stephen J. Townsend, the then commander of United States Africa Command, relayed to the Tunisian minister of defense during a telephone conversation that the United States was willing to deploy SFAB to respond to Russian regional involvement that "continues to fan the flames of the Libyan conflict."[63] However, unlike the short-term deployments experienced in other countries, the SFAT was led by an American officer with a rank of lieutenant colonel and organized around forty junior US officers and noncommissioned officers, reportedly deployed for a renewable period of six months in three main locations (i.e., Bizerte, Tunis, and Hammamet) and tasked with holistically improving TAF's operational capabilities, while providing advice and training to their special forces, training air-to-ground integration for grounded forces, and providing education on joint operations center systems at the JOCC.[64] The SFAT's deployment occurred while the Tunisian MOD was working on a fledging "2030 Vision" centered on seven priorities: reorganizing the MOD and improving its outcomes at the level of planning and foresight; modernizing the MOD and its different structures and developing its professional capabilities; developing the combat capabilities of the armed forces and establishing rules and methods of jointness; setting mechanisms to properly use human resources and upgrading defense infrastructure; developing information systems and building protection capabilities against cyber threats; modernizing equipment and supporting national military industry; and developing the national service while contributing to the national effort for development.[65] Although achieving this very ambitious vision would require substantial means, it is unlikely that BCAP, as a framework of US security assistance prioritizing combat performance against nonstate armed groups, would play any significant role in contributing to it. This vision looks coherent on paper, as it prioritizes a holistic reshuffle of Tunisia's defense sector, but would be difficult to implement due to the country's dire socioeconomic situation, which obviously impacts defense reform and related expenditures.[66]

With the United States running Tunisian security assistance, the BCAP was complemented by a ten-year Roadmap for Defense Cooperation (RFDC) signed by the Donald Trump administration's secretary of defense, Mark Esper, and his Tunisian counterpart on September 30, 2020.[67] The RFDC frames Tunisia as a regional "security exporter" of "stability and security on the African continent," while emphasizing "shared priorities . . . shared interests and shared threats" between the two signatories.[68] The RFDC focuses on the enhancement of the country's "military capabilities and training to improve interoperability" in line with "shared interests [that] include freedom of navigation, intelligence sharing, humanitarian operations and disaster relief."[69] Reportedly, the RFDC would serve as a benchmark framework for future cooperation between the United States and other African countries.[70] Interestingly, Esper linked the RFDC to the US global power competition that identifies China and Russia as both "intimidat[ing]" and "coercive" strategic forces seeking to "expanding their authoritarian influence worldwide" and in Africa.[71] Notwithstanding this clear correlation between the United States' strategic interests as the provider of security assistance and the local agenda of a recipient country in the Global South (i.e., Tunisia), Esper's Tunisian counterparts downplayed his statement by pointing out that "the RFDC doesn't stipulate any new arrangement from what already exists."[72] While the United States has framed its security assistance to Tunisia within its regional alliances to "counter its peer competitors," obviously Tunisia does not "see Chinese and Russian activities from Washington's lens. From Tunisia's standpoint, the latter wanted to buy from [them] something that doesn't exist, so [they] have sold them the nothingness."[73] Regardless of the intentions and underlying interpretations of each party to this new institutional security assistance, Tunisia—like other countries in the region—is in the process of being further integrated into the US global security complex while "assuming a new geopolitical significance and acquiring new strategic 'rents' from the United States."[74] Yet this assistance has been increasingly operating independently—and, to some extent, to the detriment—of Tunisia's sociopolitical realities in the post-2011 era.

US Security Assistance and Its Implications for Tunisia's Marginalized Border Regions

In early March 2016, the southern town of Ben Guerdane, twenty miles from the Libyan border, fell under a coordinated assault by Islamic State of Iraq and Syria (ISIS) militants against the military barracks and ISF facilities, seeking to take control of the border town. The fighting lasted three days, and the assailants failed in their enterprise, while "the support of the population for the army and ISF was critical in defeating the insurgents."[75] The assault resulted in the deaths of seven civilians, a dozen members of security forces, and more than forty fighters suspected of involvement in the attack.[76] Notwithstanding Ben Guerdane's hospitable reputation among Tunisians and foreigners for welcoming thousands of refugees who had fled Libya and for serving as a crossing point for almost one million Libyan refugees during the apex of the Libyan crisis from February to September 2011,[77] the mainstream foreign media quickly came to characterize the town as a "breeding ground of foreign fighters"[78] into which "mayhem was spilling over from neighboring Libya."[79] Yet this stigmatizing discourse toward marginalized border areas has become a constant narrative of Tunisia's governments, which have failed to address economic inequalities and social justice since 2011. Instead, they embraced a securitization discourse that framed protests and sit-ins organized by aggrieved unemployed people "in the border areas in the governorates of Medenine and Tataouine [as] doctored to cover up the smuggling of weapons and allow the passage of terrorists."[80] The depiction of unemployed protesters as facilitating terrorists' activities has enabled ruling elites to delegitimize protesters' demands in forgotten-excluded border areas situated in the margins of the Tunisian state and to prioritize a hard security-oriented approach over long-term socioeconomic solutions.[81]

Most noteworthily, Ben Guerdane belongs to the country's interior and border peripheral regions, which have been heavily discriminated against and marginalized since Tunisia's independence. The coastal ruling elites prioritized socioeconomic development of the northeastern coastal regions to the detriment of the northwestern, central-western, southwestern, and southeastern hinterlands, leading to a lack of economic opportunities and salient uneven development between regions. While Tunisia has been experiencing fits and starts in its democratization since 2011, these disparities have been further entrenched. In 2019, the national unemployment rate was estimated at 15.3 percent, but in the country's peripheral areas, it reached 22.2 percent in the southeast and 24.8 in the southwest.[82] Most strikingly, the feelings of abandonment and marginalization among locals in the border areas have deeply affected "the self-image of people in Ben Guerdane and Dhehiba with almost 90% and 98% of inhabitants, respectively, reporting a strong sense of exclusion."[83] This perception of injustice and dispossession in the country's southern hinterland is reminiscent of the history of systematic alienation that goes back to the colonial era and deepened in Tunisia's postindependence.[84]

People in Jefara—the region encompassing the Tunisian-Libyan border territory—developed intertwined economic relations and resilient tribal ties that came to rule the area extending from Matmata in Tunisia's south to east of Tripoli in Libya. The irruption of the colonial order in the nineteenth century, which arbitrarily divided this tribal territory between the French and Italian colonial powers, unsettled the web of relations dominated in Jefara by the powerful Tunisian Wherghemma tribal federation that had relentlessly resisted the central power's military expeditions seeking tax collections.[85] Notwithstanding political tensions that punctuated Tunisian-Libyan bilateral relations in the postcolonial era (i.e., in the 1970s and 1980s), local communities on both sides of the borders—mainly between Ben Guerdane and Zuwarah along the Mediterranean Libyan coast and further south between Dhehiba and the Nefusa Mountains—have built resilient trading relations, based on informal economic exchanges stemming from marginalization.[86] Although this informal economy "is not always part of formal legality," it constitutes the "visible expression of various survival strategies developed by local populations."[87] The expansion of informal trade was instrumental to Ben Ali's regime, allowing it to assert power over the country's southern border areas, including well-established local smugglers and communities, while using these activities to "absorb unemployment at a smaller cost."[88] However, the political-security disorder in Libya following the demise of Mu'ammar Gadhafi's regime and the reduction of iron-fist security in the immediate aftermath of the fall of Ben Ali's regime in Tunisia impacted the patterns and actors of cross-border smuggling. Tribal armed militias took control of the Libyan side of the border, leading to new arrangements and rivalries among fractured cross-border networks along the Wherghemma tribal lines (i.e., Twazin and Rabai'a tribes) on the Tunisian side while paving the way for new practices of informal trade infiltrated by violent nonstate actors.[89]

In the aftermath of the Bardo and Sousse attacks, Tunisia's government decided—without consulting with the parliament or civil society actors, let alone local border communities—to begin constructing of a barrier fence along the border with Libya in 2015.[90] This securitizing measure further militarized the country's periphery, contributing to the "immobiliz[ation of] flow[s] of people, good[s] and services" while "governing problematic populations."[91] The resulting formation of "clear population hierarchies" mirrored and enforced "imperial and colonial specificities."[92] This hierarchization is reflected in the discourse of the US Global War on Terror and the EU "fight against terrorism," both centered on narratives of "fear of the 'other' as a source of insecurity and uncertainty that is seen as endemic within Western society in the 21st century."[93] This "othering" is applicable to the local border communities, which some Tunisian media continue to frame both as terrorists and as posing a threat to national security and stability.

Interviewees repeatedly emphasized the "amalgamation of informal trade and terrorism" reminiscent of the French colonial policy that turned border regions in the country's south into military zones to crush the armed resistance, while Habib Bourguiba "framed the entire south as unruly and a threat to his regime after he triumphed in a bloody struggle over his rival Salah Ben Yousef in the 1960s."[94] This amalgamation is another form of "marginalization where poverty and unemployment are criminalized by the central government, as people in the country's margins struggle to survive through the informal economy."[95] One interviewee in his mid-twenties noted that

> smuggling is not a luxury for people of my age; you get in by necessity not by choice. My mother sold her jewelry to be able to send my three sisters to university. All of them graduated with no job on the horizon. I felt that I have the moral obligation to express my solidarity with my family and preserve its cohesion. I left high school one year before graduation to support my family as I don't think going to university will provide me with a job.[96]

One Zarzis interviewee, who was visiting his family in Ben Guerdane during the March 2016 ISIS attack, acknowledged:

> There is no trust whatsoever in central government among local communities in border areas. However, people's support to security forces against the assailants was crucial in defeating ISIS militants while most of the fighters were from Ben Guerdane. We backed security forces despite their involvement in cross-border extortion rackets and the disproportionate use of force against local communities. The message that we people of marginalized and stigmatized border areas wanted to send to decisionmakers in Tunis is that we belong in this country, we're willing to defend it as our ancestors did against the French, and above all we are not terrorists as we vehemently denounced and contributed to the arrest of some of ours who embraced the path of violence. Our loyalty is to Tunisia not to the ruling elites. Rather than judging us, they must understand the constraints of our social realities. . . . Undoubtedly, solidarity, kinship, blood, and marriage relations between both sides of the border transcend any sophisticated system of walls and fences that the government is building with the assistance of foreign powers.[97]

Western providers of security assistance, mainly the United States and Germany, involved in walling Tunisia's southern border with Libya, ignored these microdynamics in border areas, while this hypersecuritization "deteriorated the economic situation of local communities and led to despair among youths, thereby undermining Tunisia's long-term stability."[98] Most significantly, this discursive process of border surveillance, walling, and securitization (as Sean Yom notes in the Jordanian case) has been translated into a sophisticated militarized fortification of the Tunisian border with Libya.[99] Tunisia's militarization of its borders aims at further integrating the country into a new form of the "Global War on Terror" with its "criminalization of mobility around the world" by "investing in militarized border regimes that reach far beyond particular territorial borders to manage the movement of people from the Global South."[100] This approach is in line with the globalized nature of the counterterrorism paradigm translated into militarized borders in the US and EU contexts alongside excessive reliance on advanced technologies monitoring citizens and noncitizens alike, while leading to increasing violence at border areas and criminalization of migrants.[101] Vayl Oxford, director of the US Defense Threat Reduction Agency (DTRA), referred to the border areas as "Tunisia's inhospitable border with Libya."[102] This framing ignores the underlying socioeconomic dynamics that shape the daily lives of local people involved in cross-border trade activities, as residents in the country's eastern border "need Libya more than they need Tunis. And thus, a wall, for better or worse, will always be a simple answer to a complicated problem."[103] According to Oxford, the wall involves "stationary electro-optical/infrared cameras and radars on 16 towers along the border, a Common Operating Picture, communications links to a Border Security Operations Center [BSOC], and four regional border security headquarters."[104] DTRA outsourced the fence project to two US contractors for an initial amount of $24.9 million.[105] Germany joined DTRA in financing and equipping the border with electronic assets.[106]

So far, two regional BSOCs are operational; the first, established at the headquarters of the First Mechanized Brigade in Gabès, is responsible for the first border section from Ra's Ajdir to Dehiba, while the second operates under the First Regiment Saharan Territorial Infantry in the town of Remada and monitors the section stretching further south from Dehiba to Bir Zar. Each of these regional centers relies on Border Response Units tasked with intervention upon detection of cross-border activities by the installed sensor towers.[107] Moreover, the Tunisian MOD has repeatedly requested that DTRA finance the walling of the third section of the border from Bir Zar to the town of Borj el-Khadra bordering both Algeria and Libya.[108] In addition to these aggressive border measures, the TAF will receive two modified Cessna Caravan aircraft with ISR capabilities from the United States, expected to be delivered by the end of 2022 "to aid in Tunisia's border security efforts."[109] These complex policing efforts, which seek to reproduce engineered-militarized territorial space of governance through walling and control in a culturally and economically interconnected environment of natural mobility, have failed to seal a border that continues to be breached on a daily basis.[110] Oxford's claim that "WMD proliferation [is] one of many concerns about the border" is rhetorical,[111] as most of the seized goods include no more than tobacco, livestock, electronics, and gasoline, and their confiscation forces local communities into further deprivation and economic distress.

This attempted "Mexicanization" of the Tunisian-Libyan border, as one interviewee put it, mirrors the "securitization of local communities' livelihood and their socio-economic marginalization."[112] Although they evoke control mechanisms and security architecture, "borders are more than territorial boundaries but rather constitute a rhetorical process of demarcating and defining identity and social space."[113] In the US-Mexico context, migration and cross-border movements challenge the US militarization of its borders to "police the boundaries of the U.S. identity," while creating a sense of "We didn't cross the border, the border crossed us."[114] One takeaway from my formal and informal interviews was that local communities in southern border areas are determined to demonstrate to Tunisia's post-2011 rulers that if there is a lesson to draw from US-Mexico dynamics, it is that "borders move, migrate, and cross individuals and groups for good or ill."[115]

This broad picture of securitization and stigmatization of border communities in southern Tunisia would be incomplete without examining the nature of military curriculum training programs provided within US security assistance to many Tunisian units and their implications for border communities. The content of the Foreign Military Training Program for Fiscal Years 2018 and 2019 is a comprehensive indicator regarding the US military training programs provided to each country around the world, detailing the "purpose for the activity, the number of foreign military personnel provided training and their units of operation, and the location of training."[116] For instance, most of the courses dispensed under the US Department of Defense's Regional Defense Combatting Terrorism and Irregular Warfare Fellowship Program revolved around counterterrorism and the controversial Countering Violence Extremism (CVE) strategy. Needless to say, CVE prioritizes securitization (i.e., symptoms) over socioeconomic development (i.e., drivers) by supporting state-centered and Western-designed approaches to security while contributing to further stigmatization and marginalization of communities targeted by these programs. Most significantly, members of military personnel deployed in the peripheral border areas, such as the 17th Mechanized Battalion based in Tataouine, attended CVE courses at MacDill Air Force Base in Florida in January 2018. It is unclear how the military can promote resilience among local communities, including youth, if their primary mission is to limit their movements, further undermining their social and economic opportunities. Still, Tataouine is home to 20 percent of the country's gas and 40 percent of its oil while suffering the highest rate of unemployment, at 28.7 percent (2019); it has also been experiencing the El Kamour social protests demanding that the government prioritize the region's development and provide jobs in oil companies in accordance with an agreement signed and endorsed by the two major parties in 2017.[117] As protesters blocked oil facilities in the region several times, the army has been assigned with the task of "protecting" key oil and gas infrastructure.[118] These protests were used by the late president Mohamcd Beji Caid Essebsi to justify his decision to expand the closed military zone to include, in addition to "critical sites," large swaths of land close to border areas in Tataouine Governorate; these then "became inaccessible to landowners without a special military pass difficult to obtain,"[119] thereby establishing inner borders in this long-marginalized southern region.

Yet people's perception of US security assistance in the southern border areas reveals how border populations view the US application of its coercive hard power through a local agent (i.e., the Tunisian military) over their living space. One interviewee described the appearance of the Tunisian military that patrols on a daily basis in the border areas:

> [They] drive US-made Humvees while dressed in US-made military gear, including bulletproof jackets; many are equipped with A-4 assault rifles. They represent the facade of the American empire that is stretching its muscle and encroaching into our geography. Like in Hollywood action movies, there are more bullets and fewer dollars. Here we endure more coercion but no development. The sad side of the story is that the Tunisian military has become the coercive tool of this empire.[120]

Reportedly, the military is no longer refraining from using coercion, including opening fire on everything that moves in border areas—particularly on suspected smugglers who try to escape control. Although it is difficult to confirm such a claim, targeting and killing of locals, apparently in a closed military zone south of Remada next to the border with Libya, occurred several times, in 2016, 2020, and 2021.[121] These lethal actions, often portrayed as accidents by both ruling elites and local media, may be a sign that decisionmakers in Tunis, who have failed to improve citizens' lives through meaningful governance, are tempted to exert more pressure on border communities by criminalizing their means of subsistence without providing them with any alternative livelihood and conflating their border economy activities with terrorism. In the absence of any socioeconomic vision for the country outside the neoliberal paradigm and its ensuing asymmetric regional disparities,[122] these shortsighted tactics may backfire. In July 2021 alone, despite the perpetual state of emergency since 2011, heightened by President Saied's exceptional measures, there were 975 protest movements nationwide compared with 798 during the same month in 2020, including 491 that occurred in the country's southern hinterland.[123] Notwithstanding the securitized approach to socioeconomic issues actively supported by Western donors (i.e., United

States), the persistence of social pressure is a sign that the slogan *al-sha'b yureed* ("The People Want"), which constituted the soul of the 2010–2011 Tunisian popular uprising, is still alive.

Conclusion

Western donors, chief among them the United States, continue to assess Tunisia's democratization through the prism of "stability," with "countering terror" a prerequisite for the country's "success story." This mantra has become central to Tunisian political elites' discourse of legitimization after 2011. This discourse suggests that there is an organic link between US security assistance and the precarious transitional process in Tunisia. This framing is problematic as it tends to further incorporate Tunisian local agency into a US global security architecture, situating Tunisia's stumbling democratization in a more decreed neoliberal economic perspective through securitization that threatens marginalized segments of Tunisian society, particularly border communities.

Transferring military equipment and providing training and assistance in a complex sociopolitical context without considering the underlying local dynamics may further erode Tunisia's democratic experiment, with the real risk of destabilizing the country's marginal border areas as a result of unrelenting militarization. In the absence of any valuable economic resources and regular jobs, Tunisia's southern borders remain a key site for informal trade and economic activity, allowing people to meet their immediate needs while surviving the precariousness of their "spatial, economic, social and political marginalization."[124] The conflation of informal cross-border activities with terrorism, as depicted in Tunisian governmental discourse backed by transnational security actors, chief among them the United States, has further contributed to the exclusion and dispossession of border communities while possibly subverting the security resilience that US security assistance seeks to achieve in the first place. The United States should reassess the strategic implications of its patronage security policies for recipient countries in the Global South (i.e., Tunisia), where poverty, a lack of opportunity, and populism are on a sharp rise, and where the marginalized of Tunisia's peripheries are more likely to believe that Tunisia's democratic experiment is flawed and will not benefit them. Thus, it is time for the United States to demystify the "Tunisian exception" narrative and its underlying "stability" paradigm and to move beyond shaping Tunisia's security assistance in accordance with Washington's own preferences and agendas.

Notes

1. "Security Assistance Database."
2. Wezeman, "Saudi Arabia, Armaments and Conflict in the Middle East."
3. Hartung, *The U.S. Support for Saudi Arabia and the War in Yemen.*
4. Clinton, "Press Statement on Recent Events in Tunisia."
5. Blanton, "Instruments of Security or Tools of Repression?" 233–244; Blanton, "Promoting Human Rights and Democracy in the Developing World," 123–131.
6. Berger, "Guns, Butter, and Human Rights," 603–635.
7. Powel, "The Stability Syndrome," 57–73.
8. Ibid., 68.
9. Ibid., 69.
10. Santini and Cimini, "The Politics of Security Reform in Post-2011 Tunisia," 225–241; Youssef, "Beyond Performance."
11. Jebnoun, *Tunisia's National Intelligence*, 58–90.
12. Santini and Cimini, "The Politics of Security Reform in Post-2011 Tunisia."
13. Pogodda, "Revolutions and the Liberal Peace," 352.
14. Buzan, Waever, and de Wilde, *Security*, 25.
15. Ibid., 5.
16. Presidential Decree 2021-69; Presidential Decree 2021-80.
17. Since July 25, 2021, President Kais Saied has been ruling and legislating by decree. He issued a series of controversial decrees aimed at consolidating his power by paving the way for one-man rule while deepening Tunisia's unfolding democratization crisis. On September 22, 2021, President Saied issued Presidential Decree 2021-117 maintaining suspension of the legislative body's activities and reiterating the lifting of parliamentary immunity. On February 12, 2022, he issued Presidential Decree 2022-11 suspending the Supreme Judicial Council and establishing a Provisional Council, ending any judicial independence. On March 30, 2022, Saied announced through Presidential Decree 2022-309 the dissolution of the parliament after a majority of members (121 out of 217) took part in a virtual session to repeal Saied's decrees that gave him full power since July 25, 2021. In the process, he ordered the minister of justice to investigate and prosecute these parliamentarians for "conspiring against state security." On April 21, 2022, Saied issued Presidential Decree 2022-22 allowing him to appoint members of the Independent High Authority for Elections, thus calling into question the credibility of the commission as well as future elections. On May 19, 2022, Saied issued Presidential Decree 2022-30 creating an advisory body calling for the establishment of a "new republic." On May 25, 2022, he promulgated Presidential Decree 2022-506 abolishing the 2014 constitution and organizing a referendum for a new constitution that was held on July 25, 2022, which granted the president with expansive and unchecked powers and consolidated his one-man rule. On June 1, Saied tightened his grip over the judiciary by issuing Presidential Decree 2022-516, not subject to any form of appeal, that arbitrarily dismissed fifty-seven judges with no due process of law, further weakening the independence of the judiciary. All of these decrees are in flagrant violation of the 2014 constitution and its article 80 on "imminent perils" invoked by Saied on July 25, 2021.
18. Agamben, *State of Exception*, 1.
19. Human Rights Council, "Visit to Tunisia."
20. Mullin, "Tunisia's 'Transition.'"
21. Furness, "Strategic Policymaking and the German Aid Programme," 6.
22. Couzens Hoy, *Critical Resistance*, 3.
23. Congressional Research Service, "U.S. Foreign Assistance to the Middle East," 15.

24. Gates, "Helping Others Defend Themselves," 1.
25. Baker, "Obama Upgrades Tunisia as a U.S. Ally."
26. Jebnoun, "Tunisia: Patterns and Implications of Civilian Control," 116.
27. Coon, "Support Tunisia."
28. US House of Representatives, Committee on Foreign Affairs, *Tunisia's Struggle for Stability, Security, and Democracy*, 6.
29. US Senate Committee on Appropriations, Subcommittee on State, Foreign Operations, and Related Programs, *State, Foreign Operations and Related Programs Appropriations for Fiscal Year 2018*.
30. Recommendation of Dr. Amna Guellali, deputy regional director for Middle East and North Africa, Amnesty International, to US Representative Tom Malinowski (7th District of New Jersey), during a hearing before the US House Foreign Affairs Subcommittee on Middle East, North Africa, and Global Counterterrorism.
31. Congressional Research Service, "U.S. Foreign Assistance to the Middle East," 12.
32. Personal communication via call phone with a former Tunisian defense attaché in Washington, DC, September 18, 2020, supplemented by data available through the Security Assistance Monitor (http://securityassistance.org).
33. Security Assistance Monitor (http://securityassistance.org).
34. Initially, Tunisia ordered twelve Black Hawks under the FMS program worth $700 million in 2014. Later, the number was reduced to eight (Valine, "Tunisia Accepts Delivery of Last of Eight Black Hawks"). Further information on the initial sale and the characteristics of these helicopters are provided by the Defense Security Cooperation Agency (DSCA), "Tunisia—UH-60 M Black Hawk Helicopters."
35. DSCA, "Tunisia—OH-58 Kiowa Warrior Aircraft Equipment and Support"; Flight International's *World Air Forces 2021* lists (p. 31) only eighteen OH-58D Kiowas so far operational within the Tunisian air force.
36. DSCA, "Tunisia—AT-6 Light Attack Aircraft."
37. All three DSCA press releases emphasize these objectives.
38. Security Assistance Monitor (http://securityassistance.org).
39. Hensler, "Security Assistance in Focus."
40. Ibid.
41. Personal communication with a high-ranking Tunisian military officer on active duty, location undisclosed, June 12, 2019.
42. Jebnoun, *Tunisia's National Intelligence*, 80–81.
43. For instance, see military activities undertaken by Tunisia's military within the frame of security cooperation listed in US Department of Defense and US Department of State, *Foreign Military Training Program FY 2018 and 2019*.
44. According to a document internal to Tunisian Air Force titled *New Approach to Counterterrorism*, the air force integrated counterterrorism as one of its key missions using airpower both to provide forces engaged in operations against armed groups with better situational awareness through air-ground integration and to target these groups' infrastructures (i.e., training camps) and decisive points (i.e., observation posts, ambush sites).
45. Jebnoun, *Tunisia's National Intelligence*, 62–68; Entous and Ryan, "U.S. Has Secretly Expanded Its Global Network." Photos of US military presence inside the Tunisian air force base of Sidi Ahmed in Bizerte were widely circulated on social media: "#Tunisia: Photos circulating on social media allegedly showing #US troops & material at the Sidi Ahmed TAF base, #Bizerte," posted to Twitter by MENASTREAM at 4:08 p.m. on November 1, 2016, https://twitter.com/MENASTREAM/status/793454646329274369.
46. Personal communication with a high-ranking Tunisian military officer on active duty and confirmed by a US military official who previously served at the US

embassy in Tunis. The US decision to end its ISR presence in Bizerte seems to be lessening the friction between Algiers and Tunis that rose up in the aftermath of the deployment of the US drones in Tunisia in 2016.

47. Gibbons-Neff and Schmitt, "After Deadly Raid, Pentagon Weighs."
48. Mattis, "Summary of the 2018 National Defense Strategy of the United States of America."
49. "DoD Personnel, Workforce Reports, and Publications."
50. See, e.g., Savell et al., "United States Counterterrorism Operations"; Turse and Naylor, "Revealed"; US House of Representatives, Office of the Law Revision Counsel, "10 USC 127e: Support of Special Operations to Combat Terrorism."
51. Szoldra, "Exclusive"; Nsaibia, "America Is Quietly Expanding Its War in Tunisia"; Blaise, Schmitt, and Gall, "Why the U.S. and Tunisia Keep Their Cooperation Secret."
52. Morgan, "Behind the Secret U.S. War in Africa."
53. Ibid.
54. Jebnoun, "Tunisia," 131–134.
55. This trend has become obvious. For example, in January 2022, the Tunisian Land Army added a new battalion to its Special Forces Group and renamed it a Special Forces Brigade. The unit's expansion from the size of a task force to a brigade—though a light brigade with three battalions so far—implies that the priority is given to counterterrorist and counterinsurgency elite units at the expense of the bulk of the armed forces, which retain aged arms, vehicles, and jets and different types of obsolete military hardware.
56. Vest, "Can Anything Stop the Flow of Advanced Weapons into Libya?"
57. Reuters Staff, "Eastern Libyan Forces Warplane Makes Emergency Landing in Tunisia." The Libyan L-39 Albatros from General Khalifa Haftar's Libyan National Army landed on a road in the southern town of Beni Khadash about sixty miles from Tunisia's border with Libya. Although the statement of the Tunisian MOD claimed that the Libyan L-39 was detected by the radar system and that "the Tunisian air force planned to intercept the jet after it violated the country's airspace, but it landed before they could do so," sources within the MOD confirmed to the author that the statement tried to downplay serious shortcomings within the Tunisian air force to respond in real time to such incidents, as the radar had failed to detect the Libyan jet.
58. According to a US military official who previously served at the US embassy in Tunis, the BCAP was initially an American framework discussed among US defense officials in Tunis in 2016. The BCAP aimed at capturing "the strategic security cooperation goals for U.S. and Tunisian security cooperation efforts" by allowing the Tunisian counterpart to "focus on the desired capability to all-encompassing shared objectives, rather than become fixated on a specific resource or type of equipment."
59. Personal communication via call phone with a retired high-ranking military officer actively involved in the establishment of the Joint Operations Control Center, October 22, 2020.
60. Ibid.
61. Ibid.
62. Ibid.
63. See "AFRICOM Commander Reaffirms Bilateral Partnership with Tunisia."
64. Personnel communication via email, October 13, 2021. Undisclosed source.
65. Internal draft to the Tunisian MOD on the "2030 Vision."
66. In 2020, Tunisia's public debt reached 88 percent of GDP. However, the "debt burden exceeds 100 percent of GDP once government guarantees and SOE

[state-owned enterprise] debts are included." See Micro Poverty Outlook–World Bank, "Tunisia," 176–177.

67. US Department of Defense, "Readout of Secretary of Defense Dr. Mark T. Esper's Meeting."
68. Garamone, "U.S., Tunisia Sign a Road Map for Defense Cooperation."
69. Ibid.
70. Ibid.
71. Garamone, "Esper's Africa Visit Aims to Encourage Stability, Interoperability."
72. Personal communication via call phone with a high-ranking Tunisian military officer on active duty involved in the process of negotiation and conception of the RFDC, October 3, 2020.
73. Ibid.
74. Henry, "Reverberations in the Central Maghreb of the 'Global War on Terror,'" 297.
75. Jebnoun, "Tunisia," 130.
76. MEE and Agencies, "Tunisian Forces Kill Seven in Fresh Fighting on Libya Border."
77. Executive Committee of the High Commissioner's Programme, "Update on UNHCR's Operations in the Middle East and North Africa."
78. Bryant, "Inside Tunisia's Extremist Breeding Ground."
79. Samti and Walsh, "Tunisian Clash Spreads Fear That Libyan War Is Spilling Over."
80. "In a Two-Hour Meeting."
81. In early February 2015, inhabitants of the small town of Dhehiba, less than two miles from the Libyan border, organized peaceful protests demanding that local and regional authorities prioritize employment and economic development of their town, which relies on a cross-border economy. The governor of Tataouine rejected any dialogue with locals, who were already portrayed in the official discourse as "barons of smuggling and terrorists." He ordered the overwhelming deployment of security forces that besieged Dhehiba for several days, undertaking a campaign of brutal arrest of protesters, who were harshly oppressed through the use of expired tear gas canisters, gunshot pellets, and live ammunition. For further details, see Tunisian Forum for Economic and Social Rights, "Dhehiba's Incidents."
82. National Institute of Statistics, "Employment and Unemployment Indicators."
83. Lamloum, *Marginalization, Insecurity and Uncertainty on the Tunisian-Libyan Border*.
84. Ibid.
85. Anderson, *The State and Social Transformation in Tunisia and Libya*, 66; Guillaume, *Entre désertification et développement*, 198.
86. Kartas, *On the Edge?*
87. Ayeb, "Après Ben Guerdane."
88. Lamloum, *Marginalization, Insecurity and Uncertainty on the Tunisian-Libyan Border*, 16.
89. Kartas, *On the Edge?*
90. MEE Staff, "Tunisia to Build a Border Wall with Libya."
91. Pallister-Wilkins, "Bridging the Divide," 438–459.
92. Ibid., 450.
93. Baker-Bell, "The Discursive Construction of the EU Counter-Terrorism Policy," 189.
94. Interview with a high school math teacher, Ben Guerdane, May 11, 2019.
95. Ibid.

96. Interview with B, Ben Guerdane, May 14, 2019.
97. Interview with K, a mechanic in his twenties, Zarzis, May 12, 2019.
98. Stahl and Treffler, "Germany's Security Assistance to Tunisia," 40.
99. "Washington Consolidates Tunisia-Libya Electronic Border Surveillance Wall."
100. Besteman, "Border Regimes and the New Global Apartheid."
101. Jones and Johnson, "Border Militarization and the Re-articulation of Sovereignty," 187–200.
102. Oxford, *Reviewing Department of Defense Strategy, Policy, and Programs*, 9.
103. *Le Monde*, "A Troubling New Wall Rises at the Tunisia-Libya Border."
104. Oxford, *Reviewing Department of Defense Strategy, Policy, and Programs*, 9.
105. Public Affairs Section, "U.S. Support for Tunisian Border Security Project"; Nkala, "U.S. Army Awards Contract for Installation of Surveillance System on Tunisia-Libya Border."
106. Monroy, "Germany Funds New Border Control Technology in Tunisia."
107. Personnel communication, undisclosed source.
108. Ibid.
109. Martin, "Tunisia Getting Cessna Caravans for Intelligence, Surveillance and Reconnaissance."
110. Personnel communication, undisclosed source.
111. Oxford, *Reviewing Department of Defense Strategy, Policy, and Programs*, 9.
112. Interview with a physician, Tataouine, June 3, 2019.
113. Cisneros, *The Border Crossed Us*, 3.
114. Ibid., 2.
115. Ibid.
116. US Department of Defense and US Department of State, *Foreign Military Training Program FY 2018 and 2019*.
117. Meddeb, "Life on the Edge."
118. "Video-Les militaires mobilisés à Tataouine face à l'assaut des sit-inneurs d'El Kamour."
119. Interview with S, Guermessa, June 16, 2021.
120. Interview with a construction engineer, Tataouine, June 3, 2019.
121. "Tataouine: Grève générale à Remada;" "Remada: Anger Among Inhabitants"; Ghanem and Jrad, *When the Margins Rise*, 26. There are many videos on social media showing the army deploying Turkish-made Mine-Resistant Ambush Protected vehicles in downtown Remada during local protests. See, e.g., https://m.facebook.com/ayebbechir.ayeb/posts/pcb.3377980842264905/?.
122. See *Programme de réformes pour une sortie de crise*. This leaked confidential document of the Tunisian government encapsulates its agenda of negotiations with the International Monetary Fund and international donors. The document clearly endorses an economic vision revolving around neoliberalism by promoting fiscal austerity, further deregulation, and privatization, as well as lifting subsidies, freezing wages, and cutting government spending. Tunisian technocrats drafted the document without consulting about these déjà-vu "reforms" with social actors, mainly labor unions, chief among them the Tunisian General Labor Union.
123. Tunisian Forum for Economic and Social Rights, "Report of July 2021."
124. Ayeb, "Social and Political Geography of the Tunisian Revolution," 467.

5
Lebanon: Assessing US-Led Capabilities Development

Aram Nerguizian

> *The [Lebanese Armed Forces are] manned by officers and soldiers who are hardworking, innovative and motivated by national pride and unity. However, the LAF is not currently equipped or trained to succeed in anything but the most basic tactical missions against minimal and irresolute opposition and is still fragile due to a cultural loyalty along confessional lines. . . . [The] LAF conventional forces must undergo a sustained period of intense [training]—lasting several years, to reach a point where the LAF can sustain its readiness and [fulfill] its responsibilities of exerting Lebanese government control within its borders.*[1]
>
> —Lieutenant General Joseph Martz, US Army, 2006

After Lebanon's 1975–1990 civil war, Syria's security and intelligence apparatus regulated state-society and civil-military relations, largely relegating the Lebanese Armed Forces (LAF) to a limited internal security role. The withdrawal of Syrian troops in 2005 led to renewed Western interest in the LAF as a regional military partner. That year also marked the resumption of relatively large-scale US security assistance and security cooperation with Lebanon and the LAF after the de facto suspension of aid programs in the mid-1980s.

US policy toward Lebanon is a function of far broader US strategic imperatives in the Middle East, including the regional contest with Iran.

How the United States goes about providing security assistance to its Lebanese allies is also dependent on, and held back by, this overarching top-down approach to security politics in the Levant. From a US perspective, military aid to Lebanon was clearly expected to help reduce the country's footprint in regional instability and its role as a regional confrontation state against Israel. In short, military assistance to Lebanon became the latest addition to US-Iranian proxy warfare in the Levant.

US military planners believed that LAF personnel had relatively high morale, force cohesion, professionalism, adaptability, and, critically, a will to fight when given the order to do so. Security assistance and cooperation by the United States—in addition to efforts by allied nations such as the United Kingdom, France, and other Western states—over the 2005–2020 period would upgrade both special forces units and larger regular formations and propel the LAF along a gradual but substantial process of military recapitalization and force development.

In strictly operational and tactical terms, the effort was a relative success. Ten years after the LAF's drawn-out and costly 2007 battle against Fatah al-Islam militants near the northern city of Tripoli, the LAF's 2017 Fajr al Jurud ("dawn of the hills") combined-arms military campaign decisively led to the defeat and expulsion of heavily armed Islamic State in Iraq and the Levant (ISIL) militants from Lebanese soil. Five years on, the LAF remains one of the only credible and popular postwar national security institutions—if not the only one.

These achievements and milestones are not, in and of themselves, sufficient to characterize US and Western military assistance to Lebanon as an unqualified success. First, throughout the 2005–2021 period, US preferences and priorities would take time to align with the reality of what was, is, and might be achievable in Lebanon. Second, it would become clear early on that US assistance to the LAF was separate from providing aid to a Lebanese government comprised of a divided mix of domestic political and sectarian factions that disagreed on almost everything but a common aversion to a strong, professional, and credible national military. Supporting and building the LAF would prove a critical and persistent challenge to the long-term priorities and effectiveness of any external aid effort. Lastly, the United States and other partners of the LAF must learn from Iran's own successful model of "security assistance" to its local nonstate ally Hezbollah.

This chapter first provides a brief overview of the postwar LAF. It then unpacks the multisectarian character of Lebanon's military before describing Lebanese civil-military relations. Next, it describes some of the broader touchstones of US Lebanon policy before describing some of the key drivers of current patterns of US security assistance/cooperation to the LAF. The chapter proceeds to describe some of the principal lines of effort the United States is engaged in with the LAF. It then assesses some of the main limits of US security assistance/cooperation to the LAF before conversely exploring some of the LAF's challenges in absorbing aid from the United States. The chapter then looks at Iran's own parallel effort to support its own local ally Hezbollah, followed by concluding observations.

The main focus of this chapter is US aid, and for clarity's sake, it principally describes US assistance as "security assistance/cooperation." This will serve as an amalgamated abbreviation of Title 22 Department of State–funded "security assistance" and Title 10 Department of Defense–funded "security cooperation." This chapter also limits its focus to the Lebanese Armed Forces and does not address Lebanon's other national security institutions: the Internal Security Forces (Quwa al-Amn al-Dakhili), the General Directorate of General Security, also commonly referred to as General Security (al-Amn al-'Am), and the State Security Directorate (Mudiriyat Amn al-Dawla).

The Post–Civil War Lebanese Armed Forces

The LAF that emerged from the war in 1990 was a divided fighting force composed of Christian and Muslim personnel serving in brigades that were mainly homogenous along confessional lines.[2] Nevertheless, many of the LAF's postwar officers and noncommissioned officers, regardless of their sectarian affiliations, continued to subscribe to the Huntingtonian premise of military professionalism tied to expertise, corporateness, and responsibility.[3] This was the case even though these principles were not always followed by all of the LAF's military personnel and institutions, let alone reinforced by either the Syrian security and intelligence apparatus between 1990 and 2004 or by the country's sectarian/political elite since 2005.

The LAF's postwar officer corps remained broadly competent, professional, and adequately trained over the 1990–2005 period, despite the often overbearing politics of Syrian military fiat over Lebanon—but more on this topic later in this chapter. In the wake of the withdrawal of Syrian troops from Lebanon, the LAF—supported by the United States, the United Kingdom, France, and other Western states—underwent a gradual but substantial process of military recapitalization and force development. In 2005, the military transitioned to an all-volunteer force that no longer relies on mandatory military service. This shrank the size of the force from an active total of 61,803 in 2005 to 49,062 by 2006.[4]

In the years that followed, a procession of new and emerging national security challenges forced the LAF to adapt and expand both its capacity and military capabilities. By 2020, the LAF had grown to 81,707 military personnel,[5] driven by the need to expand internal stability operations, secure the deployment of troops to the south after the 2006 Israel-Hezbollah conflict for the first time since 1968, and meet the threat posed by militant Sunni Islamist groups like Fatah al-Islam, Jabhat al-Nusra, and ISIL. The need to adequately resource new intervention and land border regiments, pressures from Syria, and the rehabilitation of the Lebanese navy and air force also drove manpower trends.[6]

The resulting LAF is a joint force without an independent or separate structure at present for either the Lebanese navy or air force. The Lebanese army stood at 78,328 men and women under arms, including eleven mechanized infantry brigades, six intervention regiments, three elite special operations units, and four dedicated land border regiments.[7] The LAF is a textbook case of top-down military command and control where the commander of the force operates essentially as the de facto commander in chief of the armed forces. Furthermore, despite the existence of military commands based in the country's governorates—Beirut, Mount Lebanon, the North, the Beqa', Nabatiyé, and the South—how the LAF commander orients and manages the combat units spread across Lebanese territory remains heavily centralized.

All four postwar LAF commanders have been relatively "hands-on" military commanders, often with a high tendency to micromanage military and civil-military matters that in other militaries are relegated to officers with the rank of brigadier general, colonel, or lieutenant colonel. In extreme cases, the LAF commander was also known to bypass much of the chain of command, and while this may be conducted with the best of intentions, it may compromise the military chain of command.[8]

As discussed later in this chapter, with increased and sustained US-led security assistance/cooperation over the 2006–2021 period, the postwar and post-Syria LAF finds itself an increasingly capable national military. While still lacking key maritime and aerial capabilities, the LAF nonetheless counts in its ranks some of the most capable, motivated, and battle-tested special operations forces (SOF) components of any Arabic-speaking Middle Eastern country. Lebanese SOFs are held in such high regard by their US counterparts that this alone has become one of the critical drivers of the US-Lebanon bilateral military relationship.[9]

The LAF leverages these emerging capabilities to meet overlapping national security priorities. The first focus is containing the effects of instability in Syria. This has meant focusing on an area that successive Lebanese governments hitherto had ignored: creating a real-world security and border regime along the Lebanese-Syrian border. Second, the LAF sought to manage the risk of intermittent volatility along the UN Blue Line between Israel and Lebanon.[10] The third core national security focus pertains to internal stability in what the LAF has described as "high intensity internal stability and counterterrorism operations."[11]

The Multisectarian Makeup of the Postwar LAF

Sectarian considerations and efforts to become a nationally representative security institution were critical to the composition of the postwar LAF. Attaining these goals entailed recasting the sectarian composition of the officer corps and the rest of the military to better reflect the composition of Lebanese society at any given time. Moreover, units were now rotated periodically so that no formation can become too interconnected with the local sociodemographics and sectarian affiliations of a given area.[12]

One key tool in reshaping the makeup of the postwar LAF is a sectarian quota system within the officer corps that strives to maintain a 1:1 parity between Christians and Muslims. While the quota system is essential to maintaining equity and stability within most institutions in postwar Lebanon, it is nonetheless in dissonance with the Huntingtonian precept that "any given officer will adhere to the [professional military] ethic only to the extent that it is professional, that is, to the extent that it is shaped by functional rather than societal imperatives."[13]

Sectarian quotas also shape the allocation of LAF flagstaff positions, albeit in different ways throughout the organization's history. Just as the LAF commander is traditionally a Maronite, so too is the LAF chief of staff traditionally a Druze with a rank of major general. Meanwhile, the deputy chiefs of staff (DCoSs)—who nominally hold the rank of brigadier general in the postwar LAF—are also subject to similar sectarian calculations, and a quota system shapes DCoS appointments. Nominally, the post of DCoS for personnel is a Sunni, the DCoS for operations is a Shi'a, and the DCoS for logistics is a Christian, as is the DCoS for planning. Between 2008 and 2015, for example, the DCoS for planning was either a Greek Catholic or a Maronite, while the post of

DCoS for logistics was held by Maronite and—for the first time—Armenian Catholic officers.[14]

It is also important to note that second-order or deputy positions can at times be at least as important as leadership-level posts; consequently, most deputy-level posts are filled by officers from different sects than their superiors. For example, the director of operations—a post usually reserved for Christians—is central to battlefield operations and tactics, playing a far more immediate role than the officeholder's direct superior, the DCoS for operations, a position reserved for Shi'a officers.[15] Similarly, the deputy director of military intelligence—a post often reserved for Shi'a officers—has proven to be crucial throughout the postwar history of the LAF, at times overshadowing the Maronite-held post of director of military intelligence. However, the character, professionalism, and capabilities of senior flag officers inform many of these dynamics, and it is entirely possible for perceived power dynamics between commanders and their deputies to reverse themselves altogether.[16]

Just as key posts in the LAF command abide by considerations tied to sectarian balance and distribution, the same applies to officer appointments to lead the LAF's fighting units.[17] Unlike in the officer corps, however, a clearly defined sectarian quota is not enforced with regard to the rest of the postwar LAF. As a result, snapshots of the LAF's sectarian makeup at any given time shed light on which sectarian community or communities are vying for service in the military more broadly and within which specialized units more narrowly.

Intriguingly, when studying the military beyond the officer corps, scholarship on the composition of the postwar LAF exaggerated the representation of the Shi'a community within the force. For example, one study estimated that the Shi'a community's share in the LAF accounted for 60 percent of the rank and file.[18] The data presented below suggests otherwise, however. Internal LAF statistics showed that of a total force of 64,592 in 2014, 71.17 percent were Muslims, and 23.64 percent were Christians. The Sunni community had the highest level of representation within the force, accounting for 22,931 military personnel, or 35 percent of the LAF. The second-largest demographic was the Shi'a community, which accounted for 17,674, or 27 percent of the total force. The LAF had 8,261 Maronites, or 13 percent; the Druze and Greek Orthodox were 6 percent, Greek Catholics were 4 percent, and the balance was a mix of other smaller sectarian demographics.[19]

Ultimately, almost thirty years after the launch of efforts to create Christian-Muslim demographic parity in the postwar military, and in raw sectarian terms, the LAF finds itself a Muslim-majority force, with Sunnis constituting the dominant minority within it. The officer corps still abides by the precept of Christian-Muslim parity. By contrast, the rest of the force reflects key demographic trends with sectarian implications: over the 2005–2021 period, a growing intake of Sunnis on an annual basis has largely outpaced the intake from communities, including Maronites and Shi'a, whose annual intake rates appear to be in decline.[20]

Lebanese Civil-Military Relations

Lebanon has a long history of precarious civil-military relations. Weak state institutions serve as arenas for contestation between competing members of the sectarian/political elite. Although it has enjoyed more episodes of relative autonomy than other state institutions, the postwar LAF is no exception to an otherwise stubborn trend.

Soon after independence in 1943, the LAF acquired the role of arbiter between rival sectarian and political alliances in 1958 when it intervened directly to neutralize the political imbalance created by a short-lived civil war. The ensuing counterstruggle by confessional elites to restore their patronage networks culminated in the defeat of the military-backed political establishment in the 1970 presidential election and the dismantling of the Deuxième Bureau, the LAF's military intelligence apparatus. The long 1975–1990 civil war consequently fragmented the LAF along sectarian lines and gave way to the sectarian militia order of the civil war years.

As part of Lebanon's postwar political settlement under the Ta'if Agreement (1989), militias successfully underwent disarmament, demobilization, and partial reintegration. The Pax Syriana era transformed the LAF substantially. Syria's security and intelligence apparatus in Lebanon worked to recast the LAF into an impenetrable pro-Syrian institution, disconnected from government oversight and control. The former achieved this by interposing itself between the Lebanese military and the country's political system, thereby quickly penetrating and regulating Lebanese civil-military affairs until the departure of Syrian forces from Lebanon in 2005.

The 2005–2021 period was defined by two competing trends in hybrid security governance in postwar Lebanon. On the one hand, the LAF attempted to maintain and develop its military credibility and autonomy. On the other, competing political factions rapidly reasserted themselves after the withdrawal of Syrian security and intelligence personnel and were eager to penetrate and regulate the post-Syria LAF.

First, between 2005 and 2008, the pro-Western 14 March alliance sought to marginalize officers who had either trained in Syria or had ties to pro-Syrian political forces. The rival 8 March alliance, aligned with Syria and Iran, similarly sought from 2008 to 2010 to sideline officers who had received US military education or were suspected of supporting US policies in the region. Both political camps solicited officers seen to be ideologically sympathetic and strove to promote their professional advancement.

Initially, the LAF's post-2010 posture in the national security arena seemed poised to erode the rationale for hybrid security arrangements in postwar Lebanon, and the need to contain the worst effects of Syria's civil war prompted an unprecedented increase in LAF military development between 2010 and 2016. However, the LAF's thrust to assert national security primacy over groups like Hezbollah would soon begin to stall. An unprecedented military leadership crisis between August 2016 and March 2017 proved especially detrimental: a protracted stalemate in Lebanon's sectarian political system led to the retirement of key senior officers, botched critical transitions in key command-level posts, and the advancement of officers who were either unwilling or ill-equipped to sustain the arc of the LAF's 2010–2016 military transformation.

Ultimately, Lebanon's 2016–2017 military leadership crisis demonstrated that Lebanon's sectarian/political elite chose their short-term factional and communal interests over the military professionalization that is paradoxically necessary to preserve Lebanon's postwar and post-Syria political stability. History tells us that it is in the sectarian system's nature to undermine the military. For a time, the system afforded the LAF some breathing room as the military worked to defeat ISIL and other radical forces born out of civil conflict in Iraq and Syria. However, with ISIL defeated, these same sectarian/political elites—be they Hezbollah or allies of the West—feel they can once again focus all their attention on their narrow clientelist instincts, which may have significant negative consequences for both the LAF and Lebanon.

The United States and Lebanon Policy

Lebanon has been the chronic problem child in US foreign policy in the Levant since the Dwight Eisenhower administration. In the aftermath of the US-led invasion of Iraq, US policy toward Lebanon became primarily a by-product of US attempts to deny regional opponents, such as Syria and Iran, the means to undermine US strategic interests in the wider region. These included preserving a regional order that favored broader US interests in the region and safeguarded Israel's national security. Lebanon's centrality to regional security politics and Iran's support for the Shi'a militant group Hezbollah all but assured that Lebanon would serve as one arena of competition with Iran in the broader Levant.

Since 2005, the United States has sought to consolidate its gains by trying to ensure that Lebanon following Syria's exit would not become an arena for proxy competition yet again. After Syria left in 2005, Iran began to play a more proactive role in Lebanon. While Iran has always had a vested interest in defending Shi'a interests across the Middle East, there is little indication that Iranian foreign policymaking differs much from that of the United States in terms of a desired end state. Iran's ambitions in Lebanon are simply to secure its regional hegemonic interests and to continue to act on the Arab-Israeli stage in order to shore up its broader regional position in a mainly Sunni Arab Middle East. Having a role to play in Lebanon also meant that Iran could use the small country as a means of foiling US strategic and political interests in the broader Levant.

In broad and consistent terms, the current mix of US policy priorities has centered on five principal areas of interest.[21] First, the United Sates continues to seek ways to weaken Iran's principal proxy in Lebanon, the Shi'a militia Hezbollah, short of direct and open competition in ways that could threaten Lebanon's stability, including by supporting the LAF as Lebanon's sole legitimate national security institution.[22] This in turn informs the second priority, assisting Lebanon in securing its border with Syria, which ties into the third: assisting more than a million Syrians in Lebanon displaced by the now ten-year conflict in Syria. The US government's fourth and fifth priorities in Lebanon are strengthening government institutions and their capacity and encouraging reform in a country that is one of the most chronically corrupt in the world.[23]

Drivers of US Security Assistance and Security Cooperation to the LAF

In the wake of Hezbollah's military operations against the group's mainly Sunni rivals in May 2008, it became clear to successive US administrations that supporting a politically neutral and cross-confessional LAF so that it might confront Hezbollah was unrealistic. In the wake of regional protests starting in 2011 and the outbreak of Syria's civil war, the US-Lebanese bilateral relationship became increasingly defined by both countries' need to cooperate on regional security, intelligence sharing, and dealing with emerging and common threats from militant groups inspired by al-Qaeda and ISIL with operational links to Lebanon, Syria, and Iraq.

It is not easy to draw lessons from the achievements and limitations of the US security assistance and cooperation programs in Lebanon or to tie this assistance to US competition with Iran—and Syria and Hezbollah. From a US perspective, military aid to Lebanon was clearly expected to help reduce the country's footprint in regional instability and its role as a regional confrontation state against Israel. In short, military assistance to Lebanon became the latest addition to US-Iranian proxy warfare in the Levant.

As the previous section attempted to articulate, in the wake of Syria's withdrawal from Lebanon in 2005 and spurred on by the LAF's counterterrorist efforts against the al-Qaeda-inspired Fatah al-Islam terrorist group, the US government hoped that the LAF, which was popular across the country's sectarian divisions, could gradually take on an increasingly important national security role, largely at the expense of Iran's main nonstate regional ally, Hezbollah.

Many in the US Congress supported US efforts to build up the LAF based on the hope that the military could one day confront Hezbollah and serve as a bulwark against Iranian influence along Israel's northern flank. However, there is a consensus among US security assistance/cooperation personnel familiar with Lebanese civil-military dynamics in postwar Lebanon that US military aid to Lebanon at the levels maintained between 2006 and 2021 has so far had only limited impact on the balance of force between the LAF and Hezbollah.

It is far clearer, however, that in the eyes of US civilian and military planners focused on security assistance/cooperation, they had found something rare: an emerging military in the Arabic-speaking Middle East that saw the US military as the military it wished to emulate on a path to future interoperability with the United States and other western European states tied to the North Atlantic Treaty Organization (NATO).[24] This stands in contrast to other regional states that remained focused on the transactional nature of ties to the United States, as opposed to perceived shared military values, principles, and objectives.[25]

US-Supported Efforts and Outcomes

A critical area of focus of US security assistance/cooperation programming was helping the LAF plan for its own modernization and military development. An unclassified but unpublished US government assessment of the LAF—commonly referred to as the "Martz Report" after its principal author, retired brigadier general Joseph E. Martz—accurately captured the state of Lebanese national security and defense planning in late 2006, noting that "the most . . . critical deficiency within the [LAF] is the lack of strategic guidance at a national level. There is no single coherent document describing what the Lebanese [national security strategy] is and what the [LAF] are supposed to do to support the security strategy."[26]

The 2006 Martz Report and subsequent US assessments helped frame and shape an ongoing series of joint capability reviews (JCRs) between the US military and the LAF starting in 2009. On the US side, the working meetings brought together personnel from the Defense Security and Cooperation Agency (DSCA), Central Command (CENTCOM), the US embassy's Office of Defense Cooperation, and other civilian and military personnel tasked with supporting the LAF. In parallel, personnel from the LAF representing the army, navy, air force, communications, intelligence, protected mobility, and special operation forces were tasked to support the JCR process. LAF internal joint meetings took place monthly in anticipation of the next bilateral round of JCRs with their US counterparts.

The US JCR effort laid the groundwork not only for regular US-LAF bilateral engagements in the form of security assistance management reviews, joint staff talks, and joint military commissions, but they also enabled the United States to put in motion other forms of aid to support planning. One such effort was the defense institution building (DIB) initiative, known previously as the defense institution reform initiative. Efforts like DIB allowed the US government to work in tandem across multiple lines of effort to assess, evaluate, and plan for current and future LAF requirements in concert with LAF planning staff.

Assessing the Limits of US Security Assistance and Security Cooperation to the LAF

The US military-to-military relationship with the LAF has led to an LAF that is increasingly self-assured and capable. By the same token

US civilian and military partners have shown growing confidence in their investment in the LAF. Be that as it may, several obstacles remain on both the US and the Lebanese sides of the security assistance/cooperation equation, and they have severely limited the United States' ability to compete with Iran and Syria in Lebanon, as well as efforts to strengthen Lebanon's moderates and its democracy. Some of these problems are also the result of US policies and expectations.

First, the US continues to struggle with the reality that it cannot significantly modify Lebanese civil-military dynamics, given the primacy of sectarian politics in the wake of Syria's withdrawal in 2005. In the US-Lebanese principal-agent dynamic, the agent is the LAF itself and not the government of Lebanon. Lebanese civil-military relations are such that few if any Lebanese political stakeholders have any meaningful investment in the institutional success of the LAF, let alone the success of the US effort to support it. US civilian and military planners increasingly take Lebanese internal dynamics for what they are and try to extract the outcomes most favorable to Washington's interests. However, this ability to adapt to internal Lebanese dynamics is often at the mercy of changes in US administrations and the congressional balance of power.

Second, the quality of US assistance will continue to be determined by preexisting core US interests. Chief among them is the US commitment to Israel's security. To US civilian and military planners, on the one hand, there is understanding that US assistance can only "stand up" the LAF and bolster its national security legitimacy by turning it into a force that the Shi'a can respect and that can dissuade Israel from future military confrontations. On the other hand, they also understand that such an effort would create an untenable policy paradox as far as Washington's commitment to Israel's qualitative military edge (QME) and other US regional interests are concerned.

Third, the US Congress is playing a growing role. Successive administrations have argued—to varying degrees—in favor of continued support to the LAF. However, calls for maintaining or upgrading security assistance/cooperation to the LAF are increasingly falling on deaf ears. This reflects a deepening domestic political polarization when it comes to any form of security assistance/cooperation to external states and the frustration of a congressional body with a country that continues to be a source of difficulty for US policy in the Levant. The fact that aid to Lebanon has done little to shift the balance of forces in favor of the United States against Iran in the Levant is another core driver of congressional criticism. However, how the United States can suspend military aid to Lebanon without handing over the country to Syria and Iran remains unclear.

A fourth challenge, which is by no means unique to Lebanon, is the timing and pace of US security assistance and cooperation programs. Unlike those of other states such as Russia or China, US security assistance/cooperation programs generally enjoy far more transparency, accountability, and oversight. Major arms sales must go through a congressional notification process, and the DSCA must explain why and how the sale or provision of a given defense article meets the US national interest. However, this process and its complexities also serve to slow down the pace and timing of aid. This too is not unique to Lebanon. However, in a space where Iran actively supports Hezbollah with financial resources and aid on an annual basis, the optics of the US effort are often lost on a Lebanese public that is far more focused on the presumed "glitter factor" of external aid.[27]

Lastly, it is important to note that, ultimately, US security assistance/cooperation is a choice and not a necessity. While successive US administrations have made the case that engaging in security assistance/cooperation to the LAF is in the US national interest, doing so is nonetheless an exercise in providing aid to a partner who is one among many in a region where the United States has other priorities viewed as far more strategic in the eyes of US planners and legislators alike. While US interlocutors such as the US military's CENTCOM are some of the most ardent advocates of aid to the LAF, countries like Israel, Egypt, and Jordan are viewed as more critical aid targets and as far more institutionalized.

Assessing the Limits of the LAF's Ability to Absorb US Assistance

While the previous section unpacked some of the key contradictions in how the United States can and cannot effectively support the LAF, all the security assistance in the world cannot counteract domestic factors that actively work to negate military and capabilities development in any given country.[28]

A first key challenge is how the LAF has internalized its own lessons learned when it comes to confronting Lebanon's sectarian political order. Every time the military has tried to stabilize or regulate contentious internal politics in Lebanon, normally competing sectarian factions and elites have de facto bandwagonned against the LAF.

Much like an immune system fighting off a virus, Lebanon's sectarian political actors are deeply intolerant of any state structure that challenges their domestic autonomy—a lesson that the LAF has internalized well.

The second challenge—the kinds of military leaders the Lebanese sectarian political order allows to emerge—is intertwined with the first. It has always been clear what kind of leadership the LAF needs to advance Lebanese military development: officers who stand apart from the country's patronage networks, who have a proven track record and the courage required to lead soldiers into harm's way, and who have the ability to unite a multiconfessional military and lead by example, to lead beyond the LAF as a "coalition leader" and an agent of national unity, and to think strategically both about the future development of the LAF and how to navigate Lebanon's precarious political, bureaucratic, and operational challenges.

While Lebanon's competing factions have chosen LAF commanders with some of those attributes, they have never selected one with all of them. That is not for lack of choice; rather it is by design. In 2016, the Lebanese political establishment had the opportunity to advance at least one such officer (Brigadier General Maroun Hitti, at the time the deputy chief of staff for planning and one of the driving forces behind the LAF's bilateral and multilateral engagements, including with the United States) to become the new LAF commander. However, advancing any officer with these combined characteristics presented Lebanon's competing elites with the shared threat of an LAF led by a chief of defense whom they could not control.

While selecting less disruptive officers for command is in keeping with Lebanon's postwar civil-military dynamics, doing so can come at the cost of the LAF's bilateral and multilateral relationships. The United States has worked well with successive generations of Lebanese military leaders. However, the depth and breadth of the US effort in Lebanon might also be far more dynamic if the LAF had the kind of leadership that was openly willing to challenge a political status quo—to include Hezbollah—that is increasingly associated with many if not most of Lebanon's socioeconomic and political ills.

The third challenge also ties in to the first two in what is a pattern of Lebanese civil-military incoherence on strategy. In Lebanon, the concept of a national defense strategy has been removed from its traditionally technical context. Instead, it is often articulated in terms of internal political brinksmanship or the foreign policy preferences of key external allies and patrons. This atomization precludes defining a commonly held set of national interests or foreign policy prerogatives. The absence of such a definition prevents the emergence of real-world strategic policymaking centered on ways and means.

The LAF has worked to bridge part of this gap by producing thus far the 2013–2017 and 2018–2022 capabilities development plans (CDPs), and a third is currently in development. However, the LAF's CDPs are at most "force upgrading plans," not a national military strategy.[29] Given the polarized nature of Lebanese politics and the general absence of effective postwar civil-military coordination, it will be difficult for the LAF to produce the kind of strategic guidance document that partners like the United States expect.

A fourth challenge that derives from the previous two is civilian leadership's complicity in maintaining a resourcing gap tied to military development. On the surface, Lebanese defense expenditures appeared to increase over the 2005–2021 period. However, when adjusted for inflation, defense expenditures were broadly flat during that period, even showing more than minor reductions in actual defense spending. More critically, the bulk of authorized funding by successive governments in Beirut has emphasized current expenditures tied to wages and entitlements. By contrast, successive governments have refused to sign off on LAF-requested levels tied to capital expenditures that are critical to force recapitalization, acquisition, and sustainment.

Taken together, Lebanon's internal civil-military relations and the LAF's own institutional dynamics are a critical challenge to any external partner providing security assistance/cooperation to the LAF. On balance, this means that civilian political leaders are agnostic if not indifferent to military aid and capabilities development; able to disrupt or compromise the Lebanese military's credibility as a national security actor; largely antagonistic to the military regardless of their regional geopolitical alliances; and willing to shape the kind of military leadership that will struggle to push back against a political system that it feels it cannot control.

Lessons from Iran's Military Support for Hezbollah

The previous sections focused on US priorities and challenges tied to Lebanese civil-military relations. However, the Iranian model of "security assistance" also bears important lessons for any future US engagement with Lebanon—particularly in the context of the problems in US efforts to build up the LAF in a divided Lebanon.

First, the United States is invested in Lebanon as part of a broader multifaceted effort to shape stability and outcomes from the Mediterranean to Afghanistan. Meanwhile, Iran looks at Lebanon and Hezbollah as central to its prerogatives, not only in the Levant but also in the broader Arab Muslim Middle East. Prior strategic commitments and policy choices make it difficult for the United States to bring its tremendous national resources to bear effectively. Washington is concerned with maintaining Israel's QME and ensuring that no regional player poses an imminent threat to its regional ally. Iranian policy toward Lebanon is not burdened by competing geopolitical priorities, which means that, unlike the United States, it can provide its allies with as much assistance as they need.

Second, despite its revolutionary rhetoric, Iran recognizes that Lebanon's sectarian system is to Hezbollah's advantage, given the group's level of organization, unique military capabilities, and unrivaled intelligence-gathering capabilities. Iran does not need to "capture the state" or build a "state within a state" in Lebanon to further its interests. The same goes for Hezbollah, which has increasingly accepted the benefits of the autonomy granted by eschewing the fragile and hollow postwar Lebanese state structure.

In contrast, the United States continues to focus on trying to rehabilitate Lebanese state institutions that, by virtue of the primacy of sectarian politics in the post-Syria period, are very resistant to change or reform. The United States also continues to face difficulties in dealing with sectarian and feudal rather than true reform-minded national leaders. Pursuing US policies predicated on dealing with Lebanon for what it is will allow the United States to recalibrate its reform agenda to find more meaningful avenues for future reform.

Third, time is a critical factor in building up truly capable regional allies. Iran has spent the past twenty-five years and tens of billions of dollars, by even low estimates, to build up Hezbollah, and it has done so without any qualitative reservations and without the burden of a transparent bureaucratic interagency process. The United States has been conducting security assistance to the LAF for fourteen years with relatively fewer resources and under the watchful eye of an often cumbersome and ill-directed interagency effort.

Lastly, even if the United States were able or willing to provide the LAF with capabilities and training that could change the balance of force between it and Hezbollah, the US approach is not focused on either creating an authoritarian military or aggressively trying to reshape divided domestic politics tied to Lebanese civil-military affairs.

By contrast, coercion and intimidation of domestic rivals are critical to Hezbollah's domestic success and not discouraged by its international sponsors in Tehran.

Is it unclear how many of these lessons can be integrated, and how well, in future US and allied efforts in Lebanon or elsewhere, to build up and support local allies. The Iranian approach has clearly been successful, while the US effort has been defined more by good intentions than measurable geopolitical outcomes.

Conclusion

After fifteen years of sustained military assistance led by the United States, the Lebanese Armed Forces is considered by the military personnel who advised its officers and trained its soldiers to be among the most capable militaries in the region. At the operational level, LAF personnel and units are cohesive, professional, capable under fire, and innovative in their ability to integrate and frugally maintain even more complex battle and battle-management systems.

The challenge is not the military in Lebanon; rather it is the civilian enabling and disabling environment. If a Lebanese civilian leadership emerges that credibly supports national strategic direction, professionally plans and rebalances funding on defense, and works with rather than against the military, then US and allied efforts will serve to empower and sustain those trends. However, should Lebanese governance structures and civil-military relations remain largely unchanged, transformational change in the role of the military nationally—let alone vis-à-vis Hezbollah—is at best wishful thinking. The most the United States and its partners could hope for from their time and effort would be a partial success in keeping a lid on a chronic headache in US Middle East policy.

Notes

1. See Martz, "Executive Summary," 1–2.
2. See Barak, "Towards a Representative Military?"; Baylouny, "Building an Integrated Military in Post-Conflict Societies."
3. See Huntington, *The Soldier and the State*, 7–18, and author's interviews with LAF senior officers, Beirut, July 1–2, 2013; October 10, 2013; January 2–3, 2014; and January 6, 2015.
4. Official LAF data collected from author's interviews with LAF senior officers, Beirut, March 29–30, 2021.
5. Ibid.

6. Author's interviews with LAF senior officers, Beirut, July 1–2, 2013; October 10, 2013; January 2–3, 2014; and March 29–30, 2021.

7. This does not include two smaller elite counterterrorism units attached to the LAF's Military Intelligence Directorate; author's interviews with LAF senior officers, Beirut, July 1–2, 2013; October 10, 2013; January 2–3, 2014; and March 29–30, 2021.

8. To illustrate this, LAF commander general Jean Kahwaji was in direct contact with junior officers and platoon leaders during the LAF's confrontation with Jabhat al-Nusra and ISIS militants in 'Arsal in August 2014. Author's interview with LAF senior officer, Beirut, August 28, 2014.

9. Author's interview with US Task Force 5 officers, names withheld, March 28–30, 2021.

10. Author's interview with UNFIL civil and military personnel, August 10, 2010; author's interview with an LAF senior officer, July 7, 2011; and "Ambassador DiCarlo's June 30 Meeting with IDF BG Heymann on Implementation of UNSCR 1701."

11. Author's interviews with LAF senior officers, Beirut, July 1–2, 2013; October 10, 2013; and January 2–3, 2014.

12. See *al-Hayat*, February 15, 1991; *al-Hayat*, March 29, 1991; and Emile Lahoud in *al-Jaysh* 71 (March 1991): 4–5.

13. Huntington, *The Soldier and the State*, 61–62.

14. It is noteworthy that for the first time in the LAF's history, the post of deputy chief of staff for logistics (J-4) was held at the time of writing by Brig. Gen. Manuel Kirejian, an Armenian Catholic.

15. The current director of operations, Brig. Gen. Ziad al-Homsi, is Christian but not a Maronite.

16. Author's interviews with LAF senior officers, Beirut, July 1–2, 2013; October 10, 2013; and January 2–3, 2014.

17. Ibid.

18. See Gaub, "Merging Militaries."

19. Author's interviews with LAF senior officers, Beirut, May 2, 2014.

20. Author's interviews with LAF senior officers, Beirut, May 2, 2014, and March 30, 2021.

21. See Humud, "Lebanon."

22. See US Department of State, "Daily Press Briefing by Spokesperson John Kirby"; US Department of State, "Background Briefing."

23. See "Lebanon," Corruption Perceptions Index.

24. Author's interview with US foreign area officer, name withheld, March 10, 2021.

25. Ibid.

26. See Martz, "Executive Summary."

27. Author's interviews with US foreign area officers, names withheld, March 29–30, 2021.

28. See Nerguizian, "The Five Wildcards."

29. Author's interview with Brig. Gen. (Ret.) Maroun Hitti, former deputy chief of staff for plans in the LAF and architect of the first 2013–2017 Capabilities Development Plan, February 10, 2021.

6

Egypt: Reconsidering the Political Value of US Assistance

Zeinab Abul-Magd

THIS CHAPTER INVESTIGATES THE IMPORTANT PLACE THAT SECURITY assistance occupies in shaping principal-agent relations in international relations today by focusing on the case of Egypt and its ties to the United States. For the past four decades, US military aid to Egypt has played a pivotal role in constructing and restructuring the relationship between the two countries. Since the 1980s, Egypt has largely depended on US aid for procurement of heavy weapons and technologically advanced equipment and consequently maintained its position as a reliable American ally in the Middle East. However, this chapter shows the current military regime in Egypt has complicated its relations with consecutive US administrations in reaction to the declining value of this aid. On the one hand, Egypt's ruling officers today continue to use prestigious US armaments to boost the public image of the army, as they occasionally showcase the freshly received items in propaganda campaigns publicized in both traditional and online social media. On the other hand, they evidently view the shrinking economic worth of this aid as reason to revise their relationship with Washington.

In 1986, the Egyptian minister of defense complained that the annual $1.3 billion in US military aid was no longer enough and intended to ask for a raise of several hundred million dollars. Egypt had started to receive US security assistance initially in the form of loans seven years earlier, after signing the 1979 peace treaty with Israel, and this turned into annual aid in the fixed amount of $1.3 billion in 1985–1986. The then-influential minister, Field Marshall Abd al-Halim Abu Ghazala, who enjoyed good relations with Washington, explained that global prices of arms had already increased.[1] In the 1980s, he obtained F-16 fighter jets that each cost about $36 million.[2] If Abu Ghazala were still alive, he would be surprised to learn that today the same aircraft costs $122 million. Similarly, the price of an M1A1 Abrams battle tank almost doubled from $6 million to $11 million in 2011, and that of an Apache helicopter increased almost sixfold from $11 million for the AH-64A in 1995 to $61 million for the AH-64D in 2020. These are the three most prestigious and famous items in the aid package that Egypt has regularly received for the past three decades.

In the summer of 2013, another influential minister of defense overthrew an Islamist president and took power. The Barack Obama–Joe Biden administration disapproved of this political move, informally considering it a military coup, and unsuccessfully attempted to change its outcomes by using security assistance. In July, a *Washington Post* article then asserted that Egypt's generals had "ignored" Washington's political advice to manage a democratic transition after taking control of the state in the wake of the 2011 uprisings. The article described this as a "collapse of U.S. prestige and influence in Cairo." More importantly, it criticized the administration for not using the US military aid's "leverage" by possibly suspending it.[3] Obama did suspend that aid three months later, in October of the same year, but this decision failed to place pressure on the new military regime of then minister of defense Abdel Fattah al-Sisi. The administration restored the aid package less than a year and a half later, in March 2015, shortly after Sisi swept the presidential election and concluded large procurement deals with Russia and other arms manufacturers outside the United States.

This chapter has bad news for the makers of US foreign policy: American security assistance to Egypt, whose nominal dollar amount of $1.3 billion hasn't change for the past thirty-five years, has lost most of its economic value. With this, especially after 2011, the United States also has lost much of its influence over the current military regime's domestic policies, especially regarding democratization, human rights violations, and regional expectations, mainly in terms of relations to other nondemocratic systems in and outside the Middle East, from Saudi Arabia to Russia. General F. C. "Pink" Williams compellingly points out (see Chapter 14) that US influence over Egypt has declined, and the security assistance program is a main factor in changing the relation between the two countries.

The Jimmy Carter administration started Egypt's Foreign Military Sales program in 1979, after President Anwar Sadat signed the Camp David peace accord with Israel. Congress then approved providing Egypt loans to buy US weapons in the amount of $1.5 billion to be received over the course of three years.[4] In postwar hard times, the Egyptian government was almost bankrupt, with a population of forty-one million people to feed. Thus, US military aid then constituted a considerably welcome contribution to Sadat's state budget of only $4.8 billion. However, the situation is fundamentally different in 2022: the Egyptian population is more than 100 million people, and the state budget is $118.4 billion. More importantly, the Egyptian military's budget itself has multiplied and earned tens of billions of dollars in off-budgetary cash through different sources since 2013. The contribution of US aid to the budget of the Egyptian armed forces has become less vital over time.

Throughout three and a half decades of economic struggle, inflated state budgets, fundamental political changes, and ever-expanding military-owned business enterprises in the country, US security assistance to Egypt remained the same—$1.3 billion. Similarly, the United States' self-image about its abilities to politically influence the country's military regimes did not change. It is time to revisit this evidently less effective assistance and explore means to reform it for the benefit of both countries.

This chapter traces the steadily shrinking value of US military aid to Egypt from the 1980s until the present day—under the governments of Hosni Mubarak (1981–2011) and Abdel Fattah al-Sisi (2014–present). It chronologically follows the Egyptian state and military budgets from the 1980s until today and examines how, based on the value of US military aid to Cairo, different US administrations successfully or unsuccessfully pressured Egypt's military presidents to respond to Washington's domestic or regional expectations. Since 1986, Egypt has uninterruptedly (except briefly between 2013 and 2015) received the same amount of cash annually to use to purchase arms from American manufacturers, when the government's expenditure and military spending have been steadily multiplying between the early years of Mubarak's tenure and then Sisi's. In Fiscal Year (FY) 1985/1986, the Egyptian state budget was only $9 billion and the official budget of the Egyptian Armed Forces (EAF) was $2.6 billion. In Sisi's first budget as president, FY 2014/2015, the state budget reached $142 billion, and the military one mounted to $5.2 billion.

In addition, the chapter shows how since 2013, under Sisi, the Egyptian military has had access to unusual flows of cash that allowed it to reduce its dependency on US arms and diversify its sources of procurement away from American manufacturers. Thanks to the Egyptian military institution's gigantic and profitable civilian business empire and donations of tens of billions of dollars from Arab Gulf states, especially Saudi Arabia and the United Arab Emirates, the regime has been able to finance its ambitious arms deals with European suppliers for the past seven years. Based on Sisi's official statements, the Egyptian military's business enterprises generate at least $2 billion to $3 billion in annual profit, and his regime received at least $32 billion in donations from oil-producing allies between 2013 and 2015 alone. Apparently, a considerable part of this extra cash went to an active policy of purchasing non-US weapons whose prices way exceed US annual aid. In 2017, Egypt jumped into the rank of the third-largest importer of weapons, and France has already replaced the United States as the largest exporter of weapons to the country (see below).

Thus, this chapter presents two main arguments. First, it argues that a clear correlation exists between a shrinking percentage of US aid in the Egyptian state and military budgets, on the one hand, and a diminishing foreign-policy influence for the United States over the Egyptian state, on the other hand, over the past thirty-five years. This is especially affecting US ability to pressure the Egyptian military regime to undertake democratic reforms and to end human rights violations against civilian citizens and civil society organizations. Second, it argues that the Egyptian military's access to swelling amounts of off-budgetary cash in the last seven years has further contributed to the shrinking value of US aid in its unpublished budget and allowed it to diversify its arms exporters and significantly reduce its dependency on American imports.

The chapter is divided into three sections. The first section chronologically traces the Egyptian state and military budgets in relation to US military aid, and investigates the degrees of success of US foreign policy in Egypt based on this, from 1985 until 2020. The second section follows the regime's access to tens of billions of dollars in the past seven years that way exceed what Egypt receives or has received in US aid for decades. It also details the regime's recent arms deals with European suppliers worth billions of dollars—also way exceeding the stagnated amount of annual US aid. Finally, the third section attempts to propose policy recommendations for US policymakers to revisit the security assistance package to Egypt. For the Egyptian side, it will discuss revisions in the context of utilizing the aid leverage to help democratize civil-military relations in the country.

Shrinking Value, Losing Influence?

Table 6.1 tracks the steadily increasing figures of the Egyptian state and military budgets from 1985 until 2020 and presents the percentage of an unchanging amount of US military aid in proportion to them.[7] Before delving into these figures and their analysis, it is important to note that, as a matter of fact, US aid does not appear in the officially published Egyptian state or military budgets. The Ministry of Finance (MOF) usually releases a detailed budget in June of every year, and it includes an elaborately itemized section for "aid received from foreign governments and organizations." US military aid is never listed underneath this section. It is similarly never listed in the section for "defense and national security," which includes the income/expenditure of the Ministry of Defense (MOD) and the Ministry of Military Production (MOMP). The military budget always appears as one number in the state budget anyway, so there is no room to mention any sources of income there.[5] But clearly US military aid has been never counted toward this one number since its onset: it did not get reflected in the military budgets of the late 1970s through the late 1980s, which remained almost constantly stable before and after receiving the aid.[6] Thus, the percentages calculated in the table are the percentages of US military aid in proportion to, and not as a part of, Egyptian state and military annual spending.

In the 1980s, during the last decade of the Cold War when Egypt was a part of the US camp, US security assistance constituted a significant percentage in relation to the Egyptian national and military budgets. In 1986, Washington's military aid to Egypt was converted from fluctuating loans that were difficult to pay back into an annual grant in the fixed amount of $1.3 billion.[8] In FY 1985/1986, this amount made up a full 50 percent of a military budget of $2.6 billion and 13.2 percent of a state budget of $9.8 billion. Arguably, as a result, the degree of Egyptian responsiveness to the Ronald Reagan administration's foreign policy requests at a regional level was high. Egypt showed great commitment to Reagan's Cold War expectations across the Arab world—especially with regard to neighboring countries that were or could fall under Soviet influence as well as the oil-producing Gulf states. As Abu Ghazala received his routine shipments of F-16 fighter jets and Apache helicopters and concluded a coproduction agreement to assemble M1A1 Abrams tanks at a Cairo-based military factory, he exerted his efforts to counter the radical Mu'ammar Gadhafi of Libya, contain the militant resistance in the Palestinian Liberation Organization, watch the Syria of Hafiz al-Assad, pledge

Table 6.1 Egyptian State Budget, EAF's Budget, and US Military Aid, 1985–2020

Fiscal Year	Egyptian State Budget (US$ Billion)	EAF's Budget (US$ Billion)	EAF's Percentage of State Budget	US Military Aid (US$ Billion)	US Military Aid as Percentage of EAF's Budget	US Military Aid as Percentage of Egyptian State Budget
1985/1986	9.8	2.6	26.5	1.3	50.0	13.2
1986/1987	10.1	2.7	26.7	1.3	48.0	12.9
1987/1988	11.7	2.5	21.4	1.3	52.0	11.1
1988/1989	14.1	2.3	16.3	1.3	56.5	9.2
1989/1990	22.5	3.2	14.2	1.3	40.6	5.7
1990/1991	25.2	3.3	13.0	1.3	39.4	5.1
1991/1992	16.9	1.9	11.2	1.3	68.4	7.7
1992/1993	N/A	1.9	8.5	1.3	76.0	
1993/1994	17.0	2.0	11.8	1.3	65.0	7.6
1994/1995	19.1	2.2	11.5	1.3	59.0	6.8
1995/1996	22.7	2.4	10.5	1.3	48.0	5.7
1996/1997	22.7	2.3	10.1	1.3	56.5	5.7
1997/1998	26.9	2.7	10.0	1.3	48.0	4.8
1998/1999	26.8	2.8	10.4	1.3	46.4	4.8
1999/2000	29.3	3.0	10.2	1.3	43.3	4.4
2000/2001	32.36	3.3	10.2	1.3	39.3	4.0
2001/2002	31.8	3.1	9.7	1.3	42.0	4.0
2002/2003	30.5	2.8	9.2	1.3	46.4	4.3
2003/2004	26.0	2.4	9.2	1.3	54.1	5.0
2004/2005	28.5	2.4	8.4	1.3	48.1	4.5
2005/2006	36.8	2.7	7.3	1.3	48.1	3.5

continues

Table 6.1 Continued

Fiscal Year	Egyptian State Budget (US$ Billion)	EAF's Budget (US$ Billion)	EAF's Percentage of State Budget	US Military Aid (US$ Billion)	US Military Aid as Percentage of EAF's Budget	US Military Aid as Percentage of Egyptian State Budget
2006/2007	47.3	3.0	6.3	1.3	43.0	2.7
2007/2008	46.6	3.3	7.1	1.3	39.3	2.8
2008/2009	70.7	4.0	5.7	1.3	32.5	1.8
2009/2010	63.0	4.0	6.4	1.3	32.5	2.0
2010/2011	85.3	4.4	5.1	1.3	29.5	1.5
2011/2012	99.2	4.3	4.2	1.3	30.2	1.3
2012/2013	88.0	4.5	4.3	1.3	29.0	1.5
2013/2014	76.0	4.3	6.1	1.3	30.2	1.7
2014/2015	142.0	5.4	3.9	1.3	24.0	0.9
2015/2016	150.0	5.6	3.8	1.3	23.2	0.86
2016/2017	142.0	5.3	3.75	1.3	24.5	0.9
2017/2018	82.0	2.9	3.5	1.3	44.8	1.6
2018/2019	97.0	3.34	3.4	1.3	39.0	1.3
2019/2020	118.4	4.0	3.5	1.3	32.5	1.0

Gulf security, and so forth. More importantly, he aided Iraq in its war with the Islamic Republic of Iran through the 1980s.

In the early 1990s, Egypt's responsiveness to US expectations regarding the security of oil-producing Gulf states reached its peak. Shortly after the Cold War came to an end and the United States asserted its role as the sole hegemon globally and in the region, Egypt participated in the American-led international coalition to liberate Kuwait from Iraqi occupation, the "Desert Storm" operation of 1991, and it supported the US-sponsored peace process between the Palestinians and the Israelis. The George H. W. Bush administration continued Reagan's military aid to Mubarak, and in FY 1990/1991 its percentage of the military and state budgets remained significant: 39.4 and 5.1 percent, respectively. When Saddam Hussein, no longer a US ally after the end of the Iran-Iraq War, posed a great threat to the militarily vulnerable Gulf states by invading Kuwait in August 1990, the Egyptian army was among the largest forces recruited in the US-led coalition to terminate the invasion. Moreover, Mubarak aided the Bill Clinton administration's sponsorship of the peace process to tame Palestinian resistance, which brought about the 1993–1995 Oslo Accords and the Camp David summit in 2000. During the first half of the 1990s, US military aid reached the highest percentages of the Egyptian military budget ever: it jumped to 68.4 percent in FY 1991/1992 and increased again to 76 percent in a military budget of $1.9 billion in FY 1992/1993. It reached 7.6 percent of a state budget of $17 billion in FY 1993/1994.

In the early 2000s, in the wake of the September 11, 2001, attack, the United States needed Egypt again for regional counterterrorism activities, and Mubarak did deliver as a historically reliable ally. The percentage of US aid of the military budget fluctuated but overall remained high. In FY 2000/2001, the percentage shrank slightly to 39.3 percent of the military budget but soon rose back to 42 percent in FY 2001/2002. The year the George W. Bush administration occupied Iraq, it rose again to 54 percent of the military budget and 5 percent of the state budget in FY 2003/2004.

However, a political rift took place between Mubarak and the Bush administration during the second half of the 2000s, which affected the military's dependence on the aid. With the overthrow and execution of the dictator of Iraq, Bush's "Democracy Doctrine" threatened other dictators in the region—including Mubarak. US political pressure on Egypt to liberalize the political sphere and transition the political system into a pluralistic one in both the presidential and parliamentary elections met with reluctance and resentment from Mubarak's regime. Mubarak only introduced decorative reforms in the electoral system and modified the constitution in a way that barely allowed civil forces to wrest power away from the strong grip of his security apparatus. Meanwhile, Mubarak pursued new coproduction agreements with non-US arms manufacturers, hoping for less dependence on American firms. According to Shana Marshall, he attempted to form ties with less-ranked or smaller manufacturers and engage in small-scale projects with them with a goal of technology transfer.[9] In the latter half of the 2000s, Mubarak increased the military budget and allowed it to expand gigantic business conglomerates that generated hundreds of millions of off-budgetary profits from sales in the civilian market (see below). By the end of a decade full of tense relations, in FY 2009/2010, the official military budget rose to $4 billion in a state budget of $63 billion. The percentage of US military aid in both automatically shrank to only 32.5 and 2 percent, respectively.

In 2011, the year of the Arab Spring, Egyptian military and state financial dependence on US aid further diminished. Arguably, this might explain why the Egyptian army, which took control of the state after Mubarak's abdication from February 2011 to June 2012, was barely responsive to US political pressure during these tumultuous months. In FY 2010/2011, state expenditure was estimated at $85.3 billion, with $4.4 billion in military spending—not including the army's increasing profits from its widely stretching business enterprises. With this, US military aid's contribution shrank to 29.5 percent of military spending and only 1.5 percent of the national budget. Under the transitional government of the Supreme Council of Armed Forces (SCAF), protests were brutally crushed by security forces, and human rights conditions deteriorated. Evidently, the political leverage of the Obama-Biden administration to support the process of democratic transition and civil society organizations suffering from a wide crackdown was far from effective under SCAF.[10]

Signaling an almost complete loss of influence over the Egyptian military during 2011–2012, the Obama-Biden administration even failed to save four American nongovernmental organizations promoting democracy in Egypt whose offices were raided and closed. Between the domestically tumultuous months of December 2011 and March 2012, dozens of the workers of these American organizations—including about sixteen US citizens—were interrogated or detained, placed on prolonged trial, and sentenced to prison. Ironically, one of the tried Americans was the son of Obama's own secretary of transportation. After Obama's secretary of state, Hillary Clinton, threatened to withdraw the annual military aid to Egypt, the American workers were allowed to flee the country, but their trial continued until their conviction, and they received their sentences in absentia. Clinton approved the aid package for 2012 upon their departure, amid concerns about her overlooking alarming issues with democratic transition under SCAF in the country. Some officials then asserted that military aid to Egypt had to be resumed for mainly US domestic considerations tied to the economic and electoral interests of the administration. Delaying or cutting it would have mainly harmed American arms manufacturers that had contracts with Egypt, such as Lockheed Martin and General Dynamics, amid Obama's reelection campaign.[11]

In the summer of 2013, when mass protests erupted against the regime of the Muslim Brotherhood, Minister of Defense Sisi overthrew their president. The Obama-Biden administration this time made the unprecedented decision to suspend military aid. Although Obama did not classify the events as a military coup, he did request restoration of democratic measures in the country and halted shipments of equipment in October. However, Sisi's interim government, which included prominent civilian forces from the liberal and leftist camps, did not comply with Obama's demand. Sisi was elected president the following summer. Arab Gulf oil-producing states backing his new regime granted it billions of dollars to support its budget. Realizing again that the decision was ineffective and only harmed US weapon manufacturers with binding contracts with Egypt, the Obama administration resumed the overdue shipments sixteen months later, in March 2015. Moreover, Secretary of State John Kerry visited Egypt to attend Sisi's international economic conference to join Arabian Gulf allies in supporting his plans to develop the country.

Thus, deploying military aid to influence domestic politics failed in 2013. In FY 2012/2013, the Egyptian public expenditure was estimated at $88 billion, with $4.5 billion allocated to the military. In that year, the value of US military aid declined to 29 percent of the military budget and only 1.5 percent of the state budget. Afterward, the value of US military aid to Sisi's spending continued to shrink noticeably, and Sisi's regime resented repeated US pressure regarding human rights violations and crackdowns on civil society organizations. In Sisi's first budget as an elected president, that of FY 2014/2015, US military aid diminished to only 0.9 percent of the state budget and 24 percent of the military budget, and it shrank again in FY 2015/2016 to only 0.86 percent of a state budget of $150 billion and 23.2 percent of an officially published military budget of $5.6 billion.

Ending Dependency on US Arms?

There is another equally decisive side to the above story of the shrinking economic value of US military aid. Since 2013, the Egyptian military has had access to unusual and exceptionally large flows of off-budgetary cash that further diminished American contributions. There are two sources of this irregular but substantial capital amounting to tens of billions of US dollars. The first is profits gained from a gigantic business empire, which was already established under Mubarak but has been massively overstretched with monopolistic qualities under Sisi. The second is the billions of dollars recently received from Arabian Gulf oil-producing allies that have strategic interests in the new military regime's stability and survival. The 2013 crisis involving the unprecedented suspension of US security assistance undoubtedly alarmed the Egyptian military and triggered it to reduce its decades-old dependence on American arms imports. The new military regime has adamantly determined to diversify its sources of procurement, and since then it has been actively pursuing multiple non-US suppliers. Apparently the availability of considerable flows of extra cash has facilitated this ambitious and seemingly effective plan.

According to the latest Stockholm International Peace Research Institute (SIPRI) "Trends in International Arms Transfers" report, Egypt is the third-largest importer of weapons for the short period between 2016 and 2020, coming only after Saudi Arabia and India. It accounted for 5.8 percent of global sales, doubling its 2.4 percent during the 2011–2015 period. More importantly, the United States has fallen to the rank of the third-largest supplier of weapons to Egypt during these four years, providing only 8.7 percent of what the country purchased in this period, while Russia comes first, with 41 percent, and France second, with 28 percent.[12] During the same years, namely in 2017, Egypt was the largest importer of German weapons.[13] This section of the chapter claims that Sisi's regime is able to finance its expensive scheme to move away from US arms manufacturers because of quick access to the army's accumulated profits over the course of many decades from its business conglomerates that sells consumer goods and services in civilian markets. Besides, it claims that the considerable financial support that Saudi Arabia and the UAE gave to the new regime in its first few years helped with certain transactions that seem beneficial to the security of the Red Sea and the Gulf.

Before delving into more detail about the matter, let's take a glance at two of the regime's recent arms deals and how they were financed. In one of the early and major deals of 2015, Egypt purchased twenty-four

Rafale combat jets and other French military equipment at the huge price of €5.2 billion ($5.6 billion)—that's four times the amount of annual US aid. To finance the transaction, MOMP, which purchased the items, obtained a loan from a number of French banks in the amount of €3.37 billion ($3.65 billion). The Egyptian parliament approved the loan agreement, and the presidential decree authorizing it asserted that MOMP would pay back this loan, which would be guaranteed by MOF.[14] Aside from its arms manufacturing lines, MOMP is a massive and rich business conglomerate for profitable civilian goods and certainly qualifies to apply for such a huge foreign loan. According to its website, it owns twenty companies that invest in producing goods such as home appliances, pharmaceuticals, agricultural machinery, chemicals, engines, and much more.[15]

Still, as part of the early deals of 2015, Egypt again purchased from France a Mistral warship at $1 billion. Egypt planned, according to the state-owned *Al-Ahram* newspaper, to deploy this advanced helicopter carrier in the Red Sea, at the same time that Saudi Arabia started the war in Yemen. "The Mistral contract . . . is seen as crucial given the threats emanating from the Red Sea and the civil war in Yemen."[16] French sources then claimed that the transaction was this time financed by Saudi Arabia to boost the two countries' power in the Red Sea and the Mediterranean.[17] In the same year (and before concluding the deal with France), Sisi, Crown Prince Mohammed bin Salman, and the Saudi defense minster signed a "Cairo Declaration," the first goal of which was "development of the military cooperation and working towards establishing the Joint Arab Force."[18]

After these two quick glimpses, this section will provide more data on the subject as follows. It begins with a brief historical background on the roots and evolution of the Egyptian military business from Mubarak to Sisi. Afterward, it traces Sisi's endeavors to diversify his procurement and seek new coproduction agreements since 2013. Without any transparency on the Egyptian side, it is impossible to identify the sources of funding that the regime used to finance these costly deals. Nonetheless, they took place at a time when the military institution was extensively enlarging its business enterprises and establishing monopolies in certain sectors of the economy. They also happened after rich Arab allies, namely Saudi Arabia and the UAE, backed the new regime with tens of billions of dollars in donations.

The roots of military-owned business conglomerates that exist in Egypt today go back to the 1950s and 1960s, and they were substantially expanded in the 1980s—especially with a coproduction agreement for

M1A1 tanks with the United States.[19] In the early 1990s, their plants were financially and technologically struggling, and Mubarak's regime had to convert considerable parts of their production lines to civilian manufacturing. At this point, Egypt had at least twenty-five publicly known military factories: sixteen functioned under MOMP and nine under the military-run Arab Organization for Industrialization (AOI). By 2010, 40 percent of MOMP's production had turned civilian, and the other 60 percent was still military.[20] The situation was more drastic at AOI. By 2009, 70 percent of AOI's outcome was civilian, and the remaining 30 percent was still military.[21] Military factories that once produced heavy ordinance were now heavily utilizing their facilities and labor to produce goods such as washing machines, fridges, TVs, kitchenware, fertilizers, pesticides, cars, trucks, and more. In addition, MOD had already started to develop civilian enterprises a decade before under its National Services Products Organization, which was established after the 1979 peace treaty with Israel in order to assimilate the officers' energy in noncombat activities.[22]

In the 2000s, Mubarak allowed the military to add to these plants many more new ventures and to benefit from his ongoing economic liberalization and privatization plans. The military seized many public-sector enterprises that were up for sale, and they partnered with foreign technology providers to embark on new projects. By the time Sisi reached power, the Egyptian military owned companies in almost every economic sector in the country. It owned manufacturing plants for cement, steel, automotive products (cars, railway wagons, tractors, and spare parts), mining, agrochemicals (especially fertilizers), and energy (petroleum) and provided services in public construction, logistics, and retail. In addition, it owned factories for pharmaceuticals, water desalination, processed food, home appliances, kitchenware, computers, optics, and much more. Its agribusiness reclaimed farms of hundreds of thousands of acres over the years. It constructed bridges, hotels with lucrative wedding halls, sea resorts with luxury summerhouses, apartment buildings, and lavish villas. It ran gas stations, shipping firms, domestic cleaning companies, and spacious parking lots. The state allocated it thousands of miles of land to construct toll highways to collect their daily fees.[23]

Under Sisi since 2013, the economic dominance of military-owned civilian enterprises has been remarkably spiking with conspicuous monopolies. Besides all business activities listed above, the military has recently become the monopolistic contractor for public construction of roads, bridges, highways, public schools, and public hospitals across the country, in addition to taking charge of the mega New Suez Canal and the New Administrative Capital projects. It has paid more attention to manufacturing of and trading in pharmaceuticals and controlling Mediterranean-coast fisheries. It owns shares in or controls IT firms providing wireless telecommunications and internet services. It manages private security firms that serve university campuses and other public spaces. It has also recently ventured into the financial sector by controlling investment firms, mortgage companies, and the newly created "Sovereign Wealth Fund." Above all this, the military now controls media production companies that fund TV satellite channels, online news websites, and cinema companies.[24]

It is impossible to estimate how much of this military business profit is directed to financing procurement from countries other than the United States. The records of military companies and subsidiaries are largely considered "national security secrets" and not accessible to the civilian public or government accountability authorities. Thus data on the amount of profit they make annually and how much of it is directed to buying weapons on the global market are clandestine. However, in 2016 Sisi stated that the size of military business was around 1 to 1.5 percent of the country's gross domestic product (GDP). Attempting to calculate its exact value based on the president's official statement, a *Mada Masr* report by Mohamed Hamama stated, "In the first nine months of the 2015–16 Financial Year, Egypt's GDP was LE2 trillion, according to the Planning Ministry. Using Sisi's calculations, this would put their [military] activities at between LE20 and LE30 billion."[25] These 20 billion to 30 billion EGP converted to around $2.24 billion to $3.37 billion in 2016. This might not be enough to finance the above-mentioned large arms purchases from France, but it seems to constitute sufficient credit for international lenders to approve loans like, for example, the one that MOMP obtained from French banks for the transaction of $5.6 billion in 2015.

On the eve of the 2013 crisis, most of Egypt's procurement came primarily from US firms. Egypt traditionally used the aid to obtain large-scale, conventional items from major American defense manufacturers. The list of these firms included Lockheed Martin, Boeing, General Dynamics, DRS Technologies, L3 Communications, Raytheon, AgustaWestland, US Motor Works, Goodrich Corporation, and Columbia Group.[26] They shipped to Egypt items such as the F-16C/D fighter jet, the Apache AH-64D helicopter, and the Black Hawk helicopter. Besides, MOMP has continued coproduce the M1A1 with General Dynamics since the 1980s. In July 2013, the Pentagon suspended a shipment of twelve Lockheed Martin F-16 fighter jets to Egypt. This was followed by freezing the shipment of twenty Boeing Harpoon missiles and around 125 M1A1 Abrams tank kits. Furthermore, the "Bright Star" biennial joint training between the Egyptian and US armies was canceled.

A few months later, in February 2014, and in his capacity as the minister of defense, Field Marshal Sisi visited Vladimir Putin near Moscow to negotiate a $2 billion arms deal. On the same visit, Putin supported Sisi's presidential candidacy.[27] Two months later, in April 2014, the US administration partially relaxed its strict position and decided to deliver ten Apache helicopters to help with combating terrorist attacks in the Sinai Peninsula. Around the same time that the Islamic State in Iraq and the Levant (ISIL) was spreading, "U.S. Defense Secretary Chuck Hagel informed his Egyptian counterpart of the decision, which would help Egypt's counter-terrorism operations in the Sinai Peninsula, the Pentagon said."[28] Eventually, all suspended supplies were released nine months after Sisi won the presidential election.[29]

However, the Obama-Biden administration ended the weapons suspension in a way that was again deeply alarming to Sisi. As General F. C. Williams indicates (see Chapter 14), Egypt had to accept the renegotiation of the purposes of the US security assistance program and restriction of its items primarily to counterterrorism and border-control weaponry. According to a Congressional Research Service (CRS) report, the administration responded to calls from congressmen to release the aid, but this came with major changes and heavy conditions. Egypt had always liked large-scale tanks and jets that are traditionally used in conventional wars, but Obama had altered the country's procurement behavior toward facing the new realities of asymmetric combat with terrorist cells in battlegrounds such as Sinai. The CRS report explained,

> On March 31, 2015, after a phone call between President Obama and President Sisi, the White House announced that the Administration was releasing the deliveries of select weapons systems. . . . However, the White House simultaneously announced that future military assistance to Egypt would be largely reformulated: "Beginning in fiscal year 2018 . . . we will channel U.S. security assistance for Egypt to four categories—counterterrorism, border security, Sinai security, and maritime security—and for sustainment of weapons systems already in Egypt's arsenal."[30]

Therefore, the aftermath of the 2013 crisis provoked the military regime to widely and intensively pursue diversifying its suppliers and seek new coproduction contracts. In 2014, Egypt signed a major coproduction contract with France—perhaps the first since the M1A1 tanks deal that is part of the US aid package. It was with the French shipbuilder Naval Group (formerly DCNS), a partially French-state-owned defense contractor, to make the Gowind 2500 corvette, which is considered the most advanced naval technology in France. Egypt purchased four ships, and three of them were to be constructed in the Egyptian-military-owned Alexandria Shipyard. Technology transfer, included in the procurement agreement, was also to take place in the military shipyard. In 2016, Egypt received the first ship and named it ENS *El Fateh*. In 2018, Egypt completed the building of the second ship and named it ENS *Port Said*. In mid-2019, it completed and launched the ENS *Al-Moez* (981). In order to provide "in-service support," Naval Group created an Egyptian subsidiary, Alexandria Naval, to take charge of such tasks.[31]

Nonetheless, Egypt diversified much more through arms imports and very little through coproduction contracts. It purchased items from European states that were willing to deal with the new military president for mutual interests, based on counterterrorism efforts, and for the benefit of their national manufacturers. In 2016, SIPRI's "Trends in International Arms Transfers" report ranked Egypt the eleventh-largest importer of major weapons globally between 2012 and 2016. The World Bank's aggregates indicate that Egyptian imports tripled after the 2013 wave of terrorism and the need to contain ISIL in Sinai. They rapidly increased from $630 million in 2011 to $675 million in 2013 and $1.483 billion in 2016. They grew by 69 percent during this brief period.[32]

By 2016, France alone was the source of 40 percent of the country's imports—an equal percentage at this point to that of the United States. Egypt became the largest client of France with deals worth billions of euros for fighter jets and warships. It also signed many large arms deals with Russia, including contracts for fifty combat aircraft and forty-six combat helicopters.[33] In 2017, Germany "quintupled" its arms sales to Egypt, which quickly reached the rank of the first importer of German arms. Egypt then bought German equipment worth $350 million.[34] It was anticipated that China might become one of Egypt's non-US suppliers, but it did not because Egypt continued to prefer Western suppliers.[35]

By 2017, France had already replaced the United States as the largest exporter of weapons to Egypt. According to a SIPRI report, Egypt quickly jumped to the rank of the third-largest importer of weapons globally for the previous four years. As mentioned above, Egypt remained the third-largest global importer through 2019, according to the SIPRI report of that year.[36] Egyptian imports by 2017 had increased by 4.5 percent, and Egypt came third after India (12 percent) and Saudi Arabia (10 percent). Between 2008 and 2012, the United States was the main supplier, with around 45 percent of Egyptian imports. Between 2013 and 2017, France took this top place by providing Egypt with 37 percent of its procurement.[37] France, so far, has sold the Egyptian Armed Forces (namely the air force and the navy) twenty-four Rafale aircraft manufactured by Dassault Aviation, followed by the Mistral warship manufactured by Naval Group and four Gowind corvettes (coproduction) again with Naval Group.

While France has steadily grown into the largest arms supplier to Egypt, President Emmanuel Macron has repeatedly refused to respond to criticism for ignoring the country's human rights record. Sisi visited Paris in late 2017 and was received by the newly elected Macron. As journalist Jenna Le Bras explained in a report published by the Cairo-based *Mada Masr*, "The relationship between the two countries in recent years has centered on military and security cooperation and counterterrorism, while France has turned a blind eye to Egypt's worrying human rights record. Macron defended this position during Sisi's visit, saying it is not his place to 'lecture' Egypt on civil liberties."[38] Sisi paid another similar visit to Macron in December 2020, amid international criticism of the detention of civil society activists in the country. Once more, Macron agreed to sell Egypt French arms and asserted during this second visit that such exports would not be "conditional on human rights" records. Macron stated, "I will not condition matters of defense and economic cooperation on these disagreements [over human rights].... It is more effective to have a policy of demanding dialogue than a boycott which would only reduce the effectiveness of one of our partners in the fight against terrorism."[39]

There is no transparent information about whether Saudi Arabia and the UAE are involved in financing the transactions that have taken place since 2013, but these two states, along with Kuwait, donated tens of billions of dollars to the country after it removed the Islamist regime. According to Sisi's statement, Egypt received $20 billion from Gulf states in the eight months between August 2013 and May 2014.[40] A year later, after Sisi's election as president, it received another $12 billion from the Gulf states during his international economic conference. That, as officially announced, adds up to a total of $32 billion in just two years—the equivalent of twenty-four years of US military aid going back as far as 1991 and Desert Storm.

Before his first presidential election, in March 2014, Sisi visited the UAE for military cooperation purposes.[41] After he was elected, according to the state-owned newspaper *Akhbar al-Yom*, Sisi and the then Emirati Vice President Muhammad bin Zayed visited each other twelve times between 2014 and 2019, and military cooperation, mutual training, and the inauguration of new military bases were often on the agendas of these trips.[42] Egypt's contribution to the Saudi-led coalition's war in Yemen, which includes UAE troops, is taking place at a minimum level with mainly "keeping the Red Sea safe," according to *Al-Ahram*. Egypt engages in naval training with Saudi forces in this area.[43]

European media have made sporadic references to potential funding for Egyptian arms deals from these two countries. When Egypt first approached Russia in late 2013, Yasmine Farouk writes, "International media reported that Saudi Arabia and the United Arab Emirates (UAE) are to fund a $2 billion Egyptian-Russian arms deal."[44] Similar claims were made by French media about the Mistral warship deal in 2015, alleging that Saudi financed the $1 billion transaction.[45] German media closely tied huge German arms sales to Egypt with those to Saudi Arabia as they took place together. In 2017, two years into the Yemen war, *Deutsche Welle* (*DW*) revealed Germany's fivefold increase in its arms sales to both Egypt and Saudi Arabia. Amid heated criticism of Chancellor Angela Merkel's deals with two Middle Eastern "dictatorships," as *DW* stated,

> the German government approved nearly €450 million ($526 million) worth of weapons exports to Saudi Arabia and Egypt in the third quarter of 2017, more than five times the €86 million it sold in the same quarter of last year. . . . Egypt alone bought nearly €300 million worth of weapons . . . while Saudi Arabia handed over nearly €150 million. By comparison, the two countries imported €45 million and €41 million respectively in the third quarter of 2016.[46]

Deutsche Welle suggested that the large sale was "feeding the war in Yemen," and the spokesperson for a German anti-arms-trade campaign alleged that Egypt, along with Saudi Arabia, had to "answer for thousands of deaths" in this conflict.[47]

Since the start of the Russian war in Ukraine in February 2022, Egypt's plans to diversify away from the United States have been challenged but not paused. Although international sanctions prohibit importing military goods from Russia, Egypt hasn't cut economic or military ties with Moscow and barely responded to US pressure to do so. For example, Egypt ignored US warnings and apparently is proceeding with the purchase from Russia of twenty-six Su-35s.[48] According to SIPRI's data on international arms trade for the period between 2013 and 2021, Egypt was the fifth-largest importer of equipment from Russia (after India, China, Vietnam, and Algeria), with a total of $3.5 billion in various transactions during those eight years. Egypt has not made any decisions or promises that might jeopardize its pending or potential procurement contracts with Russia. In addition, Sisi already has the friendly French government of President Macron as a reliable ally to compensate for shortages that might result from increased pressure.[49] Sisi's regime apparently still maintains its maneuvering tactics in balancing ties with Western allies and Russia in order to continue its persistent strategy of breaking away from US arms dependency.

How to Reform the Aid Package to Enhance Democracy?

These concluding remarks attempt to propose policy recommendations to Washington, DC, to revise the security assistance package to Egypt. They do not recommend increasing, decreasing, or entirely cutting this aid. Rather, they suggest reforming it in ways that are beneficial to both countries. Focusing on the Egyptian side, the revisions are proposed in the context of utilizing aid to particularly help democratize the civil-military relations in the country.

To Egypt's military regime, US security assistance does not seem to be a matter of cash only, despite its lesser financial contribution to the budget. The Egyptian military clearly still values the technologically advanced equipment that comes in the American shipments and publicly takes pride in the professionalizing experience its officers are exposed to through other components of the aid package. At the propaganda and morale levels, the military-run social media and YouTube channels always celebrate and show off with elaborate footage the arrival of fresh items from the United States as well as the biennial activities of the "Bright Star" joint training with American troops.[50] For example, once the shipment of F-16 fighter jets was restored in 2015 and four of them landed on the air force's runways in Cairo, the MoD's official YouTube channel displayed the delivery in a video of a festive parade. The same video also celebrated the long history of US-Egyptian military relations.[51]

The Egyptian military similarly puts high value on the professionalization experiences that its officers have access to through education and field exercises with American soldiers. Only a small, highly qualified group of Egyptian officers is selected every year to travel to the United States to attend war colleges. These officers, who included Sisi himself and his first minister of defense in one class in the US Army War College in 2006, come back to rise to higher ranks and leadership posts. In terms of field exercises, an important example of this is how the Egyptian counterterrorism special unit, which leads the operations in Sinai, benefited from working with American elite forces. The Egyptian SEAL team, part of the al-Sa'qa units for special missions, regularly commissioned in Sinai's most threatened battalions, was created in the early

2000s on the American SEAL model. Many pioneering officers of the Egyptian SEALs traveled to train in the United States, and some of them accompanied the American SEAL force on international counterterrorism missions in places such as Afghanistan and Pakistan.[52]

As US aid to Egypt is not a question of cash only, this chapter doesn't necessarily recommend increasing it or raising it back into influential percentages of the country's budget. The Egyptian military and state annual expenditures now are too grand for any increases in the US aid's dollar amount to catch up and restore political leverage. Nor does the chapter recommend cutting aid, which still benefits both sides. Instead, it suggests reforming aid by placing more emphasis on the professionalization component of the aid package and utilizing it to introduce Egyptian officers to systematic knowledge and awareness of democratic principles in civil-military relations and encourage them to adhere to liberal values.

This chapter suggests incorporating compulsory curricula in the political sciences and other relevant social sciences for officers receiving the aid package or coming to study in the United States. Such curricula could include brief educational programs in the delivery of shipments and make it obligatory for the officers who receive technical training to operate new equipment to attend these programs either in the United States or in Egypt. Such curricula could also include obligatory courses for officers attending US war colleges on subjects such as the following:

- Civil-military relations in the United States
- Civil-military relations in democratic governments in Europe
- The history of military dictatorships and transitions to democracy in Latin American states
- Religious and ethnic equality in the armed forces (taking into consideration disproportionate admission of Christian Copts, Nubians, and the tribes of Sinai in the Egyptian military academies due to religious or political prejudices)
- Inclusion of women in the armed forces (which the Egyptian military academies don't allow)
- Military budget transparency and oversight in democratic systems
- Successful models of divestment from military business enterprises, such as in China

It is worth mentioning here that the Egyptian military has recently responded to democratization requests in one of the above subjects—at least partially. It has started to adhere to UN requirements to add female officers to its peacekeeping missions abroad. Egyptian peacekeepers receive millions of dollars in compensation every year, and not applying the recommendations of UN Security Council Resolution 1325 to include women and provide male officers with gender-streaming training might have caused financial losses, along with cutting off an important source of global prestige that stems from joining these missions. Egypt has recently opened the door for female officers and civilian workers to join its missions with the United Nations.[53] This positive example indicates that democratic reform could be feasible when pioneered by the provider of funding or aid. As Glenn Robinson affirms (in Chapter 3 of this book), reform is more likely to occur on the supply side than on the receiving end of security assistance. In Egypt's civil-military relations, US aid could potentially be usefully redeployed in this direction.

Notes

1. *Al-Mushir Abu Ghazala wa-l-Sahafa*, 250.
2. The $36 million estimate is based on an official cost of a sale to Israel presented to Congress in 1983, and it included spares, support equipment, and training. *Hearing and Markup Before the Subcommittee on Europe and the Middle East of the Committee of Foreign Affairs*, 45. For the recent price of $125 million, see Congressional Research Service, "Egypt," 11.
3. "Egypt Ignores Washington After U.S. Policy Missteps."
4. *Supplemental 1979 Middle East Aid Package for Israel and Egypt Hearings*.
5. For example, in FY 2019/2020, out of a budget of EGP 66.3 billion, EGP 66 billion are listed as "other expenditure." Aid and grants are less than EGP 1 million. In FY 2020/2021, out of a budget of EGP 76.1 billion, EGP 74.4 billion are listed as "other items of expenditure." Aid and grants are again less than EGP 1 million. See Egyptian Ministry of Finance (http://www.mof.gov.eg).
6. For the Egyptian military budget from the mid-1970s through the late 1980s, see the detailed chart in Abul-Magd, *Militarizing the Nation*, 251.
7. See Egyptian Ministry of Finance (2006–2016; http://www.mof.gov.eg); SIPRI, The SIPRI Military Expenditure Database; *The Military Balance 1965–2015*; US Department of State, "World Military Expenditures and Arms Transfers, 1972–1996"; Soliman, *The Autumn of Dictatorship*, 62.
8. See ibid., 78–93.
9. Marshall, "Egypt's Other Revolution."
10. Ezzat, "Targeting of NGOs Puts Egypt-US Relations to Test."
11. Ismail and Ahmed, "Egyptian Court Acquits 40 NGO Workers."
12. Wezeman, Kuimova, and Wezeman, *Trends in International Arms Transfers, 2020*, 1, 6.
13. Knight, "Germany Quintuples Arms Sales to Saudi Arabia and Egypt."
14. Reuters, "3.2 billion Euros of Egypt-French Arms Deal Financed by Loan from Paris"; Presidential Decree 2015-156.
15. Ministry of Military Production (www.momp.gov.eg, accessed December 12, 2020).
16. Eleiba, "Sea Power."

17. Reuters, "Egypt, Saudi Arabia 'Desperate' to Purchase Mistral Warships"; Reuters, "Egypt Takes Delivery."
18. Reuters, "Egypt, Saudi Arabia Issue 'Cairo Declaration' to Strengthen Cooperation."
19. Abul-Magd, *Militarizing the Nation*, chaps. 1 and 2.
20. Ta'lab, "Dr. Sayyid Mash'al Wazir al-Intaj al-Harbi."
21. al-'Azim, "al-Fariq Hamdi Wahiba- Ra'is al-Hay'a al-'Arabiyya li-l-Tasni'-fi Hiwar ma'a Ruz al-Yusuf."
22. Abul-Magd, *Militarizing the Nation*, chap. 3.
23. Ibid., chaps. 3 and 4.
24. Abul-Magd, Akça, and Marshall, "Two Paths to Dominance," 10–21.
25. Hamama, "Sisi Says Military Economy Is 1.5% of Egypt's GDP."
26. Reuters, "10 U.S. Companies Profiting Most from U.S. Military Aid to Egypt."
27. Reuters, "Egypt's Sissi Negotiates Arms Deal in Russia"; Reuters, "KSA, UAE to Finance Russian Arms Deal with Egypt"; Reuters, "Putin Backs Sisi 'Bid for Egypt Presidency.'"
28. Stewart and Mohammed, "U.S. to Deliver Apache Helicopters to Egypt."
29. US Department of State, "Remarks at the Opening Plenary of the Egypt Economic Development Conference."
30. Congressional Research Service, "Egypt," 7.
31. *The Military Balance 2017*, 361; Reuters, "Egypt Receives First Gowind 2500 Corvette from France."
32. "Arms Importers (SIPRI Trend Indicator Value)."
33. Ibid.
34. Knight, "Germany Quintuples Arms Sales to Saudi Arabia and Egypt."
35. See "Egypt in the News"; Nader, "UK Arms Deals with Egypt Soar"; Govindasamy and Hassan, "China Trying to Undercut Germany on Submarine Offer to Egypt."
36. Wezeman et al., *Trends in International Arms Transfers, 2016*, 6, 11; Fleurant et al., *Trends in International Arms Transfers, 2019*, 1, 6.
37. Wezeman et al., *Trends in International Arms Transfers, 2017*.
38. Le Bras, "France and Egypt."
39. Reuters, "Macron Says French Arms Sales to Egypt."
40. "al-Sisi: al-Da'm al-Khaliji li-Misr 20 Milyar."
41. Ibid.
42. Ibid.
43. Eleiba, "Keeping the Red Sea Safe."
44. Farouk, "More Than Money."
45. Reuters, "Egypt, Saudi Arabia 'Desperate' to Purchase Mistral Warships"; Reuters, "Egypt Takes Delivery."
46. Knight, "Germany Quintuples Arms Sales to Saudi Arabia and Egypt."
47. Ibid.
48. "US Warnings Ineffective on Egypt's Su-35 Plans as Pilots Train in Russia."
49. See Kandil, "Sisi, Macron Discuss Ukraine, COP27 and Regional Security."
50. See Spokesman of the Egyptian Armed Forces, official Facebook page, https://www.facebook.com/EgyArmySpox (accessed December 6, 2020).
51. Egyptian Ministry of Defense's official YouTube channel (www.youtube.com/channel/UC5AvwPA0ewLnAcNvCF8ZEhg).
52. For example, elite officer Ahmad Mansi, who was stationed in Sinai and led successful raids against ISIL between 2014 and 2017: al-Biyali, "Mansi la Yunsa."
53. "Dabitat Hifz Salam Misriyya."

7

EU and Member States' Security Assistance: Complementary or Contradictory?

Florence Gaub and Alex Walsh

EUROPE IS NOT CONVENTIONALLY SEEN AS A PROVIDER OF SECURITY assistance in what is called, in EU lingo, its "Southern Neighborhood." This is because it engages only minimally in a military fashion. A closer look reveals, however, that Europe does more than is perhaps seen: it has police missions in Libya, the Palestinian Territories, and Iraq and runs security sector reform (SSR) programs in several other states in the region. And some of its member states occasionally use a more muscular approach, including weapons deliveries and tactical training. While this might be considered a "soft touch" compared with the other approaches outlined in this book, it is still a security-oriented one. The rationale for this is simple: the two sides of the Mediterranean have also been tied by (in)security since the end of decolonization; any instability or conflict the region experiences has direct or indirect effects on Europe. Both the Israeli-Palestinian conflict and the Algerian civil war spilled over in the shape of airplane hijackings and bomb explosions in the 1970s. More recently, refugees fleeing the conflict in Syria, terror attacks by the Islamic State (IS), and the Libyan civil war all had direct impacts on European security and stability. Prospects of a proliferation of weapons of mass destruction, war between Saudi Arabia and Iran, or failed states loom over how the region features in European security thinking. Middle Eastern instability also has an economic impact on Europe, be it because of oil-price fluctuation or vulnerable shipping lanes through the Strait of

Hormuz or the Suez Canal. The strong connection between European and regional security is perhaps best summarized by France's ambassador when he stated that "Egypt's security is France's security" (also visible in NATO's thinking, outlined in Kevin Koehler's Chapter 8).[1]

Europe has broadly taken two approaches to its neighbors' security predicament: on the one hand, member states of the European Union have lent Middle Eastern and North African nations significant security assistance (such as military-to-military support, police-to-police collaboration, and training and equipping). On the other hand, and in an apparently contrasting logic, the European Union *as a whole* offers security-sector reform programs to its Southern Neighborhood. SSR is designed to change the target institution (be it military, police, gendarmerie, customs, etc.) to make it both more effective and accountable along norms of human rights and the rule of law. European member states' assistance preceded European Union reform assistance, but both picked up significantly after the Arab Spring in 2011. This acceleration has three drivers: First, the opening space for reform in some of the Southern Neighborhood's countries, most notably Tunisia but also Lebanon, gave the EU, a generally reform-minded organization in its external relations, an opportunity to become more involved in an area previously difficult to penetrate. Second, the EU's own slow but progressive transformation toward security action facilitated its pivot toward security assistance. Third, worsening security conditions in the neighborhood pushed EU member states and the EU toward a deepened engagement in security matters.

The two approaches superficially share the objective of improving security in the recipient states, but a closer look reveals that they differ in some substantial ways. Security assistance focuses on equipping, training, and strengthening security and military institutions *as they stand*, whereas SSR involves security and defense *transformation*. Whereas security assistance is therefore a status quo approach, SSR is transformational. And while member-state approaches tend to focus on material and equipment, EU approaches tend to focus on intangible matters such as doctrine, procedures, and rules. It is worth noting that this difference is in part the result of a member-state prerogative: the EU has no oversight over European arms production or exports and is not involved in procuring or exporting them itself. The two approaches differ also in that the EU's security assistance focuses almost exclusively on the police, whereas member states cooperate with both police and the military. This is because until 2015, the recipients of EU development assistance did not include military actors. While the regulation was changed subsequently to include military capacity building in third countries, so far the EU has not engaged in military capacity building in its Southern Neighborhood.[2]

The two approaches also have different time horizons: whereas European member-state support seeks to achieve an almost immediate effect of improvement, European Union support seeks the transformation of an institution, which takes close to a decade or even more. This difference in time horizon is visible, too, in the programming time frames, which are three years for member states and seven years for EU programs.

In addition, the two approaches are set at different levels. Whereas European member-state assistance is strategic in that it quickly strengthens a relationship between states, EU assistance tends to have no immediate strategic benefit. In part this is because its recipients are, by default, fragile states that often accept it despite its interfering nature as part of a larger cooperation, whereas security assistance tends to go to states that are strong in capacity but often weak on democratic credentials, such as Egypt. But EU SSR has potentially other, much longer-term strategic benefits because it is ultimately about not just security but democracy and the rule of law. Therefore EU SSR is one of several tools to establish and strengthen democracy and designed to expand the number of democracies in Europe's neighborhood, which is in itself one of Europe's main foreign policy objectives. This also explains why EU security assistance never makes it to states in the Gulf (see Zoltan Barany's Chapter 9) or Egypt: a minimum potential for democratization is a prerequisite for EU engagement in security matters.

The two approaches also differ in financial ways: whereas the European Union outspends the member states when it comes to SSR (see Figure 7.1), member states spend significantly less on transformational programs but significantly more on training and equipping, which is not considered development assistance and therefore does not feature in this calculation. For instance, the budget of the EU's mission in Iraq stands at €64.8 million per year, an amount close to what Germany alone delivered in weapons to Iraq in 2018. According to one study, 24 percent of weapons exports to the region come from European countries, with 11 percent coming from France, 5 percent from Germany, 3 percent from Italy, 2 percent from Spain, and 1.45 percent from the Netherlands.[3] With the exception of Iraq, all other recipient states are not involved in SSR programs with the EU or its member states, suggesting, as indicated above, that the choice between security assistance and SSR is linked to the recipient state's strategic posture, political system, and penetrability.

A closer look reveals that the two approaches are built on two different implicit assumptions about security and insecurity. While member

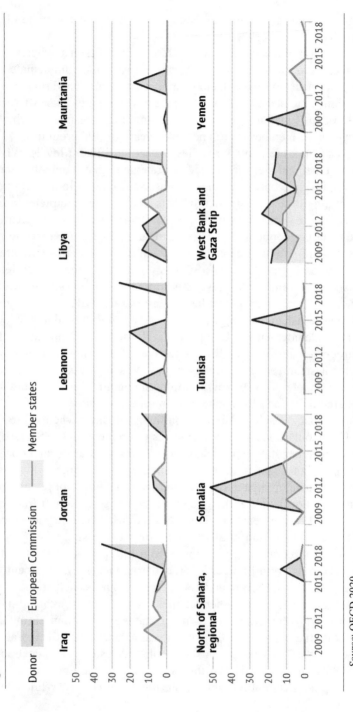

Figure 7.1 European Involvement in Security Assistance and Reform, 2009–2018 (US$ Million)

Source: OECD 2020.
Note: Official development assistance commitments by EU member states and institutions for security system management and reform.

states' approaches tackle the phenomenon of insecurity directly, the EU's approach seeks to tackle the root causes of insecurity. Whereas the former takes insecurity as a given, the latter assumes that citizen discontent is (among other things) the result of security actors' abuse. The EU's approach is therefore one of normative values: it is embedded in a wider logic of democratic norms that see the security sector as part and parcel of a system of accountability, oversight, and participatory structures. Without ever being explicit, the EU's assistance, be it security or other, is built on the assumption that its own model of governance leads to stability and prosperity in the long run—even if this means having to deal with insecurity in the short run. This longtime logic of democratic transformation explains its approaches to the Southern Neighborhood in general.

Member-state assistance, in return, tends to be shaped by a key feature of democracy: the short lifespans of electoral cycles. Decisionmakers are pressed by their constituencies to deliver not just security but also prosperity as fast as possible. Their security engagement with the Southern Neighborhood is therefore designed to deliver immediate results—even if this means creating instability or insecurity in the long run. In addition, security assistance is not just about internal security (e.g., terrorism or trafficking) but also about more strategic-level security (e.g., interstate conflict and diplomacy). Maintaining friendly relations with strategically important states is a task European heads of states will have to deliver to their constituencies to a greater extent than the European Union—at least, for now. Surveys show increasing European citizen support (more than 57 percent in favor) for more joint European action when it comes to foreign and security policy.[4]

These differences invite a reflection on whether they are complementary or contradictory: Do they ultimately reinforce or undermine each other's objectives?

Complementarity is defined as "a relationship or situation in which two or more different things improve or emphasize each other's qualities."[5] *Contradiction*, in turn, is defined as "a combination of statements, ideas, or features which are opposed to one another."

In our context, this would mean that in a complementary setting, security assistance and SSR would both help each other in achieving their respective goals of short-term security and stability by way of strengthening the security actors and long-term security and stability by way of strengthening democratic approaches to security. In turn, contradiction would mean that one undermines the other, meaning that SSR undermines stability in the short term and security assistance undermines democratic security approaches in the long run. To understand whether they are in complementarity or contradiction, we would have to focus solely on those states that receive both SSR from the EU and security assistance from European member states. This narrows the scope down considerably: the number of states that receive both is limited to Iraq, Libya, Tunisia, Jordan, Lebanon, and the Palestinian Territories. Of the EU member states, Germany, France, and the Netherlands have spent the most on SSR in these countries and in the region as a whole. From this clutch of states, we draw three cases—Iraq, Tunisia, and Libya—to compare EU member states and the EU in their security approaches to find out where and how they are either complementary or in contradiction.

Iraq, the EU, and France

Like the other states studied here, Iraq has been a weak state in terms of capacity, democratic stability, and security since the invasion of 2003. While European states were divided on the invasion itself, the EU not only developed several economic and humanitarian ties with Iraq but also operated its first integrated rule-of-law mission in Iraq, EUJUST LEX–Iraq, between 2005 and 2013. As its name indicates, it focused exclusively on aspects such as accountability, respect for human rights, and compliance and worked within the criminal justice system only (i.e., police and justice officials). Its mission was therefore not per se security in a first instance, but rather in a second instance, as it worked to improve things in the field adjacent to security: justice. In total, it trained more than 7,000 mid- and high-level Iraqi officials, but ultimately its work was severely hampered by imploding Iraqi security, political polarization, and corruption.[6] The mission ended in 2013, not because it had achieved its objective but because security conditions, as well as domestic politics in Iraq, made it increasingly difficult to operate. The justice-sector focus of the mission, too, meant that it was not equipped to address several issues of the Iraqi security sector that were outside its mandate, such as militias acting with impunity, counterterrorism, and widespread absenteeism. Nevertheless, the mission served as a blueprint for EU security assistance elsewhere: the very notion of normative reform and transformation of the security sector was first tested in Iraq.

In those years, France did not engage in substantial bilateral security assistance of any type to Iraq; even its weapons sales, six Gazelle helicopters delivered in 2010, were far below what it used to export to

Iraq during the Saddam Hussein era. It did support, however, EUJUST LEX in its training efforts through the provision of training personnel.[7] In this context, its activities were entirely focused on the operational and tactical level of security, aiming at things such as the improvement of crime-scene management or forensic sciences. In part, this was less a strategic choice by France and more a strategic constraint: France's relations with the new leadership were as much marred by its close relations with the previous regime as they were with the United States and the coalition by its very vocal opposition to the intervention in 2003.[8]

Things changed from 2014 onward for both the EU and France: the fall of Mosul and conquests of large parts of Iraqi territory turned Iraqi security into a matter of international concern.

For the EU, this meant the launch of a new advisory mission, EUAM Iraq, in 2017, following the recapture of Mosul. Its arrival in Iraq only after the formal end of the Islamic State as a territorial entity and combat action is no coincidence: the EU's missions are designed for peace and stabilization rather than war. This also explains why most of its missions—eleven at the time of writing—are civilian, and only six are military.[9] In contrast to its predecessor mission, EUAM Iraq has a broad SSR mandate. Although still very much focused on the civilian side of security, this means that the mission's approach is much broader and more strategic than EUJUST LEX. Its methodology also differs: instead of providing training, this mission advises senior Iraqi officials in the Ministry of Interior and the Office of the National Security Advisor. With a yearly budget of €65 million, this mission surpasses its predecessor by more than four times the amount in financial terms.[10] The EU's challenge is that its distinction between civilian and military security is problematic in a region like the Middle East and North Africa. Whereas in Europe *civilian* equates to the domestic and *military* to the external, this distinction is not so easily made in the region. Counterterrorism, arguably Iraq's biggest security concern, is handled at least in part by the armed forces, but the EU mission has no mandate to advise them.

France's support to Iraqi security began in earnest from September 2014 onward, when it joined all the working groups of the international coalition against the Islamic State. As part of Operation Inherent Resolve, its Operation Chammal contributed by advising and training Iraqi security forces, conducting air strikes and maritime patrols, and providing naval vessels in support of air and ground efforts. It is worth noting that this type and extent of engagement is unusual for France in the Arab world. France participates in security-sector reform in Sub-Saharan Africa—for instance, in Senegal and Djibouti. France's efforts paid off strategically as it emerged from the operation as a new geopolitical player in Iraq. In 2020, the Iraqi government wrote on its official Twitter account that "France is a comrade and friend of Iraq who has supported the Iraqi armed forces in the war against Daesh" just ahead of President Emmanuel Macron's visit to Baghdad. Two weeks later, Iraq's foreign minister traveled to Paris to discuss, among other things, the acquisition of French weapons.[11]

The security assistance relation between France and Iraq highlights how a European member state has evolved away from traditional security assistance in the shape of arms sales and operational support toward a more structural understanding of security-sector reform. While France adopted an interdepartmental concept of security system reform in 2008, this approach, which resembles that of the EU, has become visible in how it has handled Iraqi security in the years since 2014. It differs from the EU in its emphasis on the military dimension in security as well as on effectiveness. Matters such as morale of the armed forces will appear in French security-sector programming but not in the EU's.[12]

In sum, the Iraqi case shows that EU and member-state security assistance has been complementary rather than in contradiction. Whereas French support has focused on the short term, it has taken place within the (albeit weak) democratic context of Iraq; perhaps because of this, its efforts against IS have been judged as legitimate and appropriate rather than fueling more violence and extremism. At the same time, the EU's efforts have focused on the same objective but at a strategic level in the Ministry of Interior. The two approaches have therefore been intertwined and in harmony with each other. There is, however, reason to believe that this is primarily the result of Iraq's political setup as opposed to any efforts of the EU or France: both have displayed different behavior in other cases less easy to penetrate. In Egypt, for instance, France's diplomatic and material support to the security sector has been at odds with EU objectives, empowering security actors deemed overly violent and repressive at the expense of political democratic reform.

Tunisia, the EU, and Germany

After the Arab Spring, Tunisia became a prime recipient of both security assistance and SSR from European states and the EU. The main reason for this was, of course, its promising transition to democracy, which was considered a desirable trajectory to support. This, again, shows that the nature of the recipient's state political system is a crucial component in the choice of security assistance and/or SSR. Security considerations, too, played a role, primarily related to terrorism. This focus became stronger after a spree of terrorist attacks on the Tunisian mainland that killed Europeans and the involvement of Tunisians in many terrorist attacks on European soil (Paris in November 2015, Berlin in December 2016, and Nice in July 2016).[13] Alongside terrorism, the EU also has a strategic interest in combating other forms of transnational crime linking Europe and Tunisia, including money laundering and narcotics smuggling.

As elsewhere, the EU takes a wide view of Tunisian security, linking prosperity, democracy, and stability. It seeks to develop a stable, democratic, and prosperous partner in the long term and in the meantime to ensure that the process does not collapse.

The EU's security cooperation with Tunisia stretches back well into the Zine El Abidine Ben Ali era but in 2011 found fresh impetus and, most importantly, a mandate from the Tunisians themselves to play a leading role in reform. In line with its commitment to the security-development nexus, the EU weaves hard security matters into broader development areas both on paper and in practice. For instance, the EU-Tunisia Shared Strategic Priorities for 2018–2020 numbered four, covering inclusive and sustainable economic development; democracy, good governance, and human rights; bringing peoples closer together; and mobility and migration—as well as security and counterterrorism, areas couched in terms of human rights and democracy. Prosperity and democracy are viewed by the EU as the strongest counter to terrorism, while security is a requirement for prosperity.[14]

At the invitation of the transitional government, the EU was at the forefront of the SSR efforts from 2011 in Tunisia, in a country deeply cognizant of the importance of the security sector to the substance and power of the former authoritarian regime. Implementation was slow in the first couple of years but was renewed in 2015 with fresh vigor due to new counterterrorism imperatives, the advent of integrated border management, and projects designed to restore citizens' faith in the security sector by tackling corruption; support to intelligence agencies also gave it a harder edge.[15] With the formation of the G7+6 Coordinating Group, the EU works on providing independent oversight of the police and developing investigative capacity.[16] Progress in the fundamental reform of Tunisia's security sector has been frustratingly slow, but the EU remains a driving force from an SSR perspective.

In pursuit of its interests in migration control, the EU signed a mobility partnership in 2014, conceived as an instrument to facilitate regular migration, combat irregular migration, and support international protection for refugees and internal migration. Here, the EU is interested not only in Tunisians arriving and residing irregularly in the EU but also in third-country nationals arriving from Sub-Saharan Africa. The EU has interests in Tunisia to commit more strongly in terms of resources for border management and the readmission of irregular migrants to Tunisia and its neighbors. Although already signed, the mobility partnership continues to undergo negotiations to further substantiate its principles and kick off implementation. The EU has partly pursued these negotiations using the bargain of visa facilitation for Tunisians seeking to travel to the EU in exchange for greater Tunisian commitment to repelling EU-bound migrants and Tunisian and third-country readmissions. It also uses its economic weight to help negotiations.[17] This type of approach faces the critique of border externalization,[18] a claim that the EU manipulates its southern neighbors into doing its border management. If accepted, this critique places the EU's engagement on the migration aspect of security somewhat in contrast to its engagement with the Tunisian Ministry of Interior on accountability and oversight, as it casts the EU as inducing other states to be responsible for its migration policies.

At the same time, Germany is an EU member state that has been very involved in Tunisia. Its "Interministerial Strategy to Support Security Sector Reform" is a forty-page document dedicated to the normative concepts of SSR, intoning Germany's commitments to linking security, institutional oversight, transparency, and the rule of law.[19] Conceptually, it places Germany's security engagement within its overall contribution to global human development rather than as a separate packet of interests and processes. This strategy places Germany's outlook directly in line with the EU's commitment to SSR; much of Germany's security interests also overlap with those of the EU, nestling around the ambition for a prosperous and democratic Tunisian state and focusing on a strong commitment to combat irregular migration and transnational terrorism. Germany's very substantial and wide-ranging development budget bears out its commitment to human development, with focus areas including employability, the energy transition, and the environment.

However, Germany's approach to security issues is considerably less SSR driven than that of the EU. Its security engagement portfolio is funded by three major sources—an instrument known as the Ertüchtigungsinitiative (E2I), the program for Police Training and Equipping Aid (AAH-P). E2I can include lethal weapons.[20] In short, in the last five to six years the lion's share has gone to security assistance and only a fraction explicitly to SSR support by way of funding with the contribution to the North Africa trust fund used by the Tunis office of the Geneva Centre for Security Governance. This majority covers train-and-equip programs and police-to-police cooperation, with a focus on border security. (Some attention is also given to more values-based training such as combatting violence against women.)

The hardening of the Tunisian-Libyan border is perhaps the most important project (there is also assistance on the Tunisian-Algerian border). This support for border management is done in part in cooperation with the United States and includes building walls on the Tunisian-Libyan border and installing electronic surveillance systems. Germany also supports the Tunisian security forces in enhancing their supervision of Tunisian coastal waters. This pattern is reflected in the role Germany adopted in the G7, where it assumed responsibility for counterterrorism. Its approach has been characterized as "a narrow military outlook."[21]

The EU's and Germany's approaches might have been complementary (i.e., reformist and operational in tandem) if the former had been more successful to date. However, given the slow progress, there is a danger that increasing the capability of the Tunisian security sector and pumping resources into it may actually have been harming the cause of security-sector accountability and oversight—a view also outlined in Noureddine Jebnoun's Chapter 4. The security forces' support of the president's coup in 2021 could be read as a sign that this has materialized.

Indeed, Germany's and the EU's support for Tunisia's security sphere could thus be said to be rather well aligned, if not in spirit, then in terms of results. Germany's considerable expenditure on security assistance has not brought deep reform, but neither in particular has the EU's large spending on SSR. Tunisia's internal security has seen gains in effectiveness that outstrip improvements in accountability and oversight, concepts that are nonetheless kept alive by the EU. Germany's pumping of resources into the security sphere outside such strict normative conditionality may not have helped reform, but for the time being, its contribution to security-sector effectiveness is probably appreciated by the European Commission for its contribution to migration control, especially given the slow progress in substantiating the mobility partnership, particularly when it comes to leveraging Tunisian assistance in repelling irregular migration from Sub-Saharan Africa. Finally, indicating an area of coherence, German and EU investment in counterterrorism and the (rather amorphous) field of countering violent extremism seems to have met with success given the decline of terrorist attacks. Tunisia, at least, has suffered fewer terrorism-caused deaths than Germany in the past five years, a muddled if evocative measurement.

Indeed, even while Germany appears locked on a path of providing hard security assistance, it continues to wrap this in a larger security and prosperity portfolio linking security at a scale and logic comparable with EU programming.

Libya, the EU, the Netherlands, and France

The end of the Mu'ammar Gadhafi regime in 2011 saw an opportunity to reform Libya's security sector in a substantial way. Police and military forces had largely melted away during the war, leaving the country virtually bare of security-sector agents. Although all parties concerned, Libyans themselves as well as their international partners in Europe and the United States, expressed the wish to undertake security-sector reform—or rather, reconstruction—this was hampered from the outset by a number of things. First, the security void had to be filled quickly. This was done by giving provisional legitimacy to militias that had formed during the war as the Supreme Security Committee for domestic security and as the Libya Shield for military matters. Second, police and armed forces were to be rebuild and then replace these provisional structures. This plan underestimated two things from the outset: the unwillingness of the militias to bow to oversight and accountability and the extended time it would take to rebuild a security sector as hollowed out as the Libyan one.

In this context, the EU and several of its member states got involved early on in providing assistance to Libya in security matters. In May 2013, the EU launched a border assistance mission, EUBAM Libya, with the objective of assisting Libya with the creation of an effective border force in line with democratic principles. Its main activities were therefore centered on capacity building via training, mentoring, and advising Libyan officials. In the summer of 2014, the mission had to relocate to Tunisia as Libya fell into disarray. Its training activities were henceforth reduced to the Libyan coast guard.[22] The mission returned to Libya in 2019.

In addition, the EU launched EUNAVFOR MED IRINI, whose objective is to enforce the maritime dimension of the UN arms embargo. Although in place since 2011, it is considered to be "totally ineffective."[23] As secondary objectives, the mission also has noted the control of illicit petroleum trade, migration, and building capacity of the Libyan coast guard and navy.

The EU's security activities in Libya have not been without problems. In large part, this is due to the very nature of the conflict environment in which it operates. High levels of violence, the prevalence of militias acting with impunity, and weapons in the hands of the civilian population mean that security-sector reform in the traditional sense is not possible. That said, even the focus on external borders is problematic. EU missions—and indeed, European border management—are civilian by definition, whereas Libyan border guards traditionally have a military background. In addition, the chaos in Libya's security sector soon meant that the EU's counterparts were not always clearly identifiable as state actors. As a result, both missions have been accused of acting solely in the interest of the EU to prevent migration rather than actually improving Libyan security by reducing the smuggling of arms.[24]

From a more strategic point of view, the enforcement of the embargo has meant inadvertently taking sides in the Libyan conflict by making it more difficult for weapons to reach certain conflict parties.[25] As we will see below, this has led some member states, notably France, to act on their own.

One member state that is quite active in Libya, despite its geographic distance and size, is the Netherlands. When it comes to security abroad, the Netherlands does not have a single overarching SSR strategy, but its strategic papers and institutions present a blended approach that brings operational and peacekeeping commitments together with the logic of SSR as part of the international development field.[26]

This reform-minded and multilateral approach is in view in the Dutch engagement in Libya, where the Netherlands were the second-largest donor to UNSMIL/UNDP Policing and Joint Security Program (2017–2020).[27] On paper, this supports the Libyan Ministry of Interior, police, and criminal justice system in advancing security and the rule of law in Tripoli. Its program logic sees the identification of the security needs of civilians as the basis of law enforcement prioritization. This program attempts to bring human rights standards and notions of community policing into Libyan Ministry of Interior usage. While foregrounding these normative aspects, the program is not particularly emphatic on accountability and oversight measures.

The Netherlands is also an active supporter of the EU's embargo position on Libya, dating back to the embargo of 2011, when the Netherlands deployed F-16s and refueling aircraft, a minehunter, and around 200 personnel.[28] Today, it contributes to Operation Irini, and the arms embargo is even a Dutch domestic policy issue. In November 2020, a number of parties from the Netherlands' ruling coalition petitioned the government to pressure the EU to establish a weapons embargo against Turkey—linked to Turkish involvement in Nagorno Karabakh and in Libya.[29] While on the UN Security Council in 2018, the Netherlands successfully proposed a resolution to counter people smuggling and human trafficking in Libya that would "freeze all bank accounts belonging to six leaders of criminal networks and ban them from travelling internationally."[30] In sum, the Netherlands is therefore very much in line with EU approaches to Libyan security.

The problem is perhaps the fact that Libyan security is in a state in which the EU normally does not undertake security assistance. Violent conflict is the most extreme form of insecurity and is a political phenomenon first and foremost. As a result, any action undertaken in Libya's security sector will never be neutral but will take sides in a conflict regardless of intention.

This is perhaps best illustrated by the example of France in Libya. While France broadly supports EU objectives in Libya, it felt it necessary to influence the Libyan conflict by delivering weapons to those following General Khalifa Haftar.[31] This is in direct contradiction to the arms embargo the EU seeks to enforce. But it also showcases the different levels on which security assistance takes place: whereas weapons deliveries and direct operational support are almost always immediate in nature, security-sector reform is a long-term project that can come at the expense of immediate security. It is worth noting that France later joined forces with Germany and Italy to denounce weapons deliveries to Libya.[32]

Conclusion

The dichotomy described above—short-termist weapons deliveries and operational support, on the one hand, and long-termist reform endeavors, on the other—underpins how Europe approaches security assistance to the region. Whereas the latter leads to assistance designed to reform and improve, the former brings about assistance short term in nature but with almost immediate effects. Whereas the latter tends to be focused on transfer of skills and sharing of best practices, the former zeroes in on equipment and sometimes tactical assistance.

These two logics are broadly distributed between the EU, on the one hand, and those member states deeming the region a priority, on the other. Whereas the EU pursues a reform agenda largely in line with the United Nations' approach to security (i.e., shaped by socioeconomic conditions, tied to good governance and the rule of law), member states at times orient their assistance along the lines of hard security (i.e., shaped by criteria such as effectiveness against terrorism or crime). Inadvertently, the EU's approach operates with a horizon of several years, whereas member states seek to achieve immediate results.

Superficially, this would invite the conclusion that these two approaches undermine each other in effect. This does not appear to be the case, according to our case studies, which found only minor elements of contradiction, but under two conditions: First, where the EU has ongoing reform programs, its member states tend to follow its objectives broadly. Second, the recipient country is not in a state of war, a situation for which the EU's security reform programs are perhaps least suited conceptually.

Where these two conditions do not apply, member states have indeed deviated from their own norms and those of the EU. For instance, the delivery of French and German weapons to Egypt's security forces (including warships, fighter jets, armored vehicles, and surveillance and crowd-control tools) is not tied to any conditions concerning long-term reform, be it the rule of law or the protection of human rights. But we also notice that the biggest weapons recipients (Egypt and Saudi Arabia) are not those with the biggest investment in SSR and development (Palestine, Libya, and Iraq). This seems to indicate that the two approaches rarely manifest themselves jointly and more typically in an either-or fashion.

This in itself could be an indication that security-sector reform requires a degree of permissiveness and cooperation that is not found in some states. In those cases, security assistance will take the shape of weapons deliveries in order to achieve a minimum strategic objective of bilateral cooperation. This means that the decisive factor when it comes to European security approaches could very well be the recipient state rather than the division of labor between a more long-term and democracy-promotion-oriented EU and more short-term and stability-oriented member states. The dichotomy therefore lies elsewhere: states that are weak in capacity and in transition to democracy (itself often a fragile state) not only will need both security assistance and SSR but might very well see both as an asset to strengthen their capacity and relations. In turn, states that are strong in terms of capacity but weak in terms of democracy will reject SSR and focus security assistance on primarily technical assistance.

This means that both SSR and security assistance are, ultimately, decided not by security considerations but by political values in both the EU and the recipient states.

Notes

1. "France's Security Starts in Egypt."
2. "Revised EU Approach to Security and Development Funding."
3. Center for International Policy, "The Mideast Arms Bazaar."
4. "Foreign Policy."
5. "Complementarity" and "Contradiction," Oxford Languages, https://languages.oup.com/google-dictionary-en.
6. Christova, "Seven Years of EUJUST LEX."
7. "Old News in Brief"; "News in Brief."
8. Béraud-Sudreau, "French Arms Exports."
9. "Military and Civilian Missions and Operations."
10. "Iraq: EU Advisory Mission Extended and Budget Agreed."
11. "France, New Key Player in Iraq."
12. Deneckere, Neat, and Hauck, "The Future of EU Security Sector Assistance."
13. Santini and Cimini, "The Politics of Security Reform in Post-2011 Tunisia."
14. Dandashly, "EU Democracy Promotion and the Dominance of the Security-Stability Nexus."
15. Santini and Cimini, "The Politics of Security Reform in Post-2011 Tunisia."
16. El-Malki and Dworkin. "The Southern Front Line."
17. Seeberg, "Mobility Partnerships and Security Subcomplexes in the Mediterranean," 2.
18. Abderrahim, "A Tale of Two Agreements," 7.
19. "Interministerial Strategy to Support Security Sector Reform (SSR)."
20. Stahl and Treffler, "Germany's Security Assistance to Tunisia," 32–34.
21. Santini and Cimini, "The Politics of Security Reform in Post-2011 Tunisia," 235.
22. "EU-Libya Relations."
23. "Libya Arms Embargo 'Totally Ineffective.'"
24. Megerisi and Fine, "The Unacknowledged Costs of the EU's Migration Policy."
25. "The EU Is in a Muddle over Libya."
26. Deneckere, Neat, and Hauck, "The Future of EU Security Sector Assistance."
27. The other donors, in order of contribution size, were the United States, Italy, Germany, and the United Nations Development Programme. "UNSMIL/UNDP Policing and Security Joint Programme."
28. "Netherlands Help in Enforcing Libyan Arms Embargo."
29. "Dutch Coalition MPs Call for EU Weapons Embargo Against Turkey."
30. "Dutch Initiative."
31. "U.S. Missiles Found in Libyan Rebel Camp Were First Sold to France."
32. "France, Germany, Italy Threaten Sanctions over Arms for Libya."

8

The Politics of Security Assistance by "European NATO"

Kevin Koehler

SINCE THE END OF THE COLD WAR, SECURITY ASSISTANCE HAS BECOME an increasingly important tool of foreign and security policy. Security assistance funds mobilized by Organization for Economic Cooperation and Development countries as part of global official development aid flows grew by a factor of twenty-five between 2000 and 2019, even though such figures only capture a fraction of the true volume.[1] The Russian war against Ukraine has again highlighted the importance of such policy instruments, as Western governments have authorized unprecedented levels of military aid to Ukraine.[2] The North Atlantic Treaty Organization (NATO) has been active in capacity building for the Ukrainian armed forces since 2014, and the 2022 Madrid Summit adopted a strengthened assistance package to Ukraine.[3] Security assistance is thus an important tool, but is it also effective?

The answer to this question depends on how effectiveness is assessed. In academic discussions, *security assistance* is frequently defined as "training, equipping and advising allied or 'partner' militaries to enable them to defend themselves."[4] Measured against this capacity-building yardstick, most security assistance efforts are not particularly successful.[5] The collapse of parts of the Iraqi army in the face of the Islamic State (IS) offensive in 2014 and the 2021 disintegration of the Afghan National Army following the withdrawal of US and international troops highlight the limits of such an approach.[6] If security assistance does not succeed in building capacity, why do donors continue to spend scarce resources on such policies?

Security assistance can also be seen as an integral part of larger security strategies. Indeed, official definitions frequently refer directly to national security interests,[7] and it is clear that many countries use security assistance as a tool to increase their influence and to cement international alignments. As F. C. Williams and Sean Yom argue in this book, from such a geostrategic perspective, US assistance to Egypt and Jordan, respectively, could be said to achieve its aims.

These differences are important for understanding security assistance efforts by NATO, which are the focus of this chapter. On the rhetorical level, capacity building is the declared goal of security assistance through NATO. In fact, at their 2021 summit, NATO heads of state and government decided to strengthen NATO's capacity-building efforts, a decision reinforced by the new strategic concept adopted at the June 2022 Madrid Summit.[8] Compared to bilateral programs, however, NATO security assistance efforts are limited by the fact that the organization cannot provide matériel or direct financial support and is hampered by strict resource constraints. In that sense, NATO activities in this field concentrate on "softer" forms by default, even though this focus is not necessarily linked to a normative framework aimed at security-sector reform, as Florence Gaub and Alex Walsh suggest for the case of the European Union.[9] Crucially, however, NATO security assistance is inscribed in the larger political context of strategic considerations on the level of the alliance, as well as that of individual member states. I argue that this last, political level actually drives security assistance activities through NATO.

In this chapter, I substantiate this point by examining NATO security assistance efforts in the Middle East and North Africa (MENA). Given the dearth of prior research on the subject, I approach the issue in a largely descriptive manner. In a first step, I outline NATO's partnership frameworks in MENA, highlighting a number of important structural elements, in particular the partner-driven nature of NATO initiatives as well as the "costs lie where they fall" principle. In a second step, I then examine the politics of security assistance through NATO, drawing on illustrative case studies of France, Germany, and Italy. The case studies show how security assistance through NATO is driven by an interplay of national priorities and alliance politics, limiting the extent to which a multilateral organization such as NATO can hope to provide strategic direction.

This chapter proceeds as follows: The next section outlines how NATO has approached security assistance to MENA in terms of policies as well as concrete tools and institutional mechanisms. The second section examines French, German, and Italian security assistance activities in MENA, specifically in three countries that are central from a NATO perspective—namely, Jordan, Iraq, and Tunisia. The final section concludes by highlighting the limitations of NATO-led security assistance emerging from this particular process.

"When Our Neighbours Are Stable, We Are More Secure"[10]

For most of its seventy-year history, NATO has focused on its core mission of deterrence and collective defense. Only with the end of the Cold War did the alliance begin to establish formal cooperation frameworks with nonallied countries. These partnership frameworks—the Partnership for Peace, the Mediterranean Dialogue (MD), the Istanbul Cooperation Initiative, and Partners Across the Globe—comprise around forty nonallied countries and provide the formal basis for security assistance activities.

The emergence of NATO partnerships must be seen in the context of the alliance's general reorientation "out of area" after the end of the Cold War. In the course of this adaptation, the stability of the alliance's periphery—both east and south—became a core concern.[11] The 2010 strategic concept for the first time formally defined cooperative security as one core mission, next to collective defense and crisis management.[12] The 2022 strategic concept has refocused the alliance on deterrence and defense; at the same time, capacity-building efforts remain an important element of crisis management and cooperative security. The provision of security assistance through training and capacity building will thus continue to play an important role in NATO policy, not least in relation to the Southern Neighborhood.[13]

NATO has developed its own vocabulary and set of policy instruments for security assistance. On the most general level, the alliance approaches cooperation with nonallied countries under the heading of "partnership." While not all partners are necessarily also recipients of security assistance, membership in a formal partnership framework is a precondition for almost all forms of security assistance through NATO.[14] Partnership initiatives with countries in MENA started with the Mediterranean Dialogue set up in 1994. Initially, the MD was meant to capitalize on what was then perceived to be a positive regional dynamic in the wake of the Oslo Accords between Israel and the Palestinian Liberation

Organization, as well as the Madrid peace conference, which brought together Israel and a number of Arab states. This background was reflected in the initial composition of the MD, which included Israel and five Arab countries: Egypt, Jordan, Mauritania, Morocco, and Tunisia. Algeria joined the framework in 2000, and at the 2012 Chicago Summit, NATO leaders invited Libya to join as well (the country has not yet accepted the offer). A second south-facing partnership initiative was launched at the alliance's Istanbul Summit in 2004. Known as the Istanbul Cooperation Initiative, this format comprises four Arab Gulf states: Bahrain, Kuwait, Qatar, and the United Arab Emirates. Oman and Saudi Arabia were invited to join but decided to keep their distance. Reflecting their specific situations, both Afghanistan and Iraq are part of yet another partnership framework, Partners Across the Globe, together with countries such as Australia, Colombia, Japan, and Pakistan. Figure 8.1 illustrates the reach of NATO partnerships in MENA.

Security assistance within NATO's partnership frameworks is demand driven. Partners can access a range of different activities, collected in the Partnership Cooperation Menu, which currently lists around 1,400 items, more than twice the number on offer in 2011.[15] These items range from educational activities at the NATO Defense College (NDC) in Rome or the NATO School in Oberammergau, to cooperation on defense education through the Defense Education Enhancement Program (DEEP), to more targeted training activities at NATO Centers of Excellence or through dedicated mobile training teams. The NDC, for example, trained a total of 284 military officers

Figure 8.1 NATO Partners in MENA

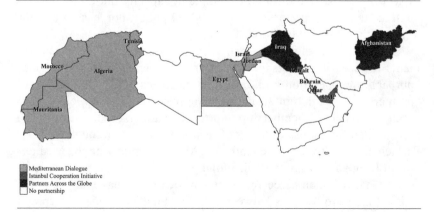

from MENA countries through its NATO Regional Cooperation Course between the inception of the course in 2009 and 2019.[16] According to the NATO Secretary General's annual report for 2020, moreover, 2,400 partner faculty and students active in professional military education were reached through DEEP during 2020 alone.[17] In general, security assistance activities through NATO focus on "softer" elements, in particular capacity building through training and education, reflecting the fact that the alliance itself cannot provide matériel or financial support. Conceptually, however, NATO places less emphasis on institutional reform—especially when compared to the European Union's more ambitious agenda (see Chapter 7)—even though dedicated programs have been developed as part of the Building Integrity approach.[18]

The intensity of cooperation within NATO's partnership frameworks differs significantly, ranging from sporadic interaction, through educational activities, to more structured cooperation based on regular planning cycles. NATO's closest security assistance partners in MENA are Jordan, Iraq, and Tunisia. Other MENA partners participate in security assistance activities as well, yet in a less structured form. Jordan, Iraq, and Tunisia are beneficiaries of the Defense Capacity Building (DCB) Initiative, which bundles security assistance to each of these countries. Currently there are only six active DCB packages. In addition to Iraq, Jordan, and Tunisia, DCB packages have been developed in support of Georgia and Moldova, as well as for the training of UN peacekeepers. Libya has submitted a request for NATO support through the DCB Initiative, but given conditions on the ground, no such package has been launched yet. The fact that three out of NATO's six DCB packages involve MENA partners illustrates the centrality of the Southern Neighborhood to NATO security assistance.

Jordan has developed the closest ties with NATO among all partners in MENA.[19] The kingdom is the only Enhanced Opportunity Partner in MENA, a status it received in 2014 in recognition of its participation in NATO operations from Afghanistan to the Balkans and Libya. This status is part of the Partnership Interoperability Initiative and signals a specific emphasis on developing interoperability between NATO and partner forces. Reflecting this close cooperation, Jordan also became the first country in the region to host a NATO exercise in 2017.[20] NATO-Jordan cooperation is also shaped by the fact that the country hosts international forces deployed in neighboring Iraq. In terms of NATO activities, the first round of training for Iraqi officers in the framework of the NATO DCB package took place at the King

Abdullah Special Operations Center in Amman, before the NATO training mission was launched in Iraq.[21] In this respect, NATO-Jordan relations are driven by some of the same factors that Yom describes for US assistance to Jordan, in particular individual NATO allies' reliance on access to Jordanian military bases.[22] Iraq, in turn, is unique in that it hosts an actual NATO mission—namely, the NATO Training Mission in Iraq (NMI).[23] This mission, established in 2018, was first led by Canada before leadership was transferred to Denmark. In February 2021, NATO decided to significantly strengthen the mission in the coming years. Leadership of NMI transitioned to Italy in May 2022.[24] Tunisia, finally, has seen an increasing volume of cooperation with NATO since 2011 and in particular after 2015.[25] Given the variety of bilateral and multilateral donors active in security assistance in Tunisia,[26] coordination of NATO and EU initiatives in Tunisia has become one item of enhanced NATO-EU cooperation.[27]

It is important to note that NATO itself does not dispose of independent resources to finance these activities. Rather, as with the organization at large, the financing of security assistance follows the "costs lie where they fall" principle, meaning that individual allies bear the costs of activities they offer through NATO. Partial exceptions to this rule are activities funded through trust funds, such as the Partnership for Peace, Afghan National Army, Iraq, and DCB trust funds. These funds are provided by allies and partners and can be disbursed by NATO. However, the bulk of NATO's security assistance activities is conducted and financed directly by individual allies and partners. In most cases, one or more countries take the lead on a specific activity, with other countries contributing to the effort either financially or through personnel.

This specific way of financing security assistance also means that the overall volume of security assistance spending through NATO remains difficult to gauge. NATO itself maintains statistics on allies' contributions; yet given their sensitive nature, these statistics remain classified.[28] Examples of NATO security assistance activities in specific countries can serve as illustrations of the general mechanism, however. In Mauritania, for example, NATO is currently implementing the Mauritania II package, which amounts to a total volume of €2 million to be disbursed over forty months. Led by the United States, the program is supported by Germany, Italy, Luxembourg, Spain, Turkey, and the United Kingdom, as well as by Switzerland as a non-NATO donor.[29] It followed a Mauritania I package of €2.1 million led by Italy and supported by the same group of nations.[30] Both of these projects received funding through the Partnership for Peace Trust Fund.

These examples also illustrate the relatively modest size of individual projects. While overall numbers are again not available, the DCB Trust Fund established in 2015 had received contributions from twenty-five allies and four partners by 2020, but total contributions amounted to a relatively meager €27 million.[31] The single-largest NATO security assistance activity was without doubt the training of the Afghan military. By early 2021, the Afghan National Army Trust Fund had reached an overall volume of $3.4 billion since its establishment in 2007, including contributions from thirty-seven different countries. The largest donor was Germany with $810 million, followed by Australia with $680 million and Italy with $508 million.[32] While being by far the largest NATO-led program, assistance to the Afghan security forces thus still amounted to an average of about $240 million per year in the 2007–2021 period. By comparison, the United States committed $3.05 billion to the Afghan Security Forces Fund in 2021 alone.[33]

Most activities conducted under the NATO umbrella, however, are provided and financed by individual allies, and their costs appear in these allies' defense budgets, not in a central NATO budget or fund. Since most countries do not publish detailed data on their security assistance spending, much less on which parts of this spending is directed through NATO channels, it is impossible to ascertain the overall volume of security assistance spending through NATO. In the absence of such systematic data, the following section looks at the security assistance strategies of France, Italy, and Germany in more detail, focusing in particular on these countries' activities in the three core recipients of NATO security assistance in the region—namely, Jordan, Iraq, and Tunisia.

The Politics of Security Assistance Through NATO

The previous section outlined the core institutional mechanisms for security assistance available to NATO. It also highlighted important structural features of the alliance's security assistance process—namely, the partner-driven nature of cooperation as well as the "costs lie where they fall" principle. These specific features interact to constrain the extent to which NATO can provide strategic direction to security assistance efforts within its larger partnership frameworks.

In this section, I substantiate this point by exploring the politics of security assistance through NATO by way of case studies of French, German, and Italian security assistance efforts in MENA. These cases are instructive because they illustrate different approaches to this issue.

While all three countries do provide security assistance, they differ significantly from each other in terms of not only the overall volume of such activities but also in the extent to which they rely on NATO channels in performing them: France has the most extensive security assistance program among these three countries, but French security assistance is overwhelmingly bilateral, and reliance on NATO mechanisms is minimal. Germany, in turn, is a relative newcomer to security assistance but clearly prioritizes multilateral channels, particularly EU mechanisms but also NATO. Italy, finally, is one of the main proponents of a "southern focus" within the alliance and consequently is particularly active when it comes to NATO security assistance activities in MENA.

France: Military Partnership

The French military has a long tradition of military cooperation, particularly with former French colonies in Africa.[34] Following their independence, French officers were closely involved in building national armies and training their officer corps.[35] This laid the basis for a series of security and defense treaties, including the stationing of French forces, but also more technical security assistance agreements. By 1980, all former French colonies in Sub-Saharan Africa, with the exception of Guinea, had some form of military cooperation agreement in place.[36] This tradition still shapes French security assistance. For example, France currently maintains sixteen regional military academies (*écoles nationales à vocation régionale*) in eleven African countries. Focusing on specific functional areas, these schools are open to participants from different countries and together reach about 1,400 officers each year from a total of thirty-five countries.[37]

On the institutional level, French security assistance has evolved. Throughout the Cold War era and up to the reorganization of French security assistance policy in the late 1990s, security assistance was directed by military cooperation missions (*missions militaire de coopération*), which came under the authority of the Ministry of Defense. Since 1998, by contrast, security assistance is coordinated by the Directorate of Cooperation of Security and Defence (Direction de la coopération de sécurité et de défense, DCSD) under the aegis of the Ministry for European and Foreign Affairs (MEAE), even though the DCSD remains led by a general.[38] Conceptually, French security assistance follows a particular model differentiating between structural cooperation (*coopération structurelle*) and operational cooperation (*coopération opérationelle*), the former conducted by the DCSD and MEAE and the latter under the Ministries of Defense or Interior.[39] The main focus of structural cooperation is the development of defense institutions, a task description that is closer to what would be called defense institution building in the NATO context.[40]

In 2021, the total budget for security and defense cooperation within MEAE amounted to €100 million,[41] even though it is important to note that this figure does not represent an adequate estimate of overall spending on security assistance. More operational forms of security assistance, in particular military-to-military cooperation, are provided by the French Ministry of Defense, the Ministère des armées. In contrast to structural cooperation, this form of security assistance, known as military operational partnership (*partenariat militaire opérationnel*, PMO), ranges from training to joint deployments with an emphasis on "operational commitment alongside partners."[42] It thus denotes a mode of security assistance that is more hands-on than what could be provided through NATO channels in most cases. In 2018, the French land forces set up a dedicated Centre terre pour le partenariat militaire opérationnel to coordinate PMO activities.[43]

Given the relatively expansive definition of security assistance as PMO, precise figures on the resources invested in this type of cooperation are not available since many activities are not listed as independent budget items but are part of the overall costs of operations or prepositioned forces.[44] Anecdotal evidence, however, suggests that PMO constitutes an important part of French military operations. In one of France's largest recent operations, Operation Barkhane in the Sahel, for example, 18,000 soldiers from the G5 Sahel armies participated in training activities.[45] Given both the nature of this operation and the concept of PMO, many of these activities consisted of training through joint deployments, in addition to more classical training activities.[46]

French security assistance continues to focus on Africa. The most recent French white paper of 2013 places security assistance in the context of the "new strategic fact" of threats emanating from state weakness.[47] The document makes clear that a "substantial part" of French development aid should be directed toward fragile states and that "security and defense cooperation [and] operational assistance to foreign armies" constitute important elements of crisis prevention.[48] French military planning for 2019 to 2025 also places particular emphasis on prevention with the "aim of locally containing potential threats for Europe" by relying on prepositioned forces in Africa, the UAE, and French overseas territories, as well as on the "reinforcement of European and international financing in support of the defense sectors of African countries."[49]

NATO does not play a major role in French security assistance activities. The military planning law (*loi de programmation militaire*) for 2019 to 2025 does not make reference to NATO or its partnership frameworks in the context of security assistance; nor does the 2013 white paper.[50] Rather, French security assistance is primarily bilateral, and French planners remain skeptical of NATO's potential to add value and thus see little reason to act through the alliance.[51] Moreover, even where multilateral channels are used, France is more likely to act through the European Union or more flexible arrangements such as the 5+5 initiative in the Mediterranean.[52] Given the French focus on Africa, part of the reason for this reluctance is the fact that NATO is not particularly active in this world region. At the same time, security assistance as PMO requires a degree of involvement on the ground that is difficult to realize within the NATO framework in the absence of a formal NATO operation.

This preference for more flexible forms of cooperation is clearly visible on the ground. France established a military cooperation agreement with Jordan in 1995. This agreement was renewed in 2014 through an exchange of letters and finally through a new formal agreement in 2017.[53] One major driver for this renewal was the need to regulate the status of French forces deployed to Jordan in the context of Operation Chammal (the French contribution to Operation Inherent Resolve in Iraq) and stationed at Prince Hassan Air Base northeast of Amman since 2014. In terms of security assistance, France provides capacity-building support and training to Jordanian officers. In 2017 alone, France offered seventy different security assistance activities to the Jordanian armed forces.[54] Beyond bilateral activities, France led a €6 million capacity-building package for Jordanian border protection through the European Union's Instrument Contributing to Stability and Peace, as well as general training to the Jordanian military.[55] The Jordanian case thus illustrates the overall dynamics of French security assistance in MENA: cooperation with Jordan is driven by the practical need to maintain a French presence and regulate the status of French forces. The bulk of security assistance provided in the context of this relationship is bilateral. EU programs play some role, but NATO and its partnership programs do not figure prominently in French security assistance to Jordan.

A similar pattern emerges in the case of Iraq as well. France has been involved in the fight against the Islamic State in Iraq and Syria since 2014 through Operation Chammal. In the context of this mission, the French armed forces have trained a total of 28,000 Iraqi troops since 2015.[56] Within this effort, a French colonel leads the Joint Operational

Command Advisory Team, which coordinates three regional advisory teams embedded with different command structures of the Iraqi armed forces.[57] A total of fifty-eight advisors from fourteen countries are deployed through this mechanism.[58] At the same time, the French contribution to the NATO Training Mission in Iraq is limited to three French liaison officers embedded in NMI. As in the Jordanian case, French security assistance to Iraq also demonstrates a preference for bilateral activities or more flexible international frameworks, as opposed to activities coordinated through NATO.

French military cooperation with postindependence Tunisia, finally, goes back to a 1973 military cooperation agreement that provided for the deployment of French military experts within the Tunisian Armed Forces and also opened French military academies to Tunisian officers.[59] Despite this tradition, Pierre Ménat, French ambassador to Tunisia between 2009 and 2011, defined military cooperation between France and Tunisia as "inconsistent" and of "little significance" at the time of the 2010–2011 Tunisian revolution.[60] Following the revolution and in particular the terrorist attacks that shook Tunisia in 2015, however, France stepped up security assistance to Tunisia.[61] Based on an exchange of letters, the two nations decided to revive the 1973 cooperation agreement and to focus assistance in particular on the training of special forces as well as intelligence in counterterrorism.[62] As a consequence of this agreement, the intensity of cooperation between France and Tunisia increased significantly, with the number of activities growing from 83 in 2015 to 200 in 2019.[63] Moreover, the French and Tunisian navies stage annual joint exercises in the framework of the 5+5 defense initiative,[64] and France coordinates its security assistance activities within the G7+, where it takes responsibility for counterterrorism together with the EU.[65] As with the previous examples, French security assistance to Tunisia is substantial and broadly in line with NATO priorities; yet NATO mechanisms do not play an important role. French security assistance, more generally, remains overwhelmingly bilateral, and even where security assistance takes place through multilateral mechanisms, France gives precedence to more flexible channels such as the anti-IS coalition in Iraq or the 5+5 initiative and the G7+ in Tunisia.

Germany: Enable and Enhance

Germany is a late arrival when it comes to most aspects of security assistance. While an Equipment Aid Program for Foreign Armed Forces (Ausstattungshilfeprogramm der Bundesregierung für ausländische

Streitkräfte) has existed since 1960, this program was mainly used in support of regional peacebuilding capacities and did not allow for the provision of weapons or ammunition. Only recently has Germany developed a new tool, the Enable and Enhance Initiative (Ertüchtigungsinitiative, E2I), which provides greater flexibility in the provision of security assistance—including in terms of providing material support. Importantly, E2I was initially proposed as a joint initiative within the European Union and was only adopted as a national policy instrument once the European Commission decided that European funds could not be used for the provision of military matériel.[66] While the EU's Instrument Contributing to Stability and Peace was reformed to allow for security assistance activities in late 2017,[67] the approach is also reflected in NATO's Defense and Related Security Capacity Building Initiative, which was formally adopted at the 2014 Wales Summit.[68] According to the German defense white paper of 2016,[69] E2I would mainly target partner countries in the Middle East and North Africa as well as the Sahel. Accordingly, the group of countries selected as E2I priority partners (*Schwerpunktländer*) were Iraq, Jordan, Mali, Nigeria, and Tunisia, while Burkina Faso and Niger were added to that list in 2017.[70] E2I is coordinated jointly by the Ministries of Defense and External Affairs and is funded through a separate title in the federal budget. Funding for E2I has increased steadily from €100 million in 2016 to €225 million in the 2021 budget.[71] The concrete activities funded through the initiative remain classified, however, and no official account of German security assistance efforts is published by either ministry.

Given this lack of transparency, it is difficult to assess the overall strategy underpinning Germany's approach to security assistance. The following illustrations therefore largely rely on information drawn from parliamentary documents to sketch the contours of German security assistance to Jordan, Iraq, and Tunisia.

Jordan is one of the focus countries of the E2I and therefore of German security assistance. The government justifies this focus with Jordan's "constructive and reliable" role in the Israel-Palestine and Syrian conflicts, as well as with the fact that Jordan hosts German and other international troops at its Al-Azraq air force base.[72] While detailed data are not publicly available, parliamentary documents reveal that Germany spent a total of €100 million on security assistance to Jordan between 2016 and 2020.[73] This amounts to an average of €20 million per year in this period, or about one-fifth to one-tenth of annual E2I spending. The activities funded include the modernization of seventy-five Marder infantry fighting vehicles by weapons manufacturer Rheinmetall for transfer to Jordan.[74] Rheinmetall also sent qualified personnel—including former German service members—to Jordan to train Jordanian soldiers in the use of the vehicle.[75] In total, German weapons exports to Jordan between 2016 and 2020 amounted to €81.6 million.[76] Within the NATO framework, Germany financially supports the Jordan III and Jordan IV packages, focused on women in the armed forces and demilitarization, respectively. The total volume of these NATO-led projects amounts to about €5 million.[77]

Germany continues to be part of the anti-IS coalition, yet recognizes the increasing importance of the NATO mission in Iraq. Currently, the German contribution to NMI is limited to a small number of staff officers serving in Baghdad. According to the German government's request for parliamentary approval to extend the mission, this limitation is due to Covid-19 restrictions,[78] but parliamentary authorization extends to up to 500 troops for both NMI and the anti-IS coalition.[79] While no breakdown is provided for these different missions, the authorization suggests that the German military will "increasingly contribute to a successful NATO mission in Iraq alongside allies."[80] The total costs budgeted for 2021 amount to €116 million to be drawn from the defense budget, separate from dedicated E2I funds.[81]

German security assistance to Tunisia, finally, focuses primarily on internal security and particularly border protection, building on cooperation with the Tunisian police, which had started before 2011.[82] As Noureddine Jebnoun suggests, the focus on border protection has contributed to the securitization of border communities and is clearly driven by European interests in regulating migration.[83] Following a 2016 security cooperation agreement,[84] this cooperation was intensified and funded with about €20 million per year through E2I and an additional €8 million through the Ausbildungs- und Ausstattungshilfeprogramm der Bundesregierung (AAH-P), an equipment and training program for foreign police forces.[85] Given this focus, coordination of German security assistance to Tunisia within NATO is minimal. Instead, Germany took the lead on coordinating border protection within the G7+ framework.[86]

In conclusion, German security assistance only recently reached the full spectrum of tools available to other actors. Since the adoption of E2I in 2016, German security assistance in MENA has broadly followed the priorities set within multilateral mechanisms, both EU (Tunisia in addition to Mali and Niger) and NATO (Jordan, Iraq, and Tunisia). While Germany contributes to several NATO initiatives, the bulk of German security assistance is provided alongside, not through, multilateral mechanisms.

Italy: Looking South

Security assistance plays an important role in Italy's foreign and security policy. Given their particular focus, Italian policymakers place specific emphasis on stabilization and crisis management in a geographic area that is sometimes referred to as the "enlarged Mediterranean" (*il Mediterraneo allargato*).[87] The 2015 white book, which remains the main reference point for Italian security and defense policy, adopts such a wider perspective by linking Mediterranean security to conditions in the Mashriq, the Sahel, the Horn of Africa, and the Gulf and by designating this area as the main focus of national Italian efforts.[88] The role of Italian defense policy in this context is defined as "ensuring targeted military cooperation with all nations in the area, by striving for better and deeper cooperation in order to build a broader context of security and stability over time,"[89] explicitly underlining the central role of security assistance activities. The document also puts these national priorities into a larger multilateral context, explicitly referring to both the European Union Common Security and Defence Policy and NATO's MD.[90]

Within the NATO context, the Italian emphasis on security assistance is reflected in different ways as well. To begin with, Italy has been a major supporter of NATO outreach activities to the south. As Minister of Defense Lorenzo Guerini emphasized in May 2021, Italy sees itself as one of the "main supporters of increased attention toward the South" within both NATO and the EU, pushing for "stronger partnerships and more concrete neighborhood policies" within both frameworks.[91] On the political level within NATO, Italy has indeed pursued the development of a more coherent approach to the alliance's Southern Neighborhood.[92]

Following the 2016 Warsaw Summit, these efforts found expression in NATO's emphasis on a "360 degree" perspective as well as in the (re)emergence of "projecting stability" in the alliance's catch-phrase dictionary.[93] Subsequently, this notion was further developed within the NATO bureaucracy, in particular within the NATO military staff of the Supreme Allied Command Transformation. A draft Military Concept for Projecting Stability (MC 0655) was developed but never officially adopted by the military council. While not making it into official policy documents, these discussions triggered important initiatives aimed at refocusing NATO security assistance activities within the alliance's larger partnership frameworks.[94] While political consensus on alliance strategy toward the south could not be reached, the 2018 Brussels Summit adopted a package for the South, including "a range of political and practical cooperation initiatives towards a more strategic, focused, and coherent approach to the Middle East and North Africa."[95]

The establishment of the NATO Strategic Direction South Hub (NSD-S Hub) at Joint Force Command Naples is one concrete initiative in this area. The hub, inaugurated in September 2017, was initially led by Italian brigadier general Roberto Angius. Among other things, the hub aimed at streamlining NATO security assistance in the South by coordinating NATO efforts with the activities of other multilateral players, in particular the EU, as well as with bilateral initiatives undertaken by individual allies.[96] The hub faced some difficulties, however, including initial staffing problems as well as a reluctance by some NATO allies to share information on their security assistance activities with the hub.[97]

Italy continues to support a southern focus in the alliance. The current NSD-S Hub director is another Italian officer, air force brigadier general Davide Re, and Italy budgeted €400,000 in Fiscal Year 2021 to specifically support NATO's Package for the South by providing additional personnel.[98] A further sign of the Italian emphasis on developing NATO's security assistance programs is the fact that Italy funds a NATO Security Force Assistance Center or Excellence, which is located in Cesano outside Rome and received NATO accreditation in December 2018. The center's mission focuses on developing NATO's security assistance activities based on lessons learned from earlier experiences.[99]

While Italy worked on the political level to strengthen NATO's institutional capacities for partnership with the South, practical cooperation is limited by resource constraints. Italy is active in security assistance to all three main NATO partners in MENA (in addition to taking an active role in maritime operations in the Mediterranean, including the training of the Libyan coastguard through EUNAVFOR MED IRINI); yet Italian assistance to Jordan, Iraq, and Tunisia is modest compared to US or even French efforts.

Cooperation with Jordan, to begin with, is based on a military cooperation agreement concluded in 2002 and ratified by the Italian Parliament in 2004. Renewed in 2015, the agreement instituted a regular planning cycle for defense cooperation between the two countries,[100] including annual coordination meetings between representatives of the respective general staffs. Initial bilateral cooperation focused mainly on information exchange in various fields, mutual visits, and joint exercises. Since 2013, Italian defense education institutions are open to participants from Jordan. In 2014, Jordan bought eighty Centauro armored vehicles from Italian army stocks—significantly under value at €40,000 a piece—and Jordanian officers were trained in the use of these vehicles in Italy.[101] In the NATO context more specifically, Italy financially supports the Jordan III project aimed at enhancing the training of female Jordanian officers.[102]

In Iraq, Italy focused its security assistance activities on training Kurdish Peshmerga forces through Operation Prima Parthica, the Italian national contribution to the anti-IS coalition, as well as the training of Iraqi forces first through the same channels and then through the NATO Training Mission in Iraq, relaunched in 2018.[103] At the February 2021 meeting of NATO defense ministers, it was agreed that Italy would take over the leadership of a significantly strengthened NATO capacity-building mission in Iraq once the mission had reached full capacity.[104] By 2022, Italy's contribution to the NATO Training Mission in Iraq had increased to 650 personnel at a cost of €77 million.[105] In 2022, moreover, the authorization explicitly foresees the transfer of assets to NMI from the anti-IS coalition,[106] which is currently funded with €230 million and comprises 900 personnel.[107] While the actual contribution to NMI thus remains limited, Italy's willingness to invest in NATO-led security assistance in Iraq is evident.

Italian security cooperation with Tunisia, finally, goes back to a 1991 agreement that instituted an annual meeting of a mixed military commission to coordinate efforts. This commission, chaired by the two ministers of defense, has met almost every year since 1991, with the twenty-second meeting having taken place via video conference in May 2021.[108] On the practical level, Italy supported the establishment of a naval training facility in Zarzis,[109] including €13 million for the acquisition of a diving support vessel produced by the Italian company Vittoria.[110] In 2019, a bilateral mission was authorized to support the establishment of three army-led regional joint operation centers in Tunisia. The mission comprised the deployment of fifteen personnel and a financial volume of €2 million in 2019 and €1 million in 2020.[111] This project was first planned as a NATO activity,[112] yet was rejected by Tunisia over concerns relating to base access by foreign forces.[113] Similar concerns also prevented the establishment in Tunisia of a NATO Intelligence Fusion Center, which had been announced by the alliance in 2016.[114] Through NATO, Italy provided support to Tunisia via the Defense Education Enhancement Program, working in particular with the Tunisian War College.[115]

While Italy is politically committed to providing security assistance through NATO, the Italian case illustrates two additional limitations. For one thing, resource constraints place clear limitations on the range of activities Italy is able to undertake and fund; second, even where resources are available, the Tunisian example demonstrates that cooperation through NATO is not always the format preferred by partner countries. This highlights the important question of the extent to which cooperation with NATO is attractive to partners, particularly given that much the same support can frequently be obtained bilaterally as well.

Conclusion: Supply, Demand, and Control

Academics, policy analysts, and NATO officials alike tend to offer rather sobering perspectives of NATO partnership in MENA. Writing in 2000, for example, Gareth Winrow, in one of the few book-length academic studies of the MD, noted, "There [was] still a deep-rooted suspicion of the West and of NATO, in particular, in the Arab world, and Arab governments, thus, [did] not want to be perceived as working too closely with NATO."[116] Some years later, writing in *NATO Review* in 2004, Chris Donelly remarked that "unlike the Partnership for Peace, the Mediterranean Dialogue has not been a great success. It has played no significant role in stabilising the region or in helping and promoting the evolution of participating countries."[117] Martin Smith and Ian Davis agree and note that a "general impression has been that [the Mediterranean Dialogue] has amounted to little more than political and diplomatic window dressing."[118] Most recently, Rolf Schwarz suggested, "The alliance's policy toward the south seems half-hearted: lofty statements, the reality of dwindling resources, and only slowly advancing practical cooperation with partners in the region—not enough to have an effect and keep instability from spreading."[119]

These overwhelmingly negative assessments are due to three fundamental limitations of security assistance through NATO's partnership framework. First, NATO suffers from problems in the supply side of security assistance, with allies frequently preferring bilateral over NATO mechanisms; second, NATO security assistance is confronted with demand-side problems as partners turn to bilateral or other multilateral donors, instead of NATO; finally, these two problems combine to limit the extent to which NATO can control and strategically use its security assistance activities. I will briefly discuss these limitations in turn.

Not only do NATO allies sometimes have different perspectives on the main challenges to alliance security, but even those allies who are active in a specific arena might prefer mechanisms other than NATO. This phenomenon is of course not limited to security assistance, but it is clearly visible in this context as well. Facing inevitable resource constraints, allies have to decide not only whether to invest in security assistance but also whether to do so through bilateral activities, the European Union, some other multilateral mechanism, or NATO. Especially "harder" forms of security assistance are more easily provided bilaterally rather than through multilateral channels. This is particularly the case if specific national security interests are at stake. Given this situation, NATO has to clearly demonstrate where it can add value beyond other mechanisms in order to gain visibility.

Second, NATO continues to suffer from a bad reputation in many partner countries, particularly in the South. The example of Tunisia clearly demonstrates how even the availability of resources and the political will to spend those resources through NATO do not always suffice. Instead, partners might be tempted to opt for more flexible bilateral modes of cooperation, especially if, as in Tunisia since 2015, there is no shortage of bilateral donors.

These problems combine to limit the extent to which NATO as an organization can give its security assistance activities strategic direction. Not only does the alliance lack a commonly agreed strategic vision for the south, but its level of control over security assistance activities is too low to use these tools in a strategic manner. This has been recognized in the NATO 2030 reflection process. The final report coming out of this exercise suggests that NATO should "outline a global blueprint for better utilizing its partnerships to advance NATO strategic interests. It should shift from the current demand-driven approach to an interest-driven approach."[120] This suggestion was taken up by the alliance and has found its way into the 2022 strategic concept, which puts partnership in the context of protecting the global commons and the rules-based international order.[121] In practical terms, NATO will reform partnership coordination mechanisms to introduce a new tool, Individual Tailored Partnership Programs, which aim to increase NATO's agency in identifying concrete areas of cooperation. While these reforms suggest that NATO recognizes the problem, it is doubtful that NATO can also solve it. The fundamental constraint remains one of political will, both on the part of allies and on the part of partners. Institutional reforms to NATO's partnership mechanisms are unlikely to tackle these limitations.

Should NATO thus give up its security assistance activities? I argue that this would be a step too far. Just as with bilateral security assistance, NATO efforts in this arena should not be measured against a capacity-building yardstick alone. While NATO security assistance activities might thus be limited in practical terms, they are an important political mechanism. Within the alliance, individual allies can, and do, attempt to shape the alliance's agenda by building consensus around their specific threat perceptions, including by investing in security assistance. What makes NATO assistance unique is thus not its practical impact on the capacity of security forces but the political signal sent by the unanimous support of an alliance of thirty sovereign states. If used strategically, such support can be a powerful political signal.

Notes

1. In absolute numbers, security assistance spending as part of overseas development assistance (ODA) grew from $183 million in 2000 to $4.7 billion in 2019, according to the OECD International Development Statistics database (https://bit.ly/3mpshAc). These figures only reflect orders of magnitude, however, since the OECD's definition of ODA excludes resources spent on cooperation with security institutions.
2. See the Ukraine support tracker maintained by the Institute for the World Economy at https://www.ifw-kiel.de/topics/war-against-ukraine/ukraine-support-tracker.
3. See "Madrid Summit Declaration."
4. Biddle, Macdonald, and Baker, "Small Footprint, Small Payoff," 90.
5. Bärwaldt, *Strategy, Jointness, Capacity*; Biddle, Macdonald, and Baker, "Small Footprint, Small Payoff"; Karlin, *Building Militaries in Fragile States*.
6. Abbas and Trombly, "Inside the Collapse of the Iraqi Army's 2nd Division"; Arabia, "The Collapse of the Afghan National Defense and Security Forces."
7. See the introduction to this book by Alaoui and Springborg for US definitions.
8. See "Brussels Summit Communiqué," paragraph 6f; "NATO 2022 Strategic Concept," para 38.
9. See Chapter 7 of this book.
10. "Projecting Stability Beyond Our Borders."
11. Moore, *NATO's New Mission*; Yost, *NATO's Balancing Act*.
12. NATO, "Active Engagement, Modern Defense."
13. "NATO 2022 Strategic Concept," paras 38 and 45.
14. An exception to this rule is the participation of nonpartners in educational activities. As part of NATO's Defence and Related Security Capacity Building Initiative, security assistance to nonpartners is possible as well.
15. Larsen and Koehler, "Projecting Stability to the South"; Lesser et al., "The Future of NATO's Mediterranean Dialogue."
16. Author's conversation with NDC personnel, March 2021.
17. Stoltenberg, "The Secretary General's Annual Report," 96.
18. "Building Integrity."
19. Ryan, "What Jordan Means for NATO."
20. "Exercise Regex 17 Concludes in Jordan."
21. "NATO Training for Iraqi Officers Starts in Jordan."
22. Chapter 11 of this book.
23. Koehler, "Projecting Stability in Practice?"
24. Di Feo, "Via gli americani, toccherà all'Italia guidare in Iraq la missione Nato."
25. Profazio, "Tunisia's Reluctant Partnership with NATO."

26. Varga, "Building Partnerships in Challenging Times."
27. NATO and European Union, "Fifth Progress Report."
28. E-mail correspondence with member of the NATO International Staff, March 2021.
29. "Mauritania II, Phase 1+."
30. "Mauritania I."
31. Stoltenberg, "The Secretary General's Annual Report," 99.
32. NATO, "Afghan National Army (ANA) Trust Fund."
33. SIGAR, "Quarterly Report to Congress," 30.
34. Charbonneau, *France and the New Imperialism*.
35. Ammi-Oz, "La formation des cadres militaires africains."
36. Luckham, "Le militarisme français en Afrique."
37. https://www.diplomatie.gouv.fr/IMG/pdf/2022.08.05.brochure_presentation_envr_maquette-finale_cle88f1c9.pdf .
38. Charbonneau, *France and the New Imperialism*, 78.
39. Brousse, "La coopération structurelle de sécurité et de défense du XXIe siècle"; Moroney et al., *Lessons from U.S. Allies in Security Cooperation with Third Countries*.
40. "Defence Institution Building."
41. "Budget de l'État."
42. Vidal, "Le partenariat militaire opérationnel aujourd'hui," 2.
43. https://www.emsome.terre.defense.gouv.fr/index.php/fr/cpmo.
44. Charbonneau, *France and the New Imperialism*, 80.
45. Ministère des Armées, "Opération Barkhane," 31.
46. Ibid, 21.
47. Ministère des Armées, "Livre blanc sur la défense et la sécurité nationale," 39.
48. Ibid, 98.
49. Journal Officiel, LOI no 2018-607 du 13 juillet 2018 relative à la programmation militaire pour les années 2019 à 2025 et portant diverses dispositions intéressant la défense.
50. Ibid.; Ministère des armées, "Livre blanc sur la défense et la sécurité nationale."
51. Confidential conversation with colonel in the French army, 2021; Varga, "Building Partnerships in Challenging Times," 22.
52. 5+5 Defence Initiative (www.5plus5defence.org).
53. Allizard, "Rapport," 8.
54. Ibid., 11.
55. IcSP Map (https://icspmap.eu).
56. Ministère des Armées, "Opération CHAMMAL"; also see Chapter 7 of this book.
57. https://www.defense.gouv.fr/operations/actualites/chammal-joint-operational-command-advisory-team-iraq-unite-premier-plan-assister-larmee.
58. Bussoletti, "Iraq."
59. See the text of the agreement at "2 mai 1973: Convention de coopération technique militaire."
60. Quoted in Ekovich, "Les États-Unis et le Maghreb," 68.
61. *Le Monde*, "L'aide militaire de la France à la Tunisie multipliée par quatre."
62. "Conférence de presse conjointe."
63. For 2015, "Conférence de presse conjointe"; for 2019, "Mission de défense."
64. 5+5 Defence Initiative (www.5plus5defence.org).
65. Peinaud, "La coopération bilatérale UE-Tunisie en matière sécuritaire."
66. Puglierin, "Germany's Enable and Enhance Initiative."

67. See "Regulation (EU) 2017/2306 of the European Parliament and of the Council."
68. See "Defence and Related Security Capacity Building Initiative."
69. Bundesregierung, "Weißbuch zur Sicherheitspolitk und zur Zukunft der Bundeswehr."
70. Bundesregierung, "Drucksache 19/8592."
71. See Titel 687 03-032 in the respective budget documents, which can be consulted at www.bundeshaushalt.de.
72. Bundesregierung, "Drucksache 19/30202."
73. DIE LINKE, "Drucksache 19/29414."
74. https://web.archive.org/web/20191115084230/https://www.rheinmetall-defence.com/en/rheinmetall_defence/public_relations/news/archiv/2017/aktuellesdetailansicht_7_15616.php.
75. DIE LINKE, "Drucksache 19/29414," 2.
76. Bundesregierung, "Drucksache 19/30202," 5.
77. NSPA, "Jordan III"; NSPA, "Jordan IV."
78. Bundesregierung, "Drucksache 19/22207," 8.
79. Bundesregierung, 5.
80. Bundesregierung, 8.
81. The exact time frame is November 2020 to January 31, 2021; see Bundesregierung, 8.
82. Stahl and Treffler, "Germany's Security Assistance to Tunisia," 31.
83. Chapter 4 of this book; see also Chapter 7 of this book.
84. Bundesregierung, "Drucksache 18/11509."
85. Stahl and Treffler, "Germany's Security Assistance to Tunisia," 31.
86. Stahl and Treffler, "Germany's Security Assistance to Tunisia," 22.
87. Marrone, "La politica di sicurezza nel vicinato meridionale," 4.
88. Repubblica Italiana, "Libro bianco per la sicurezza internazionale e la difesa," para 50 and 51.
89. Ibid., para 71.
90. Ibid., para 72.
91. "Colloquio tra il Ministro Guerini e il Ministro della Difesa tunisino Bartagi."
92. Taylor, "Molto agitato," 55.
93. Díaz-Plaja, "Projecting Stability"; Koehler, "Putting the Horse Back Before the Cart."
94. Author's conversations at the NATO Military Strategic Partnership Conference (MSPC), Dead Sea Marriott Hotel, Jordan, March 2019.
95. NATO, "Brussels Summit Declaration Issued by the Heads of State and Government."
96. Briefing at NSDS-Hub, JFC Naples, October 2017.
97. Author's conversations with Hub personnel, Naples, October 2017, and Rome, March 2018.
98. Camera dei Deputati, "Autorizzazione e proroga missioni internazionali nell'anno 2021," 82.
99. Author's conversations at the SFA COE launching event, Centro Alti Studi per la Difesa (CASD), Rome, December 8, 2018.
100. "Accordo tra il Governo della Repubblica italiana ed il Governo del Regno Hascemita di Giordania sulla cooperazione nel settore della difesa."
101. "Blindati Centauro per la Giordania"; Taylor, "Molto agitato," 67; "Militari giordani si addestrano in Italia."
102. NSPA, "Jordan IV."

103. Koehler, "Projecting Stability in Practice?"
104. Credi, *L'Italia alla guida della missione Nato in Iraq*; Di Feo, "Via gli americani, toccherà all'Italia guidare in Iraq la missione Nato."
105. Camera dei Deputati, "Autorizzazione e proroga missioni internazionali e interventi di cooperazione e sviluppo per l'anno 2022 – DOC. XXV, n. 5 e DOC. XXVI n. 5, 10.
106. Camera dei Deputati, "Autorizzazione e proroga missioni internazionali nell'anno 2021," 51.
107. Ibid., 50.
108. "Colloquio tra il Ministro Guerini e il Ministro della Difesa tunisino Bartagi."
109. "Italia-Tunisia."
110. "Vittoria consegna alla Tunisia la nave scuola Zarzis."
111. Camera dei Deputati, "Delibarazione del Consiglio dei Ministri in merito alla partecipazione," 6; Ministero della Difesa, "Documento Programmatico Pluriennale per la Difesa per il Triennio 2020–2022," C–XXXIX.
112. In fact, the 2019–2021 DPP still represents the activity as a NATO project; see Ministero della Difesa, "Documento Programmatico Pluriennale per la Difesa per il Triennio 2019–2021," map on 14.
113. Profazio, "Tunisia's Reluctant Partnership with NATO."
114. "Quasi pronto il Nato-Tunisian Intelligence Fusion Centre."
115. "Nato DEEP."
116. Winrow, *Dialogue with the Mediterranean*, 167.
117. Donelly, "Building a NATO Partnership for the Greater Middle East."
118. Smith and Davis, "NATO's Mediterranean Dialogue in the Wake of the Arab Spring."
119. Schwarz, *NATO and the Middle East*, 5.
120. Reflection Group, "NATO 2030."
121. "NATO 2022 Strategic Concept," para 42.

9

The Gulf Monarchies: Security Consumers and Providers

Zoltan Barany

As CHAPTER 1 AND MANY OTHER CHAPTERS IN THIS BOOK ATTEST, THE Middle East and North Africa (MENA) may well be the most vulnerable region on the planet and is the largest recipient of foreign, especially US, security assistance. Even a brief consideration of the five primary physical regions of the Arab Middle East—the Northern Tier, the Fertile Crescent, the Nile Valley, the Maghreb, and the Arabian Peninsula—suggests that the last is very different indeed from the others. Arabia is home to six wealthy and stable absolute monarchies and one failed state, the Republic of Yemen, which has been the victim of a multitude of tragic ills, some caused by civil war and foreign intervention over the past decade. This chapter focuses on Arabia's kingdoms that make up the Gulf Cooperation Council (GCC) member states (Bahrain, Kuwait, Oman, Qatar, Saudi Arabia, and the United Arab Emirates). Even though their regional neighborhood has faced political turmoil and violent conflicts, aside from a few upheavals—including the Iraqi occupation of Kuwait and the First Gulf War (1990–1991)—the monarchies of Arabia have remained remarkably calm. Moreover, unlike most other states of the wider region, the GCC countries have themselves paid for the security assistance they receive from abroad.

The political and economic clout and strategic weight of the GCC member states have steadily increased in recent decades. All too often, studies on MENA still ignore the states on the Arabian Peninsula or fail to recognize the differences between Arab monarchies and republics. From the perspective of domestic military-security issues, the key disparities between them are that, unlike in republics, in monarchies the army as an institution has not played a political, let alone state-building, role, the generals' political influence has been negligible, and the GCC armies have not been involved in their national economies. Another difference is that some GCC states—primarily the UAE and to a lesser extent Saudi Arabia and Qatar—are not just consumers of regional security but also contributors to it, or at least perceive themselves as such. (One may, of course, wonder with good cause whether, for instance, Emirati and Qatari involvement in Libya has promoted stability there, and most experts would concur that the Saudi's war in Yemen has been disastrous to all but Iran—precisely the outcome Riyadh wanted to avoid.)

This chapter seeks to answer several fundamental questions. What political imperatives have guided the development of Gulf armed forces? What primary factors explain the patterns of military expenditure in the GCC? In what way have some Gulf states—primarily consumers of security assistance—become providers of security themselves?

I propose three broad arguments. First, the Gulf countries' geographical and natural endowments act as a double-edged sword: on the one hand, their strategic position and abundant fossil fuel resources allow them to realize high living standards; on the other hand, these attributes also make them vulnerable to security threats from inside and outside the region. Therefore, they are characterized by a large latent demand for military spending, combined with a high capacity to spend militarily, especially on a per capita basis. Second, just as a number of chapters on other Arab countries note, the absence of institutionally balanced civilian oversight in the Gulf over defense-strategic issues often results in corruption, which reinforces the aforementioned latent demand for military spending and distorts incentives in military procurement. Political calculation and institutional and/or individual vanity have often motivated or even determined defense-spending patterns in general and armaments acquisitions in particular. These factors, in turn, contribute to and help explain the ineffectiveness and general underperformance of Arabia's armies.

Finally, and most importantly, because the Gulf militaries are incapable of defending the monarchical regimes, they largely rely on the United States (and, to a far lesser degree, the United Kingdom) for their own protection. The Gulf armies do not quite function as conventional armies but rather actually help to buy the services of the regimes' real protectors through the purchase of vast quantities of often unneeded, superfluous, and expensive weapons that are inappropriate for their defense. They are not just rentier states but rentier militaries. Procurement decisions closely reflect the ruling families' perception of the level of support they can expect from their allies and are accordingly reassessed as needed. That in the past decade and a half some GCC states paid more attention to elevating their defense capacities is in large measure explained by their growing anxiety regarding America's unconditional commitment to their defense.

The Domestic Political Environment

The Gulf monarchies are authoritarian states that fit comfortably into H. E. Chehabi and Juan Linz's conceptualization of the "sultanistic" regime subtype.[1] Gulf rulers allow virtually no political debate, they embrace what may well be described as the "cult of personality," and their power is anything but well defined. To be sure, the royal families of the Gulf are constrained by some "soft factors," such as Islamic norms (i.e., ruling as Islam requires), attention to consensus building, and including family members and other elites in decisionmaking. Still, they view themselves as the owners rather than the rulers of their countries.

In the Gulf monarchies no decision of consequence is made and no policy is devised, let alone implemented, without the rulers' agreement. They make the laws, which they need not justify, for the rulers are not accountable to anyone even if they consult family members and advisors. If there is some sort of pseudo-parliament, as in Kuwait, it may "enact" these laws, but that endeavor is really just a nicety because the legislative organ itself exists at the pleasure of the ruler. Members of the royal family and their close tribal allies hold the vast majority of key public-sector jobs, especially in sensitive areas, like defense.

An essential attribute of autocracies is the centralization, or even "hypercentralization," of authority in the hands of the king and his closest family members. Decisions are made by an extremely small circle of people. More generally, hypercentralized decisionmaking, overlapping jurisdictions of central and local governments, and other bureaucratic challenges often cause the failure to put ambitious public policies, such as Saudi Crown Prince Mohammed bin Salman's Vision 2030, into action. Furthermore, even at the top of institutional hierarchies, information tends to be compartmentalized, and areas of competence and responsibility are carefully guarded because they are a source of power and guarantee one's continued relevance. Even senior bureaucrats and military officers often know little outside their narrow specializations.

Historically, the major threats to the Gulf chieftains and monarchs have been assassinations or coups from within the ruling families. These have been relatively rare in recent decades, though succession paths have not always been smooth. The Gulf monarchies have to contend with little domestic opposition—with the exception of the systematically suppressed Shia majority in Bahrain—that, at least to an outside observer, would represent a credible threat to their safety, let alone survival. In the early 2000s al-Qaeda operatives became active in Saudi Arabia and managed to radicalize a number of young men willing to carry out a domestic bombing campaign.[2] After 2004, however, the danger of terrorist attacks inside the kingdom had greatly diminished, owing to the effective counterterrorism operation led by later crown prince Mohammed bin Nayef.

The upheavals in 2011 frightened the ruling families into stepping up security measures against potential adversaries, no matter how improbable or weak the challenge they posed. Their perception of waning American interest in Arabia during the Barack Obama and Donald Trump administrations and the former's nuclear policy accord with Iran, the GCC's archenemy, also added to their sense of vulnerability. As a result, since 2010 we have witnessed a militarization of the Gulf signaled by elevated defense budgets, a sharpening focus on counterterrorism, and new policies to deepen a sense of nationhood among Gulf citizens. Mandatory military service was recently introduced in Qatar and the UAE and reintroduced in Kuwait, military parades have been staged on national holidays, and military museums and memorials have been opened in several Gulf countries.[3] In the realm of foreign policy, several Gulf countries took the step of normalizing their relations with Israel, with which they share an archenemy and from whom they hope to purchase not just security- and defense-related equipment and services but also nonmilitary technologies and assistance.[4]

The Gulf Economies and the Burden of Defense Spending

Even among authoritarian states, military regimes and monarchies have the highest defense spending.[5] Considering the lackluster performance of Gulf armies, the question of how effectively their military budgets have been used is inescapable. What did they get for their enormous expenditures? What has been the rationale behind their choice of vendors and the weapon systems they decided to purchase?

There are considerable economic disparities between the three richer and the three less-endowed GCC countries. In 2018 the per capita gross domestic product (GDP) in current US dollars of all six Gulf states was well above the World Bank's "upper middle income" average of $9,205: Bahrain's was $24,050, Oman's $16,415, and Saudi Arabia's $23,339, while Kuwait's was $33,994, Qatar's $68,793, and the UAE's $43,005.[6] In terms of the Arab World (average: $6,608), even the figure for Oman was far above that of all non-Gulf Arab states (e.g., Algeria: $4,114; Egypt: $2,519; Iraq: $5,834; Jordan: $4,241; Libya: $7,241; Morocco: $3,237; Tunisia: $3,447). Iran's GDP in 2017, at $5,627, was similar to Iraq's.

It is important to note that the figures above are per capita numbers for the entire population and thus considerably underestimate the living standards for GCC citizens, who earn much more on average than migrant or expatriate workers. The latter comprise a large majority of the population in the UAE (87.4 percent), Qatar (87.3 percent), and Kuwait (69.8 percent), a small majority in Bahrain (54.9 percent), and a large minority in Oman (44 percent) and Saudi Arabia (37.8 percent).[7] A more comprehensive picture can be gleaned from Table 9.1, which presents data from the UN Development Programme (UNDP) Human Development Index (HDI). In this table the six Arabian monarchies are complemented by the seventh state on the peninsula, the Republic of Yemen, which, as can be readily appreciated, is in a different league than its neighbors in every measured variable.

Different gauges of economic wealth and health would impart more or less the same basic message: by global standards all GCC states are very prosperous, and in the context of North Africa and the Middle East, all of them may be considered extremely affluent. The six Gulf countries account for about 60 percent of the Arab world's GDP but

Table 9.1 GCC Countries and Yemen UNDP HDI Rank

Rank	Country	HDI (value)	Life Expectancy at Birth	Mean Years of Schooling	GNI per Capita ($)
35	UAE	0.866	77.8	11.0	66,912
36	Saudi Arabia	0.857	75.0	10.2	49,338
41	Qatar	0.848	80.1	9.7	110,489
45	Bahrain	0.838	77.2	9.4	40,399
47	Oman	0.834	77.6	9.7	37,039
57	Kuwait	0.808	75.4	7.3	71,164
177	Yemen	0.463	66.1	3.2	1,433

Source: Data for 2019 from "Human Development Insights."

only about 6 percent of its population, if foreign workers are excluded.[8] Four Gulf states—Kuwait, Qatar, Saudi Arabia, and the UAE—hold more than $2 trillion—that is, over a quarter—of the world's sovereign-wealth funds.[9]

The GCC countries' wealth, however, still overwhelmingly relies on the export of oil and gas, even after decades of putative efforts to diversify their economies. Oil prices dropped sharply in mid-2014, however, and, owing to saturated markets and unsteady demand, have been projected to stay low for several years followed by a gradual recovery.[10] The decline of demand for oil and the additional impact of the Covid-19 pandemic have dealt bitter blows to every Gulf economy, even if their preparation to deal with this distress has varied greatly. With the end of the pandemic, oil prices largely recovered, and the war in Ukraine served to further raise them. In fact, in early October 2022 the Saudi-led OPEC voted to reduce oil production by 2 million barrels a day in order to ensure that oil prices would remain high. Table 9.2 collects the break-even oil prices for the GCC countries in April 2020. It shows both the fiscal break-even price (the price required to balance the budget) and the external break-even price (the price required to keep the current account at zero).

Long-term forecasts, however, often do not play out. How could forecasters have foreseen, after all, Russia's invasion of Ukraine in February 2022? Moscow's action upended oil markets with massive economic consequences worldwide that benefited oil producers but detrimentally affected all other countries. In fact, the price of Brent crude oil per barrel increased from a May 2020 low of $29.38 to $68.53 in May 2021 (surpassing the fiscal break-even point of Kuwait and Qatar) and to $74.17 in December 2021. As the prewar crisis created by President Vladimir Putin unfolded, prices rose further to $97.13 in February 2022

Table 9.2 GCC Break-Even Oil Prices per Barrel, 2020

GCC State	Fiscal Break-Even Oil Price (US$)	External Break-Even Oil Price (US$)
Bahrain	95.6	80.8
Kuwait	61.1	50.6
Oman	86.8	62.1
Qatar	39.9	37.6
Saudi Arabia	76.1	44.2
UAE	69.1	32.0

Source: Cahill, "Gulf States."
Note: Price per barrel on October 15, 2020: $42.15.

(the month of the invasion), rising yet higher in March to $117.25—a price point well above the production costs of even the most expensive (Bahraini) barrel of crude among the Gulf kingdoms.[11] Although prices since then have fluctuated, they have remained in comfortably profitable territory for all GCC states. Still, there can be little doubt that, for a multitude of reasons, future world demand for hydrocarbons is going to diminish, which, at the very least, ought to continue to motivate the Gulf monarchies to reduce their dependence on them.

In any event, the Gulf states' extravagant defense expenditures make little economic sense. Even if some of their military spending may be considered unwise, Kuwait, Qatar, and the UAE are prosperous enough to weather the consequences of questionable investments. They also have their own grand programs for economic diversification (i.e., Qatar National Vision 2030), implementation of which has been, politely put, unhurried. The poorer GCC states, however, have already been forced to tighten their belts. They have sold state assets, reduced subsidies on fuel, electricity, and water, introduced a value-added tax on some classes of goods (e.g., tobacco, sweetened drinks), and, in Oman, required high earners to pay income tax starting in 2022.

Defense Budgets Prior to 2011

From the moment of their independence (Saudi Arabia, 1932; Oman, 1951; Kuwait, 1961; Bahrain, Qatar, and the UAE, 1971), Bahrain, Kuwait, Qatar, and the UAE have been both rich and vulnerable to regional security threats. One way to deter potential challengers was to build up formidable arsenals purchased from would-be protectors, the United States and Britain. Even prior to the 1979 Iranian Revolution, military outlays in the Gulf were high by almost any measure and growing rapidly. Increases continued in the 1980s, then slightly diminished in the early 1990s, before beginning to rise again toward the end of that decade. Saudi military expenditures, for instance, went from $26.5 billion in 1997 to $32 billion in 2001 (a 20.7 percent surge), while the UAE boosted its defense spending in the same four-year period by a whopping 66 percent (from $6 billion to $10 billion).[12]

Between 1997 and 2009 the annual combined defense expenditures of the GCC states more than doubled.[13] In the last four years of this period, the United States alone had sold nearly $37 billion worth of armaments to the Gulf nations.[14] Since 2007 the UAE has been second only to Saudi Arabia in acquiring American military hardware. Table 9.3 illustrates the rapid acceleration of defense spending since 2000—

Table 9.3 GCC Weapons Imports from the United States, 1970–2014

Country	Amount (US$ Billion)
Bahrain	3.267
Kuwait	36.252
Oman	27.830
Qatar	57.771
Saudi Arabia	263.986
UAE	74.670
Total	473.775

Source: Anthony, "GCC Arms Imports," 29.

considering that of the over $470 billion invested in US weapons in the Gulf countries from 1970 to 2014, only about $74 billion (constant dollars) was spent in the three decades between 1970 and 2000 and nearly $400 billion in the fourteen years thereafter.

Not surprisingly, the largest spender in the Gulf has been Saudi Arabia, but all six Arabian monarchies devote far more resources on defense than most countries of similar size and economic capacity. As Table 9.4 reveals, between the overthrow of Saddam Hussein's regime and the eve of the Arab upheavals, all GCC states, with the exception of Kuwait, significantly increased their defense spending.

Increasing Military Spending After the Arab Spring

In all GCC states, defense budgets dramatically rose following the Arab Spring even though, aside from the one major Shia-dominated uprising in Bahrain and ongoing protests in Saudi Arabia's Eastern Province, disturbances were minor (in Kuwait and Oman) or virtually nonexistent (in Qatar and the UAE). The rising military outlays were a reaction to five security concerns in the second decade of the twentieth century: the threat of domestic upheaval, the deepening of mutual distrust and growing conflict between the GCC (especially Saudi Arabia, the UAE, and Bahrain) and Iran, concern about America's commitment to the unconditional defense of the peninsula, the discord between the same GCC states and Qatar, and the war in Yemen (2014–present).

Saudi defense expenditures rose from $54 billion in 2011 to $87 billion in 2017, notwithstanding a significant decrease in the world market price of oil, the government's main source of revenue. By 2014, Saudi Arabia was third in the world in terms of military outlays and maintained that rank even in 2018 (the last year for which data is available). Such

Table 9.4 Defense Spending in the GCC, 2004–2010

Country	2004 (US$ Million)	2010 (US$ Million)	Change (%)
Bahrain	677	915	35.15
Kuwait	5,500	5,000	−9.09
Oman	4,300	5,300	23.25
Qatar	1,300	2,100	61.53
Saudi Arabia	31,000	52,000	67.74
UAE	10,500	18,500	80.95

Source: Jarzabek, "GCC Military Spending in Era of Low Oil Prices," 3.

massive defense spending, of course, is also reflected in GDP terms. No country spent more in the 2011–2017 period than Oman, the least prosperous GCC state, devoting over 12 percent of its GDP to defense every year from 2014 to 2017. One may speculate that the sultan, like King Abdullah of Jordan, justified such a high level of defense spending with the imperative to distribute economic favors to tribal allies. (For comparison's sake: the United States' defense spending in the same period hovered between 3 and 4 percent of its GDP.) According to data from the Stockholm International Peace Research Institute (SIPRI), in 2016 Saudi Arabia had the fourth- and in 2017 the third-largest defense budget in the world ($69.4 billion); the UAE was second in the entire Middle East and sixteenth overall (SIPRI 2018, 2, 7).[15]

Table 9.5, based on data from the International Institute for Strategic Studies (IISS), suggests that Omani defense spending relative to GDP was actually above Saudi Arabia's in every year between 2012 and 2018, and in 2013 and 2014 it was significantly higher—presumably as a response to the protests in the sultanate in 2011. Although the UAE has not published data regarding its military outlays in the last several years, analysts believe that the amount would certainly place it somewhere in the world's top fifteen.

Remarkably, Iran, the GCC's main adversary, devoted proportionately fewer resources to defense in the same decade than most GCC states and much less than Saudi Arabia, Bahrain, and, presumably, the UAE. Finally, by the end of the decade, the share of defense outlays as a proportion of the GDP had decreased in several GCC states, likely, again, as a response to plummeting revenues from hydrocarbon exports.

In much of MENA, real change in defense spending from 2017 to 2018 has been mostly negative (Saudi Arabia and Bahrain registering a decrease of between 10 and 20 percent, while Kuwait and Oman saw a

Table 9.5 Military-Expenditures-to-GDP Ratio for the GCC States, 2011–2018 (percentage)

Country	2011	2012	2013	2014	2015	2016	2017	2018
Bahrain	3.63	3.84	4.94	3.90	4.95	4.77	4.19	3.76
Kuwait	2.50	2.64	2.56	2.70	3.60	5.17	4.83	4.26
Oman	5.90	8.40	11.73	11.95	16.40	13.72	12.08	10.95
Qatar	2.00	2.03	2.15	2.42	2.84	2.80	—	—
Saudi Arabia	8.12	7.79	7.98	10.38	12.90	12.60	11.20	10.70
UAE	2.72	2.60	3.46	3.60	—	—	—	—

Source: Military Balance Annual Reports, 2011–2019. https://www.iiss.org/en/publications/military-s-balance.

more modest drop of 3 to 10 percent).[16] According to SIPRI data, Saudi military spending fell by 6.5 percent in 2018 to $67.6 billion.[17] In 2019 and 2020 these changes continued, particularly in response to the Covid-19 pandemic. Defense outlays in Arabia declined by nearly 10 percent to $90.6 billion in 2021 and were expected to drop further to $89.4 billion in 2022 before rebounding to prepandemic levels by 2024.[18]

In the last decade, GCC countries have committed to major purchases of American arms. In 2008 to 2011, $5.8 billion (from a total of $13 billion) worth of the weapons Saudi Arabia took delivery of originated in the United States, while in 2012 to 2015 America sold $10.5 billion (from a total of $17.7 billion) of the weapons purchased by the kingdom.[19] In 2009 to 2016 the GCC imported about $200 billion worth of American arms. Under Barack Obama's presidency, within a five-year period (October 2010 to November 2015), Saudi Arabia purchased $111 billion worth of American weapons.[20] In 2017 alone, the US Department of State approved arms agreements with Bahrain ($4 billion), Kuwait ($800 million), Qatar ($12 billion), and the UAE ($2 billion).[21] The largest deal, however, was apparently reached with Saudi Arabia in May 2017. The total amount, $110 billion, was revealed with much hype by President Donald Trump in Riyadh, but the agreement does not commit the Saudis to actually procuring these weapons, and it is at best doubtful that they will find the money for such a large purchase. Indeed, two years after the "agreement"—which Anthony Cordesman has called "little more than speculative nonsense and empty political spin"—was reached, it had generated only $14 billion in confirmed purchases.[22]

These figures, it ought to be recognized, are unlikely to reveal the entirety of the GCC states' defense spending. For instance, military expenditure is only a portion of total Saudi defense outlay, which, as the Saudi budget statement for 2018 notes, is spread between the security and regional administrations sector (whose budget includes allocations for new projects and expanding already existing ones) and the military sector. Also, though the work IISS and SIPRI do is extremely valuable—their methodologies are reasonably consistent and offer fresh data annually—it is unclear how much their figures take into account such items as operations, maintenance, repair, and personnel costs (including training). In other words, one should exercise caution before accepting Riyadh's—or, for that matter, any other authoritarian government's—budget figures as reflecting the true extent of Saudi defense expenditures.

One large-ticket item these budget data do not reflect is the cost of hiring foreign contract soldiers (a.k.a. mercenaries).[23] Not surprisingly, the highest proportion of foreign contract soldiers serve in the Gulf's three richest states—Qatar (about 85 percent), the UAE (less than 80 percent), and Kuwait (less than 65 percent)—where few young men have any economic incentive to sign up for enlisted positions. Conversely, Oman has the smallest number of contract soldiers, most of whom are British noncommissioned officers who work as training instructors and advisors seconded to the Sultan's Armed Forces. The vast majority of contract soldiers serving in the Gulf are Sunni Muslims from the Arab world and South Asia. Since independence, the Gulf states have also employed a large number of British, American, and other (mostly Western) advisors, instructors, and technicians to provide much-needed services ranging from strategic planning to weapons maintenance.

Armaments Acquisition

In the Gulf, where only members of the ruling family have the authority to condemn improprieties, arms sales are ordinarily accompanied by little or no transparency. Weapons procurement has often gone hand in hand with corruption or, as one Transparency International expert has put it, referring to Saudi Arabia, has been "theft on a grand scale."[24] The wide-ranging embezzlement in the defense sector has impaired the effectiveness of the GCC armies: when the princes pocket their "share" of the transactions, army units do not get what they are supposed to get. The lack of information on the accounting basics and the general absence of transparency of Gulf military-security companies also make it "difficult to access the economic effectiveness of developing a defense technological and industrial base."[25] At a time when oil revenues are down, the desirability of fiscal prudence increases, and the scourge of corruption becomes a more readily recognized issue. The Saudi government—along with other GCC regimes, particularly Kuwait's—has pursued a selective and partial anticorruption drive of sorts. An important feature of Mohammed bin Salman's much-touted defense transformation "boils down to better cash control" in Saudi military affairs: "Controlling money as a way to deepen both political control and domestic credibility is a hallmark of the present Saudi leadership."[26]

The United States has been and, for the foreseeable future, may be expected to remain the largest source of armaments for the Gulf. At the same time, much of the GCC states' weapons acquisition has been primarily motivated by political considerations and the desire for prestigious, top-of-the-line equipment rather than the armaments their armed forces need to respond to or prepare for real-world threats. Not only has Washington been the largest exporter of major arms in the world in every year since 1991, but the gap between the United States and other leading exporters—Russia, France, Germany, and China—has actually widened.[27] By far the largest recipient of US armaments in 2014 to 2018 was Saudi Arabia, which accounted for 22 percent of Washington's total arms exports (the Middle East accounted for 52 percent); in fact, US weapons exports to Saudi Arabia grew by 474 percent between 2009 and 2018.[28]

Though the United States continues to dominate Gulf arms markets, GCC countries have been, in fact, spreading their risk and hedging their bets; that is, they have widened their weapons procurement around a variety of vendors, most of them—though by no means all—American allies and Western democracies. The Gulf states have used arms purchasing not only as a way of shoring up bilateral relations but also to make sure they have alternative sources of weapons: if relations with one country go cold, they will not be without supplies. If US and western European vendors close the tap of arms owing to, for instance, their concerns about human rights violations, the Gulf states can always turn to China or Russia, which are not troubled by such considerations.

The majority of the aircraft in Qatar's air force, for instance, are French (Mirage and Rafale). Not surprisingly though, in 2017, when Qatar needed to cement US support soon after finding itself isolated by Saudi Arabia, Bahrain, and the UAE, Doha quickly dispatched a delegation to Washington to purchase thirty-six F-15 fighter jets.[29] Britain has also been a major arms supplier to the Gulf. In 2018 alone, it concluded agreements with Saudi Arabia for a variety of weapons sales and sold Qatar twenty-four Typhoon jets valued at almost $7 billion (Saudi Arabia already operated seventy-two Typhoon jets).[30] In 2017 Australia, eager to expand its defense exports, agreed to sell armaments to Saudi Arabia, while in 2018 the German government authorized further arms sales to Riyadh (four artillery positioning systems) and Doha (170 warheads and engines for Meteor missiles).[31]

The procurement choices of GCC states frequently have little to do with achieving or maintaining combat readiness, let alone improving combined arms or warfare capabilities. They often bear no relationship to pragmatism or cost-effectiveness, ignore budgetary trade-offs, and address no pressing need. Interoperability of armaments is seldom a consideration; it seems more important to have fancy weapons that can be reported about and shown off in *Jane's Defence Weekly*. Instead of building effective forces through training and development, the wealthy Gulf states have been known to privilege what Cordesman has dubbed the "glitter factor" and "the shiniest toys for the boys."[32]

More generally, it should be recognized that, regardless of how dazzling, cost-effective, or necessary the weapons Gulf leaders buy, they first and foremost should be viewed as an indirect cost of the security guarantee, the premium on the security insurance policy they pay primarily to the United States and United Kingdom. In a regional conflagration the GCC cannot defend itself from the likes of Iraq or Iran. According to Stephanie Cronin, by the twenty-first century Saudi Arabia had essentially "abandoned the goal of creating an army strong enough to defend its borders from external aggression."[33] The many billions of dollars' worth of American and British weapons, training, bases, and so on help to ensure that American and British soldiers will protect them if the need should arise. Whether the United States would sell its most advanced weapons to Arab countries—owing to Washington's primary alliance with Israel and its commitment to the Jewish state's qualitative military superiority in the Middle East—has been a serious consideration in recent decades.[34] More recently, one condition the UAE set on normalizing its relations with Israel was Jerusalem's agreement to the Emirati acquisition of F-35 combat aircraft from the United States.[35]

Providing Security

Some GCC states actually contribute to regional security, or, as noted above, think of themselves as doing so, in a variety of ways. In this section, I briefly outline their provision of bases for the United States and the United Kingdom as well building facilities and offering security assistance abroad.

Bases at Home and Abroad

In 1945 there were three US bases in the Gulf (one in Saudi Arabia and two in Bahrain), all with less than thirty personnel. After the end of the Cold War and the withdrawal of most American troops from Saudi Arabia in 2003, numerous US bases remained in the region, several were expanded and modernized, and some new ones were constructed. In 2015 Kuwait made ten bases or other military-related physical assets available for US forces, Qatar seven, Bahrain ten, and the UAE three, and American soldiers could use four small facilities in Saudi Arabia.[36] According to the British weekly the *Economist* and the US Congressional Research Service, in early 2020 there were approximately 41,600 American military personnel stationed in the GCC states (6,000 in Bahrain; 14,000 in Kuwait; 600 in Oman; 13,000 in Qatar; 3,000 in Saudi Arabia; and 5,000 in the UAE).[37]

The largest bases have been provided by Bahrain, Kuwait, and Qatar for the American navy, army, and air force, respectively. Bahrain has since 1971 leased to the US Navy part of the former British naval base, which has lately been home to about 6,000 US military personnel. The most important Pentagon asset in the country, however, is Naval Support Activity Bahrain (NSAB), which serves as the headquarters of the US Navy's Fifth Fleet. The base could not be more strategically situated to enable American warships to guarantee the safety of maritime traffic and to check Iran's interference with the transportation of oil and gas from the Gulf.

Kuwait is home to two large US Army bases—Camp Arifjan and Camp Buehring—and the Ali Al Salem Air Base. It has become a key staging area and logistical center for American ground troops. Nowadays there are 14,000 to 16,000 American soldiers there—about half the number that were stationed there in the last stages of the large-scale US military presence in Iraq. Together with NSAB, the Al Udeid Air Base is the largest and most important American military facility in the entire Middle East. Since 2002, Al Udeid has been home to the US Central Command's forward headquarters, the Combined Air and Space Operations Center with representatives from twenty nations, and the 379th Air Expeditionary Wing.[38] The facility is home to nearly 10,000 American servicemen, accommodates their more than 120 aircraft, and has the longest runway in the Gulf.

Since its withdrawal from the region, the United Kingdom has maintained its military influence mainly through hundreds of seasoned advisors and trainers in every Gulf state. In 2015, however, the United Kingdom began construction on its first permanent naval base abroad since 1971. Located at the Mina Salman Harbor in Manama, virtually next door to the US navy's facility, the new Royal Navy base, HMS Juffair, was tasked with helping to battle the Islamic State and other jihadist and extremist groups in the region.[39] In 2019 the United Kingdom opened a £1 billion joint support base near Duqm, Oman, that can accommodate up to 500 military personnel and will be used as a training facility for the Omani armed forces.[40] The new bases suggest that the United Kingdom seeks to expand its influence and take on more responsibility in the Gulf. By continuing to provide facilities to their protectors, the Gulf countries foster security cooperation with them and promote stability in the region.

Since 2010, the UAE and Saudi Arabia have expanded their military influence over the Horn of Africa (Sudan, Eritrea, Djibouti, and Somalia). This region is critical for controlling the sea traffic from the Mediterranean Sea to the Suez Canal and the Red Sea, through the Bab el-Mandeb Strait to the Gulf of Aden and the Arabian Sea. Since the beginning of the war in Yemen in 2014, the four-country coastal zone has become all the more important strategically owing to its location just across the sea from Yemen. The Saudis and the Emiratis have long maintained a military relationship with Sudan and pledged financial aid for the poverty-stricken country after its army ousted the long-reigning dictator Omar al-Bashir in April 2019.[41] Sudan actually deployed 15,000 troops to Yemen to augment the Saudi-led coalition. Khartoum drew down its forces to 5,000 by mid-June 2019 and to as few as 657 troops by January 2020, greatly diminishing one of the most important sources of revenue for the Sudanese Rapid Support Forces.

Eritrea has been the beneficiary of a diplomatic spat between the UAE and Djibouti, the latter optimally situated to control the Bab el-Mandeb Strait. Following a 2015 altercation between the chief of the Djibouti air force and Emirati diplomats, the African state evicted Saudi and Emirati troops from the facility they used and broke off diplomatic relations with Abu Dhabi. On the same day they were pushed out, however, the Gulf troops found a welcome haven in Eritrea. The Eritrean government soon completed a thirty-year lease agreement with the Emiratis on the Port of Assab with an airfield nearby that can accommodate even large military transport aircraft.[42] The Emiratis have used the airfield to train Yemeni pilots and developed Assab into a major expeditionary base, the first outside the UAE.[43] They also trained and equipped the Hadrami Elite Forces and Security Belt Forces there—all told, some 4,000 Yemeni fighters.[44]

Before relations between them deteriorated, the UAE had maintained close military ties with Somalia and even trained, equipped, and (for a four-year period) paid the salaries of Somalia's national army and some of its counterterrorist units.[45] But Emirati policies have deepened rather than bridged the chasm between Somalia's weak central authorities in Mogadishu and the semiautonomous or self-declared states such as Somaliland, Jubaland, and Puntland. In 2017 Somaliland signed an agreement with the UAE to build and lease a military and naval base in its port city of Berbera for twenty-five years; Abu Dhabi reached a similar deal with Puntland.[46] Qatar's ties to Somalia have been dominated by humanitarian aid and stepped-up investment rather than military cooperation.

Foreign Deployments and Nascent Defense Industries

The UAE is the only Gulf state that has accumulated considerable experience deploying its forces to combat zones abroad, assisting its allies in faraway places from Afghanistan to Bosnia. Zayed bin Sultan Al Nahyan, the UAE's founding father, well understood that his small nation was unlikely ever to become a great military power, but he also recognized—alone among his fellow Gulf monarchs—the international respect to be gained from developing a credible fighting force capable of contributing to its allies' campaigns. To that end, the UAE's forces began to participate in international peacekeeping missions in East Africa and in the former Yugoslavia in the 1990s and have since continuously and ever more intensively taken part in multinational military operations in environments as varied as Afghanistan, Bosnia, Kosovo, Libya, Lebanon, Kuwait, Somalia, and, of course, Yemen.[47]

In the spring of 2011, UAE air force jets joined NATO and non-NATO forces helping to enforce the no-fly zone and attacking targets in Libya to help unseat Colonel Mu'ammar Gadhafi's regime in Libya. This action was the first offensive operation the UAE conducted outside its borders. Some Emirati military personnel have been stationed in Libya and have provided support to Khalifa Haftar and his eastern-Libya-based Libyan National Army (LNA). Notwithstanding a UN arms embargo, the UAE has shipped large amounts of weapons to the LNA.[48] Qatar also participated in the air strikes against Gadhafi's regime. Doha not only helped give NATO political cover but sent six of its Mirage fighter jets 3,000 miles from home—an unprecedented feat in Qatar's history—and, near the end of the campaign, it dispatched some of its special forces to train rebels in Libya and later even in Qatar.[49]

The UAE's is the only GCC military to have participated in major foreign deployments prior to the war in Yemen. Bahrain sent a small (125-person) special security force to Afghanistan in 2009. Its contingent was supposed to have done well there—mostly securing coalition bases like the conjoining Camp Bastion and Camp Leatherneck, a British and an Afghan airbase, respectively, in Helmand Province. Bahrain's air force also deployed some F-16 fighter jets and crews to Jordan to support the anti–Islamic State air campaign in Syria. While symbolic in the big picture, the deployment was certainly an effort of a small country and was duly appreciated by the US-led coalition.[50] The Royal Saudi Air Force also flew some sorties against IS targets in Iraq and Syria, though its contribution to the campaign was insignificant.[51]

Finally, Saudi Arabia and the UAE have also begun to build up their defense industries and have been able to sell their products to some MENA countries and even to conclude licensing agreements (for the production of the Emirati Nimr armored carriers with Algeria).[52] Still, for *any* country, entry into the highly competitive world of the arms market, full of mature and experienced producers, is a profoundly difficult and risky proposition. For indigenous defense industries to be able to stand on their own without major state subsidies, they need, at the very least, a highly skilled labor force, enormous financial resources, and (often niche) products that possess a qualitative or price advantage over those of rival producers. Few small countries aside from Sweden and Israel—with far better starting conditions than the UAE, let alone Saudi Arabia—have been able to succeed in this market.

Conclusion

In spite of the enormous sums Gulf countries have spent on defense, the gap between their armaments and actual capabilities to deter aggression and defend themselves has narrowed but little in recent decades. The GCC member states continue to rely on the protection of the United States, though the experiences of the last decade—the policies of the Obama and Trump administrations suggesting that their support of the Gulf monarchies was not unconditional—have motivated them both to expand their search for allies (e.g., the rapprochement with Israel) and to take their own defense more seriously (e.g., the emphasis on increasing Emirati and Saudi power-projection capabilities). These two Arabian states have also been involved in providing security in various ways, although their activities have been mostly self-serving and intended to ensure that their allies prevail in the conflicts they are involved in.

Military expenditures have signified a major burden on the economies of the less well-endowed Gulf monarchies. Especially since the 2014 fall in world market prices of oil and the likely long-term diminution of demand for it—a major development that may reorder the social contract of the rentier states—the governments of Arabia will have to rethink their outsized defense outlays. Saudi Arabia will need to follow more prudent foreign and security policies and avoid expensive and unwise entanglements—such as its reckless and counterproductive six-year (and counting) involvement in the Yemen war with a price tag of $2 billion to $5 billion.[53] Relatively poorer countries, like Oman and Bahrain, as well as Kuwait, which has evidenced no regional strategic ambition, may be expected to reduce and rationalize their military budgets. As in recent decades, Oman and Kuwait may be expected to continue their widely recognized regional mediation activities. Qatar, owing to its massive natural gas resources, may be anticipated to weather the coming changes in the Gulf's energy markets most comfortably. Doha certainly aspires to play a larger role in the region, but its tiny citizenry (a little over 300,000) will moderate its strategic ambitions.[54]

Notes

1. Chehabi and Linz, "A Theory of Sultanism."
2. See Hegghammer, *Jihad in Saudi Arabia*, esp. 130–142, 186–198.
3. Barany, "Soldiers of Arabia," 118–140.
4. Barany, "The Gulf Monarchies and Israel."
5. See Bove and Brauner, "The Demand for Military Expenditure in Authoritarian Regimes."
6. All data in this paragraph come from Barany, *The Political Economy*, 20–21.
7. "GCC Total Population and Percentage of Nationals and Non-nationals in GCC Countries."
8. "A Wild Ride," 4.
9. "Sovereign Wealth, Sovereign Whims," 40.
10. Bahgat, "Lower for Longer," 39–40.
11. All data in this paragraph are sourced from "Average Monthly Brent Crude Oil Price from May 2020 to May 2022."
12. Jarzabek, "GCC Military Spending in Era of Low Oil Prices."

13. Cordesman, *Gulf Military Balance*, 36.
14. Cordesman, Shelala, and Mohamed, *The Gulf Military Balance*, Vol. 3.
15. *SIPRI Yearbook 2019*, 194.
16. IISS, *The Military Balance 2019*, 325.
17. *SIPRI Yearbook 2019*, 186.
18. Darasha, "GCC Defence Spending."
19. Cordesman, "Military Spending," 11.
20. Blanchard, *Saudi Arabia*, 39.
21. Harb, "The United States and the GCC," 50.
22. Cordesman, "Military Spending," 11.
23. For more detail, see Barany, "Soldiers of Arabia," 123–133.
24. Katherine Dixon cited in Kulish and Kirkpatrick, "In Saudi Arabia."
25. Gaub and Stanley-Lockman, "Defense Industries in Arab States," 10.
26. Partrick, "Saudi Arabia's Elusive Defense Reform."
27. *SIPRI Yearbook 2019*, 230.
28. *SIPRI Yearbook 2019*, 231–234.
29. Coates Ulrichsen, *Qatar and the Gulf Crisis*, 209, 214–216.
30. Perez-Peña, "Britain to Sell Jets to Saudis Despite Conduct of Yemen War."
31. "Saudi Arabia to Acquire Australian Military Equipment"; "Germany Approves Arms Sales to Gulf, Mideast Countries."
32. See Cordesman, Gold, and Berntsen, *The Gulf Military Balance*, 1:50.
33. Cronin, *Armies and State-Building*, 239.
34. For some illustrative examples, see Riedel, *Kings and Presidents*, 60–61, 87; Entous, "The Enemy of My Enemy," 34.
35. Barany, "The Gulf Monarchies and Israel," 577.
36. Byman, "Assessing Current US Policies and Goals in the Persian Gulf," 61–63.
37. "After the Assassination," 41.
38. This paragraph draws on Karlin and Dalton, "It's Long Past Time."
39. See "British Navy Begins Construction on New Base in Bahrain."
40. Browne, "Britain Announces New Military Base in Oman."
41. Al Sherbini, "UAE Defends Contacts with Sudan Military."
42. Mello and Knights, "West of Suez."
43. Meyer Kantack, "The New Scramble for Africa"; Mello and Knights, "West of Suez."
44. Hussein, "The UAE's Military."
45. Mello and Knights, "West of Suez."
46. Hussein, "The UAE's Military."
47. For a list of the Emirati forces' foreign deployments, see Yates, *The Evolution of the Armed Forces of the United Arab Emirates*, 329–332.
48. Irish and Siebold, "U.N. Says Libya Arms Embargo a 'Joke.'"
49. Roberts, *Qatar*, 129.
50. Singh Grewal, "Bahraini Jets Join Syria Strikes."
51. Interview with a US Air Force colonel involved in the campaign (Manama, December 4, 2015); Hubbard, "Saudis Cast Net for ISIS Sympathizers."
52. For a more detailed examination of this issue, see Barany, *The Political Economy*, 57–62.
53. See Ottaway, "Saudi Arabia's Yemeni Quagmire"; Riedel, "In Yemen."
54. See, e.g., Miller and Verhoeven, "Overcoming Smallness," 1–20.

10

Regional Entanglements: MENA States as Providers of Security Assistance

Simone Tholens

SECURITY ASSISTANCE (SA) HAS EVOLVED SIGNIFICANTLY IN THE MIDDLE East over the last decade. Violent political upheavals and shifting geopolitics since 2011 have paved the way for intensification and diversification of regional actors looking to shape the political and economic landscape. Security assistance has offered an opportunity to do so while largely keeping below the threshold of direct confrontation with competitors and adversaries. The conflicts in Iraq, Libya, Syria, and Yemen have been particularly prone to external competition over political and economic control, with regional states engaging in training and equipping of local partners for tactical, strategic, and political motivations. In this book, security assistance is treated as both a specific US Joint Chief of Staff definition (falling under Title 22 authorities) and broader security cooperation.[1] As set out in Chapter 1, other actors, notably Russia and Iran, operate on the "dark side," actively integrating "grey zone operations" into their versions of security assistance.[2] In this chapter, I bring a broad contextualization of security assistance practices, including those targeting nonstate recipients. I do so to reflect the reality on the ground in the Middle East and North Africa (MENA) region, where the state/nonstate binary is often unhelpful in understanding security dynamics and political developments. I also widen the analysis so to include constitutive dimensions of regional MENA security assistance, with the aim of providing an alternative and more grounded perspective to the study of security assistance, which may be of particular importance when analyzing the behavior of regional states and their view of what SA offers as a distinct foreign policy strategy.

Iran is often highlighted as one of the most successful providers of security assistance in the Middle East.[3] The post-2011 period has offered new opportunities for Iran to capitalize on its long-term cultivation of covert resistance to US hegemony through regional networks of nonstate or quasi-state partners relying on asymmetric capabilities. Tehran's training and equipping of Hezbollah in Lebanon, Shia militias in Iraq, and, albeit on a lesser scale, Houthis in Yemen and Palestinian groups, including Hamas in Gaza, indicate the breadth of Iran's security assistance repertoire. Yet the relationship with these partners is complex, and the strategy of disruption has simultaneously enabled and isolated Iran's international diplomacy and status as a regional player.

Turkey, meanwhile, has since the Arab uprisings in 2011 taken a more active role in molding the regional MENA security environment, arguably part of a neo-Ottoman revival, including through its use of security assistance in its "strategic hinterland."[4] It first began arming and equipping Islamist rebels in Syria in 2013, eventually taking the lead in supporting the Free Syrian Army (FSA) and the subsequent National Syrian Army. Its engagement in Syria has since been coupled with direct action, increasingly developing into competition and schisms with other actors present in the country, notably Russia and Iran. Turkey's main thrust into the practice of security assistance outside its immediate neighborhood came with the 2020 parliamentary bill that authorized noncombat troops to act as advisors and trainers for Libya's Government of National Accord (GNA). Ankara's overt entry into the Libyan war theater through the provision of training, arming, and tactical support, including by members of the Free Syrian Army, in the GNA's fight against the Tobruk-based coalition led by General Khalifa Haftar not only demonstrated Turkey's forward posture in the region but also the extent to which security assistance has become a mainstream practice by previously noninterventionist states in the MENA region.

This chapter surveys the practice of regional MENA actors training and equipping local security forces in the Arab Middle East and discusses the evolution of security assistance as a means of shaping the competition over influence and leverage building. Analyzing regional states with a track record of providing security assistance as part of broader regional engagement, the chapter contributes to discussions of the *entangled* dimensions of widespread security assistance in intraregional relations. The chapter discusses the development of security assistance as a shared and coproduced site, where temporally and spatially interdependent dynamics fundamentally challenge binary logics of patron/client, international/local, and state/nonstate. By analyzing Iran and Turkey as two regional states that have accelerated their security assistance engagements considerably since 2011, the chapter highlights how security assistance practices can be analyzed as *entanglements* that traverse these binaries. This makes for an alternative reading that underscores the way in which the practice has evolved significantly and requires new theoretical lenses. The chapter concludes by observing that security assistance is no low-cost fast track to influence and that, for regional states with integrated stakes in the long-term politics of their neighborhoods, the lure of leverage may easily turn into political conundrums with implications for both domestic and regional stability.

Existing Approaches to the Study of Security Assistance Practices

The Middle East is not just a site of global competition but is both reproducing and coproducing these geopolitics. Security assistance by regional Middle Eastern actors is an increasingly complex and multifaceted field of such contention and competition. The practice has evolved considerably, creating its own set of internal logics. This is not least important because so much of Western security assistance to the region is provided as a response to non-Western "support to terrorist groups" or "state-sponsored terrorism," as Nathan A. Sales, the US ambassador-at-large and coordinator for counterterrorism, said in his remarks at the US Virtual Embassy Iran: Iran's support to proxies offers "an extraordinary compendium of evil," which is why the United States will "continue to target Iran's terrorist proxies."[5] Yet we don't have adapted theoretical lenses for how this practice is constituted, in particular because much of the work on security assistance originates from two distinct traditions: on the one hand, patron-client approaches that heavily influence the US security assistance research agenda and, on the other, peacebuilding and security-sector reform (SSR) literature that informs much of the European approaches to the subject.

First, much strategic studies literature on SA analyzes the relationship between the delivery of security assistance and the attainment of specific foreign policy goals. Some of these analyses offer strong prescriptive narratives—SA, and specifically US SA, should be more, better, or otherwise enhanced based on long-term strategic commitments, more resources, and best practices.[6] Political science approaches to states' support of foreign armies or rebel groups seek to "bring politics back in." Here, there is a recognition of the politics at play when states use SA as a foreign policy instrument.[7] Drawing on principal-agent (PA) problems, these approaches seek to capture how states' support to other states or nonstate groups may forego some of the costs of large-scale troop deployments and also how the relegation implies the loss of a degree of foreign policy autonomy.[8] Stephen Biddle and colleagues apply the PA approach in their analysis of how effective SA is in increasing military effectiveness, finding that on the whole "[security assistance] is much harder in practice than often assumed" and that "small footprints means small payoffs."[9] The "loss of autonomy dilemma" is also reflected in recent theories of proxy warfare, which seek to draw lineages from the Cold War concept to the practice of using surrogate forces today.[10] In this literature, there is a tendency to provide models that capture the various strategic challenges involved, such as time, power, and delegation problems.[11] Other contributions apply modifications to the principal-agent framework so as to accommodate for the construction of "identities" in determining the US approach to enlisting local allies and to explain SA providers' response to recipients of military aid in the face of violations of human rights norms.[12]

While the above studies brought attention to the global practice of SA, principal-agent thinking rests on assumptions that, this chapter argues, eschew important elements of how SA is practiced by regional actors. First, such thinking obfuscates the *experimental* nature of SA. SA providers work in composite spaces, where multiple other actors compete and collude, which in turn influences the contents and direction of SA engagements. All these context-specific factors impact the way we conceive of the actors involved, to the point where identifying principals and agents becomes a highly blurred exercise. This is evident, for example, in Amos C. Fox's "In Pursuit of a General Theory of Proxy Warfare," where it becomes clear that despite personal field experience and close scrutiny of events in Iraq in 2017, he is hardly able to determine who was the principal and who was the agent as the Iraqi Security Forces, supported by the US-led coalition, attacked positions held by the Islamic State in Iraq and Syria (ISIS).[13] Second, the contractual premise of principal-agent theory, as per its origins in economic theory, is hard to reconcile with the complexities and fluidity of SA. While weapons, equipment, and training pass from one actor to another as part of SA practices, there is very little of the contractual and agreed-upon to guide expectations of such "transactions." Rarely does the provider have assurances from the recipient that certain objectives will be met; nor are there legal instruments to enforce breaches of contract. The recipient, meanwhile, is likely to have a very different view of the "contract," and officials on both sides will know that the terms of the engagement will constantly change and appear more as a multidimensional, ontologically fluid, and decentered relationship than as a situation resembling any familiar model of transaction. As such, the patron-client framework is perhaps more of a burden than a meaningful analytical tool when scrutinizing security assistance today, particularly when it comes to regional MENA SA providers, who will have all sorts of multifarious interests and associated legitimizing narratives for getting in on messy engagements.

The second set of literature tackling security assistance practices stems from the short-lived European experience in exporting security governance. In particular, the work on security-sector reform is influential. Central to SSR was the creation of functioning and legitimate security structures. SSR emphasized at least three key features: first, the role of external militaries in leading the reform process in partnership with local security forces; second, the assumed postconflict environment, locating SSR in a conflict settlement that had provided the terms for reconstruction; and third, a strong embeddedness in good governance and liberal democratic norms.[14] Arguably, all of these conditions have been modified in later iterations of security governance, leaving the similarities with contemporary SA to come to the fore.[15] This has also been recognized by recent work on the MENA region, which stays faithful to the belief that SSR still exists,[16] even if it may in practice be nothing more than a "string of bilateral approaches."[17] Arguably, "European" work on SSR rectifies some of the problems with PA theory and the "proxy" literature for what concerns the purely interest-based aspect of security assistance, but, at the same time, much of it has outplayed its capacity to provide meaningful analyses of ongoing SA practice, which is inherently more "pragmatic." For example, it has exposed the importance of local agency and how "hybrid" systems emerge as international actors intervene in local contexts.[18] Yet it is still largely wedded to analyses of the spread of good norms, or "capacity building" in its latest iteration, which nonetheless is based on a certain underlying theory of change. This is not least relevant in many studies of the EU and, to a similar extent, the North Atlantic Treaty Organization (NATO) as providers of "soft" forms of security assistance under headings such as SSR. As Florence Gaub and Alex Walsh show in Chapter 7, this largely undercuts the considerably "harder" forms of SA provided by some member states of these IOs, not least France and the United Kingdom, but also Italy, heavily involved in covert action, arms sales, and training and equipping of nonstate actors.

The literatures on both *patron-client thinking* and *normative governance/SSR* suffer from hierarchical assumptions as to the relationships at work in security assistance practice; pregiven interests or norms as drivers; and analyses of effects that are limited to effectiveness and state governance. They both fail to capture the multidimensional, often short-term, partly political and partly economic motives, the considerable autonomy of "clients"/"recipients," and above all the *jointly constituted space of interaction* so characteristic of security assistance, in particular at the intraregional MENA level. This chapter proposes a broader frame for analyzing security assistance as entangled practices and develops two types of *entanglements* for this purpose.

Entanglements of Security Assistance

I take inspiration from postcolonial security studies, where *entanglement* has been used to demonstrate the participation of "subaltern" actors in the production of global security complexes.[19] Entanglements connect spatially and temporally dispersed elements and consider complex global processes not as impositions of particular "imperial" wills but as coproduced "irrespective of the apparent power-asymmetries between the involved actors operating in these fields."[20] They are in some ways akin to global security assemblages but focused less on constellations of actors and more on the temporary stabilization of heterogenous material, human, and discursive parts, such as those required for security assistance engagements to materialize.[21] Seen in this light, security assistance is not a linear undertaking by actors with predefined interests and identities but becomes a constitutive practice that produces subjectivities and relationships, particularly so at the regional level, where longtime and transnational interconnectedness defines relations. In the Middle East, security assistance is increasingly entangled, both spatially and temporally; that is, it cannot be analyzed as simple costs and benefits but is deeply interlinked with the practice of others, coproduced by conglomerates of different types of actors, and accompanied by existential narratives of the past and projections for the future. Instead, therefore, of analyzing security assistance as per binary typologies (state/nonstate actors, conflict/nonconflict contexts, patrons/clients, costs/benefits), it might be purposeful to identify *entangled practices* that could open up fresh analyses of security assistance in general and regional actors specifically.

I propose two such forms of entanglements through which regional security assistance can purposefully be analyzed:

First, *spatial entanglements* bring our attention to the way dispersed territorial spaces are connected and interdependent in ways that do not map neatly with sovereign power.[22] Spatial politics has been brought to the fore in recent iterations of security studies, in particular in the context of the War on Terror, in which violent geographies advanced a deterritorialization that was already underway with globalization.[23] Spatial analyses, particularly of territoriality, are concerned with how dispersed geographies shape and control in ways that eschew sovereignty, yet also reterritorialize relations of power. Security assistance is much concerned with such spatial politics. Some have described it as "governing from afar" or "remote warfare,"[24] while others have sought to capture the "liquidity" of intervention practices and the unfixed role of territoriality in contemporary forms of interventions.[25] In regional MENA security assistance contexts, the role of territory is important but undertheorized. On the one hand, security assistance as a model of doing foreign policy is precisely *not* designed for holding territory or making territorial claims to other states. But on the other hand, security assistance practices connect fragmented spaces in ways that challenge fixed territorial definitions of sovereignty and establish transversal fields that connect dispersed spatial locations and weave them together in a certain logic. Providers think about geography, but security assistance practices often connect geographies in rearticulated ways. Below, examples show how territorial entanglements in Iranian and Turkish security assistance produce a regional understanding based on "depth" and "influence" rather than control and sovereignty. Territoriality becomes both a function of security assistance and a product of it.

Second, *temporal entanglements* bring attention to the way time—past, present, future—features into regional security politics. Security assistance providers draw on historically grounded experiences of war, domination, threats, and interference to justify and rationalize often costly and risk-prone engagements overseas.[26] Recipients also construct historically informed narratives that justify the support they receive by often controversial regional actors. Sometimes they abandon their backer. Sometimes, the external support runs dry and new alliances are made. The narratives supporting these fluid relationships are core to establishing temporal entanglements that make sense of the past and—crucially—provide pathways for the future. This is why, in entangled perspectives, *narratives* form important components in the weaving together of a sense of purpose, of a rationale, for an otherwise controversial and costly practice.

For the United States and partners, the War on Terror and its unending, dispersed, and global characteristics have served such a purpose. For Iran and Turkey, narratives are, this chapter argues, equally important, but also more composite: narratives centered on neo-Ottomanism, in the case of Turkey, and resistance, in the case of Iran, serve as legitimizing vehicles around which ontological security is established and enduring political pathways are meted out, but there are variations over time, and the narratives are challenged politically. Crucially, whereas actors external to the region can—or think they can—eclipse such narrative construction by working on assumptions of "strategic utility" or "norm promotion," regional actors are perhaps even more keenly aware of the importance of building narratives that provide pathways between the past, present, and future. The nature of these relationships can be discerned in such narratives, as they carve out geographies of control that traverse national boundaries and actor status. Instead of treating discourses as post hoc justifications, a focus on what narratives *enable and prevent* regional actors from doing in the field of security assistance allows for analysis that considers both the agency of the "recipients" and the wider political purpose of SA practice.

The term *security assistance* is often used to describe "rational" Western approaches to shaping the Middle East, whereas non-Western support to local partners is described in various derogatory terms. Recently, scholars have begun treating Russian and Iranian security assistance as comparable to that of Western countries and provided sound starting points for thinking about similarities and differences in their practice.[27] There is also important work on the role of the Gulf states as parts of the bricolage of global security assistance assemblages, in particular the role of the United Arab Emirates as simultaneously a recipient and a provider.[28] In the next sections, I depart from analyses of the effectiveness of various actors' approach to security assistance and provide a transversal approach to the carving out of fields of influence by regional states, using the inroads to conceptualizing the entanglements identified above.

Entanglements in Iran's Security Assistance Practices

How then can one make sense of the function of security assistance in Iran's engagement with its neighborhood? In the following, I propose a reading that builds on the aforementioned entanglements.

Spatial Entanglements: Reterritorialization and the "Campfire Strategy"

Spatial entanglements are transnational constructions serving as belts to navigate both domestic and international audiences, and narratives are core to this end. Narratives are harnessed domestically to derive legitimacy for arming and equipping partners in the region but are also coproduced to varying degrees by partners and shape security assistance practices in constitutive ways. They matter for what can and cannot be done under the bracket of security assistance and produce subjectivities and identities set in regional hierarchies.

Iran's support to partners across the Middle East is one of the most contentious practices in the region. The labeling of this practice as funding "terrorists," "proxies," or "nonstate groups" is indicative of the West's threat perception of what is often referred to as Iran's "campfire strategy," that is, a strategy of diversion to prevent threats to the state's territory, population, and interests.[29] In this light, Iran externalizes its first line of defense through asymmetrical warfare strategies and effectively outsources its strategic defense to theaters in Lebanon, Syria, Iraq, and Yemen.[30] The campfire strategy also connects dispersed territories into a temporally stable geography, which is governed and ruled in particular ways. This reterritorialization is vital to upholding a perception of threat and a projection of "strategic depth." It is perhaps precisely because of this ability to weave together a fragmented but territorially widespread project that Iran is described as successful in utilizing security assistance to its advantage, despite the isolation it suffers internationally.

There is, however, an interesting tension in the literature, which is divided on whether Iran's support to local partners in the region is propelled by defensive or offensive strategic considerations. According to Andreas Krieg and Jean-Marc Rickli, Iran's notion of "mosaic defense" has prompted a strategy of "surrogate warfare" to externalize its defense and disrupt US assets in the region in order to protect the Iranian homeland from an attack by the United States.[31] Such a view is furthermore supported in principle by analyses of the multiple formative events in the history of postrevolutionary Iran, not least the Iran-Iraq War, where Iraq had vast international support from regional and global actors, leading to a sense of alienation and injustice that cemented the necessity for military self-reliance in regional affairs.[32] But others, agreeing in principle with these formative moments, consider Iran's security assistance to "militant clients" a rational and effective strategy to achieve its essentially offensive goal of regional dominance.[33] This offensive dimension is also highlighted in studies of the Islamic Revolutionary Guard Corps (IRGC), which point to how this military force, created out of militias that had overthrown the shah in the Islamic Revolution of 1979, was by nature revolutionary and saw mobilization in its neighborhood as critical to Iran's national security.[34]

This offense-defense debate highlights tension over Iran's "true intent," but it also highlights different geographies of control. Important for a focus on narratives is what the spatial entanglements allow an actor with a given identity to do—in our case, how and to whom Iran provides security assistance. Ariane Tabatabai is in many ways in disagreement with the perspective of Iran as principally concerned with exporting the Islamic Revolution and disrupting its enemies by providing security assistance to nonstate groups whose main aim is to challenge the sovereignty of Arab states. As she writes, "While today Iran is certainly a revolutionary state with an Islamic ideology, its first aim is far from the promotion of the revolution abroad. Instead, the security apparatus's main aim is to preserve internal stability and security."[35] She demonstrates how historical narratives and experiences with war and domination would push the country to develop a particular brand of security assistance based on the "campfire strategy."[36] She also shows how this externalization of defense and support to partners in the region has been far from static but rather evolved significantly over the years. In particular, whereas the early rhetoric by the Islamic Republic of a "revolution without borders" was noteworthy, the practice took on low-key and covert operations up until the 2001 US War on Terror, escalating further in the post-2011 period.[37] The United States's enlarged presence in the region and, in particular, the Arab uprisings and the instability that followed created new opportunities to reinforce and expand Iran's networks, as well as formalize the narratives of Iran as a counterforce in the region. Tabatabai shows how this formalization was produced by the government's effort to wrestle engagement with external partners away from the exclusive and clandestine control of the IRGC and nationalize the narrative of security assistance so as to meet the demands from a series of popular protests under conditions of sanctions and economic hardship.[38] The myth of the IRGC–Quds Force commander Qassem Soleimani must be seen as feeding into such narrative construction that simultaneously seeks to appease domestic public sentiments and project steady support to external partners. Soleimani's symbolic power rested on the image of a calm-and-collected, down-to-earth commander who would project brotherhood and equality with Iran's external partners, not a hierarchical command-and-control relationship.[39]

The spatially dispersed community of resistance has become an important vehicle also for the varieties of partners across the Middle East, who have also been more vocal about their affiliation with Iran after the 2011 Arab uprisings and ensuing armed conflict in the region. Hezbollah in Lebanon is effective at coproducing the narratives of an "axis of resistance" against US hegemony and the presence of Israel in the region,[40] while also maintaining its own entrenchment in the Lebanese state. Both Hezbollah in Lebanon and the Badr Corps and subsequently the Popular Mobilization Units in Iraq have skillfully maneuvered into positions of co-optation of these respective states, so much so that sovereignty has become entangled with their existence. As Marina Calculli argues in the case of Lebanon, Hezbollah's gradually moving into formal politics and "hedging" the state has reproduced the sectarian architecture in which it is part.[41] This in turn has allowed for the reproduction also of Iran's patronage of Hezbollah in ways that render it inseparable from, or entangled with, the Lebanese state. Much the same can be said about Iraq, where Shi'ite armed groups have been subsumed under the formal Iraqi army, thereby blurring and in fact dismantling the distinction between "Iranian supported terrorist groups" and the state. Iran's long-term support of Shia groups in Iraq can be seen as producing spatial entanglements that commentators often refer to as a "source of leverage over Western powers."[42] I would argue that rather than viewing the effects of SA as "leverage," security assistance practices is spatially entangled by design. This is particularly so in the case of regional states, which are interested mainly, perhaps, in forging long-term relationships that are constitutive of their own being in the region. In this light, the campfire strategy is not producing clear or direct political benefits to Iran and must be seen as an expression of an approach to regional relations that eclipse territorially as in and through sovereign states and rather forge communities that extend spatially and allow for a host of entangled dynamics, including religion, economics, ideology, and security. This stands in contrast to most efforts by Western SA providers, who consider leverage as dependent primarily on influence over state institutions. However, in the contemporary Middle East, processes of reterritorialization—the reconfiguration of relationships between sovereignty and territoriality—are profound and intense, and the jury is still out as to whether the two approaches are significantly different in terms of "leverage" creation.

Temporal Entanglements: The Enduring Logic of Resistance

Iran has embedded support to partners in its defense policies in ways that are deeply linked to its own ontological security and indeed appear to be projecting and externalizing its defense through security assistance.

Its foreign policy is argued to be based on three main pillars: Iran as a protagonist of the Islamic Revolution; opposition to US imperialism and by proxy Israel and the Arab allies; and a disregard for sovereignty inasmuch as it sees the Arab states as currently upholding an international order based on liberal US values and worldviews.[43] Recent scholarship has demonstrated that there is, however, more continuity with prerevolutionary Iran at work than is often assumed and that revolutionaries often drew on the past to inform and explain their security thinking.[44] Moreover, we may also include visions for the future in these temporal entanglements and consider Iran's security assistance practices as providing reasoning that can help navigate the future course of action at both national and regional levels. This resonates with observations on the use of long-term Iranian liaison officers, who will spend years working alongside their Lebanese or Iraqi "brothers,"[45] manifesting the continuity and commitment required for "success" and for harvesting the benefits of security assistance in the Middle East.

Taken together, the past and the future interlocks in what may be described as a logic of "responsibility to resist" in the case of Iranian SA.[46] This logic connects dispersed temporal elements in ideological narratives that supply guidance for behavior in the contexts in which it operates.

According to Stockholm International Peace Research Institute data, Iran spends far less on defense than its neighboring rivals.[47] Its economic and military inferiority to regional rivals and Western powers is usually used to explain why Iran has turned to asymmetric warfare in general and security assistance to regional partners in particular. If, however, we go beyond the notion of the costs and benefits of security assistance and rather consider its constitutive effects, then the effect is more concerned with status and identity in international politics than relative gains. And this is arguably an area where Iran has been able to become a considerable player.

On the one hand, Iran's partners have significant military capabilities in their home states and have contributed militarily to further Iran's interests in the region, notably to export the revolution and construct a powerful "Shi'ite crescent" that would reinforce anti-American positions in the Middle East.[48] On the other hand, the practice of supporting partners across the Middle East has not only produced intense counter-Iran strategies on the part of the United States and allies, particularly Israel and the Gulf monarchies, but also made Iran an international "pariah" more generally. The isolation and sanctions regime imposed on it have no doubt inflicted great hardship on Iranians. But this polarized context has also further militarized the response to Iran's security assistance and certainly produced more staunch opposition and rivalry regionally. It is then no wonder that most analysts evaluate the costs as considerable and perhaps unproportionate.

At a regional level, Iran's revolutionary narrative effectively produces a disregard for national sovereignty and abridges the stateness of the countries in which its partners operate.[49] Iran effectively uses asymmetric means to challenge the comparative strength of Arab states and erode their rivals' state capacities. Here, the narrative of the IRGC as by nature dislocated from the state provides an important logic to the antistateness of Iran's security assistance. Such an antistate narrative offers pathways to reject the status quo of US "friendly" Arab states, something that Iran has successfully capitalized on in its regionalization of the conflict with its main regional competitor, Saudi Arabia. This "grey status" of a regional power with the means and the will to destabilize the status quo has yielded influence through support to the Houthi rebels in the conflict in Yemen and to Hamas in Gaza, none of which share the notion of a "Shi'ite crescent."

Spatial and temporal entanglements make Iran an inevitable force that must be reckoned with and negotiated in Middle East politics. Through reterritorialization processes, Iran is able to use its SA networks to shape "facts on the ground" and informally pressure concessions in the states that it operates in. Yet it is hardly willing to take on responsibility for sovereign states' militaries and rather combines narratives of spatial and temporal entanglements to build transversal communities of "resistance" in postsovereign ways.

Entanglements in Turkish Security Assistance

Turkey's foreign and security policy has undergone considerable changes in the post–Cold War period. From a strategic partner of NATO, with secularism and noninterference as core commitments, domestic politics and regional outlook have shifted in tandem. Domestically, the rise of a more active and less EU-oriented foreign policy under Recep Tayyip Erdogan from 2003 onward and the major changes in the Middle East and its security architecture since 2001 and then 2011 have contributed to shaping an understanding of Turkey's purpose in the region as "order building," replete with more active engagement as a party in the armed conflicts in its neighborhood.[50] Such order building points us in the direction of deeply entangled dynamics with regard to Turkey's support to local security forces in Syria and Libya. Not unlike Iran, Turkey has been the object of increasing isolation in recent years and has found itself with few allies and many competitors. Also not unlike Iran, it seems to view security assistance increasingly as a means to unlock hegemonic potential while keeping with strategic, ideological, and historical notions of Turkish ontological security. Contrary to Iran, whose main strategy is to deliver SA to long-term partners, carefully building rapport and local entanglement, Turkey has demonstrated a seemingly more erratic or at least inconsistent use of SA to partners for the purpose of projection and reterritorialization of power.

Spatial Entanglements: Geographies of Control and Influence

Turkey's use of security assistance has effectively expanded its territorial reach and articulated domestic and international politics in new ways. Turkey has three main concerns through which its security assistance provision must be seen: (1) its long-standing efforts to prevent Kurdish mobilization and claims of autonomy within Turkey and in adjacent territory in northern Syria; (2) ambitions to expand its economic interests, especially in the maritime and energy areas in the eastern Mediterranean; and (3) the protection of enthopolitical communities, the generally favorable view of the Muslim Brotherhood specifically, and Ankara's support for "moderate Islam" more generally, as well as support for ethnic Turkish brethren, especially in the Caucasus but also among Libyan elites. Each of these elements has brought it on a collision course with its neighbors in recent years, and its status of "precious loneliness" appears unlikely to end soon.[51] Loneliness increases the importance of imaginaries of belonging, and in Turkey's security assistance engagements, we can observe at least two ways in which spatial entanglements are at work.

First, Turkey's internal concern with territorial sovereignty has entangled its foreign policy and security assistance engagements since 2011. Already in 2011, Turkey had sent clandestine shipments of arms to rebel groups in Syria with the aim of regime change. Secret bases were established in Turkey's border provinces of Gaziantep and Hatay in 2012 to train and equip Syrian rebels, as a part of US-Turkey intelligence cooperation.[52] This clandestine arms trade, which included the Free Syrian Army and other Islamist rebels, some of whom later went on to join ISIS, was gradually made public, culminating in the "MIT trucks" court case in 2014, in which the Turkish National Intelligence Organization, or MIT, was intercepted by border guards and subsequently prosecuted for involvement in illegal arms trade.[53] Only after this public exposure were new narratives deployed by the Turkish government to make the practice more palatable to the public opinion, and it began reframing Turkish Syria policy as a campaign to prevent the emergence of a "Kurdish belt" along its border. This appeased the opposition and brought about political consensus on Turkey's operations in Syria.[54] This mobilization against a "Kurdish belt" indicates entanglements with domestic security concerns as well as with territorial imaginaries. In this image, arming and training the FSA, from 2016, as well as the coalition force the National Syrian Army (NSA), amounted to counterterrorism, as the People's Defense Units (YPG) in Syria was equated with the Kurdistan Workers' Party (PKK) in Turkey and designated a terrorist organization by Turkey. As can be seen through Turkey's training and equipping of the FSA and NSA, in conjunction with its major military operations Euphrates Shield (2017), Olive Branch (2018), and Peace Spring (2019), narratives of establishing a "safe zone," where it would also be possible to resettle some of the 3.6 million Syrian refugees living in Turkey, have increasingly been deployed.[55] These linkages between security assistance, "counter-terrorism" and migration resettlement have offered domestic legitimacy, but Turkey's continued presence in Syria has also contributed to regional and international tension.

The spatial entanglement of security assistance is lastly of considerable significance in Turkey's Libya engagement. Turkey has supported many of the Arab movements that sought to topple governments since the 2011 Arab uprisings, but these have largely failed, leading to a sense of "imprisonment" between hostile Middle Eastern neighbors, not least Egypt and the UAE and, to a lesser extent, Saudi Arabia. In addition, a sense that Greece and Cyprus, and by extension the EU, as well as Israel, seek to box Turkey into a corner in the Mediterranean has produced a desire to break through barriers that would see it excluded from energy projects as well as geopolitically.[56] Spatially, Libya offers a way of demarcating the eastern Mediterranean in terms of gas explorations, while also redrawing the geopolitical map of the region in its favor.[57]

While Ankara had supported various Libyan groups clandestinely and in contravention of the UN arms embargo imposed on Libya since 2011, the big shift in SA delivery came in 2019 when a maritime demarcation agreement and a military cooperation agreement were signed between Turkey and the internationally recognized government in Tripoli, the Government of National Accord, then led by Fayez al-Sarraj—himself of

Turkish origin, with his grandfather apparently having served in the Ottoman army.[58] This was followed in early 2020 by a bill passed by the Turkish Parliament that authorized Turkey to overtly train, equip, and support the GNA as it sought to prevent General Khalifa Haftar and his coalition forces, the Libyan National Army, from gaining control of the country.[59] Turkey's role in Libya is not based primarily on political allegiance, and it is mainly seen to be relying on individual networks through its business clites or prior relationships with local militias, some of whom have ties to the Muslim Brotherhood or other elements of Islamist intelligentsia that relocated to Istanbul after Qatar reduced its regional footprint in 2014.[60] Its capacity building has mostly taken the form of train-and-equip programming rather than institutionalization and reform, and its own use of Syrian and Turkmen mercenaries—which it has so far failed to fully remove as per the terms of the UN-sponsored Libyan Political Dialogue Forum and the associated ceasefire agreement—is rather replicating the fragmented politico-security landscape in Libya than offering pathways for unity.[61]

Temporal Entanglements: A Neo-Ottoman Revival

Deeply linked with spatial entanglements, temporal entanglements allow for concepts and narratives of the past to provide a sense of direction and purpose in foreign policy. Where Iran draws on enduring logics of the Islamic Revolution and logics of resistance as a temporal trajectory and compass, Turkey's hegemonic drive in the Middle East is connected with a process of reconciliation with and reinvigoration of its Ottoman legacy, which has ceased to be depicted as a distant and bothersome past and instead has come to serve as an important source of linkage to its neighborhood and the Middle East in particular.[62] Breaking with the Kemalist tradition of modern Turkey with its emphasis on fixed borders and sovereignty, the surrounding areas around Turkey have increasingly been the subject of its foreign policy ambitions.[63] This historical reinterpretation is a product of the combined efforts by neoliberal, neo-Ottoman, and political Islamist movements, and the historical trajectory that it offers is powerful in terms of regional unity between Turkey and its surroundings, which are imagined as areas of influence in this revised paradigm.[64] Turkish foreign policy underwent a gradual transformation from Kemalist anchoring in principles of noninterference, secularism, and nationalism to neo-Ottoman visions during the 1990s, but it was first with the appointment of Ahmet Davutoğlu as foreign minister in 2008 that a revival of ideas of Pax Ottomanica took hold of Turkish foreign policy.[65] Based on Davutoğlu's book titled *Strategic Depth*, a series of neo-Ottoman principles that were to guide Turkey's reinvigorated role in the Middle East were set out, allowing for renewed interest in molding its adjacent geographies. From its post–Cold War profile as an unexciting and reactive actor, it now set out to engineer a new course based on imaginaries from its glorious past, aimed at the possibility of extending "Turkey's renewed influence on the former imperial territories."[66] Not least was this based on the peace ethos of Pax Ottomanica and the role of Turkey as a "peace-bringing" descendant of the Ottoman Empire, as well as ideals of multiculturalism and the caliphate as the symbol of an alternative world order.[67] Erdogan's active use of the language of neo-Ottomanism, a designated policy for a "virtuous Turkey" in Sub-Saharan Africa, and soft power in the form of hugely popular Turkish television dramas exported to Arab societies together indicate a continued presence of the past in Turkey's engagement with its wider region.[68]

Turkey's endeavors into security assistance practices epitomize these temporal entanglements in Turkish foreign policy discourse based on neo-Ottomanism, even if they have also challenged and subsequently recalibrated that discourse. A growing belief by elites in the repeatedly elected, AKP-led government that Turkey's role in the world was one of importance and influence produced expansionist policies also in the security realm. Such expansionist foreign policy brought Turkey to be increasingly engaged in the conflict in Syria from 2011, though ever more so on an interventionist and Sunni-sectarian basis rather than due to grand visions of "multicultural" peace.[69] Moreover, its belief in its own importance in the Caucasus and the eastern Mediterranean can only be taken as an indication that reimagination of its imperial legacies has promoted constitutive ideas about its trajectory as a regional power. Security assistance comes across as low-cost in this regard—even if it often proves costlier as mission creep sets in. In Libya, we can identify a reinvigorated Turkey with an appetite for a role in the endgame, even if recent overtures toward conciliation with Egypt and the UAE in particular may condition this strategy. In May 2021, there were about 500 Turkish soldiers stationed in Libya involved in training military and police units affiliated with the newly launched Government of National Unity, headed by Abdul Hamid Dbeibeh, who took office as part of a UN-backed initiative to take the country to elections in December 2021.[70]

Turkey appears to be in it for the long haul in Libya. And it is digging into its positions in Syria, while supporting Azerbaijan in its conflict with Armenia. Weaving these ad hoc security assistance practices together brings about an understanding of temporal and spatial entanglements that eclipse domestic/foreign policy, and that in turn brings about a practice that rests on constitutive ideas about who Turkey is and what it needs to be doing in its neighborhood, especially vis-à-vis the Arab Middle East. Whether security assistance is translated into political and economic gains may be rather secondary in this image. What appears to be core is a postimperial pathway, coupled by postsovereign entanglements, through which navigation of the Middle East and wider region becomes possible and Turkish importance is restored, even if, for all intents and purposes, it appears rather chimeric.

Conclusions:
Security Assistance and Entangled Geographies of Control in the Middle East

Entanglements offer a way to analyze how MENA providers are enabled but also hampered by their security assistance practice, which brings about an awareness that SA is not a low-cost instrument of domination but rather requires tactful diplomatic skills in order to translate into international political gain. In the case of Iran, findings point to antagonism rather than influence as the main outcome, although disruption cannot be fully excluded as a means in itself. Supported by accompanying narratives that provide legitimacy at home and project capabilities abroad, security assistance practices are as much about *the production of actorness* in international relations as about obtaining direct rewards and influence in particular contexts. Status is here seen as embedded in and through social practices rather than "measurable" parameters.[71] Despite SA often being denied and responsibility deferred, the practice generates a certain type of status and membership in a "club" of middle-sized powers with capabilities to shape the strategic environment through external partnerships. Seen in this light, security assistance entanglements also produce certain lock-in effects, as they become symbolically potent and therefore harder to undo or scale back without implicating the status of their providers.

Iran's security assistance practices produce regional entanglements that are enduring and constitutive. Turkey, on the other hand, seems to be more erratic in its SA engagements. Thinking in terms of entanglements may provide an alternative lens though which we can make sense of middle-sized regional powers' security assistance practices and SA's potency for their ontological security. Yet this optic also exposes how security assistance, as it is practiced today, significantly complicates neighborly relations and creates enduring interdependencies that are difficult to undo. Indeed, the "investment-return" perspective is fraught with misperceptions and should be revisited for a more accurate understanding of the deeply constitutive role of security assistance in broader Middle East imaginaries.

Notes

1. Chapter 1 of this book.
2. Ibid.
3. Ostovar, "The Grand Strategy of Militant Clients," 159; Krieg and Rickli, *Surrogate Warfare*, 164.
4. Badi, "To Advance Its Own Interests"; "Turkey Wades into Libya's Troubled Waters."
5. Sales, "Tehran's International Targets."
6. Karlin, *Building Militaries in Fragile States*; Matisek, "The Crisis of American Military Assistance"; Paul et al., *What Works Best When Building Partner Capacity and Under What Circumstances?*
7. Biddle, Macdonald, and Baker, "Small Footprint, Small Payoff."
8. Salehyan, "The Delegation of War to Rebel Organizations."
9. Biddle, Macdonald, and Baker, "Small Footprint, Small Payoff," 94–95.
10. Mumford, *Proxy Warfare*; Krieg and Rickli, *Surrogate Warfare*.
11. Fox, "In Pursuit of a General Theory of Warfare."
12. Rittinger, "Arming the Other," 398; Burchard and Burgess, "US Training of African Forces and Military Assistance," 349.
13. Fox, "In Pursuit of a General Theory of Warfare," 8, footnote.
14. Ehrhart and Schnabel, *Security Sector Reform and Post-Conflict Peacebuilding*.
15. See the special issue on Second Generation SSR introduced by Jackson, "Introduction," 8.
16. Cellino and Perteghella, "Conflicts, Pandemics and Peacebuilding."
17. Cf. Jackson, "Introduction," 4.
18. Mac Ginty, "Hybrid Peace," 395; see Jarstad and Belloni, "Introducing Hybrid Peace Governance," 3; Richmond, "The Dilemmas of a Hybrid Peace," 54.
19. Barkawi and Laffey, "The Postcolonial Moment in Security Studies" 334; Hönke and Müller, "Governing (in) Security in a Postcolonial World," 384.
20. Hönke and Müller, "Governing (in) Security in a Postcolonial World," 389.
21. Abrahamsen and Williams, "Security Beyond the State," 9.
22. Sassen, *Territory, Authority, Rights*; Agnew, "Sovereignty Regimes."
23. Elden, *Terror and Territory*, xxviii.
24. Knowles and Watson, *Remote Warfare*.
25. Demmers and Gould, "An Assemblage Approach to Liquid Warfare," 365–366.
26. See Watling and Reynolds, *War by Others' Means*, for an account of British "defense capacity building," drawing heavily on references to imperial pasts and imperial commanders in their "how-to guide" for delivering modern-day capacity building to UK partners.
27. Springborg, Williams, and Zavage, "Security Assistance in the Middle East."
28. Krieg, "The UAE's 'Dogs of War'"; Zoltan Barany in Chapter 9 of this book.

29. Tabatabai, *No Conquest, No Defeat*.
30. Krieg and Rickli, *Surrogate Warfare*, 175.
31. Ibid., 173.
32. Tabatabai and Samuel, "What the Iran-Iraq War Tells Us," 293.
33. Ostovar, "The Grand Strategy of Militant Clients."
34. Ostovar, *Vanguard of the Imam*, 102–107; see also Byman, "Confronting Iran," 122.
35. Tabatabai, *No Conquest, No Defeat*, 182.
36. Ibid., 253.
37. Ibid., 254.
38. Ibid., 260.
39. Ibid., 261.
40. See Norton, *Hezbollah*; Khan and Zhaoying, "Iran-Hezbollah Alliance Reconsidered," 113; Daher, *Hezbollah*.
41. Calculli, "Self-Determination at All Costs," 97.
42. Younis, "Iraqis' Vote to Restrain Armed Groups."
43. Ostovar, "The Grand Strategy of Militant Clients," 162–163.
44. Tabatabai, *No Conquest, No Defeat*, 5.
45. Watling and Reynolds, *War by Others' Means*, 46.
46. Rudolf, "The Popular Shadow over the US-Iraq Strategic Dialogue."
47. Ostovar, "The Grand Strategy of Militant Clients," 170.
48. Seliktar and Rezaei, "Conclusion," 235–239.
49. Springborg, Williams, and Zavage, "Security Assistance in the Middle East."
50. Aydın, "Turkish Foreign Policy," 374.
51. Gormus, "Why Is the End of Turkey's 'Loneliness' Now Precious?"
52. Tastekin, "Turkish Mobster's Revelations Extend to Arms Shipments to Syria."
53. Reuters, "Turkish Intelligence Helped Ship Arms to Syrian Islamist Rebel Areas."
54. Tastekin, "Turkish Mobster's Revelations Extend to Arms Shipments to Syria."
55. Seeberg, "Neo-Ottoman Expansionism Beyond the Borders of Modern Turkey."
56. Badi, "To Advance Its Own Interests."
57. "Turkey Wades into Libya's Troubled Waters."
58. Kabalan, "Outrage, Rift and Resignations over Erdogan's Libya Plan." Note that this is widely cited but unverified.
59. Haftar, "Turkey's Parliament Approves Military Deployment to Libya."
60. Badi, "To Advance Its Own Interests."
61. "United Nations Support Mission in Libya (UNSMIL)"; Badi, "To Advance Its Own Interests."
62. Aydın, "Turkish Foreign Policy," 373.
63. Seeberg, "Neo-Ottoman Expansionism Beyond the Borders of Modern Turkey."
64. Aydın, "Turkish Foreign Policy," 380.
65. Ataç, "Pax Ottomanica No More!"
66. Furlanetto, "Imagine a Country," 176.
67. Ataç, "Pax Ottomanica No More!" 54.
68. Langan, "Virtuous Power Turkey in Sub-Saharan Africa," 1409; Kraidy and Al-Ghazzi, "Neo-Ottoman Cool."
69. Ataç, "Pax Ottomanica No More!" 57.
70. Gurcan, "Libyan Conflict Stands Out as Key to Turkey-Egypt Normalization."
71. Wohlforth et al., "Moral Authority and Status in International Relations."

11

US Security Assistance in Jordan: Militarized Politics and Elusive Metrics

Sean Yom

AMONG THE THEMES GIRDING THIS BOOK IS THAT WESTERN SECURITY assistance in the Middle East trips over frequent tensions between competing goals. As many other chapters showcase, security assistance intends to achieve *operational* objectives to improve the "partner capacity" of allied Arab militaries. The official doctrine of such programming revolves around a common terminology about battlefield efficacy, modernized weaponry, force cohesion, internal professionalism, civil-military relations, combat readiness, and other desiderata of modern military affairs. Hence, security assistance aims to make Middle East armies much better fighting forces.

However, when those friendly armed forces fail to meet lofty expectations, then proponents of security assistance fall back upon *geopolitical* imperatives. Western powers like the United States need to maintain robust relationships with client states like Jordan, Saudi Arabia, and Egypt, and security assistance is a useful tool to attain that. A steady tide of aid and arms not only bolsters these regimes but also ensures that the US enjoys political access to their rulers because such external support sends a strong signal of confidence. Security assistance, then, seeks to upgrade the physical resources and skill sets of partner militaries; but if that fails, then it at least keeps recipient regimes afloat while strengthening bilateral relations at a strategic level.

Ideally, these goals work in tandem, with security assistance accomplishing some concrete measures as a starting point. In cases like

Egypt, as Chapter 14 by General F. C. Williams makes clear, one can detect at least modest improvements in the Egyptian armed forces from the decades-long provision of American military support. But what if few operational ambitions are satisfied, leaving only the geopolitical justification of retaining the loyalty or friendship of a client state, no matter how ineffective its military may be? The Hashemite Kingdom of Jordan represents such a case of extreme imbalance. Here, US security assistance since the late 1950s has officially aimed to turn the Jordanian Armed Forces (JAF) into a sleek military that can independently defend its borders, mitigate regional conflicts, and win the battles it must fight. Having such a potent Jordanian military, as the US Department of State envisages, synergistically contributes to "a stable, secure, and prosperous Middle East."[1]

By its own stated goals on this operational front, however, US security assistance to Jordan has failed. For all its American backing, the JAF remains a glorified garrison force, more accustomed to policing society to maintain authoritarian order at home than undertaking sophisticated operations as a proficient military might be expected to do. Its checkered performance clashes with its vaunted reputation as a ferocious and Spartan-like strike force. The real payoff for Washington tilts entirely to the geopolitical side. US aid and arms help the JAF—and thus also the pro-Western monarchy it serves—survive. And so long as it survives, the JAF can augment domestic repression while keeping Jordan's tribal communities, the historic bastions of monarchical rule, indebted to the state through its payrolls and services. By buttressing the coercive guardian of a nondemocratic regime, US security assistance therefore sustains the stability of autocratic rule in a client state.

It is not hard to see why Jordanian stability ranks high on the list of Middle East priorities. The kingdom has been central to the United States's war making in the Middle East for several decades and today remains an integral component of its regional framework for dealing with Palestine, monitoring Syria and Iraq, fighting terrorism, containing Iran, and engaging other security challenges. In Washington, pundits on a bipartisan basis praise Jordan as America's "unsung ally" in the Arab world.[2] They celebrate it as the "little kingdom that could," its pro-Western monarchy uncannily persisting despite having little oil and being surrounded by regional turmoil.[3] They acclaim the kingdom as an "oasis of moderation"—an indefatigable peace partner of Israel and supposed democratic reformer.[4] And they describe Jordan as an "island of stability," its tribal soldiers preventing the raucous revolutions and civil wars wracking neighbors like Syria and Iraq from spreading onto their land.[5]

Such applause suggests a perverse policy scenario. Operational goals and geopolitical interests are not working in tandem within the US-Jordanian security assistance relationship; rather, the former is being used as cover for the latter. Washington needs the pretense of bolstering the JAF's capabilities on a military-to-military basis in order to rationalize, more broadly, the enormity of all its diplomatic, economic, and security resources flowing to Amman in order to keep alive a compliant authoritarian regime. The stakes are far higher than whether the Jordanian military can become an effective fighting force; they implicate whether a pro-Western dictatorship that facilitates American hegemony continues to rule at all. And yet, operational justifications about partner capacity persist in US policy discourse and within the corridors of Washington, DC, suffusing endless policy papers, military discussions, and training manuals about the JAF.

Unraveling the elusiveness of these metrics drives this chapter, which follows in three sections. First, the chapter theoretically shows how domestic politics and authoritarian logic collide within the militaries of client states. In many states, the armed forces are not merely purveyors of coercive violence but also bellwethers of popular support and thus pillars of political order. Second, it zooms into Jordan to unpack the JAF as an institution. It demonstrates that regardless of its military carapace, the JAF's primal role has always been domestic—to enforce the monarchy's writ upon society and to supply economic and social goods to tribal communities, which are both essential aspects of Jordanian stability. Finally, it reviews the scope and impact of US security assistance on the JAF. While US-Jordanian military ties are strong, on almost every count—successful combat, border defense, operational competency—the JAF has not performed to the level expected of a client military that has enjoyed American backing for nearly three-quarters of a century. What is left, the chapter argues, is the geopolitical rationale.

Theoretical Precepts About Recipient Dynamics of Security Assistance

The sprawling policy literature on security assistance pays little attention to recipient dynamics or how the absorption of security assistance affects domestic politics in foreign states. Yet as Glenn Robinson's Chapter 3 argues, domestic factors are first-order concerns for recipient regimes. Almost always, requests for security assistance from US allies are driven by a desire not to wage war but rather to stay in power by securing fungible resources like weaponry and money. It is therefore worth rehearsing what we know about security sectors from theories of authoritarianism and why foreign support is so central to these bulwarks of autocratic rule.

First, in authoritarian states, the aim of regime organizations that specialize in the use of violence is to ensure their political stewards stay in power. Usually, those threats emanate not from distant lands but from their own society; militaries and security forces therefore can be expected to spend inordinate time surveilling, monitoring, and repressing domestic opposition.[6] None of the magnificent goals cited in most discussions of security assistance, from military professionalization to encouraging good governance, matter if these pro-Western regimes cannot stay in power in the first place.

Second, coercion is a necessary but insufficient condition for most autocracies to endure. For one, their coercive sentinels can themselves covet power, forcing leaders to engage in "coup proofing" and other insulating tactics to ensure the masters are not overthrown by their guardians.[7] Beyond this, dictatorships must also capture the support of at least some subset of their population. They cannot rule from a bunker, threatening to kill anyone who disobeys. Scholars of authoritarianism have used many terms to describe the process of securing popular backing in the absence of elections (e.g., finding legitimacy, co-opting opponents, building coalitions, inducing loyalty, sharing power, and making credible commitments).[8] All these optics boil down to the following: since there are no free and fair elections to guarantee that rulers embody a plurality, if not an outright majority, of popular preferences, autocrats must find other ways to convince some citizens that, all else being equal, they are better off with the status quo rather than rolling the dice with a coup or revolution. Shrewd dictators woo rivals, convince doubters, and seduce standpatters; they turn citizens into subjects and subjects into supporters.

Often, rallying such a social foundation requires making implicit bargains that target supporters with specialized arrangements such as jobs, services, and other privileges. Cases like Jordan stand out by showing how ties between a rulership and its supporters are not contingent deals but may harken back to the founding of political order itself. In the Hashemite Kingdom, a simple equation suffices: no tribal support, no monarchy. The Jordanian state coalesced following its 1921 inception after its British-installed military pacified the tribal residents of this scrubby territory known as Transjordan, or the East Bank (of the

Jordan River). While the 1948 and 1967 Arab-Israeli wars gave Jordan a Palestinian majority, the Transjordanian tribes remained the core constituency of Hashemite rule.[9] The security sector has been a crucial part of this tribal-state alliance. The army and other security institutions not only curbed dissent in society but also almost exclusively employed Transjordanians—and not, for the most part, Palestinians. They also furnished education, health care, and other services to these tribal communities, bringing them into proximity with the monarchy.

This does not mean that all Transjordanian tribes are loyal or that Palestinian Jordanians comprise all political opposition. Ideology, class, and clientelism crosscut the Transjordanian-Palestinian divide, and the Hashemite monarchy counts plenty of Palestinian backers and a growing number of disgruntled tribal dissidents. Nonetheless, the historical use of Jordan's security sector as a *material* linkage to Transjordanians leaves an important implication. The Hashemite regime has always considered the tribes as its most legible subjects, and their incorporation through the army reifies this perception. The JAF hence serves as an indispensable mechanism for Jordanian authoritarianism, the building block without which its artificial political order could never have existed.

Finally, because security-related institutions can play a dual role in suppressing domestic threats and absorbing regime supporters, successful dictatorships prioritize their material well-being. Foreign aid has an obvious role to play here. Economic assistance can keep local militaries afloat by subsidizing their regimes' budgets, which ensures their personnel continue receiving all the pecuniary rewards to which they are accustomed—prestige, salaries, pensions, and so forth.[10] At a logistical level, high-tech kit from Western defense firms can improve the morale of the officer corps, while enhanced training from Western militaries can deepen the capabilities of the indigenous rank and file.

Resource-poor countries like Jordan provide a poignant window into this dynamic. In purest terms, US security assistance provided through military-to-military channels delivers weaponry, skills, and services to the JAF. Yet it is prudent to consider *economic* aid given through nonmilitary conduits as part of security assistance, because it boosts the "budget security" of the Jordanian regime—and a bankrupt autocracy can field no armies.[11] Economic aid that comes as fungible fiscal grants allows client states to fulfill their ordinary nonmilitary spending items, such as civil service salaries and social services, freeing the rest of its budget for the security sector.

This characterizes the US-Jordanian aid relationship. Historically, the biggest part of US economic aid to Amman has been not project-specific or humanitarian aid (such as food shipments or development funding) but rather cash grants that pad government revenues and thus enable it to afford its vast security sector. Of the nearly $26 billion in total US foreign aid that Jordan received from 1957 through 2022, about three-quarters has manifested as economic support; of that, nearly 70 percent has comprised cash-based grants to support Jordan's national budget. During the 1960s and 1970s, such annual financing often exceeded all the domestic revenues collected by the Jordanian state, and even as late as 2020, those budgetary grants equaled 14 percent of Jordan's internal tax haul. Put another way: in aggregate terms, one out of every ten dinars spent by the Jordanian state since the late 1950s has originated from Washington. The seven-year US-Jordanian aid agreement signed in September 2022 perpetuates this pattern: of the total $10.15 billion to be provided to Amman from 2023–2029, at least $7.3 billion will materialize as economic assistance, of which nearly $5 billion will consist of direct budgetary support.

These suppositions bear upon contemporary debates about security assistance. Coercive institutions must be understood not only as wielders of battlefield competencies but as domestic political actors. They carry out internal functions, from repressing opposition to enmeshing regime constituencies, and their organizational health is inseparably linked to their regimes and states. This sheds light not only upon why Western security assistance programs often fail to build partner capacity but, more importantly, on the fact that this may not matter: more important is ensuring that those armed forces, and the regimes that command them, simply exist.

Jordan's Security Sector and the JAF

Jordan's security sector comprises a tripod of institutions, namely the Jordanian Armed Forces, the General Intelligence Directorate (GID), and the Interior Ministry's various civil-policing and gendarme forces.[12] The JAF is the national military, led by the chairman of the Joint Chiefs of Staff and adjuvant command structures. The GID is a combination of spy agency and secret police that squashes political threats against the monarchy. The Interior Ministry's policing and gendarmerie enforce laws and regulate public behavior. All report to the palace. They are not directly accountable to any other stakeholder within the Jordanian political system, from the elected (and largely toothless) parliament to the royally appointed cabinet led by the prime minister.

As a national military, the JAF encompasses about 110,000 personnel, who staff a land army supplemented by a small air force, tinier coast guard, and specialized units such as its special operations and counterterrorism divisions. That the Jordanian public consistently ranks the JAF as the most respected national institution in surveys, drawing trust ratings of over 90 percent that dwarf that of parliament (21 percent) or even the government (54.2 percent), gives some indication of its gargantuan footprint in domestic society.[13] Another is how Jordan's other security institutions reflect militaristic influences. The Interior Ministry's policing agencies—the Public Security Directorate (i.e., civil police) and the General Directorate of Gendarmerie Forces, the latter of which merged into the former in 2019—have systems of promotion that mirror JAF ranks, and their directors have always come from the JAF's senior staff rather than civilian law enforcement. Even the GID was born under the JAF's shadow, emerging in the 1960s to supplement military intelligence efforts to eliminate domestic opposition.[14]

It is little surprise, then, that the JAF represents the largest, costliest, and most prominent element of Jordan's security sector, garnering almost all official US security assistance.[15] Its highly sequestered nature means that few have investigated its innards, compared to the richer corpus of literature on Jordanian politics and society. A handful of studies focus on the JAF's early years, particularly its role in subduing Arab Nationalist unrest in the 1950s and 1960s.[16] Rigorous academic analysis generally stops in the 1970s, and most published works since then are bland tributes that glorify the JAF as a cohesive fighting force.[17] During this middle period of the Cold War, for instance, commentators celebrated the JAF as a Spartan-like army, whose "tribesmen in uniform" represented "fighting material *par excellence*" given their rugged Bedouin backgrounds and atavistic loyalties to the Hashemite crown.[18] Upon King Abdullah's enthronement in 1999, Western analysts counted the JAF as a net plus for his reign—it was "one of the best trained armed forces in the region" and a "crack force" from whose ranks the new young king had emerged.[19] If the Hashemite Kingdom is "Fortress Jordan," an oasis of stability housing Western forces and facilitating American interests,[20] then the JAF stands as its fearless—and peerless—defender.

Political Realities

Such neo-Orientalist homages obscure two fundamental realities that govern Jordan, one political and the other economic. First, in domestic terms, the JAF plays a primal role in maintaining authoritarian rule; it is the monarchy's institutional backbone. It historically descends from the Arab Legion, the British-officered constabulary that forged Jordan's embryonic statehood during the British Mandate (1921–1946) by transposing the authority of the newly implanted Hashemite monarchy upon the reticent tribes of the East Bank. From then on, the army operated as a public warden of sorts, with few legal injunctions against the deployment of soldiers to wipe out internal strife. In Jordan, the military preceded state building.

The 1950s represented a minor inflection point, as the regime dealt with Arab Nationalist sympathies among the officer corps that dovetailed with rising domestic opposition, until the monarchy and the army's loyal majority cracked down to restore order.[21] From the latter part of that decade through the 1980s, the rapidly expanding military served as a pillar of governance under martial law. Dissidents from this period recall the brutality with which the JAF helped the government smash leftist parties, muzzle critical media, and suffocate civil society.[22] The army also defeated Palestinian Liberation Organization commandos during the bloody 1970 Black September civil war.[23]

Even after tepid, quasi-democratic reforms began in 1989, which ended martial law, the JAF kept a brooding presence upon the public sphere. It occasionally mobilized to curb popular unrest waged around social and economic discontent—as it did with riots in 1989, 1996, and 2002—and during the 2020–2021 coronavirus pandemic, troops imposed nationwide lockdowns that ranked among the world's most draconian. The GID carries a more dreaded reputation in ordinary social life, given its sweeping authority to surveil, arrest, and prosecute all threats ranging from Salafists to students. Yet the army casts the longest silhouette by virtue of its synonymy with the Jordanian state. The regime did not deploy the JAF to deal with the thousands of Arab Spring protests during 2011 and 2012 for a simple reason: it did not have to, because almost every demonstration was peaceful and called for reforms rather than revolution. There lingers little doubt that if rioters ever besieged the palace, the sledgehammer of the army would fall upon them.

Second, the Hashemite monarchy has brassbound control over the JAF, mirroring its grip on foreign policy. Excepting for the Arab Nationalist–inspired grumbling of the mid-1950s and a small mutiny involving the 40th Armored Brigade in 1974, the JAF has never rebuffed the palace. Professional norms of loyalty permeate its internal culture and training programs, and the political affinity between state and soldier is popularly enshrined in lavish royal ceremonies and commemorative holidays. The frequent public appearances by which King Hussein (r. 1953–1999) and King Abdullah (r. 1999–present) have donned military garb also symbolize this connection. To foreclose internal politicization, JAF personnel also cannot vote in elections and are otherwise discouraged from openly discussing political issues. For all these reasons, the JAF poses no threat of coup mongering against the monarchy.[24] It was telling that when King Abdullah rounded up his half-brother, former crown prince Hamzah, and a dozen other alleged conspirators in a palace crackdown during April 2021, he assigned the army to do the work.

Jordan, then, exemplifies the sort of civil-military relations that situate the armed forces not as servants of revolutionary parties and tinpot dictators but instead as handmaidens of political order under firm guidance of a royal center.[25] The organizational signs of monarchical control are evident in how JAF priorities are legislated. There is no functional Ministry of Defense; since the 1970 Black September civil conflict against Palestinian militant groups, the prime minister has held the dual (and meaningless) position of defense minister. Neither the prime minister nor elected parliamentarians can investigate military affairs such as the JAF's budget, arms procurements, or operations. Sensitive topics like manpower and strategy are debated only in the palace or within JAF command; so too are issues related to security assistance and foreign aid. Programmatic priorities, including technological needs and weaponry requests, are concocted through internal consultations between JAF command, high-level auditors, the royal palace, and Western representatives. Military expenditures, much like GID and the Interior Ministry's spending, remain shrouded from popular scrutiny, with the parliament only knowing the top-line JAF budget rather than itemized breakdowns (such as, for instance, what portion of military spending is devoted to actual equipment versus retiree pensions).[26]

While most Jordanians do not know how the JAF operates, more clear is how costly it has been. As Table 11.1 shows, since 1965, military and security spending (which includes the police) has seldom dipped below 30 percent of the government's total budget and as recently as 2015 consumed nearly 40 percent. As the next subsection describes, such steep expenditures have a purpose beyond equipping soldiers for combat, for the JAF is as much a welfarist institution as it is a coercive one.

Table 11.1 The Costs of Coercion in Jordan, 1965–2020 (in Jordanian dinars, millions)

Year	Military and Security (total[a] [JAF])	Total Public Spending	Military and Security as Percentage of Total Public Spending
1965	22.2 (18.8)	35.8	62.0
1970	38.1 (33.1)	59.0	64.6
1975	58 (48.3)	125.7	46.1
1980	140 (118.2)	336.1	41.7
1985	229.5 (190.2)	542.5	42.3
1990	263.2 (205)	841.4	31.3
1995	400.9 (296)	1,225.2	32.7
2000	631.8 (531.2)	2,187.1	28.9
2005	973.4 (698.8)	3,181.8	30.6
2010	2,215.4 (1,699.3)	5,055.2	43.8
2015	2,765.7 (1,987.5)	7,045.0	39.3
2020	2,633.2 (1,390.4)	9,606.9	27.4

Source: Central Bank of Jordan, *Annual Statistical Bulletin*, various years; General Budget Department, *Summary of General Budget*, various years.

Note: a. Includes reported official expenditures for JAF and all policing agencies under the Interior Ministry but not the GID, whose budget is not publicly disclosed.

Welfarism Through Militarism

The second reality is economic. The JAF has long been one of Jordan's biggest welfarist agencies, designed to enmesh tribal constituencies with financial and social benefits. Starting in the colonial dawn of the 1920s and 1930s, military service brought not only salaries to Transjordanian recruits but also a host of other targeted services, including education, food relief, housing, and health care. Such material provisions proved a lifeline to many precarious tribal communities, both Bedouin and settled alike. Officer promotions and command positions were allocated to candidates from leading tribes, a careful balancing game to assuage the demands of competing Transjordanian groups. Through its training and education, the Jordanian army in the colonial period hence helped create a distinctive national identity for the new kingdom's tribal residents, one that saw military service to the crown as the ultimate expression of citizenship.[27]

These early policies remained entrenched following Jordan's independence in 1946, as the JAF evolved from the Arab Legion. Thereafter, the story of the JAF is also one of social reconfiguration, in which militarization continued interweaving the lives and productivity of many Transjordanians into the state.[28] While the entire public sector, including the mushrooming civil service, served as an ethnocratic shelter for Transjordanian labor, it was army personnel who often guided economic policies. For instance, the regime made concerted efforts to more closely appeal to tribal interests after the Black September civil war and subsequent fears of Palestinian rebellion. Among its innovations was the creation of the Ministry of Supply in 1974, which instituted basic price controls for food, petrol, and other necessities.[29] While universal measures like wheat and fuel subsidies benefited the entire populace, such initiatives intended to first maintain the modest purchasing power of tribal families against then raging inflation. For many Transjordanian communities, particularly in rural areas where old modes of Bedouin pastoralism and subsistence cultivation were no longer viable, military employment remained a basic means of livelihood. Military patronage covered almost every aspect of these communities' well-being: cheap foodstuffs ensured sufficient caloric intake, specialized housing gave secure quarters, educational funds allowed for some upward mobility, and medical services became so well-equipped that military hospitals had superior equipment to most private clinics in the civilian sector.

Such welfarism was, and remains, multigenerational and lifelong. Most JAF personnel need only attain sixteen years of service to qualify for their pensions, which the king frequently raises in times of economic distress; in addition, military benefits such as health care continue to be available to veteran families long after their service is over. More targeted benefits also abound. As a quotidian example, tourists passing through Amman's Queen Alia International Airport will find that every official airport taxi is driven by a veteran, as military retirees enjoy a monopoly on this service. At the same time, such domestic protectionism has spawned very sticky redistributive preferences among tribal communities, which have long seen employment within state institutions like the JAF as a matter of entitlement. Thus, in the late 2000s, when King Abdullah's neoliberal policies had succeeded in privatizing a considerable number of state-owned enterprises while pruning the bloated public sector, hundreds of military retirees protested to reprimand the regime for seemingly violating its social contract with its tribal base.[30] Indeed, wider discomfiture among Transjordanians over the king's embrace of market-oriented economics over traditional state-led development partly explains the burst of grassroots activism seen in many tribal communities since the Arab Spring.[31]

Growing fissures between tribal constituencies and the monarchy, however, obscure the material realities that still tie Transjordanians to the regime and state. Today, over 250,000 Transjordanian men are military pensioners. This, added to the roughly 110,000 active-duty personnel, means that more than a quarter of all Transjordanian males alive today in Jordan have served in uniform. The number becomes starker when accounting for employees of the intelligence directorate and policing agencies. In 2020, out of Jordan's 1.38 million citizens with registered formal jobs, over 210,000 drew salaries from the JAF, the GID, and the Interior Ministry's civil police and gendarmerie.[32] This means that out of all formally employed Jordanian males (including Palestinians) at the start of the coronavirus pandemic, *nearly one in five made a living by soldiering, policing, or spying for the state.* If we assume that Palestinians compose two-thirds of this formal labor force, reflecting their overall demographic majority, then the more startling figure is that almost half of all Transjordanian men with registered jobs still work for institutions that specialize in the use of violence. By contrast, virtually no Palestinian Jordanians serve in these institutions—a product of the anti-Palestinian chauvinism that inundated political discourse after Black September, which also extirpated most Palestinian employment in the public sector. Modest plans unveiled in 2020 to open conscription in the JAF to all citizens will not change this, as the new policy is little more than a short-term effort to curb skyrocketing youth unemployment through temporary work rather than permanently diversifying the JAF's ranks.

A final wrinkle related to the JAF bears mention—namely, its tentacular extension into economic and social life. For instance, Army Day, which falls on June 10, is among Jordan's most revered national holidays; never mind that it celebrates not the combat prowess of the Jordanian military over the past century of the kingdom's existence but rather the start of the 1916 Great Arab Revolt, which predates the creation of Jordan, the arrival of the Hashemites to Amman, and thus the inception of the JAF itself. As another example, much as the Public Security Directorate runs its own terrestrial radio station (Amen FM), the JAF funds its own radio broadcasting branch, including FM stations like Bliss, Hala, and the sensibly named Jaysh (Arabic for *army*). Criticizing the JAF is expressly forbidden by Jordanian law, constituting a red line whose sensitivity is exceeded only by the lèse-majesté rules protecting the monarchy itself.

Insulated from public scrutiny, the military under King Abdullah has branched out to help create a small but profitable defense industry, tying together a cryptic web of foreign suppliers and local middlemen.[33] One outcome is the King Abdullah II Design and Development Bureau, created in 1999, which sells small arms and war matériel to regional buyers like Iraq and the Gulf kingdoms. Another is the King Abdullah Special Operations Training Center, built partly with American funding, which sells counterterrorism training services to private clients and foreign militaries.[34] Real estate development has also loomed large. Mawared, a secretive state-owned firm created in 2001 to manage army-owned lands, has piloted some of Amman's most glamorous megaprojects, such as the $5 billion 'Abdali Boulevard luxury corridor.[35] Mawared has seen its share of controversy, including the 2011 arrest of a former director on charges of corruption, but it has also reaped immense profits, which quietly accrue to the subset of military and regime elites assigned to manage its portfolio.

The JAF's imbrication into these networks of social production and capital accumulation go hand in hand with its rising prominence in the side business of military outsourcing. For decades, several Gulf kingdoms have hired the Jordanian military and, to a lesser extent, the gendarmerie to supplement their indigenous militaries and police ranks. The Gulf armies "hold Jordanian soldiers in the highest regard" given their reputation for "solid training, professionalism, and discipline," and they either advise local forces or else serve as contract soldiers.[36] For political reasons, Jordan likely understates the extent to which its personnel have served in some Gulf states, which pay handsomely for their services. In December 2014, for instance, a Jordanian gendarme was killed in Bahrain in a purported bombing attack.[37]

The preceding analysis has blunt ramifications for how security assistance should be read in the Jordanian context. The JAF is central to Hashemite rule in Jordan. Discussions about US foreign aid should therefore take into account how equipping, training, and financing this military apparatus has far-reaching political and economic consequences. From the Jordanian perspective, the goal of procuring Western security assistance is not to field a sophisticated war-making machine but rather to guarantee that the entire militarized ecology of its political order stays solvent and functional.

The Ends of US Security Assistance

The United States has served as Jordan's predominant patron and donor since 1957, when the Dwight Eisenhower administration replaced the fading British.[38] While the alliance has waxed and waned over the decades, the post–Cold War era has seen Jordan situate itself as an unapologetic US client state, partly through its peace treaty with Israel and partly because it has furthered the ends of American war making in the region. For example, after 9/11, the kingdom participated in the US-led War on Terror through extraordinary renditions and other counterterrorist programs. It facilitated the invasion of Iraq in 2003. During the Syrian civil war, Jordan hosted not only the multinational military coalition against

ISIS but also the corruption-ridden, Central Intelligence Agency (CIA)–led Timber Sycamore program, which funneled weapons and training to Syrian rebels through Jordanian intermediaries. Since 2010, the United States has also conducted an expensive, if perfunctory, military training exercise in Jordan—Eager Lion—which rates as the largest annual American noncombat exercise in the Middle East.[39]

Now, hence, Jordan reaps deep sustenance from Washington. Unlike some of America's other strategic Arab allies, such as Saudi Arabia and Egypt, Jordan almost never garners criticism from either Congress or the White House, regardless of which political party holds power. US policymakers support Jordan on a bipartisan basis, repeating all the neo-Orientalist tropes invoked earlier in this chapter.[40] Under the current US-Jordanian Memorandum of Understanding (2018–2022), Jordan receives a baseline of $1.275 billion in aid annually. Of this, over $850 million is typically allocated as economic assistance, of which the biggest part is direct budgetary grants—in State Department parlance, Economic Support Fund (ESF) payments—that serve as cash revenues for the Jordanian government.[41] These allow a perennially broke Jordanian treasury to meet state expenditures, including the JAF's upkeep. For instance, in 2010 the United States provided $460.9 million in ESF, a sum equivalent to nearly 20 percent of the JAF's budget; in 2020 Washington furnished nearly $1.1 billion in ESF, equal to a staggering 55.6 percent of Jordan's military expenditures. While the numbers vary, the magnitude does not: the United States bankrolls a political regime whose perennial flirtation with insolvency partly stems from its gigantic defense-related outlays, but which can sidestep fiscal calamity thanks to American dollars.

Outside economic aid, Jordan currently receives around $350 million to $400 million in conventional military assistance from the US annually—a volume set to increase in the near future, thanks to a new seven-year aid agreement inked by the two countries in September 2022. For decades, the largest element of American military assistance has consisted of weaponry and equipment transferred on a grant, credit, or occasionally commercial basis (via the Foreign Military Financing, Foreign Military Sales, and Excess Defense Articles programs). As a result, much of the JAF's combat-ready gear (e.g., F-16 fighter jets, Black Hawk helicopters, field electronics, rocket launchers, surveillance equipment, and infantry weaponry) comes from the US arsenal.[42] Other security components include the International Military Education and Training program, which has brought thousands of JAF officers to the United States, as well as subsidies for specialized programs, such as counterterrorism, crisis mitigation, and combat readiness (the latter of which is vividly portrayed by John Zavage's Chapter 15). Perhaps the most understated aspect of US support has been border defense: Jordan's irregular boundaries with Syria and Iraq, long seen as indefensible, have been secured with a US-funded and Raytheon-built border-security system. Small but notable military-to-military engagements also abound. For example, since 2004 the Pentagon has facilitated cooperation between the Royal Jordanian Air Force and the Colorado National Guard, while quietly providing some funding to allow JAF troops to carry out UN peacekeeping operations abroad.

Signaling the intensifying of this bilateral partnership, the 2021 US-Jordanian Defense Pact formalized the increasingly broad slice of sovereign rights that Amman has transferred to Washington since the 1996 Status-of-Forces Agreement. The pact not only provided US military personnel visa-free entry rights into the kingdom but also legalized the transfer of territory for the prepositioning of US forces. Essentially the kingdom has been cleared to become a giant terrestrial aircraft carrier in the heart of the Mashriq, which could serve as a major hub of future US war making. To that end, the kingdom is open for military business: since "Western military personnel will have a greater likelihood of operating inside Jordan," one practitioner's guide for visiting soldiers states, they should know that "the JAF is a well-trained and educated force," as well as a "gracious host" that will make their time in Jordan a "rewarding" one.[43]

What Capacity? What Goals?

In official American policy discussions, the doctrine of security assistance is frequently predicated upon the standard aim of building partner capacity so that the JAF can become a more proficient military. The JAF needs to develop more operative capabilities to secure Jordan from external threats and mitigate regional conflicts, and Washington's aid squares that circle. And indeed, at a granular level, the experiences of some American officers who have worked with JAF personnel suggest such help has been quite successful. Zavage's chapter in this book, for instance, describes a very positive live-fire training exercise in which American officers worked fastidiously to nurture a "warrior ethos" in Jordanian troops, where basic soldierly virtues like courage and determination were on full display in realistic combat scenarios.

The problem is that while Jordanian military forces may exhibit impressive readiness and skills at the level of individual troops, there is little evidence that at an aggregate scale they can be an effective national fighting force. Western perceptions of the JAF stem more from a positive reputation shrouded in historical memory than from objective, empirical measurements of battlefield success. But when unpacked, that reputation becomes extremely checkered. In terms of interstate conflict, the Jordanian army's lone unambiguous victory came in the 1948 Arab-Israeli War, when the British-led Arab Legion captured the West Bank and East Jerusalem from Israel. It lost those territories in the 1967 Arab-Israeli War; both before and after that conflict, the JAF also fought indeterminate border skirmishes with Israel. It did emerge victorious in the 1970 Black September civil war, but only with serious losses—and that was a domestic campaign waged on home soil against disunited Palestinian guerillas who had far fewer numbers and cruder arms.[44] By then, with neighboring militaries far outpacing it in either quality (i.e., Israel) or quantity (i.e., Syria, Iraq), the JAF settled into a posture that still holds today. The army "stands no chance" of resisting any invasion launched by a hostile country and so operates with a defensive doctrine that seeks to deter—or at least delay—any foreign aggression long enough until the United States can intervene to save the monarchy.[45]

In recent years, some of Jordan's most vaunted security successes have occurred not because of American assistance but because the United States has entirely appropriated the task from the JAF. For instance, it was not until 2015, when the Raytheon-built border defense system came online, that the JAF could finally claim a secure monopoly over the kingdom's craggy borders with Syria and Iraq. American assessments of how the kingdom dealt with the regional troubles wrought by the Syrian civil war—accepting nearly a million refugees, for instance, and participating in a multinational campaign to eradicate ISIS—emphasize US-led efforts to manage the conflict through an American-led forward command structure, relegating the Jordanians to little more than subordinates who served the proverbial tea for their Western superiors.[46] Areas where Jordanian authorities had more direct command, such as counterterrorist interdiction, show a more checkered record. Security forces halted numerous ISIS-inspired terrorist attacks, but the country was also rocked by a spate of militant bombings, public shootouts, and arms-smuggling discoveries, resulting in the JAF and GID blaming one another for these defense failures.[47]

Moreover, in the post–Cold War era, the JAF has projected its power outward only in tiny windows and always as part of multinational coalitions. For instance, Jordanian soldiers have participated in numerous UN peacekeeping duties, but these have been partly funded by the United States—and in any case, they have little bearing on the JAF's operational capabilities as a combat force. (Over 125 countries now lend their soldiers to UN peacekeeping missions, including Djibouti, Togo, and Papua New Guinea.) It quietly contributed nearly 1,000 troops to NATO's security force in post-Taliban Afghanistan, but even normally sanguine American observers conceded that those units had "mixed results" and struggled with basic combat procedures—an uneasy outcome chalked up to the absence of a well-trained, noncommissioned officer corps within the JAF.[48] Jordanian special forces units also deployed in Syria and Libya against ISIS, but the results of those excursions are unknown.

The Jordanian air force, for its part, shows a similarly inauspicious record. One of its first operations came in 1962, when Jordan sent a squadron of planes to help the flailing monarchy of North Yemen during its civil conflict. That had tragicomic consequences; several pilots defected to Egypt, the remaining force proved ineffectual, and the cost of that entire operation upended that year's national economic development plan.[49] Apart from fleeting involvement in the Saudi-led intervention in Yemen, its last confirmed combat missions came through air strikes against ISIS units in Syria throughout 2014 and 2015, conducted with ammunition and funds consigned by the United States and with its strike jets escorted by American fighters. The campaign against ISIS coincidentally also revealed how little such paltry contributions mattered to Western strategists, who instead valued Jordan as a command center rather than for what the JAF could accomplish as the leading Arab edge of a multinational alliance.

Even more startling than the JAF's spotty record of military action are the internal conclusions quietly murmured by US observers in previous years behind closed doors and far from the public limelight of Congress. One 1988 CIA assessment complained that "management problems, corruption, poor planning, and insufficient technical expertise" haunted "all levels of the military."[50] The coast guard was a "case study in ineptitude," with many sailors proving unable to swim or operate their vessels.[51] A 1977 State Department cable likewise concluded that US military assistance should not revolve around making the JAF a credible, legitimate army—which was impossible—but instead focus on very basic goals, such as enhancing troop morale. The latter, of course, still required American dollars and arms so that the monarchy could satisfy its military payrolls and keep its soldiers happy.[52]

In sum, these observations suggest that the JAF cannot be what some American military strategists envision, because its institutional purpose remains that of a royal constabulary that protects an autocratic regime and sustains its tribal supporters. Converting it to a proficient, twenty-first-century assemblage of combatants would mean remaking the Jordanian military itself and prioritizing external security functions over its internal policing and welfarist roles. Such an outcome will not transpire without corollary shifts within Jordanian political order, which may require a diminished role for the Hashemite monarchy and the rise of a genuinely democratic—and hence elected—government that oversees the security sector.

Conclusion

No matter the era, the Middle East news cycle frequently draws Jordan into its maws. In summer 2022, for instance, King Abdullah evinced support for a Middle East–style NATO military alliance, following secret meetings with Israeli, Saudi, Qatari, Emirati, and Bahraini officials that sketched out what a US-guided regional defense platform might entail.[53] The JAF would ostensibly be a proud member of such a project, which would further justify the profuse influx of American security assistance and will continue to broadcast its periphrastic lexicon about building partner capacity, strengthening operational capabilities, and ensuring combat readiness among Jordanian troops.

Yet, in practice, US support simply incites a self-perpetuating cycle of foreign patronage, deepening authoritarianism, and military subsistence. Washington cares less about whether the JAF becomes an effective and capable military and more about whether a stable Jordan can support wider strategic goals. That American security assistance has become embedded in this snake pit of geopolitical theater is hardly exceptional to Jordan, of course; Aram Nerguizian's Chapter 5, for example, parses out how US support for the Lebanese Armed Forces has become "proxified" as the latest front in the region-wide conflict against Iran. What *is* exceptional to Jordan is how wide the gap appears between the official doctrine of building partner capacity versus the reality of merely keeping alive an authoritarian client state. The JAF's long-standing function since the Arab-Israeli wars has been not to step onto any battlefield but to protect Hashemite rule at home by defending public order and delivering economic and social goods to tribal constituencies. These are the organizational tasks of the JAF, inscribed into its historical origins and expressed in its vast institutional presence throughout Jordanian society. And these, ultimately, are the true ends of US security assistance.

What might change this state of affairs? One political variable is whether Jordan ever transitions to a more democratic regime. In that case, the JAF and other elements of the Jordanian security sector would no longer need to police society or keep tribal communities tied to a ruling monarchy. But democracy in Jordan would also pose an inconvenience to US grand strategy, which requires a reliably pro-Western autocracy in the heart of the Levant that willingly houses Western troops, defends American strategic interests, expedites future war making, and keeps peace with Israel.

For US policymakers, however, there exists a danger to anchoring security assistance purely to preserving the stability of an authoritarian ally. Consider prominent cases of other US client states, such as Pahlavi-era Iran, El Salvador under José Duarte, South Vietnam, and the post-9/11 Afghan state prior to 2021. In those contexts, the mantra of building partner capacity was repeatedly invoked by American policymakers too. When these regimes collapsed, all the arms and training invested in client militaries also melted away, and new reactionary governments had little appetite for cultivating the same alliance with Washington as their predecessors. Such lessons of the past remain regnant as ever in a Middle East still defined by contentious waves of popular protests, economic disarray, and demands for democracy.

Notes

1. US Department of State, "Fact Sheet."
2. Dowd, "Jordan."
3. Wright, "Beyond ISIS Turmoil."
4. US Agency for International Development, *Jordan*, 7.
5. Schenker, "The Growing Islamic State Threat in Jordan."
6. Davenport, "State Repression and Political Order"; DeMeritt, "The Strategic Use of State Repression and Political Violence."
7. Quinlivan, "Coup-Proofing"; Greitens, *Dictators and Their Secret Police*.
8. See, e.g., de Mesquita et al., *The Logic of Political Survival*; Magaloni, "Credible Power-Sharing and the Longevity of Authoritarian Rule"; Gerschewski, "The Three Pillars of Stability"; Albertus, Fenner, and Slater, *Coercive Distribution*.
9. Yom, "Bread, Fear, and Coalitional Politics in Jordan."
10. Bellin, "The Robustness of Authoritarianism in the Middle East."
11. Brand, *Jordan's Inter-Arab Relations*. For the converse example of Tunisia, whose more dilapidated and underfunded military institution proved unwilling to defend a republican autocracy facing mass protests during the Arab Spring, see Bou Nassif, "A Military Besieged."
12. Tell, "Jordanian Security Sector Governance."
13. "Jordanians Overwhelmingly Have More Trust in Army, Police." It should be noted, however, that the military, much like the intelligence and policing institutions, is also protected by ironclad laws that forbid public criticism of its operations and role.
14. Moore, "A Political-Economic History of Jordan's General Intelligence Directorate."

15. The GID and the Interior Ministry's policing agencies also receive American assistance, albeit either in covert form (e.g., the GID's close relationship with the CIA) or through civilian channels (e.g., police equipment, counterterrorism training).
16. Vatikiotis, *Politics and the Military in Jordan*; Heller, "Politics and the Military in Iraq and Jordan."
17. See, e.g., El-Edroos, *The Hashemite Arab Army*.
18. Axelrod, "Tribesmen in Uniform"; Dann, *King Hussein and the Challenge of Arab Radicalism*, 13.
19. "King Abdullah Inherits a Strong Fighting Force."
20. This quoted—and appropriate—phrase comes from Barakat and Leber, *Fortress Jordan*.
21. Tal, *Politics, the Military, and National Security in Jordan*.
22. Murad, *Al-dawr al-siyaasi lil-jaysh al-urduni*.
23. For more on Black September, see Nevo, "September 1970 in Jordan"; Hattar, *Dhikriyat 'an ma'rika aylul*.
24. Ryan, "The Armed Forces and the Arab Uprisings."
25. Cook, *Ruling but Not Governing*; Bou Nassif, *Endgames*.
26. US Embassy–Amman, "Re: Transparency of Budgets/Military Spending."
27. Massad, *Colonial Effects*.
28. Tell, *The Social and Economic Origins of Monarchy in Jordan*.
29. Baylouny, "Militarizing Welfare," 291.
30. Tell, "Early Spring in Jordan."
31. Yom, "Tribal Politics in Contemporary Jordan."
32. Figures from the Jordanian Department of Statistics.
33. Marshall, "Jordan's Military-Industrial Sector."
34. Schuetze, "Simulating, Marketing, and Playing War."
35. Hourani, "Urbanism and Neoliberal Order," 642–644.
36. Barany, "Foreign Contract Soldiers in the Gulf."
37. "Gendarmerie Officer Killed in Bahrain."
38. Yom, *From Resilience to Revolution*, 165–170.
39. Yoke, "Eager Lion Exercise a 'Keystone Event' in US-Jordan Partnership."
40. See, e.g., Riedel, *Jordan and America*.
41. There are many other ways the United States finances the Jordanian state aside from economic aid. For instance, the US Treasury has backed several multibillion-dollar offerings of Jordanian Eurobonds on international markets, thereby allowing its government to secure new streams of external capital while shielding it from the nominal risk of defaulting on these debts.
42. Britain is the second-largest supplier of military hardware to Jordan.
43. Deegan and Moreno, "A Military Practitioner's Guide to Jordan."
44. Plapinger, "Insurgent Recruitment Practices and Combat Effectiveness."
45. Bligh, "The Jordanian Army," 17.
46. Cole, "Learning and Innovation," 74–91.
47. Yom and Sammour, "Counterterrorism and Youth Radicalization in Jordan."
48. Rank and Saba, "Building Partnership Capacity 101," 27.
49. Shair, *Out of the Middle East*, 133.
50. Central Intelligence Agency, *Jordan's Military Modernization*.
51. Ibid.
52. US Embassy–Amman, "Assessment of US Security Assistance Programs."
53. Echols, "Wait, Is There Really a New US-Led Defense Alliance in the Middle East?"

12
Security Assistance and Public Support for Arab Militaries

Lindsay J. Benstead

A THEME OF THIS BOOK IS THAT SECURITY ASSISTANCE HAS THE POTENtial to contribute to improved governance but is unlikely to democratize. In this chapter, I explore the relationship between the perceived effectiveness of the military and demand for democracy. The evidence suggests that, while US security assistance strengthens authoritarianism in recipient countries, it also contributes to building institutional trust among citizens, an outcome that could support democratic consolidation in the future.

Despite decades of US engagement with and support of military institutions in the Middle East and North Africa (MENA), we know little about the factors that shape support for Arab militaries across societies with different sectarian dynamics and relationships with the United States and other external actors. Studies of Arab public opinion toward international relations and security assistance have been limited, despite their theoretical importance and interest to policymakers and the general public.[1] Several studies consider the relationship between citizens' perceived insecurity, confidence in the military, and support for democracy.[2] Other research examines societal polarization when it comes to views of US influence in their countries,[3] but few studies shed light on Arab citizens' views of their security providers.

Drawing on data from the Arab Barometer Wave IV surveys conducted in seven countries in 2016, this chapter explores how individual and contextual-level factors shape confidence in the military and in turn relate to confidence in having freer elections. Extending a consequence-based approach, I argue that citizens' views of the military are shaped by the context in which they live, including their assessments of how their country's armed forces impact them and their social group. When citizens regard the military as contributing to their well-being, relative to other institutions, they will develop greater confidence in the armed forces.

The findings are consistent with this approach. I find that citizens in countries with stronger armed forces—due in part to US security assistance—and those in countries in which protests occurred, regardless of the role the armed forces played, are more supportive of the military. This may be because heightened civil unrest causes citizens to be concerned about instability and increases their willingness to look to the armed forces to maintain order.

Consistently with other research, higher confidence in the military also supports greater confidence in having a democratic system of government. This suggests that as a foreign policy tool, US military assistance has diverse impacts on the societies receiving aid and that some of these impacts are consistent with US national security interests. It also suggests that the armed forces have positioned themselves to benefit both from regional insecurity over the past few decades and from the Arab Spring protests, as shown by growing confidence in the military and declining support for civilian institutions and democracy.[4]

What Explains Support for the Military? Consequence-Based Approach

A consequence-based approach sees attitudes toward democracy as shaped by beliefs about the political, economic, and religious consequences of democracy, including what sectarian or national groups might gain or lose if freer elections were implemented.[5] Support for the military is a key dimension of institutional trust that develops as a result of perceiving that the armed forces deliver on keeping the peace. Like support for democracy, attitudes toward the military are not determined by unchanging culture but by the contextual circumstances in which citizens live and by their assessments of how the military affects them and their identities.

Since the Arab Barometer began fielding in 2006, there has been a general decline in confidence in civilian institutions and in democracy.[6] The military enjoys higher trust than any other state institution asked about in the Arab Barometer survey.[7] To be sure, many citizens have incentives to falsify their preferences by overreporting their confidence in the military.[8] But even overreporting is unlikely to account for the discrepancy between support for militaries as compared to that for civilian institutions such as legislatures and political parties. Strong support for militaries may reflect their being perceived as more effective than other institutions, or, in a more manipulative interpretation, their undertaking public relations campaigns effectively.

Measuring Confidence in the Military

Yet confidence in the military fluctuates across time and also varies substantially within and across countries. Overall, depending on the context, it has remained constant in some countries and declined or increased in others.

A consequence-based theory allows for a nuanced understanding of how winners and losers—and more or less vulnerable segments of society—perceive the military and allow for both individual and contextual factors to be considered.[9] Not all citizens benefit equally from the public good provided by the military. Those who work in the army or in the government may benefit directly from rents. Religious minorities may benefit from feelings of increased security, or they may feel excluded or threatened by the military. For instance, Gürsoy finds that political affiliation is important for trust in the military in Turkey.[10] Social identity, in the form of group identity, also shapes attitudes toward the military. And women may be more prone to feelings of insecurity, leading them to have more confidence in the institutions that provide security. For example, women have been found to have higher anxiety in seven Arab and Western countries (except the United Kingdom) as measured on the Arabic Scale of Death Anxiety.[11]

Individual-Level Hypotheses

Accordingly, I hypothesize that citizens who are advantaged by the political economy will have higher confidence in the military such that

> H1: Higher government satisfaction will be positively related to confidence in the military.
> H2: Citizens who work in the military and in the government will have higher support for the military than those who do not work or work in other sectors.

H3: Those with higher incomes will have higher support for the military.

Citizens' views of the military, while they may be shaped by specific interactions with security services (e.g., at a protest), are shaped by how citizens believe their well-being is affected by the military. Citizens' assessments of their well-being are also shaped by their group identity, especially in countries with diverse sectarian divides such as Lebanon, where major changes in the balance of power between the groups could radically alter not only economic and political outcomes but also individuals' security. Even in more homogenous cases like Tunisia, many citizens identify as Islamist or secular and are more or less affluent. These differences relate to how reforms in the army could affect them and their group because the military provides a critical link to a past era of stability under the authoritarian regime of Zine El Abidine Ben Ali and Habib Bourghiba.

I hypothesize that religious minorities, women, and those who support the regime (rather than the opposition) are more likely to be more supportive of the military than those who are from the dominant group, men, and political Islam because the former have most to lose from political instability. Those who support the opposition are less likely to support the military such that

H4: Those who support non-Islamist parties will have higher confidence in the military.
H5: Those with anti-American attitudes will have lower confidence in the military.

Those who are from groups that are well represented in the military or protected by it will be more supportive of the military than those who are from marginalized sects:

H6: Christian and Druze minorities—and the Sunni majorities—will be more supportive of the military than will the Shi'a.

Even though the Shi'a in Lebanon are well represented in the Lebanese Defense Forces (LDF), they may be less supportive of the LDF than Christians and Druze because the Shi'a also look to Hezbollah to protect their interests.[12]

Moreover, those who are from socially more marginalized groups will be more confident in the military than those who are not:

H7: Those in rural areas will be more supportive of the military than those in urban areas.
H8: Females will have more confidence in the military than males.
H9: Older generations will have more confidence in the military than younger generations.

Contextual Hypotheses

Citizens' views of their armed forces are likely related to the perceived capacity of the military and its role in recent protests, which in turn are shaped by the degree of US military assistance.[13] According to Nicholas Lotito,[14] the high level of resources enjoyed by the military contributes to high public trust in military institutions. US military assistance to the Arab countries has been substantial over the past few decades and varies across countries. US military support—which is high in Egypt, Jordan, and Lebanon, moderate in Morocco and Tunisia, and low in Algeria and Palestine—may enhance social polarization across social groups. While citizens have incentives to falsify their preferences, these findings nevertheless underscore that support for the military is high in the Arab world. Indeed, many prefer military rule to democracy, not only in the Arab world, where insecurity is substantial, but in other regions as well.[15]

How the military intervenes at unstable times is also important. Dana Alkurd shows that confidence in the military in Algeria and Sudan depended on domestic conditions, including the military's reaction to protests.[16] During and in the years following the outbreak of protests in Tunisia in December 2010, protests occurred in most Arab countries, and when they did, the armed forces were in a position to side with either the protesters or the regime.[17] Seeing the military acting to maintain order strengthens citizens' confidence in the military. This translates to institutional trust and supports confidence in freer elections.

H10: Citizens in countries whose military supported the people over the regime will be more supportive of the military than those in countries with limited protests or whose military sided with the regime.
H11: Citizens in countries with militaries that receive more US support will be more supportive of the military than those who do not.

A consequence-based approach also predicts that those with greater confidence in their security forces will also have higher confidence in democracy. Mark Tessler and Ebru Altinoglu found that trust in institutions of order in Turkey was positively related to support for democracy.[18]

> H12: Higher confidence in the military will be positively related to stronger demand for democracy.

The Data

To test these hypotheses, I use data from the Arab Barometer (Wave IV).[19] The surveys were conducted by local teams using samples that are representative of the national populations. Because the dependent variable examined in this chapter, confidence in the military, was not asked in every country in Wave V, at the time the most recent wave, I use Wave IV (2016) for the regression analysis in this chapter. The countries included are Morocco, Algeria, Tunisia, Egypt, Jordan, Palestine, and Lebanon.[20]

These cases are varied in terms of contextual factors, including the degree of US support for the military and the role of the military in protests since the Arab Spring. For example, Jordan and Egypt enjoy a high level of bilateral assistance funds for their security sectors,[21] while Tunisia receives less direct funding but has long participated in training programs and is a non–North Atlantic Treaty Organization ally of the United States.[22]

Measurement

The dependent variables are support for the military and belief that democracy is a suitable form of government. To measure support for the military, I use an item measured on a four-point Likert scale: "I'm going to name a number of institutions. For each one, please tell me how much trust you have in them. The armed forces. A great deal, quite a lot, not much, and none at all."[23] To measure the belief that democracy is suitable, I use an eleven-point scale with the following prompt: "Suppose there was a scale from 0 to 10 measuring the extent to which democracy is suitable for your country, with 0 meaning that democracy is absolutely inappropriate for your country and 10 meaning that democracy is completely appropriate for your country. To what extent do you think democracy is appropriate for your country?"[24]

Individual-Level Variables

I include several individual-level factors. To measure government satisfaction, I use a similar scale with the following prompt: "Suppose that there was a scale from 0 to 10 to measure the extent of your satisfaction with the government, in which 0 means that you were absolutely unsatisfied with its performance and 10 means that you were completely satisfied. To what extent are you satisfied with the government's performance?"

To measure sector of employment, I used two questions asking respondents about their work and that of their spouses.[25] In the sample as a whole, 11 percent of families have a spouse working at a government ministry, while 3 percent have one in the army; 87 percent live in families in which neither spouse works in the army or a government ministry.[26]

Income is measured using the standardized income measure in the Arab Barometer, which dichotomizes lower and higher income in order to maximize response rates before later asking for more specificity. For example, in Lebanon, the question reads, "What is the total monthly income for all household members? Is it less than or greater than 500 US dollars?" To measure support for non-Islamist parties, I use an indicator measuring the respondent's preferences for religious or nonreligious parties: "Which of the following sentences is the closest to your point of view? Choose sentence 1 or sentence 2. First sentence: I prefer a religious political party over a nonreligious political party. Second sentence: I prefer a nonreligious political party over a religious political party. (1) I strongly agree with the first sentence. (2) I agree with the first sentence. (3) I agree with the second sentence. (4) I strongly agree with the second sentence."

To measure attitudes about the United States, I ask, "Irrespective of the foreign policy of their governments, would you say that most people from the following countries are very good people, good people, bad people, or very bad people? Agree/Disagree." While this is not a perfect measure, it is a reasonable proxy.

I also include a variable measuring religious identity: Sunni Muslim, Christian, Shi'a, and Druze/other. I include an indicator for whether the respondent is located in a rural or urban area and for gender. Age is measured in four categories: thirty years or younger, thirty-one to thirty-nine years, forty to forty-nine years, and fifty or more years. I include country-fixed effects and, in some models, indicators of the role that the military played in the Arab Spring protests and its level of assistance from the United States.

Contextual Variables

To measure US security assistance, I use average obligated funding from 2014 to 2019 in three levels. Assistance is low (less than $10 million per year) in Algeria, the Palestinian Territories, and Yemen.[27] Funding is moderate ($10 million to $250 million per year) in Bahrain, Kuwait, Libya, Morocco, Sudan (significant increase in 2019 to new government), and Tunisia. Funding is high (greater than $250 million per year) in Egypt, Iraq, Jordan, Israel, Lebanon, Saudi Arabia, Qatar, and the United Arab Emirates (Table 12.1).

As an example, Iraq has the most types of US assistance, with seven of the eight possible: training and education, tech support, matériel, advisory, US military presence, direct support, and military humanitarian assistance/disaster response (HA/DR; i.e., funds, supplies, construction, delivery of aid for the host-state civilian populace, and disaster relief). The only type of support that Iraq does not receive is military to military (mil-mil) (i.e., periodic visits by US military units for bilateral, multinational, or hosted unilateral exercise and training).[28]

To measure the role of the military in protests, I use Timothy Hazen's categorization of this involvement. There were minimal protests in the Palestinian Territories and Jordan. In Lebanon, Morocco, and Algeria, the military had a minimal role because the internal security forces were successful. In Egypt and Tunisia, the military was disloyal (Table 12.2).[29]

Table 12.3 summarizes the contextual factor—the level of US security assistance and the role of the military in the uprisings.

Descriptive Statistics

An analysis of the descriptive statistics finds that confidence in the military is highest in Jordan, followed by Tunisia, Morocco, and Egypt (Figure 12.1). Support for the military is lower in Lebanon, Algeria, and Palestine.

I told respondents, "I'm going to name a number of institutions. For each one, please tell me how much trust you have in them. The armed forces (the army). A great deal of trust (= 4); quite a lot of trust (= 3); not very much trust (= 2); no trust at all (= 1)." The highest level of trust in the national military is in Jordan, where 90 percent have a great deal of trust, followed by Tunisia, where 79 percent have a great deal of trust. Between 60 and 69 percent have a great deal of trust in Egypt, Lebanon, and Morocco, while only 45 percent in Algeria and 9 percent in Palestine have high trust.

Table 12.1 US Security Assistance to MENA States, 2019

State	Level of Support	Arms Transfers (1)[a]	Other Assistance	Total US Security Assistance	Training and Education	Tech Support	Matériel	Advisory	US Military Presence	Direct Support	Mil-Mil	Military HA/DR
Algeria	Low	$0.00	$1,825,570.00	$1,825,570.00	X							
Bahrain	Moderate	$10,000,000.00	$491,726.00	$10,491,726.00	X		X	X	X			
Egypt	High	$48,000,000.00	$1,009,322,963.00	$1,057,322,963.00	X	X	X	X				
Iran	None	$0.00	$0.00	$0.00								
Iraq	High	$0.00	$615,089,232.00	$615,089,232.00	X	X	X	X	X	X		X
Israel	High	$482,000,000.00	$3,295,820,273.00	$3,777,820,273.00	X	X	X	X			X	
Jordan	High	$25,000,000.00	$511,746,763.00	$536,746,763.00	X	X	X	X			X	X
Kuwait	Moderate	$7,000,000.00	$2,315,361.00	$9,315,361.00	X		X				X	
Lebanon	High	$60,000,000.00	$274,027,216.00	$334,027,216.00	X	X	X	X				X
Libya (GNA)	Moderate	$1,000,000.00	$25,303,973.00	$26,303,973.00	X							
Morocco	Moderate	$26,000,000.00	$19,055,934.00	$45,055,934.00	X	X	X	X			X	
Palestine (West Bank/Gaza)	Low	$0.00	$4,877,500.00	$4,877,500.00	X			X				

continues

Table 12.1 Continued

State	Level of Support	Arms Transfers (1)[a]	Other Assistance	Total US Security Assistance	Training and Education	Tech Support	Matériel	Advisory	US Military Presence	Direct Support	Mil-Mil	Military HA/DR
Qatar	High	$531,000,000.00	$79,396.00	$531,079,396.00	X	X		X	X		X	X
Saudi Arabia	High	$3,138,000,000.00	$621,528.00	$3,138,621,528.00	X	X	X	X	X		X	X
Sudan	Moderate	$0.00	$184,937,791.00	$184,937,791.00								
Tunisia	Moderate	$15,000,000.00	$125,697,864.00	$140,697,864.00	X	X	X	X			X	
Turkey	High	$128,000,000.00	$1,784,747.00	$129,784,747.00	X	X	X	X	X		X	
UAE	High	$383,000,000.00	$805,841.00	$383,805,841.00	X			X			X	
Yemen	Low[c]	$0.00	$2,481,639.00	$2,481,639.00	X			X		X[b]		X

Sources: Stockholm International Peace Research Institute 2018, 2019, SIPRI Arms Transfers Database, https://www.sipri.org/databases/armstransfers. Obligated USG funds for "peace and security" or "multisector-unspecified" in FY 2019. US Government 2020, ForeignAssistance.gov, US Government Foreign Assistance. Categories of assistance are derived from multiples sources, including ForeignAssistance.gov.

Notes: Level of Support (Average obligated funding 2014–2019): Low = <$10,000,000/yr; Moderate = $10,000,000–$250,000,000/yr; High = >$250,000,000/yr. Training and Education = Scholarship to the United States, multinational schools; US training teams in recipient state. Tech Support = Equipment expert familiarization, integration, troubleshooting. Matériel = Equipment and supplies. Advisory = Consultation on recipient state's unit, HQ, or system operation, effectiveness, and efficiency; defense reform assistance. US Military Presence = US military forces or headquarters based in/operating out of recipient state. Direct Support = Combat support or combat service support provided during recipient state operation(s). Mil-Mil = Periodic visits by US military units for bilateral, multinational, or hosted unilateral exercises and training. Military HA/DR = Funds, supplies, construction, delivery of aid for host state civilian populace; disaster relief provided by US military.

a. Includes direct transfers (US expense), receipt of US financing to purchase US weapons systems, and weapons purchased at recipient state expense.
b. Support to Saudi Arabia-led coalition not included in US security assistance to Yemen figures.
c. Figures do not include US support to Saudi-led coalition.

Table 12.2 Five Types of Military Responses During the Arab Spring

Disloyal	Fractured	Loyal	Minimal Role—Success of Internal Security Forces	Minimal Role—Limited Protests
Egypt, Tunisia	Libya, Yemen	Bahrain, Iraq	Algeria, Iran, Jordan, Kuwait, Lebanon, Morocco, Saudi Arabia, Iran	Israel, Palestine, Qatar, Turkey, UAE

Source: Hazen, "Explaining Middle Eastern and North African (MENA) Military Responses During the 2011–2012 Arab Uprisings," tab. 1 (abridged).

Table 12.3 Contextual Factors

Country	Arab Spring Transition	Role of Military in Arab Spring Protests	US Military Aid
Algeria	Substantial protests	Minimal role—success of internal security forces[a]	Low
Egypt	Regime change	Disloyal[b]	High
Jordan	No	Minimal role—limited protests[a]	High
Lebanon	Substantial protests	Minimal role—success of internal security forces[b]	High
Morocco	No	Minimal role—success of internal security forces[b]	Moderate
Palestine	No	Minimal role—limited protests[a]	Low
Tunisia	Regime change	Disloyal[b]	Moderate

Notes: a. Author's records.
b. Hazen, "Explaining Middle Eastern and North African (MENA) Military Responses During the 2011–2012 Arab Uprisings."

Support for democracy is highest in two countries with high confidence in the military: Morocco (7.15) and Jordan (6.51). That support for democracy is lowest in Tunisia (4.89) is striking because it has transitioned to a minimalist democracy and also has high confidence in the military (Figure 12.2). Countries falling in the middle of the spectrum on support for democracy are Lebanon (6.20) and Algeria (5.44), with Egypt (5.02) and Palestine (4.91) scoring on the lower end.

I asked respondents, "Suppose there was a scale from 0 to 10 measuring the extent to which democracy is suitable for your country, with 0 meaning that democracy is absolutely inappropriate for your country and 10 meaning that democracy is completely appropriate for your country. To what extent do you think democracy is appropriate for your country?" (In Lebanon the scale ranged from 1 to 10).

Confidence in the military is also higher in countries where the military was disloyal to the regime in support of the protesters than in countries where the internal security forces successfully diffused protesters or where there were limited protests ($p < .001$) (see Table 12.4).

Figure 12.1 Mean Confidence in the Army in Seven Countries (Wave IV, 2016–2017)

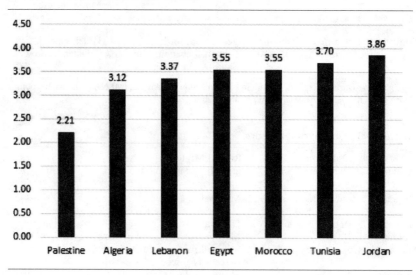

Figure 12.2 Mean Belief that Democracy Is Suitable in Seven Countries (Wave IV, 2016–2017)

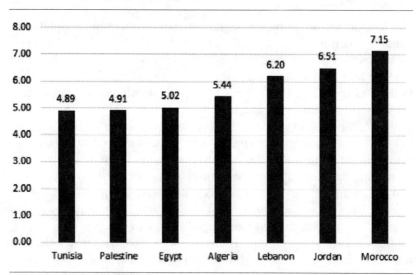

Table 12.4 Mean Confidence in the Armed Forces by Independent Variable

Government Satisfaction	Mean Confidence in Armed Forces
0 = absolutely none	2.95
1	2.96
2	3.08
3	3.22
4	3.25
5	3.45
6	3.51
7	3.57
8	3.59
9	3.62
10	3.78
	Pearson $\chi 2$ (30) = 711.2607[a]
Work sector of respondent and spouse	
Does not work in ministry or army	3.35
Works in army	3.20
Works in ministry	3.38
	Pearson $\chi 2$ (6) = 12.2893†
Income	
Low	3.37
High	3.32
	Pearson $\chi 2$ (3) = 45.7891[a]
Prefers secular parties	
Strongly prefers religious parties	3.31
Prefers religious parties	3.26
Prefers nonreligious parties	3.34
Strongly prefers nonreligious parties	3.49
	Pearson $\chi 2$ (9) = 102.9154[a]
Anti-American attitudes	
Strongly agree Americans are good people	3.39
Agree Americans are good people	3.36
Disagree Americans are good people	3.20
Strongly disagree Americans are good people	3.13
	Pearson $\chi 2$ (9) = 75.3515[a]
Religion	
Christian	3.33
Sunni Muslim	3.55
Shi'a Muslim	3.21
Druze	3.20
	Pearson $\chi 2$ (9) = 63.9544[a]
Residence	
Rural	3.45
Urban/refugee camp	3.29
	Pearson $\chi 2$ (3) = 52.232[a]
Sex	
Male	3.32
Female	3.37
	Pearson $\chi 2$ (3) = 12.0673[b]

continues

Table 12.4 Continued

Government Satisfaction	Mean Confidence in Armed Forces
Age	
Less than thirty years	3.24
Thirty to thirty-nine years	3.31
Forty to forty-nine years	3.37
Fifty years and older	3.46
	Pearson χ^2 (9) = 87.1034[a]
Country	
Algeria	3.12
Egypt	3.55
Jordan	3.86
Lebanon	3.37
Morocco	3.55
Palestine	2.21
Tunisia	3.70
	Pearson χ^2 (18) = 2.6e+03[a]
Military role	
Minimal protests	3.05
Internal security forces controlled protests	3.35
Army disloyal to regime/protected protesters	3.63
	Pearson χ^2 (6) = 573.2953[a]
US security assistance	
Low	2.67
Moderate	3.63
High	3.59
	Pearson χ^2 (6) = 1.7e+03[a]

Notes: a. $p < .001$.
b. $p < .01$.

At the individual level of analysis, higher government satisfaction is related to higher confidence in the government ($p < .001$), while work sector is not related. Those with higher incomes have lower confidence in the military ($p < .001$), while those who prefer nonreligious parties or have pro-American views are more supportive of the army ($p < .001$).

Across sects, the Druze followed by the Shi'a are the least supportive of the military, followed by Christians, with the Sunni Muslim respondents having the most confidence in the army ($p < .001$). Citizens who live in rural areas and females ($p < .01$) are more favorable toward the army, as are older citizens ($p < .001$).

Results and Discussion

I use ordered logistic regression for the models predicting higher confidence in the military, measured on a four-point Likert scale (models 1 to 4) and ordinary least squares regression in the model predicting support for democracy, measured on an eleven-point scale from 0 to 10 (model 5). Because of the small number of nations, the level 2 variance is not large enough for a mixed-level model. Due to the brevity of this chapter, I present pooled results.

Confidence in the Military

First, I present four models of higher confidence in the armed forces. I include measures of groups that are winners in a system with a stronger military and those who are threatened by—or may perceive themselves to be harmed by—strong armed forces. These models differ in terms of how the contextual factors are measured. Model 1 includes country-fixed effects to control for country-level variation in confidence in the military. This facilitates a direct cross-country comparison of overall levels controlling for other factors. Model 2 includes a variable measuring the role of the military in protests—that is, whether internal security forces diffused protests (= 2) or the army was disloyal to the regime and supported protesters (= 3). The comparison category is minimal protests (= 1). Model 3 includes a variable measuring whether the role of the United States in providing military aid is moderate (= 2) or high (= 3) compared to low (= 1). Finally, model 4 includes both the role of the military in protests and the level of US security assistance. The results, while similar across the models, show a few minor differences. The best-fitting model is model 1, which explains 18.6 percent of the variation in the dependent variable, followed by model 4, which explains 15.1 percent of the variation, and model 3, which explains 14.6 percent. Model 2 only explains 8.0 percent of the variation in the dependent variable, suggesting that the role of the military in the protests alone has limited explanatory power for citizens' confidence in the military. Unless otherwise indicated, the results of model 1 are presented.

Winners and losers. Across the four models, in support of H1, there is a consistent relationship between higher satisfaction with the government and higher confidence in the military ($p < .001$ in all four models). Those who work in the military are also more likely, on average, to have confidence in the military relative to those who are unemployed or work at a nongovernment job ($p < .05$ or less) in three of the four models. The exception is model 2, which is also the least well-fitting model of confidence in the military, with an R2 of only .0822. In the best-fitting model (model 1), those who work in the military are also more supportive of the armed forces than those who work at a government ministry ($p < .05$, Wald test) and those who have other employment ($p < .01$). This provides support for H2.

Surprisingly, those who are advantaged in terms of higher income are less likely across the four models to have confidence in the military ($p < .05$), contrary to H3. This may suggest that the military holds much of its popularity by supporting the more vulnerable segments of society through physical protection and patronage.

Only in model 3 are those who prefer secular parties more confident in the armed forces than those who prefer Islamist parties ($p < .01$), in support of H4. Generally, the relationship is more mixed and statistically insignificant across the cases. Yet those who hold more anti-American views—that is, those who might be more oppositional to their regime due to the US support of militaries throughout the region—are less supportive of their armed forces ($p < .05$), in support of H5.

Vulnerable social groups and controls. The data also show some but not all vulnerable minority groups are more likely to have confidence in the military. In model 1, Sunni Muslims and Christians are not significantly different from one another in their attitudes about the armed forces, but they are more supportive than the Shi'a ($p < .01$) and the Druze ($p < .01$), though the Shi'a and Druze are not significantly different from one another (Wald test 3). These sectarian differences provide broad support for H6, which expects that Christian minorities and the Sunni majority will be more supportive of the military than the Shia or the Druze.

Even in Lebanon, where the army has succeeded in transcending to a considerable degree the sectarian politics that plague the police and society writ large,[30] there are sectarian differences in attitudes toward the military. The Druze are the least confident in the military, a significant difference relative to the Sunni ($p < .05$), Christians ($p < .001$), and Shi'a ($p < .001$). The Shi'a are also significantly less trusting of the army than Christians ($p < .01$) and the Sunni ($p < .05$).

Contrary to H8, there is no evidence of gender differences in confidence in the military, on average, but in support of H9, older generations are more supportive than younger generations in two models ($p < .05$). Those in urban areas are, across the four models, more likely than those in rural areas to have high confidence in the military ($p < .05$), contrary to H7.

Contextual factors. In model 1, the district-fixed effects show significant differences in confidence levels between most country pairs. Jordan, then Tunisia, and then Egypt have the highest average confidence levels when it comes to the armed forces, controlling for other factors, with Morocco, Lebanon, Algeria (the comparison category), and Palestine following them. Model 2 shows that countries in which the army was disloyal to the regime (i.e., loyal to the protesters) have the highest average level of trust in the military, followed by those where the army supported the regime or there were minimal protests. The groups are significantly different from one another ($p < .001$), providing some support for H10.

In support of H11, the highest confidence in the military is in countries with a high level of US security assistance, followed by those with a moderate level of support. The groups are different from one another and from those with low security assistance (models 3 and 4). This suggests that the military has used protests to position itself to directly benefit from its response, whether that response is to quell protests or—especially—to contribute to order while siding with protesters. US security assistance also contributes to support of the national military via the strong capacity of the military. This resonates with the observations of a US army colleague's view that years of US assistance and relationship building have helped to build society's trust in the military little by little over time.[31]

Model 4 includes both sets of contextual regressors. While the results are similar, they underscore the point that the military is a winner when protests occur, regardless of its role. Citizens in countries with a military (or internal security sector) that intervened to quell protests, as well as those in countries in which the military overtly sided with protesters and was disloyal to regime incumbents, are more supportive of the military on average than those in countries with limited protests ($p < .001$). The differences between the two involvement groups—whether for or against the protests—are not significant (Wald test). This suggests that many citizens value the stabilizing role that the military plays, regardless of which side ultimately wins the contest. In this model, higher levels of US assistance are consistently related to higher levels of support for the military, on average. The patterns in the data stand in contrast to anecdotal evidence. For example, in Sudan, civilian protesters are resuming demonstrations against the military, suggesting that lower confidence in the military—at least among protesters—is related to higher support for democracy. (See Table 12.5.)

Support for Democracy

While an in-depth discussion is beyond the scope of this chapter, model 5 predicting a stronger belief in democracy shows that confidence in the

Table 12.5 Factors Predicting Confidence in the Military and Support for Democracy

	Confidence in the Military				Support for Democracy
	Model 1	Model 2	Model 3	Model 4	Model 5
Higher confidence in the military					.12 (.04)[b]
Higher government satisfaction	.20 (.01)[c]	.21 (.01)[c]	.18 (.01)[c]	.18 (.01)[c]	.39 (.01)[c]
Works in military[d]	.50(.17)[b]	.00(.16)	.37(.17)[a]	.48(.17)[b]	.07(.20)
Works for government ministry[d]	.11(.09)	−.11(.09)	.25(.09)[b]	.20(.09)[a]	.14(.10)
Higher income	−.15(.06)[a]	−.13(.06)[a]	−.11(.06)†	−.17(.06)[b]	.01(.08)
Prefers non-Islamist parties	.06(.03)†	.03(.03)	.08(.03)[b]	.02(.03)	−.10(.04)[b]
Anti-American attitudes	−.10(.04)[a]	−.17(.04)[c]	−.13(.04)[c]	−.12(.04)[b]	−.06(.04)
Religion					
Christian[e]	.13(.17)	.27(.14)[a]	−.56(.15)[c]	−.73(.15)[c]	.43(.20)[a]
Shi'a[e]	−.58(.20)[b]	−.33(.15)[a]	−1.33(.16)[c]	−1.62(.17)[c]	.76(.24)[c]
Druze[e]	−.96(.28)[c]	−.73(.24)[b]	−1.68(.26)[c]	−1.89(.26)[c]	−.14(.36)
Urban residence	.19(.07)[b]	.16(.06)[a]	.25(.07)[a]	.16(.07)[a]	.08(.08)
Female	.02(.06)	−.03(.06)	.04(.06)	.04(.06)	.13(.07)†
Higher age	.02(.03)	.07(.02)[b]	.05(.03)[b]†	.06(.03)[a]	.05(.03)
Country					
Egypt[f]	1.07(.11)[c]				−.54(.13)[c]
Jordan[f]	2.51(.15)[c]				.70(.14)[c]
Lebanon[f]	.69(.16)[c]				−.46(.20)[a]
Morocco[f]	.85(.11)[c]				1.44(.14)[c]
Palestine[f]	−1.55(.10)[c]				−.14(.13)
Tunisia[f]	1.76(.11)[c]				−.48(.12)[c]
Constant					3.40(.24)[c]
Role of military in protests					
Minimal role		.66(.07)[c]		.62(.08)[c]	
Disloyal to regime		1.65(.08)[c]		.50(.10)[c]	
US military aid					
Medium			2.09(.08)[c]	1.85(.10)[c]	
High			2.29(.08)[c]	2.30(.09)[c]	

continues

Table 12.5 Continued

	Confidence in the Military				Support for Democracy
	Model 1	Model 2	Model 3	Model 4	Model 5
Wald/linear tests					
Christian-Shi'a	13.20[c]	10.25[b]	16.75[c]	21.23[c]	2.05
Christian-Druze	15.61[c]	13.81[c]	16.44[c]	17.50[c]	2.62
Army-government	4.13[a]	0.39	0.46	2.37	.10
Minimal role—disloyal to regime		158.80[c]		1.72	
Medium-High			4.89[a]	21.61[c]	
Egypt-Jordan	80.06[c]				77.68
Egypt-Lebanon	4.64[a]				.15
Egypt-Morocco	3.15[†]				187.43
Egypt-Palestine	528.39[c]				8.00
Egypt-Tunisia	30.92[c]				.23
Jordan-Lebanon	80.07[c]				30.87
Jordan-Morocco	109.60[c]				25.51
Jordan-Palestine	724.34[c]				33.54
Jordan-Tunisia	22.32[c]				80.28
Lebanon-Morocco	0.79				82.14
Lebanon-Palestine	178.98[c]				2.38
Lebanon-Tunisia	37.20[c]				.01
Morocco-Palestine	473.24[c]				116.22
Morocco-Tunisia	56.82[c]				201.53
Palestine-Tunisia	856.06[c]				6.19
N	5,148	5,148	5,148	5,148	5,057
χ^2/F	2137.71[c]	921.80[c]	1671.95[c]	1733.66[c]	78.89[c]
Pseudo R2/R2	.1860	.08022	.1455	.1509	.2293

Notes: † $p < .10$; a. $p < .05$; b. $p < .01$; c. $p < .001$; d. does not work for the military or the government; e. Sunni Muslim; f. Algeria.

military is positively related to support for democracy, in support of H12 and existing literature.[32] This relationship is also consistent in each of the countries. There is no relationship in Egypt, Lebanon, Palestine, and Tunisia. However, there is a positive and significant relationship in Algeria ($p < .05$), Jordan ($p < .01$), and Morocco ($p < .001$).

Conclusion

The results suggest that citizens of countries with stronger armed forces—due in part to US security assistance—and those in which protests occurred are more supportive of the military because they see it as contributing to their security. Consistently with other research, higher trust in the military also supports greater confidence in having a democratic system of government, should free and fair elections be implemented. As this chapter shows, many citizens are reticent about implementing freer elections, making good governance and stability crucial outputs in and of themselves.

These observed relationships should not be taken to mean that US assistance promotes democratization directly; indeed, worldwide, there is a negative relationship between US alliances and democracy.[33] Yet the findings suggest that when citizens see their military as effective and fair, they may experience these outputs as good governance and are more likely to develop deeper institutional trust, even if their leaders are enabled by the military assistance to maintain authoritarian rule.[34]

It is also important to note that support for democratic rule is flagging in the MENA region, in part due to increases in perceived insecurity. Yet the evidence presented here suggests that US military assistance has mixed impacts on the societies receiving aid, some of which are consistent with US national security interests. While it stymies democratization in the short and medium term, security assistance may contribute to creating conditions that support democratization in the long term.

Sean Yom (see Chapter 13) also grapples with this tension between promoting security and democracy. The military provides a form of economic and social welfarism to tribal constituencies deemed critical to the social foundations of Hashemite rule. Yet, the military is the guarantor of authoritarian rule under the Hashemite monarchy through opposition.

One concrete solution for assuaging this tension is to pursue a more human-centered definition of security by shifting organizational resources on the US side to diplomacy and development;[35] this is similar to the approach that some European programs take (see Gaub and Walsh in Chapter 7). This is easier said than done, but it suggests that the United States and other resource-rich countries have the power to take steps that maximize the benefits of aid while minimizing its potential drawbacks.

Another solution, following Yezid Sayigh's prescriptions (Chapter 13), is to actively support civilian oversight of the military in the form of democratic accountability. He suggests that defense-institution capacity building and democratization are not at odds with one another but rather are mutually reinforcing goals.

The findings in this chapter also add weight to Aram Nerguizian's (Chapter 5) conclusions by underscoring the difficulty of building a truly national force in a deeply sectarian society. The Shi'a are not substantially underrepresented in Lebanon's military; indeed, all groups use it for social advancement. Yet the data presented suggest that the Shi'a have lower confidence in the military than do Sunni and Christian citizens, with the Druze voicing the least support. This may be because the Shi'a see Hezbollah as even more capable than the Lebanese Armed Forces of protecting their interests.[36]

Future research should explore Wave VI data, which had not been released at the time of writing. Even though conditions are likely to remain insecure in the region—and this has benefited the armed forces—research might explore whether this remains the case. Such an approach may allow for a test of these propositions in other country cases. Research might also explore the factors that shape support for the military in contrast to other police and security agencies, many of which are seen as repressive or incompetent by some segments of the population.[37]

Further research should build a comparative framework that includes cross-regional cases and also explore the extent and determinants of preference falsification around one's support for the military and other public and private institutions.[38] For instance, it is notable that the military is also the most trusted institution in the United States, but trust has declined significantly in the recent years and trust in the military is declining more rapidly than trust in other institutions.[39]

Additionally, it is worth exploring the low level of support for the military in Tunisia and Jordan, given the sensitivity of asking respondents about their views of the military. Through this and related research, scholars can better understand the complex factors that shape public opinion, particularly those that stem from international dynamics.

Notes

I would like to thank the Hicham Alaoui Foundation for funding this chapter; the book editors and other chapter authors for helpful feedback; the Arab Barometer and its team for conducting the survey; and Patri Bartausky, Sucdi Ahmed, Elif Sari Genc, and Chris Owens for excellent research assistance.

1. Nachtwey and Tessler, "The Political Economy of Attitudes Toward Peace"; Nugent, Masoud, and Jamal, "Arab Responses to Western Hegemony"; Tessler and Warriner, "Gender, Feminism, and Attitudes"; Benstead, "Differentiation and Diffusion."

2. Al-Ississ and Diwan, "Individual Preferences for Democracy in the Arab World"; Benstead, "Why Do Some Arab Citizens See Democracy as Unsuitable?"; Benstead and Snyder, "Is Security at Odds with Democracy?"

3. Haddad, "Islam and Attitudes Toward U.S. Policy in the Middle East"; Benstead and Reif, "Polarization or Pluralism?"; Corstange and Marinov, "Taking Sides in Other People's Elections."

4. Lotito, "Public Trust in the Arab Armies"; Alkurd, "Public Opinion and the Army."

5. Benstead, "Why Do Some Arab Citizens See Democracy as Unsuitable?"; Cammett, Diwan, and Vartanova, "Insecurity and Political Values in the Arab World."

6. Kilavuz and Sumaktoyo, "Hopes and Disappointments"; Alkurd, "Public Opinion and the Army"; Benstead and Synyer, "Is Security at Odds with Democracy?"

7. Lotito, "Public Trust in the Arab Armies."

8. Koehler, Albrecht, and Grewal, "Who Fakes Support for the Military?"

9. Benstead, "Why Do Some Arab Citizens See Democracy as Unsuitable?"

10. Gürsoy, "The Changing Role of the Military in Turkish Politics."

11. Abdel-Khalek et al., "The Arabic Scale of Death Anxiety."

12. Nerguizian, "Lebanon at the Crossroad."

13. Gourevitch, "The Second Image Reversed"; Waltz, "Theory of International Relations"; Waltz, *Man, the State, and War.*

14. Lotito, "Public Trust in the Arab Armies."

15. Wike and Fetterolf, "Global Public Opinion in an Era of Democratic Anxiety."

16. Alkurd, "Public Opinion and the Army."

17. Lotito, "Public Trust in the Arab Armies."

18. Tessler and Altinoglu, "Political Culture in Turkey."

19. The Arab Barometer (www.arabbarometer.org, accessed May 29, 2021).

20. Wave V has been released. However, confidence in the armed forces was not asked about in all countries in Wave V, and when it is, it appears to be asked about with different question wording. Thus, I use Wave IV in this chapter for the multivariate analysis.

21. Congressional Research Service, "U.S. Foreign Assistance to the Middle East."

22. Military-military training programs are important points of contact between the US and Arab militaries, and the two regions mutually rely on one another to promote their national security goals.

23. The Arab Barometer also asks about trust in the police. While trust in police and military are positively correlated in every country, it is not sufficiently high to justify creating a scale measure: Algeria ($r = .63$), Egypt ($r = .36$), Jordan ($r = .71$), Lebanon ($r = .37$), Morocco ($r = .54$), Palestine ($r = .79$), and Tunisia ($r = .30$). Citizens often have differing levels of trust in these institutions. For instance, Wood and Boswell, "We Do the Police's Job," highlights the low confidence that Lebanese

citizens have in the Internal Security Forces, or *darak*, in contrast to their higher confidence in the military.

24. In Lebanon the scale is from 1 to 10. There is no 0 category.
25. If the respondent stated that they or their spouse worked in the military, I coded this variable as 2. If they stated that they or their spouse worked at a government ministry, I coded the employment variable as 1, unless the variable was already coded 2. All other respondents who stated that they and/or their spouse worked in any other sector, was unemployed, or was a housewife, I coded as 1, unless the variable was already coded as 2 for military or 1 for government ministry.
26. Jobs such as teacher and lawyer are coded as nonarmy and non–government ministry, even though many workers in these positions are public employees.
27. Does not include assistance to Saudi-led coalition.
28. For more information related to the analysis presented in this chapter, see "Optional Online Appendix," Academia, https://www.academia.edu/79097601.
29. In Jordan there were limited protests compared with other states during the Arab Spring, with suppression done primarily or totally by police forces rather than by the military; similarly, in Palestine, there were minimal protests and no military involvement (Hazen, "Explaining Middle Eastern and North African [MENA] Military Responses"; Yom, "Tribal Politics in Contemporary Jordan"). In Algeria, the military supported the regime but showed restraint toward protesters—mainly using preventative measures and management during protests that involved limited involvement; the internal security forces were largely successful in suppressing protests (Volpi, "Algeria"). Morocco was similarly restrained; it limited protests controlled by internal security agencies. In Lebanon, limited protests were controlled by internal security agencies (Hazen, "Explaining MENA Military Responses"). In Tunisia and Egypt, the military sided with the protesters but in Egypt later violently suppressed Islamist movements (Dunne, "Fear and Learning in the Arab Uprisings"). In Tunisia, the traditionally neutral military was unwilling to use high levels of violence against protesters (Anderson, "Demystifying the Arab Spring"). During the violence that ensued after President Ben Ali resigned, the military fought against security forces loyal to the former regime (Hazen, "Explaining MENA Military Responses"; Shah and Dalton, "The Evolution of Tunisia's Military").
30. Nerguizian, "Lebanon at the Crossroad."
31. Col. John Zavage, workshop discussion, November 2021.
32. Tessler and Altinoglu, "Political Culture in Turkey"; Benstead and Snyder, "Is Security at Odds with Democracy?"
33. Fisher, "U.S. Allies Drive Much of World's Democratic Decline."
34. Benstead, "Why Do Some Arab Citizens See Democracy as Unsuitable?"
35. Wehrey and Dunne, "From Hardware to Holism."
36. Nerguizian, "Lebanon at the Crossroad."
37. Wood and Boswell, "We Do the Police's Job."
38. Koehler, Albrecht, and Grewal, "Who Fakes Support for the Military?"
39. Wike and Fetterolf, "Global Public Opinion in an Era of Democratic Anxiety."

13
Civilians in Arab Defense Affairs: Implications for Providers of Security Assistance

Yezid Sayigh

THERE IS A PARADOX AT THE HEART OF INTERNATIONAL SECURITY ASSIStance to Arab armed forces: the latter have for decades received some of the highest levels of foreign defense equipment and training flows in the world, but external providers have remained almost uniformly unable to generate commensurate levels of either transformation in the capabilities of recipient militaries or gains in their actual combat performance.[1] While recipient ability to absorb and utilize international security assistance effectively is the outcome of several factors, one factor that routinely escapes scrutiny is the minimal level of integration of civilians into defense sectors in most Arab countries. Academic and advocacy studies often note the weakness of civilian oversight and control over national armed forces and the lack, in particular, of democratic governance, but this addresses only the political dimension. Little or no attention is paid, in contrast, to the striking absence of civilian professionals in all areas of defense—strategy and policy development, planning, budgeting, resource management, and development of technology or doctrine—and in providing the kind of informed public debate that can also be critical to building capable and professional armed forces.

As the introduction to this book argues, security assistance has repeatedly contributed to the consolidation of authoritarian governance, privileged national militaries in the external relations of recipient countries, and fueled proxy wars and the emergence of nonstate armed actors. For the most part, additionally, it has not even adequately served the objectives of its providers. This chapter confirms these broad takeaways, touching on them in passing, but focuses on civil-military integration as a missing—or at best underdeveloped—pillar of defense modernization and transformation in most Arab countries. Integrating civilians into defense affairs is not a sufficient condition to ensure better outcomes, but it is necessary, as the evolution of advanced militaries in both democratic and authoritarian systems worldwide has shown.

This chapter first discusses the limitations inherent in security assistance that impede its effectiveness, followed by a discussion of the impact of political factors in recipient countries and defense sectors—above all, their civil-military relations—and of cultural explanations. The chapter next moves to the principal focus, which is the importance of integrating civilians in defense affairs for improving defense outcomes, and then uses this lens to assess the challenges facing internationally supported defense institution building (DIB) and the potential for enhancing it. A final section illustrates the importance of civil-military integration for the development, absorption, and utilization of up-to-date military technology through a case study of Arab defense industry. The conclusion touches briefly on the dilemmas and politics of civil-military integration and its part in democratic governance of the military.

Hobbling Security Assistance

On the surface, the often-limited effectiveness of international security assistance appears to be a consequence of the marked bias among providers toward supplying military hardware and related technical skills, to the exclusion of building the systemic requirements and intangible determinants of combat effectiveness. This is at least partly true. Major providers of security assistance, such as the United States, may recognize the importance of building cohesion, capacity, and integrated defense functions, but they find it difficult to induce recipients to undertake requisite changes in the institutional culture, organizational logic, and social ethos of their armed forces. Getting "boots on the ground" is considerably easier; generating genuine military professionalism and improving outcomes are exponentially harder. Providers of security assistance do what they can, but mainly take the easy route.

Indeed, problems on the provider side are integral to the often poor effectiveness of international security assistance to Arab countries. A long-standing legacy of poor coordination between providers—despite their repeatedly going through the motions of lesson learning—has not helped matters. In fact, it has weakened their leverage and encouraged a shopping-list approach among recipients. The bureaucratic politics and legacies of international providers of security assistance are also at fault. A highly critical assessment of US assistance published in the wake of the spectacularly swift collapse of the Afghan security forces in the summer of 2021 shows that, although "what the [US] military calls 'security force assistance,' 'building partner capacity,' or 'train-and-equip operations' remains a pillar of U.S. defense strategy," rosy progress reports are frequently self-serving, change the goal posts of what is actually being measured, and skew assessments of recipient capabilities to justify a business-as-usual approach.[2]

Furthermore, although the volume of international security assistance may represent a significant proportion of recipient defense spending and military capital investment, providers rarely invest enough political, human, or material capital to acquire serious leverage. Small footprints usually mean small payoffs. But the harsh reality is that even an intervention on the scale of the 2003 US invasion of Iraq, in which the United States both invested massively and exercised overweening, unilateral decisionmaking, may lead to minimal, if not counterproductive, results. The United States brought about a whole-sale transformation of Iraqi state institutions (including the armed forces), the constitutional framework (reshaping the political system), and civil-military relations, and yet failed dismally to engineer the specific kinds of changes in Iraqi military capabilities and government capacity to oversee, manage, and sustain the defense sector that US policy planners sought.[3] Provider leverage has never been so great in other Arab countries, but as Rachel Tecott argues regarding the US approach to Afghanistan, providers are invariably loath to use the leverage they have.[4]

In fairness, even if they were willing to exert themselves further, external powers have exceedingly little ability to induce the kinds of changes in the political, institutional, and social frameworks that shape the formation of recipient defense capabilities. The case may be made that Iran was far more successful in bringing about exactly this kind of transformation in the Lebanese Hezbollah in part by "entangling" itself in the party, to use Simone Tholens's formulation in this book, but this is a fairly rare exception.[5] More common is for leaders in the weak or failed states to prioritize their personal and political survival over strengthening national militaries and to use them for patronage or as a cudgel against their domestic political opponents. And with Arab defense sectors among those most at risk of corruption worldwide, the stakes are high in maintaining opacity regarding defense affairs generally, and defense finances and procurement particularly, and in excluding anyone who is not a member of narrow ruling coalitions from any role in or access to these domains.[6]

Political and Cultural Explanations

Clearly, for ruling elites in recipient countries and often also for their defense leaders, domestic politics trumps all. Whereas a fundamental challenge facing external providers is to ensure effective absorption and utilization of their security assistance, the counterpart for heads of state is to coup-proof themselves against the very armed forces that underpin their power, or at least to ensure they are not controlled by political rivals.[7] This is not to suggest that civilian control is shaky across the Arab region or that the problem is uniquely one of activist armed forces bullying civilian authorities (though this is true in countries such as Egypt, Algeria, and Sudan). Often the contrary is true: civilian leaders such as Iraq's Saddam Hussein, Syria's Bashar al-Assad, and Saudi Arabia's Mohammed bin Salman have all demonstrated their ability to decapitate and restructure their officer corps and defense sectors, largely at will. Rather, authoritarian systems shape all relationships—political, institutional, social, and market—within which the armed forces fit.

External providers are caught in something of a catch-22: no matter how apolitically or incrementally they strive to enhance defense effectiveness and efficiency, they are, in effect, modifying the single most important instrument of power in a group of predominantly authoritarian states. The challenge is especially complicated in countries mired in armed conflict or that remain at risk of relapsing into it. Arguably, this is partly because their "field" of military affairs, to borrow Hazem Kandil's use of the term, is poorly institutionalized. Furthermore, while it might appear to outsiders that enhancing the capability of national armed forces is desirable for state leaders in these countries, political and institutional logics actively impede developing the ability of their armed forces to absorb and utilize security assistance fully. Security assistance is moreover highly contentious and polarizing in these settings and almost inevitably becomes a vector for the emergence of nonstate armed actors, resumption of conflict, and state breakdown.[8]

Indeed, it is often also hard to deliver security assistance effectively to Arab countries that are at peace. Their defense sectors may observe a greater degree of formal hierarchy, yet have fluid internal relations as officer cliques and factions reflect wider political and social allegiances or respond to a mixed political and moral economy of incentives and expectations. As John Zavage's Chapter 15 shows, many officers are "consumed with political influence," and competent defense leaders may be sidelined by political or communitarian biases that affect their "organization's effectiveness more than the competence of its leaders."[9] Aram Nerguizian hammers home a similar message in Chapter 5 on the Lebanese sectarian political order, which appoints commanders who have some but not all key attributes of effective leadership: an ability to stand apart from patronage networks, to unite and lead by example, to act as an agent of national unity, and to think strategically about future development while navigating political, bureaucratic, and operational challenges.[10]

Behavior that is inimical to defense needs is moreover a general feature of most Arab countries in which "the military institution [is] maintained in an otherwise weak institutional environment characteristic of enduring authoritarianism," to borrow Philippe Droz-Vincent's perceptive observation.[11] This allows the military both to expand institutionally and to position itself below the "threshold of the regime," emphasizing its role as a crucial political actor while diminishing the importance of evolving as a capable and professional national defense force.[12] Even in the politically stable and socially cohesive civil-military relationships of the Gulf monarchies, as Zoltan Barany argues in Chapter 9, defense-related "information tends to be compartmentalized and areas of competence and responsibility . . . carefully guarded" because they are a source of power, often leaving senior officers and bureaucrats knowing "little outside their narrow specialization."[13]

These factors, rather than the kind of sociocultural analysis proffered in Kenneth Pollack's well-known *Armies of Sand*, explain the inherent shortcomings and often poor combat performance of Arab militaries.[14] This is not to say that their social nature and institutional culture are not immensely important—quite the contrary. But these are formed by the political framework of state and regime building within which military bodies and minds are formed and by the moral economy of incentives, expectations, and perceived obligations that derives from it. This also offers an answer to the counterfactual question: What to do if the executive or legislative branches of government permit civilians to get involved in defense affairs, but they do not step forward? Low civilian take-up of opportunities is to be expected given political frameworks in most Arab countries that actively discourage or expressly forbid discussion of defense affairs, collection of related data, or interaction with military personnel in professional settings.

In this context, it is especially noticeable that officers and civilians occupy what, by US and European standards, are separate universes, whether in terms of their residences, educations, places of recreation, or, increasingly, families.[15] There are few if any genuine Arab counterparts to the US Naval Postgraduate School or National Defense University, where both civilians and officers mix, or to the Chinese People's Liberation Army (PLA), which draws approximately half of all new officers from civilian universities and recruits civilians to defense science parks.[16] In other words, addressing the issue of integrating civilians into Arab defense affairs is not just a matter of personnel policies but rather involves a more profound social adjustment: away from what is often a palpable sense of military contempt toward civilians seeing their involvement as equal partners in defense affairs as both normal and rightful.

In any case, as a growing body of military sociology suggests, national armed forces tend to be conservative everywhere in the world, resistant to doctrinal, organizational, and technological change and to lesson learning—usually until a harsh shock such as a battlefield defeat compels a rethink.[17] Some of the more advanced armed forces seek nonetheless to routinize lesson learning into a "culture of military innovations," as Russia undertook following its military expedition to Syria from 2015 onward, or to institutionalize it, as has the US Army with its *Journal of Military Learning* and the Department of Defense (DOD) with the quasi-autonomous Military Operations Research Society. The abysmal performance of Russian forces in the first two months of the 2022 invasion of Ukraine does not contradict this observation; rather, it reveals that Russian failure derived both from "not following its doctrine" and from a fundamentally flawed civil-military relationship that obscured (if not encouraged) false reporting, corruption, and poor training and motivation.[18]

Crucially, defense innovation implies a deliberate "technological, organisational and doctrinal change away from the status quo," as Simona Soare and Fabrice Pothier argue, as well as the "redesigning and implementing [of] a new relationship between defence establishments and societies, particularly expert communities in private industry and academia."[19] But there are no known equivalents in the Arab case.[20] Path dependency is additionally at play: the powerful political and institutional legacies of Arab defense sectors are especially difficult to shift given the resilience of the wider governing systems within which they are embedded.[21] All of this impedes efficient absorption and utilization of assistance.

The Civilian Handicap

Besides highlighting the importance of politics and the logic governing civil-military relations to the effectiveness of international security assistance, the preceding background sketch also reveals a staggeringly low level of civilian expertise and participation in the defense affairs of most Arab countries, if not all of them. This works both ways. On one hand, civilians—not only civil society organizations and independent researchers but also civil servants in relevant government agencies, cabinet ministers, and legislators and their staff—lack professional understanding of defense issues to an unparalleled extent compared to other world regions. But on the other hand, civilians are systematically kept out of defense affairs. Most Arab countries wrap defense spending and procurement decisions in secrecy and prohibit, often formally, public discussion of any aspect of defense affairs or transmission of any security-related information not issued by official military spokespersons.

Consequently, civilians play a minimal role in shaping defense policy or governing Arab defense sectors (as will be discussed in greater detail in the next section). Civilian integration and oversight are not a sufficient condition for democratic governance, but they are necessary for it.[22] The issue is not only one of civilian oversight and control, however, or even of the authority to take the country to war or to determine its national security goals and defense strategies. As importantly, civilians make almost no contribution to the development of the core defense competences and capacities relating to warfare—the actual conduct of war—depriving national armed forces of key inputs and resources they need to keep up with global trends in military technology and doctrine.[23]

The near-total absence of civilians from defense affairs is part and parcel of the generally low level of exploitation of overall experience and weak culture of military innovation within Arab armed forces. It moreover reinforces the impediments to effective absorption and utilization of international security assistance. Integration of civilians is not a panacea, but their deliberate nonintegration is symptomatic of systemic shortcomings in defense sectors that for the most part have failed, despite decades of external assistance, to develop indigenous capacity to apply, adapt, and innovate technological, organizational, and associated doctrinal solutions in light of local conditions and experience. Arab military transition has remained elusive and sustained, internally driven defense development and transformation more the exception than the norm. Impact, that holy grail of foreign donors across a wide spectrum of fields, has similarly remained low in proportion to the volume and quality of international security assistance.

Hamstringing Defense Institution Building

It was largely in response to the limited impact of their security assistance that the United States and other Western providers recognized the need to focus more on "building partner capacity" over the past two decades. Specifically, they sought increasingly to resolve what Alexandra Kerr calls "the short-term capability, long-term capacity disconnect": the realization that "major investments in time, money, and personnel had not resulted in corresponding increases in institutionalized and sustainable partner capacity—and in some cases, overall security had even diminished."[24] This has taken the form of defense institution building, a separate discipline and distinct tool adopted by the North Atlantic Treaty Organization in 2004 and formally articulated by the US DOD in its DOD Directive 5205.82 of 2016.[25]

As Kerr notes, DOD Directive 5205.82 defined DIB as empowering recipient defense institutions "to establish or re-orient their policies and structures to make their defense sector more transparent, accountable, effective, affordable, and responsive to civilian control." The principal emphasis here is normative, which is both commendable and necessary in equal measure, but DOD Directive 5205.82 also committed to

> creating or improving the principal functions of effective [partner] defense institutions, including:
> (a) Strategy, planning, and policy.
> (b) Oversight of policy implementation.
> (c) Resource management (including budgeting and finance).
> (d) Human-resource management.
> (e) Logistics and acquisition.
> (f) Administration, information management, audit, and inspector general.
> (g) Intelligence policy, organization, and professionalization.
> (h) Defense education.
> (i) Other authorities and systems necessary to the effective functioning of the defense sector and its operations.[26]

Crucially, DOD Directive 5205.82 also singled out improving "the sustainability, effect, and value of other U.S. security cooperation" as a goal, along with broadening the effect and sustainability of other US security cooperation and assistance programs.[27] What this has meant concretely is neither consistent nor wholly clear, however, especially for recipient countries in the Arab region that do not already have reasonably proactive and responsive defense institutions to begin with. In large measure, as noted at the outset, this is due to recipient politics.

Providers of international security assistance certainly understand this and repeatedly try to engage with local dynamics. Russian efforts to enhance the authority of the Syrian armed forces command and improve the quality and accountability of officers since the 2015 intervention tipped the ongoing conflict decisively in the Damascus government's favor certainly reflect awareness of regime and officer politics and of Iran's parallel influence, for example.[28] US officers assisting the Tunisian defense and internal security agencies are equally aware of the political and bureaucratic dynamics that impede information sharing between them, while their counterparts in Iraq had previously shaped their triage of which army units to stand up after the Mosul debacle in 2014 on a similar understanding.[29]

Clearly, there is a very real problem of leverage: providers of international security assistance either lack it or are unable to exercise it without running the risk of not only alienating partners and clients, but also of disrupting local political governance and military command arrangements to the extent of destabilizing the very institutions they seek to assist. The post-2003 experience of the United States in Iraq and that of Russia in Syria post-2015 both testify to this limitation (albeit in diametrically opposite ways), as does the fundamentally transactional relationship that first the Soviet Union and then the United States had with the Egyptian Armed Forces over more than half a century.

This is where the absence of additional parties to the renegotiation of civil-military relationships and discussion of defense policy and of defense affairs more broadly is most felt. The exclusion of civilians from this field, coupled with their own poor readiness to engage in it, which together form a self-reinforcing vicious circle, narrows the political margin within which external actors must approach their counterparts. It is also where the DIB approach does not go far enough, by omitting to factor in the need to integrate civilians on a significant scale across the spectrum of defense affairs. All significant providers of international security assistance are guilty of this omission, or at most they relegate it to the bottom of their list of priorities in official government-to-government and military-to-military dialogues and allocate minimal resources to programs intended to enhance civilian capabilities.

A narrower focus is understandable for a policy document such as DOD Directive 5205.82, which restricts the scope of DIB within recipient defense sectors to "the ministerial, joint or general staff, or service headquarters levels."[30] This is indeed where what Kerr calls the fundamental "pillars" of defense (strategy and policy development, strategic human resources management, logistics, and resource management) come together, but as the list of principal defense functions cited above underlines, achieving success at the command level assumes an ability across the defense sector to engage effectively with policy directives and prompts—translating these into concrete measures, observing and assessing implementation, and generating lateral and upward information flows.

In short, DIB needs to be extended across the board in defense sectors that do not yet have this kind of institutional habitus, which is the case in numerous Arab countries. The shortfall is even more obvious in areas that are acquiring increasing importance in defense affairs globally, foremost of which is the ability to undertake and drive military technological innovation, generate and utilize data effectively in an information-intensive era, and mainstream the participation of women in armed forces—in all of which civilian integration offers especially significant potential for added value in defense.

That civilians are essential to this effort is suggested powerfully by the sheer scale of civilian participation in the US defense sector: the DOD employed some 800,000 civilians as of Fiscal Year 2020, more than half as many as the 1.4 million active-duty personnel in the armed forces.[31] This, of course, is besides the hundreds of thousands of civilians who work in the defense industrial sector or in organizations working on military-related research and those who enable federal and state legislatures, government audit bodies, and the like to fulfil their responsibilities in allocating and overseeing defense appropriations, assessing effectiveness and efficiency, and ensuring the United States gets the maximum bang for its buck.

The Efficiency of Civil-Military Relations

Thomas Bruneau argues that the absence of "the fabric or tissue" for the United States to relate its DIB efforts "to civilians and civilian-led institutions" leads it instead "to link with the armed forces, thereby strengthening them relative to the civilians."[32] This is also true of other major providers of international security assistance. But the fabric or tissue is nearly as weak in the defense sectors of most Arab countries too. Nowhere is this more evident than in Arab defense ministries, virtually all of which are "colonized" by officers, to use Hazem Kandil's apt turn of phrase.[33] More to the point, a majority of defense ministries function as clerical appendages to the armed forces, dealing with pay, supply, and lower-end procurement. Furthermore, if these ministries represent the "torso" of defense management, then the "head"—comprising the official posts, committees, and routinized policy reviews that form the interface between defense sectors and the executive branches of governments that provide (or are supposed to provide) political direction, ratification of laws and command appointments, and, above all, budgets—is mostly nonexistent or, at best, embryonic.

The institutional capacities of Arab defense sectors vary quite widely, but the impediments are broadly similar. Inefficient civil-military relationships mean that decisionmaking in defense affairs is very rarely subjected to internal review, let alone debate, even when taken by civilian leaders. This is due to predominantly autocratic modes of governance that stifle questioning and accountability and subject defense affairs primarily to regime maintenance considerations. Another consequence of this inefficiency is the exclusion of civilians from involvement in defense affairs—whether through direct employment of civilians or procurement of specialist services from them or through their expert contributions to discussion of policy issues based on publicly accessible information—thus depriving defense sectors of critical human resources and intellectual assets.

Efficiency, in this context, is defined as the ability of civilian and military actors to negotiate, formulate, and coordinate coherent policies in the sphere of national defense, in ways that further effective governance of the defense sector, assist its professional development, and ensure maximum effectiveness for lowest cost. This definition borrows directly from Tawazun: Index of Arab Civil-Military Relations, the first platform of its kind to offer quantitative measures of the efficiency of Arab civil-military relations.[34] Its first edition, launched in 2020, surveyed precisely what DOD Directive 5205.82 called for: "government-wide systems," within which defense sectors function (including the executive, legislative, and judicial branches), and their particular synchronization across other government sectors (particularly security, justice, and finance).[35] In the initial sample of four Arab countries covered (Egypt, Lebanon, Syria, and Tunisia), the Tawazun index scores revealed a preponderance of "low" to "intermediate" efficiency across five main domains: governance, military professionalism, social perceptions and cultural attitudes, defense finances and economics, and civilian competences. Only one score of "high" was recorded, for Tunisia, and that in relation to governance.

While there is no room to discuss the results in detail, they demonstrate that proposing integration of civilians into Arab defense affairs is of considerably more than declaratory or normative importance. The foremost illustration of this is strategic planning for defense: because it brings together so many core capacities, it is the truest measure of the overall health and functionality of the defense system as a whole. Precious few Arab defense sectors are capable of developing what Hugh F. T. Hoffman labels a "strategy-to-plans-to-requirements system" that informs force design, acquisition, manning, and budget expenditures.[36] There is no a priori reason why officers could not deliver effective planning with no civilian participation whatsoever, but in the Arab case we know definitively that, with one or two exceptions, they do not. The United Arab Emirates is a notable exception: its approach to force building reveals coherence in defining national goals and designing strategies, enabling it to identify precisely what assistance it needs and how to use it.[37] While it still lacks indigenous capacity in key areas, it has a higher potential ability to utilize its graduates from the United States and other defense colleges to develop its strategic planning and analysis capabilities.[38]

Capabilities analysis and budget planning and execution, a special subset of planning, are often equally problematic. As Hoffman details in relation to post-2003 Iraq, for instance, what passes as planning is little more than "shopping lists of equipment untethered to either real threats, doctrine, force design, or budgetary realities."[39] Of course, providers of international security assistance are at fault too, as they provide a supermarket for military hardware and services. Meaningful coordination is rare; the bespoke capabilities development plans to assist the Lebanese Armed Forces (LAF)—led by the United States on the donor side and supported by the United Kingdom, France, Canada, Italy, and UN agencies—are very much the exception. A positive outcome is that the LAF has started to internalize the concept and tools of strategic planning, but as defense expert Aram Nerguizian notes, this capacity has not yet become entrenched within the defense sector. It moreover remains vulnerable to the country's problematic civil-military relations and lack of "even the most basic elements of national security guidance" from civilian decisionmakers.[40] As a result, "donor coordination mechanisms such as the [Executive Military Commission] and the newly formed Directorate of International Military Cooperation are either inactive or underutilized."

As the preceding suggests, the preparation of national security strategies and doctrines and defense white papers is crucial to guide planning. This is an area where civilian contributions are especially important, since these core documents depend entirely on integrated assessments of long-term trends—in threats, resources, funding, and science and technology—and therefore inform strategic planning in the defense sector. Debates about specific defense choices—such as acquiring a high-tech or low-tech arsenal and introducing, repealing, or modifying military conscription—are of course tied to national strategies and doctrines, always involve nonmilitary factors, and may rely on inputs from civilian sources.

Civil-Military Integration: The Case of Defense Industry

A particularly pertinent illustration of the importance of civilian input is the need for civil-military integration in developing, absorbing (that is, using and adapting), and updating military technology. Countries with highly advanced economies and industrial bases such as Japan have yet to achieve this goal, as the Japanese defense white paper published in the summer of 2021 acknowledges, but the fact that Japan already has high levels of civilian involvement across the defense sector and in defense affairs generally, as well as a highly advanced civilian industrial and technology base, means that it can more readily jump-start civil-military integration in this field.[41]

In contrast, no Arab country can claim to invest sufficiently in indigenous (as opposed to imported) research and development, and none has anything approaching a genuine science and technology strategy.[42] With a growing number of Arab countries seeking to build their own defense industries, such as Algeria, Jordan, the UAE, and Saudi Arabia, or to upgrade existing ones—most prominently, Egypt—the need for a fundamental rethink of approach is clear.[43] Indeed, with the exception of Algeria, the newcomers have already adopted a more mixed civil-military approach to designing and developing their capabilities.[44]

Whether democratic governance and full freedom of research and public discussion of defense affairs are absolutely necessary for developing and incorporating the military technology solutions that a country's armed forces need is debatable. China's success in enhancing the capabilities of the People's Liberation Army argues otherwise, but its authoritarian one-party system is complemented by a thriving semicapitalist technology market, an extensive industrial base, and a central position in global value chains.[45] As important are the processes of internal review and lesson learning within the PLA and the ruling Communist Party that guide strategic policy and lead to changes in defense equipment, doctrine, and deployment.

Again, in contrast, the rapid development and crash expansion of Iraq's defense industry during its 1980–1988 war with Iran shows that although much was achieved in terms of generating indigenous production (and some adaptation), this was highly inefficient in terms of capital and human outlay.[46] Nor could it be sustained or converted after the war's end, given the weakness of Iraqi industry generally and the resulting lack of means and opportunities to integrate defense factories and research centers into the wider civilian economy (even before the start of the 1990 sanctions).

This and subsequent Arab experiences confirm the need to open up defense affairs to counteropinions and innovative thinking. The list of these experiences is long: complete disintegration of the Iraqi defense industry after 1990; agonizingly slow deployment of Egyptian troops and armor to Saudi Arabia ahead of the 1991 Gulf War and less-than-stellar combat performance of the Arab contingents of the US-led military coalition in liberating Kuwait; degradation of massive stores of weapons that were surplus to need in Libya between the 1980s and 2000s; failure of successive heavy-handed counterinsurgency campaigns by the Egyptian Armed Forces in Sinai since 2008; poor cohesion, initiative, and combined arms operations displayed by the Syrian Arab Army over a decade of armed conflict since 2011; collapse of the Iraqi army in northern Iraq in 2014; lackluster performance of Saudi forces in Yemen since 2015; and enduring technological constraints and production inefficiencies that continue to hobble the Egyptian defense industry more than sixty years after its establishment.

In each and every preceding case, and in others, national leaders and military commanders in Arab countries eschewed contributions that a wider range of civilian actors outside the defense sector could make to evolving doctrinal, organizational, and management solutions, among others, let alone to providing the scientific know-how to develop or upgrade hardware. Paradoxically, integrating civilians into defense affairs does not necessitate a radical transformation of civil-military relationships (even though this would make their role more effective), but it is necessary if national armed forces are to become more professional and accountable.

Conclusion: Plus ça Change?

Shifting deep-seated aversion to the involvement of civilians in Arab defense affairs is difficult and will remain so for the foreseeable future. The few defense sectors that have opened up to civilians have done so cautiously and in a limited number of select areas. More to the point, they did so after identifying needs they could not meet effectively or quickly without the assistance of civilians. This was done on their own initiative or that of competent political leaderships, rather than as a result of advocacy or support by providers of international security assistance.

These cases demonstrate that the best performers—and reformers—are already predisposed to problem solving and lesson learning on their own and have sufficient autonomy and interest to take the initiative. And it is almost exclusively in these cases that providers of international security assistance have had any demonstrable traction in relation to capacity building. They have remained unable to insert themselves meaningfully in defense institution building processes in other Arab countries.

It is no coincidence that the Arab countries whose defense sectors are most resistant to change, even when the objective need for it is apparent and assistance is available, have tended also to be more notably characterized by unbalanced civil-military relationships, visibly authoritarian domestic politics, and political instability or armed conflict than the better performers/reformers. Zoltan Barany is absolutely right in arguing, unequivocally, that "building democratic civil-military relations may be the most fundamental prerequisite of the transition to and the consolidation of democracy."[47] The integration of civilians into defense affairs is a necessary condition for this transition to take place, even if it is an insufficient one on its own.

The preceding underlines that the scope for integrating civilians into defense affairs is highly context specific, contingent on conjunctures of political, institutional, and security factors that allow shifts in attitude and, consequently, in practice. This also reveals two additional conclusions. First, it is important to build supporting arguments and constituencies for civil-military integration, in anticipation of opportunities that may arise to achieve it. Second, the diversity of civil-military relationships and of politico-military and institutional cultures across Arab countries—even between ones that otherwise appear very similar in key respects, for example, Qatar and the UAE—means that the manner and timing of achieving integration will vary considerably and will not follow a single path or model.

A legacy of worsening economic and financial conditions in most Arab countries over the past two decades, compounded by the long-term impacts of the Covid-19 pandemic, will affect how they manage their defense affairs. Severe cutbacks in defense spending may become unavoidable in coming years, reinforcing shortfalls in virtually every area of defense needs, straining civil-military relations, and potentially undermining the loyalty of national armed forces. At the same time, their increasing salience as political actors over the past two decades—highlighted by their responses to the popular uprisings during and since the Arab Spring and their direct interventions in several Arab countries—has unfolded in the specific context of the ongoing redefinition of authoritarian social contracts.[48] And so for now, doubling down to preserve existing governing arrangements and power elites is more likely, as is increased encroachment by Arab defense sectors into the civilian economies of their countries. But although prospects for the integration of civilians into defense affairs look as grim as ever over the medium term, the eventual erosion of authoritarian pacts may generate openness to change wherever state leaders and officer corps seek genuine improvement to their national defense capabilities.

Notes

1. The Bonn International Center for Conversion's Global Militarisation Index (http://gmi.bicc.de) ranks the Middle East and North Africa as the most militarized region worldwide.
2. Tecott, "Why America Can't Build Allied Armies."
3. This point is made powerfully in Hoffman, "Lessons from Iraq."
4. Tecott, "Why America Can't Build Allied Armies."
5. Chapter 10 in this book.
6. Transparency International's Government Defense Anti-Corruption Index for 2015 revealed that sixteen out of the seventeen Arab countries reviewed receive the lowest scores in terms of safeguards against corruption, placing them in the highest risk category. "Why It Matters."
7. The dominance of coup-proofing in relations between political regimes and national armed forces in autocracies is the focus of Bou Nassif, *Endgames*.
8. Kandil, *The Power Triangle*.
9. Chapter 15 in this book.
10. Chapter 5 in this book.

11. Droz-Vincent, *Military Politics of the Contemporary Arab World*, 15.
12. Ibid., 16.
13. Chapter 9 in this book.
14. Pollack, *Armies of Sand*.
15. I owe much of this paragraph to Robert Springborg, email, September 1, 2021.
16. On the Chinese example, see Lee, "Swords to Ploughshares," 19.
17. Examples of this literature include Hasselbladh and Ydén, "Why Military Organizations Are Cautious About Learning?"; Dyson, "The Military as a Learning Organisation; Farrell and Terriff, *The Sources of Military Change*.
18. Quote from Christopher Dougherty, a former planner for the Pentagon, in "How Deep Does the Rot in the Russian Army Go?"
19. Soare and Pothier, *Leading Edge*.
20. Quote and Russian example from Adamsky, "Russian Lessons from the Syrian Operation and the Culture of Military Innovation." The US *Journal of Military Learning* was launched in 2017 (www.armyupress.army.mil/Journals/Journal-of-Military-Learning). The Military Operations Research Society was incorporated in 1966 and receives funding from the US Navy, Army, Air Force, and Marine Corps, the Office of the Secretary of Defense, and the Department of Homeland Security.
21. For additional reviews of the state of Arab civil-military relations, see Kårtveit and Gabrielsen, *Civil-Military Relations in the Middle East*; Gaub, *Civil-Military Relations in the MENA*.
22. Zoltan Barany, in *The Soldier and the Changing State*, 353, is one of the rare authors to recommend civilian participation in defense affairs as a means of contributing to democratic civil-military relations.
23. The distinction between war and warfare is underlined by Nikolić, "On New Military Technologies and Concepts."
24. Kerr, "Introduction," xvi.
25. Noted in ibid., xvi. DOD Directive 5205.82 is publicly available, for example at https://www.esd.whs.mil/Portals/54/Documents/DD/issuances/dodd/520582p.pdf?ver=2019-02-04-144847-587. Another, related US program designed to improve security-sector governance and core management competencies in partner countries is the Defense Security Cooperation Agency's Institutional Capacity Building (https://www.dsca.mil/institutional-capacity-building). The Ministry of Defense Advisors program commissions US Department of Defense civilian experts to assist foreign counterparts in building core ministerial competencies such as personnel and readiness, logistics, strategy and policy, and financial management.
26. DOD Directive 5205.82, 4.
27. Ibid., 5.
28. For a discussion, see Sayigh, "Syrian Politics Trump Russian Military Reforms."
29. On Tunisia, see Wehrey, "Tunisia's Wake-Up Call."
30. DOD Directive 5205.82, 5.
31. Daniels, "Assessing Trends in Military Personnel Costs," 3.
32. Bruneau, "Challenges in Building Partner Capacity," 436.
33. Kandil, *The Power Triangle*, 156.
34. Tawazun's Index of Arab Civil-Military Relations (http://tawazun.net/english/index.php; Arabic version: http://tawazun.net/arabic/index.php) is an independent platform launched in 2020 by the Program on Civil-Military Relations in Arab States of the Malcolm H. Kerr Middle East Center in Beirut, Lebanon (https://carnegie-mec.org/specialprojects/arabcivilmilitaryrelations/?lang=en; Arabic version: https://carnegie-mec.org/specialprojects/arabcivilmilitaryrelations).

35. DOD Directive 5205.82, 4.
36. Hoffman, "Lessons from Iraq," 345.
37. An explanation of UAE success is Roberts, "Bucking the Trend."
38. Dalton and Shah, "Evolving UAE Military and Foreign Security Cooperation."
39. Ibid., 345.
40. Nerguizian, "The Five Wildcards." A discussion of the need for national security guidance is in Hitti, "Nonstate Actors and Lebanese National Security Documents."
41. Kishi, *Defense of Japan 2021*; Koshino, "Is Japan Ready for Civil-Military 'Integration'?"
42. On the poor levels of R&D investment and flaws in science and technology strategies in Arab countries, see Zahlan, *Technological Illiteracy and Its Impact on Arab Development*; *Arab Human Development Report 2003*.
43. For a discussion of emerging Arab defense industries, see Gaub and Stanley-Lockman, "Defence Industries in Arab States." For a review and assessment of Egypt's defense industry, see Sayigh, *Owners of the Republic*.
44. On newcomer defense industries in the Gulf, see Borchert, "The Arab Gulf Defense Pivot; Samaan, "The Rise of the Emirati Defense Industry."
45. China's integration into global value chains is discussed extensively, for example, in Kee and Tang, "How Did China Move Up the Global Value Chains?"
46. For an assessment of the Iraqi defense industry up to 1990, see Sayigh, *Arab Military Industry*.
47. Barany, *The Soldier and the Changing State*, 10–11.
48. For an excellent discussion of the redefinition of authoritarian social contracts, see Heydemann, "Rethinking Social Contracts in the MENA Region."

14

US Security Assistance to Egypt: The Importance of Framing a Relationship

F. C. "Pink" Williams

THE DECADES-LONG SECURITY ASSISTANCE (SA) RELATIONSHIP BETWEEN the United States and Egypt illustrates many of the limitations of SA as a means of achieving national objectives, while also offering an example of significant strategic success. The initial strategic goals—cementing an Israeli-Egyptian peace and bringing Egypt at least partially into the Western orbit—were unquestionably accomplished, at least in part because those goals were clear, achievable, and agreed upon by all parties. Over time, however, stated objectives multiplied and goals diverged without an attendant re-calibration of the program or the relationship. Although the introduction of the "four pillars" in 2018 resulted in a sharper focus, it remains to be seen whether this approach will be successful.

The United States has provided economic aid to Egypt since World War II,[1] but the current era of military cooperation began in 1975 when Egypt secretly requested Northrop F-5 fighter aircraft from the United States, and Egyptian pilots and maintenance personnel began training on the F-5 in Saudi Arabia. In 1976 President Gerald Ford announced the sale of six C-130 cargo airplanes to Egypt.[2] Ford later stated, since Egypt had severed its military relationship with the Soviet Union, "I think it makes it at least responsible for us to take a look at Egypt's military needs."[3] In 1977 Congress approved $750 million for Egypt to support budget outlays as part of the foreign aid bill. This was followed in 1979, subsequent to the Camp David Accords, by a $4.8 billion treaty aid package for Israel and Egypt,[4] including $3.7 billion in guaranteed loans, of which $2.2 billion of was earmarked for Israel and the remaining $1.5 billion committed to Egypt.[5] Egypt's original request for F-5s had foundered when in the wake of the Camp David Accords the Saudis withdrew their offer to fund the project.[6] In any case the Egyptians, knowing that Israel was acquiring a fleet of the much more capable F-15 fighters and that a request for their own F-15 fleet would not be approved, held out for the F-16, the newest fighter in the US inventory at the time.[7] In March President Jimmy Carter refused this proposal, again offering F-5s, but by May a compromise of sorts had been reached resulting in an agreement for the United States to provide two squadrons of F-4s, an aging but still capable fighter that could be delivered quickly and at reduced cost.[8]

President Anwar Sadat asked that the first delivery occur before Egypt's commemoration of the 1973 war in order "to show other Arab nations that the peace treaty is yielding results for Egypt."[9] Accordingly, in September 1979 the first F-4s arrived, along with fifty armored personnel carriers (APCs) and seventy-five US technicians.[10] The new era of US security assistance to Egypt had begun.

The F-4 delivery perfectly encapsulated the disconnect between strategic objectives and operational outcomes that often occurs in security assistance programs. Undoubtably the offer of significant US aid was a factor in bringing both Egypt and Israel to the peace table[11] and, as one US lawmaker said when briefed on the initial agreement, "If that's a fair estimate of the cost, it's a bargain."[12] Conversely, the F-4, while a proven and successful aircraft with significant combat success in both the US and Israeli forces, was difficult to employ effectively and especially to maintain properly compared to most of the Soviet equipment the Egyptian air force then possessed. At least initially, the Egyptians lacked the training and infrastructure to support the aircraft. As a result, even with significant US technical assistance, mission capable rates—defined as the percentage of aircraft possessed by a unit that are capable of executing the unit's mission set—were consistently low.[13] In one infamous case an aircraft remained on the ground unused for so long that the jet fuel congealed in its tanks,[14] and at one point in the early 1980s, only 25 percent of the Egyptian F-4 fleet was mission capable.[15] (At the time, average US Air Force fighter aircraft mission capable rates ranged from 64 to 76 percent.)[16] Increased US technical assistance and more rigorous training resulted in better mission capable rates by the mid-1980s, but the Egyptian F-4 fleet was never a significant combat asset.

Throughout the 1980s, high-tech American armaments continued to pour in, at first in the form of older US equipment such as the F-4 that could be delivered quickly. A portion of the $1.5 billion approved by Congress in 1979 funded 11 Improved Hawk ground-to-air missile batteries and 800 APCs among other items. The Pentagon approved transfer of 244 M60 tanks in early 1980, and in May it offered 40 F-16 fighters and 600 Maverick air-to-ground missiles, representing a progression to state-of-the-art equipment.[17] Training, organizational, and infrastructure limitations continued to hamper effectiveness, especially in situations involving technologically advanced equipment. F-16 maintenance and operational facilities were rudimentary, for instance, often lacking windows, furniture, and sometimes electricity. Entrances to Mig-21 aircraft shelters had been modified to accept the larger F-16 by the simple expedient of hammering the concrete arches until they collapsed. Successful daily operations depended heavily on the advice and assistance of US technicians.

Three characteristics of this successful yet flawed early effort would shape the relationship. The first was the linkage between US assistance and the Egyptian acceptance of the Camp David Accords. Even as the prospect of an Egyptian-Israeli conflict became increasingly remote, and in spite of the obvious advantages to Egypt of the peace agreement, Egyptians continued to regard the annual allotment of US aid as their just reward for good behavior. As time went on, the United States attempted to place more conditions on the aid while the Egyptians invariably insisted that their adherence to the accords was justification enough for continued US support.

The second characteristic was the bias of both parties toward weapons systems that supported conventional warfare capability. Understandably there was a desire in the early days for Egypt to be seen as benefiting from the accords and from its decision to switch partners from the Soviets to the Americans, just as there was a desire for the United States to be seen as a reliable ally. An additional factor was the hope among at least some Americans that the weapons would bolster support for Sadat within the Egyptian Armed Forces (EAF).[18] In this environment main battle tanks and tactical fighters were bound to have more symbolic impact than new communications gear or improved training, and in any case, Egypt could justify a period of rearmament given the age of its Soviet equipment. As time went on the Egyptian conventional arsenal grew ever larger, while the potential dangers shifted increasingly toward insurgency, terrorism, and other unconventional threats. Numerous attempts by the Americans to change the Egyptian emphasis were unsuccessful, in part because there was no policy consensus among the US agencies concerned. In the face of this disjointed approach the Egyptians stood firm, continually reminding American officials that their conventional force was necessary to "defend the borders of Egypt."[19]

The third attribute of the early effort concerned the boundaries of the military relationship. While several teams were dispatched to Egypt during the late 1970s to survey military requirements, and even though Sadat impressed more than one US official with his strategic vision for the Middle East and Africa,[20] there is no evidence of extensive discussions focusing on military objectives or strategy. Once American trainers arrived in Egypt, numerous technical assistance field teams (TAFTs) were established to organize training, logistics, maintenance and operations functions for each weapons system. American advisors on these teams worked closely with their Egyptian counterparts, and had access to Egyptian military facilities and personnel as required in order to ensure the successful administration of each program. Joint oversight of the larger effort was vested in the Office of Military Cooperation (OMC) at the US Embassy and the Egyptian Armament Authority (EAA) in the Ministry of Defense. Coordination between the two occurred regularly up to the general officer level, but was focused almost exclusively on processing Egyptian requests, updating the status of deliveries, and other aspects of program management.

No similar cooperative mechanism was established at higher echelons, and US personnel were not privy to the broader workings of the EAF. Insight into Egyptian strategic thinking, threat analysis, and doctrine was limited, as was knowledge of Egyptian deliberate and contingency planning methodology and the products thereof. As a result, most training opportunities were restricted to the tactical echelon, with little to no engagement at the operational, staff, or strategic level. US advisors were embedded in the fighter squadron or the tank company, not in the wing or the division, not among the senior staff and certainly not at the command or Ministry of Defense level. Among other things this lack of access would hamper US efforts to monitor the usage and security of equipment. In addition, the occasional US efforts to wean the Egyptians away from their emphasis on conventional warfare were difficult to sustain since the United States had scant knowledge of Egyptian war planning and thus could not credibly argue for a significant change in equipage. Of course, nothing in the initial agreements mandated that the United States would necessarily have engagement across the EAF, but this lack of access resulted in a relationship whose breadth and depth, even after many years of partnership, was less than might be expected.

By the end of the 1980s, the United States had supplied Egypt with 82 F-16s,[21] 42 F-4s,[22] approximately 785 M-60A3 tanks, 1,000 M-113A2 APCs,[23] and 12 batteries of Improved Hawk surface-to-air missiles.[24]

In 1984 the US agreed to finance a tank factory (Factory 200) outside Cairo and subsequently authorized Egypt to co-produce the state-of-the art M1A1 Abrams main battle tank at the plant.[25] The biennial "Bright Star" exercise, first conducted in 1980 between US and Egyptian land forces, had grown into a joint operation including land, sea, and air components.[26] Annual security assistance funds appropriated for Egypt, which had fluctuated significantly in the late 1970s and early 1980s, had by 1987 stabilized at $1.3 billion a year. Egypt was one of a handful of countries allowed to use these funds to make purchases directly through commercial companies. Further, Egypt was permitted to exercise "cash flow financing," which permitted payment over time for goods and services purchased in any given fiscal year.[27]

As the amount of American equipment increased and the quality improved, the norms established early on held. Egypt continued to link American assistance directly to the Camp David Accords. While some deliveries supported other types of military operations, the emphasis was overwhelmingly on tanks, APCs, air defense systems, and aircraft, especially tactical fighters. Egypt did not feel compelled to outline the operational requirement for the equipment, nor did the United States require it to do so. The primary limitation on arms deliveries was the need to maintain Israel's qualitative military edge (QME), intended to ensure Israel retained the ability to deter or defeat numerically superior adversaries and embraced by the United States since the Lyndon Johnson administration.[28] As long as QME could be assured, the United States generally acquiesced to any reasonable Egyptian request.

As each major weapons program was added or expanded, additional TAFTs were established. American military and contract civilian personnel were vital to operations at a variety of EAF bases and installations, and their assistance remained critical to effective training. This arrangement was beneficial to both parties, but as a consequence cooperation continued to occur primarily at the small-unit level, and the resultant training retained its tactical focus. Broader engagement between the two militaries remained largely off limits, and that which did occur was mostly scripted and ceremonial.

The Bright Star exercise, for instance, would eventually include participants from a dozen countries, as well as observers from over thirty more, and comprise tens of thousands of personnel from air force, army, and navy components.[29] Certainly, this offered numerous opportunities for multinational training and cooperation, but even here such exchanges were primarily at the small-unit level. Cooperative logistical and operational planning was focused almost exclusively on executing the exercise, not on working together within the construct of the exercise to simulate combat conditions. Actual maneuvering and decisionmaking were highly scripted, the outcomes preordained, and the postexercise critique designed more to avoid hurt feelings than to reveal lessons learned. While the symbolic benefits of Bright Star cannot be denied, the lack of free play limited opportunities for meaningful operational training and staff-level engagement.

Eventually the Military Cooperation Committee (MCC) was established to conduct an annual review of the program. This committee was comprised of senior officials from both countries, including the EAF chief of staff and the American deputy secretary of defense for international security affairs. According to the US embassy in Cairo, "The MCC is the premier bilateral defense forum for coordinating defense cooperation, identifying shared security objectives, and consulting on a wide array of strategic issues."[30] In practice the MCC is almost entirely concerned with coordinating defense cooperation. Although strategic issues and shared objectives are often on the agenda, discussion is usually limited to vague pronouncements and broad generalities.

Even though enhancing interoperability between Egyptian and American forces was repeatedly cited as a US objective,[31] after ten years in Egypt interoperability hardly extended beyond similarity of equipment. Discussions of doctrine, organization, and planning methodology—all aspects of "interoperability"—were not on the table. Nor were realistic planning or maneuver exercises.

At the end of the 1980s then, the EAF possessed a significant amount of US equipment, much of it state-of-the-art and right off the production line. While a broader Middle East peace settlement remained elusive and Egyptian-Israeli relations were frosty, the Camp David Accords were firmly in place and respected by both parties. Russian influence in Egypt and the wider region had been greatly diminished. Egypt had been readmitted to the Arab League. Sadat's broader objectives at Camp David had failed to come to fruition, but Egypt itself had benefited from the much-needed peace, received significant economic aid, and enjoyed a nonstop stream of equipment deliveries. The strategic gains for the United States had been significant and at little cost. That the military relationship remained largely transactional could therefore be seen as an acceptable downside. However, American objectives and expectations had begun to change, and those of Egypt had not. As the possibility of an Egyptian-Israeli conflict became ever more unlikely, many on the American side felt that whatever the initial benefits, US security assistance was no longer reaping rewards commensurate with its cost. The Egyptians of course disagreed.

This divergence would increase over time, making the differences more difficult to address. An opportunity was missed in the late 1980s to formally reassess the objectives of the program and the expectations for the relationship.

If the strategic value of the relationship was immediately apparent, the operational benefits came to the fore with the initiation of Operation Desert Shield in 1990. The pattern of frequent US overflights and Suez Canal transits had begun and continue to the present day. At the same time the forces Egypt deployed in support of US operations, if insignificant militarily, were important from a diplomatic perspective. The Egyptian II Corps, comprising the 3rd Mechanized Infantry Division and the 4th Armored Division, was positioned on the eastern third of the allied line facing Kuwait and operated under Saudi command. The Egyptians "looked the best" of the Arab forces, according to some sources, but in the event the Egyptians and Syrians both failed to move forward as scheduled, opening a large gap in the coalition line.[32] While the EAF's performance under fire has been rightfully questioned,[33] its 40,000-man corps was the largest of the Arab contingents and second only to the US force in size. Egypt's participation unquestionably bolstered the credibility of the coalition.[34]

Perhaps even more important were the overflight privileges and Suez Canal priority granted by Egypt. During the first days and weeks of the crisis, Iraq held the initiative and controlled the tempo of events. Amid concerns about an Iraqi incursion into Saudi Arabia, the United States rapidly deployed forces that were of necessity lightly armed and equipped. The logistical effort to reinforce and resupply these initial units was complex and time sensitive and would have been impossible without access to Egyptian airspace and expedited passage through the canal. As Norman Friedman notes, "It helped enormously that Egypt, through whose Suez Canal the ships had to pass enroute to the Gulf, was a coalition partner."[35]

Even in this successful partnership, the problems inherent in the relationship were manifest. Its transactional nature was apparent in the $7 billion in Egyptian debt forgiven by the United States as an inducement to participate.[36] As to interoperability, there had been "precious little real accomplishment"[37] toward this goal, not only where Egypt was concerned but also among the United States and its NATO allies. With little ability to share supplies and equipment among forces in the theater, the United States was forced to rely on long supply lines from North America or Europe, making Egypt all the more crucial to success.

In the wake of the Desert Storm success and the end of the Cold War, the United States once again missed an opportunity to formally address the assumptions and agreements that underpinned the relationship. In retrospect, this failure was particularly important as Egyptian-American diplomatic relations probably peaked in 1991.[38] Instead things proceeded much as before. Egypt ordered an additional forty-seven F-16s in 1990, and delivery began in 1991. Forty-six more aircraft were ordered in 1993, another twenty-one in in 1996, and an additional twenty-four in 1999.[39] The United States supplied 700 M60 main battle tanks free of charge beginning in 1990. The first co-produced M1A1 rolled out of Factory 200 in 1992.[40] Four Perry class frigates were added to the Egyptian navy in 1996, and the United States upgraded the weapons control systems on Egypt's aging Romeo class submarines. As the new millennium dawned, the EAF possessed approximately 2,000 M113 APCs,[41] 1,700 M60s, and 555 M1A1s.[42] A total of 196 F-16s had been delivered, although several had been lost to attrition.[43] Egypt had increased its armored divisions from two to four and its mechanized divisions from three to eight. Over twenty years the United States had supplied $35 billion in economic and military aid, and by 1999 Egypt's military was "arguably the Arab world's most sophisticated armed force."[44] As interoperability, higher echelon cooperation, and access were all limited, however, whether Egypt could effectively employ this force was difficult to judge.

The issue of access grew more problematic when US personnel were required to evaluate the "end use" of US equipment. In 1996 Congress mandated that a program be established to reasonably assure that recipients of US defense articles and services "comply with restrictions imposed by the US government on the use, transfer, and security of defense articles and defense services and that such articles and services are being used for the purposes for which they are provided."[45] As a result, end-use monitoring was required for all defense articles and services included in security assistance programs. Routine end-use monitoring does not require special access and can be performed in parallel with normal duties. Enhanced end-use monitoring is mandated for equipment or technologies that have been designated "sensitive" by the United States. Periodic access to these items is required in order to check inventory, evaluate physical security, and determine how the items are used. These functions are performed by in-country personnel (in the case of Egypt, OMC), but in both cases—routine and enhanced monitoring—occasional inspections by visiting teams may occur. Such requirements are agreed to in writing at the beginning of the equipment-transfer process. Violations of end use can occur when a recipient country—whether accidently or otherwise—fails to safeguard equipment, sells it to a third party or country without authorization, or uses it in a manner contrary to US policy. For instance, as early as 1977 end-use concerns arose when Egypt used recently transferred US C-130s to transport Soviet arms to Somalia during the Ogaden War.[46]

In Egypt, lack of access limited routine monitoring opportunities, and even though enhanced monitoring had been previously agreed to by both parties, the Egyptians sometimes restricted access. As an example, on at least two occasions in the mid-2000s, OMC personnel were denied entry to a storage facility housing night vision devices (NVDs) that were subject to enhanced monitoring. The Egyptians instead brought the devices to a central location where they could be inventoried. This prevented OMC personnel from conducting a required security assessment of the storage facility. In addition, a 2016 US government report found that "the Egyptian government's incomplete and slow responses to some inquiries limited US efforts to verify the use and security of certain equipment, including NVDs and riot-control items."[47]

Other legislation "prohibits the United States from providing assistance under the Foreign Assistance Act or the Arms Export Control Act to any unit of the security forces of a foreign country if the Secretary of State has credible information that such unit has committed a gross violation of human rights."[48] Once again, the gathering of such information is expected to occur during the performance of normal duties, but given the opacity of the EAF, this was, and continues to be, a challenge.

Meanwhile, as Zeinab Abul-Magd details in Chapter 6, several factors were at work that decreased the value of US aid in both real and nominal terms. A tacit agreement promising Egypt two-thirds of the aid that Israel received had been in place since the days of Camp David, but by 1996 discussions had begun to reduce aid to both countries. With Israel's economy much improved, the United States proposed reducing the economic portion of that country's package. The Israelis quicky suggested that the economic aid be rolled into military assistance, and the Americans agreed. The Egyptians assumed this would also hold true in their case, but they were mistaken. Instead, the Congress proposed reducing economic support funds (ESF) to Egypt by 70 percent over ten years while keeping military assistance constant.[49] As a result, ESF assistance decreased from over $833 million in Fiscal Year (FY) 1998, to approximately $315 million in 2008, to just over $112 million in FY 2019. Total US aid in current dollars decreased from almost $2.6 billion at its peak in 1979 to $2.2 billion in 1999, to just over $1.5 billion in 2011.[50] The real value of the $1.3 billion in military aid was continually eroded by inflation, prompting the periodic observation from the head of the EAA that "one point three billion just doesn't buy what it used to!"[51] At the same time, Egyptian gross domestic product (GDP) in current US dollars grew from $18 billion in 1979 to almost $91 billion in 1999, and would increase to over $300 billion by 2019.[52]

US aid, therefore, had decreased in both real and nominal terms and as a percentage of Egypt's GDP, while the two-to-three ratio of Egyptian to Israeli aid had been abandoned.

After 9/11, the operations tempo of American forces in the region increased dramatically, and the relationship with Egypt offered substantial operational advantages. Even though Egypt strongly opposed the invasion of Iraq in 2003 and refused to participate in the US-led coalition, it nonetheless provided priority canal transit, overflight permission as required, and emergency basing options. These advantages became all the more important when Turkey refused overland access and initially refused to permit overflight as well, rendering the two carrier battle groups in the eastern Mediterranean ineffective. Not only were the carrier-based aircraft unavailable, but so were the scores of ship-launched cruise missiles targeted at northern Iraq through Turkish airspace. The impact on operations in northern Iraq was severe, and the only way to salvage some capability was to move the carrier task force swiftly through the Suez Canal and into the Red Sea. Rarely had the ability to rapidly transit the canal been more valuable. In the event, the Turks relented at the last moment and permitted overflight, although not overland transit. In consequence the US 4th Infantry Division was shifted from the Mediterranean to the Persian Gulf via the Suez Canal.

In the aftermath of the invasion, the proliferation of unconventional threats in the region made Egypt's continued emphasis on conventional capability ever more difficult to justify. As John Zavage notes in his analysis of security assistance, in response to the extremist threat US security assistance increasingly focused on *building partner capacity,* a "term that refers to a broad set of missions, programs, activities, and authorities intended to improve the ability of other nations to achieve those security-oriented goals they share with the United States."[53] In the case of Egypt, unfortunately, the shared goals remained elusive. The EAF continued to purchase F-16s, manufacture main battle tanks, and emphasize its role as the defender of Egypt's borders. Publicly, at least, the possibility of an insurgency within those borders was discounted or the difficulty of dealing with it minimized. Nor were the Egyptians interested in discussing the hard lessons the United States had learned while battling insurgents in Iraq. When asked how the EAF would conduct counterinsurgency operations, an Egyptian general replied, "We will just get some tanks, some troops, and some aircraft, put them together and go do it."[54]

At the same time, the George W. Bush administration significantly stepped up efforts to promote human rights and democracy in the Middle East, believing this was the best way to secure American interests. Although a similar agenda had been pursued for years by various administrations with varying degrees of emphasis, the campaign now became more strident and public. It was not surprising that this effort quickly became tied to security assistance, but in fact the Americans had now added another condition to the aid, and a very significant one, even as the leverage conveyed by that aid continued to decrease. Inevitably more friction resulted as the Americans were frustrated by the lack of progress, while the Egyptians were offended at being publicly lectured.[55]

Meanwhile the Egyptian military's ever-widening involvement in commercial enterprises represented another source of friction, as the search for profit sometimes led to end-use violations. One ongoing problem was the US-funded military hospital outside Cairo, which the EAF promoted across the region as a "medical tourism" destination. Thus a facility funded by Americans for the use of the Egyptian military oftentimes provided treatment for profit to patients who were neither military nor Egyptian. Another recurring issue involved the synchrolift, an apparatus that raises ships out of the water so maintenance or repairs can be accomplished. OMC personnel often discovered that the Egyptian navy was leasing its synchrolift in Alexandria to private shipping companies. The commercial enterprises were pervasive and the competition fierce. During one meeting, an Egyptian three-star general complained that other generals made more money than he. When the OMC visitor observed that American generals were all paid the same amount, the Egyptian answered, "It's not the salary I'm worried about, it's the profits!"[56] As Hicham Alaoui and Robert Springborg note in Chapter 1, these commercial activities, at least partially enabled by US aid, enhance the power and prestige of the military establishment to the detriment of other state and civil institutions.

In the aftermath of 9/11, the altered strategic situation in the region, the increase in asymmetric threats, the decreasing value of US aid, and the emphasis on human rights as an objective all argued for a joint reevaluation of the relationship especially as Egypt was considered a key regional partner in the "War on Terror."

During the 2011 revolt the primary US military objective was to restrain the EAF and the Ministry of Interior security forces, a foremost concern being that the EAF would fire on the demonstrators using US equipment. Daily communications between Washington and Cairo were conducted at echelons from the Department of Defense/Ministry of Defense level to the respective chiefs of staff, service chiefs, senior staff, and relevant combatant commanders. Most of this effort was coordinated through OMC, and the years of building relationships paid dividends as Egyptian officials were consistently accessible, no small concession given the crisis they confronted. Access is not the same as influence, however, and while the EAF did in fact exercise restraint, it had numerous sound reasons for doing so other than US desires. Thus the extent to which the EAF's discipline is attributable to US influence is debatable.

After the "Day of Rage" on January 28, 2011, the EAF moved quickly to protect the US embassy, which, while not a specific target of the demonstrators, was inevitably threatened due to its proximity to Tahrir Square and its visibility as a symbol. The EAF established an enhanced security cordon outside the embassy and allowed additional armed US military personnel into the country to bolster security inside the compound. In sovereignty-obsessed Egypt, such a concession was noteworthy.

In any case, after 2011 the relationship was fundamentally altered. Lack of US support for President Hosni Mubarak during the revolt and perceived US encouragement of the Muslim Brotherhood in the aftermath resulted in deep suspicion among many Egyptian officials.[57] Even when US aid was at its peak, Egypt had procured weapons systems and support from other countries. These activities accelerated dramatically after US deliveries were withheld in response to the 2013 coup,[58] reducing America to a still important but decidedly less significant security assistance provider. The insurgency in the northern Sinai revealed how woefully ill-prepared the EAF was for unconventional operations, which were conducted with typical secrecy and circumspection, limiting the ability of US personnel to advise and assist. In 2018 the United States finally forced a redirection of the Egyptian program by limiting military aid, other than sustainment funds for existing equipment, to the "four pillars"—counterterrorism, border security, maritime security, and Sinai security—a task no doubt made easier by the EAF's struggles in the Sinai. In addition, beginning in FY 2018 Egypt was no longer offered the option of cash flow financing.[59] Cairo has continued to purchase arms from other countries, including France, Italy, and, most problematically, Russia, from which it ordered over two dozen Su-35 tactical fighters in 2018 in spite of US sanctions threats. Production delays as a result of sanctions on Moscow[60] and the recently announced US intention to finally supply Egypt with F-15s may scupper this deal, however.[61]

Meanwhile repression in Egypt worsened. Fostering respect for democracy, human rights, and civilian control of the military is one objective of US security assistance.[62] Exposure to the American professional military education system will, it is hoped, inculcate these values.

Most of the EAF senior leadership through 2011 had Soviet roots, but the subsequent transition to a younger, American-trained cadre seemed to offer an opportunity for change, especially since President Abdel Fattah al-Sisi was a graduate of the US Army War College.[63] Events swiftly dashed these hopes, and it must be said that the US effort to promote democracy in Egypt through security assistance has failed.

Both Egypt and the US have benefited from their relationship over the years. The strategic advantages as a result of the Camp David Accords were enormous and attained at modest cost. Certainly, a grand strategic bargain can be torpedoed by focusing excessively on details, and the parties at Camp David were no doubt wise to avoid this pitfall. In the early days, keeping the peace was more than sufficient reason to justify US expenditures, and if the hardware was canted toward conventional capability, Egypt's desire to rearm and modernize its force was understandable after many years of warfare. After a decade of strategic success, the "details" had become too important to ignore, but ignored they were. There was little discussion of or agreement on joint national objectives beyond the Egypt-Israeli peace. There was no consensus regarding how much and how long the United States was willing to pay for that peace. There was no acknowledgment that keeping the peace was demonstrably in Egypt's best interest and no further incentives were required.

For their part the Egyptians clung to the cloak of Camp David far too long. Their concern with sovereignty and their penchant for secrecy undermined trust. While they gained some advantage by playing one US agency against another, this made them seem devious. Their dislike of direct confrontation sometimes caused them to dissimulate or deflect when in fact they should have just disagreed. This caused misunderstandings and further erosion of trust.

The early 1990s represented the pinnacle of the relationship both militarily and diplomatically. Taking advantage of these relatively warm ties at a crossroads in the relationship offered the best opportunity to reset the program to the satisfaction of both parties. Once this chance was missed, recalibration became ever more difficult. Even so, several lesser opportunities were missed as time went on. Had the relationship been strengthened by periodic reviews and updates it might have been better able to withstand the upheaval of 2011 to 2013, and the US position would be stronger today.

After some years of drift, Nabil Fahmy, former Egyptian foreign minister and ambassador to the United States, summed up the Egyptian-American relationship: "The former assumed that the assistance was provided for Egypt being the pioneer of Arab-Israeli peace and would not entail further demands. The Americans, however, assumed that because they had been providing substantial assistance for several decades, Egypt should be at America's beck and call."[64]

Ambassador Fahmy's apt summation points up the difficulty in assessing the effects of the security assistance program. As US goals have proliferated and become more ambitious, not just success but the definition of success has become more elusive. The first and most important objective, maintaining the Egyptian-Israeli peace, has unquestionably been achieved to date. The second, leveraging the aid to gain preferential access to the Suez Canal and Egyptian airspace and bases, has resulted in significant operational advantages to the US military. A third group of objectives includes the broader governance and human rights goals introduced over time by the United States. These have not been achieved. The civil-military balance in Egypt has only tilted more strongly towards the military, and US aid, far from mitigating the problem, may well have exacerbated it. In addition, despite increased US emphasis on democracy and human rights as qualifying conditions for the aid, Egypt's performance in both areas has failed to improve and has arguably deteriorated.[65]

Finally, there is the relationship itself, which many in the United States believed would deepen over time, resulting in increased influence. This has generally not been the case. For instance, the United States has trained thousands of EAF personnel in areas ranging from technical and job-related disciplines to broader subjects such as leadership, strategy, organization, civil-military relations, and the laws of armed conflict. In the decade from 2009 alone, over 7,000 personnel were trained at a cost nearly $57 million.[66] EAF technical and tactical training has probably improved as a result, but the hoped-for embrace of Western organizational and leadership concepts, and especially of the Western approach to civil-military relations, has not occurred. As an institution the EAF remains rigid, top-heavy, without an effective noncommissioned officer corps, distrustful of initiative, too often focused on appearance at the expense of substance, and fundamentally opposed to any hint of civilian control or oversight.

Further, even though security assistance has made Egyptian leaders more accessible, there is scant evidence that their subsequent actions have been influenced in any appreciable way. Egypt has supported the United States when doing so furthered Egyptian goals, but it has also opposed US policy on numerous occasions. The example of EAF conduct during the 2011 demonstrations has already been cited: the EAF exercised restraint primarily because this course was in its best interest, not because of US urging. In 1990 Egypt joined the Desert Shield/Storm coalition in spite of its aversion to expeditionary operations, but supporting Saudi Arabia was no doubt at least as important to Egyptian interests as supporting the United States, especially since Egypt had only been readmitted to the Arab League in 1989, and presumably wished to bolster its credentials as a valuable member—if not again the leader—of the Arab world. For years, in spite of US entreaties, the Egyptians downplayed the significance of smuggling in the Red Sea and the Sinai,[67] which supplied the Gaza Strip with weapons and commodities. Only after unrest erupted in the Sinai itself did Egypt decide it could no longer tolerate an unbridled Hamas and crack down on the border.[68] Egypt feared the invasion of Iraq in 2003 would stoke regional instability, and therefore opposed it. In Libya, concerned about a possible Islamist threat on the border, Egypt supported Field Marshal Khalifa Haftar in Tobruk while the United States backed the Government of National Accord in Tripoli.[69] Egyptian policy regarding Syria,[70] Iran,[71] and especially North Korea[72] has often been at odds with that of the United States.

It should come as no surprise, then, that Egypt pursues its own course regarding the war in Ukraine. It is heavily reliant on imported wheat; in 2020 over 60 percent of that wheat came from Russia and approximately 24 percent was sourced from Ukraine.[73] Economic, military, and political ties between Russia and Egypt have deepened in recent years. Between 2016 and 2020 Russia supplied over 40 percent of Egypt's arms imports. Russia has promised a $25 billion loan to largely finance Egypt's first nuclear power plant.[74] Russian and Egyptian strategic objectives in Libya and Syria roughly coincide and are certainly more compatible than are those of Egypt and the United States.[75] Egypt is therefore reluctant to antagonize Moscow but at the same time does not want to jeopardize relations with the West. In an effort to remain neutral, Egypt voted with the UN General Assembly to demand an end to the war and protection for Ukrainian civilians and infrastructure, but it also abstained from the UN Human Rights Council's vote to suspend the Russians,[76] refused to enact sanctions,[77] and has mostly ignored Ukraine's requests for assistance.[78]

Egypt, not for the first time, is caught between two more powerful entities and is steering a typically independent course based on self-interest. Rather than deplore the fact that Egypt is doing so despite significant US aid, Western leaders should recognize that absent such aid, Egypt might be firmly in the Russian camp.

The US experience in Egypt suggests several lessons in framing a security assistance relationship.

First, establish a horizon. Avoid open-ended programs. Set milestones, whether temporal or goals based, when progress will be checked, objectives refined, and expectations discussed. In Egypt, for example, the United States might have stipulated that after three fighter wings had been established or 500 tanks had been manufactured, the nature and number of weapons deliveries would be reevaluated, or that after ten years a general reassessment would occur.

Next, measure progress. This seems fundamental, but as late as 2006 the US Government Accountability Office found that "although officials and several experts assert that the FMF [Foreign Military Sales] program to Egypt supports US foreign policy and security goals, State and DOD do not assess how the program specifically contributes to these goals"; that "DOD has not determined how it will measure progress in achieving key goals such as interoperability and modernizing Egypt's military"; and that this determination is complicated in part by "the lack of a common definition of interoperability."[79] Thus a key US objective in Egypt had not, after almost thirty years, been precisely defined, and progress toward it had not been measured.

Third, manage expectations. Security assistance is not a solution for every diplomatic problem or the best method of achieving every national objective. The goals of any specific SA program should be reasonably achievable, coordinated among US agencies, and understood by all US officials as well as those of the recipient country. US expectations in Egypt became ever more unrealistic as time went on, all the more so since these increasing expectations coincided with decreasing influence. Whatever the merits of fostering democracy and human rights, there is a vast difference between negotiating operational concessions, such as overflight privileges, and attempting to restructure a country's political system. There is a certain arrogance in thinking one can buy a country, especially one as old and proud as Egypt, for $1.3 billion a year. Yet this is very close to the attitude displayed by many official American visitors to Cairo.

Finally, understand differing perspectives. This extends from strategic outlook to operational procedures to cultural mores. It is a mistake, but a surprisingly common one, to graft American values and opinions onto recipient countries. In Egypt, a proud country very much aware of its history, its conquests, its place in the Arab world, and its humiliation at the hands of a long string of occupying powers, the issue of sovereignty is vital, touchy, and always present in a way that Americans, given their history, struggle to understand. The EAF was never likely to open its defense establishment to the Americans, and American expectations that a deeper relationship would evolve simply as a result of monetary aid was unrealistic. In the same vein, in a proud culture obsessed with status, public lecturing is unlikely to be effective.

The relationship has endured four decades of shocks and changes. An initial effort focused on strategic gains set the tone, but a much-needed reassessment of goals and guidelines was left until far too late. US expectations escalated significantly over the decades even as its leverage decreased. Targeting further aid to specific mission sets such as counterterrorism and border security may be a step in the right direction, but only if these focus areas are agreed upon by both parties. The revolution of 2011, and the coup in 2013, sounded the death knell for the old relationship, and there is every reason to believe that as Egypt diversifies its weapons suppliers, US influence will remain at a reduced level for some time to come. Expectations must reflect this reality. The glory days of the relationship are long over, but the benefits of cooperative engagement built on mutual understanding are still substantial.

Notes

1. Congressional Research Service, "Egypt," 29, 30.
2. Stork and Reachard, "Chronology," 29.
3. "Dinitz: U.S. Sale of C-130s."
4. Stork and Reachard, "Chronology," 30.
5. "Public Law 96-35—July 20, 1979," 3.
6. "Phantom with Egypt."
7. Burt, "Carter Is Said to Put New U.S. Aid."
8. Stork and Reachard, "Chronology," 30.
9. "Egypt Airmen to Study in U.S."
10. Stork and Reachard, "Chronology," 30.
11. Burt, "Carter Is Said to Put New U.S. Aid."
12. Oberdorfer, Russell, and Walsh, "The Price of Peace."
13. "Phantom with Egypt."
14. Senior USAF Official.
15. "Phantom with Egypt."
16. Conetta and Knight, "The Readiness Crisis."
17. Stork and Reachard, "Chronology," 31.
18. Ibid.
19. Senior Egyptian officials.
20. Stork and Reachard, "Chronology," 30.
21. "Egypt," F16.net.
22. "Phantom with Egypt."
23. "Egypt—Army Equipment—Introduction."
24. "Egypt—Air Defense Force."
25. "M1A1 Abrams."
26. Montgomery, "Operation Bright Star."
27. Congressional Research Service, "Ending Cash Flow Financing for Egypt."
28. Wunderle and Biere, "U.S. Foreign Policy and Israel's Qualitative Military Edge," 1.
29. Montgomery, "Operation Bright Star."
30. "U.S. and Egypt Hold 31st Military Cooperation Committee Meeting."
31. US General Accounting Office, "Security Assistance: State and DOD."

32. Schubert and Kraus, *The Whirlwind War*, 130, 131, 173, 183.
33. Pollack, "The U.S. Has Wasted Billions."
34. Hundley, "Egyptians Abandoned by Gulf War Allies."
35. Friedman, "Gulf War."
36. US General Accounting Office, "Operation Desert Storm/Shield."
37. Conrad, "Moving the Force," 19.
38. Fahmy, *Egypt's Diplomacy*, 163.
39. "Egypt," F16.net.
40. "M1A1 Abrams."
41. Ibid.
42. Honig, "A Mighty Arsenal."
43. "Egypt F-16 Peace Vector."
44. Honig, "A Mighty Arsenal."
45. US General Accounting Office, "Security Assistance: U.S. Government," 7.
46. Stork and Reachard, "Chronology," 30.
47. US General Accounting Office, "Security Assistance: U.S. Government," 1.
48. Ibid.
49. Fahmy, *Egypt's Diplomacy*, 164.
50. Congressional Research Service, "Egypt," 30, 31.
51. Senior Egyptian Official.
52. "GDP (Current US$)—Egypt, Arab Rep."
53. Congressional Research Service, "What Is 'Building Partner Capacity'?"
54. Senior Egyptian Official.
55. Fahmy, *Egypt's Diplomacy*, 172, 173.
56. Senior Egyptian Official.
57. Fahmy, *Egypt's Diplomacy*, 193.
58. Congressional Research Service, "Egypt," 19.
59. Congressional Research Service, "Ending Cash Flow Financing for Egypt."
60. Lionel, "Production of Egypt's Su-35s Almost Complete."
61. O'Brien, "U.S. Plans to Sell F-15 Fighters to Egypt."
62. US Department of State, Bureau of Democracy, Human Rights, and Labor, "Security and Human Rights."
63. Kenner and Lubold, "Sisi's Year Abroad."
64. Fahmy, *Egypt's Diplomacy*, 200.
65. "Egypt: UN Experts Report Worsening Crackdown on Protest."
66. Hartung and Binder, "US Security Assistance to Egypt."
67. "Smuggling Weapons from Iran into the Gaza Strip."
68. Amer, "Arms Supplies to HAMAS."
69. Hartung and Binder, "US Security Assistance to Egypt."
70. Ibid.
71. Hellyer, "Egypt's Stance on The Iran Talks."
72. Leone, "Egypt's North Korea Connection."
73. "Share of Wheat Imported to Egypt."
74. Anani, "Russia's War on Ukraine."
75. Hamzawy et al., "What the Russian War in Ukraine Means for The Middle East."
76. Salah, "Shoukry's DC Charm Offensive."
77. "Russia's War on Ukraine."
78. "Ukraine Asks Egypt for Weapons, Humanitarian and Medical Aid."
79. US General Accounting Office, "Security Assistance: State and DOD," 2.

Bibliography.

15

Subjectivity and Objectivity in Assessing Security Assistance

John J. Zavage

"THE QUARREL BETWEEN . . . RIVAL TYPES OF KNOWLEDGE—THAT WHICH results from methodical enquiry, and the more impalpable kind that consists in the 'sense of reality,' in 'wisdom'—is very old."[1] Thusly Isaiah Berlin captures, in his renowned essay *The Hedgehog and the Fox*, the tension between opposing methods of observation and drawing conclusions. This chapter's use of such tension to characterize US security assistance (SA) programs illuminates two of this book's recurring themes: first, that building partner capacity (BPC) competes with strengthening long-term relationships as provider nations' key SA objectives; and second, that provider nations struggle to diagnose SA problems as "upstream" (strategy or policy centered) or "downstream" (tactical or implementation centered).

What is this tension as it pertains to assessing SA programs, and why should scholars and policymakers be concerned with it now, if not before? How and why does the provision of SA employ both "methodical" and "impalpable" approaches to gaining knowledge? Assuming it's possible to clarify the significance of these two opposing approaches to SA, such clarity will prove instructive toward understanding the themes of this book.

Addressing these questions, this chapter proposes that the United States's recent policy emphasis on systematized assessment of recipient nations' suitability for security assistance programs creates an intriguing tension between, on one hand, objective data gained via regimented assessment frameworks and, on the other, subjective understanding gleaned through long-term relationship building, both personal and institutional. The United States's ability or inability to strike the right balance between these two competing approaches—or as Berlin's work might suggest, to coexist with the tension—is crucial not only to understanding competing objectives of SA as a policy tool but also to diagnosing upstream versus downstream challenges of SA.[2] Indeed, recent events demonstrate, at best, indeterminate results of large-scale US SA endeavors. Acknowledging that Ukraine's resilience, as of this writing, in the face of overwhelming Russian invasion offers indications that US SA there has contributed to Ukraine's survivability, it is also impossible to deny that the Taliban's 2021 takeover of Afghanistan confirms the futility of over $80 billion in US Department of Defense (DOD) SA alone.[3]

The chapter proceeds along the following lines: First, it presents historical context to identify key milestones in the development of US SA and how changes in policy and approach displayed a progression in SA objectives from relationship strengthening toward building partner capacity, as well as marked increases in SA expenditure. Second, the chapter describes how increased spending, coupled with dubious results of capacity-building programs—dubious results being possible indicators of the "interest misalignments" of Stephen Biddle's principal-agent problem, noted in Chapter 1—prompted both upstream/policy-centric changes and downstream/implementation-centric changes. Through a number of developments, US policymakers sought to address possible interest misalignments and anchor SA policy to better implementation by mandating data-driven, methodical frameworks for assessing recipient nations' suitability for SA programs. Third, this chapter juxtaposes the "impalpable" method with the "methodical" by using the author's personal experiences as a US military SA practitioner in Middle East and North Africa (MENA) nations to display the value of subjective understanding and perception facilitated by sustained institutional and personal relationship building. Finally, the chapter offers projections about the tension between objective and subjective assessments and how that tension might instruct SA policymakers as they navigate the balance between competing objectives for SA and address policy-centric and implementation-centric challenges to SA.

US Historical Context

Moving from Relationship-Building to Build Partner Capacity

The events of 9/11 reshaped the way the United States envisioned and implemented SA. Prior to 9/11, SA as large-scale, government-funded provision of arms and services began in 1947 and continued through the 1950s with the intent of strengthening allies to stop the encroachment of Soviet communism.[4] The 1960 Draper Commission, whose research informed and helped create the outline of the 1961 Foreign Assistance Act (FAA), which served as the central piece of SA legislation for forty years, offered conclusions that colored US SA for years afterward. Responding to what it perceived as an undesirable divorce between foreign policy and the implementation of military advisors on the ground, the commission recommended that the US government assign policy ownership of all SA policy to the Department of State (DOS) before obligating funds to SA implementors.[5] This idea—that SA activity ought to be an instrument of the nation's chief diplomat and international relationship builder and ought to align with the nation's foreign policy vision of partnerships and alliances, remained a, if not the, guiding principle for US SA policy until 9/11. Indeed, Lindsay Benstead's skillful correlation in Chapter 12 between public support for recipient-nation regimes and US SA to those regimes strengthens the idea that SA may indeed offer generational benefits based on sustained strengthening of bilateral relationships.

Despite its merits, this principle had at least one effect that may not have been apparent to the framers of the 1961 FAA. With the alignment of SA under the DOS, before 9/11 most SA efforts—particularly those in MENA—generally emphasized the strengthening of foreign policy relationships over the building of effective military capability with the provided aid. This had the effect of marginalizing the recipients' actual military performance, which often took on a desirable, yet secondary objective.[6] Such situations may have been tolerable until policy priorities arose requiring that recipient nations demonstrate capable military performance.

The 9/11 attacks created such a requirement. The post-9/11 fear that fragile states might become terrorist breeding grounds forced a reprioritization of threats and resources. New fears motivated US policymakers to emphasize SA programs that prioritized the actual military capabilities of SA recipients so that they might independently defeat threats to their and America's interests, particularly in MENA, where many terrorist threats originated.[7] A manifestation of this change arose in the creation of specifically titled "building partner capacity" programs, where—in a diversion from the foreign policy vision set by the 1961 FAA—Congress authorized the DOD, in greater scale, to lead some efforts to train, equip, and improve the capabilities of recipient-nation allies. This marked not only a policy change by authorizing the DOD to implement SA programs to a greater extent than it had ever done but also a shift in approach and objectives by prioritizing recipients' military performance over foreign policy relationships. US policy now needed MENA recipient-nation security forces to perform well, in order to assist the United States by independently defeating terrorist threats in places where US combat troops did not deploy.[8]

Examples abound of this tendency toward BPC over relationship building. General F. C. Williams's excellent Chapter 14 on the US-Egypt strategic relationship details one such example. As he describes, the United States provided more than $30 billion in SA grant aid to Egypt before 9/11 without asking Egypt for evidence of measurable increases in military capability—that is, until the presence of an al-Qaeda-linked violent extremist organization (VEO) in the Sinai Peninsula motivated US policymakers to scrutinize how well Egyptian military forces might combat VEOs within their borders.[9]

Similarly, US SA activities in Iraq, Afghanistan, and elsewhere after 9/11 took on a capabilities-based focus. The US-led coalition force effort to develop Iraq and the Iraqi Security Forces cost more than $53 billion, including roughly $27 billion in BPC programs.[10] The twenty-year US effort to improve the capabilities of the former Afghan National Defense and Security Forces (ANDSF) witnessed expenditure of over $80 billion between 2001 and 2019.[11] In contrast to pre-9/11 approaches, the United States intended primarily to improve recipient-nation security capabilities.[12] Iraq and Afghanistan are not the only recipient nations for this policy change; indeed, the chapters in this book by Noureddine Jebnoun on Tunisia, Aram Nerguizian on Lebanon, Zeinab Abul-Magd on Egypt, and Sean Yom on Jordan all detail, from unique perspectives, the travails of US efforts to build military capabilities in these allied states.

New Approach and Objectives Cost More Than the Old

After years of burgeoning post-9/11 SA and BPC budgets, US policymakers had little more to show for the effort to combat extremists and stabilize potential terrorist breeding grounds than that very increase to said security assistance budget. The historical trend in US security assistance spending between 1961 and the present day demonstrates this significance. In 2003, when the United States removed the Saddam Hussein regime in Iraq and doubled DOD-funded security programs in Afghanistan, US security assistance funding trends began to emphasize BPC programs.[13] Between 1961 and 2002, the annual aggregate of federal security assistance funding obligated through all US departments (including DOS, DOD, and others) averaged approximately $11 billion, measured in 2019 dollars. Between 2003 and 2019, this same aggregate averaged nearly $15.5 billion, representing a 50 percent annual average increase.[14]

Further inspection into the substance of this 50 percent annual average increase reveals more telling details. In the years between 1961 and 2002, funding obligated to the Department of Defense averaged approximately 25 percent of total SA spending. After 2003, funding obligated to the Department of Defense, which included BPC programs, averaged closer to 33 percent of the security assistance funding total, revealing an upstream/policy-centric decision to center a significant portion of the post-9/11 cost increase on DOD-led BPC and similar programs to improve recipient-nation capabilities.[15] Government watchdogs Special Inspector General for Iraq Reconstruction and Special Inspector General for Afghanistan Reconstruction (SIGAR) routinely published reports detailing the spending associated with SA missions to Iraq and Afghanistan. Through these and other reports, congressional appropriators realized how easily costs increased as the Defense Department gained unprecedented authority to combat terrorist threats and stabilize fragile states.[16] The United States undertook not only a more measurable and performance-based SA objective, but a vastly more resource-intensive one.[17]

Recent events like the collapse of the US-supported ANDSF in Afghanistan—whether or not they confirm Biddle's principal-agent problem—do confirm that recipient-nation security performance often offers little justification for such high expenditures. Estimates vary, but most indicate the United States spent well more than $80 billion in efforts to improve the former ANDSF, nearly all of which the ANDSF's precipitous collapse rendered futile.[18] Place this next to the 2014 collapse of the Iraqi Security Forces at the hands of the Islamic State—after the aforementioned $53 billion US taxpayer investment—and there exists a damning and embarrassing trend that calls into question the upstream/policy-centric decision to shift toward BPC: huge sums of money and national treasure intended to improve recipient-nation security performance has been radically wasted.[19]

SA Develops an Objective Methodology

Upstream Approach:
Improving Policy Effectiveness for Sustainable Cost

That the US government sought—and continues to seek—to rectify this embarrassing trend speaks to the difficulty not only in diagnosing causes of failure in BPC programs but in setting appropriate goals for SA programs writ large. Interestingly, policymakers appear equally ready to attribute BPC failure to both upstream/policy-centric and downstream/implementation-centric causes. One might call the methodology created to address BPC failure a layered attempt to address principal-agent challenges by instituting a policy fix through improved implementation.

At the upstream/policy level, the US government began this effort to respond to such exorbitant and ineffective expenditures through, among other things, the Barack Obama administration's 2013 Presidential Policy Directive 23 (PPD-23). PPD-23 brought SA policy into focus by introducing the term *security-sector assistance* (SSA) to gather all variants of security assistance under one umbrella. With that term, the United States attempted to consolidate, if only nominally, DOS control of SA policy together with DOD control of a similar but differently designed constellation of military cooperation programs known as security cooperation (SC), which included BPC programs. Additionally, PPD-23 defined an order of priority for US SSA policy and programs, bringing pre-9/11 SA philosophy into alignment with post-9/11 philosophy. Indeed, PPD-23 aspired not only to streamline what was a dual-department system but also to synthesize those two competing objectives (namely, relationship building versus BPC) whose competition this book seeks to unpack. While "promot[ing] partner support for U.S. interests" would remain a top priority of SSA programs, another leading priority ought to be to "help partner nations build sustainable capacity to address common security challenges."[20]

Following PPD-23 Congress directed US departments to systematize objective methods for measuring foreign assistance program success, creating mandates focused on the downstream/implementation level. A leading example, the 2017 National Defense Authorization Act

(NDAA), mandated that the US Department of Defense formally assess, monitor, and evaluate (commonly referred to as AM&E) specified DOD-funded BPC programs to reduce waste and improve effectiveness in building partner-nation security capabilities.[21] This and other laws led to systematic knowledge collection intended to hold policymakers accountable by mandating that implementors of federal assistance programs assess, measure, and evaluate how well they accomplished goals of US policy. In the case of broad SA, which for the purposes of this chapter includes how the US defines all SA, SC, and BPC programs, the first step toward measuring this effectiveness would be the assessment phase: assessing recipient-nation suitability for receiving SA.

Downstream Approach: Addressing Implementation with Objective Measures and Assessment Frameworks

Responding to these congressional mandates, DOS and DOD both created frameworks to define and standardize measuring SA and BPC programs' success.[22] Both departments direct SA implementers toward objective assessments, tangible indicators, and logical, results-based reasoning sequences. Through a myriad of guiding policy documents, both the DOD and the DOS identify assessment of the recipient nation as the foundational step in the objective methodology. The DOD defines the assessment as "a systematic analysis to provide an understanding of the context, conditions, partner capabilities, and requirements to inform security cooperation planning and implementation."[23] The DOD goes on to direct BPC program implementors to format assessments by first "identify[ing] gaps between current and desired results," and, after analysis, deciding how to "address gaps and move toward desired results." Immediately one sees the DOD's underlying assumption is that such gaps can be tangibly identified and measured.

Continuing, the DOD instructs practitioners to unpack the critical task of identifying gaps by focusing on "results first and solutions second" and to "define needs as gaps in results."[24] Note the guidance focuses the implementor on a results-based observation: define the desired results, observe the current results, and measure the gap between them. This data-driven exercise intends to make the process as objective as possible by focusing on measurable, reportable data. Many DOD assessment teams categorize data in terms of, among other frameworks, the "DOTMLPFP" construct, a model that helps determine "acceptability, suitability and feasibility" of proposed assistance programs by aligning data against the following functions: *d*octrine, *o*rganizational structure, *t*raining, *m*atériel, *l*eadership and education, *p*ersonnel, *f*acilities, and *p*olicy framework.[25] While the collection process of this data may vary from team to team, the DOD instructs implementors to collect the data via interviews, questionnaires, and other perspectives, implying assessment teams must make deliberate, scheduled arrangements with recipient-nation leaders and stakeholders to collect specifically targeted information.[26]

The United States has focused partner-nation assessments on results-based measurables, which indicates an objective, methodological approach to SA. In a larger sense, however, the results-based assessments are emblematic of the United States's effort not only to improve the effectiveness of BPC by striking a balance of upstream and downstream improvements but also to justify the transition from relationship-building to BPC as a primary goal of SA. If SA implementors measure well and make accurate assessments, so the thinking goes, the United States will reduce waste in BPC programs and justify future BPC endeavors as pillars of SA policy.

Long-Term Relationship Building: A Subjective Approach to SA

The challenge to centering improved BPC policy upon such assessments is that the frameworks designed to collect objective data at prearranged intervals according to set checklists will struggle to incorporate valuable intangibles. While methodological objectivity understandingly gained momentum in the United States after 2013, the US government historically centered (and still does, to a great extent) SA recipient-nation assessments upon the subjective perceptions of skilled diplomats and military leaders assigned to build long-term, sustainable relationships with recipient-nation security leaders. These personnel include military leaders and diplomats assigned to embassies, as well as those assigned to overseas positions pursuant to operational deployments.[27] From the personal trust engendered by consistent, protracted side-by-side bilateral working arrangements, year in and year out, these relationships produce invaluable subjective assessments: firsthand appreciation of tactical soldier strengths, better clarity of entrenched loyalties and biases, and deeper understanding of leadership traits and nuanced context. Such valuable perceptions and appreciation can be difficult to gain via formally scheduled, structured, arguably "snapshot" assessments.

This author's own experience as a US military officer working in relationship-building billets in MENA offers an opportunity to examine personal interactions between US leaders and recipient-country counterparts for extended periods. Personal reflections show how sustained relationships with recipient-nation leaders build valuable insights. For comparison's sake, we can categorize these insights under the same "DOTMLPFP" construct used for more methodological assessments: (1) intangible warrior traits reveal insights into *training*; (2) leader personality traits reveal insights into quality of *leadership*; (3) ethnic, social, or political biases reveal insights into *leadership* and *policy*; (4) observation of real-time and unexpected changes in external circumstances also reveal insights into *leadership, organizational structure*, and *doctrine*; and finally (5) unique multilateral arrangements maximize regional *policy* benefit. Each forthcoming anecdote illustrates how long-term relationships, absent methodological frameworks, can enable qualitative assessments of recipient-nation suitability for SA and BPC programs. Given the systemic and temporal restrictions associated with the frameworks, it is precisely the nuances and subtleties illustrated below that SA provider nations should incorporate into SA program assessment procedures. While the anecdotes recount details of personal, individual relationships, such relationships would not have been possible without the generational benefit of SA that began as the 1961 FAA prioritized relationship building as a primary goal of SA. The anecdotes will point to how individual and long-term institutional relationships transcend methodical attempts to assess recipient nations.

Assessing Tactical Intangibles Through Sustained Cooperation

Eight weeks alongside soldiers in a small-unit tactical training course in Jordan helped clarify the effect of individual soldier intangibles upon combat readiness. Experience at this tactical level offered insight into soldier aggressiveness, courage, and stamina—or what we might call the warrior ethos. Additionally, these traits point to strategic capabilities in the training category, such as institutional training philosophy and training logistics.

Soldiers in this training course exhibited a high degree of personal aggressiveness, courage, and physical stamina. For example, each day of field training required a one-mile foot movement from cantonment to training area. Dressed in military gear with helmet, boots, individual load equipment, and a rifle, soldiers were not content to simply walk. Not only did they run the length of the movement, both to and from, but each day brought a new opportunity to race fellow soldiers for bragging rights.

Additionally, soldiers excelled in scenario-driven live ammunition exercises. Trainers required students to demonstrate proficiency by assaulting a one-room building in two-person teams, using individual fire and maneuver. Given rocky terrain and use of live bullets, some degree of hesitation on the part of soldiers would have been understandable. In contrast, the students approached this exercise with determination, excitement, and a high degree of aggression and combat realism. While trainers expected soldiers to demonstrate such an ethos, teaching it was not part of the course—the soldiers manifested it because of personal expectations and collective esprit de corps.

In addition to the soldierly qualities on display, the training demonstrated philosophical and logistical strengths of the collective Jordanian training institution. For example, the course demonstrated an emphasis on combat realism. Trainers expected soldiers to fire live bullets in relative proximity to each other, often with fellow soldiers as close as thirty feet from the line of rifle fire. That trainers implemented few, if any, visual or auditory fire-control mechanisms that might have tempered realism for safety's sake indicates a collective expectation that soldiers demonstrate combat readiness to the most realistic extent possible. While demonstrating a need for improved risk management, this institutional expectation points to a noteworthy expectation in the nation's training philosophy for combat readiness.

Additionally, this course demonstrated consistent logistical capability that enabled training to occur on a predictable basis. Predictability allows leaders to orchestrate appropriate preparatory activities to maximize the training's benefit and hinges on dependable logistical provision of critical support items: food and water, ammunition, and personal equipment. The course involved a frequent schedule of live-fire exercises, and each soldier in the course received a predictably sufficient degree of support needed to benefit from training.

Gaining such granular insight required eight continuous weeks of shared physical and emotional experiences. Such insight enables one to draw nuanced conclusions about the character of the nation's training institution and, by extension, its combat readiness. SA providers must acknowledge that regimented assessment processes, governed by a checklist or formalized data collection, may struggle to incorporate the nuance critical for understanding a recipient nation's true capabilities.

Personality and Leadership Traits Take Time to Manifest

Senior ground commander during civil conflict. Throughout a yearlong tour with US forces in Baghdad, a senior operational commander appeared inappropriately preoccupied by political concerns above his pay grade. On the heels of a national parliamentary election that witnessed over sixty terrorist attacks nationwide and over twenty-five Iraqi civilians killed, I expected a senior commander of his level to emphasize security challenges and make improvements for future elections. Instead, he spent a disproportionate amount of time discussing Iraq's postelection process of government formation and how the Kurdish bloc might influence the choice of prime minister (PM). He often seemed unfocused and out of touch, undervaluing his duties as military operational commander and instead becoming distracted by political circumstances outside his control.[28]

Additionally, this commander exhibited a reactive approach to leadership. On numerous occasions, while watching interaction with US leadership, I observed him emphasize what he perceived as inequities or instances of unfairness perpetrated by actors external to his organization and appeal for help. In one instance he indicated a belief that the Iraqi Ministry of Defense (MOD) leadership became "jealous" when US forces provided his troops with equipment the MOD had previously withheld. At times he complained he hadn't received the right information or been included in the right conversations at high levels, in apparent attempts to curry favor with the counterpart with whom he may have been speaking. His insistence on waiting and reacting to unfortunate circumstances rather than taking a proactive approach to problems made him conspicuous among Iraqi military leaders at high levels.

This may have decreased more senior military and political leaders' trust and confidence in him. One example of such a lack of trust may have appeared when he did not assume an influential role in a postelection review hosted by senior MOD leadership. The MOD and PM's office invited leaders to share challenges and successes from an election security operation. Despite this commander's senior rank, event organizers omitted significant input from him, instead favoring input from subordinate regional commanders. If senior MOD leadership also noticed the tendency I noted regarding his distracted and reactive approach to leadership, that may have explained the smaller role assigned him in this senior-level meeting.

Senior maritime commander during civil conflict. An opposite but relevant observation from time spent working with the Yemeni Armed

Forces (YAF) emphasizes the importance of personality traits.[29] While I was serving as senior US military liaison to the YAF, a ranking member of Yemen's security forces explained to me the predicament of the Yemeni coast guard and recommend it receive US SA or BPC programs. The facts he presented would have demanded a failing assessment by any structured, quantitative assessment process. Since the beginning of the Yemeni civil conflict in 2014, attacks by Houthi rebels had contributed to significant degradation of the coast guard's operational capability. Division of Yemeni military formations along political fault lines split what coast guard vessels remained into distinct fighting forces commanded by different Yemeni factions; this leader, representing the legitimate YAF, exercised control over only one of these. This leader effectively controlled merely a handful of vessels that secured barely a sliver of Yemen's coastline.

The leader knew the United States would not solve all, if any, of his problems immediately. Yet he persisted with humility, professionalism, and realism. Over the course of a year meeting with and coming to know this officer, I found him to be a competent leader, a patient planner, and an astute observer of the Yemeni political and security landscape. He distinguished himself from peers consumed with political influence amid the turmoil of a nation in crisis, advocating calmly and professionally for the strategic and operational benefits of training and equipping the small force he led. He also astutely lobbied with appropriate Yemeni and other external regional military leaders, including leaders from Saudi and Emirati forces who exercised influence over Yemeni political and military affairs.

As US resources and priorities evolved, opportunities emerged to use US SA authorities to provide small, inexpensive programs for the benefit of the Yemeni maritime forces. Absent the humility, professionalism, patience, and competence of this leader, such resources would likely have gone elsewhere.

Personality traits are critical to assessing SA recipient leadership capabilities, but they often manifest not in the course of one or several meetings but rather over time as relationships develop. If a senior commander finds himself marginalized due to distraction and passivity, critical functions may suffer from collective marginalization of a central leadership node. Conversely, if a senior commander demonstrates competence through patience, persistence, and calm professionalism, the organization he leads may be more capable than a mere lack of equipment might imply. Because personality-based insights like these gained from long-term relationships remain difficult to capture via questionnaires administered in a circumscribed time frame, the objective approach toward SA assessments will benefit from balance with subjective assessments.

Ethnic, Social, or Political Biases Emerge over Time

Few leaders displayed the type of competence, intelligence, and professional optimism displayed by a particular senior civilian in the Iraqi Ministry of Defense.[30] While he did have a military background, he was likely chosen more for his ethnic background than his military record, as he came from a Sunni Arab region and was a political representative of one of the leading moderate Sunni Arab political parties. Given the rise to power of Shi'ite parties after the removal of Sunni dictator Saddam Hussein, naming a Sunni to a top post helped enable the Shi'ite leadership to maintain power by creating a facade of reconciliation toward the often-disenfranchised Sunni voting bloc.

That said, meetings with this leader in early 2010 revealed him to be articulate and understanding of not only policy but military imperatives also. He understood operational challenges like fusing intelligence with operations, protecting critical terrain across the country, and addressing obstacles to transition between coalition forces and Iraqi security forces. He displayed acute appreciation of the organizational complexity of mixing new Iraqi security formations with the same faces who had run the show for decades under Ba'ath rule. He recognized a need for US help in the use of air reconnaissance assets, and his understanding of Iraq's weaknesses in these areas offered confidence that if the United States provided SA in these areas, Iraqi use of the assets might be successful. He demonstrated unbiased appreciation of Iraq's ethnosectarian political frictions. Regarding the sensitive issue of cooperation between the Kurdish Peshmerga and the Iraqi army, he patiently advocated for a political agreement on the organizational and financial relationship between the two forces. He praised pragmatists from other groups and sects, while condemning radicals from his own.

Despite his competence, the handcuffs of bias that the Iraqi levers of power placed upon him became apparent over time. At a conference with far-reaching implications for the future of Iraq's national defense, this leader attended but did not appear to be the most influential person in the room. That distinction belonged to a lesser-ranking military officer from the prime minister's personal staff. This lesser-ranking officer responded more frequently, offered more critiques, and provided more guidance about the way forward than did the MOD leader. From an outside observer's perspective, the lesser-ranking officer held more decisionmaking authority in this forum than did the nominally senior MOD leader. A likely explanation points to how ethnic and political bias can affect an organization's effectiveness more than the competence of its leaders. The officer from the PM's office, a Shi'ite Arab like the prime minister, shared a history of political and military cooperation with the PM and likely enjoyed professional and political trust that the Sunni Arab MOD leader did not. The MOD leader's competencies were, at that time, called into question, since it became clear that at the crucial moments, he did not enjoy the full trust of Iraq's command authority.

The hindrance to leadership and policy effectiveness created by political and ethnic bias needs little elaboration. Notable here is the time and effort required by an SA provider nation to gain appreciation of the subtleties and nuances of how bias works inside a recipient nation's organization. It required multiple contacts spanning weeks if not months, with different contexts and interactions surrounding each meeting, to reveal the cumulative effect of bias at work. If an SA implementor had written an assessment after only one meeting with the MOD leader, or a few meetings over the course of a few days, it might have championed the strengths noted above with little to no mention of the weaknesses created by political bias. The value of perceptions gained through protracted relationships will assist provider nations in deciphering conditions like these and assigning them relevance in recipient-nation assessments.

Real-World Crises Affect Performance, Often for the Better

In my observation, a real-world crisis revealed competence in the categories of leadership, doctrine, and organizational structure that otherwise might not have emerged.[31] Understanding this requires noting non-crisis observations and juxtaposing them with observations made later, during a crisis.

A meeting with a senior Iraqi army leader on the MOD staff revealed his notable discomfort with perceived intelligence failures that facilitated election-day attacks. He struggled to articulate analysis, commensurate with his rank, regarding intelligence operations. Additionally, he appeared embarrassed that Iraqi information and US information were dissimilar, and this incongruence led to self-consciousness on his part. It struck me as noteworthy that a leader, expected to lead his own formations, seemingly dealt with the embarrassment of laying bare his weaknesses for a larger, more powerful provider nation. From this observation it appeared hesitation and self-consciousness defined his personality more than did expertise and assertiveness.

Over a month later, a real-world crisis emerged: extremists demonstrated intent to destroy selected religious shrines. A meeting with this leader under these conditions led to a constructive conversation about counterair and counterground security measures intended to protect shrines from asymmetric attacks. He demonstrated assertiveness, confidence, knowledge, and foresight about potential courses of action. He articulately discussed strategic and operational aspects of security activities: preventing terrorist aircraft from entering airspace, shooting down terrorist aircraft if they did enter airspace, streamlining reporting procedures, deconflicting friendly fires, and maximizing weapons capabilities. The difference in my perception of this leader's competence at the earlier meeting and at this later crisis meeting was dramatic. The increase in exuded confidence, assertiveness, and competence on this leader's part was likely linked to energy he derived from his perception of a potential real-world crisis.

This crisis revealed strengths in leadership, organizational structure, and doctrinal understanding that did not emerge in earlier meetings under noncrisis conditions. Only the access and trust enabled by the relationship alongside this and other leaders provided this unique view of what may otherwise have been concealed competencies. Observations about how recipient nation strengths manifest in crisis situations can lead to better assessments and decisions about how provider nations provide SA.

Achieving Multilateral Policy Objectives Through Limited Training Programs

As liaisons worked to coordinate a US-funded program training Yemeni border soldiers in 2018 while the Republic of Yemen Government (RoYG) worked from Riyadh, an interesting multilateral policy dynamic manifested between the United States, Yemen, and the Kingdom of Saudi Arabia (KSA).[32] In most cases, US-funded programs would be a bilateral issue, involving only provider and recipient. Indeed, as the senior US military liaison to Yemen at the time, I expected and looked forward to this arrangement. However, due to political, security, and logistical obstacles presented by the Yemeni civil conflict, both the RoYG and the US diplomatic mission to Yemen relied on logistical and institutional support from KSA. The KSA MOD used this arrangement to its advantage in the case of US-Yemeni bilateral training. Because the strengthening of Yemeni border capabilities served both US and Saudi strategic objectives, it made sense for KSA to support the training and even offer logistical support to host it inside KSA's borders. Moreover, working through a temporary trilateral military coordinating committee, KSA ministry officials insisted on exercising influence on key details of the training, such as dates, and providing Saudi military with day-to-day oversight of the training.

In other situations, a US military liaison may have been justified in refusing such third-party influence over an otherwise bilateral issue. However, regional circumstances presented an opportunity to advance the United States's bilateral and regional objectives concurrently by allowing KSA to exercise unique influence in this case. The Yemeni civil conflict and the inability of the Yemeni Armed Forces to secure the training in Yemen made KSA the logical training location. In terms of regional dynamics, by exercising influence KSA enhanced cooperation with the Yemeni Armed Forces, thus strengthening the Saudi-led coalition, whose success against the Yemeni Houthi rebellion was so critical to resolving the civil conflict in a manner amenable to Saudi and US interests.

From this perspective, the training program took on a regional and multilateral benefit that transcended its bilateral scope. The program trained mere tens of Yemeni border soldiers, a drop in the bucket in terms of measurable capabilities. This may have been enough to drive SA assessors to conclude that US SA resources might be better spent elsewhere. However, US military-liaison involvement helped uncover the additional, multilateral benefit of KSA support and oversight of the training initiative. In this way KSA, as the self-proclaimed supporter and overseer of the training, also became the target of a beneficial US multilateral policy effort. The time spent planning the program spanned nearly six months. US military-liaison personnel used that time in multiple face-to-face engagements with Saudi and Yemeni officials to discuss, coordinate, troubleshoot, and ultimately approve implementation of the training, leveraging personal relationships. The personal insights and trust required to enable such a multilateral benefit would not have been apparent, or accessible, to a visiting assessment team charged with completing a preformatted assessment framework.

Going Forward

The effort to hold SA policymakers accountable is valid and should continue—especially in the wake of the US 2021 policy catastrophe in

Afghanistan that witnessed the Taliban inherit unheard of amounts of US-funded assistance. Additionally, while this chapter has not addressed human rights violations by US SA recipient nations, seeking to limit SA intended for potential human rights abusers, as the Joe Biden administration's new conventional arms transfer policy review attempts to do, is also a valid effect of holding SA policymakers accountable.[33] With these justifications for accountability frameworks in mind, some like Andrew Natsios caution current policymakers against processes that champion centralized quantitative frameworks and measurable short-term returns at the expense of more valuable localized decisionmaking and long-term outlooks.[34] Similarly, Zach Gold critiques those who would reduce evaluation of SA programs to simple return-on-investment analysis, instead calling for a "mixed methods" quantitative and qualitative evaluation framework.[35] Both authors acknowledge a dialectic similar to that which defines this chapter—namely, that accepting the challenge of assessing and evaluating SA projects forces policymakers to wrestle with objective versus subjective methods. While Natsios and Gold make compelling claims about how to do just that, this chapter's intent is not binary—it acknowledges benefits of both approaches. The hope is that by juxtaposing the rigor of the assessment rubric with the nuanced and unpredictable insights gained through long-term personal and institutional relationships, the chapter provides readers with an enlightened appreciation of the dialectic balance required of SA policymakers and implementors, especially in the face of enduring principal-agent challenges.

The objective/methodical approach represents a reasonable response by a government aiming to be a better steward of taxpayer resources and follows from well-funded, well-researched analysis by government and private research agencies.[36] Formalized assessment frameworks introduce a level of accountability that heretofore had not existed; even if they only capture a fraction of what they seek, they succeed in achieving at least a measure of the intended accountability.

Accountability notwithstanding, it will be important for provider nations committed to objective methodologies to consider whether objective assessments miss the forest for the trees. Each anecdote here illustrates how extended time and personal trust enabled a provider-nation liaison to gain valuable insight into strengths and weaknesses of respective recipient-nation military capabilities. Of the anecdotes recounted, the minimum time required to gain observed insights was four weeks; one case required eight weeks and another several months. Each activity observed arose naturally, the result of strategic, operational, or tactical motivators. In all cases, additional time for reflection proved critical to a more accurate understanding of all influences at play. Additionally, the author did not build relationships from scratch; each relationship had existed previously for years among predecessors on both sides, the result of bilateral institutional ties between the respective nations, strengthened in most cases by generations of US SA programs. Conversely, objective methodology tends toward a more targeted and necessarily less comprehensive data-collection model. Rarely will assigned assessors be permitted to spend weeks on end with recipient-nation partners. They will carry targeted checklists into hours-long or, at most, days-long meetings and strive to "check all the boxes" in the allotted time. Partners will surely cooperate, but interactions likely will be sanitized of spontaneous influencers observable in long-term relationships.

Provider nations can account for these challenges with nuanced changes at both the upstream and downstream levels. At the downstream level, the DOD framework already calls for the collection of subjective data, gleaned or inferred through analysis of relevant economic, political, sociological, cultural, and other factors that may impact the implementation of a program in a specific country. The framework calls for assessors to use the subjective data to estimate a partner's political stability and willingness to pursue the objective.[37] The frameworks remain vague regarding how to measure the subjective data and integrate it with the more tangible data. To maximize accurate insertion of this critical subjective data, SA provider nations must—and indeed, the US strives to—ensure those diplomats and military assigned to enduring relationship-building posts serve as primary sources of insight and nuance.[38] Those assigned to embassies or operational deployments should develop close working relationships with visiting assessment teams in order to contribute subjective assessments on the basis of deeper knowledge of enduring bilateral relationships.

At the upstream level, policy or even legal reforms may offer an appropriate pathway to achieve necessary course corrections. Just as 2013's PPD-23 rightly attempted, with only marginal success, to rebalance a US SA enterprise whose center of gravity had shifted from the DOS to the DOD, more current proposals may continue such movement toward reemphasizing bilateral institutional relationships. A 2022 US legislative effort proposes to regain for the DOS a measure of SA primacy it lost to the DOD after 9/11. It seeks to increase personnel to make DOS more competitive in the policy space and eliminate some generational obligations to improve DOS's flexibility in parceling out billions in SA funding.[39] While uncertain and still in planning phases, such efforts justify significant consideration if capable of helping provider nations find the sweet spot between objective and subjective approaches to SA.

That said, the United States's national embarrassment in Afghanistan proves it's not enough to simply draw upon insight and nuance from the proper sources; decisionmakers must use that insight to make sound decisions. SIGAR has described with great accuracy since 2008 the short-sighted, uninformed decisionmaking process at the heart of twenty years' worth of ineffective nation-building programs in Afghanistan; yet the exorbitant spending continued year after year.[40] SIGAR's effective reporting revealed—beginning in 2008 and continuously until 2021—the cultural nuances, ANDSF limitations, and other obstacles to BPC success in Afghanistan. Yet, instead of effectively integrating such insights, decisionmakers continued the appalling annual expenditures, which 2021's tragic culmination confirms as largely futile. From a programmatic perspective, the waste in Afghanistan eludes the main thrust of this chapter because, ironically, the primary funding source for SA programs there, the Afghan Security Forces Fund, does not require the same accountability regimen that the 2017 NDAA mandates in many current BPC programs.[41] One might cite principal-agent challenges, but the embarrassing result only emphasizes the need to get preprogram assessments right, one way or another. Indeed, it might appear the United States wasted $80 billion in Afghanistan without thoughtfully incorporating available objective or subjective assessments. Comparable in scale but different in scope and purpose, the sizeable SA commitment the United States has made thus far in Ukraine bears watching for similarities to and differences from Afghanistan. If Ukraine remains independent and US SA proves helpful to that end, policymakers will have struck upon a unique set of circumstances that may prove instructive for future BPC and SA efforts.

Stepping back from what will hopefully be onetime anomalies and assuming a 30,000-foot view, the most penetrating approach to integrating objective methodologies with subjective understanding requires a philosophical rearrangement and revisits the earlier mentioned themes of this book. Just as the practice of framework-based methodological assessments risks missing the forest for the trees, so a policy focus on BPC programs in the first place risks emphasizing the short-term goals of military capabilities over the generational benefits of SA. The policy momentum for SA accountability emanated from justified alarm at outrageous sums going toward improving recipient capabilities, only to witness failures of those capabilities. That said, policymakers should not allow embarrassing results of short-term, short-sighted BPC efforts to mislead them into thinking they can "get it right" with just a bit more rigor. Rather, these ill effects ought to motivate policymakers to avoid the internal competition between upstream-focused and downstream-focused diagnoses of BPC's associated problems and, more importantly, to limit emphasis on BPC-focused policies altogether. Instead, policymakers ought to turn their gaze back to the transcendent benefit gained by generational commitment engendered when provider nations use SA simply to improve relationships. Egypt's and Jordan's steadfast support, and even Iraq's lukewarm support, of US regional objectives is an immeasurable asset in a turbulent region. The Abraham Accords, the largest regional diplomatic achievement in a generation, likely would not have occurred without steadfast US political and financial commitment to Saudi Arabia, Bahrain, and the United Arab Emirates, not to mention Israel, spanning generations. Like the objective methodologies that assess them, BPC programs are a tool, not the goal in and of themselves. In this sense a core concept of the Draper Commission ought to remain intact: SA is a tool of foreign policy, with strengthened relationships the goal of foreign policy. Leaning too heavily on BPC programs, even those handrailed by methodical frameworks, risks placing the tool ahead of the goal. In keeping with Isaiah Berlin's observation that Leo Tolstoy lived his life in constant tension between one intellectual mode and the other, SA provider nations' ability to sustain a healthy tension between methodological assessment frameworks and subjective nuance hinges on their ability to maintain the proper philosophical relationship between SA's short-term goals and its generational benefits.[42]

Notes

The views and opinions in this work are those of the author alone and do not necessarily represent the policies or views of the Defense Security Cooperation University, the Defense Security Cooperation Agency, or the Department of Defense.

1. Berlin, *The Hedgehog and the Fox*, 112–114.

2. Will Waddell, PhD, US Air War College, Maxwell AFB, Alabama, January 2017. My assertion that there is benefit to coexisting with tension and applying that benefit to the dialectic expressed by Berlin rests on many conversations with Dr. Waddell while a student in his war theory class at the Air War College.

3. Baldor and Corder, "US Sending $1 Billion More Military Aid to Outgunned Ukraine"; "Foreign Aid Explorer" (accessed September 15, 2021).

4. Clarke, O'Connor, and Ellis, *Send Guns and Money*, 1–5.

5. Overfield, "The Draper Report."

6. Congressional Research Service, "U.S. Foreign Assistance to the Middle East," 1–5.

7. Bergman and Schmidt, "A Plan to Reform U.S. Security Assistance."

8. Congressional Research Service, "What Is 'Building Partner Capacity'?"
9. Ibid., 4–5.
10. SIGIR, "Learning in Iraq," 92.
11. SIGAR, "Divided Responsibility."
12. Blanchard, "Iraq," 32.
13. "Foreign Aid Explorer," accessed September 11, 2021.
14. "Foreign Aid Explorer," accessed March 1, 2021.
15. Ibid.
16. SIGIR; SIGAR.
17. "Foreign Aid Explorer."
18. Arabia, "The Collapse of the Afghan National Defense and Security Forces."
19. Francis, "How the U.S. Lost Billions over 9 Years in Iraq."
20. White House, Office of the Press Secretary, "Fact Sheet."
21. Other laws with similar effect included the Foreign Aid Accountability and Transparency Act of 2016 and the Program Management Improvement Accountability Act of 2016.
22. US Department of Defense, "Assessment, Monitoring and Evaluation"; US Department of State, "Program and Project Design, Monitoring, and Evaluation Policy."
23. US Department of Defense, "Assessment, Planning and Design, Monitoring, and Evaluation Overview for Security Cooperation," 7.
24. US Department of Defense, "Principles for Security Cooperation (SC) Assessment," 4–5.
25. Ibid., 10.
26. Ibid., 5.
27. Karas, "Reconciling Defense and State Department Cultures at Embassies."
28. Written journal notes of author, March-April 2010.
29. Personal reflections of author.
30. Written journal notes of author, March-April 2010.
31. Ibid.
32. Personal reflections of author.
33. Cohen, "Biden's Conventional Arms Transfer Policy Review."
34. Natsios, "Foreign Aid in an Era of Great Power Competition," 112–117.
35. Gold et al., "A Better Way to Measure Returns."
36. RAND Corporation and the Center for Strategic International Studies have published extensive reports between 2013 and 2020 that have contributed to the base of research and discussion upon which current activity for assessment, monitoring, and evaluation for SA is grounded. Examples include, but are not limited to, Moroney, Thaler, and Hogler, *Review of Security Cooperation Mechanisms Combatant Commands Utilize to Build Partner Capacity*; Thaler et al., "From Patchwork to Framework"; Dalton et al., *Oversight and Accountability*.
37. US Department of Defense, "Assessment, Monitoring and Evaluation," 14.
38. Plaster and Howk, *Culture Shock*. This book provides an excellent and value-added compilation of military leaders' abilities to strengthen institutional foreign policy relationships from overseas postings.
39. Gould, "For America's Security Aid Programs."
40. Ward, "Government Watchdog."
41. Arabia, "The Collapse of the Afghan National Defense and Security Forces"; US Defense Security Cooperation University, *Security Cooperation Programs Handbook*, 38–39, 58–59.
42. Berlin, *The Hedgehog and the Fox*, 113–116.

16
Quit Trying, or Try to Cure?

Hicham Alaoui and Robert Springborg

THE WEST HAS FAILED EFFECTIVELY TO COUNTER OPPONENTS' STRATE-gies designed to reduce Western influence in the Middle East and North Africa (MENA). First Iran, then Russia, and now China has developed a distinctive approach based on its own national strengths. Iran's strategy of subverting Arab states by mobilizing and arming Shi'i fifth columns has capitalized on that religious affinity coupled with technical capacities to wage asymmetric warfare at a distance from its own borders. Russia has drawn upon its ample military resources and diplomatic sophistication to exploit MENA actors' desires to counter or reduce Western influence.[1] The success of that strategy is reflected in MENA states' reactions to Russia's invasion of Ukraine, which have overwhelmingly been to hedge their bets by taking neutral positions, distancing themselves from their traditional Western allies. China has relied on its economic strength to cultivate relations with MENA actors—relationships that are beginning to serve its geopolitical as well as its economic interests.

As for developments within the region, they have generated their own challenges for the West, of which the most direct and publicized are terrorism and emigration. Being structural and likely enduring, the underlying trend of declining state coherence and capacities, exacerbated by rapidly growing populations, stagnation of the regional monocrop oil economy, and increasing political repression, will continually test the West's abilities to interact effectively with the region.

Faced with growing competition in an ever more unstable, fractious region labeled as the "axis of failed states," the West has yet to devise effective responses.[2] Strategies to counter these threats have been so inadequately developed that selling them to reluctant publics has yet to even be seriously attempted, with sloganeering substituting for formulating and explaining the ways, means, and ends from which effective strategies would be formulated.[3]

Many and Difficult Choices

The sheer range of policy options proposed in Western capitals and especially Washington suggests disarray. At one end are quitters, those who advocate or just foresee the inevitability of a strategic withdrawal from MENA.[4] The usual reasoning behind this recommendation or prognosis is that the region has lost its geostrategic centrality, largely because of the alleged declining centrality to the global economy of MENA hydrocarbons, but also because the region is essentially broken and too difficult and expensive to fix. That is best left to others, as US neglect of Syria seems to exemplify. A related observation, one typically made by aspiring politicians across the political spectrum, is that too much Western blood and treasure have already been wasted in MENA, so it is past time to retrench and invest in development and democracy at home. Yet another argument is that security assistance to MENA has concentrated on counterterrorism, consuming a disproportionate amount of total US security assistance, distorting the entire program and rendering it less capable of confronting more important threats posed by China and Russia, an argument the latter's invasion of Ukraine has underscored.[5]

At the opposite end of the policy spectrum are those who advocate hanging in there, either carrying on as before but with greater commitment, or fighting fire with fire.[6] They argue that MENA remains strategically located (so a key transit route or potential choke point in global trade); that hydrocarbons are fungible and cheaply produced in MENA (so the region will remain vital to the global energy economy); that it is central symbolically, strategically, and as a weapons testing ground for global contestation for power between authoritarianism and democracy (just as it was central to European imperial competition in the colonial era and to the conduct of both world wars, as well as the Cold War); and that the West, with its thumb pressed more firmly on the scale, can correct the present imbalance that favors authoritarian forces. These arguments have also been reinforced by the war in Ukraine.

As for how to add more weight to the balance between evil and good in MENA, one approach is to double down on traditional security assistance, while another is to learn from the success of one's opponents, imitating and improving their methods. *Grey zone, asymmetric, hybrid,* and *full spectrum* are some of the labels that have been given to Iranian and Russian strategies to be emulated. Their tactics include applications of both hard and soft power, ranging from use of weaponry that facilitates stealth and deniability, such as unmanned arial combat vehicles, to deployment of mercenaries, to assassinations, to cyberwarfare, to disinformation campaigns and the use of economic rewards and punishments.[7]

This strategy and its associated tactics, which some analysts urge the West to imitate, amount to technically and politically updated coercive diplomacy, an approach developed during the Cold War, intellectually primarily by Alexander George.[8] It entails the threat or actual use of selective and limited force to induce an opponent to change its objectionable behavior or in some cases "to make fundamental changes in its government."[9] In other words, it signals to opponents by reference to or use of coercion. According to Michael Eisenstadt, because it was developed during the protracted Cold War in which total victory was unimaginable and only marginal gains within an overall strategy of containment possible, it is particularly appropriate in the contemporary Middle East.[10] Decisive, final victory by any actor is virtually impossible there as well, so commitment to protracted contestation, coupled with use of threatened or actual coercive signaling, is preferable to either preparing for all-out war, which is unlikely to occur, or abandoning the field to enemies.

Between the positions of quitting or doubling down on security assistance to MENA, there are two other recommended fixes. One is offshore balancing; the other is correcting what is claimed to be disproportionate emphasis on security assistance at the expense of what might be termed "3D," by which is meant diplomacy, democratization, and development. John Mearsheimer and Stephen Walt's advocacy of offshore balancing rests on their critique of building partner capacity (BPC) on the grounds it was oversold as a cure to expensive boots-on-the-ground approaches to security assistance.[11] The West has permanent interests in MENA, not permanent alliances, in part because of profoundly different values and systems. The West can best pursue its interests not by seeking to bolster the armed forces of presumed partners but by selective, direct interventions designed to preserve an overall balance of power by depriving aggressive actors of the prospect of total victory. American capacity to project power is, in Mearsheimer and Walt's view, sufficient to implement such offshore balancing.

Among prominent figures urging at least the addition to security assistance of a more "3D" approach is former secretary of defense Robert Gates.[12] He argues that America's victory in the Cold War relied not on "military might but on subtler tools of power." Since then, the United States "has become overly dependent on military tools and has seriously neglected its nonmilitary instruments of power, which have withered as a result."[13] He identifies those instruments as the Department of State (DOS), the US Agency for International Development (USAID), and the onetime US Information Agency, the vital tasks of which are the conduct of diplomacy, fostering economic development, promoting liberty and freedom, and public messaging as well as cyberwarfare. Not only should these institutions be upgraded, according to Gates, but they need to be integrated into a whole-of-government approach.

The former defense secretary is preaching to a large and growing choir, among whose voices are various of America's prominent think tanks. The RAND Corporation, for example, released in April 2021 its prescription for US strategy in the Middle East, in which it argued that "reliance on military instruments of power is escalating—rather than reducing—regional conflict."[14] It recommended shifting resources from "heavy reliance on military tools to economic investments, governance, diplomacy, and programs focused on people." This should be in cooperation with global and regional partners and conducted within a long-term time horizon "even at the cost of short-term risks." Some two months later the Center for a New American Security issued its strategy for the Middle East, stating as its lead recommendation, "The U.S. assistance mix in the Middle East must be rebalanced away from security assistance and toward development, democracy, humanitarian, and stabilization programs as part of a broader strategy emphasizing civilian rather than military tools."[15] To do this, it urged, the US government should reduce "large-scale conventional weapons sales to the region" and focus on "elite forces capable of conducting counterterrorism and irregular warfare missions instead of trying to fundamentally reshape regional militaries." It further noted that improving governance is a prerequisite for economic growth in the region. Several years previously, in "Modernizing US Security and Development Assistance in the Middle East," the Center for Global Development noted, "US investment in regional security institutions has failed to produce capable allies" and "placed a thumb on the scale in support of security institutions." Its recommendations were to "promote civilian oversight through increased transparency," to "elevate and amplify local voices pushing for reform," and to "establish a Middle East and North Africa Fund to address constraints to economic growth."[16] Focusing specifically on security assistance to Egypt, the Project on Middle East Democracy led its recommendations with a call for a reduction of $300 million in annual security assistance followed by more robust reactions to human rights violations and increasing transparency in military aid.[17]

Brookings lead analysts of security assistance to MENA advocated in late 2020 a mixed version of "quitting" MENA and "3D." They identified the key problem as the presence of too many US boots on the ground and on ships' decks in the region and called for a reduction of 20,000 soldiers and sailors, which, according to them, "could help streamline and partly demilitarize U.S. strategy for a part of the world that, while still important, should no longer be a center of American foreign policy."[18] Alexandra Stark, a Middle East analyst at New America, contends, "The proxy approach to Middle East conflicts has failed. It's time to focus on a new strategy centered on major investments in development and diplomacy."[19] Frederic Wehrey and Michele Dunne of the Carnegie Endowment recommend shifting "financial and human resources on the U.S. side—from privileging military-to-military ties to diplomacy and development," which "almost certainly would cost far less in financial and human terms."[20] The Stockholm International Peace Research Institute (SIPRI) urged the EU in 2020 to "rethink, refocus, and reform" its strategy toward MENA to take "the needs of the populations as the starting point" and support "economic diversification."[21] In the wake of America's abrupt, unilateral withdrawal from Afghanistan in August 2021, *Foreign Affairs* published an article by Dalia Dassa Kaye, titled "America Is Not Withdrawing from the Middle East," arguing that "the United States is not going to abandon the Middle East. In fact, it may be facing a different problem—not that it is leaving, but that it is staying in all the wrong ways." The right way, in her view, is to "dial down military commitments and increase economic and development assistance. The United States needs to refocus its attention and resources on the challenges affecting the day-to-day lives of people."[22]

While most observers of Western security assistance to MENA agree that its costs are high and its benefits few, their prescribed cures stretch over such an expansive policy range that even attentive, intelligent decisionmakers would find it difficult to formulate from them and then articulate a clear, concise MENA security assistance strategy. The range extends from abandoning the region or security assistance to it, to tweaking security assistance such as by reducing bases and personnel, to redirecting at least some funding for security assistance to the 3Ds, to overhauling the machinery responsible for national-security-related policies toward the region, to substituting for security assistance a people-centric or human-needs approach to relations with MENA. Clearly there is no simple solution. Even a George Kennan, were his equivalent present today, would have a hard time boiling this complexity down to the equivalent of a single word, *containment*, which rendered Cold War strategy understandable even to mass publics. Anthony Cordesman's suggested shift in the lexicon and practice of security assistance from "long wars" to "long engagements" is precisely the change that needs to occur, both to put the political curse of "forever wars" behind us and to prepare for the long haul ahead.[23] But useful as this alternative characterization may be, and much as Russia's invasion of Ukraine points to the need for more robust efforts to counter Moscow militarily, at least in eastern Europe, it will still be a hard sell to skeptical publics and wary policymakers. Moreover, virtually all recommended fixes are not without problems and critics, as a brief review suggests.

Many Guns, No Silver Bullet

The existential issue of whether to leave or remain in MENA can be dismissed on the grounds that abandonment is unlikely to happen. That engagement by Western powers has a long history; that it is a key area for intensifying global competition between Great Powers; that it may pose direct security threats to its neighbors, especially Europe; and that it remains the world's preeminent source of oil and gas while sitting astride primary trade routes between Asia and Europe all suggest Western engagement will continue for the foreseeable future. As Cordesman states in Chapter 2, the US military and defense civilian presence in most MENA countries other than Iraq and Syria has not declined and appears unlikely to do so in the foreseeable future.[24]

The halfway house of offshore balancing in which the West monitors the region from afar, intervening only when inherent self-balancing tendencies between contesting indigenous forces falter, is indicted on varying grounds, summed up by one critic as follows: "Offshore balancers' hearts are in the *offshore* part—the *balancing* part is secondary for them. Hence their inattention to the mechanics of intervening in Eurasian rimlands."[25] Not defining a clear strategy to guide the timing and methods of intervention, undermining capacities for power projection by withdrawal and alarming regional allies by so doing, and downplaying the threatening role of competitive global actors, offshore balancing, like the argument for comprehensive retreat, seems destined to remain more an academic exercise than a guide to foreign policy.[26] While further development of precision weapons launched from the United States and capable of striking small targets in MENA may eventually enhance prospects for offshore balancing, deployment of such weapons is not imminent.

Seeking to augment or supplant security assistance by more energetic pursuit of one or more of the Ds in the 3D approach shares some of the pie-in-the-sky quality of abandonment or rigorous offshore balancing. MENA is probably the world's least receptive region to fullbore 3D treatment. Democratization has made less progress there than in any other region, despite disproportionately large allocations of official development assistance to achieve it.[27] Economic development has lagged growth rates of other regions. The Middle East economy is more dependent now on hydrocarbon production and export than it was a generation ago. More development assistance is unlikely to speed economic growth, and in fact, there is an inverse relationship between the two.[28] Underlying the region-wide deficiencies of democratization and development are "limited access orders," which characterize virtually all MENA regimes.[29] State capture by elites intent on maintaining power and extracting rents while subordinating regime outsiders to their control is a method of rule extremely difficult to change, as contemporary Lebanon attests. Despite its responsibility for bringing about one of the three worst national economic collapses in the last 150 years, according to the World Bank, the political elite that brought on Lebanon's disaster remains in power.[30]

Two primary objectives of diplomacy in the region—arms control and creation of formalized security systems—have abysmal track records dating back to World War II. Western efforts to impose arms control in the wake of the 1948 Arab-Israeli War were shattered by the so-called Czech arms deal of 1955, never to be reinstated. The regional zone free of weapons of mass destruction first called for by Egypt in 1990, then adopted as part of the 1995 indefinite extension of the Nuclear Nonproliferation Treaty, is characterized by the Arms Control Association as having "garnered broad international support," although "practical progress has since been elusive."[31] Of the five regions in North Africa that were intended to create standby peace and security forces according to the terms of the 2003 African Peace and Security Architecture Agreement, "nothing has eventuated."[32]

As for creation of a regional security framework, a veritable library of works exists on the topic, but no such framework exists.[33] A recent Chatham House study calling for renewed efforts to create one paradoxically illustrates the obstacles. Noting that "the process for getting to a regional security framework should begin now, as conditions are—counterintuitively—favourable," it continues by observing that "not only does Iran need to recognize the counterproductive impact of its financial and military support for proxy groups across the region: Arab states also have to acknowledge that they too bear responsibility in driving conflict."[34] The failure of the six Arab Gulf Cooperation Council states, since the founding of their organization more than forty years ago, to create a security system limited to them alone suggests how slim chances are for success of this larger venture urged by Chatham House. The likely fate of current diplomatic efforts to create arms control and security systems in the region is suggested by that of a previous US-led effort to do both. The Madrid Conference of 1991, initiated by George H. W. Bush and James Baker, created a working group on arms control and regional security to complement bilateral negotiations between Israel and its Arab neighbors. According to the zombie website of that organization, which has not been updated since 2003, "Thirteen Arab States, Israel, a Palestinian delegation, and a number of extra-regional entities participated in plenary and intercessional meetings focusing on both conceptual and operational confidence-building and arms control measures applicable to the Middle East."[35]

US signaling of intent to reduce its footprint in MENA, combined with Russia's invasion of Ukraine, has stimulated intensified negotiations between various regional states. They have been accompanied by growth in arms transactions and cooperative military exercises, even including Israel alongside Arab states. While they may ultimately prove to be initial steps on the road to constructing one or more regional security frameworks, they may also just be false starts down that track, stimulated by transitory circumstances, whose passing will remove the stimulus for cooperation. Strong Arab criticism of the Joe Biden administration's efforts in the summer of 2022 to create a North Atlantic Treaty Organization (NATO)–like alliance including Israel, the United States, and four Arab states indicated the difficulties facing that initiative.[36]

If the objectives of Western diplomacy are to be arms control and security systems in MENA, then clearly it is advisable not to abandon security assistance unless and until tangible progress is made. In the meantime, there is much to recommend coercive diplomacy, even though that is not necessarily the type those seeking to substitute diplomacy for security assistance advocate. Its relative success in the Cold War attests to its utility, while its foremost practitioners within MENA—Iran and Russia—demonstrate its applicability there. In fact, reading between the lines, some advocacy for revitalization of US diplomacy, such as that by former secretary Gates, suggests that it may well be a plea for coercive diplomacy more than an injunction to pursue through diplomacy difficult-to-realize, idealistic objectives.[37] But to be effective, coercive diplomacy requires close cooperation between diplomats and warriors within a whole-of-government approach, something easier to achieve in centralized authoritarian systems such as those of Iran and Russia. Whether the presently fragmented, politicized, and "overmilitarized" US government, to say nothing of the dysfunctional broader political system, could regain the coherence, unity of purpose, and coordination maintained during the Cold War is an open question.[38] Coercive diplomacy, at least if it is to be practiced by the United States, might be almost as difficult to conduct as that focused on arms control and security systems.

Another debate over curing what ails security assistance to MENA turns on the issue of the relative costs and benefits of grey-zone as opposed to traditional forms of it. Three contributors to this book—F. C. Williams, John Zavage, and Robert Springborg—have argued elsewhere that despite downsides of traditional approaches and some advantages of grey-zone activities, it would be premature to discount benefits of traditional security assistance, which derive, primarily, from the relative "stateness" of recipients and the shaky but still intact Metternichian system of MENA states and, secondarily, from association with global order and rule of law.[39] The West, after all, is the status quo external power operating in the region. To undermine the very state system it helped to create in order to better fight its challengers by adopting their methods is a risky, possibly counterproductive undertaking. Fragile they may be, but most MENA states have capacities that separately and jointly undertake more effective collective action than that by nonstate actors, although it is fair to say that in the case of Lebanon, Hezbollah may have more capacities than the government, but this is debatable and a special case. It also begs the question of values and their role in security assistance. If values are to be largely or entirely disregarded in favor of methods and interests, then justifications for protecting and projecting Western-supported values in the region become dubious.[40] If Western actors are to become equivalent to militias contesting for power and spoils in MENA, as in effect Russia has done by supplying various dictatorial regimes with mercenaries, typically in return for actual or the equivalent of "blood diamonds," then their reason for being there will be more open to question among their own citizens, to say nothing of those in MENA.

The search for a silver bullet to eliminate the shortcomings of security assistance to MENA or to provide substitutes for it is, in sum, likely to be fruitless. In the meantime, the lethality and numbers of weapons and those utilizing them in MENA increase as quality of governance and rates of the region's overall economic growth deteriorate, rendering the challenges facing security assistance ever greater. While the search for less harmful and more effective solutions to problems facing security assistance should proceed, that search should supplement but not displace efforts to reform existing practices. The contributions to this book, combined with lessons from the history and contemporary political economy of security assistance, suggest some potentially useful reforms.

Escaping Historical Legacies and Contemporary Pressures

The dominant forces shaping today's security assistance are embedded in its history and in the contemporary political economies of providers and recipients. The overwhelming predominance of militaries in MENA states, according to Stephanie Cronin, is the legacy of dialectical interaction from the late eighteenth century between the region's defensive modernizers and the European powers called upon by them to transform their militaries.[41] Local rulers sought to expand the size and scope of the new conscript armies to have them buttress their own power and serve as pillars of their states. European assistance providers generally sought to build smaller, more professional, capable fighting forces through which, maybe not incidentally, they could exert influence. "These origins indelibly stamped Middle Eastern armies as instruments primarily for the enforcement of domestic political power."[42] Among the contradictions of this dialectic was that rulers' appetites for large, expensive militaries inevitably outran the resources of their states, resulting in ruinous national debt. Military modernization, "intended to protect sovereignty and enhance centralized domestic political power," led to "exactly the opposite results."[43] Cronin concludes her comparative study by noting that in MENA, "the era of state-building and national consolidation is far from complete," as evidenced by the failure of representative institutions to address ethnic, sectarian, and other tensions. "Inevitably, into the vacuum created by the mass popular challenge offered to discredited regimes has stepped the army, once again presenting itself as a uniquely pre-eminent national institution."[44]

She might have added that as was the case some two centuries ago, today's MENA armies are keen to leverage that assistance into influence over or direct control of their states. Neither side seems to have learned from this lamentable, unique history, encompassing as it does most states in the region and profoundly distorting them. Viewed in this light, security assistance has been the handmaiden of MENA's authoritarianism, militarization, and misallocation of national resources.[45] While this is a severe indictment, there is sufficient truth in it to merit careful reexamination of the dialectic between providers and recipients of security assistance with an eye to at least reducing, if not eliminating, negative consequences.

Careful assessments of motivations and consequences of security assistance for both providers and recipients, combined with recommendations for how to reduce harm and increase benefits, are notably absent. This is due in part to the dearth of careful historical analyses—Cronin's work being an exception—but is more the result of contemporary interests embedded in both sides of the relationship that have been more thoroughly baked into security assistance since World War II, so much so they are simply taken for granted.[46] Provider interests consist of economic benefits, such as those accruing to arms manufacturers and to militaries, for which procurement costs are lowered because of larger production runs, and political ones, including geostrategic positioning. Moreover, economic interests within provider countries are translated into political ones, resulting, in US parlance, in the notorious military-industrial complex or, more accurately, the military-industrial-political complex. The distribution of weapons-manufacturing facilities in the United States, for example, is influenced by corporate intent to influence votes of representatives of congressional districts, while American arms manufacturers are leading contributors to political campaigns.[47] Political influence within their respective countries is similar for European armaments manufacturers, while their Russian equivalents are vital to that country's economy and to the continued incumbency of its political elite.[48]

As for recipient countries, the mix of economic and political interests is similar, if yet cruder. Whether constituting the regime itself or a crutch for it, MENA militaries need resources to build and maintain loyalties not only within their organizations but between them and rulers, on the one hand, and among citizens, on the other. These political needs explain in large part why the average expenditure on militaries of MENA countries is presently 4.8 percent of gross domestic product (GDP), double the global average.[49] But magnitude of expenditures is only part of the problem, another being that they are hidden, disguised, or downplayed. Transparency International's Government Defense Integrity Index documents the two features of lack of transparency: corruption and nonprovision of definitive financial information.[50] All MENA countries other than Tunisia are rated as having "very high" or "critical" levels of corruption risk. Tunisia is rated as "high." Only two countries, Tunisia and Kuwait, allow for even limited parliamentary oversight of military finances. Several MENA countries criminalize unauthorized scrutiny of those finances.[51] Examples of cover-ups exist throughout the region. Algeria does not disaggregate its annual military budget, reporting it as a lump sum. Egypt does not include procurement in its budgets or the financial activities of the military economy. Qatar did not release any budget figures for the defense and security sector between 2010 and 2020. Since 2014 the United Arab Emirates has not provided data on total military spending.[52] Only four Arab countries have made their military budgets publicly available over the past five years. SIPRI notes that the data on military spending in Algeria, Egypt, and Iraq is "highly uncertain" and that the lack of transparency regarding it in Saudi Arabia, Bahrain, Lebanon, and Oman requires "SIPRI to estimate their annual military spending."[53]

Extensive and debilitating as corruption and inadequate reporting and oversight are in MENA, yet worse for the prospects of development are the proliferation of military-owned enterprises and the subordination of entire civilian economies and relevant state instrumentalities to militaries and their officers.[54] Militarization of MENA political economies has expanded the scope of corruption and imposed drag effects throughout entire economies, as Yezid Sayigh has so carefully documented for Egypt.[55] While civilian dictatorships in MENA have failed to manage adequate economic growth, the prospects for military ones, such as in Egypt, Algeria, and Sudan, are yet worse. According to Ishac Diwan, "Compared to military dictatorships, civilian rulers can enlarge the economic pie by cooperating with the civilian economy more than military dictatorships can—to caricature, civilian elites use carrots and sticks, and armed forces use only sticks." Among other depredations, armed forces "have a direct interest in reducing political competition by potential opposition movements," so they deny "opponents access to finance from the private sector." In Egypt, for example, "as the army's involvement in the economy rose, private investment has fallen to 6 percent of GDP, less than its level under former president Gamal Abdel Nasser." Diwan sums up the economic capacities of political elites from the military, saying, "It is likely that they are less able than civilian elites to manage basic economic relations, let alone complex economic reforms."[56]

The Democratic Paradox

The combined effect of legacies of security assistance and their contemporary political economy drivers results in a paradox that bedevils relationships, especially those of security assistance, between Western and MENA countries. That paradox is that Western democratic states are the prime external supporters of authoritarian, antidemocratic MENA regimes. It is this paradox that underlies the emphasis by American critics of contemporary security assistance on the need to reconceptualize security policy to "more closely align with American values."[57] In addition to stimulating criticism at home of providers of security assistance to MENA, the democracy paradox undermines providers' leverage, hence the geopolitical value of their assistance. Seeking to avoid pressures from those democratic providers to liberalize their regimes, to respect human rights, and to democratize, MENA rulers, whether monarchs or civilian or military dictators, turn to authoritarian states as counterbalances, especially through provision of security assistance. The paradox thus accounts for much of Russia's success in reentering MENA and presages that likely to be enjoyed by China.

Resolving, or at least reducing, the democratic paradox is thus essential to the long-term strategic success of Western security assistance. Otherwise, competition with authoritarian providers of it will intensify as MENA regimes become progressively more repressive in the face of rising political and economic demands from their citizens. Addressing the democratic paradox, however, poses a huge challenge. It is rooted in some two centuries of security assistance and its consequences for MENA recipients. It is driven by powerful actors in both provider and recipient political economies. Sudden, substantial efforts to liberalize and democratize could easily result in strong counterreactions, as they have since 2011 in many Arab countries, or in state collapse, as in Libya and Yemen, or in a mix of the two, as in Syria.

Resolving the democratic paradox thus should be a long-term rather than immediate goal of security assistance providers. In the shorter term, improving the quality of governance is a useful goal in its own right. It might also serve as a stepping-stone toward subsequent democratization. An obvious good-governance reform would be reducing military influence over MENA political economies while expanding civilian oversight of those militaries. That would require strengthening relevant civilian institutions and capacities, presumably to some degree at the direct expense of militaries and security assistance provided to them. This presents to security assistance providers the challenge of carefully anticipating how their actions will impact recipients' civil-military relations and adjusting those actions accordingly. While the long-term objective of resolving, or at least reducing, the democratic paradox is being pursued, immediate security threats and challenges must also be addressed.[58] The dilemma of preventing short-term threats and reactions to them from dictating long-term strategy thus must also be resolved. The remainder of this chapter addresses these challenges.

Downsizing Militaries

Reducing the magnitude and effects of the democratic paradox requires a rebalancing of civil-military relations. Overgrown MENA militaries will have to be shrunk and repurposed, a task that Western security assistance providers have failed to achieve over some two centuries, suggesting just how difficult it is for them to counter MENA rulers' preferences for sprawling armed forces as regime props. On the other side of the equation, effective civilian states, essential to the welfare of the region and its citizens as well as to the West's strategic interests, have not been built. Moreover, Western appetites for state building in MENA have been jaded by misfired attempts to do so in Iraq and Afghanistan. Given the magnitude of these twin tasks and the dismal track records of achieving them, one is tempted to conclude they simply lie beyond the West's manageable interests in MENA.

This book, which documents and analyzes the difficulties of grappling with the democratic paradox, suggests ways and means to address them. They are found on both sides and in interactions between providers and recipients in security assistance relationships. Among the latter, Cordesman's label, "axis of failed states," aptly describes the inherent weakness of the region's nation-states, the multiple causes and resulting complications of which have thus far exceeded the abilities of Western security assistance providers to formulate effective strategies in response. Glenn Robinson's investigation of how regime rather than national interest drives contemporary demands for security assistance reinforces Cronin's point about the historical continuity of MENA rulers' desires for armed forces to prop up their regimes more than to serve as shields of their nations. General Williams and Zeinab Abul-Magd describe in behavioral and numerical terms, respectively, the limits of US influence over the Egyptian military and that country's national security policies in general, despite the remarkably generous US security assistance to it over the past almost half century. Colonel Zavage provides firsthand examples of the difficulties of creating professional, competent officer corps in Arab armies cleaved by subnational loyalties, which also divide the societies and polities those armies are meant to defend. In so doing he renders further support to Jason Lyall's well-established proposition that militaries whose composition reflects severe inequalities between national social forces will fare worse in battle than those built on more inclusive social and political structures.[59] Noureddine Jebnoun's analysis of the tensions resulting from US pressure on Tunisia's military to narrow its focus to counterterrorism and border control provides another example of problems that beset principal-agent relations.[60] Interestingly, Aram Nerguizian's account of security assistance to the Lebanese Armed Forces reveals its favorable impacts on military capacities but also underscores that those capacities cannot easily be broadened to support a state in peril, which is *a* if not *the* major reason for Western security assistance to Lebanon. Unintended consequences also plague principal-agent relations. Sean Yom describes how security assistance to Jordan has beefed up its repressive security services in tandem with or even more than the military. Lindsay Benstead's review of public opinion data reveals the abiding popularity of Arab militaries, an outcome eagerly sought by them and in many cases assisted directly or indirectly by security assistance.

In sum, this book is replete with examples of disconnects between the objectives of principals on the one hand and agents on the other and how these differences plague the effectiveness of security assistance. There is no case in this book or in real life of security assistance to MENA having had direct, positive impacts on the democracy paradox, either by reducing the clout of militaries or by increasing that of civilians. If, however, the definition of effect is relaxed and the implications of at least some of these chapters carefully considered, the prospects for security assistance contributing to the shrinking, repurposing, or internal restructuring of MENA militaries seem better. The Egyptian military, for example, has responded favorably to US urgings to emphasize border control and counterterrorism, rather than the long-outdated strategic focus on war with Israel, as is noted in General Williams's chapter and elsewhere.[61]

Jahar Matisek and William Reno make a case against providing security assistance to armed forces as a whole in weak states, where "leaders lack the political willpower and capacity to utilize the benefits of SFA [security force assistance] in this context, at least beyond distributing SFA as patronage." Accordingly, "the best the U.S. military can do in these situations is to build a militia that is insulated from the bad politics of the state and to use that militia for counterterrorism or other specific tasks that serve American national interests."[62] Focus on subunits of larger militaries appears to be a strategy that Iran has adopted. "It has hand-picked hundreds of trusted fighters from among the cadres of its most powerful militia allies in Iraq, forming smaller, elite and fiercely loyal factions in a shift away from relying on large groups with which it once exerted influence. The new covert groups were trained last year in drone warfare, surveillance and online propaganda and answer directly to officers in Iran's Quds Force."[63] US security assistance in Iraq and Lebanon is also selective in that it has targeted specially chosen units, which, as a result, have outperformed the armed forces of which they are components.[64] The likely explanation of the success of such units is the greater control exerted over them by the assistance provider. In the case of Iran, "The new factions are linked directly to the Iranian Revolutionary Guards Corps. They take their orders from them, not from any Iraqi side."[65] Direct Russian control of handpicked units of the Syrian military, such as the Fourth and Fifth Corps, accounts for their superior performance, as does US control of Syrian Democratic Forces.[66] Mara Karlin's comparative analysis of outcomes of US security assistance concludes that the single most important correlate of success is degree of control exerted by US armed forces.[67]

However effective in strictly military terms building capacities of specialized units may be, it only nibbles at the edges of the problem of overly large militaries and their drag effects on democratization and development. Moreover, as Anthony Cordesman notes with reference to Afghanistan, drilling down on selected units of larger armed forces does not guarantee successful military outcomes, undermines the effectiveness of those larger forces, and does little if anything to develop the capacities of defense institutions or contribute to improved governance more generally.[68] In reviewing security assistance to fragile states as a whole, Oystein Rolandsen, Maggie Dwyer, and William Reno observe that fragmented security forces frequently cause providers to "single out small units for specialist training to make them 'good enough' to fight insurgents. Such pragmatism can exacerbate the fragmentation of armed forces." They further note that providers can easily be "drawn into violent competition among the recipients' domestic political factions and play a direct role in further blurring lines between state and 'non-state' actors."[69] The temptation to achieve immediate battlefield success by bolstering specialized forces may thus impede downsizing and professionalizing militaries and exacerbate their internal divisions and those of the polity.

A more directly relevant security assistance approach to downsizing militaries, or at least to changing their character, is to promote professionalization. The International Military Education and Training (IMET) program is the primary US vehicle for so doing. It has been relatively sparsely funded in MENA. Its annual allocation within the bilateral military aid program to Egypt, for example, has for years been $1.6 million out of the $1.3 billion total.[70] Numerous studies have found positive correlations between participation in IMET programs and favorable outcomes, such as reduced probabilities of coup attempts, higher levels of acceptance of professionalization, and reduction in state fragility.[71] A recent big-data study of the impact of US security assistance in the Middle East and Africa found that "programs geared toward education and training are more positively correlated with stability than programs oriented toward providing hardware."[72] A parallel effort supported by the US Department of Defense (DOD) is to upgrade the administrative capacities of ministries of defense. Jomana Amara, a faculty member in the Defense Resources Management Institute at the Naval Postgraduate School, has noted that the importance of this undertaking for Arab militaries has been increased by recent expansions in their size due in part to the reintroduction of conscription in several of them. She concludes by observing that "to free up the military to focus on their professional expertise," it is necessary not just to empower ministries of defense with legal authority, financial responsibility, and personnel resources but for them to develop competencies "in budgets, personnel, acquisition, and definition of roles and responsibilities."[73] These capacities are necessary but not sufficient conditions for formulating effective military strategies, which Thomas Bruneau observes is a missing element in efforts to build partner capacities, in part because the United States itself has been so poor at strategy formulation since the end of the Cold War.[74]

Direct efforts to use security assistance to reconfigure and downsize militaries have been recommended, as for example by the United States to Egypt when it commenced its security assistance program under President Anwar Sadat, but not implemented. One such method is to use positive rather than negative conditionality, so that "instead of punishing partners that don't live up to their end of the bargain, the United States should reward those that do."[75] Specifically it is recommended that the United States "draft a memorandum of understanding with the partner nation that articulates a road map for the relationship" and then provide incentives for its implementation. Rachel Kleinfeld urges the Biden administration to be yet tougher to ensure that recipients of security assistance adopt best practices in the governance of their security sectors. "That means the United States cannot be afraid to say no. Ending foreign military sales, loans, security sector assistance, or cooperation may occasionally mean that a country will look to a competitor for military goods. But if an ally is so quick to turn to Russia or China, the United States must ask whether the partner could have been counted on when the chips were down."[76]

Military downsizing coupled with professionalization is more difficult to achieve in MENA than in other authoritarian settings. Possibly the best comparators are Russia and China, whose military modernization programs over the past thirty years have been veritable models of best practice. In the latter, between 1990 and 2012, three major reductions were imposed on the People's Liberation Army (PLA), coupled with raising recruitment standards. The goal was set in 2009, for example, for 60 percent of PLA officers to be civilian university graduates by 2020. Fringe activities, such as sports and entertainment, were stripped away from the PLA "so that it [could] better concentrate on the business of war."[77] In Russia's case professionalization has included converting a Chechen-originating "military police" corps of some 20,000 into an instrument to project both soft and hard power in Syria by combining security and humanitarian assistance functions.[78] That force was subsequently deployed in Ukraine. Tellingly, both the Chinese and Russian regimes prepared the grounds for downsizing and professionalization by ensuring in advance effective political control of their militaries. In China this was achieved through the Communist Party, while in Russia it resulted from party control, succeeded by personalistic manipulation of the officer corps—initially by Boris Yeltsin, then by Vladimir Putin—coupled with counterbalancing by the security services.[79] The more pronounced sultanistic characteristics of MENA regimes, or their outright domination by militaries, render it more difficult for those at the center of them to be sufficiently confident of their control to impose what might appear to officers to be sacrifices imposed on them and the armed forces they command.[80]

This brief review indicates that shrinking MENA militaries is presently a step too far for security assistance providers, which in turn suggests three alternative approaches. One is to let inexorable pressures to downsize take their course. Those forces include increasing budget constraints, greater needs for skilled recruits to operate and maintain ever more sophisticated weaponry, and the reduced likelihood of major wars between states. Admittedly there are counterforces at work as well, such as the need to absorb growing numbers of unemployed youths. This approach, therefore, might be equivalent to waiting for Godot. Possibly his unexpected arrival could result from emulation, induced or otherwise, not of the United States but of the Russian or Chinese experiences of downsizing and professionalization, which would be paradoxical, to say the least. An alternative is to nibble away at the edges of the existing military behemoths through professionalization, repurposing, and upgrading of selected units. A third method would be to bolster counterbalances to militaries, or, in other words, to address civil-military relations, which necessarily involves strengthening state capacities.

Strengthening States

As noted above, nation building has become a political albatross in the United States, so could only be attempted in limited, incremental fashion, such as through relevant USAID, Middle East Partnership Initiative, and other governance programs. Those are unlikely to have dramatic, immediate effects, however, almost regardless of funding levels. Hope lies, therefore, in the linkages between militaries and states and elements of the latter most directly relevant to the former. These are the domains of efforts to improve civil-military relations and security-sector governance.

European governments, the EU, and NATO have been more active in this area than the US Departments of Defense or State, as indicated in the chapters by Florence Gaub and Alex Walsh and Kevin Koehler.[81] The United Nations has also been closely associated with the development and evolution of security-sector reform (SSR), which is broader than civil-military relations as it refers to the overall governance and conduct of the security sector, so in addition to the military includes intelligence services, police, border guards, customs and immigration, and legal/judicial systems. Legal constraints on the involvement of US foreign assistance providers with some of these instrumentalities is partly responsible for America's comparative reluctance to engage.[82]

But policy preferences appear also to play a role, as suggested perhaps by the relatively minor support for IMET and by the funding patterns of the Defense Department's Center for Civil-Military Relations. The overwhelming portion of that center's funding is directed to foreign militaries, largely for the purpose of professional training, thus duplicating IMET's function. The differential treatment by that center of civil-military relations in Latin America, as opposed to those in MENA, may reflect its hesitancy to deeply engage with the latter. The center, for example, provided financial support to the Buenos Aires–based RESDAL (Latin America Security and Defense Network), comprised of civilian activists against military rule from various Latin American countries, in order to publish its *Defense Atlas for Latin America and the Caribbean*, which enjoyed extensive distribution and had positive impact, including within South American military establishments.[83] When approached to support a similar undertaking for the Arab world, the center declined. So too did USAID. Funding for that program, which ultimately was hosted by the Carnegie Endowment's Beirut office and labeled the Program on Civil-Military Relations in the Arab States, was provided by numerous non-American donors, including Canada's International Development Research Center, the United Kingdom's Department for International Development, the EU, the Federal Foreign Office of Germany, the Swiss Federal Department of Foreign Affairs, the Rockefeller Brothers Fund, and the Friedrich Nauman Foundation. The program produced among other outputs a website titled Tawazun [Balance]: Index of Arab Civil-Military Relations, modeled on RESDAL's *Defense Atlas*, albeit more extensive.[84] The diversity of funding sources, which include various European governments and private American foundations but no US government agency, may reflect Washington's reluctance to directly address civil-military relations in MENA. Whether that hesitancy could be due to disinterest, to fear of backlash, or to a belief that the objective of improving MENA civil-military relations is unattainable is unknown. But we can say with certainty that US government support for activities to enhance civilian control of MENA militaries or to improve security-sector governance pales into financial insignificance when compared to its support for traditional security assistance to militaries. It also is relatively pecunious in these areas as compared to other Western governments.

Amazingly enough, Iran's activities in Iraq suggest it is more concerned with the legal-judicial system there and its relevance to security issues than is the United States, albeit not to reinforce but to undermine the rule of law. According to an investigation of involvement by elements of the Iran-backed Popular Mobilization Forces (PMFs) in the Iraqi legal system, they are doing so as part of a tripartite strategy not to implement SSR but to conduct "lawfare" against opponents, including the United States, to facilitate state capture, and to bolster their self-conception as defenders of Iraqi sovereignty and somehow reconcile that with their advocacy of the doctrine of *wilayat al-faqih* (guardianship of the Islamic jurist), which implies subordination to the rulers of Iran.[85] This targeting of the Iraqi legal-judicial system has already paid substantial dividends, as evidenced by the judicial decision in June 2021 to release PMF leader Qasim Muslih, who had been accused of murdering a protest leader.[86]

Clearly the West is neither united in support of, nor strongly committed to developing, civilian state capacities to oversee and control MENA militaries. Western states have for the most part left this so-far thankless task, and other aspects of developing and exerting soft power as described by Gaub, Walsh, and Koehler, to NATO and the EU, presumably suggesting its secondary importance or hopelessness in their view. This begs the question of whether a more unified, strongly supported approach would achieve what scattered efforts have failed to accomplish. Certainly, the prospects for success of a coordinated, substantial effort to impact MENA civil-military relations and effect SSR would be better than the present, sporadic undertakings.

Provider Reforms

The substantial library on US security assistance includes more works on how to improve its delivery by American institutions responsible for it than on recipients' use of it or on coordination with other security assistance providers. Secretary Gates's lament, cited above, over deterioration of America's diplomatic and development assistance institutional capacities is a case in point. These oft-expressed views have had some impacts, as suggested, for example, by Section 333 of the National Defense Authorization Act of 2017, which calls for "synchronization and joint planning between DOS and DOD." Because of this legal initiative, the secretary of defense has been compelled to seek the agreement of the secretary of state before initiating some types of security assistance programs.[87] Reforms within the DOD include efforts to empirically evaluate security assistance activities, presumably reflecting congressional and broader political pressure for financial accountability. As Zavage observes in his chapter, this effort has had mixed results. Numbers and the method of their gathering do not in his view adequately capture nuances of personal attributes and relationships and their implications for performance. Moreover, these check-list assessments focus overwhelmingly on strictly military capacities, thus excluding the broader goals of security assistance, of which relationship building is the most vital.

Efforts such as these to encourage whole-of-government approaches and improve existing delivery mechanisms are unlikely to produce either immediate or profound benefits. As Secretary Gates and others have noted, deterioration of the size, budgets, morale, and functioning of DOS and USAID is such that it would take years to rebuild those agencies even if a major commitment were made to do so. Moreover, DOD has such inherent advantages over civilian institutional participants in security assistance that the balance of power between them is unlikely to be substantially shifted. The comparatively generous budget of the DOD is a key element, but so too are the structure and operations of DOD as compared to DOS and USAID. The existence of regional commands enables military officers, who are less confined by security restrictions than DOS or USAID personnel, to interact relatively freely in host countries. They necessarily become the go-to persons for those on the other side, who in any case frequently consider these US officers to have more clout in Washington than their civilian counterparts. Moreover, unlike DOS and USAID, the US Army's Foreign Area Officer (FAO) Program has created substantial cadres of regional specialists with relevant language skills. Systematically enhancing FAOs' diplomatic and other relevant soft-power skills might in fact have more benefits than seeking to upgrade DOS and USAID.

Whatever gains might be made by tinkering with the governmental apparatus charged with providing security assistance, in the absence of change to its objectives and means such reforms are likely to have little effect. The crux of the matter is not the balance between hard and soft power or between personnel in uniform and those in civies. It is the willingness to commit to resolving the democratic paradox by working both sides of civil-military relationships with the intent of not just empowering the former better to control the latter but of converting MENA subjects into citizens. These necessarily are long-term goals, achievement of which would require more collaboration with other security assistance providers than currently exists. That is a necessary but not sufficient condition to empower MENA civilians and their institutions, with other requirements being shifts in the balance of public expenditures away from militaries, reduction of military involvement in many MENA economies, enforcement of respect for human and political rights, and lessening levels of insecurity in much of MENA.

It would be foolhardy and probably counterproductive to suddenly and dramatically reorient security assistance and relevant diplomacy and development assistance to achieve these objectives. Both recipient and provider countries and relevant stakeholders in both, including publics and political champions, need to be convinced and then drawn into reform-supporting activities. Moreover, as Rachel Kleinfeld observes with regard to US security assistance, "If it pushes too hard on governance, it will simply push potential allies straight into the arms of China and Russia."[88] Yet Emile Hokayem's cogent point that, for at least the Gulf Arab states, "prosperity may come from the East, but their best bet for security is in the West" implies that the West's leverage is substantial and can be used to support governance reform, including that to civil-military relations.[89]

Division of Tasks

Improving security assistance to MENA while the democratic paradox remains unresolved may depend upon a clearer division of labor between providers and recipients. Military heavy lifting should be done primarily by providers, with recipients operating at more tactical levels. The cost and technical complexity of state-of-the-art weapons systems impose ever greater financial and personnel burdens on recipients. The ratio between purchase and sustainment costs is shifting steadily toward the latter, rendering it ever more challenging for recipients to maintain operability, even with external assistance. By contrast, so-called Costco drones—meaning less sophisticated weapons that are inexpensive and relatively easy to operate and maintain—which are at the heart of hybrid warfare, offset many advantages of frontline weapons, as both Iran and Turkey have demonstrated.[90] Evolving military technology, in sum, is rendering high-cost weapons systems vulnerable to simpler, lower-cost ones, while bifurcating them between those affordable and manageable by Western providers but much less so by MENA recipients.

It is appropriate, therefore, for the security roles and responsibilities of the two to be more sharply differentiated but better linked. In terminology previously drawn upon in this chapter, Western powers should rely upon their arsenals of sophisticated weapons for offshore balancing, by which is meant defining the military parameters within which intraregional tactical power struggles occur. But to be effective, this offshore balancing should be coupled with coercive diplomacy, for which advanced weapons systems need to be complemented with mainstays of hybrid warfare, most especially drones, missiles, cyberwarfare, and disinformation. Western powers presently and no doubt into the future will use hybrid weaponry, but the region's militaries have some advantages in its application, including proximity, deniability, familiarity with opponents and terrain, language, and lower cost. Chapters in this book, especially those by Zoltan Barany and Simone Tholens, point to even more complex divisions of labor between providers and recipients, with some MENA militaries serving as intermediate security assistance providers.[91] But whether bilateral or trilateral, relationships between providers and recipients are likely to become steadily more important, complex, and affected by the relative technological sophistication of countries' weapons systems. Management of those relationships will thus become more important and difficult, paralleling the evolving nature of hybrid warfare in the region. The Russian-Turkish relationship of "adversarial collaboration," which refers to bilateral cooperation on tactical, case-by-case bases, is likely to displace strategic, long-term alliances.[92] UAE military cooperation with Russia in Libya appears to be another example of this and illustrates how demanding management of these relationships is.[93]

Implications of the widening divergence of roles and responsibilities between providers and recipients of security assistance, coupled with changes in weapons technology, are that large-scale Western military presence, such as US bases in Qatar and Bahrain, will become less relevant, while the components of hybrid warfare, soft-power projection, and joint operations will grow in importance.[94] This in turn underscores the relevance, among other things, of Western multilateralism, including the roles of NATO and the EU not only as coordinators but as soft-power projectors into the region. The divergence of security roles also emphasizes the need for effective coordination between military and nonmilitary decisionmakers in the making and implementation of national security policies on virtually a country-by-country basis.

Clouded Future of Security Assistance to MENA

The democratic paradox that bedevils Western security assistance to MENA will not be resolved easily or quickly. Unless and until it is, Western political systems, especially in the United States, will struggle to maintain public support for security assistance, which will also be increasingly difficult and complex to provide while facing increasing challenges from authoritarian states. While Western security assistance can be modified to help reduce the paradox, both by reconfiguring assistance to militaries to enhance their broader institutional capacities and by addressing civil-military relations more directly and consistently, substantial positive effects will take time to develop. In the meantime, security assistance needs to be reconfigured to accommodate the increasingly differentiated roles and responsibilities of providers and recipients that is made necessary by technological developments, economic constraints, and a general shift from strategic to tactical alliances between regional and extraregional states. This in turn requires effective and close cooperation between key actors, military and civilian, within provider states in order to ensure effective cooperation with recipients, especially for coercive diplomacy. None of this will be simple or straightforward; nor will mobilizing and sustaining political support for security assistance to MENA.

The challenge of providing more effective security assistance while simultaneously seeking to induce MENA recipients to reform their political economies is difficult, as is its political packaging. Appropriate carrots and sticks will have to be presented to recipients to induce them to reform rather than to run to the Russians or just hunker down in their own authoritarian mini-worlds. The goal-oriented Pentagon, to use General Williams's term, will need to accept the idea that containment, not victory, is an appropriate objective.[95] Political audiences in provider countries will need to be convinced that the paradox of supporting nondemocratic states to reduce threats to the West is ultimately resolvable—and in the meantime acceptable. Moreover, they will have to be made to believe that the "go long, not big" approach, as Michael Eisenstadt characterizes the nascent containment strategy in MENA, is in pursuit of a sufficiently vital cause for American security to merit the open-ended commitment.[96]

These political sales jobs will be easier if the threats posed by authoritarian states to the MENA region and the West's roles in it continue to escalate. Effective, sustained reform of security assistance to MENA may thus depend as much or even more on what the Russians, Chinese, and Iranians do than on the preferences and choices of Western security assistance providers. Western reactions to the invasion of Ukraine may ultimately include much stronger resolve to provide security assistance to the Middle East and to do so with serious strings attached regarding civil-military relations and governance more generally. It would be preferable were the unfolding "Great Game" in MENA to be replaced by effective security systems and arms controls, but if the past is a guide to the future, it is advisable to assume that the players of the "Great Game" will not soon tire of it.

Notes

1. On Russia's military upgrading, see "Putin's New Model Army," 45–46. On the limits of Russia's influence due to its economic weakness, see Pritchett, "Less Than a Full Deck."

2. Cordesman, "The Greater Middle East." For an indictment of US security assistance, see Wehrey and Dunne, "From Hardware to Holism."
3. Winnefeld, Morell, and Allison, "Why American Strategy Fails."
4. For a debate on the utility of "quitting," see Manning and Preble, "Reality Check #8," and the rebuttal, Wechsler, "No, the US Shouldn't Withdraw from the Middle East." For an analysis of the quitting option, see Yom, "US Foreign Policy in the Middle East," arguing that the quitting option is prevailing because "the Middle East no longer generates credible threats against the US." Freeman, "The Fadeout of Pax Americana in the Middle East," contends that the US will "quit" the region because it is consumed with internal dynamics rather than with Great Power rivalries.
5. Tankel and Ross, "Retooling U.S. Security Sector Assistance."
6. Eisenstadt, "Deterring Iran in the Gray Zone."
7. On Russia's utilization of these tactics, see Fridman, *Russian Hybrid Warfare*.
8. George, *Forceful Persuasion*.
9. George, "Coercive Diplomacy," 7.
10. See, e.g., Eisenstadt, "Deterring Iran in the Gray Zone."
11. Mearsheimer and Walt, "The Case for Offshore Balancing."
12. Gates, *Exercise of Power*. For a condensed presentation of the book's argument, see Gates, "The Overmilitarization of American Foreign Policy," 121–132.
13. Gates, "The Overmilitarization of American Foreign Policy," 122, 126.
14. Kaye et al., *Re-imagining U.S. Strategy in the Middle East*.
15. Goldenberg et al., *A People-First U.S. Assistance Strategy for the Middle East*.
16. Ash and Grossman, "Modernizing US Security and Development Assistance in the Middle East."
17. Hartung and Binder, "US Security Assistance to Egypt."
18. Riedel and O'Hanlon, "How to Demilitarize the US Presence in the Middle East."
19. Stark, "Give Up on Proxy Wars in the Middle East."
20. Wehrey and Dunne, "From Hardware to Holism."
21. Bourhrous et al., "Protest and State-Society Relations," 61.
22. Kaye, "America Is Not Withdrawing from the Middle East."
23. Cordesman, "The Biden Transition and Reshaping U.S. Strategy."
24. According to Brumberg, "U.S. Middle East Influence in Afghanistan's Shadow," "As of December 2020, there were some 42,000 troops, but when including the regular rotation of air and naval forces, the figure is closer to 65,000. This puts the United States' deployment in the Middle East nearly on a par with Europe, where there are 70,000 US troops." In assessing the status of US forces in MENA in the wake of withdrawal of troops from Afghanistan in July 2021, Brumberg concludes that "vague talk of 'demilitarizing' the US presence in the Middle East is not grounded in reality."
25. Holmes, "Why Offshore Balancing Won't Work."
26. This, for example, is the argument of Deudney and Ikenberry, "Misplaced Restraint."
27. Hamid, "The Struggle for Middle East Democracy"; Congressional Research Service, "Democracy Promotion."
28. Zuaiter, "The Middle East's Addiction to Foreign Aid."
29. On MENA limited access orders, see Springborg, *Political Economies of the Middle East and North Africa*.
30. "Lebanon Sinking into One of the Most Severe Global Crises Episodes."
31. "WMD Free Middle East Proposal at a Glance."
32. Robinson, "Political and Military Obstacles to the North African Regional Capability."
33. For a historical overview and the prospects of efforts to create such a framework, see Congressional Research Service, "Cooperative Security in the Middle East."

34. Vakil and Quilliam, "Steps to Enable a Middle East Regional Security Process," 2.
35. Arms Control and Regional Security in the Middle East (ACRS).
36. Ahmed Eleiba, "No Arab NATO," *Ahram Online* (July 1, 2022); al-Shayji, "Biden's Principle and the Challenges of the NATO Middle East Initiative."
37. Gates, "The Overmilitarization of American Foreign Policy."
38. Brooks, Golby, and Urben, "America's Broken Civil-Military Relationship Imperils National Security."
39. Springborg, Williams, and Zavage, "Security Assistance in the Middle East."
40. For a discussion of the relationship of employment of mercenaries in MENA and democratic values, see Guzansky and Marshall, "Outsourcing Warfare in the Mediterranean."
41. Cronin, *Armies and State-Building*; Cronin, "State and Army in the Middle East and North Africa."
42. Cronin, "State and Army in the Middle East and North Africa," 111.
43. Ibid., 112.
44. Cronin, *Armies and State-Building*, 254.
45. That security assistance supporting overly large, politically powerful militaries is a major determinant of MENA's lack of democracy is suggested by the fact that militaries in other regions have generally had less negative impacts on democratic development. See Kuehn, *The Military's Impact on Democratic Development*.
46. Koehler, "Officers and Regimes," 34–53, investigates the historical origins of Arab political-military relations, but only since independence.
47. Munsil and Wright, "Is Lockheed Martin Too Big to Fail?"
48. On the importance of the armaments industry to the Russian political economy, see Fridman, "Russia," 159–174.
49. "Trends in World Military Expenditure." For a summary of relevant data drawn from this report, see Kuimova, "Opaque Military Spending."
50. See http://government.defenceindex.org/list.
51. For a review of corruption in MENA militaries, see Vittori, "Mitigating Patronage and Personal Enrichment in U.S. Arms Sales."
52. Kuimova, "Opaque Military Spending."
53. Binder, "Black Box."
54. Abul-Magd and Grawert, *Businessmen in Arms*.
55. Sayigh, *Owners of the Republic*; see also Sayigh, "Egypt's Military as the Spearhead of State Capitalism"; Sayigh with Toronto, "Politics of Military Authoritarianism in North Africa"; Abed, *The Egyptian Economy*.
56. Diwan, "Armed Forces in Power and in Business."
57. Wehrey and Dunne, "From Hardware to Holism," 1.
58. On "threatism" driving security assistance strategy, see Kaye et al., *Re-imagining U.S. Strategy in the Middle East*.
59. Lyall, *Divided Armies*.
60. US security assistance, according to Elias Yousef, succeeded in developing the counterterrorism capacities of the military and security services but tended to empower them at the expense of civilian institutions and democratization. See Yousef, "Beyond Performance." On the politicization of the security sector, see Boussen, "The Unfinished Revolution."
61. Springborg and Williams, "The Egyptian Military."
62. Matisek and Reno, "Getting American Security Force Assistance Right."
63. Davison and Rasheed, "In Tactical Shift, Iran Grows New, Loyal Elite."
64. In Iraq the Counter Terrorism Service, backed by US Special Forces, became the hero of the 2017 battle for Mosul and remains the most popular and

effective unit of the Iraqi military. Ignatius, "Mustafa al Khadhimi's Government in Iraq Has a Long Way to Go."

65. Ibid.

66. Lavrov, "The Efficiency of the Syrian Armed Forces"; Williams, "In Syria, US Commanders Hold the Line."

67. Karlin, *Building Militaries in Fragile States*.

68. Cordesman, "Learning from the War," 34.

69. Rolandsen, Dwyer, and Reno, "Security Force Assistance to Fragile States," 565.

70. Congressional Research Service, "U.S. Foreign Assistance to the Middle East."

71. The IMET program for Tunisia, which received $1.8 million annually between 2001 and 2010, almost 10 percent of total US security assistance to the country, served as an effective bridge-building mechanism between Tunisian and American officers, which was useful in general and in the transition away from Ben Ali's rule in 2011. See Yousef, "Beyond Performance," 6–7.

72. Childs, "Granting Security?" 157–182. Childs cites studies of IMET impacts on 167–168.

73. Amara, "Reality vs. Fantasy."

74. Bruneau, "Challenges in Building Partner Capacity."

75. Tankel and Dalton, "How to Improve Return on Investment for Security Assistance."

76. Kleinfeld, "Why Supporters of Democracy."

77. Ji, *China's Military Transformation*, 60. On Russia, see Tsypkin, "Lessons Not to Learn"; Fridman, "Russia."

78. Trad, "In Its Battle for Influence."

79. Tsypkin, "Lessons Not to Learn"; Fridman, "Russia."

80. On the relevance of the Weberian notion of sultanism to MENA, see Davidson, *From Sheikhs to Sultanism*.

81. Samaan, "The Limitations of a NATO–Middle East Military Cooperation," underscores Koehler's assessment of NATO's principal contribution to security assistance as lying in the area of security architecture rather than bolstering of hard power.

82. For a discussion of US support for SSR and the legal constraints on it, see US Agency for International Development, US Department of Defense, and US Department of State, *Security Sector Reform*.

83. RESDAL (www.resdal.org/ing/index.html).

84. Program on Civil-Military Relations in Arab States (https://carnegie-mec.org/specialprojects/ArabCivilMilitaryRelations/?lang=en); "About Us," Tawazun: Index of Arab Civil-Military Relations, http://www.tawazun.net/english/about.php.

85. Smith, Malik, and Knights, "Team of Legal Gladiators?"

86. Knights, "Iraq's Judiciary Weak Link."

87. Saab, "What Does America Get for Its Military Aid?"

88. Kleinfeld, "Why Supporters of Democracy."

89. Hokayem, "Reassuring Gulf Partners While Recalibrating U.S. Security Policy."

90. Stalacanin, "The Middle East's Game of Drones."

91. See also Ardemagni, "The UAE's Military Training-Focused Foreign Policy."

92. Yildiz, "Turkish-Russian Adversarial Collaboration in Syria, Libya, and Nagorno-Karabakh."

93. Mackinnon, "Pentagon Says UAE Likely Funding Russia's Shadow Mercenaries in Libya."

94. Matisek, "Shades of Gray Deterrence."

95. Private communication, F. C. Williams to authors.

96. Eisenstadt, "Deterring Iran in the Gray Zone."

Acronyms

AAH-P	Police Training and Equipping Aid
ANDSF	Afghan National Defense and Security Forces
AOI	Arab Organization for Industrialization
APC	armored personnel carrier
BCAP	Bilateral Country Action Plan
BPC	building partner capacity
BSOC	Border Security Operations Center
CDPs	capabilities development plans
CENTCOM	Central Command
CIA	Central Intelligence Agency
CRS	Congressional Research Service
CT	counterterrorism
CVE	Countering Violence Extremism
DCoS	deputy chief of staff
DCSD	Directorate of Cooperation of Security and Defence [Direction de la coopération de sécurité et de défense]
DEEP	Defense Education Enhancement Program
DIB	defense institution building
DISA	Defense Intelligence and Security Agency
DOD	Department of Defense
DOS	Department of State
DSCA	Defense Security and Cooperation Agency
DTRA	Defense Threat Reduction Agency

DW	*Deutsche Welle*
E2I	Enable and Enhance Initiative [Ertüchtigungsinitiative]
EAA	Egyptian Armament Authority
EAF	Egyptian Armed Forces
ESF	Economic Support Fund
FAA	Foreign Assistance Act
FAO	Foreign Area Officer
FID	foreign internal defense
FMS	Foreign Military Sales
FSA	Free Syrian Army
FY	Fiscal Year
GAO	General Accounting Office
GCC	Gulf Cooperation Council
GDP	gross domestic product
GID	General Intelligence Directorate
GNA	Government of National Accord
GNU	Government of National Unity
HDI	Human Development Index
IFC	Intelligence Fusion Cell/Center
IISS	International Institute for Strategic Studies
IMET	International Military Education and Training
IRGC	Islamic Revolutionary Guard Corps
IS	Islamic State
ISF	Internal Security Forces
ISIL	Islamic State in Iraq and the Levant
ISIS	Islamic State of Iraq and Syria
ISR	intelligence, surveillance, and reconnaissance
JAF	Jordanian Armed Forces
JCPOA	Joint Comprehensive Plan of Action
JCRs	joint capability reviews
JOCC	Joint Operations Control Center
JRC	Joint Reconnaissance Center
KSA	Kingdom of Saudi Arabia
LAF	Lebanese Armed Forces
LDF	Lebanese Defense Forces
LNA	Libyan National Army
LRCA	limited revamped capabilities approach
MCC	Military Cooperation Committee
MD	Mediterranean Dialogue
MEAE	Ministry for European and Foreign Affairs
MENA	Middle East and North Africa

MNNA	major non-NATO ally
MOD	Ministry of Defense
MOF	Ministry of Finance
MOMP	Ministry of Military Production
MOU	memorandum of understanding
NATO	North Atlantic Treaty Organization
NDAA	National Defense Authorization Act
NDC	NATO Defense College
NMI	NATO Training Mission in Iraq
NSA	National Syrian Army
NSAB	Naval Support Activity Bahrain
NSD-S Hub	NATO Strategic Direction South Hub
NVD	night vision device
ODA	overseas development assistance
OMC	Office of Military Cooperation
PA	principal-agent
PLA	People's Liberation Army
PLO	Palestinian Liberation Organization
PM	prime minister
PMFs	Popular Mobilization Forces
PMO	military operational partnership [partenariat militaire opérationnel]
PPD-23	Presidential Policy Directive 23
QME	qualitative military edge
RFDC	Roadmap for Defense Cooperation
RoYG	Republic of Yemen Government
SA	security assistance
SC	security cooperation
SCAF	Supreme Council of Armed Forces
SFAB	Security Force Assistance Brigade
SFAT	security force assistance team
SIGAR	Special Inspector General for Afghanistan Reconstruction
SIPRI	Stockholm International Peace Research Institute
SOF	special operations forces
SSA	security-sector assistance
SSR	security-sector reform
TAF	Tunisian Armed Forces
TAFT	technical assistance field teams
UAV	unmanned aerial vehicle
UCAV	unmanned combat aerial vehicle

UNDP	UN Development Programme
USAID	US Agency for International Development
USSOCOM	US Special Operations Command
VEO	violent extremist organization
YAF	Yemeni Armed Forces

Bibliography

"A Wild Ride." *Economist*. Special Report on the Gulf. June 23, 2018, 4.
Abbas, Yasir, and Dan Trombly. "Inside the Collapse of the Iraqi Army's 2nd Division." *War on the Rocks*. July 1, 2014. https://warontherocks.com/2014/07/inside-the-collapse-of-the-iraqi-armys-2nd-division.
Abdel-Khalek, Ahmed M., David Lester, John Maltby, and Joaquin Tomás-Sábado. "The Arabic Scale of Death Anxiety: Some Results from East and West." *OMEGA—Journal of Death and Dying* 59, no. 1 (August 2009): 39–50.
Abderrahim, Tasnim. "'A Tale of Two Agreements: EU Migration Cooperation with Morocco and Tunisia." EuroMeSCo. May 2019. www.euromesco.net/wp-content/uploads/2019/04/EuroMeSCo-Paper_A-tale-of-two-agreements.pdf.
Abed, George T. *The Egyptian Economy: In the Clutches of the Deep State*. Carnegie Middle East Center. October 26, 2020. https://carnegie-mec.org/2020/10/26/egyptian-economy-in-clutches-of-deep-state-pub-83027.
Abrahamsen, Rita, and Michael C. Williams. "Security Beyond the State: Global Security Assemblages in International Politics." *International Political Sociology* 3, no. 1 (2009): 1–17.
Abul Magd, Zeinab, İsmet Akça, and Shana Marshall. "Two Paths to Dominance: Military Businesses in Turkey and Egypt." Carnegie Middle East Center. June 3, 2020. https://carnegie-mec.org/2020/06/03/two-paths-to-dominance-military-businesses-in-turkey-and-egypt-pub-81869.
Abul-Magd, Zeinab. *Militarizing the Nation: The Army, Business, and Revolution in Egypt*. New York: Columbia University Press, 2017.
Abul-Magd, Zeinab, and Elke Grawert. *Businessmen in Arms: How the Military and Other Armed Groups Profit in the MENA Region*. Lanham, MD: Rowman & Littlefield, 2016.
"Accordo tra il Governo della Repubblica italiana ed il Governo del Regno Hascemita di Giordania sulla cooperazione nel settore della difesa." *Gazetta Ufficiale*. January 10, 2017.
Adamsky, Dmitry (Dima). "Russian Lessons from the Syrian Operation and the Culture of Military Innovation." George C. Marshall European Center for Security Studies. February 2020. www.marshallcenter.org/en/publications/security-insights/russian-lessons-syrian-operation-and-culture-military-innovation.
"AFRICOM Commander Reaffirms Bilateral Partnership with Tunisia." US Africa Command. May 29, 2020. www.africom.mil/pressrelease/32888/africom-commander-reaffirms-bilateral-partner.

"After the Assassination." *Economist.* January 11, 2020, 41.
Agamben, Giorgio. *State of Exception.* Chicago: University of Chicago, 2005.
Agnew, John. "Sovereignty Regimes: Territoriality and State Authority in Contemporary World Politics." *Annals of the Association of American Geographers* 95, no. 2 (2005): 437–461.
Al Sherbini, Ramadan. "UAE Defends Contacts with Sudan Military." *Gulf News.* June 12, 2019.
al-'Azim, Ahmad 'Abd. "Al-Fariq Hamdi Wahiba- Ra'is al-Hay'a al-'Arabiyya li-l-Tasni'- fi Hiwar ma'a Ruz al-Yusuf." *Ruz al-Yusuf.* November 3, 2009.
al-Biyali, Nansi. "Mansi la Yunsa." *Masrawi.* August 16, 2017.
Al-Ississ, Mohammed, and Ishac Diwan. "Individual Preferences for Democracy in the Arab World: Explaining the Gap." Working Paper 981. Economic Research Forum. http://erf.org.eg/wp-content/uploads/2016/03/981.pdf.
Al-Mushir Abu Ghazala wal-Sahafa [Interviews with Minister of Defense and Military Production (Field Marshall Abu Ghazala)]. Cairo: al-Ahram, 1996.
al-Shayji, Abdullah Khalifa. "Biden's Principle and the Challenges of the NATO Middle East Initiative" (in Arabic). *al Quds.* June 26, 2022.
Albertus, Michael, Sofia Fenner, and Dan Slater. *Coercive Distribution.* New York: Cambridge University Press, 2018.
Alkurd, Dana. "Public Opinion and the Army: The Cases of Algeria and Sudan." *AlMuntaqa* 2, no. 2 (2019): 103–109.
Allizard, Pascal. "Rapport fait au nom de la commission des affaires étrangères, de la défense et des forces armées sur le projet de loi autorisant l'approbation de l'accord entre le Gouvernement de la République française et le Gouvernement du Royaume hachémite de Jordanie relatif au statut de leurs forces." Paris: Sénat, 2017.
Amara, Jomana. "Reality vs. Fantasy: Transforming the Arab States' Military Force Structure." *Middle East Policy* 24, no. 3 (fall 2017): 104–116.
"Ambassador DiCarlo's June 30 Meeting with IDF BG Heymann on Implementation of UNSCR 1701." 09USUNNEWYORK646_a. Wikileaks. July 2, 2009. https://wikileaks.org (last accessed October 22, 2014).
Amer, Adnan. "Arms Supplies to HAMAS." *Al-Monitor.* October 16, 2013. www.al-monitor.com/originals/2013/10/gaza-arms-smuggling-tunnels-hamas.html.
Ammi-Oz, Mosché. "La formation des cadres militaires africains lors de la mise sur pied des armées nationale." *Revue française d'études politiques africaines* 12, no. 133 (1977): 84–99.
Anani, Khalil. "Russia's War on Ukraine." Arab Center Washington DC. April 6, 2022. https://arabcenterdc.org/resource/russias-war-on-ukraine-egypts-limited-room-for-maneuver.
Anderson, Lisa. "Demystifying the Arab Spring: Parsing the Differences Between Tunisia, Egypt, and Libya." *Foreign Affairs* 90, no. 3 (2011): 2–7.
———. *The State and Social Transformation in Tunisia and Libya, 1830–1980.* Princeton, NJ: Princeton University Press, 1987.
Anthony, John Duke. "GCC Arms Imports: Strategic Assessment and Economic Benefits to the United States." In *The Arms Trade, Military Services, and the Security Market in the Gulf States: Trends and Implications,* edited by David B. Des Roches and Dania Thafer, 23–43. Berlin: Gerlach, 2016.
Arab Human Development Report 2003: Building a Knowledge Society. New York: United Nations Development Programme, 2003.
Arabia, Christina L. "The Collapse of the Afghan National Defense and Security Forces: Implications for U.S. Security Assistance and Cooperation." Report IN11728. Congressional Research Service. August 23, 2021. https://crsreports.congress.gov/product/pdf/IN/IN11728.
Ardemagni, Elenora. "The UAE's Military Training-Focused Foreign Policy." Carnegie Middle East Center. October 22, 2020. https://carnegie-mec.org/sada/83203.
Arendt, Hannah. *The Origins of Totalitarianism.* New York: Harcourt Brace, 1973.
"Arms Imports (SIPRI Trend Indicator Value)." World Bank. https://data.worldbank.org/indicator/MS.MIL.MPRT.KD?end=2016&start=2011&year_high_desc=true (accessed June 10, 2018).

Bibliography 347

Ash, Nazanin, and Allison Grossman. "Modernizing US Security and Development Assistance in the Middle East." Center for Global Development. December 5, 2015. www.cgdev.org/sites/default/files/whw-middle-east-n-africa.pdf.

Ataç, C. Akça. "Pax Ottomanica No More! The 'Peace' Discourse in Turkish Foreign Policy in the Post-Davutoğlu Era and the Prolonged Syrian Crisis." *Digest of Middle East Studies* 28, no. 1 (2019): 48–69.

"Average Monthly Brent Crude Oil Price from May 2020 to May 2022." Statista.com. www.statista.com/statistics/262861/uk-brent-crude-oil-monthly-price-development (accessed on June 29, 2022).

Axelrod, Lawrence. "Tribesmen in Uniform: The Demise of the Fida'iyyun in Jordan, 1970–71." *Muslim World* 68 (1978): 25–45.

Aydın, Mustafa. "Turkish Foreign Policy, 1923–2018." In *The Routledge Handbook of Turkish Politics*, edited by Alpaslan Özerdem and Matthew Whiting. London: Routledge, 2019.

Ayeb, Habib. "Après Ben Guerdane: Dépossessions, déstructurations et insécurité alimentaire dans le sud-est tunisien." *Jadaliyya*. April 23, 2016. www.jadaliyya.com/Details/33192/Apr%C3%A8s-Ben-Guerdane—d%C3%A9possessions,-d%C3%A9structurations-et-ins%C3%A9curit%C3%A9-alimentaire-dans-le-Sud-est-tunisie.

———. "Social and Political Geography of the Tunisian Revolution: The Alfa Grass Revolution." *Review of African Political Economy* 38, no. 129 (2011): 467–479.

Azoulay, Rivka. *Kuwait and Al-Sabah: Tribal Politics and Power in an Oil State*. London and New York: I. B. Tauris, 2020.

Badi, Emadeddine. "To Advance Its Own Interests, Turkey Should Now Help Stabilize Libya." *War on the Rocks*. May 24, 2021. https://warontherocks.com/2021/05/to-advance-its-own-interests-turkey-should-now-help-stabilize-libya.

Bahgat, Gawdat. "Lower for Longer: Saudi Arabia Adjusts to the New Oil Era." *Middle East Policy* 23, no. 3 (fall 2016): 39–48.

Bahgat, Hosam. "Tafasil Istihwaz al-Mukhabarat al-'Amma 'Ala 'I'lam al-Misriyyn." *Mada Masr*. December 20, 2017.

Baker, Peter. "Obama Upgrades Tunisia as a U.S. Ally." *New York Times*. May 21, 2015.

Baker-Bell, Christopher. "The Discursive Construction of the EU Counter-Terrorism Policy: Writing the 'Migrant Other,' Securitization and Control." *Journal of Contemporary European Research* 5, no. 2 (2009): 188–206.

Baldor, Lolita C., and Mike Corder. "US Sending $1 Billion More Military Aid to Outgunned Ukraine." *Associated Press*. June 15, 2022. https://apnews.com/article/russia-ukraine-zelenskyy-sweden-finland-jens-stoltenberg-1feb3640d59b05aceca62766d7d4f74d.

Barak, Oren. "Towards a Representative Military? The Transformation of the Lebanese Officer Corps Since 1945." *Middle East Journal* 60, no. 1 (2006): 75–93.

Barakat, Sultan, and Andrew Leber. *Fortress Jordan: Putting the Money to Work*. Doha: Brookings Doha Center, 2015.

Barany, Zoltan. *Armies of Arabia: Military Politics and Effectiveness in the Gulf*. New York: Oxford University Press, 2021.

———. "Foreign Contract Soldiers in the Gulf." Carnegie Middle East Center. February 5, 2020. https://carnegie-mec.org/2020/02/05/foreign-contract-soldiers-in-gulf-pub-80979.

———. "The Gulf Monarchies and Israel: From Aversion to Pragmatism." *Middle East Journal* 74, no. 4 (winter 2020–2021): 559–578.

———. *The Political Economy of Gulf Defense Establishments*. New York: Cambridge University Press, 2021.

———. *The Soldier and the Changing State: Building Democratic Armies in Africa, Asia, Europe, and the Americas*. Princeton NJ: Princeton University Press, 2012.

———. "Soldiers of Arabia: Explaining Compulsory Military Service in the Gulf." *Journal of Arabian Studies* 8, no. 1 (July 2018): 118–140.

Barkawi, Tarak, and Mark Laffey. "The Postcolonial Moment in Security Studies." *Review of International Studies* 32, no. 2 (2006): 329–352.

Bärwaldt, Konstantin, ed. *Strategy, Jointness, Capacity: Institutional Requirements for Supporting Security Sector Reform*. Berlin: Friedrich-Ebert-Stiftung, 2018.

Baylouny, Anne Marie, 2012. "Building an Integrated Military in Post-Conflict Societies: Lebanon." Calhoun: The NPS Institutional Archive. https://calhoun.nps.edu/bitstream/handle/10945/57118/Baylouny_Building%20an%20Integrated.pdf.
———. "Militarizing Welfare: Neo-liberalism and Jordanian Policy." *Middle East Journal* 62 (2008): 277–303.
Bellin, Eva. "The Robustness of Authoritarianism in the Middle East: Exceptionalism in Comparative Perspective." *Comparative Politics* 36, no. 2 (2004): 139–157.
Benstead, Lindsay J. "Differentiation and Diffusion: Shifting Public Opinion Attitudes Toward Foreign Policy in North Africa." *Journal of North African Studies* 24, no. 4 (2019): 628–639.
———. "Why Do Some Arab Citizens See Democracy as Unsuitable for Their Country?" *Democratization* 22, no. 7 (2015): 1183–1208.
Benstead, Lindsay J., and Megan Reif. "Polarization or Pluralism? Language, Identity, and Attitudes Toward Western Culture Among Algeria's Youth." *Middle East Journal of Culture and Communication* 6, no. 1 (2013): 75–106.
Benstead, Lindsay J., and Ethan Snyder. "Is Security at Odds with Democracy? Evidence from the Arab World." Paper presented at the North African Studies Workshop, Oregon State University, Corvallis. November 4, 2016.
Ben-Youssef, Nadia, and Sandra Samaan Tamari. "Enshrining Discrimination: Israel's Nation-State Law." *Journal of Palestine Studies* 48, no. 1 (2018).
Béraud-Sudreau, Lucie. "French Arms Exports: The Business of Sovereignty." International Institute for Strategic Studies. March 2020. www.iiss.org/blogs/analysis/2020/03/french-arms-exports-introduction.
Berger, Lars. "Guns, Butter, and Human Rights—the Congressional Politics of US Aid to Egypt." *American Politics Research* 40, no. 4 (2012): 603–635.
Berger, Miriam. "Invaders, Allies, Occupiers, Guests: A Brief History of U.S. Military Involvement in Iraq." *Washington Post*. January 11, 2020. www.washingtonpost.com/world/2020/01/11/invaders-allies-occupiers-guests-brief-history-us-military-involvement-iraq.
Bergman, Max, and Alexandra Schmidt. "A Plan to Reform U.S. Security Assistance." Center for American Progress. March 9, 2021. www.americanprogress.org/article/plan-reform-u-s-security-assistance.
Bergman, Ronen, and Farnaz Fassihi. "The Scientist and the A.I.-Assisted Remote Control Killing Machine." *New York Times*. September 18, 2021. www.nytimes.com/2021/09/18/world/middleeast/iran-nuclear-fakhrizadeh-assassination-israel.html.
Berlin, Isaiah. *The Hedgehog and the Fox*. Princeton, NJ: Princeton University Press, 2013.
Besteman, Catherine. "Border Regimes and the New Global Apartheid." *MERIP* 290 (spring 2019).
Biddle, Stephen D. "Building Security Forces and Stabilizing Nations: The Problem of Agency." *Daedalus* 146, no. 4 (fall 2017): 126–138.
Biddle, Stephen, Julia Macdonald, and Ryan Baker. "Small Footprint, Small Payoff: The Military Effectiveness of Security Force Assistance." *Journal of Strategic Studies* 41, no. 1–2 (2018): 89–142.
Binder, Seth. "Black Box: Military Budgets in the Arab World." Project on Middle East Democracy. May 12, 2020. https://pomed.org/black-box-military-budgets-in-the-arab-world.
———. "Report: Back to Business as Usual—President Biden's First Foreign Affairs Budget for the Middle East. Project on Middle East Democracy. September 23, 2021. https://pomed.org/fy22-budget-report.
Blaise, Lilia, Eric Schmitt, and Carlotta Gall. "Why the U.S. and Tunisia Keep Their Cooperation Secret." *New York Times*. March 2, 2019. www.nytimes.com/2019/03/02/world/africa/us-tunisia-terrorism.html.
Blanchard, Christopher M. "Iraq: Issues in the 116th Congress." Report R45633. Congressional Research Service. July 17, 2020. https://fas.org/sgp/crs/mideast/R45633.pdf.
———. "Saudi Arabia: Background and U.S. Relations." Congressional Research Service. April 22, 2016. https://sgp.fas.org/crs/mideast/RL33533.pdf.
Blanton, Shannon L. "Instruments of Security or Tools of Repression? Arms Imports and Human Rights Conditions in Developing Countries." *Journal of Peace Research* 36, no. 2 (1999): 233–244.

———. "Promoting Human Rights and Democracy in the Developing World: U.S. Rhetoric Versus U.S. Arms Exports." *American Journal of Political Science* 44, no. 1 (2000): 123–131.
Bligh, Alexander. "The Jordanian Army: Between Domestic and External Challenges." *Middle East Review of International Affairs* 5 (2001): 13–20.
"Blindati Centauro per la Giordania." Analisi Difesa. February 5, 2014. www.analisidifesa.it/2014/02/blindati-centauro-per-la-giordania.
Borchert, Heiko. "The Arab Gulf Defense Pivot: Defense Industrial Policy in a Changing Geostrategic Context." *Comparative Strategy* 37, no. 4 (February 2019): 299–315.
Bou Nassif, Hicham. "A Military Besieged: The Armed Forces, the Police, and the Party in Bin 'Ali's Tunisia, 1987–2011." *International Journal of Middle East Studies* 47 (2015): 65–87.
———. *Endgames: Military Response to Protest in Arab Autocracies*. New York: Cambridge University Press, 2020.
Boucek, Christopher. "War in Saada." In *Yemen on the Brink*, edited by Christopher Boucek and Marina Ottoway. Washington, DC: Carnegie, 2010.
Bourhrous, Amal, Meray Maddah, Shivan Fazil, and Dylan O'Driscoll. "Protest and State-Society Relations in the Middle East and North Africa." Policy Paper 56. Stockholm: SIPRI. October 2020.
Boussen, Zied. "The Unfinished Revolution: Police Brutality at the Heart of the 10th Anniversary of the Tunisian Revolution." Arab Reform Initiative. July 13, 2021. www.arab-reform.net/publication/the-unfinished-revolution-police-brutality-at-the-heart-of-the-10th-anniversary-of-the-tunisian-revolution.
Bove, Vincenzo, and Jennifer Brauner. "The Demand for Military Expenditure in Authoritarian Regimes." *Defense and Peace Economics* 27, no. 5 (2016): 609–625.
Bowen, Andrew. "Russian Arms Sales and Defense Industry." Congressional Research Service. October 14, 2021. https://crsreports.congress.gov/product/pdf/R/R46937.
Bradley, Matt. "Analysis: Erdogan's Purge to Coup-Proof Turkey's Military May Backfire." *NBC News*. August 16, 2016. www.nbcnews.com/storyline/turkey-military-coup/analysis-erdogan-s-purge-coup-proof-turkey-s-military-may-n630791.
Brand, Laurie. *Jordan's Inter-Arab Relations: The Political Economy of Alliance-Making*. New York: Columbia University Press, 1994.
"British Navy Begins Construction on New Base in Bahrain." *Gulf News Journal*. November 3, 2015.
Brooks, Risa, Jim Golby, and Heidi Urben. "America's Broken Civil-Military Relationship Imperils National Security." *Foreign Affairs* 100, no. 3 (May–June 2021): 63–75.
Brousse, Didier. "La coopération structurelle de sécurité et de défense du XXIe siècle." *Les champs de Mars* 32, no. 1 (2019): 111.
Browne, Gareth. "Britain Announces New Military Base in Oman." *National*. November 5, 2018. www.thenationalnews.com/world/gcc/britain-announces-new-military-base-in-oman-1.788284.
Brumberg, Daniel. "U.S. Middle East Influence in Afghanistan's Shadow." *Responsible Statecraft*. July 17, 2021. https://responsiblestatecraft.org/2021/07/17/us-middle-east-influence-in-afghanistans-shadow.
Bruneau, Thomas. "Challenges in Building Partner Capacity: Civil-Military Relations in the United States and New Democracies." *Small Wars & Insurgencies* 26, no. 3 (March 2015): 429–445.
"Brussels Summit Communiqué." NATO. Last updated July 1, 2021. www.nato.int/cps/en/natohq/news_185000.htm.
Bryant, Lisa. "Inside Tunisia's Extremist Breeding Ground." *Voice of America*. June 6, 2016. www.voanews.com/middle-east/inside-tunisias-extremist-breeding-ground.
"Budget de l'État." Ministère de l'Économie, des Finances et de la Souveraineté Industrielle et Numérique. www.budget.gouv.fr/budget-etat/ministere?ministere=34846&programme=27928.
"Building Integrity." NATO. Last updated December 9, 2021. www.nato.int/cps/en/natohq/topics_68368.htm?selectedLocale=en.
Bundesregierung. "Antwort der Bundesregierung auf die Kleine Anfrage der Abgeordneten Sevim Dağdelen, Heike Hänsel, Christine Buchholz, weiterer Abgeordneter und der Fraktion DIE LINKE—Drucksache 19/8592." Berlin: Deutscher Bundestag, 2019.

———. "Antwort der Bundesregierung auf die Kleine Anfrage der Abgeordneten Sevim Dağdelen, Heike Hänsel, Dr. Diether Dehm, weiterer Abgeordneter und der Fraktion DIE LINKE—Drucksache 19/30202." Berlin: Deutscher Bundestag, 2021.

———. "Entwurf eines Gesetzes zu dem Abkommen vom 26. September 2016 zwischen der Regierung der Bundesrepublik Deutschland und der Regierung der Tunesischen Republik über die Zusammenarbeit im Sicherheitsbereich—Drucksache 18/11509." Berlin: Deutscher Bundestag, 2017.

———. "Fortsetzung des Einsatzes bewaffneter deutscher Streitkräfte—Stabilisierung sichern, Wiedererstarken des IS verhindern, Versöhnung fördern in Irak und Syrien—Drucksache 19/22207." Berlin: Deutscher Bundestag, 2020.

———. "Weißbuch zur Sicherheitspolitk und zur Zukunft der Bundeswehr." Berlin: Bundesministerium der Verteidigung, 2016.

Burchard, Stephanie, and Stephen Burgess. "US Training of African Forces and Military Assistance, 1997–2017: Security Versus Human Rights in Principal-Agent Relations." *African Security* 11, no. 4 (2018): 339–369.

Burt, Richard. "Carter Is Said to Put New U.S. Aid for Israel and Egypt at $4 Billion." *New York Times*. March 15, 1979. www.nytimes.com/1979/03/15/archives/carter-is-said-to-put-new-us-aid-for-israel-and-egypt-at-4-billion.html.

Bussoletti, Francesco. "Iraq: JOCAT and OCATs, Latest Anti-Isis Weapon, Are Almost Fully Up and Running." *Difesa & Sicurezza*. November 20, 2020. www.difesaesicurezza.com/en/defence-and-security/iraq-jocat-and-ocats-latest-anti-isis-weapon-are-almost-fully-up-and-running.

Buzan, Barry, Ole Waever, and Jaap de Wilde, *Security: A New Framework for Analysis*. Boulder, CO: Lynne Rienner, 1998.

Byman, Daniel. "Assessing Current US Policies and Goals in the Persian Gulf." In *Crude Strategy: Rethinking the US Military Commitment to Defend Persian Gulf Oil*, edited by Charles L. Glaser and Rosemary A. Kelanic, 49–78. Washington, DC: Georgetown University Press, 2016.

———. "Confronting Iran." *Survival* 60, no. 1 (2018): 107–128.

Cahill, Ben. "Gulf States: Managing the Oil Crash." *CSIS Commentary*. May 7, 2020.

Calculli, Marina. "Self-Determination at All Costs: Explaining the Iran-Syria-Hezbollah Axis." *Annals of the Fondazione Luigi Einaudi* 54 (2020): 95–118.

Camera dei Deputati. "Autorizzazione e proroga missioni internazionali nell'anno 2021." Roma: Camera dei Deputati, 2021.

———. "Delibarazione dei Consiglio dei Ministri in merito alla partecipazione dell'Italia a ulteriore missioni internazionali, adottata il 23 Aprile 2019." Roma: Camera dei Deputati, 2019.

Cammett, Melani, Ishac Diwan, and Irina Vartanova. "Insecurity and Political Values in the Arab World." *Democratization* 27, no. 5 (2020): 699–716.

Cellino, Andrea, and Annaline Perteghella, eds. *Conflicts, Pandemics and Peacebuilding: New Perspectives on Security Sector Reform in the MENA Region*. DCAF-ISPI Report 6. Geneva Centre for Security Sector Governance. www.dcaf.ch/conflicts-pandemics-and-peacebuilding-new-perspectives-security-sector-reform-mena-region.

Center for International Policy. "The Mideast Arms Bazaar: Top Arms Suppliers to the Middle East and North Africa, 2015–2019." September 2020. https://3ba8a190-62da-4c98-86d2-893079d87083.usrfiles.com/ugd/3ba8a1_c035cc647bb84e3aad535bfdc342abd7.pdf.

Central Bank of Jordan. *Annual Statistical Bulletin*. Amman: Central Bank of Jordan, various years.

Central Intelligence Agency. *Jordan's Military Modernization: One Step Forward, Two Steps Back*. July 1988, accessed via CREST, General CIA Records, Document Number CIA-RDP89S01450R000400390001-1, released July 30, 2012.

Charbonneau, Bruno. *France and the New Imperialism: Security Policy in Sub-Saharan Africa*. Aldershot, UK: Ashgate, 2008.

Chehabi, H. E., and Juan J. Linz. "A Theory of Sultanism 1: A Type of Nondemocratic Rule." In *Sultanistic Regimes*, edited by H. E. Chelhabi and Juan J. Linz, 3–25. Baltimore: Johns Hopkins University Press, 1998.

Childs, Steven J. "Granting Security? U.S. Security Assistance Programs and Political Stability in the Greater Middle East and Africa." *Journal of the Middle East and Africa* 10, no. 2 (2019): 157–182.

Christova, Alina. "Seven Years of EUJUST LEX: The Challenge of Rule of Law in Iraq." *Journal of Contemporary European Research* 9, no. 3 (2013).
Cisneros, Josue David. *The Border Crossed Us: Rhetorics of Borders, Citizenship, and Latina/o Identity.* Tuscaloosa: University of Alabama Press, 2014.
Clarke, Duncan, Daniel B. O'Connor, and Jason D. Ellis. *Send Guns and Money.* Westport, CT: Praeger, 1997.
Clinton, Hillary Rodham. "Press Statement on Recent Events in Tunisia." US Department of State. January 14, 2011. https://2009-2017.state.gov/secretary/20092013clinton/rm/2011/01/154684.htm.
CMRAS. "Program on Civil-Military in Arab States." Carnegie Middle East Center. https://carnegie-mec.org/specialprojects/ArabCivilMilitaryRelations/?lang=en (accessed July 29, 2022).
Coates Ulrichsen, Kristian. *Qatar and the Gulf Crisis.* New York: Oxford University Press, 2020.
Cohen, Jordan. "Biden's Conventional Arms Transfer Policy Review Could Be a Turning Point." *War on the Rocks.* November 29, 2021. https://warontherocks.com/2021/11/bidens-conventional-arms-transfer-policy-review-could-be-a-turning-point.
Cole, Beth. "Learning and Innovation: Jordan at the 'Crossroads of Armageddon.'" *PRISM: Journal of Complex Operations* 7 (2018): 74–91.
"Colloquio tra il Ministro Guerini e il Ministro della Difesa tunisino Bartagi." Ministero della Difesa. May 27, 2021. www.difesa.it/Primo_Piano/Pagine/Colloquio%20tra%20il%20Ministro%20Guerini%20e%20il%20Ministro%20della%20Difesa%20tunisino%20Bartagi.aspx.
Conetta, Carl, and Charles Knight. "The Readiness Crisis of the U.S. Air Force: A Review and Diagnosis." Briefing Report #10. The Commonwealth Institute and Project on Defense Alternatives. April 22, 1999. http://comw.org/pda/afread02.html.
"Conférence de presse conjointe de MM. Jean-Yves Le Drian, ministre de la défense, et Farhat Horchani, ministre tunisien de la Défense nationale, sur la coopération militaire franco-tunisienne et sur l'intervention militaire française en Syrie, à Tunis le 5 octobre 2015." République française. www.vie-publique.fr/discours/196562-conference-de-presse-conjointe-de-mm-jean-yves-le-drian-ministre-de-la.
Congressional Research Service (CRS). "Cooperative Security in the Middle East: History and Prospects." CRS. April 11, 2019. www.everycrsreport.com/reports/IF11173.html.
———. "Democracy Promotion: An Objective of U.S. Foreign Assistance." Federation of American Scientists. January 4, 2019. https://fas.org/sgp/crs/row/R44858.pdf.
———. "Egypt: Background and U.S. Relations." RL33003. CRS. September 30, 2021. www.everycrsreport.com/files/2020-05-27_RL33003_e42b422c63cfee10e5053b8b5dcbe18af9c5762e.pdf.
———. "Ending Cash Flow Financing for Egypt: Issues for Congress." R44060. CRS. Updated June 4, 2015. www.everycrsreport.com/reports/R44060.html.
———. "U.S. Arms Sales and Human Rights: Legislative Basis and Frequently Asked Questions." CRS. April 30, 2021. https://fas.org/sgp/crs/weapons/IF11197.pdf.
———. "U.S. Foreign Assistance to the Middle East: Historical Background, Recent Trends, and the FY2021 Request." R46344. CRS. May 5, 2020. https://crsreports.congress.gov/product/pdf/R/R46344/3#:~:text=It%20comprises%3A%20Algeria%2C%20Bahrain%2C,Bank%2FGaza%2C%20and%20Yemen.
———. "What Is 'Building Partner Capacity'? Issues for Congress." R44313. December 18, 2015. www.everycrsreport.com/reports/R44313.html.
Conrad, Scott W. "Moving the Force: Desert Storm and Beyond." McNair Paper 32. Institute for National Strategic Studies. December 1994. www.cc.gatech.edu/~tpilsch/INTA4803TP/Articles/Moving%20the%20Force-Chapter%202-excerpt=Conrad-McNair32.pdf.
Cook, Steven A. *Ruling but Not Governing: The Military and Political Development in Egypt, Algeria, and Turkey.* Baltimore: John Hopkins University Press, 2007.
Coon, Chris. "Support Tunisia, the Arab Spring Sole Success." *The Hill.* November 19, 2015. https://thehill.com/blogs/congress-blog/foreign-policy/260603-support-tunisia-the-arab-springs-sole-success.
Cordesman, Anthony H. "The Biden Transition and Reshaping U.S. Strategy: Long Engagements vs. Long Wars." Center for Strategic and International Studies. December 9, 2020.

www.csis.org/analysis/biden-transition-and-reshaping-us-strategy-long-engagements-vs-long-wars.

———. "The Greater Middle East: From the Arab Spring to the Axis of Failed States." Center for Strategic and International Studies. August 24, 2020. www.csis.org/analysis/greater-middle-east-arab-spring-axis-failed-states.

———. *Gulf Military Balance*. Washington, DC: Center for Strategic and International Studies, 2010.

———. "Learning from the War: 'Who Lost Afghanistan?' Versus Learning 'Why We Lost.'" Center for Strategic and International Studies. July 21, 2021. www.csis.org/analysis/learning-war-who-lost-afghanistan-versus-learning-why-we-lost.

———. "The Longer-Term Impact of the Ukraine Conflict and the Growing Importance of the Civil Side of War." Center for Strategic and International Studies. June 6, 2022. www.csis.org/analysis/longer-term-impact-ukraine-conflict-and-growing-importance-civil-side-war.

———. "Military Spending: The Other Side of Saudi Security." Burke Chair Report. Center for Strategic and International Studies. March 11, 2018. www.csis.org/analysis/military-spending-other-side-saudi-security.

Cordesman, Anthony H., Robert M. Shelala, and Omar Mohamed. *The Gulf Military Balance*. Vol. 3: *The Gulf and the Arabian Peninsula*. Boulder, CO: Rowman & Littlefield/Center for Strategic and International Studies, 2014.

Cordesman, Anthony H., with the assistance of Bryan Gold and Garrett Berntsen. *The Gulf Military Balance*. Vol. 1: *The Conventional and Asymmetric Dimensions*. Boulder, CO: Rowman & Littlefield/Center for Strategic and International Studies, 2014.

Corruption Perception Index." Transparency International. 2020. www.transparency.org/en/cpi/2020/index/lbn.

Corstange, Daniel, and Nikolay Marinov. 2012. "Taking Sides in Other People's Elections: The Polarizing Effect of Foreign Interventions." *American Journal of Political Science* 56, no. 3 (2012): 655–670.

Couzens Hoy, David. *Critical Resistance: From Poststructuralism to Post-Critique*. Cambridge: Massachusetts Institute of Technology Press, 2004.

Credi, Ottavia. *L'Italia alla guida della missione Nato in Iraq*. Roma: Istituto affari internazionale, 2021.

Cronin, Stephanie. *Armies and State-Building in the Modern Middle East: Politics, Nationalism, and Military Reform*. London: I. B. Tauris, 2014.

———. "State and Army in the Middle East and North Africa: Reflections on the Past and Future." In *The Future of Regional Security in the Middle East*, edited by Erika Holmquist and John Rydqvist, 91–116. Stockholm: Swedish Defense Research Agency. April 18, 2016.

Czulda, Robert. "Is Iran Going on an Arms Shopping Spree in Moscow." Atlantic Council. November 10, 2021. www.atlanticcouncil.org/blogs/iransource/is-iran-going-on-an-arms-shopping-spree-in-moscow.

"Dabitat Hifz Salam Misriyya." *UN News*. April 16, 2019. https://news.un.org/ar/story/2019/04/1031161 (accessed November 10, 2019).

Daher, Aurélie. *Hezbollah: Mobilization and Power*. Oxford: Oxford University Press, 2019.

Dalton, Melissa, and Hijab Shah. "Evolving UAE Military and Foreign Security Cooperation: Path Toward Military Professionalism." Carnegie Middle East Center. January 12, 2021. https://carnegie-mec.org/2021/01/12/evolving-uae-military-and-foreign-security-cooperation-path-toward-military-professionalism-pub-83549.

Dalton, Melissa G., Hijab Shah, Shannon N. Green, and Rebecca Hughes. *Oversight and Accountability in U.S. Security Sector Assistance: Seeking Return on Investment*. Boulder, CO: Rowman & Littlefield Publishers/Center for Strategic and International Studies. February 2018.

Dandashly, Assem. "EU Democracy Promotion and the Dominance of the Security-Stability Nexus." *Mediterranean Politics* 23, no. 1 (January 2, 2018): 62–82.

Daniels, Seamus P. "Assessing Trends in Military Personnel Costs." Center for Strategic and International Studies. September 2021. www.csis.org/analysis/assessing-trends-military-personnel-costs.

Dann, Uriel. *King Hussein and the Challenge of Arab Radicalism, 1955–1967*. Oxford: Oxford University Press, 1989.

Darasha, Brinda. "GCC Defence Spending Set to Decline 10% to $91bln This Year." *Zawya.* February 18, 2021.
Davenport, Christian. "State Repression and Political Order." *Annual Review of Political Science* 10 (2007): 1–23.
Davidson, Christopher M. *From Sheikhs to Sultanism: Statecraft and Authority in Saudi Arabia and the UAE.* London: Hurst, 2021.
Davison, John, and Ahmad Rasheed. "In Tactical Shift, Iran Grows New, Loyal Elite from Among Iraqi Militias." *Saltwire.* May 21, 2021. www.saltwire.com/nova-scotia/news/exclusive-in-tactical-shift-iran-grows-new-loyal-elite-from-among-iraqi-militias-100590844.
De Mesquita, Bueno, Alastair Smith, Randolph Siverson, and James Morrow. *The Logic of Political Survival.* Cambridge: Massachusetts Institute of Technology Press, 2005.
Deegan, Michael, and Joseph V. Moreno. "A Military Practitioner's Guide to Jordan." *Small Wars Journal.* March 13, 2015. https://smallwarsjournal.com/jrnl/art/a-military-practitioner %E2%80%99s-guide-to-jordan.
"Defence and Related Security Capacity Building Initiative." NATO. Last updated June 9, 2021. www.nato.int/cps/en/natohq/topics_132756.htm.
"Defence Institution Building." NATO. Last updated May 9, 2018. www.nato.int/cps/en/natohq /topics_50083.htm.
Defense Security Cooperation Agency (DSCA). "Tunisia—AT-6 Light Attack Aircraft." DSCA. February 26, 2020. www.dsca.mil/press-media/major-arms-sales/tunisia-6-light -attack-aircraft.
———. "Tunisia—OH-58 Kiowa Warrior Aircraft Equipment and Support." DSCA. May 3, 2016. www.dsca.mil/press-media/major-arms-sales/tunisia-oh-58d-kiowa-warrior-aircraft -equipment-and-support.
———. "Tunisia—UH-60 M Black Hawk Helicopters." DSCA. July 24, 2014. www.dsca .mil/press-media/major-arms-sales/tunisia-uh-60m-black-hawk-helicopters.
DeMeritt, Jacqueline H. R. "The Strategic Use of State Repression and Political Violence." In *Oxford Research Encyclopedia of Politics.* Oxford: Oxford University Press, 2018.
Demmers, Jolle, and Lauren Gould. "An Assemblage Approach to Liquid Warfare: AFRICOM and the 'Hunt' for Joseph Kony." *Security Dialogue* 49, no. 5 (2018): 364–381.
Deneckere, Matthias, Ashley Neat, and Volker Hauck. "The Future of EU Security Sector Assistance: Learning from Experience." Discussion Paper 71. ECDPM. May 2020. https:// ecdpm.org/wp-content/uploads/ECDPM-Future-EU-Security-Sector-Assistance-Learning -Experience-Discussion-Paper-271.pdf.
Deudney, Daniel, and G. John Ikenberry. "Misplaced Restraint: The Quincy Coalition Versus Liberal Internationalism." *Survival* 63, no. 4 (July 27, 2021): 7–32.
Di Feo, Gianluca. "Via gli americani, toccherà all'Italia guidare in Iraq la missione Nato." *La Repubblica.* February 22, 2021. www.repubblica.it/esteri/2021/02/22/news/iraq_la_missione _nato_presto_a_comando_italiano-301052228.
Díaz-Plaja, Ruben. "Projecting Stability: An Agenda for Action." *NATO Review.* March 13, 2018. www.nato.int/docu/review/articles/2018/03/13/projecting-stability-an-agenda-for -action/index.html.
"Dinitz: U.S. Sale of C-130s to Egypt Is Dangerous Course of Action." *Jewish Telegraphic Agency.* March 9, 1976. www.jta.org/1976/03/09/archive/dinitz-u-s-sale-of-c-130s-to -egypt-is-dangerous-course-of-action.
Diwan, Ishac. "Armed Forces in Power and in Business." Carnegie Middle East Center. October 26, 2020. https://carnegie-mec.org/2020/10/26/armed-forces-in-power-and-in-business -pub-83036.
DOD Directive 5205.82, DEFENSE INSTITUTION BUILDING (DIB), Office of the Under Secretary of Defense for Policy, 2016.
"DoD Personnel, Workforce Reports, and Publications, Military and Civilian Personnel by Service/Agency by State/Country (Update Quarterly)." DMDC. https://dwp.dmdc.osd .mil/dwp/app/dod-data-reports/workforce-reports.
Donelly, Chris. "Building a NATO Partnership for the Greater Middle East." *NATO Review.* January 1, 2004. www.nato.int/cps/en/SID-9905866F-2A80F2E9/natolive/opinions_21329.htm.
Dougherty, Christopher. "How Deep Does the Rot in the Russian Army Go?" *Economist.* April 27, 2022. www.economist.com/briefing/how-deep-does-the-rot-in-the-russian-army-go/21808989.

354 Bibliography

Dowd, Alan W. "Jordan: An Unsung Ally." *American Legion.* February 21, 2014. www.legion.org/landingzone/218585/jordan-unsung-ally.
Droz-Vincent, Philippe. *Military Politics of the Contemporary Arab World.* Cambridge: Cambridge University Press, 2020.
Dunne, Michele. "Fear and Learning in the Arab Uprisings." *Journal of Democracy* 31, no. 1 (2020): 182–192.
"Dutch Coalition MPs Call for EU Weapons Embargo Against Turkey." DutchNews.nl. November 11, 2020. www.dutchnews.nl/news/2020/11/dutch-coalition-mps-call-for-eu-weapons-embargo-against-turkey.
"Dutch Initiative: UN Sanctions Against Human Traffickers in Libya." Ministerie van Algemene Zaken. June 7, 2018. www.government.nl/latest/news/2018/06/07/dutch-initiative-un-sanctions-against-human-traffickers-in-libya.
Dyson, Tom. "The Military as a Learning Organisation: Establishing the Fundamentals of Best-Practice in Lessons-Learned." *Defence Studies* 19, no. 2 (January 2019): 107–129.
Echols, Connor. "Wait, Is There Really a New US-led Air Defense Alliance in the Middle East?" *Responsible Statecraft.* June 29, 2022. https://responsiblestatecraft.org/2022/06/29/wait-is-there-really-a-new-u-s-led-air-defense-alliance-in-the-middle-east.
"Egypt." F-16.net. www.f-16.net/f-16_users_article4.html (accessed February 19, 2021).
"Egypt—Air Defense Force." GlobalSecurity. Last modified January 1, 2020. www.globalsecurity.org/military/world/egypt/adf.htm.
"Egypt—Army Equipment—Introduction." GlobalSecurity. Last modified June 11, 2016. www.globalsecurity.org/military/world/egypt/army-equipment-intro.htm.
"Egypt: UN Experts Report Worsening Crackdown on Protest." *UN News.* May 9, 2016. https://news.un.org/en/story/2016/05/528742-egypt-un-experts-report-worsening-crackdown-protest.
"Egypt Airmen to Study in U.S. Before F-4 Sale." *New York Times.* June 1, 1979. www.nytimes.com/1979/06/01/archives/egypt-airmen-to-study-in-us-before-f4-sale.html.
"Egypt F-16 Peace Vector." GlobalSecurity. www.globalsecurity.org/military/world/egypt/f-16.htm (accessed February 19, 2021).
"Egypt Ignores Washington After U.S. Policy Missteps." *Washington Post.* July 17, 2013.
"Egypt in the News." Campaign Against Arms Trade. www.caat.org.uk/resources/countries/egypt/news (accessed June 10, 2018).
Egyptian Ministry of Finance 2006–2016. http://www.mof.gov.eg.
Ehrhart, Hans Georg, and Albrecht Schnabel, eds. *Security Sector Reform and Post-Conflict Peacebuilding.* Tokyo: United Nations University Press, 2005.
Eisenstadt, Michael. "Deterring Iran in the Gray Zone: Insights from Four Decades of Conflict." Washington Institute for Near East Policy. April 14, 2021. www.washingtoninstitute.org/policy-analysis/deterring-iran-gray-zone-insights-four-decades-conflict.
Ekovich, Steven. "Les États-Unis et le Maghreb: Une très longue histoire:" *Revue défense nationale* 786, no. 1 (January 1, 2016): 67–71.
Elden, Stuart. *Terror and Territory: The Spatial Extent of Sovereignty.* Minneapolis: University of Minnesota Press, 2009.
El-Edroos, Syed Ali. *The Hashemite Arab Army, 1908–1979: An Appreciation and Analysis of Military Operations.* Amman: Publishing Committee, 1980.
Eleiba, Ahmed. "Keeping the Red Sea Safe: Egypt and Saudi Arabia Wrapped Up the Morgan-16 Joint Naval Drill on 30 January." *Al-Ahram.* February 4, 2020.
———. "Sea Power: The Significance of Egypt's Mistral Deal." *Ahram Online.* October 4, 2015.
———. "No Arab NATO." *Ahram Online.* July 1, 2022.
El-Malki, Fatim-Zohra, and Anthony Dworkin. "The Southern Front Line: EU Counter-Terrorism Cooperation with Tunisia and Morocco—European Council on Foreign Relations." ECFR. February 15, 2018. https://ecfr.eu/publication/the_southern_front_line_eu_counter_terrorism_cooperation.
Emmott, Robin. "EU to Aim for Rapid Deployment Force Without U.S. Help by 2025 Document Says." *Reuters.* November 16, 2021. www.reuters.com/business/aerospace-defense/eu-aim-rapid-deployment-force-without-us-assets-by-2025-document-says-2021-11-16.
Entous, Adam. "The Enemy of My Enemy." *New Yorker.* June 18, 2018, 30–45.

Bibliography 355

Entous, Adam, and Missy Ryan. "U.S. Has Secretly Expanded Its Global Network of Drone Bases to North Africa." *Washington Post*. October 26, 2016. www.washingtonpost.com/world/national-security/us-has-secretly-expanded-its-global-network-of-drone-bases-to-north-africa/2016/10/26/ff19633c-9b7d-11e6-9980-50913d68eacb_story.html.

"The EU Is in a Muddle over Libya." *Financial Times*. June 1, 2020. www.ft.com/content/b9ab9060-a1cb-11ea-94c2-0526869b56b0.

"EU-Libya Relations." European External Action Service. March 2, 2021. https://eeas.europa.eu/headquarters/headquarters-homepage_en/19163/EU-Libya%20relations.

Executive Committee of the High Commissioner's Programme. "Update on UNHCR's Operations in the Middle East and North Africa (MENA)—2011." UNHCR. September 29, 2011. www.unhcr.org/4e85836f9.pdf.

"Exercise Regex 17 Concludes in Jordan." Allied Joint Force Command Naples. https://jfcnaples.nato.int/newsroom/news/2017/exercise-regex-17-concludes-in-jordan.

Ezzat, Dina. "Targeting of NGOs Puts Egypt-US Relations to Test." *Al-Ahram Weekly*. February 7, 2012.

Fahmy, Nabil. *Egypt's Diplomacy in War, Peace, and Transition*. Cham, Switzerland: Palgrave Macmillan, 2020.

Farouk, Yasmine. "More Than Money: Post-Mubarak Egypt, Saudi Arabia, and the Gulf." GRC Gulf Papers. Gulf Research Center. April 2014. www.files.ethz.ch/isn/179860/Egypt_Money_new_29-4-14_2576.pdf.

Farrell, Theo, and Terry Terriff, eds. *The Sources of Military Change: Culture, Politics, Technology*. Boulder, CO: Lynne Rienner, 2002.

Fisher, Max. "U.S. Allies Drive Much of World's Democratic Decline, Data Shows." *New York Times*. November 16, 2021. www.nytimes.com/2021/11/16/world/americas/democracy-decline-worldwide.html.

Fleurant, Aude, Alexandra Kuimova, Diego Lopes da Silva, Nan Tian, Siemon T. Wezeman, and Pieter D. Wezeman. *Trends in International Arms Transfers, 2019*. Stockholm: SIPRI, 2019.

Fleurant, Aude, Alexandra Kuimova, Nan Tian, Siemon T. Wezeman, and Pieter D. Wezeman. *Trends in International Arms Transfers, 2018*. Stockholm: SIPRI, 2018.

Flight International. *World Air Forces 2021*. Flight Global. www.flightglobal.com/download?ac=75345.

"Foreign Aid Explorer." United States Agency for International Development. US Foreign Aid by Country (usaid.gov). https://foreignassistance.gov/.

"Foreign Policy." European Parliament Research Service. June 2019. www.europarl.europa.eu/RegData/etudes/BRIE/2019/635534/EPRS_BRI(2019)635534_EN.pdf.

Fox, Amos C. "In Pursuit of a General Theory of Warfare." *Land Warfare Paper* 123. Arlington, VA: US Army Institute of Land Warfare, 2019.

"France, Germany, Italy Threaten Sanctions over Arms for Libya." *Reuters*. July 18, 2020. www.reuters.com/article/us-libya-security-sanctions-idUSKCN24J0SH.

"France, New Key Player in Iraq." *Atalayar*. September 22, 2020. https://atalayar.com/en/content/france-new-key-player-iraq.

"France's Security Starts in Egypt: French Ambassador." *Al-Ahram*. February 17, 2021. https://english.ahram.org.eg/NewsContent/1/64/404295/Egypt/Politics-/Frances-security-starts-in-Egypt-French-ambassador.aspx.

Francis, David. "How the U.S. Lost Billions over 9 Years in Iraq." *Fiscal Times*. June 19, 2014. www.thefiscaltimes.com/Articles/2014/06/19/How-US-Lost-Billions-Over-9-Years-Iraq.

Freeman, Charles W. "The Fadeout of Pax Americana in the Middle East." Remarks to the Institute of Peace and Diplomacy. May 19, 2021. https://chasfreeman.net/the-fadeout-of-the-pax-americana-in-the-middle-east.

Freer, Courtney, and Andrew Leber. "The 'Tribal Advantage' in Kuwait Politics and the Future of the Opposition." Brookings. April 19, 2021. www.brookings.edu/blog/order-from-chaos/2021/04/19/the-tribal-advantage-in-kuwaiti-politics-and-the-future-of-the-opposition.

Fridman, Ofer. "Russia: The Armed Forces as Patriotic Glue." In *Civil-Military Relations: Control and Effectiveness Across Regimes*, edited by Thomas C. Bruneau and Aurel Croissant, 159–174. Boulder: Lynne Rienner, 2019.

———. *Russian Hybrid Warfare: Resurgence and Politicisation*. London: Hurst & Co., 2018.
Friedman, Norman. "Gulf War: The War at Sea." Defense Media Network. Last modified January 17, 2011. www.defensemedianetwork.com/stories/gulf-war-the-war-at-sea.
Furlanetto, Elena. "'Imagine a Country Where We Are All Equal': Imperial Nostalgia in Turkey and Elif Shafak's Ottoman Utopia." In *Post-Empire Imaginaries? Anglophone Literature. History and the Demise of Empires*, edited by Barbara Buchenau and Virginia Richter. Leiden: Brill, 2015.
Furness, Mark. "Strategic Policymaking and the German Aid Programme in the MENA Region Since the Arab Uprisings." DIE Discussion Paper. Bonn: German Development Institute. May 2018.
Gabuev, Alexander. "Russia and Turkey—Unlikely Victors of Karabakh Conflict." BBC Viewpoint. November 12, 2020. www.bbc.com/news/world-europe-54903869.
Gallegos, Raul. *Crude Nation: How Oil Riches Ruined Venezuela*. Dulles, VA: Potomac Books, 2016.
Garamone, Jim. "Esper's Africa Visit Aims to Encourage Stability, Interoperability." *DoD News*. October 5, 2020. www.defense.gov/Explore/News/Article/Article/2372663/espers-africa-visit-aims-to-encourage-stability-interoperability.
———. "U.S., Tunisia Sign a Road Map for Defense Cooperation." *DoD News*. October 1, 2020. www.defense.gov/Explore/News/Article/Article/2368982/us-tunisia-sign-road-map-for-defense-cooperation.
———. "U.S. Complete Troop-Level Drawdown in Afghanistan and Iraq." Department of Defense. January 15, 2021. www.defense.gov/News/News-Stories/Article/Article/2473884/us-completes-troop-level-drawdown-in-afghanistan-iraq.
Gates, Robert M. *Exercise of Power: American Failures, Successes, and a New Path Forward in the Post–Cold War Period*. New York: Knopf, 2020.
———. "Helping Others Defend Themselves." *Foreign Affairs* 89, no. 3 (May/June 2010): 2–6.
———. "The Overmilitarization of American Foreign Policy." *Foreign Affairs* (July/August 2020): 121–132.
Gaub, Florence. *Civil-Military Relations in the MENA: Between Fragility and Resilience*. European Union Institute for Security Studies. October 2016. www.iss.europa.eu/content/civil-military-relations-mena-between-fragility-and-resilience.
———. "Merging Militaries: The Lebanese Case." In *Merging Competing Military Forces After Civil Wars*, ed., Roy Licklider. Washington, DC: Georgetown University Press, 2014.
Gaub, Florence, and Zoe Stanley-Lockman. "Defense Industries in Arab States: Players and Strategies." Chaillot Papers #141. European Union Institute for Security Studies. March 2017. www.iss.europa.eu/content/defence-industries-arab-states-players-and-strategies.
Gause, F. Gregory, III. "Should We Stay or Should We Go? The United States and the Middle East" *Survival* 61, no. 5 (September 17, 2019).
"GCC Total Population and Percentage of Nationals and Non-nationals in GCC Countries (National Statistics, 2017–2018) (with Numbers)." Gulf Labor Markets, Migration and Population Program. Gulf Research Center. https://gulfmigration.grc.net/gcc-total-population-and-percentage-of-nationals-and-non-nationals-in-gcc-countries-national-statistics-2017-2018-with-numbers.
"GDP (Current US$)—Egypt, Arab Rep." World Bank. https://data.worldbank.org/indicator/NY.GDP.MKTP.CD?locations=EG (accessed March 1, 2021).
"Gendarmerie Officer Killed in Bahrain." *Jordan Times*. December 9, 2014.
General Budget Department. *Summary of General Budget*. Amman: General Budget Department, various years.
George, Alexander L. "Coercive Diplomacy: Definition and Characteristics." In *The Limits of Coercive Diplomacy*, edited by Alexander L. George and William E. Simons. Boulder, CO: Westview Press, 1994.
———. *Forceful Persuasion: Coercive Diplomacy as an Alternative to War*. Washington, DC: US Institute of Peace, 1991.
"Germany Approves Arms Sales to Gulf, Mideast Countries." *Al Defaiya*. September 26, 2018.
Gerschewski, Johannes. "The Three Pillars of Stability: Legitimation, Repression, and Co-optations in Autocratic Regimes." *Democratization* 20 (2013): 13–38.

Ghanem, Dalia, and Eya Jrad. *When the Margins Rise: The Case of Ouargla and Tataouine.* Tunis: Konrad-Adenauer-Stiftung, 2021.
Gibbons-Neff, Thomas, and Eric Schmitt. "After Deadly Raid, Pentagon Weighs Withdrawing Almost All Commandos from Niger." *New York Times.* September 2, 2018. www.nytimes.com/2018/09/02/world/africa/pentagon-commandos-niger.html.
Global Militarization Index. Bonn International Centre for Conflict Studies, 2021. "GMI Ranking Table." Global Militarization Index. https://gmi.bicc.de/ranking-table.
Gold, Zach, Ralph Espach, Nicholas Bradford, and Douglas Jackson. "A Better Way to Measure Returns on U.S. Security Cooperation Investments." *Defense One* (June 16, 2021). www.defenseone.com/ideas/2021/06/better-way-measure-returns-us-security-cooperation-investments/174742.
Goldenberg, Ilan, Daphne McCurdy, Kaleigh Thomas, and Sydney Scarlata. *A People-First U.S. Assistance Strategy for the Middle East.* Center for a New American Security. June 10, 2021. www.cnas.org/publications/reports/a-people-first-u-s-assistance-strategy-for-the-middle-east.
Gormus, Evrim. "Why Is the End of Turkey's 'Loneliness' Now Precious in the Eastern Mediterranean?" *ISPI.* May 27, 2021. www.ispionline.it/en/pubblicazione/why-end-turkeys-loneliness-now-precious-eastern-mediterranean-30511.
Gould, Joe. "For America's Security Aid Programs, Who Will Run the Show?" *DefenseNews* (April 11, 2022). https://www.defensenews.com/global/the-americas/2022/04/11/for-americas-security-aid-programs-who-will-run-the-show/.
Gürsoy, Yaprak, "The Changing Role of the Military in Turkish Politics: Democratization through Coup Plots?" Democratization 19, no. 4 (2012): 735–760.
Gotowicki, LTC Stephen H. (US Army). "The Role of the Egyptian Military in Domestic Society." Department of Defense Foreign Military Studies Office, National Defense University, 1997.
Gourevitch, Peter. "The Second Image Reversed: The International Sources of Domestic Politics." *International Organization* 32, no. 4 (1978): 881–912.
Govindasamy, Siva, and Ahmed Mohamed Hassan. "China Trying to Undercut Germany on Submarine Offer to Egypt." *Reuters.* September 15, 2015. www.reuters.com/article/us-china-egypt-submarines-exclusive-idUSKCN0RF2NR20150915#.
Greitens, Sheena Chestnut. *Dictators and Their Secret Police: Coercive Institutions and State Violence.* New York: Cambridge University Press, 2016.
Grewal, Sharan. "Ten Years In, Tunisian Democracy Remains a Work in Progress." Brookings Institution. January 22, 2021. www.brookings.edu/blog/order-from-chaos/2021/01/22/ten-years-in-tunisian-democracy-remains-a-work-in-progress.
Guillaume, Henri. *Entre désertification et développement: La Jeffara tunisienne.* Tunis: Cérès Editions, 2006.
Gurcan, Metin. "Libyan Conflict Stands Out as Key to Turkey-Egypt Normalization." *Al-Monitor.* May 10, 2021. www.al-monitor.com/originals/2021/05/libyan-conflict-stands-out-key-turkey-egypt-normalization#ixzz7E0umspd3.
Guzansky, Yoel, and Zachary A. Marshall. "Outsourcing Warfare in the Mediterranean." *Mediterranean Politics.* May 7, 2021.
Haddad, Simon. "Islam and Attitudes Toward U.S. Policy in the Middle East: Evidence from Survey Research in Lebanon." *Studies in Conflict & Terrorism* 26, no. 2 (2003): 135–154.
Haftar, Khalifa. "Turkey's Parliament Approves Military Deployment to Libya." *Al-Jazeera.* January 2, 2020. www.aljazeera.com/news/2020/1/2/turkeys-parliament-approves-military-deployment-to-libya.
Hamama, Mohamed. "Sisi Says Military Economy Is 1.5% of Egypt's GDP, but How Accurate Is This?" *Mada Masr.* November 2, 2016.
Hamid, Shadi. "The Struggle for Middle East Democracy." Brookings Institution. April 26, 2011. www.brookings.edu/articles/the-struggle-for-middle-east-democracy.
Hamzawy, Amr, Karim Sadjadpour, Aaron David Miller, Frederic Wehrey, Zaha Hassan, Yasmine Farouk, Kheder Khaddour, Sarah Yerkes, Alper Coşkun, Maha Yahya, and Marwan Muasher. "What the Russian War in Ukraine Means for The Middle East." Carnegie Endowment for International Peace. March 24, 2022. https://carnegieendowment.org/2022/03/24/what-russian-war-in-ukraine-means-for-middle-east-pub-86711.

Harb, Imad K. "The United States and the GCC: A Steep Learning Curve for President Trump." In *Trump and the Arab World: A First Year Assessment*, edited by Zeina Azzam and Imad K. Harb, 49–56. Washington, DC: Arab Center, 2017.

Hartung, William. *The U.S. Support for Saudi Arabia and the War in Yemen*. Washington, DC: Center for International Policy. November 2018. https://docs.wixstatic.com/ugd/3ba8a1_5e9019d625e84087af647e6cb91ea3e2.pdf.

Hartung, William D., Christina Arabia, and Elias Yousif. *The Trump Effect: Trends in Major US Arms Sales, 2019*. Washington DC: Center for International Policy. May 2020.

Hartung, William D., and Seth Binder. "U.S. Security Assistance to Egypt: Assessing the Return on Investment." Project on Middle East Democracy and Center for International Policy. May 2020. https://pomed.org/report-u-s-security-assistance-to-egypt-examining-the-return-on-investment.

Hasselbladh, Hans, and Karl Ydén. "Why Military Organizations Are Cautious About Learning?" *Armed Forces & Society* 46, no. 3 (July 2020): 475–494.

Hattar, Jihad. *Dhikriyat 'an ma'rika aylul: al-urdun 1970* [Memories of the September struggle: Jordan 1970]. Beirut: Ittihad al-'am lil-kuttab wa al-suhufiyin al-filistiniyyin, 1977.

Hausmann, Ricardo. "How Afghanistan Was Really Lost." *Project Syndicate*. November 9, 2021. www.project-syndicate.org/commentary/failed-western-economic-strategy-in-afghanistan-by-ricardo-hausmann-2021-11.

Hazen, Timothy A. "Explaining Middle Eastern and North African (MENA) Military Responses During the 2011–2012 Arab Uprisings." *Democracy and Security* 15, no. 4 (2019): 361–385.

Hearing and Markup Before the Subcommittee on Europe and the Middle East of the Committee of Foreign Affairs of House of Representatives: Economic and Military Aid Programs in Europe and the Middle East. Washington, DC: US Government Printing Office, 1983.

Hegghammer, Thomas. *Jihad in Saudi Arabia: Violence and Pan-Islamism Since 1979*. New York: Cambridge University Press, 2011.

Heller, Mark. "Politics and the Military in Iraq and Jordan, 1920–1958: The British Influence." *Armed Forces & Society* 4 (1977): 75–99.

Hellyer, H. A. "Egypt's Stance on the Iran Talks." RUSI. February 22,2022. https://rusi.org/explore-our-research/publications/commentary/egypts-stance-iran-talks-positive-pragmatic.

Henry, Clement M. "Reverberations in the Central Maghreb of the 'Global War on Terror.'" In *North Africa: Politics, Region, and the Limits of Transformation*, edited by Yahia H. Zoubir and Haizam Amirah-Fernández, 294–310. New York: Routledge, 2008.

Hensler, Amy. "Security Assistance in Focus: Tunisia's Tier 1 Counterterrorism Company." *Security Assistance Monitor / U.S. Security Assistance in Focus*. Series 1, no. 5 (November 2019).

Herb, Michael. *The Wages of Oil: Parliaments and Economic Development in Kuwait and the UAE*. Ithaca, NY: Cornell University Press, 2014.

Heydemann, Steven. "Rethinking Social Contracts in the MENA Region: Economic Governance, Contingent Citizenship, and State-Society Relations After the Arab Uprisings." *World Development* 135 (November 2020): 1–10.

Hitti, Maroun. "Nonstate Actors and Lebanese National Security Documents." *Tawazun*. December 9, 2020. www.tawazun.net/english/blog1.php?id=119-tw.

Hoffman, Hugh F. T. "Lessons from Iraq." In *Effective, Legitimate, Secure: Insights for Defense Institution Building*, edited by Alexandra Kerr and Michael Miklaucic, 329–358. Washington, DC: Institute for National Strategic Studies, National Defense University, 2017.

Hokayem, Emile. "Reassuring Gulf Partners While Recalibrating U.S. Security Policy." In *From Hardware to Holism: Rebalancing America's Security Engagement with Arab States*, edited by Frederic Wehrey and Michelle Dunne. Carnegie Endowment for International Peace. May 18, 2021. https://carnegieendowment.org/2021/05/18/reassuring-gulf-partners-while-recalibrating-u.s.-security-policy-pub-84522.

Holmes, James. "Why Offshore Balancing Won't Work." *National Interest*. July 18, 2016. https://nationalinterest.org/feature/why-offshore-balancing-wont-work-17025.

Honig, David. "A Mighty Arsenal: Egypt's Military Build-Up, 1979–1999." Policy Watch 447. Washington Institute for Near East Policy. March 21, 2000. www.washingtoninstitute.org/policy-analysis/mighty-arsenal-egypts-military-build-1979-1999.

Bibliography 359

Hönke, Jana, and Markus-Michael Müller. "Governing (in) Security in a Postcolonial World: Transnational Entanglements and the Worldliness of 'Local' Practice." *Security Dialogue* 43, no. 5 (2012): 383–401.
Hourani, Najib. "Urbanism and Neoliberal Order: The Development and Redevelopment of Amman." *Journal of Urban Affairs* 36 (2014): 634–649.
Hubbard, Ben. "Saudis Cast Net for ISIS Sympathizers." *New York Times*. July 18, 2015.
"Human Development Insights." UNDP. 2019. http://hdr.undp.org/en/content/2019-human-development-index-ranking (accessed July 14, 2020).
Human Rights Council. "Visit to Tunisia—Rapport of the Special Rapporteur on the Promotion and Protection of Human Rights and Fundamental Freedoms while Countering Terrorism." A/HRC/40/52/Add.1. December 12, 2018. https://documents-dds-ny.un.org/doc/UNDOC/GEN/G18/362/41/PDF/G1836241.pdf?OpenElement.
Humud, Carla E. "Lebanon." R44759. Congressional Research Service. April 21, 2021. https://crsreports.congress.gov/product/pdf/R/R44759/20.
Hundley, Tom. "Egyptians Abandoned by Gulf War Allies." *Chicago Tribune*. July 7, 1991. www.chicagotribune.com/news/ct-xpm-1991-07-07-9103170485-story.html.
Huntington, Samuel P. *The Soldier and the State: The Theory and Politics of Civil-Military Relations*. Cambridge, MA: Harvard University Press, 1985.
Hussein, Rahma. "The UAE's Military and Naval Reliance on Eritrea Makes the War in Yemen Even Riskier for the U.S." *Just Security*. May 31, 2017. www.justsecurity.org/41450/uaes-military-naval-reliance-eritrea-war-yemen-riskier-u-s.
Ignatius, David. "Mustafa al Khadhimi's Government in Iraq Has a Long Way to Go, but At Least It's a Start." *Washington Post*. July 17, 2021. www.washingtonpost.com/opinions/2021/07/17/mustafa-al-kadhimis-government-iraq-has-long-way-go-least-its-start.
IISS. *The Military Balance*. London: International Institute for Strategic Studies, 1965–2021.
"In a Two-Hour Meeting with Them, Essid Discusses Several Issues with Journalists and Reveals Some Secrets." Hakaekonline.com. May 11, 2015. www.hakaekonline.com/article/28564/ديدع-نييفحصلا-عم-شقاني-يدصلا-نيتعاس-نمهب-هعمج-هءاقل-يف-ىلملاتافلمل-ا-يفشكيوضعب-نعرارسألا-quot-.quot.
Institute for Economics & Peace. *Global Peace Index 2021*. Vision of Humanity. www.visionofhumanity.org/wp-content/uploads/2021/06/GPI-2021-web-1.pdf.
"Interministerial Strategy to Support Security Sector Reform (SSR)." German Foreign Office. July 2019. www.auswaertiges-amt.de/blob/2298386/44c6eebba11f48b74243f2434535943d/sicherheitssektorreform-en-data.pdf.
International Crisis Group. "Silencing the Guns in Syria's Idlib." Middle East Report No. 213. May 15, 2020. https://d2071andvip0wj.cloudfront.net/213-silencing-the-guns-idlib.pdf.
International Institute for Strategic Studies (IISS). *The Military Balance 2019*. London: IISS, 2019.
"Iraq: EU Advisory Mission Extended and Budget Agreed." Council of the European Union. October 15, 2018. www.consilium.europa.eu/en/press/press-releases/2018/10/15/iraq-eu-advisory-mission-extended-and-budget-agreed.
Irish, John, and Sabine Siebold. "U.N. Says Libya Arms Embargo a 'Joke,' Demands Accountability." *Reuters*. February 16, 2020. www.reuters.com/article/us-germany-security-libya-idUSKBN20A09X.
Ismail, Amina, and Haitham Ahmed. "Egyptian Court Acquits 40 NGO Workers Whose Case Strained Ties with U.S." *Reuters*. December 20, 2018. www.reuters.com/article/us-egypt-usa-idUSKCN1OJ0WR.
"Italia-Tunisia: Amb. Fanara incontro Ministro Difesa su cooperazione militare." *Giornale Diplomatico*. April 30, 2020. www.giornalediplomatico.it/Italia-Tunisia-amb-Fanara-incontroministro-Difesa-su-cooperazione-militare.htm.
Jackson, Paul. "Introduction: Second-Generation Security Sector Reform." *Journal of Intervention and Statebuilding* 12, no 1 (2018): 1–10.
Jarstad, Anna, and Roberto Belloni. "Introducing Hybrid Peace Governance: Impact and Prospects of Liberal Peacebuilding." *Global governance* 18, no. 1 (2012): 1–6.
Jarzabek, Jarosław. "GCC Military Spending in Era of Low Oil Prices." Middle East Institute. Policy Focus Series. August 2016. www.mei.edu/sites/default/files/publications/PF19_Jarzabek_GCCmilitary_web.pdf.

Jebnoun, Noureddine. "Tunisia: Patterns and Implications of Civilian Control." In *Civil-Military Relations: Control and Effectiveness Across Regimes*, edited by Thomas C. Bruneau and Aurel Croissant, 119–140. Boulder, CO: Lynne Rienner, 2019.
———. *Tunisia's National Intelligence: Why "Rogue Elephants" Fail to Reform*. Washington DC: New Academic Publishing, 2017.
Ji, You. *China's Military Transformation: Politics and War Preparation*. Cambridge, UK: Polity Press, 2016.
Johnsen, Gregory D. *The End of Yemen*. Washington, DC: Brookings, 2021.
Jones, Reece, and Corey Johnson. "Border Militarization and the Re-articulation of Sovereignty." *Transactions-Institute of the British Geographers* 41, no. 2 (2016): 187–200.
Jones, Seth, Danika Newlee, Edmund Loughran, Jason Gresh, Brian Katz, and Nicholas Harrington. "Moscow's War in Syria." Center for Strategic and International Studies. May 12, 2020. www.csis.org/analysis/moscows-war-syria.
"Jordanians Overwhelmingly Have More Trust in Army, Police over Other Agencies." *Jordan Times*. January 9, 2018.
Journal Officiel. "LOI no 2018–607 du 13 juillet 2018 relative à la programmation militaire pour les années 2019 à 2025 et portant diverses dispositions intéressant la défense." Légifrance. www.legifrance.gouv.fr/jorf/id/JORFTEXT000037192797#.
Kabalan, Nidal. "Outrage, Rift and Resignations over Erdogan's Libya Plan." *Inside Over*. January 1, 2020. www.insideover.com/politics/outrage-rift-and-resignations-over-erdogans-libya-plan.html.
Kandil, Amr. "Sisi, Macron Discuss Ukraine, COP27 and Regional Security." *Al-Ahram Online*. May 5, 2022. https://english.ahram.org.eg/News/465692.aspx.
Kandil, Hazem. *The Power Triangle: Military, Security, and Politics in Regime Change*. Oxford: Oxford University Press, 2016.
Karas, Mark, Col., US Army (Ret.). "Reconciling Defense and State Department Cultures at Embassies: A FAO Survival Guide to Working on a U.S. Country Team." *Foreign Area Officer Journal of International Affairs*. October 23, 2020. https://faoajournal.substack.com/p/reconciling-defense-and-state-department.
Karl, Terry Lynn. *The Paradox of Plenty: Oil Booms and Petro-States*. Berkeley: University of California Press, 1997.
Karlin, Mara E. *Building Militaries in Fragile States: Challenges for the United States*. Philadelphia: University of Pennsylvania Press, 2018.
Karlin, Mara, and Melissa Dalton. "It's Long Past Time to Rethink U.S. Military Posture in the Gulf." *Brookings*. August 4, 2017. www.brookings.edu/blog/markaz/2017/08/04/its-long-past-time-to-rethink-u-s-military-posture-in-the-gulf.
Kartas, Moncef. *On the Edge? Trafficking and Insecurity at the Tunisian-Libyan Border*. Geneva: Small Arms Survey, Graduate Institute of International and Development Studies, 2013.
Kårtveit, Bård, and Maria Gabrielsen. *Civil-Military Relations in the Middle East: A Literature Review*. Chr. Michelsen Institute. June 2014. www.cmi.no/publications/file/5188-civil-military-relations-in-the-middle-east.pdf.
Kaye, Dalia Dassa. "America Is Not Withdrawing from the Middle East." *Foreign Affairs*. December 1, 2021. www.foreignaffairs.com/articles/united-states/2021-12-01/america-not-withdrawing-middle-east.
Kaye, Dalia Dassa, Linda Robinson, Jeffrey Martini, Nathan Vest, and Ashley L. Rhoades. *Reimagining U.S. Strategy in the Middle East: Sustainable Partnerships, Strategic Investments*. Santa Monica, CA: RAND Corporation, 2021 www.rand.org/content/dam/rand/pubs/research_reports/RRA900/RRA958-2/RAND_RRA958-2.pdf.
Kee, Hiau Looi, and Heiwai Tang. "How Did China Move Up the Global Value Chains?" *VoxDev*. June 5, 2019. https://voxdev.org/topic/firms-trade/how-did-china-move-global-value-chains.
Kenner, David, and Gordon Lubold. "Sisi's Year Abroad." *Foreign Policy*. August 5, 2013. https://foreignpolicy.com/2013/08/05/sisis-year-abroad.
Kerr, Alexandra. "Introduction: Defense Institution Building: A New Paradigm for the 21st Century." In *Effective, Legitimate, Secure: Insights for Defense Institution Building*, edited by Alexandra Kerr and Michael Miklaucic. Washington, DC: Institute for National Strategic Studies, National Defense University, 2017.

Khalili, Laleh. *Sinews of War and Trade: Shipping and Capitalism in the Arabian Peninsula*. London: Verso, 2020.
Khan, Akbar, and Han Zhaoying. "Iran-Hezbollah Alliance Reconsidered: What Contributes to the Survival of State-Proxy Alliance?" *Journal of Asian Security and International Affairs* 7, no. 1 (2020):101–123.
Kilavuz, M. Tahir, and Nathanael Gratias Sumaktoyo. "Hopes and Disappointments: Regime Change and Support for Democracy After the Arab Uprisings." *Democratization* 27, no. 5 (2020): 854–873.
"King Abdullah Inherits a Strong Fighting Force." *Irish Times*. February 8, 1999.
Kishi, Nobuo. *Defense of Japan 2021*. Ministry of Defense. www.mod.go.jp/en/publ/w_paper/wp2021/DOJ2021_Digest_EN.pdf.
Kleinfeld, Rachel. "Why Supporters of Democracy and Security Both Need to Care About Security Sector Governance." *Just Security*. June 4, 2021. www.justsecurity.org/76768/why-supporters-of-democracy-and-security-both-need-to-care-about-security-sector-governance.
Knight, Ben. "Germany Quintuples Arms Sales to Saudi Arabia and Egypt." *DW*. November 14, 2017. www.dw.com/en/germany-quintuples-arms-sales-to-saudi-arabia-and-egypt/a-41370500.
Knights, Michael. "Iraq's Judiciary Weak Link." Washington Institute for Near East Policy. June10, 2021. www.washingtoninstitute.org/policy-analysis/iraqs-judiciary-weak-link.
Knowles, Emily, and Abigail Watson. *Remote Warfare: Lessons Learned from Contemporary Theatres*. London: Oxford Research Group, 2018.
Koehler, Kevin. "Officers and Regimes: The Historical Origins of Political-Military Relations in Middle Eastern Republics." In *Armies and Insurgencies in the Arab Spring*, edited by Holger Albrecht, Aurel Croissant, and Fred H. Lawson, 34–53. Philadelphia: University of Pennsylvania Press, 2016.
———. "Projecting Stability in Practice? NATO's New Training Mission in Iraq." *NDC Policy Brief* No. 2 (October 2018).
———. "Putting the Horse Back Before the Cart: NATO's Projecting Stability in the South." In *Projecting Stability: Elixir or Snake Oil?* edited by Ian Hope, 41–51. NDC Research Paper 1. Rome: NATO Defense College, 2018.
Koehler, Kevin, Holger Albrecht, and Sharan Grewal. "Who Fakes Support for the Military? Experimental Evidence from Tunisia." *Democratization* 29, no. 6 (2022): 1055–1076.
Koshino, Yuka. "Is Japan Ready for Civil-Military 'Integration'?" International Institute of Strategic Studies. August 3, 2021. www.iiss.org/blogs/analysis/2021/08/japan-civil-military-integration.
Kraidy, Marwan M., and Omar Al-Ghazzi. "Neo-Ottoman Cool: Turkish Popular Culture in the Arab Public Sphere." *Popular Communication* 11, no. 1 (2013): 17–29.
Krieg, Andreas. "The UAE's 'Dogs of War': Boosting a Small State's Regional Power Projection." *Small Wars & Insurgencies* 33, no. 1–2 (2022).
Krieg, Andreas, and Jean-Marc Rickli. *Surrogate Warfare: The Transformation of War in the Twenty-First Century*. Washington, DC: Georgetown University Press, 2019.
Kuehn, David, ed., *The Military's Impact on Democratic Development: Midwives or Gravediggers of Democracy?* London: Routledge, 2018.
Kuimova, Alexandra. "Opaque Military Spending and Middle East Insecurity." *Tawazun*. June 8, 2021. www.tawazun.net/english/blog1.php?id=621-tw.
Kulish, Nicholas, and David D. Kirkpatrick. "In Saudi Arabia, Where Family and State Are One, Arrests May Be Selective." *New York Times*. November 7, 2017. www.nytimes.com/2017/11/07/world/middleeast/saudi-arabia-royal-family-corruption.html.
Lamloum, Olfa. *Marginalization, Insecurity and Uncertainty on the Tunisian-Libyan Border*. London: International Alert, 2016.
Langan, Mark. "Virtuous Power Turkey in Sub-Saharan Africa: The 'Neo-Ottoman' Challenge to the European Union." *Third World Quarterly* 38, no. 6 (2017): 1399–1414.
Larsen, Jeffrey A., and Kevin Koehler. "Projecting Stability to the South: NATO's 'New' Mission?" In *Projecting Resilience Across the Mediterranean*, edited by Eugenio Cusumano and Stefan Hofmaier, 37–62. New York: Palgrave Macmillan, 2020.
Lavrov, Anton. "The Efficiency of the Syrian Armed Forces: An Analysis of Russian Assistance." Carnegie Middle East Center. March 26, 2020. https://carnegie-mec.org/2020/03/26/efficiency-of-syrian-armed-forces-analysis-of-russian-assistance-pub-81150.

Le Bras, Jenna. "France and Egypt: Allies of Convenience." *Mada Masr*. October 28, 2017.
Le Monde. "A Troubling New Wall Rises at the Tunisia-Libya Border." *Le Monde* (English Edition). August 31, 2015. https://worldcrunch.com/world-affairs/a-troubling-new-wall-rises-at-the-tunisia-libya-border/c1s19493#.
———. "L'aide militaire de la France à la Tunisie multipliée par quatre." *Le Monde*. October 5, 2015.
"Lebanon." Corruption Perceptions Index, Transparency International. www.transparency.org/en/cpi/2020/index/lbn.
"Lebanon Sinking into One of the Most Severe Global Crises Episodes, Amidst Deliberate Inaction." World Bank. June 1, 2021. www.worldbank.org/en/news/press-release/2021/05/01/lebanon-sinking-into-one-of-the-most-severe-global-crises-episodes.
Lee, Dongmin. "Swords to Ploughshares: China's Defence Conversion Policy." *Defence Studies* 11, no. 1 (March 2011): 1–23.
Leone, Daniel. "Egypt's North Korea Connection." Project on Middle East Democracy. August 10, 2017. https://pomed.org/egypts-north-korea-connection.
Lesser, Ian, Charlotte Brandsma, Laura Basagni, and Bruno Lété. "The Future of NATO's Mediterranean Dialogue: Perspectives on Security, Strategy, and Partnership." German Marshall Fund of the United States. June 2018. www.gmfus.org/sites/default/files/The_future_of_NATO%2527s_MD_INTERACTIVE_FINAL_1705.pdf.
Levitsky, Steven, and Lucan A. Way. *Competitive Authoritarianism: Hybrid Regimes After the Cold War*. New York: Cambridge University Press, 2010.
"Libya Arms Embargo 'Totally Ineffective': UN Expert Panel." *UN News*. March 17, 2021. https://news.un.org/en/story/2021/03/1087562.
Lionel, Ekene. "Production of Egypt's Su-35s Almost Complete." Military.africa. May 31, 2022. www.military.africa/2022/05/production-of-egypts-su-35s-almost-complete.
Lotito, Nicholas J. "Public Trust in the Arab Armies." Carnegie Middle East Center. October 30, 2018. https://carnegie-mec.org/sada/77610.
Luckham, Robin. "Le militarisme français en Afrique." *Politique africaine*, no. 5 (1982): 95–110.
Lyall, Jason. *Divided Armies: Inequality and Battlefield Performance in Modern War*. Princeton, NJ: Princeton University Press, 2020.
Lynch, Marc. "The End of the Middle East: How an Old Map Distorts a New Reality." *Foreign Affairs* (March/April 2022).
"M1A1 Abrams." Army-Guide. www.army-guide.com/eng/product1160.html (accessed February 15, 2021).
Mac Ginty, Roger. "Hybrid Peace: The Interaction Between Top-Down and Bottom-Up Peace." *Security Dialogue* 41, no. 4 (2010): 391–412.
Mackinnon, Amy. "Pentagon Says UAE Likely Funding Russia's Shadow Mercenaries in Libya." *Foreign Policy*. November 30, 2020. https://foreignpolicy.com/2020/11/30/pentagon-trump-russia-libya-uae.
"Madrid Summit Declaration." NATO. Last updated July 22, 2022. www.nato.int/cps/en/natohq/official_texts_196951.htm.
Magaloni, Beatriz. "Credible Power-Sharing and the Longevity of Authoritarian Rule." *Comparative Political Studies* 41 (2008): 715–741.
Manning, Robert A., and Christopher Preble. "Reality Check #8: Rethinking US Military Policy in the Greater Middle East." Atlantic Council. June 24, 2021. www.atlanticcouncil.org/content-series/reality-check/reality-check-8-rethinking-us-military-policy-in-the-greater-middle-east.
Marrone, Alessandro. "La politica di sicurezza nel vicinato meridionale: A View from Rome." Friedrich Ebert Stiftung. June 2020. https://library.fes.de/pdf-files/bueros/rom/16276.pdf.
Marshall, Shana. "Egypt's Other Revolution: Modernizing the Military-Industrial Complex." *Pambazuka News*. February 16, 2012. www.pambazuka.org/governance/egypts-other-revolution-modernizing-military-industrial-complex.
———. "Jordan's Military-Industrial Sector: Maintaining Institutional Prestige in the Era of Neoliberalism." In *Businessmen in Arms: How the Military and Other Armed Groups Profit in the MENA Region*, edited by Elke Grawert and Zeinab Abul-Magd, 119–134. Lanham, MD: Rowman & Littlefield, 2016.

Marten, Kimberly. "Russia's Use of Semi-State Security Forces: The Case of the Wagner Group." *Post-Soviet Affairs* 35, no. 3 (2019): 181–204.
Martin, Guy. "Tunisia Getting Cessna Caravans for Intelligence, Surveillance and Reconnaissance." defenceWeb. November 3, 2021. www.defenceweb.co.za/aerospace/aerospace-aerospace/tunisia-getting-cessna-caravans-for-intelligence-surveillance-and-reconnaissance.
Martz, Joseph E. "Executive Summary." *The Lebanese Armed Forces: Assessment of 8–13, 2006.* Unpublished manuscript.
Massad, Joseph. *Colonial Effects: The Making of National Identity in Jordan.* New York: Columbia University Press, 2001.
Matisek, Jahara. "Shades of Gray Deterrence: Issues of Fighting in the Gray Zone." *Journal of Strategic Security* 10, no. 3 (2017): 1–26.
———. "The Crisis of American Military Assistance: Strategic Dithering and Fabergé Egg Armies." *Defense & Security Analysis* 34, no. 3 (2018): 267–290.
Matisek, Jahara, and William Reno. "Getting American Security Force Assistance Right: Political Context Matters." *Joint Force Quarterly* 92 (January 23, 2019): 65–73.
Mattis, James. "Summary of the 2018 National Defense Strategy of the United States of America: Sharpening the American Military's Competitive Edge." Department of Defense. https://dod.defense.gov/Portals/1/Documents/pubs/2018-National-Defense-Strategy-Summary.pdf?mod=article_inline.
"Mauritania I." SALW & MA Information Sharing Platform. https://salw.hq.nato.int/Project/Details/tf_11.
"Mauritania II, Phase 1+." SALW & MA Information Sharing Platform. https://salw.hq.nato.int/Project/Details/tf_9.
Mearsheimer, John, and Stephen Walt. "The Case for Offshore Balancing: A Superior U.S. Grand Strategy." *Foreign Affairs.* July/August 2016. www.foreignaffairs.com/articles/united-states/2016-06-13/case-offshore-balancing.
Meddeb, Hamza. "Life on the Edge: How Protests in Tataouine Force Tunis to Back Down." Malcom H. Kerr Carnegie Middle East Center. February 2021. https://carnegieendowment.org/files/Meddeb-Tunisian-inequalities.pdf.
MEE and Agencies. "Tunisian Forces Kill Seven in Fresh Fighting on Libya Border." *Middle East Eye.* March 9, 2016. www.middleeasteye.net/news/tunisian-forces-kill-seven-fresh-fighting-libya-border.
MEE Staff. "Tunisia to Build a Border Wall with Libya." *Middle East Eye.* July 10, 2015. www.middleeasteye.net/news/tunisia-build-border-wall-libya-0.
Megerisi, Tarek, and Shoshana Fine. "The Unacknowledged Costs of the EU's Migration Policy in Libya—European Council on Foreign Relations." *ECFR.* July 25, 2019. https://ecfr.eu/article/commentary_unacknowledged_costs_of_the_eu_migration_policy_in_libya.
Mello, Alex, and Michael Knights. "West of Suez for the United Arab Emirates." *War on the Rocks.* September 2, 2016. https://warontherocks.com/2016/09/west-of-suez-for-the-united-arab-emirates.
Meyer Kantack, Jacqulyn. "The New Scramble for Africa." *Critical Threats.* February 26, 2018.
Micro Poverty Outlook–World Bank. "Tunisia." April 2021. https://thedocs.worldbank.org/en/doc/642149f5f762c2c7cdf6fa45da5e7b49-0280012021/original/16-mpo-sm21-tunisia-tun-kcm2.pdf.
"Militari giordani si addestrano in Italia." Esercito. December 11, 2020. www.esercito.difesa.it/comunicazione/Pagine/blindo-centauro_201211.aspx.
"Military and Civilian Missions and Operations." European External Action Service. May 3, 2019. https://eeas.europa.eu/headquarters/headquarters-homepage/430/military-and-civilian-missions-and-operations_en.
Miller, Greg, Missy Ryan, Sudarsan Raghavan, and Souad Mekhennet. "At the Mercy of Foreign Powers: Libyans Ousted a Dictator, but an Ensuing Civil War Has Drawn in Russia, Turkey and Others with a Thirst for Control." *Washington Post.* February 27, 2021. www.washingtonpost.com/world/interactive/2021/libya-civil-war-russia-turkey-fighter-planes.
Miller, Rory, and Harry Verhoeven. "Overcoming Smallness: Qatar, the United Arab Emirates, and Strategic Realignment in the Gulf." *International Politics* 57 (2020): 1–20.

Ministère des Armées. "Livre blanc sur la défense et la sécurité nationale." Paris: Direction de l'information légale et administrative, 2013.
———. "Opération Barkhane." Paris: Bureau relation médias de l'état-major des armées, 2021.
———. "Opération CHAMMAL." Paris: Bureau relation médias de l'état-major des armées, 2021.
Ministero della Difesa. "Documento programmatico pluriennale per la difesa per il triennio 2019–2021." Roma: Ministero della Difesa, 2019.
———. "Documento programmatico pluriennale per la difesa per il triennio 2020–2022." Roma: Ministero della Difesa, 2020.
"Mission de défense." Ambassade de France en Tunisie. https://tn.ambafrance.org/Mission-de-defense.
Monroy, Matthias. "Germany Funds New Border Control Technology in Tunisia." Matthias Monroy Security Architectures and Police Collaboration in the EU. December 20, 2017. https://digit.site36.net/2017/12/20/germany-funds-new-border-control-technology-in-tunisia.
Montgomery, Spc. Jonathan. "Operation Bright Star: A History of Multinational Forces Cooperation." Defense Visual Information Distribution Service. Last modified September 20, 2005. www.dvidshub.net/news/3070/operation-bright-star-history-multinational-forces-cooperation.
Moore, Pete. "A Political-Economic History of Jordan's General Intelligence Directorate: Authoritarian State-Building and Fiscal Crisis." *Middle East Journal* 73, no. 2 (2019): 242–262.
Moore, Rebecca R. *NATO's New Mission: Projecting Stability in a Post–Cold War World.* Westport, CT: Praeger Security International, 2007.
Morgan, Wesley. "Behind the Secret U.S. War in Africa." *Politico.* July 2, 2018. www.politico.com/story/2018/07/02/secret-war-africa-pentagon-664005.
Moroney, Jennifer D. P., Celeste Gventer, Stephanie Pezard, and Laurence Smallman. *Lessons from U.S. Allies in Security Cooperation with Third Countries: The Cases of Australia, France, and the United Kingdom.* Santa Monica, CA: RAND, 2011.
Moroney, Jennifer D. P., David E. Thaler, and Joe Hogler. *Review of Security Cooperation Mechanisms Combatant Commands Utilize to Build Partner Capacity.* Santa Monica, CA: RAND Corporation, 2013.
Mullin, Corinna. "Tunisia's 'Transition': Between Revolution and Globalized National Security." *Pambazuka News.* October 12, 2015. www.pambazuka.org/global-south/tunisia's-"transition"-between-revolution-and-globalized-national-security.
Mumford, Andrew. *Proxy Warfare.* London: Polity Press, 2013.
Munsil, Leigh, and Austin Wright. "Is Lockheed Martin Too Big to Fail?" *Politico.* August 12, 2015. www.politico.com/story/2015/08/is-lockheed-martin-too-big-too-fail-121203.
Murad, 'Abbas. *Al-dawr al-siyaasi lil-jaysh al-urduni* [The political role of the Jordanian army]. Beirut: PLO Research Center, 1973.
Myers, Steven Lee. "Once Imperiled, U.S. Aid to Egypt Is Restored." *New York Times.* March 23, 2012. www.nytimes.com/2012/03/24/world/middleeast/once-imperiled-united-states-aid-to-egypt-is-restored.html.
Nachtwey, Jodi, and Mark Tessler. "The Political Economy of Attitudes Toward Peace Among Palestinians and Israelis." *Journal of Conflict Resolution* 46, no. 2 (2002): 260–285.
Nader, Emir. "UK Arms Deals with Egypt Soar amid Warming Diplomatic Ties." *Daily News Egypt.* August 1, 2015.
National Institute of Statistics (INS). "Employment and Unemployment Indicators: Second Quarter 2019." INS. www.ins.tn/sites/default/files/publication/pdf/Note_ENPE_2T2019_F2.pdf.
NATO. "Active Engagement, Modern Defense." Brussels: NATO, 2010.
———. "Afghan National Army (ANA) Trust Fund." Brussels: NATO, 2021.
———. "Brussels Summit Declaration Issued by the Heads of State and Government Participating in the Meeting of the North Atlantic Council in Brussels 11–12 July 2018." Brussels: NATO, 2018.
NATO and European Union. "Fifth Progress Report on the Implementation of the Common Set of Proposals Endorsed by EU and NATO Councils on 6 December 2016 and 5 December

2017." NATO. June 16, 2020. www.nato.int/nato_static_fl2014/assets/pdf/2020/6/pdf/200615-progress-report-nr5-EU-NATO-eng.pdf.
"Nato DEEP: Cooperazione militare Italia Tunisia." Ministero della Difesa. February 5, 2020. www.difesa.it/SMD_/Eventi/Pagine/Nato_DEEP_Cooperazione_militare_Italia_Tunisia.aspx.
"NATO Training for Iraqi Officers Starts in Jordan." NATO. April 2, 2016, www.nato.int/cps/en/natohq/news_129666.htm.
"NATO 2022 Strategic Concept." NATO. June 29, 2022. www.nato.int/nato_static_fl2014/assets/pdf/2022/6/pdf/290622-strategic-concept.pdf.
Natsios, Andrew S. "Foreign Aid in an Era of Great Power Competition." *PRISM* 8, no. 4 (June 6, 2020): 112–117.
Nerguizian, Aram. "The Five Wildcards of Lebanese Military Capability Development." *Tawazun*. April 20, 2021. www.tawazun.net/english/blog1.php?id=591-tw.
———. "Lebanon at the Crossroad: Assessing the Impact of the Lebanon-Syria Insecurity Nexus." Center for Strategic and International Studies. February 26, 2014. www.csis.org/analysis/lebanon-crossroad-assessing-impact-lebanon-syria-insecurity-nexus.
"Netherlands Help in Enforcing Libyan Arms Embargo." Ministerie van Defensie. March 30, 2011. www.government.nl/latest/news/2011/03/30/netherlands-help-in-enforcing-libyan-arms-embargo.
Nevo, Joseph. "September 1970 in Jordan: A Civil War?" *Civil Wars* 10 (2008): 217–230.
"News in Brief." European External Action Service. September 25, 2013. https://eeas.europa.eu/archives/csdp/missions-and-operations/eujust-lex-iraq/news/index_en.htm.
Nikolić, Nebojša V. "On New Military Technologies and Concepts Explored from the Syrian Conflict Experience." *Vojnotehnički glasnik / Military Technical Courier* 69, no. 3 (July–September 2021): 638–655.
Nkala, Oscar. "U.S. Army Awards Contract for Installation of Surveillance System on Tunisia-Libya Border." defenceWeb. April 5, 2016. www.defenceweb.co.za/security/border-security/us-army-awards-contract-for-installation-of-surveillance-system-on-libya-tunisia-border.
Norton, Augustus Richard. *Hezbollah: A Short History*. Princeton, NJ: Princeton University Press, 2007.
Nsaibia, Héni. "America Is Quietly Expanding Its War in Tunisia." *National Interest*. September 18, 2018. https://nationalinterest.org/blog/middle-east-watch/america-quietly-expanding-its-war-tunisia-31492.
NSPA. "Jordan III." Capellen: NATO Support and Procurement Agency, 2021.
———. "Jordan IV." Capellen: NATO Support and Procurement Agency, 2021.
Nugent, Elizabeth, Tarek Masoud, and Amaney A. Jamal. "Arab Responses to Western Hegemony: Experimental Evidence from Egypt." *Journal of Conflict Resolution* 62, no. 2 (2016).
Oberdorfer, Don, Mary Russell, and Edward Walsh. "The Price of Peace: Treaty Seen Costing U.S. $5 Billion in Aid." *Washington Post*. March 15, 1979. www.washingtonpost.com/archive/politics/1979/03/15/the-price-of-peace-treaty-seen-costing-us-5-billion-in-aid/023be1b1-c3d5-45d8-92cf-265904e1c07d.
Office of the Director of National Intelligence. *Annual Threat Assessment of the U.S. Intelligence Community*. Washington, DC: Office of the Director of National Intelligence, 2021.
"Old News in Brief." European External Action Service. December 5, 2011. https://eeas.europa.eu/archives/csdp/missions-and-operations/eujust-lex-iraq/news/archives/index_en.htm.
Omelicheva, Mariya, Brittnee Carter, and Luke B. Campbell. "Military Aid and Human Rights: Assessing the Impact of U.S. Security Assistance Programs." *Political Science Quarterly* 132, no. 1 (March 2017): 119–144.
Onley, James. *The Arabian Frontier of the British Raj: Merchants, Rulers, and the British in the Nineteenth Century Gulf*. New York: Oxford University Press, 2008.
Ostovar, Afshon. "The Grand Strategy of Militant Clients: Iran's Way of War." *Security Studies* 28, no. 1 (2019): 159–188.
———. *Vanguard of the Imam: Religion, Politics, and Iran's Revolutionary Guards*. New York: Oxford University Press, 2016.
Ottaway, David. "Saudi Arabia's Yemeni Quagmire." Viewpoints #89. Wilson Center. December 2015. www.wilsoncenter.org/publication/saudi-arabias-yemeni-quagmire.

Overfield, Andrew. "The Draper Report: The Birth of the Foreign Assistance Act and Modern Security Assistance." Unpublished paper, 2019.
Oxford, Vayl. *Reviewing Department of Defense Strategy, Policy, and Programs for Countering Weapons of Mass Destruction (CWMD) for Fiscal Year 2019*. Emerging Threats and Capabilities Subcommittee on Armed Services United States House of Representatives. March 22, 2018. https://docs.house.gov/meetings/AS/AS26/20180322/108018/HHRG-115-AS26-Wstate-OxfordV-20180322.pdf.
Pallister-Wilkins, Polly. "Bridging the Divide: Middle Eastern Walls and Fences and the Spatial Governance of Problem Populations." *Geopolitics* 20 (2015): 438–459.
Patrick, Neil. "Saudi Arabia's Elusive Defense Reform." Carnegie Endowment for International Peace. May 31, 2018. https://carnegieendowment.org/sada/80354.
Paul, Christopher, Colin P. Clarke, Beth Grill, Jennifer D. Stephanie Young, P. Moroney, Joe Hogler, and Christine Leah. *What Works Best When Building Partner Capacity and Under What Circumstances?* MG-1253/1-OSD. Santa Monica, CA: RAND, 2013.
Peinaud, Franck. "La coopération bilatérale UE-Tunisie en matière sécuritaire." *Revue défense nationale* 821, no. 6 (June 1, 2019): 149–154.
Perez-Peña, Richard. "Britain to Sell Jets to Saudis Despite Conduct of Yemen War." *New York Times*. March 9, 2018. www.nytimes.com/2018/03/09/world/middleeast/uk-saudi-arms-jets-yemen.html.
"Phantom with Egypt." F4 Phantom II. Last modified April 1, 2000. www.f-4.nl/f4_42.html.
Plapinger, Samuel. "Insurgent Recruitment Practices and Combat Effectiveness in Civil War: The Black September Conflict in Jordan." *Security Studies* 31 (2022): 251–290.
Plaster, Graham, and Jason Criss Howk, eds. *Culture Shock: Leadership Lessons from the Military's Diplomatic Corps*. Mt Vernon, VA: Foreign Area Officer Association, 2022.
Pogodda, Sandra. "Revolutions and the Liberal Peace: Peacebuilding and Counterrevolutionary Practice?" *Cooperation and Conflict* 55, no. 3 (2020): 347–364.
Pollack, Kenneth M. *Armies of Sand: The Past, Present, and Future of Arab Military Effectiveness*. Oxford: Oxford University Press, 2019.
———. "The U.S. Has Wasted Billions of Dollars on Failed Arab Armies." *Foreign Policy*. January 31, 2019. https://foreignpolicy.com/2019/01/31/the-u-s-has-wasted-billions-of-dollars-on-failed-arab-armies.
Powel, Brieg Tomos. "The Stability Syndrome: US and EU Democracy Promotion in Tunisia." *Journal of North African Studies* 14, no. 1 (2009): 57–73.
Presidential Decree 2015-156. *National Gazette of the Republic of Tunisia*, No. 14 (April 2, 2015).
Presidential Decree 2021-69. *National Gazette of the Republic of Tunisia*, No. 64 (July 26, 2021): 2072.
Presidential Decree 2021-80. *National Gazette of the Republic of Tunisia*, No. 67 (July 29, 2021): 2092.
Presidential Decree 2021-117. *National Gazette of the Republic of Tunisia*, No. 86 (September 22, 2021): 2282–2284.
Presidential Decree 2022-11. *National Gazette of the Republic of Tunisia*, No. 16 (February 13, 2022): 450–455.
Presidential Decree 2022-22. *National Gazette of the Republic of Tunisia*, No. 45 (April 22, 2022): 1183–1185.
Presidential Decree 2022-30. *National Gazette of the Republic of Tunisia*, No. 56 (May 20, 2022): 1614–1615.
Presidential Decree 2022-309. *National Gazette of the Republic of Tunisia*, No. 35 (March 30, 2022): 897.
Presidential Decree 2022-506. *National Gazette of the Republic of Tunisia*, No. 59 (May 25, 2022): 1753.
Presidential Decree 2022-516. *National Gazette of the Republic of Tunisia*, No. 63 (June 1, 2022): 1842–1843.
Pritchett, Joanna. "Less Than a Full Deck: Russia's Economic Influence in the Mediterranean." Carnegie Endowment. July 2021. https://carnegieendowment.org/files/Pritchett%20RussiaMed_Econ_final.pdf.
Profazio, Umberto. "Tunisia's Reluctant Partnership with NATO." IISS. April 6, 2018. www.iiss.org/blogs/analysis/2018/04/tunisia-reluctant-partnership-nato.

Bibliography   367

"Programme de réformes pour une sortie de crise. Confidentiel [Reform program for a way out of the crisis. Confidential]." I WATCH. January 2022. www.iwatch.tn/ar/article/905.

"Projecting Stability Beyond Our Borders: Speech by NATO Secretary General at the Graduate Institute Geneva." NATO. Last updated March 3, 2017. www.nato.int/cps/en/natohq/opinions_141898.htm.

Public Affairs Section. "U.S. Support for Tunisian Border Security Project." US Embassy–Tunis. March 25, 2016. https://tn.usembassy.gov/u-s-support-for-tunisian-border-security-project.

"Public Law 96-35—July 20, 1979." US Code. https://uscode.house.gov/statutes/pl/96/35.pdf.

Puglierin, Jana. "Germany's Enable and Enhance Initiative: What Is It About?" Berlin: Bundesakademie für Sicherheitspolitik, 2016.

"Putin's New Model Army." *Economist*. November 7, 2020, 45–46.

"Quasi pronto il Nato-Tunisian Intelligence Fusion Centre." Analisi Difesa. April 14, 2017. www.analisidifesa.it/2017/04/quasi-pronto-il-nato-tunisian-intelligence-fusion-centre.

Quinlivan, James. "Coup-Proofing: Its Practice and Consequences in the Middle East." *International Security* 24 (1999): 131–165.

Rank, Joseph, and Bill Saba. "Building Partnership Capacity 101: The New Jordan Armed Forces Noncommissioned Officer Corps." *Military Review*. September–October 2014, 24–35.

Recchia, Stefano, and Thierry Tardy. "French Military Operations in Africa: Reluctant Multilateralism." *Journal of Strategic Studies* 43, no. 4 (June 6, 2020): 473–481.

Reflection Group. "NATO 2030: United for a New Era." NATO Defense College. December 9, 2020. www.ndc.nato.int/news/news.php?icode=1509#.

"Regional Security in the Middle East (ACRS)." NTI. 2003. www.nti.org/learn/treaties-and-regimes/arms-control-and-regional-security-middle-east-acrs.

"Regulation (EU) 2017/2306 of the European Parliament and of the Council of 12 December 2017 Amending Regulation (EU) No 230/2014 Establishing an Instrument Contributing to Stability and Peace." EUR-Lex.europa.eu. https://eur-lex.europa.eu/legal-content/EN/TXT/PDF/?uri=CELEX:32017R2306&qid=1518011229122&from=en.

"Remada: Anger Among Inhabitants After the Army Killed a Young Man in the Closed Military Zone." *Mosaique FM*. July 9, 2020. www.mosaiquefm.net/ar/أخبار-تونس-ت‍‍وقناقاحت-فيـ-صفـولا-يلاـه‍‍ا‍‍-يلع-خلـفـةم-تـلـباش-ـنـدع-دوحلا-دودلاـةيبيللا‍/766901.

Repubblica Italiana. "Libro bianco per la sicurezza internazionale e la difesa." Roma: Ministero della Difesa, 2015.

Reuters. "al-Ra'is al- Sisi wa Muhammad bin Zayid . . . 12 Ziyara Mutbalada Khilal Khamas Sanawat." *Akhbar al-Yom*. November 14, 2019.

———. "al-Sisi bi-Ziyara 'Askariyya Bahta li-l-Imarat." CNN. March 12, 2014. https://arabic.cnn.com/middleeast/2014/03/12/egypt-sisi-uae-visit.

———. "al-Sisi: al-Da'm al-Khaliji li-Misr 20 Milyar." *Al-Imarat 71*. November 30, 2014.

———. "Egypt and U.S. Agree on a Joint Tank Plan." *New York Times*. November 2, 1988. www.nytimes.com/1988/11/02/world/egypt-and-us-agree-on-a-joint-tank-plan.html.

———. "Egypt Receives First Gowind 2500 Corvette from France." *Egypt Today*. September 22, 2017. www.egypttoday.com/Article/1/24042/Egypt-receives-first-Gowind-2500-Corvette-from-France.

———. "Egypt, Saudi Arabia 'Desperate' to Purchase Mistral Warships." *France 24*. August 7, 2015. www.france24.com/en/20150807-france-mistral-warship-egypt-saudi-arabia-repurchase.

———. "Egypt, Saudi Arabia Issue 'Cairo Declaration' to Strengthen Cooperation." *Ahram Online*. July 30, 2015. https://english.ahram.org.eg/NewsContent/1/64/136591/Egypt/Politics-/Egypt,-Saudi-Arabia-issue-Cairo-Declaration-to-str.aspx.

———. "Egypt Takes Delivery of Second French Mistral Warship." *Reuters*. September 16, 2016. www.reuters.com/article/us-france-egypt-deals-idUSKCN11M153.

———. "Egypt's Sissi Negotiates Arms Deal in Russia." *Times of Israel*. February 13, 2014. www.timesofisrael.com/egypts-sisi-negotiates-arms-deal-in-russia.

———. "Export Briefs . . . Egypt, US Sign Pact." *Journal of Commerce*. November 4, 1988.

———. "KSA, UAE to Finance Russian Arms Deal with Egypt." *Egypt Independent*. February 7, 2014. https://egyptindependent.com/ksa-uae-finance-russian-arms-deal-egypt.

———. "Macron Says French Arms Sales to Egypt Will Not Be Conditional on Human Rights." *France 24*. July 12, 2020. www.france24.com/en/france/20201207-live-macron-and-egypt-s-sisi-hold-joint-press-conference-in-paris.

368 Bibliography

———. "Putin Backs Sisi 'Bid for Egypt Presidency,'" *BBC*. February 13, 2014. www.bbc.com/news/world-middle-east-26171142.

———. "10 U.S. Companies Profiting Most from U.S. Military Aid to Egypt." *Huffington Post*. August 22, 2013. www.huffpost.com/entry/10-us-companies-profiting_n_3780973.

———. "3.2 Billion Euros of Egypt-French Arms Deal Financed by Loan from Paris: Sisi." *Reuters*. March 1, 2015. www.reuters.com/article/us-egypt-france-loan-idUSKBN0LW0ZN20150228.

———. "Turkish Intelligence Helped Ship Arms to Syrian Islamist Rebel Areas." *Reuters*. May 21, 2015. www.reuters.com/article/us-mideast-crisis-turkey-arms-idUSKBN0O61L220150521.

Reuters Staff. "Eastern Libyan Forces Warplane Makes Emergency Landing in Tunisia, Pilot Held: LNA." *Reuters*. July 22, 2019. www.reuters.com/article/us-libya-security-tunisia/eastern-libyan-forces-warplane-makes-emergency-landing-in-tunisia-pilot-held-lna-idUSKCN1UH13I.

"Revised EU Approach to Security and Development Funding." European Parliament. November 20, 2019. www.europarl.europa.eu/legislative-train/theme-europe-as-a-stronger-global-actor/file-revised-eu-approach-to-security-and-development-funding.

Rich, Paul. *Creating the Arabian Gulf: The British Raj and the Invasions of the Gulf*. Washington DC: Lexington Books, 2009.

Richmond, Oliver P. "The Dilemmas of a Hybrid Peace: Negative or Positive?" *Cooperation and Conflict* 50, no. 1 (2015): 50–68.

Riedel, Bruce. "In Yemen, Iran Outsmarts Saudi Arabia Again." Brookings. December 6, 2017. www.brookings.edu/blog/markaz/2017/12/06/in-yemen-iran-outsmarts-saudi-arabia-again.

———. "It's Time to Stop US Arms Sales to Saudi Arabia." Brookings. February 4, 2021. www.brookings.edu/blog/order-from-chaos/2021/02/04/its-time-to-stop-us-arms-sales-to-saudi-arabia.

———. *Jordan and America: An Enduring Friendship*. Washington, DC: Brookings Institution Press, 2021.

———. *Kings and Presidents: Saudi Arabia and the United States Since FDR*. Washington, DC: Brookings, 2018.

Riedel, Bruce, and Michael E. O'Hanlon. "How to Demilitarize the US Presence in the Middle East." Brookings. November 6, 2020. www.brookings.edu/blog/order-from-chaos/2020/11/06/how-to-demilitarize-americas-presence-in-the-middle-east.

Rittinger, Eric. "Arming the Other: American Small Wars, Local Proxies, and the Social Construction of the Principal-Agent Problem." *International Studies Quarterly* 61, no. 2 (2017): 396–409.

Roberts, David B. "Bucking the Trend: The UAE and the Development of Military Capabilities in the Arab World." *Security Studies* 29, no. 2 (February 2020): 301–334.

———. *Qatar: Securing the Global Ambitions of a City-State*. London: Hurst & Co., 2017.

Robinson, Colin D. "Political and Military Obstacles to the North African Regional Capability." *Middle East Journal* 74, no. 3 (August 2020): 379–398.

Robinson, Glenn E. *Global Jihad: A Brief History*. Palo Alto, CA: Stanford University Press, 2021.

———. "Syria's Long Civil War." *Current History* 111, no. 749 (December 2012).

Roblin, Sebastien. "You Missed This: There Is a Strange Air War Raging over Libya." *National Interest*. April 20, 2019. https://nationalinterest.org/blog/buzz/you-missed-there-strange-air-war-raging-over-libya-53372.

Rolandsen, Oystein, Maggie Dwyer, and William Reno. "Security Force Assistance to Fragile States: A Framework of Analysis." *Journal of Intervention and Statebuilding* 15, no. 5 (2021): 563–579.

Ross, Michael L. *The Oil Curse: How Petroleum Wealth Shapes the Development of Nations*. Princeton, NJ: Princeton University Press, 2012.

Rowe, Edward Thomas. "Aid and Coups d'Etat: Aspects of the Impact of American Military Assistance Programs in the Less Developed Countries." *International Studies Quarterly* 18, no. 2 (June 1974): 239.

Rudolf, Inna. "The Popular Shadow over the US-Iraq Strategic Dialogue." ISPI. September 4, 2020. www.ispionline.it/en/pubblicazione/popular-shadow-over-us-iraq-strategic-dialogue-27275.

Ryan, Curtis. "The Armed Forces and the Arab Uprisings: The Case of Jordan." *Middle East Law and Governance* 4 (2012): 153–167.
———. "What Jordan Means for NATO (and Vice Versa)." Milan: Istituto per gli studi di politica internazionale, 2018.
Saab, Bilal. "What Does America Get for Its Military Aid?" *National Interest*. February 22, 2018. https://nationalinterest.org/feature/what-does-america-get-its-military-aid-24605.
Saini Fasanotti, Frederica. "The Biden Administration Inherits a Rapidly Deteriorating Libya." Brookings. January 19, 2021. www.brookings.edu/blog/order-from-chaos/2021/01/19/the-biden-administration-inherits-a-rapidly-deteriorating-libya.
Salah, Eshan. "Shoukry's DC Charm Offensive." MADA. April 14, 2022. www.madamasr.com/en/2022/04/14/feature/politics/shoukrys-dc-charm-offensive-complicated-by-human-rights-concerns.
Salame, Ghassan. Address to the Mediterranean Dialogue Conference of the Italian Institute for International Studies, Rome, December 6, 2019.
Salehyan, Idean. "The Delegation of War to Rebel Organizations." *Journal of Conflict Resolution* 54, no. 3 (2010): 493–515.
Sales, Nathan. "Tehran's International Targets: Assessing Iranian Terror Sponsorship." Washington Institute for Near East Policy. November 13, 2018. www.washingtoninstitute.org/policy-analysis/tehrans-international-targets-assessing-iranian-terror-sponsorship.
Samaan, Jean-Loup. "The Limitations of a NATO–Middle East Military Cooperation." Carnegie Endowment. May 7, 2020. https://carnegieendowment.org/sada/81740.
———. "The Rise of the Emirati Defense Industry." Carnegie Endowment. May 14, 2019. https://carnegieendowment.org/sada/79121?utm_source=rss&utm_medium=rss.
Samti, Farah, and Decan Walsh. "Tunisian Clash Spreads Fear That Libyan War Is Spilling Over." *New York Times*. March 7, 2016. www.nytimes.com/2016/03/08/world/africa/attack-tunisia-libya-border.html.
Santini, Ruth Hanau, and Giulia Cimini. "The Politics of Security Reform in Post-2011 Tunisia: Assessing the Role of Exogenous Shocks, Domestic Policy Entrepreneurs and External Actors." *Middle Eastern Studies* 55, no. 2 (March 4, 2019): 225–241.
Sassen, Saskia. *Territory, Authority, Rights*. Princeton, NJ: Princeton University Press, 2008.
"Saudi Arabia to Acquire Australian Military Equipment." *Al Defaiya*. March 30, 2017.
Savage, Jesse Dillon. "Foreign Military Training and Coups d'État." In *Oxford Research Encyclopedia of Politics*. Oxford: Oxford University Press, 2021.
Savage, Jesse Dillon, and Jonathan D Caverley. "When Human Capital Threatens the Capitol: Foreign Aid in the Form of Military Training and Coups." *Journal of Peace Research* 54, no. 4 (July 2017): 542–557.
Savell, Stephanie, with Rachel McMahon, Emily Rockwell, and Yueshan Li. "United States Counterterrorism Operations: 2018–2020." *Cost of War*. Watson Institute for International and Public Affairs-Brown University. February 2021. https://watson.brown.edu/costsofwar/files/cow/imce/papers/2021/US%20Counterterrorism%20Operations%202018-2020,%20Costs%20of%20War.pdf.
Sayigh, Yezid. *Arab Military Industry: Capability, Performance and Impact*. London: Brassey's, 1992.
———. "Egypt's Military as the Spearhead of State Capitalism." Carnegie Middle East Center. October 26, 2020. https://carnegie-mec.org/2020/10/26/egypt-s-military-as-spearhead-of-state-capitalism-pub-83010.
———. *Owners of the Republic: An Anatomy of Egypt's Military Economy*. Washington, DC: Carnegie Endowment for International Peace, 2019.
———. "Syrian Politics Trump Russian Military Reforms." Carnegie Middle East Center. March 26, 2020. https://carnegie-mec.org/2020/03/26/syrian-politics-trump-russian-military-reforms-pub-81149.
Sayigh, Yezid, with Nathan Toronto. "Politics of Military Authoritarianism in North Africa." Carnegie Middle East Center. March 17, 2021. https://carnegie-mec.org/2021/03/17/politics-of-military-authoritarianism-in-north-africa-pub-84072.
Schenker, David. "The Growing Islamic State Threat in Jordan." PolicyWatch 2747. Washington Institute for Near East Policy. January 10, 2017. www.washingtoninstitute.org/policy-analysis/growing-islamic-state-threat-jordan.

Schubert, Frank N., and Theresa L. Kraus, eds. *The Whirlwind War: The United States Army in Operations DESERT SHIELD and DESERT STORM.* Washington, DC: Center of Military History, 1995.
Schuetze, Benjamin. "Simulating, Marketing, and Playing War: US-Jordanian Military Collaboration and the Politics of Commercial Security." *Security Dialogue* 48 (2017): 431–450.
Schwarz, Rolf. *NATO and the Middle East: In Search of a Strategy.* Boulder, CO: Lynne Rienner, 2020.
"Security Assistance Database." Center for International Policy, Security Assistance Monitor. https://securityassistance.org/security-sector-assistance.
Security Cooperation. Joint Publication 3-20. Washington, DC: Joint Chiefs of Staff, May 23, 2017.
Seeberg, Peter, "Mobility Partnerships and Security Subcomplexes in the Mediterranean: The Strategic Role of Migration and the European Union's Foreign and Security Policies Towards the MENA Region." *European Foreign Affairs Review* 22, no. 1 (January 1, 2017): 91–100.
———. "Neo-Ottoman Expansionism Beyond the Borders of Modern Turkey: Erdoğan's Foreign Policy Ambitions in Syria and the Mediterranean." *De Europa* 4, no. 1 (2021): 107–123.
Seliktar, Ofira, and Farhad Rezaei. "Conclusion: The Success of the Proxy Strategy and Its Limits." In *Iran, Revolution, and Proxy Wars*, edited by Seliktar Ofira and Farhad Rezaei. Cham, Switzerland: Palgrave Macmillan, 2020.
Shah, Hijab, and Melissa, Dalton. "The Evolution of Tunisia's Military and the Role of Foreign Security Sector Assistance. Carnegie Middle East Center." Carnegie Middle East Center. April 29, 2020. https://carnegie-mec.org/2020/04/29/evolution-of-tunisia-s-military-and-role-of-foreign-security-sector-assistance-pub-81602.
Shair, Kamal. *Out of the Middle East: The Emergence of an Arab Global Business.* London: I. B. Tauris, 2006.
Shanif, Mona. "Strategic Maneuvering: The Gulf States amid US-China Tensions." Middle East Institute. January 20, 2022. www.mei.edu/publications/strategic-maneuvering-gulf-states-amid-us-china-tensions.
"Share of Wheat Imported to Egypt in 2020, by Country of Origin." Statista. www.statista.com/statistics/1309988/share-of-wheat-imports-by-country-to-egypt (accessed June 10, 2022).
Singh Grewal, Sandeep. "Bahraini Jets Join Syria Strikes." *Gulf Daily News* (Bahrain). December 1, 2014.
Smith, Crispin, Hamdi Malik, and Michael Knights. "Team of Legal Gladiators? Iraqi Militias' Tortured Relationship with the Law." Washington Institute for Near East Policy. April 12, 2021. www.washingtoninstitute.org/policy-analysis/team-legal-gladiators-iraqi-militias-tortured-relationship-law.
Smith, Martin A., and Ian Davis. "NATO's Mediterranean Dialogue in the Wake of the Arab Spring: Partnership for Peace or Succour for Despots?" NATO Watch Briefing Paper 19. June 27, 2011.
"Smuggling Weapons from Iran into the Gaza Strip." Shabak. www.shabak.gov.il/english/publications/Pages/SmugglingWeapons.aspx (accessed June 10, 2022).
Soare, Simona R., and Fabrice Pothier. *Leading Edge: Defence Innovation and the Future of Operational Advantage.* London: International Institute for Strategic Studies. November 2021.
Soliman, Samer. *The Autumn of Dictatorship: Fiscal Crisis and Political Change in Egypt Under Mubarak.* Stanford, CA: Stanford University Press, 2011.
"Sovereign Wealth, Sovereign Whims." *Economist.* June 15, 2019, 40.
Special Inspector General for Afghanistan Reconstruction (SIGAR). "Divided Responsibility: Lessons from U.S. Security Sector Assistance Efforts in Afghanistan." SIGAR. July 2019. www.sigar.mil/interactive-reports/divided-responsibility/index.html.
———. "Learning in Iraq: Final Report." March 2013.
———. "Quarterly Report to Congress." Washington, DC: Special Inspector General for Afghanistan Reconstruction, 2021.
Springborg, Robert. *Political Economies in the Middle East and North Africa.* Cambridge, UK: Polity Press, 2021.

Springborg, Robert, and F. C. Williams. "The Egyptian Military: A Slumbering Giant Awakes." Carnegie Middle East Center. February 28, 2019. https://carnegie-mec.org/2019/02/28/egyptian-military-slumbering-giant-awakes-pub-78238.
Springborg, Robert, F. C. "Pink" Williams, and John Zavage. "Security Assistance in the Middle East: A Three-Dimensional Chessboard." Carnegie Middle East Center. February 6, 2020. https://carnegie-mec.org/2020/02/06/security-assistance-in-middle-east-three-dimensional-chessboard-pub-80993.
Stahl, Anna, and Jana Trefflet. "Germany's Security Assistance to Tunisia: A Boost to Tunisia's Long-Term Stability and Democracy?" European Institute of the Mediterranean. November 7, 2019. www.iemed.org/publication/germanys-security-assistance-to-tunisia-a-boost-to-tunisias-long-term-stability-and-democracy.
Stalacanin, Stasa. "The Middle East's Game of Drones." *The New Arab*. July 4, 2022. https://english.alaraby.co.uk/analysis/middle-easts-game-drones.
Stark, Alexandra. "Give Up on Proxy Wars in the Middle East." *Foreign Policy*. August 7, 2020. https://foreignpolicy.com/2020/08/07/united-states-give-up-on-proxy-wars-middle-east.
Stewart, Phil, and Arshad Mohammed. "U.S. to Deliver Apache Helicopters to Egypt, Relaxing Hold on Aid." *Reuters*. April 23, 2014. www.reuters.com/article/us-usa-egypt-apaches-idINBREA3M03L20140423.
Stockholm International Peace Research Institute (SIPRI). The SIPRI Military Expenditure Database (1988–2005). www.sipri.org/databases/milex (accessed January 5, 2017).
———. *SIPRI Yearbook 2019*. Oxford: Oxford University Press, 2020.
———. "UN Arms Embargo on Iran." https://www.sipri.org/databases/embargoes/un_arms_embargoes/iran
Stoddard, Philip H. "Egypt and the Iran-Iraq War." In *Gulf Security and the Iran-Iraq War*, edited by Thomas Naff, Washington, DC: National Defense University Press, 1985.
Stoltenberg, Jens. "The Secretary General's Annual Report 2020." NATO. 2020. www.nato.int/nato_static_fl2014/assets/pdf/2021/3/pdf/sgar20-en.pdf.
Stork, Joe, and James Paul. "Arms Sales and Militarizing the Middle East." *MERIP* 3 (January/February 1983).
Stork, Joe, and Danny Reachard. "Chronology: US-Egypt Military Relationship." *MERIP Reports*, no. 90 (1980): 29–31.
Supplemental 1979 Middle East Aid Package for Israel and Egypt Hearings, Ninety-Sixth Congress, First Session April 26; May 1, 2, 8, and 9, 1979, 96th Con. 1-17, 35-36 (1979).
Szoldra, Paul. "Exclusive: 2 Marines Received Valor Awards for Secret Gunfight Against Al Qaeda in North Africa." *Task & Purpose*. August 15, 2018. https://taskandpurpose.com/code-red-news/marine-raiders-firefight-north-africa.
Ta'lab, Ibtisam. "Dr. Sayyid Mash'al Wazir al-Intaj al-Harbi li-l-Masry al-Yuom (2-2)." *al-Masry al-Youm*. September 15, 2010.
Tabatabai, Ariane M. *No Conquest, No Defeat: Iran's National Security Strategy*. Oxford: Oxford University Press, 2020.
Tabatabai, Ariane M., and Annie Tracy Samuel. "What the Iran-Iraq War Tells Us About the Future of the Iran Nuclear Deal." *International Security* 42, no. 1 (2017): 293.
Tal, Lawrence. *Politics, the Military, and National Security in Jordan, 1955–1967*. New York: Palgrave Macmillan, 2002.
Tankel, Stephen, and Melissa G. Dalton. "How to Improve Return on Investment for Security Assistance." *Lawfare*. August 27, 2017. www.lawfareblog.com/how-improve-return-investment-security-assistance.
Tankel, Stephen, and Tommy Ross. "Retooling U.S. Security Sector Assistance." *War on the Rocks*. October 28, 2020. https://warontherocks.com/2020/10/reforming-u-s-security-sector-assistance-for-great-power-competition.
Tastekin, Fehim. "Turkish Mobster's Revelations Extend to Arms Shipments to Syria." *Al-Monitor*. June 2, 2021. www.al-monitor.com/originals/2021/06/turkish-mobsters-revelations-extend-arms-shipments-syria#ixzz7Dzc2gvuH.
"Tataouine: Grève générale à Remada suite au décès d'un contrebandier." *African Manager*. July 25, 2016. https://africanmanager.com/11_tataouine-greve-generale-a-remada-suite-au-deces-dun-contrebandier.
Taylor, Paul. "Molto agitato: L'Italia e la sicurezza mediterranea." Brussels: Friends of Europe, 2019.

Tecott, Rachel. "Why America Can't Build Allied Armies: Afghanistan Is Just the Latest Failure." *Foreign Affairs*. August 26, 2021. www.foreignaffairs.com/articles/united-states/2021-08-26/why-america-cant-build-allied-armies.

Telci, Ismail Numan, and Tuba Ozturk Horoz. "Military Bases in the Foreign Policy of the United Arab Emirates." *Insight Turkey* 20, no. 2 (spring 2018).

Tell, Nawaf. "Jordanian Security Sector Governance: Between Theory and Practice." Paper presented at the Workshop on Challenges of Security Sector Governance in the Middle East, Geneva Centre for the Democratic Control of Armed Forces, Geneva, Switzerland, July 12–13, 2004.

Tell, Tariq. "Early Spring in Jordan: The Revolt of the Military Veterans." Civil-Military Relations in Arab States Working Paper. Carnegie Middle East Center. November 4, 2015. https://carnegieendowment.org/files/ACMR_Tell_Jordan_Eng_final.pdf.

———. *The Social and Economic Origins of Monarchy in Jordan*. New York: Palgrave Macmillan, 2013.

Tessler, Mark, and Ebru Altinoglu. "Political Culture in Turkey: Connections Among Attitudes Toward Democracy, the Military and Islam." *Democratization* 11, no. 1 (2004): 21–50.

Tessler, Mark, and Ina I. Warriner. "Gender, Feminism, and Attitudes Toward International Conflict: Exploring Relationships with Survey Data from the Middle East." *World Politics* 49, no. 2 (1977): 250–281.

Thaler, David E., Michael J. McNerney, Beth Grill, Jefferson P. Marquis, and Amanda Kadlec. "From Patchwork to Framework: A Review of Title 10 Authorities for Security Cooperation." Santa Monica, CA: RAND Corporation, 2016.

Tiezzi, Shannon. "What's in the China-Iran Strategic Cooperation Agreement?" *The Diplomat*. March 30, 2021. https://thediplomat.com/2021/03/whats-in-the-china-iran-strategic-cooperation-agreement.

Trad, Ruslan. "In Its Battle for Influence, Russia's Soft Power Strategy Seeks to Reshape Syria's Future." *New Arab*. April 15, 2021. https://english.alaraby.co.uk/analysis/how-russias-soft-power-strategy-seeks-reshape-syria.

"Trends in World Military Expenditure, 2020." SIPRI. April 2021. www.sipri.org/sites/default/files/2021-04/fs_2104_milex_0.pdf.

Tsypkin, Mikhail. "Lessons Not to Learn: Post-Communist Russia." In *The Routledge Handbook of Civil-Military Relations*, edited by Thomas C. Bruneau and Florina Cristiana Matei, 110–122. London: Routledge, 2013.

"Tunisia: Examining the State of Democracy and Next Steps for U.S. Policy." Video posted to YouTube by House Foreign Affairs Committee on October 14, 2021. www.youtube.com/watch?v=VS2iiN4t6qc.

Tunisian Air Force. *New Approach to Counterterrorism*. Unpublished document.

Tunisian Forum for Economic and Social Rights (FTDES). "Dhehiba's Incidents: Report of the Independent Commission to Investigate Events in Dhehiba." FTDES. February 2015. http://ftdes.net/rapports/dehiba.pdf.

———. "Report of July 2021: Collective Protests, Suicide and Attempts of Suicide, and Migration." FTDES. July 2021. https://ftdes.net/en/ost-rapport-juillet-2021-des-mouvements-sociaux-suicides-violences-et-migrations.

Tunisian Ministry of Defense. *2030 Vision*. Unpublished document.

"Turkey Wades into Libya's Troubled Waters." International Crisis Group. April 30, 2020. www.crisisgroup.org/europe-central-asia/western-europemediterranean/turkey/257-turkey-wades-libyas-troubled-waters.

Turse, Nick, and Sean D. Naylor. "Revealed: The U.S. Military's 36 Code-Named Operations in Africa." *Yahoo! News*. April 17, 2019. www.yahoo.com/entertainment/revealed-the-us-militarys-36-codenamed-operations-in-africa-090000841.html.

"2 mai 1973: Convention de coopération technique militaire." France-États Arabes. http://fothman.free.fr/Accbitxt/Pol/tn_pol/tnpol020573mil/tnpol020573mil.html.

"U.S. and Egypt Hold 31st Military Cooperation Committee Meeting." US Embassy in Egypt. Last modified March 28, 2019. https://eg.usembassy.gov/u-s-and-egypt-hold-31st-military-cooperation-committee-meeting.

"U.S. Missiles Found in Libyan Rebel Camp Were First Sold to France." *New York Times*. July 9, 2019. www.nytimes.com/2019/07/09/world/middleeast/us-missiles-libya-france.html.

"Ukraine Asks Egypt for Weapons, Humanitarian and Medical Aid." *Middle East Monitor.* March 9, 2022. www.middleeastmonitor.com/20220309-ukraine-asks-egypt-for-weapons-humanitarian-and-medical-aid.

"United Nations Support Mission in Libya (UNSMIL) Welcomes Agreement Between Libyan Parties on Permanent Country-Wide Ceasefire Agreement." UNSMIL. October 23, 2020. https://unsmil.unmissions.org/unsmil-welcomes-agreement-between-libyan-parties-permanent-country-wide-ceasefire-agreement.

"UNSMIL/UNDP Policing and Security Joint Programme: UNDP in Libya." UNDP. 2020. www.ly.undp.org/content/libya/en/home/projects/UNSMIL-UNDP-Policing-and-Security-Joint-Programme.html.

US Agency for International Development (USAID). *Jordan: Country Development Cooperation Strategy.* Washington, DC: USAID, 2015.

US Agency for International Development, US Department of Defense, and US Department of State. *Security Sector Reform.* US Agency for International Development. February 2009. www.usaid.gov/sites/default/files/documents/1866/State-USAID-Defense%20Policy%20Statement%20on%20Security%20Sector%20Reform.pdf.

US Defense Security Cooperation University. *Security Cooperation Programs Handbook.* https://www.dscu.edu/documents/publications/security-cooperation-programs-handbook.pdf.

US Department of Defense (DOD). "Assessment, Monitoring and Evaluation for the Security Cooperation Enterprise." Instruction 5132.14. DOD. January 13, 2017.

———. "Assessment, Planning & Design, Monitoring, & Evaluation Overview for Security Cooperation." (2019): 7.

———. "DoD Concludes 2021 Global Posture Review." DOD. November 29, 2021. www.defense.gov/News/Releases/Release/Article/2855801/dod-concludes-2021-global-posture-review.

———. "Principles for Security Cooperation (SC) Assessment." (2019): 4–5.

———. "Readout of Secretary of Defense Dr. Mark T. Esper's Meeting with Tunisian Minister of Defense Ibrahim Bartagi." DOD. September 30, 2020. www.defense.gov/Newsroom/Releases/Release/Article/2367327/readout-of-secretary-of-defense-dr-mark-t-espers-meeting-with-tunisian-minister.

US Department of Defense and US Department of State. *Foreign Military Training Program FY 2018 and 2019.* Joint Report to Congress. US State Department. www.state.gov/wp-content/uploads/2019/12/FMT_Volume-I_FY2018_2019.pdf.

US Department of State. "Background Briefing: Updating on Secretary Tillerson's Trip to Amman, Jordan; Ankara, Turkey; Beirut, Lebanon; Cairo, Egypt; and Kuwait City, Kuwait." US Department of State. February 14, 2018. https://2017-2021.state.gov/background-briefing-updating-on-secretary-tillersons-trip-to-amman-jordan-ankara-turkey-beirut-lebanon-cairo-egypt-and-kuwait-city-kuwait/index.html.

———. "Daily Press Briefing by Spokesperson John Kirby." US Department of State. March 8, 2016.

———. "Fact Sheet: U.S. Security Cooperation with Jordan." US Department of State. May 21, 2021. www.state.gov/u-s-security-cooperation-with-jordan.

———. "Program and Project Design, Monitoring, and Evaluation Policy." US Department of State. November 2017.

———. "Remarks at the Opening Plenary of the Egypt Economic Development Conference. John Kerry, Secretary of State, Sharm el-Sheikh, Egypt, 13 March 2015." US Department of State. www.state.gov/secretary/remarks/2015/03/238872.htm (accessed October 10, 2015).

———. "World Military Expenditures and Arms Transfers, 1972–1996." US Department of State. www.state.gov/t/avc/rls/rpt/wmeat (accessed January 5, 2017).

US Department of State, Bureau of Democracy, Human Rights, and Labor. "Security and Human Rights." US State Department. www.state.gov/key-topics-bureau-of-democracy-human-rights-and-labor/human-rights (accessed March 1, 2021).

US Embassy–Amman. "Assessment of US Security Assistance Programs." Cable: 1977AMMAN03716_c. Wikileaks. July 5, 1977. https://wikileaks.org/plusd/cables/1977AMMAN03716_c.html.

——. "Re: Transparency of Budgets/Military Spending." Cable: 04AMMAN9370. Wikileaks. November 24, 2004. https://wikileaks.org/plusd/cables/04AMMAN9370_a.html.
US General Accounting Office (GAO). "Operation Desert Storm/Shield Costs and Funding Requirements." Report to the Chairman, Committee on Armed Services, House of Representatives, GAO/NSIAD 91-304. GAO. September 1991. www.gao.gov/assets/220/215041.pdf.
——. "Security Assistance: State and DOD Need to Assess How the Foreign Military Financing Program for Egypt Achieves U.S. Foreign Policy and Security Goals." Report to the Committee on International Relations, House of Representatives, GAO-06-437. GAO. April 11, 2006. www.govinfo.gov/content/pkg/GAOREPORTS-GAO-06-437/html/GAOREPORTS-GAO-06-437.htm.
——. "Security Assistance: U.S. Government Should Strengthen End-Use Monitoring and Human Rights Vetting for Egypt." GAO Report to Congressional Requestors, GAO 16-435. GAO. April 2016. www.gao.gov/assets/680/676503.pdf.
US House of Representatives, Committee on Foreign Affairs. *Tunisia's Struggle for Stability, Security, and Democracy: Hearing Before the Subcommittee on the Middle East and North Africa of the Committee on Foreign Affairs, House of Representatives, One Hundred Fourteenth Congress, Second Session, May 25, 2016*. Serial No. 114-193. Washington, DC: US Government Printing Office, 2016.
US House of Representatives, Office of the Law Revision Counsel. "10 USC 127e: Support of Special Operations to Combat Terrorism." United States Code. https://uscode.house.gov/view.xhtml?req=granuleid:USC-prelim-title10-section127e&num=0&edition=prelim.
US Senate, Committee on Appropriations, Subcommittee on State, Foreign Operations, and Related Programs. *State, Foreign Operations and Related Programs Appropriations for Fiscal Year 2018*. GovInfo. June 13, 2017. www.govinfo.gov/content/pkg/CHRG-115shrg79104760/html/CHRG-115shrg79104760.htm.
US Senate, Subcommittee of the Committee on Appropriations. "State, Foreign Operations, and Related Programs Appropriations Fiscal Year 2018." Senate Hearing 115. GovInfo. June 13, 2017. www.govinfo.gov/content/pkg/CHRG-115shrg79104760/html/CHRG-115shrg79104760.htm.
"US Warnings Ineffective on Egypt's Su-35 Plans as Pilots Train in Russia." *Africa Intelligence*. June 8, 2022. www.africaintelligence.com/north-africa_diplomacy/2022/06/08/us-warnings-ineffective-on-egypt-s-su-35-plans-as-pilots-train-in-russia,109790434-eve (accessed June 10, 2022).
Vakil, Sanam, and Neil Quilliam. "Steps to Enable a Middle East Regional Security Process." Chatham House. April 2021. www.chathamhouse.org/2021/04/steps-enable-middle-east-regional-security-process.
Valine, Debra. "Tunisia Accepts Delivery of Last of Eight Black Hawks." Defense Visual Information Distribution Service. November 21, 2018. www.dvidshub.net/news/300860/tunisia-accepts-delivery-last-eight-black-hawks.
Varga, Gergely. "Building Partnerships in Challenging Times: The Defence Arrangements of Tunisia." EuroMeSCo. May 2017. www.euromesco.net/publication/building-partnerships-in-challenging-times-the-defence-arrangements-of-tunisia.
Vatikiotis, P. J. *Politics and the Military in Jordan: A Study of the Arab Legion*. London: Frank Cass, 1967.
Vertin, Zach. *Red Sea Rivalries: The Gulf, the Horn and the New Geopolitics of the Red Sea*. Doha: Brookings Doha Center, 2019.
Vest, Nathan. "Can Anything Stop the Flow of Advanced Weapons into Libya?" *Defense One*. December 13, 2019. www.defenseone.com/ideas/2019/12/can-anything-stop-flow-advanced-weapons-libya/161892.
Vidal, Alain. "Le partenariat militaire opérationnel aujourd'hui." *Brennus 4.0: Lettre d'information du centre de doctrine et d'enseignement du commandement*. April 2019. www.penseemiliterre.fr/ressources/30114/50/le-pmo_col-vidal.pdf.
"Video-Les militaires mobilisés à Tataouine face à l'assaut des sit-inneurs d'El Kamour." *Business News*. February 11, 2021. www.businessnews.com.tn/Vid%EF%BF%BDo—-Les-militaires-mobilis%EF%BF%BDs-%EF%BF%BD-Tataouine-face-%EF%BF%BD-l%EF%BF%BDassaut-des-sit-inneurs-d%EF%BF%BDEl-Kamour-,520,105884,3.
Vittori, Jodi. "Mitigating Patronage and Personal Enrichment in U.S. Arms Sales." In *From Hardware to Holism: Rebalancing America's Security Engagement with Arab States*,

Bibliography 375

edited by Frederic Wehrey and Michelle Dunne. Carnegie Endowment for International Peace. May 18, 2021. https://carnegieendowment.org/2021/05/18/mitigating-patronage-and-personal-enrichment-in-u.s.-arms-sales-pub-84526.
"Vittoria consegna alla Tunisia la nave scuola Zarzis." Analisi Difesa. August 6, 2016. www.analisidifesa.it/2016/08/vittoria-consegna-alla-tunisia-la-nave-scuola-zarzis.
Volpi, Frédéric. "Algeria: When Elections Hurt Democracy." *Journal of Democracy* 31, no. 2 (2020): 152–165.
Waltz, Kenneth. "Theory of International Relations." In *Handbook of Political Science: International Relations*, edited by Fred Greenstein and Nelson Polsby, 8:1–86. Boston: Addison-Wesley, 1975.
———. *Man, the State, and War*. New York: Columbia University Press, 1957.
Ward, Jon. "Government Watchdog: America's Failure in Afghanistan Driven by Hubris and Short-Term Thinking." *Yahoo! News*. August 17, 2021. https://news.yahoo.com/government-watchdog-americas-failure-in-afghanistan-driven-by-hubris-and-short-term-thinking-202100324.html.
"Washington Consolidates Tunisia-Libya Electronic Border Surveillance Wall." *Africa Intelligence*. January 2, 2021. www.africaintelligence.com/north-africa/2021/02/12/washington-consolidates-tunisia-libya-electronic-border-surveillance-wall,109642877-art.
Watling, Jack, and Nick Reynolds. *War by Others' Means: Delivering Effective Partner Force Capacity Building*. London: Routledge, 2020.
Wechsler, William F. "No, the US Shouldn't Withdraw from the Middle East." Atlantic Council. June 24, 2021. www.atlanticcouncil.org/in-depth-research-reports/issue-brief/no-the-us-shouldnt-withdraw-from-the-middle-east.
Wehrey, Frederic. "Tunisia's Wake-Up Call: How Security Challenges from Libya Are Shaping Defense Reforms." Carnegie Middle East Center. March 2020. https://carnegieendowment.org/2020/03/18/audia-s-wake-up-call-how-security-challenges-from-libya-are-shaping-defense-reforms-pub-81312?
Wehrey, Frederic, and Michele Dunne. "From Hardware to Holism: Rebalancing America's Security Engagement with Arab States." Carnegie Middle East Center. May 18, 2021. https://audia-mec.org/2020/04/29/evolution-of-tunisia-s-military-and-role-of-foreign-security-sector-assistance-pub-81602.
Wezeman, Pieter D. "Saudi Arabia, Armaments and Conflict in the Middle East." *SIPRI*. December 14, 2018. www.sipri.org/commentary/topical-backgrounder/2018/saudi-arabia-armaments-and-conflict-middle-east.
Wezeman, Pieter D., Aude Fleurant, Alexandra Kuimova, Nan Tian, and Siemon T. Wezeman. *Trends in International Arms Transfers, 2017*. Stockholm: SIPRI, 2017.
Wezeman, Pieter D., Alexandra Kuimova, and Siemon T. Wezeman. *Trends in International Arms Transfers, 2020*. Stockholm: SIPRI, 2020.
———. *Trends in International Arms Transfers, 2021*. Stockholm: SIPRI, 2021.
Wezeman, Pieter D., Siemon T. Wezeman, Dr Nan Tian and Dr Aude Fleurant. *Trends in International Arms Transfers, 2016*. Stockholm: SIPRI, 2016.
White House. "Interim National Security Strategic Guidance." White House. March 2021. www.whitehouse.gov/wp-content/uploads/2021/03/NSC-1v2.pdf.
———. "National Security Strategy of the United States of America." White House. December 2017. https://permanent.fdlp.gov/lps90878/2017/NSSFinal121820170905.pdf.
———. "White House Fact Sheet on the Middle East Arms Control Initiative." American Presidency Project. May 29, 1991. www.presidency.ucsb.edu/documents/white-house-fact-sheet-the-middle-east-arms-control-initiative.
White House, Office of the Press Secretary. "Fact Sheet: Security Sector Assistance Policy." White House: President Barack Obama. April 5, 2013. https://obamawhitehouse.archives.gov/the-press-office/2013/04/05/fact-sheet-us-security-sector-assistance-policy.
"Why It Matters." Government Defence Anti-Corruption Index. https://government.defenceindex.org/why-it-matters.
"Why It Matters." Government Defense Anti-Corruption Index for 2015. Transparency International. https://government.defenceindex.org/why-it-matters.
Wike, Richard, and Janell Fetterolf. "Global Public Opinion in an Era of Democratic Anxiety." Pew Research Center. December 7, 2021. www.pewresearch.org/global/2021/12/07/global-public-opinion-in-an-era-of-democratic-anxiety.

Williams, Katie Bo. "In Syria, US Commanders Hold the Line—and Wait for Biden." *Defense One.* March 21, 2021. www.defenseone.com/threats/2021/03/syria-us-commanders-hold-line-and-wait-biden/172808.
Winnefeld, James A., Michael J. Morell, and Graham Allison. "Why American Strategy Fails: Ending the Chronic Imbalance Between Ends and Means." *Foreign Affairs.* October 28, 2020. www.foreignaffairs.com/articles/united-states/2020-10-28/why-american-strategy-fails.
Winrow, Gareth M. *Dialogue with the Mediterranean: The Role of NATO's Mediterranean Initiative.* New York: Garland, 2000.
"WMD Free Middle East Proposal at a Glance." Arms Control Association. December 2018. https.//www.armscontrol.org/factsheets/mewmdfz.
Wohlforth, William C., Benjamin De Carvalho, Halvard Leira, and Iver B. Neumann. "Moral Authority and Status in International Relations: Good States and the Social Dimension of Status Seeking." *Review of International Studies* 44, no. 3 (2018): 526–546.
Wood, David, and Jacob Boswell. "'We Do the Police's Job': Protecting Lebanon's Most Lawless Towns." *Al Jazeera.* December 19, 2021. www.aljazeera.com/features/2021/12/19/we-do-the-polices-job-protecting-lebanons-most-lawless-towns.
Wright, Robin. "Beyond ISIS Turmoil, Jordan Is Flush with Problems." *Wall Street Journal.* February 4, 2015. www.wilsoncenter.org/article/beyond-isis-turmoil-jordan-flush-problems.
Wunderle, LTC William, and LTC Andre Biere. "U.S. Foreign Policy and Israel's Qualitative Military Edge: The Need for a Common Vision." *Policy Focus* 80 (January 24, 2008).
Yates, Athol. *The Evolution of the Armed Forces of the United Arab Emirates.* Warwick, UK: Helion & Co., 2020.
Yiftachel, Oren. *Ethnocracy: Land and Identity Politics in Israel/Palestine.* Philadelphia: University of Pennsylvania Press, 2006.
Yildiz, Gunuy. "Turkish-Russian Adversarial Collaboration in Syria, Libya, and Nagorno-Karabakh." German Institute for International and Security Affairs. March 24, 2021. www.swp-berlin.org/en/publication/turkish-russian-adversarial-collaboration-in-syria-libya-and-nagorno-karabakh.
Yoke, Sara. "Eager Lion Exercise a 'Keystone Event' in US-Jordan Partnership, Integration." US Central Command News Release. May 11, 2017. www.centcom.mil/MEDIA/NEWS-ARTICLES/News-Article-View/Article/1179543/eager-lion-exercise-a-keystone-event-in-us-jordan-partnership-integration.
Yom, Sean. "Bread, Fear, and Coalitional Politics in Jordan: From Tribal Origins to Neoliberal Narrowing." In *Economic Shocks and Authoritarian Stability: Duration, Financial Control, and Institutions,* ed. Victor Shih, 210–235. Ann Arbor: University of Michigan Press, 2020.
———. *From Resilience to Revolution: How Foreign Interventions Destabilize the Middle East.* New York: Columbia University Press, 2016.
———. "Tribal Politics in Contemporary Jordan: The Case of the Hirak Movement." *Middle East Journal* 68, no. 2 (2014): 229–247.
———. "US Foreign Policy in the Middle East: The Logic of Hegemonic Retreat." *Global Policy* 11, no. 1 (February 2020): 75–83.
Yom, Sean, and Katrina Sammour. "Counterterrorism and Youth Radicalization in Jordan: Social and Political Dimensions." *CTC Sentinel* 10 (2017): 25–30.
Yost, David S. *NATO's Balancing Act.* Washington, DC: US Institute of Peace, 2014.
Younes, Ali. "Analysis: The Divergent Saudi-UAE Strategies in Yemen." *Al-Jazeera English.* August 31, 2019. www.aljazeera.com/news/2019/8/31/analysis-the-divergent-saudi-uae-strategies-in-yemen.
Younis, Nossaibah. "Iraqis Vote to Restrain Armed Groups." European Council on Foreign Relations. October 15, 2021. https://ecfr.eu/article/iraqis-vote-to-restrain-armed-groups.
Yousef, Elias. "Beyond Performance: Lessons Learned from U.S. Security Assistance to Tunisia." Security Assistance Monitor. July 2020. https://securityassistance.org/wp-content/uploads/2020/10/Beyond-Performance-Lessons-Learned-from-U.S.-Security-Assistance-to-Tunisia.pdf.
Zahlan, Antoine. *Technological Illiteracy and Its Impact on Arab Development.* Beirut: Center for Arab Unity Studies, 2013.
Zuaiter, Ahmad. "The Middle East's Addiction to Foreign Aid—a Crippling Crutch." Linkedin. October 30, 2019. www.linkedin.com/pulse/middle-easts-addiction-foreign-aid-crippling-crutch-ahmad-zuaiter.

The Contributors

ZEINAB ABUL-MAGD is professor of Middle Eastern history at Oberlin College. She received her PhD in history and political economy from Georgetown University and her BA in political science from Cairo University. Her latest books include *Militarizing the Nation: The Army, Business, and Revolution in Egypt* (2017) and *Businessmen in Arms: How the Military and Other Armed Groups Profit in the MENA Region* (2016).

HICHAM ALAOUI is a political scientist serving on the Advisory Board of the Weatherhead Center for International Affairs, and the founding president and director of the Hicham Alaoui Foundation. He received his DPhil from the University of Oxford. His latest book is *Pacted Democracy in the Middle East: Tunisia and Egypt in Comparative Perspective* (2022).

ZOLTAN BARANY is Frank C. Erwin Jr. Centennial Professor of Government at the University of Texas. He is author of *Armies of Arabia: Military Politics and Effectiveness in the Gulf* (2021), *How Armies Respond to Revolutions and Why* (2016), and *The Soldier and the Changing State: Building Democratic Armies in Africa, Asia, Europe, and the Americas* (2012)—all have been translated into Arabic.

LINDSAY J. BENSTEAD is Public Policy Fellow in the Middle East Program at the Woodrow Wilson International Center for Scholars in

Washington, DC, and associate professor of political science and director of the Middle East Studies Center at Portland State University. She is a past Kuwait Visiting Professor at SciencesPo in Paris. Her research has appeared in *Perspectives on Politics, International Journal of Public Opinion Research, Governance*, and *Foreign Affairs*. She holds a PhD from the University of Michigan, Ann Arbor.

ANTHONY H. CORDESMAN holds the Emeritus Chair in Strategy at the Center for Strategic and International Studies in Washington, DC, where he has written and directed numerous books and studies. He has previously served in the Office of the Secretary of Defense, the National Security Council, the State Department, and the Department of Energy. He was awarded the Distinguished Service Medal by the Office of the Secretary of Defense.

FLORENCE GAUB works on all things security and conflict in the Middle East and North Africa. She has worked for the European Union and NATO Defence College and has authored numerous publications, including two books, on the subject.

NOUREDDINE JEBNOUN is adjunct associate professor at the Center for Contemporary Arab Studies–Edmund A. Walsh School of Foreign Service at Georgetown University. Previously, in Tunisia, he taught at the National War College, the Command and Staff College, and the National Defense Institute. He is author of *Tunisia's National Intelligence: Why "Rogue Elephants" Fail to Reform* (2017) and coeditor of *Modern Middle East Authoritarianism: Roots, Ramifications, and Crisis* (2013 and 2015).

KEVIN KOEHLER is associate professor of political science at the Sant'Anna School of Advanced Studies in Pisa, Italy. His research focuses on politics and security in the Middle East and North Africa, and he is the principal investigator of the Political Elites and Regime Change in the Middle East and North Africa project funded by the European Research Council.

ARAM NERGUIZIAN is chief executive officer and cofounder of The Mortons Group. He provides strategic advice and insight to the private sector, governments, and nongovernmental and international organizations on security-sector, governance, socioeconomic, and policy challenges across the Middle East and North Africa. He is senior advisor to the Program on Civil-Military Relations in Arab States at the Carnegie Middle East Center, where his work focuses on the Lebanese security sector, long-term force transformation in the Levant, and efforts to develop national security institutions in postconflict and divided societies.

GLENN E. ROBINSON is professor of defense analysis at the Naval Postgraduate School in California. He retired in 2021 after thirty years on the faculty. His most recent book, *Global Jihad: A Brief History*, was named a Best Book of 2021 by both *Foreign Affairs* and *Foreign Policy*. Robinson is also affiliated with the Center for Middle Eastern Studies at the University of California at Berkeley.

YEZID SAYIGH is a senior fellow at the Malcolm H. Kerr Carnegie Middle East Center in Beirut, Lebanon, where he works on comparative political and economic roles of Arab armed forces, the impact of war on states and societies, and the politics of postconflict reconstruction and security-sector transformation in Arab transitions, and authoritarian resurgence.

ROBERT SPRINGBORG is a research fellow of the Italian Institute of International Affairs and adjunct professor at Simon Fraser University. Formerly he was professor of national security affairs at the Naval Postgraduate School; holder of the MBI Al Jaber Chair in Middle East Studies at the School of Oriental and African Studies in London; director of the American Research Center in Egypt; and professor of Middle East Politics at Macquarie University in Sydney, Australia. His most recent books are *Egypt* (2018), *Political Economies of the Middle East and North Africa* (2020), and *The Political Economy of Education in the Arab World* (2021, coedited with Hicham Alaoui).

SIMONE THOLENS is associate professor of international relations at John Cabot University and parttime professor at the Robert Schuman Centre/European University Institute. Her main research interests are postliberal interventions, security assistance, bordering processes, and materiality of global war practices, as well as theories of contestation and practice.

ALEX WALSH works on research and implementation for the reform of security institutions in fragile, postconflict, and divided societies. He has an MPhil from the University of Cambridge in Middle Eastern studies and Arabic. He currently works at the Geneva Centre for Security Sector Governance.

F. C. "PINK" WILLIAMS is a retired major general who served as a senior defense official, chief of the Office of Military Cooperation, and defense attaché at the US embassy in Cairo from 2008 to 2011.

SEAN YOM is associate professor of political science at Temple University, senior fellow at the Project on Middle East Democracy in Washington, DC, and senior fellow at the Foreign Policy Research Institute in Philadelphia. He is a specialist on authoritarian regimes, economic development, and foreign policy in the Arab world. His books include *From Resilience to Revolution: How Foreign Interventions Destabilize the Middle East* (2016) and *The Political Science of the Middle East: Theory and Research Since the Arab Uprisings* (2022).

JOHN J. ZAVAGE is a retired colonel whose frequent overseas postings included Bosnia-Herzegovina, Korea, Jordan, Iraq, and finally Saudi Arabia, as US senior defense official and defense attache to Yemen from 2017 to 2018. He concluded his military career as instructor of national security affairs at the Naval Postgraduate School, and works as a contractor teaching security cooperation for the Defense Security Cooperation University.

Index

Abu Ghazala, Abd al-Halim, 112, 115, 118
accountability: capacity building and democratization, 251; defense institution building, 262–265; EU assistance reform and oversight, 134, 137–145; holding SA policymakers accountable, 306–310; non-US SA providers, 105; as policy objective, 11; provider reforms, 333–334. *See also* assessment of security assistance
advisory missions: EU in Iraq, 138–140
Afghan National Army Trust Fund, 155
Afghan National Defense and Security Forces (ANDSF), 294–295
Afghan Security Forces Fund, 309
Afghanistan: assessing US assistance, 292; assessment failure of nation-building programs, 309; Bahraini military deployment, 187; downsizing militaries, 328; impact of US intervention, 20; military capability building, 294; ODA and military assistance, 1–2; shifting policy objectives and funding, 295; Taliban acquisition of US assistance, 306–307
air defense weapons, 35
Algeria: Algerian revolution, 55; assessing public support for the military, 247; belief in democracy, 242(fig.); confidence in the military, 242(fig.); long-term impacts of conflict, 133; militarization, 26; military response to Arab Spring, 241(table); popular support for the military, 235, 238, 239(table); security assistance demands, 24; size of the military, 57(table); vulnerability of repressive republics, 66

annexation, Israel's, 26
Annual Threat Assessment of the U.S. Intelligence Community, 42–43
anti-US feeling: affecting confidence in the military, 233–234, 237, 243(table); Iran's foreign policy pillars, 202–203
Arab Barometer surveys, 231–232, 236–237
Arab gulf states. *See* Gulf states
Arab League, 287
Arab Legion, 218, 226
Arab Nationalists, 218
Arab Organization for Industrialization (AOI), 123
Arab Spring, 19; Algeria's political stability, 24; Egypt's diversification of procurement sources, 125–126; Egypt's military spending, 119; European security assistance, 134; European SSR to Tunisia, 141; FID demand, 58; Gulf states' defense spending following, 178–181; Jordan's lack of protest, 218; suspension of assistance to Egypt, 120; Tunisia's flawed democracy, 61; types of military responses, 241(table); US military objective in Egypt, 283–284
Arab-Israeli War (1967), 37, 226
Armies of Sand (Pollack), 259
arms control, 319
arms embargo: Libya, 144–146, 186–187, 205
arms manufacturing: Egypt's agreements with non-US providers, 119, 122–126; EU's lack of, 134–135; Jordan's defense industry, 222–223; military assistance to Egypt, 114; US financing in Egypt, 120, 276–277

381

arms race, 2–3
arms trade: Algeria's imports from Russia, 24; Cold War bilateral relations, 5; correlation to popular support for the military, 239–240(table); cost of US aid to Egypt, 112; Egyptian arms deals with Russia, 26, 121, 125–126, 128, 284; Egypt's diversification of sources, 26, 126; EU priorities and approaches, 147; extent of US aid to Jordan, 224–225; figures on Egypt's imports, 121; French-Iraqi relations, 138–139; giving regime support and legitimacy, 53; Gulf states, 29–30, 177, 178(table), 180, 182; history of US assistance in Egypt, 273–276, 278–279; interoperability with foreign infrastructure, 47; Israel's partnership with the US, 26; Italy's sales to Jordan, 163–164; military support in Libya, 25; missile defense and layered artillery, 35; political purpose of prestige weapons, 53–54; redundancy in Arab weaponry, 172–173; SA and security cooperation to the LAF, 105; short-range precision-guided and smart weapons, 35–36; statistics on MENA countries, 49; Turkey, 62; Turkey's illegal arms trade, 205; UK and France, 22; US, France, and Russia, 22; US domination of Gulf states markets, 182; US provision in Iraq, 31; vulnerability of high-cost to low-cost weaponry, 335–336; to Yemen, 32
Assad regime, 27–28
assassinations: Libya's internal instability, 24–25
assess, monitor, and evaluate (AM&E), 297, 305–306
assessment of security assistance, 11–12; accountability of SA policymakers, 306–310; end-use monitoring of US equipment in Egypt, 280–282; inability of US assistance to reach policy objectives, 257–258; leadership traits and capability, 301–303; lessons learned from Egypt, 287–289; methods of observation, 291–292; response to real-world crises, 304–305; tactical intangibles, 299–300
asymmetric warfare: grey zone warfare, 5–6; Iranian and Russian strategies, 313–315; Iran's regional SA engagements and narratives, 192, 199, 202–203, 313; real-world crises affecting SA, 304–305; reformulating Egyptian assistance, 125, 283; US policy and strategy options, 315
Australia: arms sales to the Gulf, 183
autarchy, 3
authoritarian regimes: Bush's Democracy Doctrine, 118–119; democratic paradox, 325–326; domestic politcs impeding institutional change, 258–261; effect of SA on democratization, 231, 255–256; JAF role in maintaining, 213, 218; MENA shift towards, 19; rentierism in oil monarchies, 52; SA securing and maintaining regime power, 2, 213–214, 255–256; Syria, 27–28; Turkey under Erdogan, 60–61; US policy in Lebanese politics, 108–109; Western justification for SA, 7–9
autocratic rule: effect on civil-military relations, 265–266; oil monarchies, 52; royal families' political involvement, 173; US strategic goals, 71
axis of failed states, 326–327
Azerbaijan, 207–208

Bahrain, 28; break-even oil prices, 176(table); defense spending, 179–180, 179(table); GCC arms imports, 180; GDP, 175; military deployment abroad, 187; military response to Arab Spring, 241(table); popular support for the military, 239(table); Shi'a opposition to the monarch, 174; US military bases in, 184; US military deployment, 40; weapons imports, 178(table)
Baker, James, 320
bases, military (US): presence in the Gulf, 184–186. *See also* military presence, US
Ben Ali, Zine El Abidine, 62–63, 71, 82, 233–234
Ben Guardane, Tunisia, 80–81
Berlin, Isaiah, 291
bias, leadership assessment and, 303–304
Biden administration: growing security role in MENA, 22; importance of a new global posture, 43–44; Iran's nuclear capability, 29; lack of MENA security strategy, 40–41; minimizing US presence in the MENA states, 41–42; partnership with Iraq, 31; withdrawal of forces in Afghanistan, Syria, and Iraq, 42–43
Bilateral Country Action Plan (BCAP): Tunisia, 77–80
biological weapons, 29, 38
border control and management: EU and member states assistance in Libya, 144–146; EU-Tunisian mobility partnership, 142–143; Germany's security assistance in Tunisia, 161; Jordan's military effectiveness, 226; LAF capacity, 96; Tunisia's marginalized border regions, 80–87; Turkey's neo-Ottoman revival, 206–207; US policy priorities in Lebanon, 101; US reallocation of Egyptian assistance, 125
Border Security Operations Center (BSOC), 84
Bourguiba, Habib, 82, 233–234
Bright Star joint training (Egypt), 129, 277–278
budget planning and execution, 266–267

Index   383

building partner capacity (BPC) programs: assessing failure to upstream and downstream approaches, 296–298; defining, 11; overbuilding, 294–296; SA accountability, 309–310; the spectrum of US policy options, 315–316; strengthening long-term relationships, 291
Bush (George H.W.) administration, 118, 320
Bush (George W.) administration: promoting human rights and democracy, 283; US-Egyptian rift, 118–119

Camp David Accords, 113–114, 273–275, 278, 285
campfire strategy, Iran's, 199–201
capabilities analysis, 266–267
capabilities development plans (CDPs), 107
capacity building: assessment of SA, 292; defining security assistance, 149–150; exporting security governance, 195–196; France's military coopoeration agreements with Jordan, 158; maximizing aid benefits whilte minimizing drawbacks, 251; providers' failures to improve outcomes, 256–258. *See also* building partner capacity
Carnegie Endowment, 317
Carter administration: history of US assistance in Egypt, 113, 274
cash flow financing for arms: Egypt, 277
Center for a New American Security, 316
Center for Civil-Military Relations (DOD), 331–332
Central Intelligence Agency (CIA), 224, 227
centralization of authority in Gulf monarchies, 173–174
Chatham House, 320
chemical weapons, 29, 38
China: access to advanced weapons, 36; civil-military relations, 267–268; growing regional influence, 17; impact on US policy, 23; military role in the Gulf region, 30; Red Sea subregion, 33; strategy in Syria, 28; subverting Arab states, 313; Tunisia's SA, 80
Christians: confidence in the military, 233, 244, 246; LAF composition, 98
civil society: chemical weapons use against, 39; concerns over regional security, 1; population warfare, 37–38. *See also* civil-military relations
civilian control of the state: defense institution building, 262–264; Iran, 56; self-protection from armed forces, 258. *See also* civil-military relations
civilian missions: EU in Iraq, 138–140
civilian oversight, 72, 172, 251, 255–256, 261–262

civil-military relations: authoritarian governance and, 2; civilian oversight of the military, 251, 261–262; democratic paradox, 336–337; downsizing militaries, 326–331; Egypt's declining support for, 284–285; in flawed democracies, 63; fostering civilian control of the military, 331–333; importance to democratization, 269–270; integrating civilians into Arab defense, 258–261; integrating civilians into the defense industry, 267–269; Jordan and the JAF, 219, 222; Lebanon, 99–100; Lebanon's strategy incoherence, 106–107; in oil monarchies, 54; provider reform transforming, 334; provider role in improving, 264–267; in repressive republics, 58–59. *See also* public opinion of the military
clientelism: US aid to Jordan, 223–224
Clinton administration: assistance to Egypt, 118
coercive diplomacy: division of tasks, 335–336; elements of, 315; failure of US policy in Egypt, 279–280; global power competition, 79–80; justification for, 320–321; perception of US influence in Tunisia's border regions, 86
coercive institutions: costs of coercion in Jordan, 220(table); effect of SA on Tunisia's regime survival, 62–63, 70, 73; Jordan, 216; regime survival, 59, 213–214, 216
colonialism: Algerian revolution, 55; dividing Tunisia's border regions, 81; military legacies, 322–324; rationale for European security involvement, 133–134
commercial sector: cyber and information warfare capability, 36; Egyptian military's monopolistic control, 123–124; Egypt's declining dependence on US assistance, 114, 121; Egypt's expansion into, 283; supply side of security assistance, 64. *See also* arms manufacturing; defense industry
competitive authoritarianism, 61
complementarity, 137–138
confessional states. *See* Lebanon
consequence-based approach to assessing military support, 232–233, 235–236
contingency bases, 40
contractors, 49
contradiction: defining, 137
Coons, Christopher, 74
Cooperation of Security and Defence (France), 156
Copenhagen School, 72
corruption: arms acquisition in the Gulf, 181–182; risks of SA, 324
cost/benefit analyses of SA, 3–4
Countering Violence Extremism (CVE) strategy, 85

counterproliferation, 38–39
counterterrorism (CT): conditions on aid to Tunisia, 76; elements of provided SA, 49; EU mission in Iraq, 139; European SSR to Tunisia, 141; Germany's assistance in Tunisia, 143–144; Jordan's defense industry, 222–223; repressive republics prioritizing, 57–58; Tunisia's border region, 84; Turkey arming and training the FSA, 205; US field exercises with Egyptian forces, 129–130; US policy in Lebanon, 102; US reallocation of Egyptian assistance, 125; US targeting Iran's proxies, 193; US-Egyptian alliance after 9/11, 118
coup-proofing a regime, 13, 51, 56–57, 258
coups d'état: Egypt, 112, 120, 284; Jordan's JAF preempting, 219; military personnel in repressive republics and oil monarchies, 56–57; royal families in Gulf monarchies, 174; Tunisia, 61–62, 72; Turkey, 60
cyber warfare, 36

Davutoglu, Ahmet, 206–207
Dbeibeh, Abdul Hamid, 25, 207
Defense, US Department of (DOD), 294–297; building educational capacity, 329; Center for Civil-Military Relations, 331–332; civil-military integration, 260; defense institution building, 262–264; DOTMLPFP construct, 297–298; provider reforms, 333
Defense Capacity Building (DCB) Initiative, 153
Defense Education Enhancement Program (DEEP), 152–153
defense industry: civil-military integration, 267–269; GCC states, 186–187; Jordan's, 222–223. *See also* commercial sector
defense institution building (DIB): civil-military integration, 256, 262–264, 269; division of labor, 13–14; Lebanese Armed Forces, 103; structural cooperation, 157
defense ministries, military control of, 265
defense policy (Iran): embedding SA support, 201–202
defense spending. *See* military and defense spending
Democracy Doctrine (Bush), 118–119
democratic paradox, 325–331, 336–337
democratization: assessing and correlating public support for the military, 232–233, 241, 247–250; declining support for, 250–251; Egypt's declining support for, 284–285; EU spending in MENA states, 137; factors predicting confidence in the military and support for democracy, 248–249(table); goals of SSR approaches, 147–148; importance of civil-military integration, 269–270; increase in state-society violence, 2; leveraging Egyptian assistance, 129–131; measuring public support for the military, 236–244; reforming US assistance to Egypt, 130–131; relationship to military effectiveness, 231; in rentier states, 52; trust in the military and, 236; Tunisia's Jasmine Revolution, 62–63; US policy agenda in Egypt, 283; US strategic goals, 71; US tensions with Egypt, 26
Desert Shield/Desert Storm. *See* Gulf Wars
Desrocher, John, 74
diplomacy. *See* coercive diplomacy
diplomacy, democratization, and development (3D), 315–317, 319, 334–335
division of labor in SA, 335–336
domestic politics: affect of SA absorption on authoritarian regimes, 213–216; driving demand for assistance, 51; Dutch support of the Libyan arms embargo, 146; effect on popular support for the military, 235; Gulf states' political environments, 173–174; impeding institutional transformation, 258–261; Israel's national security needs, 62; JAF political and economic roles, 213, 217–220; repressive republics' security priorities, 59–60; royal family members' involvement, 54, 173–174; supply side of security assistance, 64; Turkey's expansion of influence and control, 204–206; value of US assistance to Egypt, 120
domestic threats, 20–21, 27, 215
DOTMLPFP construct, 297–299
downsizing militaries, 326–331
downstream problems and policy objectives, 291–292, 297–298
Draper Commission, 293
drawdown of military forces: Israel's weapons assistance, 62
Druze: confidence in the military, 233, 244, 246; LAF composition, 97–98
Dunne, Michele, 317

economic aid, nonmilitary, 5, 215, 230(n41); declining value of US assistance, 281–282
economic development: EU assistance to Tunisia, 141; security assistance and, 149; Syria's collapse, 27–28; US assistance goals, 71
economic diversification: Gulf states, 177
economic growth: ODA's economic drag, 2
economic health: corruption in arms acquisitions, 181–182; Gulf states economies, 174–181; JAF role, 222; Jordan's welfarism through militarism, 220–223; military spending in MENA countries, 48–49
economic impacts of instability, 133–134

economic support funds (ESF), 281–282
education: effect on stability, 329; NATO activities, 152–153
efficiency: civil-military relations and, 265–266
Egypt: assessing policy pillars and successes, 287–289; belief in democracy, 242(fig.); biological and chemical weapons, 38–39; BPC overrelationship building, 294; Bright Star joint training, 129, 277–278; confidence in the military, 242(fig.); declining value of US assistance, 111–113, 115–120, 281–282; downsizing the military, 329–330; effect of oil price fluctuations, 66; effects of SA, 327; ending dependency on US assistance, 121–129; ethnic composition of the military, 50; EU weapons provision, 147; Gulf War, 118; history of US assistance, 273–275; leveraging aid for democratization, 129–131; low military capacity, 50; militarization, 26; military response to Arab Spring, 241(table); military support in Libya, 25; operational and geopolitical objectives of SA, 211–212; poor civilian integration into the military, 268; popular support for the military, 235, 238, 239(table), 242(fig.), 246–247; Project on Middle East Democracy recommendations, 317; Russian arms provision, 22; size of the military, 57(table); state budget, 116–117(table); strategic success of US assistance, 273–274; US end-use monitoring of military equipment, 280–282; US policy demands for assistance, 275–277; US relations after the 2011 revolt, 283–288; US security partners in the Greater Levant, 25
Egyptian Armed Forces (EAF), 275, 282–284
employment status: public confidence in the military, 245–246
Enable and Enhance Initiative (E21), 142–143, 159–161
endorsement factor of weapons provision, 65
end-use monitoring of US equipment, 280–282
entanglement, 192–193; defining, 10; Iran's institutional change in the Hezbollah, 257; temporal and spatial, 196–198
Equipment Aid Program for Foreign Armed Forces (Germany), 159–160
Erdogan, Recep Tayyip, 60–61, 66–67, 207
Eritrea: GCC military influence, 185–186; Red Sea subregion, 32–33
Ertüchtigungsinitiative (E21), 142–143, 159–161
Esper, Mark, 79–80
ethics and morals: grey zone warfare, 8–9
Ethiopia: Red Sea subregion, 32–33
ethnic biases: leadership capability in SA recipients, 303–304

ethnicity: LAF multisectarian makeup, 95, 97–99; MENA states' military populations, 50–51
ethnocracy, 61
EUNAVFOR MED IRINI, 144–145, 163
European states: impact on US MENA assistance, 21–22; LAF transition, 95–96; NATO's defense spending, 154–155; the nature of security assistance, 133–134; policy-status and priorities, 134–137; SA in Lebanon, 94; security approaches in MENA, 134; Tunisian assistance, 140–144. *See also individual states*
European Union (EU): Germany's E21, 160; justice mission in Iraq, 138–140; policy-status and priorities, 134–137; security approaches in MENA, 134; SSR in Libya, 144–146; supporting Tunisia's political stability, 71; US funding drawdown, 4
EU-Tunisia Shared Strategic Priorities, 141
Excess Defense Articles program, 75
experimental nature of SA, 194–195
external relations: negative impacts of SA, 2–3
external threats: Iran and the threat of war, 29–30
extremist organizations: impact of conflict on the populace, 37–38; policy goals in stemming, 294–296. *See also* Islamic State

Fahmy, Nabil, 285–286
failed states, 20–21, 27; prioritizing survival over transformation, 257–258. *See also* Lebanon; Yemen
Fair al Jurud campaign, 94
Fakhrizadeh, Mohsen, 8
family-run regimes, oil monarchies as, 52
Fatah al-Islam terrorist group, 102
flawed democracies, 48; political drivers for SA, 60–63; reforming SA systems, 66–67
Ford administration: history of US assistance in Egypt, 273–274
Foreign Affairs magazine, 317
Foreign Assistance Act (1961), 281, 293–294, 299
foreign internal defense (FID) assistance, 49, 51, 57–59
Foreign Military Training Program (Tunisia), 85
foreign policy: conflicting goals in Egypt, 285–286; disjointed US policy in Egypt, 274–276; Hashemite control over Jordan's, 218–219; Iran's anti-US narrative, 202–203; offshore balancing, 318–322; SA prioritizing policy over military strengthening, 293; the spectrum of options for strategies and objectives, 314–318; strategic goals informing, 193–194; Tunisia, 69–70; Turkey's expansion

of influence and control, 204–206; Turkey's neo-Ottoman revival, 206–207
Fox, Amos C., 194
fragile states: EU assistance, 135; fragmentation of armed forces, 328–329; US concerns over growing terrorism, 293–294
France: aid to Lebanon, 27; Algerian revolution, 55; Egyptian and European security, 134; Egypt's arms imports, 121–122, 126–127; Egypt's diversification of procurement sources, 125–126; EU mission in Iraq, 138–140; hard SA provision, 195–196; LAF transition, 95–96; military assistance to Egypt, 114; NATO military partnership, 156–159; SA in Lebanon, 94; Saudi arms imports, 29; security assistance in the Arab Gulf, 28; SSR in Libya, 145–146
Free Syrian Army (FSA), 192, 204–205
funding levels for SA: Egypt, 111–113, 115, 118, 120, 277, 281–282; growth between 2003 and 2019, 295; Tunisia, 74
future of SA, 336–337

Gates, Robert, 73, 316
gender: confidence in the military, 233, 235, 243(table); reforming US assistance to Egypt, 131
General Intelligence Directorate (GID), 218, 230(n15)
geopolitical imperatives of SA, 211–212
geopolitics: MENA states as SA providers, 193–194
Germany: assistance to Egypt, 121, 126, 128; Enable and Enhance Initiative, 159–161; EU spending in Iraq, 135; NATO-led programs, 155; SSR in Tunisia, 142–143
goals of security assistance, 18. *See also* military effectiveness; stability, political
governance: exporting security governance, 195; Lebanon's hybrid security governance, 99–100; strengthening states, 331–333; US policy priorities in Lebanon, 101. *See also* authoritarian regimes; democratization
government, public confidence in, 245–246
Government Defense Integrity Index (Transparency International), 324
Government of National Unity (GNU; Libya), 25
Greater Levant subregion, 25–28
grey zone operations: elements of, 5–6; implications for SA strategies, 7–9; traditional approaches and, 321; US policy and strategy options, 315, 321
gross domestic product (GDP): Gulf states defense spending, 179–180, 180(table)

Guerini, Lorenzo, 162
Gulf Cooperation Council (GCC), 28, 30, 282; corruption in arms acquisitions, 181–182; domestic political environments, 173–174; failure of arms control efforts, 320; foreign deployment and defense industries, 186–187; increasing economic and strategic power, 171–172; security provision, 183–187. *See also specific states*
Gulf states: arms imports, 180; assistance to Egypt, 121; China's interest in MENA, 23; defense budgets, 177–181; EU's policy objectives, 135; GCC states' reliance on oil wealth, 176; military assistance to Egypt, 114; NATO partnership initiative, 152. *See also specific states*
Gulf Wars, 39–40, 118, 279–280, 286–287

Hadi, Abdrabbuh Mansur, 32
Haftar, Khalifa, 25, 192, 287
hard borders: Tunisia, 143
hard power: military modernization, 330; US policy and strategy options, 315
hard security assistance, 195–196. *See also* arms trade; training programs
The Hedgehog and the Fox (Berlin), 291
Hezbollah, 101; "axis of resistance" narrative, 201; conflict with Israel, 96; institutional transformation, 257; Iranian military support, 107–109; Lebanese citizens' confidence in the military, 233; US security assistance and cooperation, 101–102
historical context: relationship-building and partnership capacity building, 293–294
historical legacies affecting SA, 322–325
Hitti, Maroun, 106
Houthi rebels (Yemen), 32; long-range precision-guided weapons, 34–35; maritime warfare, 302; Saudi Arabia's lack of progress against, 49
human rights: accountability of SA policymakers, 307; aid to Tunisia, 73; delaying US MENA strategy formation, 41; deterioration in Egypt, 119; Egypt's declining support for, 284–285; French-Egyptian relations, 127; increase in state-society violence, 2; US policy agenda in Egypt, 283; US strategic emphasis, 43; US tensions with Egypt, 26; use of strategic partnerships, 18
human-centered definition of security, 250–251
humanitarian efforts: political considerations informing US policy, 18–19
Hussein, Saddam, 118
hybrid security governance (Lebanon), 99–100
hybrid security systems, 195–196, 315
hybrid warfare, 5–6, 30, 335–336
hypercentralization of authority, 173–174

immigration: anti-West tactics in MENA, 313–314; European issues in MENA region, 21–22; European mobility partnership with Tunisia, 141–142; Germany's security assistance in Tunisia, 161
implementation, assessment and, 297–298
"In Pursuit of a General Theory of Proxy Warfare" (Fox), 194–195
information warfare, 36
innovation, military, 260–262
institutional strength: US assistance failing to implement, 257–258
institutional transformation: EU and member states, 135
intelligence, surveillance, and reconnaissance (ISR), 30, 44, 76
intelligence community: Jordan's employment statistics, 222
intelligence technology, repressive republics prioritizing, 57–58
International Military Education and Training (IMET), 329
interoperability, military: US assistance in Egypt, 278–281
interoperability of systems, 47–48
interstate relations: centrality of military power, 3; evaluating SA benefits and US strategy, 4–7; regional conflicts, tensions, and threats, 20; SA tactics and strategies, 7–9
Iran: availability of weapons platforms, 35; China's economic and security agreement, 23; coercive diplomacy against, 321; containment priorities and strategies, 7; counterproliferation, 38; defense spending, 179; institutional change in the Hezbollah, 257; long-range precision-guided weapons, 34–35; military effects of SA, 328; military response to Arab Spring, 241(table); military support in Syria, 27–28; nuclear capability, 38–39; popular support for the military, 239(table); resistance narrative, 198; as SA provider, 192; security assistance for Hezbollah, 107–109; size of the military, 57(table); spatial and temporal entanglements, 198–203; state capture in Iraq, 332–333; state-controlled mercenaries, 37; subverting Arab states, 313; threat of war with, 29; UAE purchase of prestige weapons, 53; US lack of security strategy, 40; US security policy in Lebanon, 101; Yemen's civil war, 32
Iran-Iraq War (1980), 39–40, 118, 199
Iraq: biases in SA recipient leadership, 303–304; biological and chemical weapons, 38–39; bolstering state capture, 332–333; ethnicity in the military, 50; EU justice mission, 138–140; EU spending, 135, 136(fig.); France's military partnerships, 158–159; impact of conflict on the populace, 37; impact of US intervention, 20; integrating civilians into defense affairs, 268; Iranian-US competition, 30–31; Iran's regional SA engagements, 199; Iran's SA narrative, 201; Italy's security assistance, 164; Jordan's military effectiveness, 226; leaders' response to real-world crises, 304–305; magnitude and results of US investment, 257; military capability building, 294; military ineffectiveness, 49; military response to Arab Spring, 241(table); NATO partnerships, 153–154; popular support for the military, 239(table); proxy wars, 3; SA emphasis on BPC programs, 295–296; shifting policy objectives and funding, 295; US drawdown, 42; US security policy in Lebanon, 100–101
Iraq war: Jordan's participation, 223–224; principal-agent approach to SA, 194–195
irregular forces, 36–37
irregular warfare, 76
Islamic Revolutionary Guard Corps, 56, 200, 202–203, 328
Islamic State (IS): assault on Tunisia's border region, 80–87; Egyptian-Russian arms deal, 125; France's military partnerships, 158–159; Germany's E21, 161; Iraq's military effectiveness against, 49; Jordan's military effectivness, 227; Lebanese campaign, 94, 96; near-statehood status, 5–6; principal-agent approach to the Iraq war, 194–195; US occupation of Iraq, 20; US partnership with Iraq, 31
Israel: biological and chemical weapons, 38–39; counterproliferation, 38; Gulf states relations, 174, 183; history of US assistance in Egypt, 113–114, 275; impact of conflict on the populace, 37; Iran's foreign policy pillars, 202–203; Iran's increasing threat, 29–30; LAF security priorities, 97; military effectiveness and civil-military relations, 63; military response to Arab Spring, 241(table); NATO's Mediterranean Dialogue, 151–152; popular support for the military, 239(table); reforming security assistance, 67; SA demand in flawed democracies, 60–63; US funding drawdown in the MENA, 4; US security partners in the Greater Levant, 25
Istanbul Cooperation Initiative (2004), 152
Italy: hard SA provision, 195–196; security assistance recipients, 162–165

Japan: civilian incusion in the defense industry, 267
Joint Arab Force, 122

joint capability reviews (JCRs), 103
Joint Comprehensive Plan of Action (JCPOA), 29
Joint Operations Control Center (JOCC; Tunisia), 78
Joint Reconnaissance Center (JRC; Tunisia), 78
joint warfare: MENA forces, 33–34
Jordan: assessing public support for the military, 238, 246–247; assessing tactical intangibles, 299–300; belief in democracy, 242(fig.); building partnership capacity, 225–228; confidence in the military, 235, 239(table), 241, 242(fig.); correlating confidence in the military with democratization, 241; effects of SA, 327; ethnicity in the military, 50; EU spending, 136(fig.); failed operational objectives of SA, 212; France's military coopoeration agreements, 158; Germany's E21, 160–161; the goals of US assistance, 223–228; Italy's security assistance partnerships, 163–164; military response to Arab Spring, 241(table); NATO partnerships, 153–154; nonmilitary economic aid, 215–216, 230(n41); operational and geopolitical goals of SA, 213; popular support for the military, 235, 239(table); proposed Middle East military alliance, 228; security sector and the JAF, 216–223; subregional politics, 26; tribal support for the monarchy, 214–215; US security partners in the Greater Levant, 25; welfarism through militarism, 220–223
Jordanian Armed Forces (JAF), 6; capacity building, 225–228; extent of US aid to, 224–225; failure of US policy, 212–213; internal corruption and incompetence, 227–228; military and security spending, 220(table); tribal support for the monarchy, 215
justice mission, EU, 138–140

Kaye, Dalia Dass, 317
Kerry, John, 120
King Abdullah II Design and Development Bureau (Jordan), 222–223
Kurdish belt, Turkey's mobilization against, 205
Kurdish Peshmerga, 164
Kurdish-Arab forces, 28
Kuwait: assistance to Egypt, 127; break-even oil prices, 176(table); defense spending, 179–180, 179(table); GCC arms imports, 180; GDP, 175; mercenary contracts, 181; military response to Arab Spring, 241(table); popular support for the military, 239(table); prestige weapons purchases, 54; US military bases in, 184; utilitarian political support, 52–53; weapons imports, 178(table)

Latin America: supporting civil-military relations, 332
layered artillery, 35
leadership capability: assessing, 301–303; ethnic, social, and political biases, 303–304; response to real-world crises, 304–305
Lebanese Armed Forces (LAF): ability to absorb US assistance, 105–107; civil-military relations, 99–100, 266–267; effects of SA, 327; limits of SA and security cooperation, 103–105; multisectarian makeup, 97–99; post-civil war status and command, 95–97; US security assistance and cooperation, 101–102
Lebanon: belief in democracy, 242(fig.); confidence in the military, 242(fig.), 247; EU spending, 136(fig.); European security assistance, 134; external actors in the war, 3; Hezbollah's "axis of resistance" narrative, 201; Iran's regional SA engagements, 199; military response to Arab Spring, 241(table); political and economic instability, 27; popular support for the military, 235, 238, 239(table), 242(fig.), 247; regional conflicts, tensions, and threats, 20; sectarian differences affecting confidence in the military, 246; US efforts and outcomes, 103; US policy and strategy, 93–94, 100–101; US security partners in the Greater Levant, 25
legal reforms, 308–309
legal systems, undermining, 332–333
legitimacy, political: in rentier states, 52–53
Libya: Egypt's low military capacity, 50; EU spending, 136(fig.); European SSR assistance, 144–146; ISIS assault on Tunisia's border region, 80–87; Madrid peace conference, 152; military response to Arab Spring, 241(table); political and security instability, 24–25; popular support for the military, 239(table); proxy wars, 3; regional conflicts, tensions, and threats, 20; Russian arms provision, 22; state-controlled mercenaries, 37; Tunisian military capabilities, 77; Turkey's neo-Ottoman revival, 207–208; Turkey's SA engagement, 192, 205–206; UAE military deployment, 186–187
limited revamped capabilities approach (LRCA), 77
living standards: Gulf states citizens, 175
logistical capability: assessing tactical intangibles, 299–300
long-range precision-guided weapons, 34–35

long-term goals of SA: complementarity, 137–138; defense institution building, 262–263; EU policy reform, 147–148; prescriptive narratives of SA, 193–194; recipients' motivations, 8; resolving the democratic paradox, 325–326; strategies in Tunisia, 77–78, 81

long-term relationships, strengthening: adversarial collaboration and, 338; Iraqi military, 201–202; objective and subjective approaches to SA, 291–292; subjective approach to SA, 298–306. *See also* building partner capacity

Macron, Emmanuel, 127
Madrid Conference (1991), 152, 320
major non-NATO allies status (MNNA), 74–75
mandatory military service, 174
Maranites: LAF composition, 97–99
marginalized peoples: confidence in the military, 233–234, 246; Tunisia's border regions, 80–87
maritime security, 185; assessing leadership traits, 301–303; Egypt, 125; EU and member states assistance in Libya, 144–145
Martz Report, 103
McNamara, Robert, 11
Mediterranean Dialogue (1994), 151–152
Memorandum of Understanding, US-Jordanian, 224
Ménat, Pierre, 159
mercenaries, 37; GCC contracts, 181; military support in Libya, 25
Merkel, Angela, 128
Mexicanization of the Tunisian-Libyan border, 84–85
militarism, Jordan's welfarism through, 220–223
militarization of the MENA region: authoritarian governance and, 2–3; effect of civilianizing defense institutions, 9; Gulf states, 174; Lebanon under Hezbollah, 27; SA for the creation of new military forces, 33; SA tactics and strategies, 7; statistics on, 1
military and defense spending, 67(n3); Egypt, 113, 119, 124; Gulf states, 174–175, 177–181, 180(table); Gulf states before 2011, 177–178; Iran, 202; Jordan, 219–220, 220(table); in MENA countries, 48–49; NATO security assistance, 154–155; oil monarchies, 172; political needs accounting for, 324
military capability: advanced weapons, 36; assessing tactical intangibles, 299–300; effect on confidence in the military, 235–236; effect on public support, 232; LAF, 96–97; limits of SA and security

cooperation to the LAF, 103–105; low capacity of MENA states, 49–50; SA to irregular forces, 36–37; shifting priorities for US SA, 293–294; Western security goals, 211
Military Concept for Projecting Stability (Italy), 162
Military Cooperation Committee (MCC: US and Egypt), 278
military cooperation missions (France), 156
military effectiveness: Arabia's underperformance, 172; assessment variables, 149–150; BCAP enhancing Tunisia's, 78; in flawed democracies, 63; the future of SA, 336–337; high levels of assistance failing to influence, 255–256; Jordanian Armed Forces, 225–228; in oil monarchies, 54–55; providers' failures to implement institutional change, 256–258; relationship to democratization, 231; in repressive republics, 58–59; SA failure to achieve, 255–256
military forces: ballistic and cruise missile advances, 35; colonial legacies, 322–324; composition in repressive republics and oil monarchies, 56–57; downsizing as an objective, 326–331; effect of SA on Tunisia's, 73–80; JAF composition and function, 217; long-range precision-guided weapons, 34–35; multidomain capability, 33–34; political and cultural penetration into governance, 258–261; regime support and legitimacy in rentier states, 53; royal family members, 54; SA creating new forms of, 33; securitization of Tunisia's border region, 86; size in repressive republics and oil monarchies, 57(table); US SA strategies and goals, 18. *See also* civil-military relations; *specific military groups*
military innovation, 260–262
military modernization, 322–323
military operational partnerships (PMO; France), 157
military presence, US: bases in the Gulf, 184–186; correlation to popular support for the military, 239–240(table); drawdown in Syria and Iraq, 42; elements of provided SA, 49; exporting security governance, 195–196; GCC states, 183–184; Gulf region, 40, 194–196; objectives in Egypt's 2011 revolt, 283–284; Tunisia, 76; US military relationship in Egypt, 276–277
military-to-military assistance and cooperation: EU security assistance, 157; Jordan, 213–216, 225; Lebanese Armed Forces, 103–104; US military relationship in Egypt, 276–277
militias: Lebanese sectarian militia, 99

Ministry of Defense (MOD; Iraq), 301, 303–305
Ministry of Defense (MOD; Tunisia), 79, 84
Ministry of Military Production (MOMP; Egypt), 115, 122–124
MIT trucks court case, 204–205
modernization of the military, 330
Mohamed bin Zayed Al Nahyan, 54
Mohammed bin Salman, 122, 173, 182
Morocco: assessing public support for the military, 247; belief in democracy, 242(fig.); confidence in the military, 242(fig.); correlating confidence in the military with democratization, 241; military response to Arab Spring, 241(table); North African subregional security, 24; popular support for the military, 235, 238, 239(table)
mosaic defense, Iran's, 199
Mubarak, Hosni, 71, 113, 118–119, 123, 284
Muslim Brotherhood, 206

narratives: in entangled perspectives, 197–199; Hezbollah's "axis of resistance" narrative, 201
nation building: strengthening states, 331–333
National Defense Authorization Act (NDAA; 2017), 75, 296–297, 333
National Liberation Front, 55
NATO (North Atlantic Treaty Organization): capacity building, 149; flawed democracies in, 62; France's military partnership, 156–159; Germany's security programs, 161; goals and constraints of security assistance, 150; Italy's security assistance recipients, 162–165; MENA partners, 152(fig.); partnership frameworks, 151–155; politics of security assistance, 155–165; SSR provision, 195–196; UAE military deployment abroad, 186–187; US security policy and cooperation in Lebanon, 102–103
NATO Defense College, 152–153
NATO Strategic Direction South Hub (NSD-S Hub), 163
NATO Training Mission in Iraq (NMI), 154
natural resources: China's interest in MENA, 23
naval deployment (US), 40, 184
naval forces (Egypt), 283
neoliberal development, 71–73
neo-Ottoman revival, Turkey's, 192, 198, 206–209
Netherlands: SSR in Libya, 145–146
9/11 terrorist attacks: Egyptian-US relations, 282–283; Jordanian-US relations, 223–224; reshaping SA policy, 76, 293–296; US contingency base expansion, 40. *See also* War on Terror

nongovernmental organizations (NGO): detention of workers in Egypt, 119–120
nonstate actors, 5, 35–37, 191, 258–259
North African subregion, 24–25
nuclear capability, 38; Iran, 29
Nuclear Nonproliferation Treaty, 319
nuclear threats, 38

Obama administration: GCC arms imports, 180; improving effectiveness and cutting costs, 296–297; Israel's military assistance, 62; loss of influence in Egypt, 119; response to Egypt's coup, 112; Saudi-US relations, 174; suspending Egyptian assistance, 125; Tunisia's MNNA status, 74
objective/methodical approach to assistance assessment, 292, 296–298, 307–308
offense-defense strategy over SA provision, 199–200
Office of Military Cooperation (OMC), 280–281, 283–284
offshore balancing, 315, 318–319
oil and gas: China's interest in MENA, 23; military protection of, 86; reforming SA systems, 64
oil monarchies, 48; advantages and disadvantages of oil wealth, 172; political drivers for SA, 51–55; prestige weapons systems, 58; reforming security systems provision, 65–66; size of military forces, 57(table)
oil prices, 65–66, 176, 176(table)
Oman: break-even oil prices, 176(table); defense spending, 179–180, 179(table); GDP, 175; mercenary contracts, 181; prestige weapons purchases, 53–54; US military bases in, 184; weapons imports, 178(table)
Operation Barkhane, 157
Operation Chammal, 139–140
Operation Inherent Resolve, 139–140
Operation Irini, 145–146
Operation Prima Parthica, 164
operational objectives of SA, 211–213, 303–304; SA policy failure in Egypt, 278–289
Ottoman Empire: Turkey's neo-Ottoman revival, 206–209
overseas development assistance (ODA), 1, 167(n1)

packaging security assistance, 9–12
Pakistan: nuclear capability, 38–39
Palestine: belief in democracy, 242(fig.); confidence in the military, 242(fig.); EU spending, 136(fig.); Israel as a flawed democracy, 61; Israeli politics and Palestinian violence, 26; military response to Arab Spring, 241(table); popular

support for the military, 238, 239(table), 247
Palestinian Authority (PA), 26
Palestinian Jordanians, 214–215, 222
Palestinian Liberation Organization (PLO), 151–152
paramilitary forces, 33, 36–37, 56, 59, 75–76
Partners Across the Globe framework, 152
Partnership Cooperation Menu, 152
Partnership for Peace Trust Fund, 154–155
partnership frameworks: NATO, 151–155
Partnership Interoperability Initiative, 153–154
patronage systems: Jordan's welfarism through militarism, 221; Lebanon, 99; SA to weak states, 328; US aid to Jordan perpetuating, 228–229
patron-client approaches to SA, 10, 193, 195–196
Pax Ottomanica, 207
peacebuilding approach to SA, 193
peacekeeping operations: Jordan's participation, 226–227; NATO's DCB, 153; UAE military deployment abroad, 186–187
Persian and Arab Gulf subregion, 28–31
personal security: US priorities, 19
personality traits: assessing SA recipient leadership, 301–303, 305
police missions, European, 133
Police Training and Equipping Aid (AAH-P), 142–143
policing: Jordan's assistance, 230(n15); Jordan's employment statistics, 222; public trust in, 252–253(n23)
political beliefs: public confidence in the military, 246
political considerations in SA: biases in SA recipient leadership, 303–304; continuing US assistance to Egypt, 120; demand in repressive republics, 55–60; disconnect between security and defense strategies, 48, 50–51; driving demand in oil monarchies, 51–55; in flawed democracies, 60–63; historical legacies affecting SA, 322–325; informing US policy, 18–19; LAF's ability to absorb US assistance, 105–107; NATO security assistance, 155–165; operational objectives and geopolitical imperatives, 211–212; reforming security assistance, 64–65; role of the military in Arabian monarchies, 172; spatial and temporal entanglements, 196–198; US goals in Tunisia, 69–70; US-Egyptian rift, 118–119. *See also* democratization; domestic politics; regime type
political ideas affecting confidence in the military, 233
political reform: US strategic emphasis, 43

political science approach to SA, 194
political stability. *See* stability, political
Pollack, Kenneth, 259
Popular Mobilization Forces (PMFs) in Iraq, 332–333
population growth: increase in state-society violence, 2
population hierarchization, 82–83
population warfare, 37–38
precision-guided air munitions, 32, 38
precision-strike capability, 30
predictability: assessing tactical intangibles, 299–300
Presidential Policy Directive 23 (PPD-23), 296, 308–309
prestige weapons systems, 53–54, 57–58, 64–65, 183
principal-agent (PA) approach to SA, 194–195; assessing US failure in Afghanistan, 309; exporting security governance, 195–196; policy adjustment and, 292
professionalization of the military: Egypt's benefits from US assistance, 129; in flawed democracies, 63; integrating civilians into defense affairs, 267–269; LAF composition, 95, 97; low capacity of MENA states, 49–50; military downsizing and, 329–330; providers' failures to implement, 256–258; Tunisia, 57–58, 62–63; US agenda in Egypt, 284–285
Project on Middle East Democracy, 317
protest: Gulf states after Arab Spring, 178; JAF curbing popular unrest, 218; military involvement in, 238. *See also* Arab Spring
provider reforms, 333–335
provider-recipient coordination, 256–258
proxy warfare, 3–4, 59; failure of, 317; Iran's regional SA engagements, 199; loss of autonomy dilemma, 194; SA contributing to, 255–256; US policy in Lebanon, 101
public opinion of authoritarian regimes, 214
public opinion of the military: assessment results, 244–250; belief in democracy and, 247–250; consequence-based approach, 232–233; declining support for democracy and, 250–251; effect of military capacity, 235–236; factors predicting confidence in the military and support for democracy, 248–249(table); individual factors affecting, 233–234, 243(table); measurement of data, 236–244; study data sources, 236
Putin, Vladimir, 125

Qatar, 28; arms imports, 182–183; break-even oil prices, 176(table); defense spending, 179(table); GDP, 175; mercenary contracts, 181; military response to Arab

Spring, 241(table); military support in Libya, 25; popular support for the military, 240(table); prestige weapons purchases, 54; size of the military, 57(table); US arms imports, 182–183; US military bases in, 184; weapons imports, 178(table)
qualitative military edge (QME), 104, 108, 277
quitting as policy option, 314–317
quota system: Lebanese Armed Forces, 97

RAND Corporation, 316
Raytheon, 226
Reagan administration: US assistance to Egypt, 115
real estate development: Jordan's defense industry, 222–223
real-world crises, response to, 304–305
recipient dynamics, 213–216
Red Sea subregion, 31–33
reducing demand, 65–66
reforming assistance policy, 48–49, 333–335
regime interest: driving SA demand, 48
regime type: defining political stability, 70; delineating demand for assistance, 48; domestic politics driving SA demand, 51; European SSR to Tunisia, 141. *See also* authoritarian regimes
regional security framework, 320
relationship building: lessons learned from Egypt, 287–289; provider reforms, 333–334; subjective assessment of, 298–306; US agenda in Egypt, 283–284
religious identity: assessing confidence in the military, 233–234, 237, 243(table), 246
rentierism: military effectiveness and, 54–55; oil monarchies, 51–55, 173
repressive republics, 55–60, 66
resource allocation: Italy's security assistance partnerships, 163–165
results-based assessments, 297–298
reterritorialization, 199–204
Roadmap for Defense Cooperation (RFDC), 79–80
royal families: corruption in arms acquisitions, 181–182; political involvement, 54, 173–174
rule-of-law mission in Iraq, 138–140
Russia: access to advanced weapons, 36; arms provision to Algeria, 24; arms provisions to Iraq, 31; civil-military integration, 260; coercive diplomacy against, 321; Egyptian arms deals, 26, 121, 125–126, 128, 284; Egypt's agenda in the Ukraine, 287; grey zone operations in SA, 191; growing regional influence, 17; history of US asssistance in Egypt, 278; impact on US policy, 22; military modernizing program, 330; military role in the Gulf region, 30;

military support in Libya, 25; military support in Syria, 27–28; post-Cold War regional states, 5–6; Red Sea subregion deployment, 33; strategy in Syria, 28; subverting Arab states, 313; supporting multidomain warfare, 34; Tunisia's SA, 80; Turkey's SA provision in Syria, 192. *See also* Ukraine

Sadat, Anwar, 113; history of US assistance in Egypt, 274–275
Saied, Kais, 61, 86
Sales, Nathan A., 193
al-Sarraj, Fayez, 205–206
Saudi Arabia: achieving multilateral policy objectives through limited training programs, 305–306; arms imports, 29, 183; assistance to Egypt, 121, 127–128; break-even oil prices, 176(table); corruption in arms acquisitions, 181–182; defense industry, 187; defense spending, 177–180, 179(table), 181; domestic terrorism, 174; effectiveness of US assistance, 49; EU weapons provision, 147; GDP, 175; history of US assistance in Egypt, 273–274; long-range precision-guided weapons, 34–35; military assistance to Egypt, 114; military response to Arab Spring, 241(table); political purpose of prestige weapons, 53–54; popular support for the military, 240(table); regional military influence, 185–186; Saudi-Egyptian military cooperation, 122; size of the military, 57(table); Trump's sale of prestige weapons, 64; US arms deal, 180; US military bases in, 184; weapons imports, 178(table); Yemen's civil war, 32
SEAL forces: US-Egyptian training, 130
sectarian military, Lebanon's, 97–99, 105–108
securitization: Tunisia, 71–74, 80–87
securitization theory, 72
security assistance, defining, 10–12, 149
security cooperation (SC): BCAP, 90(n58); combining US objectives with, 69–70; defining, 10–11; EU-Tunisian cooperation, 141; French-Egyptian relations, 127; German-Tunisian relations, 161–162; increasing need for, 19; institution building, 263; Italian-Tunisian cooperation, 164–165; Lebanon, 93–94, 101–105; UK fostering regional stability, 185; upstream and downstream policy approaches, 296–298
security dynamics, 17
Security Force Assistance Brigade (US Army), 78–79
security force assistance team (SFAT), 78–79
security governance, exporting, 195
security institutions: Jordan's JAF, 216–223

security sector reform (SSR), 193; complementarity and contradiction, 137–138; European approaches in MENA, 133–135; European assistance to Tunisia, 140–144; European efforts in Libya, 144–146; exporting security governance, 195; France's Sub-Saharan efforts, 139–140; German assistance in Tunisia, 142–143; key features, 195; the need for cooperation, 147; UN role in, 331–332
Shi'a Muslims: Bahrain's domestic tensions, 174; confidence in the military, 233, 244, 246; Iran's spatial entanglements, 201; Iraq's military composition, 50, 56; LAF composition, 98
Shia Popular Mobilization Forces (Iraq), 56
short-term capability, long-term capacity disconnect, 262
Sinai security, 125
al-Sisi, Abdel Fattah, 112–114, 120, 122–125, 127–130, 285
"smart" weapons, 35–36
smuggling: Tunisia's border regions, 83
social biases: leadership capability in SA recipients, 303–304
social life, JAF penetration into, 222
socioeconomic status: confidence in the military, 233–234, 243(table)
soft power: military modernization, 330; provider reform enhancing, 334; US policy and strategy options, 315
soft security assistance, 195–196. *See also* security sector reform
Soleimani, Qassem, 200
spatial entanglements, 196–198; Iran's campfire strategy, 199–201; Iran's SA engagements, 198–203; Turkey, 204–206
special forces: downsizing militaries, 328; Jordanian units, 227; in Tunisia, 76–77
Special Inspector General for Afghanistan Reconstruction (SIGAR), 295, 309
special operations: LAF capability, 96–97
stability, political: defining, 70; economic impacts of instability, 133–134; LAF in Syria, 97; prioritizing Jordanian stability, 212–213; Tunisia, 70–71, 74; US goals in Tunisia, 69–70; US priorities, 19
stabilization programs: Italy's security assistance recipients, 162–163
Stark, Alexandra, 317
State, US Department of (DOS), 293; nonmilitary instruments of power, 316; provider reforms, 333; Tunisia's bilateral assistance, 74
state capture by elites, 319, 332–333
Stockholm International Peace Research Institute (SIPRI), 22, 26, 29, 121, 126, 179, 202, 317

Strategic Depth (Davutoglu), 207
strategic environment: regional political and security shifts, 18–21
strategy. *See* tactics and strategies
strengthening states, 331–333
subjective assessment of assistance, 292, 296–306. *See also* assessment of security assistance
subregions: Greater Levant, 25–28; North Africa, 24–25; Persian and Arab Gulf, 28–31; Red Sea, 31–33
Sudan: military support in Libya, 25; popular support for the military, 235, 240(table); Red Sea subregion, 32–33
Suez Canal, 279
Suleimani, Qassem, 8
Sunni Muslims: confidence in the military, 233–234, 237, 243(table), 244, 246, 251; contract soldiers, 181; Iraqi leadership, 303–304; LAF composition, 96–99, 101–102; Syrian conflict, 207. *See also* Iraq
Supreme Council of Armed Forces (SCAF), 120
surrogate warfare, Iran's, 199
surveillance of Tunisia's border region, 84–85, 143
suspension of aid to Egypt, 112, 120, 125
Syria, 22, 27–28; chemical weapons, 38–39; defeating the ISIS caliphate, 31; ethnicity in the military, 50; impact of conflict on the populace, 37; Iran's regional SA engagements, 199; Jordan's military effectiveness, 226; Jordan's participation in the conflict, 223–224; LAF demotion, 93–94; LAF security priorities, 97; mercenary deployment, 37; military ineffectiveness, 49; military support in Libya, 25; penetration and control of the LAF, 99; proxy wars, 3; regional conflicts, tensions, and threats, 20; size of the military, 57(table); Turkey's interventionist presence, 207–208; Turkey's SA provision, 192; US drawdown, 42
Syrian refugees, 205

tactical intangibles, assessing, 299–300
tactics and strategies, 7–9; disconnect with weapons demand, 47–49; lack of a long-term US strategy, 40; NATO goals and constraints, 150; reality and rhetoric of SA, 18; the spectrum of policy options, 314–318; US security assistance adjusting to changes, 17
Ta'if Agreement (Lebanon), 99
Taliban: US assistance, 292, 306–307
Tataouine, Tunisia, 81, 85–86, 91(n80)
Tawazun (Balance) website, 332
technology transfer: Egyptian-French arms sales, 126; non-US arms provision to Egypt, 119

temporal entanglements, 196–203, 206–209
terminological ambiguities, 9–11
terrorism: anti-West tactics in MENA, 313–314; assessing leaders' responses to real-world crises, 304–305; effect on SA policy priorities, 293–294; impact of conflict on the populace, 37–38; Saudi Arabia, 174. *See also* counterterrorism; War on Terror
Timber Sycamore program (CIA), 224
top-down military command and control: Lebanon, 96
Townsend, Stephen J., 78–79
training programs: achieving multilateral policy objectives, 305–306; assessing tactical intangibles, 299–300; Bright Star joint training, 129, 277–278; correlation to popular support for the military, 238, 239–240(table); defining security assistance, 149; effect on stability, 329; Egyptian Armed Forces technical and tactical personnel, 286–287; Egypt's al-Sisi benefiting from, 285; EU expenditures, 135; EU mission in Iraq, 138; German assistance in Tunisia, 142–143; Iran as provider of, 192; Italy's security assistance in Iraq and Tunisia, 164; by MENA states, 191; NATO missions, 154; reforming US assistance to Egypt, 130–131; securitization of Tunisia's borders, 85; Tunisia, 74; Turkey's SA engagement in Libya, 206; US in Jordan, 224–225; US training of Egyptian officers, 129–130
Transjordan, 214–215, 220–222
transparency: risks of SA, 324
Transparency International, 324
tribal affiliations: Jordan's Hashemite rule, 214–215; Jordan's JAF, 217; Jordan's welfarism through militarism, 221; MENA military composition, 50; Tunisia's border regions, 81
Trump administration: GCC arms imports, 180; growing security role in MENA, 22; JCROA withdrawal, 29; lack of MENA strategy, 40–41; minimizing US presence in the MENA states, 41–42; Saudi-US relations, 174; Tunisia's RFDC, 79–80
Tunisia: aid figures, 74; assessing public support for the military, 246–247; belief in democracy, 242(fig.); confidence in the military, 233–234, 242(fig.); CT implementation, 57–58; ethnic composition of the military, 50; EU spending, 136(fig.), 140–144; European security assistance, 134; France's military partnerships, 159; Germany's security assistance, 161; impact of assistance on the military, 73–80; Italy's security

assistance, 164; marginalized border regions, 80–87; military effectiveness and civil-military relations, 62–63; military response to Arab Spring, 241(table); NATO partnership, 154; North African subregional security, 24; popular support for the military, 235, 238, 240(table); SA demand in flawed democracies, 60–63; securitization through SA, 71–73
Tunisian Armed Forces (TAF), 75, 77
Turkey: expansion of territory and control, 204–205; Gulf Wars, 282; military effectiveness and civil-military relations, 63; military response to Arab Spring, 241(table); military support in Libya, 25; neo-Ottomanism, 198, 206–209; popular support for the military, 240(table); reforming SA systems, 66–67; SA demand in flawed democracies, 60–63; as SA provider, 192; shifting stance in MENA strategy, 22; spatial and temporal entanglements in SA provision, 203–208

Ukraine: assessing US assistance, 292; effect of the conflict on oil prices, 176–177; Egyptian-Russian arms deal, 128; Egypt's agenda, 287; entanglements, 10–11; expansion of military aid to, 149; MENA states' authoritarian leanings, 8; regional state cooperation, 320; role in MENA aid, 6; Russian failure in civil-military integration, 260; Russia's attempt to reduce Western influence, 313; US focus shifting, 44; US lack of security strategy, 41
unconventional warfare: threats to Egypt, 282–283; Tunisia, 77
United Arab Emirates (UAE): assistance to Egypt, 114, 121, 127–128; break-even oil prices, 176(table); defense industry, 187; defense spending, 177, 179, 179(table); effectiveness of US assistance, 49; GDP, 175; mercenary contracts, 181; military assistance to Egypt, 114; military deployment abroad, 186–187; military response to Arab Spring, 241(table); military support in Libya, 25; political purpose of prestige weapons, 53; popular support for the military, 240(table); regional military influence, 185–186; royal family in the military, 54; size of the military, 57(table); US military bases in, 184; weapons imports, 178(table); Yemen's civil war, 32
United Kingdom: Arabia's military underperformance, 172–173; arms supplies to the Gulf, 182–183; bases in the Gulf, 185; hard SA provision, 195–196; LAF transition, 95–96; MENA assistance,

21–22; origins of the JAF, 218; SA in Lebanon, 94; Saudi arms imports, 29; security assistance in the Arab Gulf, 28
United Nations: Egypt's agenda in the Ukraine, 287; maritime security in Libya, 144–145; security-sector reform, 331
unmanned aerial vehicles (UAVs), 7, 76
unmanned combat aerial vehicles (UCAVs), 35
UNSMIL/UNDP Policing and Joint Security Program, 145
upstream problems and policy objectives, 291–292, 295–298
US Agency for International Development (USAID), 316, 332, 334
US Information Agency: nonmilitary instruments of power, 316
US Marine Corps Special Operations Forces, 76
US Special Operations Command (USSOCOM), 75
US-Jordanian Defense Pact (2021), 225
US-Tunisia Strategic Dialogue, 74
utilitarian political support, 52–53

Venezuela: democracy in rentier states, 52
Vietnam War, 11
violent extremist organizations (EOs): scrutinizing Egyptian aid, 294
volunteer military: LAF, 95–96

War on Terror: Egypt's partnership, 283–284; Iran's revolution without borders, 200; Jordan's participation, 223–224; prioritizing irregular warfare, 76; temporal and spatial entanglements, 197–198; Tunisia's marginalized border regions, 83–84; Tunisia's population hierarchization, 82–83
weak states, 20–21; arguments against security assistance, 328; EU mission in Iraq, 138–140; Lebanon's civil-military relations, 99–100; regime legitimacy in oil monarchies, 52
weapons deployment (US): targeting MENA, 318–319
Wehrey, Frederic, 317
welfarism, Jordan's, 220–223
well-being, individual: affecting confidence in the military, 233–234
Western influence, countering, 313
white papers, importance of, 267
women: confidence in the military, 233, 235, 243(table); reforming US assistance to Egypt, 131

Yemen: achieving multilateral policy objectives through limited training programs, 305–306; assessing military leadership traits, 301–303; civil war threatening US interests, 20; economic health, 175; Egypt's role in the conflict, 128; EU spending, 136(fig.); Iran's regional SA engagements, 199; military response to Arab Spring, 241(table); popular support for the military, 240(table); proxy wars, 3; Red Sea subregion, 31–32; SA to repressive republics, 56; Saudi-Egyptian military cooperation, 122; UAE's effectiveness, 49

About the Book

WHY, GIVEN THE ENORMOUS RESOURCES SPENT BY THE US AND Europe on security assistance to Arab countries, has it led to so little success? Can anything be done to change the disheartening status quo? Addressing these thorny questions, the authors of this state-of-the-art assessment evaluate the costs and benefits to the main providers and recipients of security assistance in the MENA region and explore alternative strategies to improve outcomes for both.

Hicham Alaoui is research associate at the Weatherhead Center for International Affairs, Harvard University. **Robert Springborg** is nonresident research fellow of the Italian Institute of International Affairs and adjunct professor in the School of International Studies at Simon Fraser University.